T0211578

Lecture Notes in Computer Science 10294

Commenced Publication in 1973
Founding and Former Series Editors:
Gerhard Goos, Juris Hartmanis, and Jan van Leeuwen

More information about this series at http://www.springer.com/series/7409

Fiona Fui-Hoon Nah · Chuan-Hoo Tan (Eds.)

HCI in Business, Government and Organizations

Supporting Business

4th International Conference, HCIBGO 2017
Held as Part of HCI International 2017
Vancouver, BC, Canada, July 9–14, 2017
Proceedings, Part II

 Springer

Editors
Fiona Fui-Hoon Nah
Missouri University of Science
  and Technology
Rolla, MO
USA

Chuan-Hoo Tan
National University of Singapore
Singapore
Singapore

ISSN 0302-9743   ISSN 1611-3349   (electronic)
Lecture Notes in Computer Science
ISBN 978-3-319-58483-6   ISBN 978-3-319-58484-3   (eBook)
DOI 10.1007/978-3-319-58484-3

Library of Congress Control Number: 2017939342

LNCS Sublibrary: SL3 – Information Systems and Applications, incl. Internet/Web, and HCI

Printed on acid-free paper

This Springer imprint is published by Springer Nature
The registered company is Springer International Publishing AG
The registered company address is: Gewerbestrasse 11, 6330 Cham, Switzerland

Foreword

The 19th International Conference on Human–Computer Interaction, HCI International 2017, was held in Vancouver, Canada, during July 9–14, 2017. The event incorporated the 15 conferences/thematic areas listed on the following page.

A total of 4,340 individuals from academia, research institutes, industry, and governmental agencies from 70 countries submitted contributions, and 1,228 papers have been included in the proceedings. These papers address the latest research and development efforts and highlight the human aspects of design and use of computing systems. The papers thoroughly cover the entire field of human–computer interaction, addressing major advances in knowledge and effective use of computers in a variety of application areas. The volumes constituting the full set of the conference proceedings are listed on the following pages.

I would like to thank the program board chairs and the members of the program boards of all thematic areas and affiliated conferences for their contribution to the highest scientific quality and the overall success of the HCI International 2017 conference.

This conference would not have been possible without the continuous and unwavering support and advice of the founder, Conference General Chair Emeritus and Conference Scientific Advisor Prof. Gavriel Salvendy. For his outstanding efforts, I would like to express my appreciation to the communications chair and editor of *HCI International News*, Dr. Abbas Moallem.

April 2017   Constantine Stephanidis

HCI International 2017 Thematic Areas and Affiliated Conferences

Thematic areas:

- Human–Computer Interaction (HCI 2017)
- Human Interface and the Management of Information (HIMI 2017)

Affiliated conferences:

- 17th International Conference on Engineering Psychology and Cognitive Ergonomics (EPCE 2017)
- 11th International Conference on Universal Access in Human–Computer Interaction (UAHCI 2017)
- 9th International Conference on Virtual, Augmented and Mixed Reality (VAMR 2017)
- 9th International Conference on Cross-Cultural Design (CCD 2017)
- 9th International Conference on Social Computing and Social Media (SCSM 2017)
- 11th International Conference on Augmented Cognition (AC 2017)
- 8th International Conference on Digital Human Modeling and Applications in Health, Safety, Ergonomics and Risk Management (DHM 2017)
- 6th International Conference on Design, User Experience and Usability (DUXU 2017)
- 5th International Conference on Distributed, Ambient and Pervasive Interactions (DAPI 2017)
- 5th International Conference on Human Aspects of Information Security, Privacy and Trust (HAS 2017)
- 4th International Conference on HCI in Business, Government and Organizations (HCIBGO 2017)
- 4th International Conference on Learning and Collaboration Technologies (LCT 2017)
- Third International Conference on Human Aspects of IT for the Aged Population (ITAP 2017)

Conference Proceedings Volumes Full List

1. LNCS 10271, Human–Computer Interaction: User Interface Design, Development and Multimodality (Part I), edited by Masaaki Kurosu
2. LNCS 10272 Human–Computer Interaction: Interaction Contexts (Part II), edited by Masaaki Kurosu
3. LNCS 10273, Human Interface and the Management of Information: Information, Knowledge and Interaction Design (Part I), edited by Sakae Yamamoto
4. LNCS 10274, Human Interface and the Management of Information: Supporting Learning, Decision-Making and Collaboration (Part II), edited by Sakae Yamamoto
5. LNAI 10275, Engineering Psychology and Cognitive Ergonomics: Performance, Emotion and Situation Awareness (Part I), edited by Don Harris
6. LNAI 10276, Engineering Psychology and Cognitive Ergonomics: Cognition and Design (Part II), edited by Don Harris
7. LNCS 10277, Universal Access in Human–Computer Interaction: Design and Development Approaches and Methods (Part I), edited by Margherita Antona and Constantine Stephanidis
8. LNCS 10278, Universal Access in Human–Computer Interaction: Designing Novel Interactions (Part II), edited by Margherita Antona and Constantine Stephanidis
9. LNCS 10279, Universal Access in Human–Computer Interaction: Human and Technological Environments (Part III), edited by Margherita Antona and Constantine Stephanidis
10. LNCS 10280, Virtual, Augmented and Mixed Reality, edited by Stephanie Lackey and Jessie Y.C. Chen
11. LNCS 10281, Cross-Cultural Design, edited by Pei-Luen Patrick Rau
12. LNCS 10282, Social Computing and Social Media: Human Behavior (Part I), edited by Gabriele Meiselwitz
13. LNCS 10283, Social Computing and Social Media: Applications and Analytics (Part II), edited by Gabriele Meiselwitz
14. LNAI 10284, Augmented Cognition: Neurocognition and Machine Learning (Part I), edited by Dylan D. Schmorrow and Cali M. Fidopiastis
15. LNAI 10285, Augmented Cognition: Enhancing Cognition and Behavior in Complex Human Environments (Part II), edited by Dylan D. Schmorrow and Cali M. Fidopiastis
16. LNCS 10286, Digital Human Modeling and Applications in Health, Safety, Ergonomics and Risk Management: Ergonomics and Design (Part I), edited by Vincent G. Duffy
17. LNCS 10287, Digital Human Modeling and Applications in Health, Safety, Ergonomics and Risk Management: Health and Safety (Part II), edited by Vincent G. Duffy
18. LNCS 10288, Design, User Experience, and Usability: Theory, Methodology and Management (Part I), edited by Aaron Marcus and Wentao Wang

HCI in Business, Government and Organizations

Program Board Chair(s): **Fiona Fui-Hoon Nah, USA and Chuan-Hoo Tan, Singapore**

The full list with the Program Board Chairs and the members of the Program Boards of all thematic areas and affiliated conferences is available online at:

http://www.hci.international/board-members-2017.php

HCI International 2018

The 20th International Conference on Human–Computer Interaction, HCI International 2018, will be held jointly with the affiliated conferences in Las Vegas, NV, USA, at Caesars Palace, July 15–20, 2018. It will cover a broad spectrum of themes related to human–computer interaction, including theoretical issues, methods, tools, processes, and case studies in HCI design, as well as novel interaction techniques, interfaces, and applications. The proceedings will be published by Springer. More information is available on the conference website: http://2018.hci.international/.

General Chair
Prof. Constantine Stephanidis
University of Crete and ICS-FORTH
Heraklion, Crete, Greece
E-mail: general_chair@hcii2018.org

http://2018.hci.international/

Contents – Part II

Social Media for Business

Analytics, Visualization and Decision Support

Contents – Part I

Information Systems in Healthcare, Learning, Cultural Heritage and Government

Novel Interaction Devices and Techniques

E-Commerce and Consumer Behaviour

Sharing Economy Versus Access Economy

A Critical Reflection on Social Interaction Between Peers

Sophie Altrock[1](✉) and Ayoung Suh[2]

[1] School of Creative Media, City University of Hong Kong, Kowloon, Hong Kong
saltrock2-c@my.cityu.edu.hk
[2] Department of Information Systems and School of Creative Media,
City University of Hong Kong, Kowloon, Hong Kong
ahysuh@cityu.edu.hk

Abstract. Disruptions caused by Web 2.0 and easily accessible technologies have had an impact on many thematic areas. In the economic sector these developments have resulted in the creation of a new business model: the sharing economy (SE). Despite its success in the last decade however, researchers are debating a clear definition without highlighting the key concept in terms of functions and processes that are fundamental to the SE model. Therefore, this paper focuses on functions of peers that are either consuming or providing, and elucidates the relation in accordance with business transactions in that both peers interact. Through a critical review of previous papers, we analyze the SE model by reflecting on prior definitions of sharing. We then compare motivations of peers to participate in the SE and, as a result, find discrepancies between providing and consuming peers in relation to their respective functions in the SE. Based on these findings, we introduce a theoretical framework that exemplifies the SE concept based on social interactions between peers and, thus, relates motivations of peers to transaction types and processes based on social interactions required.

Keywords: Sharing economy · Peer economy · Access economy · Business · Social interaction

1 Introduction

Since the introduction of the information communication technologies that enabled Web 2.0 and social media, research in a variety of disciplines has sought to analyze their impact on our society. In the field of business, these new technological developments have initiated the creation of a new business model, and with it, have introduced a new area of research that combines technology, economy, and society. The sharing economy (SE) is a new economy that disrupts any common idea of business. Instead of business-to-customer relations (B2C), we now create business transactions between peers (P2P). Uber (www.uber.com) and Airbnb (www.airbnb.com) are already profiting from their business models, which are anchored in the concept of sharing [1]. Hence, the SE makes use of online platforms to connect individuals interested in providing private goods or services to

© Springer International Publishing AG 2017
F.F.-H. Nah and C.-H. Tan (Eds.): HCIBGO 2017, PART II, LNCS 10294, pp. 3–15, 2017.
DOI: 10.1007/978-3-319-58484-3_1

other individuals looking for a convenient way to access these goods or services [2–4]. Fundamental to these transactions is communication between peers [2, 5]. Thus, social interaction—in an economic process once solely regulated in commercial terms—becomes an essential cornerstone of the SE model.

Previous research has largely focused on the motivations of peers to participate in the SE [5–11]. Accordingly, social interaction is not only the key to facilitating the SE, but it also serves to motivate peers to participate in this economic model. While social interactions in a virtual space are necessary in the SE to enable business transactions in the first place, the SE also offers peers the option to interact further in the physical space [4, 8]. However, two aspects deserve more clarification. First, it is unclear to what extent the driver to participate in the SE is purely for social reasons—meaning the participant's interest in social interactions with other users rather than for economic reasons. Second, the extent to which relations between peers may become more than business depends on the willingness of peers to further engage socially, after the actual business transaction is completed. Here, the SE only serves as an incentive for further social interactions, but the impetus was not social in the first place. Thus, the aim of this paper is to highlight the role of social interaction in terms of the SE model, as well as to differentiate social interactions as the foundation of, motivator for, and consequence of business transactions between peers.

Focusing on the act of sharing in the SE reveals the lack of actual sharing in many businesses that are referred to as SE [2, 10]. While many studies focus on the term sharing in the SE, conflict has increased as to its meaning [2–5, 7, 12]. Although the label itself has been debated [3, 13], no determinant can be found to alter the term and its definition [7, 10, 13]. Accordingly, many researchers overlook ambiguities and correlations among the definitions of sharing, social interactions between peers and their motivations. While research highlights the motivations of individuals, it ignores the key concept of the SE. To fill this gap in research, this paper seeks to examine social interactions between peers according to the part they take in the SE, as well as their respective motivations. Specifically, we address the following key question: Taking into account the lack of a shared definition of the SE—how does the role of social interaction define the concept of the SE?

Towards that end, this study uses an extensive literature review and critical analysis of previous studies to clarify the definition and the principles of the SE. In an attempt to justify or amend the terminology, this study compares the definitions of sharing with the findings on the motivations of peers in the SE and, accordingly, highlights discrepancies between peers relating to their respective functions. Based on our findings, we present a theoretical framework that elaborates on transaction types and transaction processes between peers in accordance with their motivations. Thus, this paper highlights transaction types based on ownership and access, relating to social interactions between peers. Consequently, the access economy (AE) is often suggested as opposite to or as replacing the SE concept. While accessing prevails actual sharing transactions we do not replace the SE label but introduce a framework that simplifies a differentiation of both. Finally, we propose further research questions based on our framework in order to derive more tailored motivations of peers in accordance with respective transactions in the SE.

2 Defining the Sharing Economy

Reviewing previous research on the SE reveals a variety of definitions, but beyond this lack of clarification, several similar terms are often equated with the principle of the SE. Researchers have listed many terms that are used synonymously with the SE [7, 10, 13]. These include inter alia, business sharing, space sharing, P2P lending, skill sharing, crowd-sourced investments, collaborative economy, and collaborative consumption, as well as P2P economy, access economy, on-demand economy, reputation economy, trust economy, and many more. While three papers mention—as referred to by Jiang— label battle, the result is still far away from a solution [7, 10, 13]. Botsman [10] prefers using the term collaborative economy, whereas Cartagena [13] is of the opinion that AE would be the correct term to describe the phenomenon.

A report published by the European Commission in 2013 describes the foundation of the SE as being "peer-to-peer platforms that enable consumers to access consumer-owned property or competencies" [14, p. 2]. Eckhardt and Bardhi [2], Samuel and Zhang [4], and Yan and Zhao [15] all agree with this description by reusing the verb "to access". Cartagena refers to the SE as a new economy that "is based on sharing, rather than owning" [13]. The same view is shared by Jiang, who highlights the principles of the SE that lie within the concept of access "rather than possession of goods and assets" [7]. Finally, an analysis of more than 30 papers and articles on the SE reveals that terms access and sharing are used equally in the SE context.

In addition to the principle of the SE, which fits somewhere between accessing and sharing goods and services, there appears to be one common denominator that divides the SE from the collaborative economy, also referred to as collaborative consumption (CC). Kamal and Chen identify the rise of the SE in technological development [8]. Lee et al. regard "advanced technologies and social media" [3, p. 2] as drivers of the SE. However, there is still disunity among researchers in terms of separating the SE from the collaborative economy. Some researchers use CC or collaborative economy synonymously to mean the SE. For example, John observes a correlation between CC, sharing, and Web 2.0 and describes CC as a "high-tech phenomenon" [16, p. 2]. Lee et al. [3], however, clarify CC as only the foundation of the technology-mediated SE. Botsman, one of the leading figures in the CC sector, also prefers the term collaborative economy, arguing it best explains "the shift from centralized institutions towards decentralized connected communities" [10]. Yet, Botsman's preference is related to the fact that she regards sharing ventures as separate from other collaborative economies [10]. Consequently, she reveals the core issue in clarifying the definition of the SE: not all SE businesses are actually based on the principle of sharing.

Thus far, it is still unclear what phenomenon we describe when referring to the SE, and whether the common definitions of the SE do, in fact, describe what we refer to as the SE. Prior attempts to choose one term to describe the phenomenon have not succeeded. Some researchers have only one objective: to divide CC from the SE. For the following sections we shall keep in mind one aspect that will be of high importance for the further discussion: we find that, on the one hand, access is a key principle: on the other hand, the act of sharing is just as relevant. To solve the continuing issue of inconsistency in the application of a label and definition of this new economic phenomenon, we will elaborate on the details of the SE concept in the following section.

3   Peer Interaction in the Sharing Economy

In the SE, social interaction is found to be the key element enabling business transactions [9]. Yet, the role of social interaction in the SE remains unclear. As seen in Fig. 1, social interaction between peers usually takes place online, enabling business transactions in the first place [16]. Social interaction may then continue in a physical place when two peers have to exchange goods or services [14]. Furthermore, social interaction may take place between parties with the same function in the form of reputation systems that enable peers to communicate experiences to other interested users [17, 27].

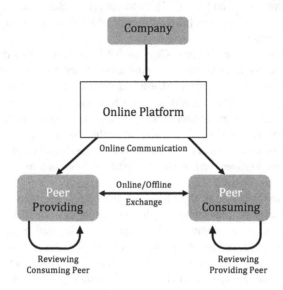

Fig. 1. Participants in the sharing economy

3.1   Different Parties in the Sharing Economy

Other than traditional business models such as B2C, the SE enables a new economy that is based on consumer to consumer (C2C) transactions. These consumers are usually referred to as peers, hence the P2P economy. However, peers per se do not yet facilitate business in the SE; thus, we have one additional intermediary that makes the SE possible. Jiang is one of few researchers who has elaborated on participating parties within the SE [7]. Accordingly, a classification scheme by Jiang reveals the role of online platforms provided by a third party that can be either an individual or business. This third party helps to connect the two other parties [7]. Further, Eckhardt and Bardhi confirm this third party in the form of a company that would serve as the regulating party in the SE [2].

Focusing on two of the three participating parties in the SE, providing and consuming peers, Schor highlights that "[those] can be on either side of a transaction" [19, p. 4]. Several researchers have defined peers according to the actions they take part in the SE. One side of peers is described as a using [4], consuming [19], buying [14, 20], demanding [7], and obtaining [21] party, whereas the other side of peers is described as a providing [5], contributing [19], selling [20], sharing [8, 21, 22], supplying [7, 14], and giving [21] party. Yet, most prior studies describe peers as consuming and providing. Figure 1 shows a brief overview of the previously described features and structures of the SE.

The new and highly important phenomenon concerning this business model, which is mainly ruled by consuming and providing peers, is the shift of power that the P2P economy enforces. Labrecque et al. [24] and Owyang [25] both mention the empowerment of consumer or customer. Thus, while the main business transaction occurs between peers, the role of the company regulating these processes becomes minor. While providing peers are now responsible for facilitating their own success in business, consuming peers also have to actively engage with the providing peers in order to make a deal. The responsibility of creating business now lies only within the willingness of peers to do so. Primary business transactions occur between two equally standing parties, as the term peer already implies. The role of peers or consumers, opposite to the role of businesses, has changed significantly. There is no obvious sign of a business or a company in the P2P economy, highlighting the novelty of business transactions between two equally standing parties using the concept of sharing.

3.2   Sharing in the Sharing Economy

In the SE, business transactions between peers enable an exchange of services or goods; however, it is debated whether the principle of the SE is actual sharing. Seeking to clarify the definition of sharing and, accordingly, the SE, two opposite views can be revealed: Whereas many researchers simply adapt to the usage of the term sharing or justify it [5, 8, 16], other researchers criticize or even try to alter it [2, 7, 10, 17, 23]. Wittel focuses in his paper on the act of sharing and the qualities of it [5]. Wittel is of the opinion that sharing exists in two forms: sharing as distribution and sharing as social exchange [5]. In his view, sharing can describe different social practices with different functions and motivations. Further, it depends on the individual's subjective reasoning and the willingness to share [5]. Kamal and Chen, too, see the roots of sharing in a broader cultural context [8]. Accordingly, sharing is anchored in humans in the form of natural instinct [8]. Kamal and Chen [8] suggest that the sharing principle in the SE has overcome the previous boundaries of only sharing between closely related people, such as family and friends.

Opposite to the views that sharing can define a large spectrum of phenomena, many more researchers tend to reject the use of the term sharing in terms of the SE. Botsman prefers the term collaborative economy, or CC, instead of SE [10]. Botsman believes that sharing is too overarching of a term for all marketplaces in this sector, and she notes the importance of discerning different forms of sharing [10]. Belk agrees with Kamal and Chen that sharing usually takes place within a close circle of acquaintances and points out the ambiguity of the act of sharing [8, 17]. Accordingly, "although giving and receiving are involved in sharing, they differ from the giving and receiving involved in commodity exchange and gift giving" [16, p. 127]. Hence, different forms of giving and receiving exist, as in gift giving and sharing, opposite to providing and consuming, as in exchange.

The most common principles used when defining the SE, are reciprocity and ownership, according to Belk [23]. Thus, giving and receiving may or may not include transfer of ownership, temporary ownership, and/or exchange in either material or immaterial forms. For example, giving someone temporary access to one's car may be a non-reciprocal act between friends, but the same act between people who are not very closely related might include expectance of compensation, or a reciprocal act. Supporting Belk, Jiang defines giving, exchanging, and sharing independently [7, 17]. Thus, gift giving is a caring act that does not involve compensation. In contrast, exchange is defined as being impersonal and includes the transfer of ownership. Finally, sharing is similar to giving and can be described as nonreciprocal and voluntarily [7]. The main difference here is that sharing, according to Jiang [7], does not involve the transfer of ownership. However, companies such as Uber and Airbnb that are commonly quoted in the SE context [22, 24, 25] are, against definition, of a reciprocal nature; drivers and hosts are being paid for their services.

Various terms are representative of the SE model. Confirming the incorrectness of the label SE for different internal processes, a few researchers have introduced new labels; these reveal that most processes are in fact not about sharing, but about accessing. Whereas Botsman [10] prefers the overarching term of the collaborative economy, Cartagena [13] and Jiang [7] share the view that the main principle of the SE is access. Thus, Jiang [7] introduces the economy of access-based distribution that is marked by balanced reciprocity and no full ownership transfer—an "alternative view of how sharing with a calculated return may actually work" [7, p. 9]. In seeking to clarify principles in the SE model, scholars have pointed to ownership and reciprocity as two main aspects that influence the relation between peers and the way in which they interact.

4   Motivations to Participate in the Sharing Economy

After analyzing the act of sharing, the definition of the SE is still unclarified. To move towards a clear description of the SE, peer motivations can help to highlight discrepancies according to the function of a peer: consuming or providing. Three main motivations of peers to participate in the SE can be identified: social, economic and environmental. This section, first, briefly examines all three motivations and, second, continues to highlight socially driven peers according to their consuming or providing function.

Recently, researchers have focused on peers' general willingness to share [3, 4, 21, 26]. Anti-capitalism, the burden of ownership, enjoyment in sharing, hedonic motivations, income, knowledge, modern lifestyle, product variety, quality, a sense of belonging, social experience, social influence, substitutability, sustainability, thriftiness, ubiquity, availability, and uniqueness have been found to be factors that positively influence participation in the SE [26]. Further, some researchers have also mentioned convenience as an important factor [2, 4, 11, 17, 27]. A study by Owyang and Samuel [11] shows that the most popular reasons to choose sharing services are convenience (78%), followed by price (68%). In terms of choosing sharing over buying though, the price is more important (53%) than convenience (30%). Another aspect here that appears to be even more important is brand (33%). The most prominent, however, are the given overarching motives—economic, social, and environmental [6, 9, 18]. Thus, some peers choose the SE for economic or environmental benefit, whereas others embrace the opportunity to socially engage. Yet, the role of a social motivator has been largely overlooked. Social interaction is a key construct on which the SE model is built. Social interaction is more than simply an impetus to participate. Taking into account the diversity of consuming and providing peers, as well as the two given acts of accessing and sharing, reveals a new dimension of the P2P economy.

4.1 Social Interaction as Motivator in the Sharing Economy

One aspect that has not yet been largely considered in terms of motivations is the prominence of three different parties in the SE: intermediaries and consuming and providing peers. While this paper focuses on the individual level [3], we highlight the relation between peers, more precisely, two different types of peers that have different functions in the SE model either providing or consuming. While a few papers specify the motivations of providing or consuming peers, others simply analyze the willingness to share [3, 4, 21, 26]. While sharing can include providing as well as consuming peers, as in sharing a car ride or rooms in an apartment, lending someone a drill clearly implies a utilitarian benefit for the consuming party but does not clearly suggest a benefit for the providing party. Thus, it is necessary to specify the motivations of different types of peers to understand the role of social interaction in the SE model.

Researchers focusing on the motivations of providing peers mostly find that economic motives drive them to provide services or goods in the SE. For example, Dillahunt and Malone are one of few researchers to specifically target providers in the SE [28]. Their research focus is on the economic benefits that the SE has to offer to providers; in this case, drivers in disadvantaged communities. A professional's report from Ernst & Young also highlights the creation of new jobs—hence, the benefits for providers. However, the findings are not consistent. Bellotti et al. [29] find that users seek convenient and valuable services, while providers "place great emphasis on idealistic motivations such as creating a better community and increasing sustainability" [29, p. 1]. Furthermore, Scholdan and Van Straaten [25] mention that social aspects motivate both providers and consumers due to "socio-demographic changes nowadays". It is likely that economic benefit is an advantage of the SE, but not all participating peers are seeking an economic benefit. Social interaction can be a significant reason to decide for or against being part of a P2P economy.

The most significant aspect when analyzing motivations is the specific occasion during which the action takes place. For example, car sharing and accommodation sharing place different requirements on both peers. The way in which interaction is required depends on this type of sharing occasion, as shown in a study by Böcker and Meelen [9]. Böcker and Meelen focus on the discrepancies between providing and consuming parties based on the three previously mentioned main motivations, which are economic, social, and environmental [9]. Their findings reveal that sociality is most important for providing and consuming parties in terms of meal sharing. The least important are social factors in the case of car sharing, which is even less important for users compared to providers, confirming the Bellotti et al.'s study suggesting that providers have a more pro-social or pro-environmental stance in the SE [29]. In contrast, accommodation sharing is the most economically driven sharing opportunity for both providers and consumers [9]. However, users appreciate the social aspect more than their providing counterparts [9]. Finally, the most environmentally driven are users in terms of ride sharing; however, providers—again mirroring the findings of Bellotti et al. [29] —regard car sharing, tool sharing, and ride sharing as the most environmentally beneficial SE types [9]. Interestingly, providers are least driven by economic factors when sharing a ride or tool [9].

Combining the findings shown in Fig. 2, the willingness to participate in the SE, and the different motivations of providing and consuming peers, we find that food sharing is not only the most social activity, but it is also the least interesting form of sharing, especially for consuming peers. Further, tool sharing is not only the most interesting form of sharing in the SE but also the most balanced one. Consumers and providers are almost equally interested in tool sharing. However, the motivations here are highly unequal. Whereas users are motivated mostly by economic reasons, providers are least motivated by economic and most influenced by environmental reasons. One last aspect that we will point out because of the highest discrepancy of willing providers opposite to willing users is accommodation sharing. As Fig. 2 shows, only 13.1% are willing to provide accommodation, while 58% would like to rent an accommodation from peers. However, adding the second findings of the motives of providers and consumers reveals that for both parties, economic reasons are the most prevalent in either providing or renting accommodation.

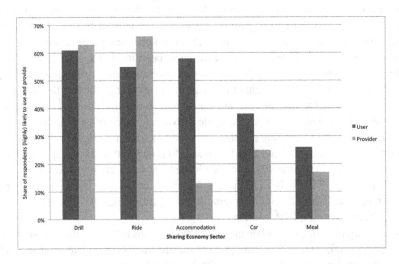

Fig. 2. Willingness of providing and consuming peers to participate in the SE by Böcker and Meelen, 2016

This section highlights the small amount of research that focuses on the different motivations between providing and consuming peers and the significant differences that these previous findings reveal. A pattern can hardly be found. An overview of the findings reveals that meal sharing is most social and least interesting. Sharing a meal means to give part of a meal away to someone else. The act of sharing a meal may be social as it might happen in the same place at the same time but it also implies a benefit for only one side of the sharing process and a loss for the giving party. Tool sharing and accommodation sharing imply temporary ownership and no final loss for the giving party. However, while using a tool is done by one party, accommodation sharing can imply use by two people at the same place at the same time, entailing possible further interactions rather than a pure transfer of business-related commonalities.

As previous studies show, motivations between providing and consuming peers can be very different. As Fig. 2 illustrates, the highest discrepancy exists among accommodation sharing, and the least interest is in meal sharing. Taking into account the required social interaction in meal sharing and accommodation sharing, it appears that purely social activities are not favoured by SE participants. Referring to the previous sections, sharing is usually a personal act between people who are known to each other. Sharing a home or a meal cannot usually be referred to as a kind act between strangers. However, giving someone a ride or lending someone a tool can happen in a short time window that does not require more interaction than necessary. Not only is the divide of consuming or providing peer important but also is the transaction occasion as well as the actual process in terms of social interactions between peers required. Böcker and Meelen argue that it is important "to not conceive the sharing economy as one coherent phenomenon" [9, p. 9]. Schor [18] also sees the importance to distinguish transaction types. Thus, to fully understand the SE concept and its participants it is fundamental to synthesize not only motivations but especially transactions types and processes.

5 Social Interaction in P2P Economies

Combining the findings that the literature review of the previous sections revealed, the lack of a uniform definition of the SE is found to be linked to an interdependence of three overlooked but significant factors; first, the divide between consuming and providing peers, second, the act of sharing in contrast to acts of accessing in relation to,

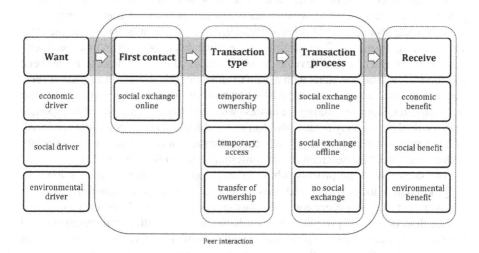

Fig. 3. Theoretical framework: social interactions between peers in the SE model

third, transactions types and processes. As a consequence, we introduce a theoretical framework (Fig. 3) that illustrates the P2P economy process focusing on peer interactions and motivations of peers.

With social media, the free culture movement [5], or maker movement [22] the SE concept originally supports the idea of a pro-social business model: An economy that uses Web 2.0 and timeless and effortless connectedness experienced through social media to develop a social economy. Schor [18] describes the origin of the SE as a "socially transformative idea" that has been disrupted ever since by for-profit platforms. Furthermore, the SE would be the "expression of a utopian" [5] image. Yet, values do not guide actions [21, 30] even if "people [may] find sustainability and sense of community important values to themselves" [30]. Although it might be that pro-social values motivate participants of the SE to provide a good or service to peers, the determinant question is the value of social interactions in contrast to economic and utilitarian benefit.

The whole transaction process in the P2P economy model can be divided into five steps while three steps define the peer interaction in detail. The first contact between peers in the SE model is based on social interaction online. In the following business transaction, thus exchange of goods or services, is defined by transaction type and process. While transaction types lay the foundation for the following exchange between peers, the transaction process results from the type of business transaction. Following Böcker and Meelen [9], we divide temporary ownership such as in accommodation sharing, car sharing or tool sharing from forms of temporary access such as in ride sharing, or accommodation sharing in terms of renting a room in a home and, finally, transfer of ownership as, for example, in meal sharing. Though, while some transactions imply on-going social exchange during the transaction process, others remain quick and easy handovers. Thus, as seen in Fig. 3, the transaction process can imply either social exchange online such as in online service exchange, social exchange offline such as in ride sharing, or no social exchange when accommodation, car, or tool are only handed over.

The peer interaction is imbedded in impetus, what either providing or consuming peer motivates, and outcome, what either peer receives from the transaction process. Though, while motivations have been researched and, thus, can be measured, the challenge when analyzing a P2P transaction is the evaluability of benefits or, more precisely, how social interaction can develop to be a benefit after the transaction has been concluded. A transaction starts with a want to either provide or consume goods or services. In this case, we can refer to the common motivations that are economic, social or environmental. However, during the process when socially engaging with the opponent peer, the final benefit may potentially change. Fundamental is that consuming peer will always satisfy a utilitarian need, whereas economic motivation or benefit equal monetary exchange and can be essential for both consuming and providing peer [23].

Transaction type and process submit information on whether the transaction is of reciprocal nature for providing and consuming peer. For example, transferring ownership will most likely imply economic loss for the providing party. However, a transaction process that consequently implies social exchange online or offline could result in social benefit. Thus, when sharing a meal, the providing party may have less of the meal, but in return, sharing the meal with the consuming party at the same time at the same place can imply a gain in sociality. On the contrary, interactions that only exchange tools, cars, or accommodation [9] with no continuing social exchange in the process do not facilitate social exchange and, with it, no social benefit. Our theoretical framework, Fig. 3, serves to illustrate social interactions between providing and consuming peers and measures the occurence and, with it, the significance of social exchange in the SE model. As a consequence, it seeks to determine when a SE model only uses social interaction as a basic instrument or when social interaction can become fundamental and predominant to the business transaction.

6 Conclusion

Reviewing more than 30 papers on the SE, we find that there is a lack of a uniform concept of the SE. The label is being criticized to a large extent and does not explain the diversity of P2P concepts. Resulting from an extensive literature review, we can find the common determinants that are new technologies, social interaction and the exchange of goods or services. Further, we divide three transaction types that consider ownership and access rather than the act of sharing as the dominant feature in the SE model, suggesting the AE label as a more tailored title. However, we do not exclude the possibility of sharing transactions but rather relate transaction types to transaction processes that define motivations and benefits. Thus, whether a transaction can be defined as a sharing transaction or an economic driven exchange is dependent on how this transaction between peers proceeds. Hence, P2P business transactions can be analyzed based on the suggested framework in order to clarify the nature of certain transactions: SE or AE.

Answering the guiding question of this paper—how the role of social interaction defines the concept of the SE—we conclude that the SE, and consequently the AE, is not only based on social interaction. Social interaction guides the definition of the P2P concept throughout, from first contact until the end of the transaction process. Thus, social interaction is a key factor in transactions between peers and can significantly affect motivations to participate in the SE. However, what remains unclear is how social interaction can transform business transactions during its process and, as a result, turns out as a social benefit. For further research we suggest to engage with the question on how social interaction during the transaction process can influence motivations of either providing or consuming peer to further participate in the SE. Further, we propose focusing on how offline social exchange during a transaction may differ from online social exchange in the P2P economy context. Lastly, empirical studies may highlight the impact of monetary compensation on perceiving social interaction with strangers as beneficial.

Concluding, this paper clarifies the SE concept, its features and determinants, elucidates the activities sharing and accessing, and, thus, creates a foundation for further research and P2P businesses to better establish customers.

Acknowledgement. This research was supported in part by grants no. CityU 21500714 from the Research Grants Council of the Hong Kong SAR awarded to the second author.

References

1. Cohen, B., Kietzmann, J.: Ride on! Mobility business models for the sharing economy. Organ. Environ. **27**, 279–296 (2014)
2. Eckhardt, G.M., Bardhi, F.: The Sharing Economy Isn't About Sharing at All. Harvard Business Review (Online) (2015). https://hbr.org/2015/01/the-sharing-economy-isnt-about-sharing-at-all. Accessed 19 Jan 2017
3. Lee, Z.W.Y., Chan, T.K.H., Balaji, M.S., Chong, A.Y.L.: Technology-mediated sharing economy: understanding user participation in collaborative consumption through the benefit cost perspective. In: PACIS Proceedings of the 20th Pacific Asia Conference on Information Systems (2016)
4. Zhang, K.Z.K., Yan, R., Zhao, S.J.: Understanding participation in sharing economy: the roles of convenience, risk, and regulatory foci. In: PACIS Proceedings of the 20th Pacific Asia Conference on Information Systems (2016)
5. Wittel, A.: Qualities of sharing and their transformations in the digital age. Int. Rev. Inf. Ethics **15**, 3–8 (2011)
6. Rude, L.: 4 Keys to a Successful Sharing Economy Business Model. Global Marketing Communications Agency Website. Text 100 (2015). http://www.text100.com/2015/05/11/sucessful-sharing-economy-business-model/. Accessed 29 Dec 2016
7. Jiang, J.: The challenges and opportunities of sharing economy - a new wrapping for doing business online? In: PACIS Proceedings of the 20th Pacific Asia Conference on Information Systems (2016)
8. Kamal, P., Chen, J.Q.: Trust in sharing economy. In: PACIS Proceedings of the 20th Pacific Asia Conference on Information Systems (2016)
9. Böcker, L., Meelen, T.: Sharing for people, planet or profit? Analysing motivations for intended sharing economy participation. Environ. Innov. Societal Trans. (2016). doi:10.1016/j.eist.2016.09.004
10. Botsman, R.: Collaborative Economy: A Transformative Lens, Not A Start-Up Trend. Collaborative Consumption (2014). http://www.collaborativeconsumption.com/2014/11/27/collaborative-economy-a-transformative-lens-not-a-start-up-trend/. Accessed 6 Jan 2017
11. Owyang, J., Samuel, A.: Collaborative Economy Report. Vision Critical, Crowd Companies, Vancouver (2015)
12. Aral, S., Chrysanthos, D., Godes, D.: Introduction to the special issue—social media and business transformation: a framework for research. Inf. Syst. Res. **24**, 3–13 (2013). doi:10.1287/isre.1120.0470
13. Cartagena, J.: Is there a Better Name for the Sharing Economy. OuiShare: Exploring the Edges. Medium (2014). https://medium.com/ouishare-connecting-the-collaborative-economy/is-there-a-better-name-for-the-sharing-economy-2d7489e1f56d. Accessed 29 Dec 2016
14. Dervojeda, K., Verzijl, D., Nagtegaal, F., Lengton, M., Rouwmaat, E., Monfardini, E., Frideres, L.: The Sharing Economy: Accessibility Based Business Models for peer-to-peer Markets. Business Innovation Observatory Case study 12. European Commission, Europe (2013)
15. John, N.A.: Sharing, Collaborative Consumption and Web 2.0. LSE Electronic Working Papers 26 (2013)
16. Belk, R.: Why not share rather than own? Ann. Am. Acad. Polit. Soc. Sci. **611**, 126–140 (2007). doi:10.1177/0002716206298483
17. Belk, R.: You are what you can access: sharing and collaborative consumption online. J. Bus. Res. **67**, 1595–1600 (2014). doi:10.1016/j.jbusres.2013.10.001

18. Schor, J.: Debating the sharing economy. Great transition initiative (2014). http://www.greattransition.org/publication/debating-the-sharing-economy. Accessed 19 Jan 2017
19. Vishnumurthy, V., Chandrakumar, S., Gun, S.E.: Karma: a secure economic framework for peer-to-peer resource sharing. In: Workshop on Economics of peer-to-peer Systems, vol. 35 (2003)
20. Samuel, A.: Established Companies, Get Ready for the Collaborative Economy. Harvard Business Review (Online) (2014). https://hbr.org/2014/03/established-companies-get-ready-for-the-collaborative-economy. Accessed 19 Jan 2017
21. Hamari, J., Sjöklint, M., Ukkonen, A.: The sharing economy: why people participate in collaborative consumption. J. Assoc. Inf. Sci. Technol. **67**, 2047–2059 (2016). doi:10.1002/asi.23552
22. Owyang, J.: Report Sharing is the New Buying, Winning in the Collaborative Economy. Web Strategy (2014). http://www.web-strategist.com/blog/2014/03/03/report-sharing-is-the-new-buying-winning-in-the-collaborative-economy/. Accessed 6 Jan 2017
23. Belk, R.: Sharing. J. Consum. Res. **36**, 715–734 (2010). doi:10.1086/612649
24. Claveria, K.: How to compete with the next Uber new rules for the collaborative, on-demand, sharing economy. Vision Critical (2015). https://www.visioncritical.com/new-rules-in-sharing-economy/. Accessed 15 Dec 2016
25. Scholdan, L., Van Straaten, N.: What are the drivers of the sharing economy and how do they change the customer behaviour? E-marketing report (2015). https://www.contextuallearning.nl/wp-content/uploads/2016/01/drivers-of-the-sharing-economy-strategie.pdf. Accessed 15 Dec 2016
26. Hawlitschek, F., Teubner, T., Gimpel, H.: Understanding the sharing economy – drivers and impediments for participation in peer-to-peer rental, pp. 4782–4791. IEEE (2016). doi:10.1109/HICSS.2016.593
27. Biswas, R., Pahwa, A., Sheth, M.: The Rise of the Sharing Economy: The Indian landscape. Ernst & Young LLP, India (2015)
28. Dillahunt, T.R., Malone, A.R.: The promise of the sharing economy among disadvantaged communities, pp. 2285–2294. ACM Press (2015). doi:10.1145/2702123.2702189
29. Bellotti, V., Ambard, A., Turner, D., Gossmann, C., Demkova, K., Carroll, J.M.: A muddle of models of motivation for using peer-to-peer economy systems, pp. 1085–1094. ACM Press (2015). doi:10.1145/2702123.2702272
30. Makkonen, J.: 3 reasons why peer-to-peer marketplaces fail (and how not to). Marketplace Academy (2014). https://www.sharetribe.com/academy/3-reasons-why-peer-to-peer-marketplaces-fail-and-how-not-to/. Accessed 19 Jan 2017

Employing Relation Visualizations to Enhance the Shopping Experience on a Used Car Trading Platform

Jianxin Chen, Dongqing Zhang, Yingjie Victor Chen[✉], and Zhenyu Cheryl Qian

Purdue University, West Lafayette, IN, USA
chenjianxin201537@126.com,
{zhan2709,victorchen,qianz}@purdue.edu

Abstract. Used car online trading is a new trend developed in the vehicle trading market recently. In this paper, we focus on user experience of car searching in a used-car website. The datasets of used vehicles are complicated and multidimensional. To find a satisfying car within the budget, the car buyer needs to compare many cars by exploring and comparing data include but not limit to car maker, type, mileage, price, and key features. Within most current e-commerce systems, to search and evaluate different cars, users often have to jump across detail pages to search pages repeatedly. Due to constraints set in the searching process, it may result in uncontrollable information overload or deficiency. With a user-centered design approach, we first analyzed the car searching behaviors through the user study, then designed a data visualization interface that helps a customer to (1) achieve an overall understanding of the used car market such as relations of car type to price, mileage/model-year to price, and features, and (2) search, filter, and compare cars of interest through simple interactions. The goal of this research is to help users to find out an ideal candidate car through an innovative interface and enhance user experience on used-car trading websites.

Keywords: Used car trading · Searching experience · Parallel coordinate plots

1 Introduction

With the rapid growth of internet users in recent decades, e-commerce of used-car has been developed rapidly and extensively. The entrepreneur team Beepi created a C2C used-car transaction mode for the first time, which has caused a close attention from the industry and investors. The principal of the company claimed that during 2014–2015, the company had realized 1000% of income growth. In this paper, we explored a new way of improving user experience in a used-car trading website by utilizing data visualization methods in the interface. Typically there are two main car-searching modes in websites. One is to search by keywords; the other is to use constraints to narrow down the range of qualified cars. While purchasing a car, users will make many comparisons. Also, we can see that most of the used car websites place a complete inspection report in a detail page. Users use the detailed contents of car performance and inspection reports

© Springer International Publishing AG 2017
F.F.-H. Nah and C.-H. Tan (Eds.): HCIBGO 2017, PART II, LNCS 10294, pp. 16–28, 2017.
DOI: 10.1007/978-3-319-58484-3_2

of cars to evaluate the car they find. Users normally should repeat the same search-comparing process for many rounds before they can make their final decisions, which is a time-consuming and inconvenient process.

The user experience of product searching is an important issue in e-commerce websites. While shopping for a product especially with many choices, the customer gradually forms his/her expectation of the product through reviewing and comparing many different products. This process can be divided into several stages [1–4]. To be specific, a user firstly forms a universal set which contains all products that are related to his/her purchasing goal. While forming the universal set, the user gradually understands the market status, realize his real demands and capacity, and create a consideration set through filtering out unfit products from the universal set. Finally the customer evaluates products within this consideration set, which is the most critical stage in products screening toward the final purchasing decision. It is impossible for a client to find the best fit product without forming a proper consideration set. To make a proper consideration set, the user has to bear a good understanding of all relevant products in the market, including their price, pros and cons, functionalities, and cost-benefit trade-off. During this process, the user will have to study and compare many products carefully. Customer's knowledge gained from previous shopping experience may not be reliable for a new shopping due to market uncertainty issues such as discount and promotions from certain products. In most e-commerce sites, including used-car platforms, customers still use the old way of studying products by examining each product. Although product data are digitalized to enable fast search, it is still a frustrating, repetitive searching-comparing process. Often consumers may have to limit their attention and evaluation to a much smaller range of products to simplify the purchasing decision, which will certainly result in less optimistic purchasing result.

In this paper, we try to employ a data visualization method to enhance user's experience on product searching via allowing users to foresee results under different parameter ranges. Through the visualization, the user can quickly get an overview of goods on the market, form a universal set, and construct his consideration set by examining product parameters with simple interactions. The customer can also consider cost-benefit trade-offs by examining relations among parameters. With this design, users can gain a quick understanding of the used cars market, recognizing relations among car make, type, price, mileage, year, and configuration packages, and thus make an optimistic purchasing decision. Car searching time will be shortened. The whole shopping process will much more effective, smooth, and convenient.

2   Literature Review

Online websites provide a great number of candidate products for users. Undoubtedly the large quantity of selections will cause difficulties on users' decision-making process [5]. Similarly, when products have plenty of parameter properties to be referred, it will result in information overloading [6]. Thus, users have to make more efforts to select products [7].

The traditional method of screening is a process of adding limiters and shrinking its range of values constantly, called as "logical product filtration". Scholars show that when users set multiple constraints, there may be an insufficient quantity of products in the result set [8]. To fix this problem, one of the solutions is to use the "soft boundary". The upper and lower boundary of the limit range could be enlarged to a certain degree. For example, if upper boundary of a limit range is 100, the broad allowable parameter is 20%, the upper boundary of the actual limit range will be 120. However, such a way may result in information overloading and increasing cognitive burdens of users. To satisfy search demands of users without significantly increasing cognitive load, researchers introduce some new methods within the soft boundary as a supplement, namely preference properties [9]. Users control these constraints, thus can be more flexible based on users' preference of the searching results. Under this search mode, however, users may still fail to anticipate searching results, and the searching process still requires users to modify limiters constantly before they could see results.

Information visualization provides an idea for solving the problems mentioned above. In an information space, utilization of sensitivity information can help to realize "movement before seeing," instead of "seeing before movement" [10]. Its presence provides clues for users to set up or modify limit ranges. Such a model may better consistent with the behavior pattern of users.

Parallel bar gram in a multidimensional and interaction techniques to support consumer-based information exploration and choice based on attributes of the items in the selection set [11]. In such an interface, each property of a car corresponds to a bar graph. It excluded cars for inconsistent with the current constraint out of the boundary of the limited range. Such a display pattern indicates that after users change the limit range, some products will be brought into the qualified range. Therefore, users have no need to obtain a reasonable amount of candidate products by modifying the filtering range through countless attempts.

One multi-dimensional data visualization method is parallel coordinate plots [12]. Parallel coordinate plots can visual enable user to see distribution on each parameter and aware correlations among parameters. Through interacting with parallel coordinate plots, a user can investigate the correlation and tendency among many parameters [13]. Users' interaction in parallel coordinate plots is direct and simple. We can utilize a select box to set up a limit range on the coordinate plots directly. Comparing with the parallel bar gram, we assume such a way can better display abundant product data, realize direct selection, and facilitate cost-benefit trade-off comparison. In this study, we first conduct a user study to understand user's behavior and needs while purchasing a used car, then designed a new interface with parallel coordinate plots and property marking function to support car-searching process on a used-car trading platform.

3   User Study

At first, to understand the problem, we conduct a user study using interviews and contextual inquiry. We recruited users by applying the "snowball" strategy. We invited six people to our study. All of them are students at Purdue University. They all have basic car knowledge and are interested in buying a 2nd car. After the interview, we invited them to conduct car-search tasks in a used-car website. Their searching and decision-making process were observed and questioned while working on the website.

3.1 Methods

We asked questions about user's previous experience of purchasing user cars and what factors they would take into consideration when they make decisions. We asked the following questions:

- Do you have any experience on purchasing a used car? If so, please describe the car picking process.
- Have you ever searched for cars information through the internet? If so, which website(s)?
- Have you ever purchased a car through C2C car-purchasing website? What is your experience? Advantage and disadvantage of the website?
- If you want to purchase a used car, what kinds of parameters will be the key factors affect your final decision? Which parameters are fixed? Which parameters are flexible? Which parameters are subject to cost-benefit trade-off?

We asked users to operate in a current used-car e-commerce websites [14]. In this way, we can investigate user's behavior and habit in detail. We asked the user to finish the following tasks:

- Browse the website freely, speak out what's your concern in the website page and why do you concern about these issues.
- For users without car purchasing experience, ask him/her to select the most preferred car as if s/he is going to buy the car.
- For users who have already purchased a car, ask him/her to finish a virtual car purchasing process.

3.2 Summary of the User Research

We found that searching and choosing a used car is a complicated process. We find that the most attractive part for novice users is the information in the detail page of cars, such as fixed parameters, every used-car's special status, inspection report and photos. Browsing such information will help novice users to form expectation on the target car gradually. Such a process means to browse, record, and summarize through many used-car detail pages constantly. Users will jump through different pages to search, record and compare. According to current websites, the information on detail pages is not able to use as constraints yet. Users can only filter unqualified used cars based on their memory. For some users with experience in car purchasing, we find that after users use traditional filters and find there are no qualified items, they will adjust constraints, observe results, repeat these two steps, and guide to acquire satisfactory results.

In summary, based on results of our interviews and contextual inquiry, we find main difficulties for users to use the current searching method on websites:

- Used car information has its inherent complexity. There are too many parameters for the user to compare. Every used car has its condition. It involves a lot of cost-benefit trade-off analysis.
- To compare candidate cars, users need to jump through many pages to find the parameters on car's detail page and need to remember these parameters. After several rounds, the user forgot previous result. Some of them have to write down the previous search using pencil and paper.
- When modifying condition ranges, there are no clues for user to predict the result. For instance, before they click the "search" button, they never know "how many candidate cars will be newly increased after the price is improved by $5000." "how much I should adjust the boundary, for the sake of acquiring other ten candidate cars". Often the user reaches a "no qualified results" due to the tight constraints. The user has to go back to lose these parameter constraints to get some result.
- Loosen the constraints often generate too many results, which causes information overload or deficiency for the user. It is very hard for the user to create a consideration set within a reasonable quantity of cars. The search either yield no result or too many results.

According to the problems defined by our study and relevant topics in the literature review, we considered the following design requirements to satisfy user's need:

- Users should easily see the overall market status, and understand how different product attributes affect his final purchase decision.
- Provide with visual clues for user to foresee search results before hit the "search button" after setting up ranges.
- Users should be able to easily conduct cost-benefit trade-offs by comparing different value combinations of product attributes.
- The user should be provided with a simple interaction method to filter our un-relevant products to create a consideration set with reasonable quantities of cars.
- In the detail page, users can mark properties, which can be used as a clue or constraint in the visualization filter.

4   Searching Interface with Data Visualization

4.1   The Visualization Design

We adopted the parallel coordinate plots into the searching interface (Fig. 1) to facilitate car searching and comparison. Using a popular car trading website [14] as a template, we implement our design in the car browsing page. It keeps the core function of the original internet site, and we added our new method to it as supplementary. For a fair comparison, we keep the similar look and feel of the original site. The data used here are real used-car data extracted from the website.

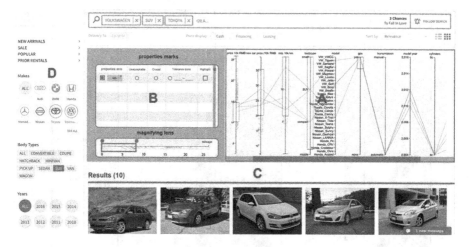

Fig. 1. A: visualization filter (parallel coordinate plots). B: Property marking system C: Searching results D: Traditional filter

Our parallel coordinate plots on the searching page will visualize main properties of each used cars in universal set (Fig. 2). Each axis stands for one parameter. We listed 11 key parameters that customers care the most, which are: car price, car type, model, transmission, mileage, model year, cylinder, engine size, new car price, skylight, and color. Some parameters carry numeric value, e.g. price, while some parameters are categorical data with limited choices, e.g. color and model. For each car, their attribute will match a position on the corresponding axis. Connecting these positions will form a polygon, which represents one car. Many cars together will form a graph like Fig. 3. We further encode one key parameter (car price) in the graph by assign each polygon a color, from blue to red, represent price from low to high.

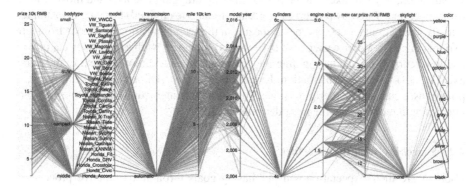

Fig. 2. Property visualization of all cars (~500 cars)

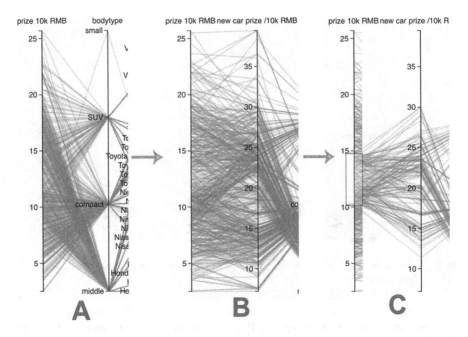

Fig. 3. The user drags and puts the property axis "new car prize" to the position next to "prize". In this way, the user can investigate two properties' correlation. (Color figure online)

One of the major advantages of this visualization tool is the visibility of different parameters' correlation. By looking the color distribution in other axes, we can see the relationship of cars' prices with other properties. For example, comparing with or without skylight option, there are more red lines connect to with skylight than without skylight, which indicates cars with skylight are mostly likely expensive cars. In this visualization, any two axes can be put together by dragging one axis and move it next to the other one. Thus any properties' correlation can be examined (Fig. 3). For example, initially, the parameter "body type" is located at the second position of all axis from left to right (Fig. 3A). When a user want to begin his purchasing with a high "new car price" and low "current price", he can drag the "new car price" and move it next to the price axis(Fig. 3B). With this interaction, he can observe the relationship between the sale price of used cars and their original price. This particular interaction execute one possible purchasing intention: find the most discounted car.

4.2 Searching with the Interface

Users aware their expectation and purchasing goals through a formative process of examining car properties. Their decision making is an iterative process with two stages, which includes general understanding the product space (universal set) and construct his/her selection (consideration set).

The first stage means to know about the distribution of cars' parameters in the universal set. At the beginning of this stage, users generally have no definite inclination and preference. They find out cars that may qualify for them in a browsing manner, make comparisons with different cars and reflect what kinds of cars, or what particular functions may meet their demands. On this stage, users will review a great number of cars and parameters that may conform to their expectation. However, it is still a stage that users just start to know about used-car properties and correlation among these properties. Users need to construct a good understanding of how parameters affect with each other through many interactions, for example, by moving axes to compare pairs of parameters. At this stage, the user only gains an overall understanding of the whole market without evaluating individual cars in detail. For a specific car, several parameters may satisfy users' demands, but other parameters may be totally unsatisfied. One impossible to fit a car satisfy on every aspect, the user has to conduct in-depth analysis on the cost-benefit trade-off among these conflicting parameters.

Through a simple interaction of using mouse to drag a small range along an axis, the user can create a "select box" and define a search range for that parameter, for example, between 100 K to 150 K RBM in price (Fig. 3C). If the user wants to adjust the range, he can drag the upper or lower boundary of the selection box, or simply move the whole box to set a new limit range. To make the use still aware about the car distribution along this axis, filtered out cars still show a short segment indicating their existence and their relation to neighboring axes. With gray outlines, the user can foresee possible result if he moves the select box (Fig. 3C). The customer may create many select boxes on several axes. The polylines remain in the visualizations forms the consideration set. The user will compare and screen out used cars on the basis of some details.

In addition to several main parameters displayed on the visualization tool, there are lots of other parameters on cars' detail pages. These parameters may not be very crucial when users construct their understanding of consideration set in the first stage. However, when user come to the second stage of evaluating cars, all the candidate cars are from consideration set selected by the constraints. The significance of properties in the detail page increases since all candidate cars are generally qualified. However, current information architecture of used cars trading website doesn't provide access for users to utilize these kinds of parameters to screen cars. Therefore, the user needs to remember these details in their mind and jump through many pages to compare values of different vehicles, which is truly inconvenient.

4.3 Use Example

Here we demonstrate how a customer construct a small consideration set using the interface. Imagine the user tried to buy a car with a high new car price but low on sale price so that he can enjoy an advance car with large discount. He finds that new car prices of cars with current prices between 100 K to 150 K RMB is ranging from 120 K to 300 K RMB (Fig. 3C). He considers new car price at more than 200 K are good choices. So he sets a constraint via the select box (Figs. 3C and 4A). Next, the user begins to explore the mileage. He does not want to buy a car with a very long mileage. Thus he set a limit of 0 to 70000 km on mileage (Fig. 4B). One more thing he cares is the car's body type. Most qualified cars are SUV and mid-sized cars. He dragged the "body type" axis to the 4th position to keep compact cars and middle cars by leaving SUV out of the select range (Fig. 4C).

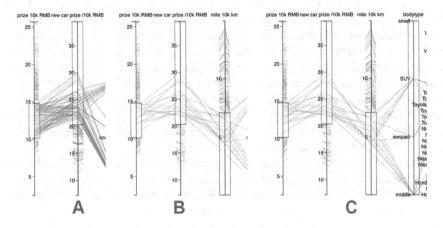

Fig. 4. Searching process

So far, the user has explored main parameters of used cars and learned a lot about the correlation among these crucial properties via the visualization tool. After setting four main constraints, the user thinks cars selected are qualified. His first stage has been finished. A consideration set for the user has been established (Fig. 5). Parameters of the car in this consideration set meet demands of the user. For the next stage, the user should evaluate and choose cars from this short list.

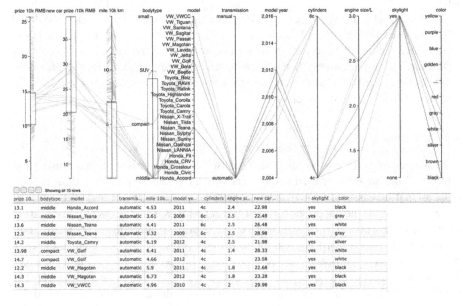

Fig. 5. Consideration set cars under four constraints.

4.4 Interaction Between Detail Page with the Visualization

In our design, we allow users to mark properties on the detail page and utilize them as new constraints. After reviewing detail pages of several candidate cars, the user realized that GPS is another useful function for him, but this property currently cannot be used as a constraint. He checks his current consideration set and finds there is only one car with GPS (Fig. 5). The available choices are very limited for him. He should go back to the searching page, modify previous constraints and let more cars come into the new consideration set for a fair comparison. To do so, he needs to mark "GPS" as a new constraint. First, he moves the mouse to text "GPS" and clicks right button on it. The property marking interface will pop out. The user then clicks "mark this property" to put this "GPS" selection into consideration. This section will also be recorded into history (Fig. 6A). Then the user can go back to the visualization to adjust select boxes to modify constraints. The "GPS" label is now in the properties marks. The user clicks the check box of "GPS" to establish a new axis on the parallel coordinate plots (Fig. 6B). Thus, a new constraint-GPS for the next round of selection has been set.

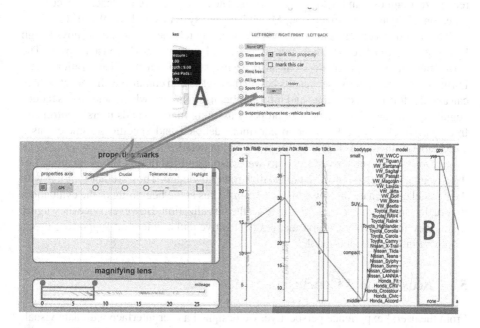

Fig. 6. A: Property marking tool in cars' detail page. Marked property will be shown on the searching page. B: Users can build a new axis to add the "GPS" as a new constraint. The "magnifying lens" will display details of the axis the user is operating on.

When the user modifies previous constraints, some gray lines on each axis outside the select box will serve as important clues. For example, as for the "new car prize" axis, gray lines below the lower boundary of the select box stand for cars that have been filtered out only because they did not meet the "new car prize" range set by user. Now, the user feels that a little lower new car prize is acceptable for him. Then he drags the lower boundary of selection box and let more cars come into new consideration set. In this way, the user can foresee the results because he can see the distribution of potential candidate cars and modify the range based on both his needs and the distribution of cars. He knows what efforts he need to do to achieve his goal.

4.5   Heuristic Evaluation

To validate our design and figure out usability problems, we built a paper based static prototype for the new searching page and a high-fidelity interactive prototype for the parallel coordinate plots. We grabbed more than 500 used cars' data from a real used car trading website [15]. After we had finished building our prototype, we recruited 5 people who work or study in user experience program at Purdue University to conduct a heuristic evaluation. We took use of 10 usability heuristics for user interface design [16] as principles to be checked. The main positive feedbacks are: Good visibility of system status; user control and freedom; Flexibility and efficiency of use; Help users recognize, diagnose, and recover from errors. The main negative feedbacks are concentrated on: Help and documentation; Match between system and the real world.

The overall feedback is positive. Most evaluators felt the new system enjoys a high Level of visibility because they can compare and screen cars in a visual space. The correlation of main parameters can also be investigated via the visualization tools. Furthermore, they can foresee results before they set search conditions. In this way, they can avoid information overload and information insufficiency, which helps users reduce cognitive load and avoid error. The property marking function adds users' control and freedom, which allows the user to add more detailed and specific parameters as a constraint on the fly while examining a product in detail.

However, some negative feedbacks were also identified during the evaluation. 4 of the five evaluators have now data visualization knowledge. They are not familiar with the parallel coordinate plots used in the design. Thus at the beginning of the evaluation, they had to spend some extra effort to learn the visualization. However, once they figure it out, they fill the visualization method is effective and efficient on supporting user's searching in large product pool.

5   Discussion and Conclusion

From the users' experience perspective, we designed a user interface with data visualization to improve the searching process on a used car e-commerce website. Began with exploring users searching behavior and define the problems via our user study, we utilized the parallel coordinate plot visualization as the main component for product searching while keeping current used car trading websites' current navigation and information hierarchy. Users can use this tool to explore the correlation among so many different cars and different properties to gain a good understand of cars, which increases user's decision quality. The process is visible, and the result is predictable. Another thing we added is the properties marking function. Since the searching page cannot display all the parameters, some of the properties on the detail page of each car cannot serve as a constraint before. Properties marking will make up this limitation.

The design provides a scheme for solving two major problems happened when user need search in a large number of products. One is how to perceive and compare products' complicated properties and make decisions on the basis of these properties. The other one is about problems of data overloading or data insufficiency caused by setting constraints when searching products with multidimensional data. By solving these two problems, this design naturally supports the two-stage model of consumers' decision making process on shopping. The visualization gives a clear overview of the universal set which includes all products with important attributes. The customer can see the distribution of products along each attribute, or examine the trade-off relations among attributes. Through simple interaction, the customer can filter and select desired products to form the consideration set. The consideration set can be easily adjusted.

The design is based on an existing website. Thus, it has high feasible for implementation. In this design, we do not abandon the conventional screening system. The new screening mode and conventional mode can co-exist, evading from risks by using sophisticated solution in the brand-new design. Though this study is focused on the used-car trade, the solution can be applied to explore other products with complicated properties. The design proposes a new way of using data visualization for multi-dimensional data screening in the e-commerce area. Also, the way of using property marking will help users choose cars among various tiny details. Multi-dimensional data screening, such as house purchasing, tourism products, electronic products, as well as other used products, can also use this combination of parallel coordinate plots and properties marking function.

We explore the way to employ relation visualization on real industry to benefit users. We try to collect various kinds of data of each used cars. Total used-car data, however, are still far less than it in the real world. The issue of scalability cannot be ignored. When the data reaches 1000 or more, it would be hard to visualize all of the data at same time, because the lines will be too intensive and overlap with each other.

The primary purpose aims to create a good searching experience for users. In the future, it is necessary to create a more high-fidelity prototype, closer data size in real trade and conduct a deeper user research. In this study, we have found that proposed data visualization method can effectively reduce searching effort and give user better understanding about the whole product space. Such interfaces are still rare in real websites. Our next effort may focus on making such interface more user-friendly so that it can be adopted broader to benefit consumers.

References

1. Roberts, J.H., Lattin, J.M.: Development and testing of a model of consideration set. J. Mark. Res. **28**(4), 429–440 (1991)
2. Shocker, A., Ben-Akiva, M., Boccara, B., Nedungadi, P.: Consideration set influences on consumer decision-making and choice: Issues, models, and suggestions. Mark. Lett. **2**(3), 181–197 (1991)

3. Holden, S.J.S.: Individual and situational influences on purchase goal specification. Adv. Consum. Res. **21**(1), 589 (1994)
4. Aurier, P., Jean, S., Zaichkowsky, J.L.: Consideration set size and familiarity with usage context. Adv. Consum. Res. **27**(1), 307–313 (2000)
5. Pu, P., Viappiani, P., Faltings, B.: Increasing user decision accuracy using suggestions. In: Proceedings of the SIGCHI conference on Human factors in computing systems (2006)
6. Todd, P., Benbasat, I.: The influence of decision aids on choice strategies–an experimental-analysis of the role of cognitive effort. Organ. Behav. Hum. Decis. Process. **60**(1), 36–74 (1994)
7. Parra, J.F., Ruiz, S.: Consideration sets in online shopping environments: the effects of search tool and information load. Electron. Commer. Res. Appl. **8**(5), 252–262 (2009)
8. Dabrowski, M., Acton, T.: Modelling preference relaxation in e-commerce. In: IEEE International Conference on Fuzzy Systems FUZZ-IEEE. IEEE, Barcelona (2010)
9. Dabrowski, M., Acton, T.: The performance of recommender systems in online shopping: a user-centric study. Expert Syst. Appl. **40**(14), 5551–5562 (2013)
10. Spence, R.: Information Visualization: Design for Interaction, 2nd edn., pp. 136–138 (2007)
11. Wittenburg, K., Lanning, T., Heinrichs, M., Stanton, M.: Parallel bar grams for consumer-based information exploration and choice. In: ACM Proceedings of UIST 2001, pp. 51–60 (2001)
12. Inselberg, A.: Multidimensional detective. In: IEEE Proceedings of Information Visualization 1997, pp. 100–107 (1997)
13. Siirtola, H.: Direct manipulations of parallel coordinates. In: IEEE Proceedings Information Visualization 2000 (IVOO), pp. 373–378 (2000)
14. Beepi: https://www.beepi.com. Accessed 15 Jan 2017
15. Renrenche: https://www.renrenche.com. Accessed 15 Jan 2017
16. Ten usability heuristics for user interface design: https://www.nngroup.com/arti-cles/ten-usability-heuristics/. Accessed 1 Feb 2017

Arousal or Not? The Effects of Scarcity Messages on Online Impulsive Purchase

Junpeng Guo, Liwei Xin, and Yi Wu[✉]

College of Management and Economics, Tianjin University, Tianjin, China
{guojp,yiwu}@tju.edu.cn, xinliwei1992@126.com

Abstract. With the proliferation of e-commerce, online promotion strategy of limited quantity and limited-time is widely used by online retailers to entice consumers' purchases. However, few research has investigated the exact effects of such a promotion strategy on consumers' online impulsive purchase. Based on the environmental psychology view, this study focuses on the mediating role of arousal in explaining the influences of scarcity messages in aspects of limited-quantity and limited-time on impulsive purchase. By building an online shop for an actual offline milk tea shop at taobao.com, an experiment with 182 participants was conducted to test our research model. The results provide strong evidence that both the limited-quantity and the limited-time scarcity messages positively influence consumers' perceived arousal, leading ultimately to impulsive purchases. Both theoretical and practical implications are discussed.

Keywords: Environmental psychology · Online impulsive purchase · Scarcity message · Arousal

1 Introduction

Singles' Day – symbolized by its single-digit heavy date, 11/11 – began seven years ago, when unattached college kids went online to hunt for bargains. Alibaba, China's largest e-commerce giant, started offering huge discounts to mark the day. Thereafter, this shopping event has grown exponentially, now being a shopping festival globally. For Singles' Day 2015, the company raked in $5 billion during the first 90 min of the sale, totaling $14.3 billion in just 24 h largely through its online shopping platforms, Taobao.com and Tmall.com[1]. Singles' Day is a shopping carnival for online consumers, and online shops utilized promotion strategy of limited-quantity and limited-time, in which a limited amount of products are on sale within a given time period, to entice impulsive purchases. The scarcity messages about limited-quantity and limited-time provide online shopping environment that might shape consumers' impulsive purchase decision-making.

Specifically, in a limited-quantity scarcity message, the promotional offer is made available for a predefined quantity of the product. In a limited-time scarcity message,

---

[1] http://www.businessinsider.com/how-alibaba-made-143-billion-on-singles-day-2015-11, accessed at May 8, 2016.

© Springer International Publishing AG 2017
F.F.-H. Nah and C.-H. Tan (Eds.): HCIBGO 2017, PART II, LNCS 10294, pp. 29–40, 2017.
DOI: 10.1007/978-3-319-58484-3_3

the offer is available for a predefined period, after which the offer becomes unavailable. Scarcity seems to create a sense of urgency among buyers that results in increased quantities purchased, shorter searches, and greater satisfaction with the purchased products, therefore, accompanying impulse buying. Prior research has shown that purchase restrictions are used as informational cues by customers to evaluate promotion strategies [1]. Although, amply studies have emphasized the influences of scarcity messages on impulsive purchases in the offline contexts, scant research has been devoted to the online shopping environment.

Comparing to the offline shopping environment, the two types of scarcity messages are more visible and timely updated. Online consumers are able to view the timely changes of decreasing supply amount and feel the time pressure by counting down the available shopping time. Patterns of manifestation of scarcity message are different in online versus offline environment. IT could easily be designed to manipulate perceptions of scarcity that could be potentially more difficult to manipulate offline. Scarcity messages create a sense of urgency and constitute the dominant stimuli in online environment. Scarcity messages manipulated by IT provide online shopping environment that might shape consumers' impulsive purchase decision-making. Therefore, to bridge the gap, this study aims to elaborate how limited-quantity information and limited-time information to online shopping environment influence the consumers' impulsive purchase.

Consumers often act impulsively when making online purchase decisions, triggered by easy access to products, easy purchasing (e.g., 1-Click ordering), lack of social pressures, and absence of delivery efforts [2]. The marketing and IS literatures show that impulse purchase can be studied from the state of mind created by the online shopping environment [3]. Prior literature has demonstrated the irrationality of impulse purchase decision-making from the online shopping environment perspective. Verhagen and van Dolen [4] suggested that the irrational decision-making of online impulsive purchase occurs without a thoughtful consideration of why and for what reason one needs the product. Specifically, there are two core elements characterizing this irrational impulse buying decision-making. First, the process is unplanned and lacks cognitive deliberation. Second, emotions dominate the impulse buying process [4]. Therefore, this study draws on the environmental psychology view and posits that arousal stimulated by online shopping environment (i.e., limited-quantity scarcity message, limited-time scarcity message) affects consumers' impulsive purchase.

To fill the above research gaps, this study aims to address the following research questions:

(1) What are the impacts of limited-quantity scarcity message and limited-time scarcity message on online consumers' arousal toward impulsive purchase?
(2) How does consumers' arousal lead to online impulsive purchase?

By answering these research questions, this study provides the following theoretical contributions. First, this proposal examines the mechanism through which online scarcity messages influence consumer impulsive responses and investigates the impacts of scarcity messages on online impulsive purchase. Second, this study enriches the irrational decision-making literature of impulsive purchase from the perspective of arousal.

In addition, this study is with its practical contributions. On one hand, it provides design guidelines on successful use of limited-quantity and limited-time promotion strategy. On the other hand, this proposal also suggests that online consumers should pay close attention on their emotional responses toward the online promotion strategy.

2   Literature Review

2.1   Online Impulsive Purchase

Impulsive purchase is defined as "a purchase that is unplanned, the result of an exposure to a stimulus, and decided on the spot" [5]. The stimulus in the definition can be an actual product, service, or the extrinsic attributes of the product, such as the shopping environment or atmosphere. On the one hand, when exposed to a stimulus, an individual experiences a sudden, spontaneous urge or desire to buy the stimulus, regardless of the impetus (e.g., individual trait or environmental cue) [6]. On the other hand, the impulsive purchase occurs only after the individual first experiences the urge to purchase impulsively [6].

Impulsive purchase is distinguished from unplanned purchase. Unplanned purchase is "the purchase of a product that was not planned prior to entering the store" [7]. The term "impulse buying" refers to a narrower and more specific range of phenomena than "unplanned purchasing" does. More importantly, it identifies a psychologically distinctive type of behavior that differs dramatically from contemplative modes of consumer choice [6]. This study focuses on impulse buying, which occurs when a consumer experiences a sudden, often powerful and persistent urge to buy something immediately.

The urge to buy impulsively (UBI) is defined as "the state of desire that is experienced upon encountering an object in the environment" [8], it is a qualified and reasonable proxy for actual impulsive purchase [9–11]. Additionally, it is suggested that not all impulsive urges are acted upon, and the greater the number of urges experienced, the higher is the likelihood that an impulse purchase will occur [8]. Although it is a qualified and reasonable proxy for actual impulsive purchase, the urge to buy impulsively, which can be restricted by many factors (e.g., money, time, product availability), is not equivalent to actual buying. Therefore, this study focuses on consumers' actual impulsive purchases as the research outcome.

Amply studies have investigated the role of environmental cues on online impulsive purchase, mainly from the perspective of website quality characteristics [e.g., 4, 9, 11–13]. With the advances of e-commerce, a new type of promotion strategy, i.e., limited-quantity and limited-time offer, is widely used by online retailers to entice consumers' impulsive purchases. For instance, Alibaba, China's largest e-commerce giant, holds sale-events utilized this limited-quantity and limited-time offer on Singles' day. The success of the limited-quantity and limited-time offer relies on e-commerce websites' capabilities in timely updating the information of quantity and time for online consumers. The information of limited-quantity and information of limited-time are viewed as scarcity messages [14], and these two types of information constitute of the online informational environment for consumers.

2.2 The Environmental Psychology View of Online Scarcity Message

The environmental psychology view proposes that environmental stimuli are linked to behavioral responses by the primary emotional responses of arousal, pleasure, and dominance [15]. Environmental psychology has been used when investigating online impulsive purchase, which extend our knowledge of online environment and impulsive purchase [12]. Environment factors (e.g., scarcity messages) influence people's affective responses to the environment, which in turn induce people to approach or avoid the environment [15]. Emotion of affective response can be classified based on three independent and bipolar dimensions: pleasantness, arousal, and dominance [16]. Subsequent research has found that pleasantness and arousal explain most of the variance in affect and behavior, and arousal is the most critical type of emotional state [17, 18]. However, few research has confirmed the connection between scarcity messages and pleasantness. Literature has also presented that there is no significant differences of pleasantness among individuals in response to scarcity condition [19]. Therefore, this study focuses on arousal as the consumers' emotional state from the online informational environment.

Arousal is defined as the neurophysiological basis underlying all processes in the human organism, ranging from sleep to excitement with intermediate states of drowsiness to alertness [16]. It is the basis of emotions, motivation, information processing, and behavioral reactions [20]. Donovan and Rossiter [18] showed that arousal-nonarousal dimension taps the degree to which a person feels alert, excited, stimulated or active in the situation. In particular, there are two types of arousal: excited arousal and competitive arousal. On one hand, excited arousal is feelings of excitement reflecting high levels of arousal combined with high levels of pleasure and joy, where environmental cues (e.g., warm color, fast music tempo, scent) would activate excited arousal [21]. On the other hand, competitive arousal is an adrenaline-laden emotional state that can arise during competitive interactions [22], where arousal based on rivalry, time pressure, and audience effects can trigger the desire to win [23].

Prior research has theorized potential theoretical connections between scarcity messages and arousal [14, 24]. Research on activation and attention explicates that arousal is typically produced by input changes to which an organism is unaccustomed, particularly when the input is scarce, surprising, and novel [24]. According to Cialdini [14], when something that people like is less available, they become physically agitated, such that their focus narrows, emotions rise, and cognitive processes are often suppressed by "brain-clouding arousal". Zhu and Ratner [19] examined the underlying mechanisms of scarcity polarizes preferences, demonstrating that the effect of scarcity salience on choices is mediated by consumers' perceived arousal.

3   Research Model and Hypotheses

The research model is presented in Fig. 1.

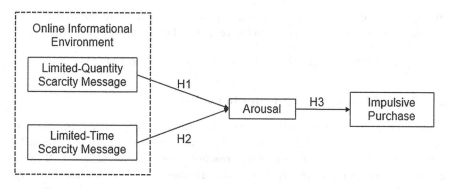

Fig. 1. Research model

3.1 Effects of Scarcity Messages on Arousal

A limited-quantity scarcity message (LQS) offer is restricted to a set number of units. Units are limited, often administered on a first-come, first-served basis, and run until sell out. This creates a sense of time pressure and uncertainty for an LQS deal. Combining to the retail auctions, consumer under time pressure are believed to elicit an excited arousal [25] and research has shown that time pressure increases arousal [26].

Furthermore, consumers compete for the advantageous inequity that accrues to the recipient of promotions [27]. The promotion of LQS, companying with time pressure and rivalry, makes a consumer feel that him- or herself in direct competition with other consumers. Such a situation will stimulate the consumer and result in competitive arousal. Prior studies show that time pressure, rivalry and audience effects increase competitive arousal that a consumer experiences [23]. As well as the similar situation in the auctions, the object is limited and bidding under time pressure with rival, which significantly stimulates competitive arousal and affects the consequences [22, 25]. Therefore, we propose that:

H1: High LQS leads to higher perceived arousal of consumers than low LQS.

In the case of limited-time scarcity message (LTS), consumers can buy the product at any moment within a period of time, and the supply is abundant but time is scarce. Consumers only have to complete the deals before the deadline. Even the consumers know the existence of vast others, there is no conflict of interest between each other and competitive arousal in consumers. However, obtaining a bargain becomes more like "winning" a bargain, where the bargain provides both utilitarian as well as hedonic fulfillment [28]. Scarce products on sale open a gate to obtain the bargain and stimulate the emotion, consumers feel excited or joy because of the utilitarian satisfaction. In addition, a festival's programme content can affect both attendees' emotions and hedonism [29]. LTS is the core feature of the online promotion strategy and motivates consumers' purchase intention as attending the event is outside the daily routine. Furthermore, scarcity appeal plays an important strategic role to create an excitement around promotions [30]. Research on activation and attention explicates that arousal is typically produced by input changes to which an organism is unaccustomed, particularly when the input is scarce, surprising, and novel [24]. Therefore, we hypothesize that:

H2:   High LTS leads to higher perceived arousal of consumers than low LTS.

3.2   Effects of Arousal on Urge to Buy Impulsively

The affective reactions to the environment will determine an individual's response, e.g., urge to buy impulsively [15]. In a traditional shopping context, a positive relationship has been found between positive affective reactions (i.e., enjoyment) and UBI [8]. In the online context, perceived enjoyment will have a positive effect on the impulsive urge to buy [9, 31]. Moreover, we focus specifically on time pressure and the inherent social competition under online promotion strategy, as these factors are considered to be the main drivers for so-called competitive arousal. In auctions, such competitive arousal may ultimately lead to auction fever [22, 23]. With respect to auction fever, competitive arousal theory suggests that arousal can impair the bidders' decision-making, and push them to bid past their limits [23]. Adam, Krämer [25] showed that affective processes have a definite influence on human decision making when bidders compete with human opponents. In addition, excitement has a positive effect on desire to stay at the mall and increases patronage intentions [32]. Therefore, we posit that:

H3:   Arousal is positively related to consumers' urge to buy impulsively.

4   Research Methodology

4.1   Experimental Design

A lab experiment with a 2 (i.e., limited-quantity: high vs. low) × 2 (i.e., limited-time: high vs. low) factorial design was conducted to test the proposed hypotheses. LQS and LTS were shown on a real online retailer webpage by manipulating the number of restricted products and time of discounts. We selected milk tea coupons as our product category due to their popularity among Chinese college students and product affordability. Particularly, all products are on sale and discount settled according to the actual situation of Tmall.com on Singles' Day. Accordingly, in our manipulation, we set the number of deals to 200 to present low scarcity in terms of quantity, and the number of promotional deals to 20 to present high scarcity in terms of quantity. Discount time was set to 1 h and 10 min on the webpage.

4.2   Sample and Experimental Procedures

Participants in this experiment were students at a large public university. Prior to the experiment, participants were asked to provide information about demographics and online shopping experience. 182 participants were recruited to take part in the experiment. Participants were randomly assigned to four experimental conditions. The random assignment was performed once for every participants. They were presented an experimental website with different experimental treatments in which they can browse the product information. Participants were told to imagine that the scenario is real and browse the website carefully. Afterwards, participants were instructed to complete a questionnaire that contained measurement items of the research variables (shown in Appendix). The measures utilized a 7-point Likert-type scale anchored by 1 (Strongly Disagree) and 7 (Strongly Agree). Finally, participants were debriefed and thanked.

5   Data Analysis and Results

5.1   Subject Demographics and Background Analysis

Among the 182 valid participants, 109 were female. The age of the participants ranged from 18 to 23, with the average online shopping experience being 3.51 years. No significant differences were found among participants assigned randomly to each of the four experimental conditions with respect to age, gender, online shopping experience, and daily plan for buying beverages, indicating that participants' demographics were quite homogeneous across different conditions.

5.2   Manipulation and Measurement

Scarcity manipulation was checked for with the questions "How available do you think are the limited-quantity products?" and "How available do you think are the limited-time products?," and the responses were based on a seven-point scale from "extremely sufficient" to "extremely insufficient" [33]. Participants in the low-quantity condition reported a mean value of 4.37 for the extent of perceived scarcity (standard deviation, 1.510), and participants in the high-quantity condition reported a mean value of 3.37 for the extent of perceived scarcity (standard deviation, 1.692). The difference was significant ($t = -4.221$, $p < 0.001$), and hence, manipulation for LQS worked as anticipated. On a seven-point Likert scale, participants in the low-time condition reported a mean value of 4.47 for the extent of perceived scarcity (standard deviation, 1.592), and participants in the high-time condition reported a mean value of 3.17 for the extent of perceived scarcity (standard deviation, 1.554). The difference was significant ($t = -5.591$, $p < 0.001$), and hence, the manipulation for LTS worked as anticipated.

Four items were adapted to measure arousal from Russell and Mehrabian [16] (Cronbach's alpha = 0.812; see Appendix). Exploratory factor analysis showed that in general, items loaded well on their intended factors and lightly on the other factor, thus indicating adequate construct validity (see Table 1). Impulsive purchase was measured by the actual number of coupons a participant bought in his/her order. If a participant did not place an order, we coded his/or impulsive purchase as "0". In addition, impulsive purchase was considered effective only if a participant had no plan to buy a beverage on the day of the experiment. If not, impulsive purchase of that participant was adjusted to "0". Data on participants' impulsive purchase was collected from the objective transactions on our Taobao shop. We included in the model several control variates that affect consumers' impulsive purchase. The literature on impulsive purchase suggests that consumers' price consciousness affects their purchase behavior [34]. In addition, gender, age, and online shopping self-efficacy are governing factors as well. To control for consumers' online shopping self-efficacy, we adapted measurements from Compeau and Higgins [35]. The correlation matrix is reported in Table 2.

Table 1. Results of factor analysis

	Perceived arousal	Price consciousness	Online shopping self-efficacy
arl1	**.813**	.012	.161
arl2	**.811**	.024	.002
arl3	**.769**	−.095	.051
arl4	**.791**	.120	.022
priCon1	.141	**.726**	.056
priCon2	.022	**.766**	−.077
priCon3	−.038	**.745**	−.002
priCon4	−.073	**.809**	−.092
onSSE1	.058	−.024	**.822**
onSSE2	.027	−.072	**.907**
onSSE3	.016	.067	**.867**
onSSE4	.118	−.090	**.758**

Table 2. Variable Correlations Matrix

	M	SD	AVE	CR	CA	Gender	Age	PC	OSSE	PA
Gender	0.599	0.492	–	–	–	–				
Age	20.132	0.850	–	–	–	0.003	–			
PC	3.188	1.043	0.585	0.849	0.768	−0.052	−0.081	**0.765**		
OSSE	5.631	1.091	0.708	0.906	0.864	0.011	−0.009	−0.083	**0.841**	
PA	4.089	1.237	0.633	0.873	0.813	−0.023	−0.056	0.012	0.148	**0.796**
IP	0.918	1.583	–	–	–	−0.092	0.107	−0.147	0.101	0.107

Notes. PC = price consciousness; OSSE = online shopping self-efficacy; PA = perceived arousal; IP = impulsive purchase; M = mean; SD = standard deviation; AVE = average variance extracted; CR = composite reliability; CA = Cronbach's alpha.

5.3   Results Pertaining to Perceived Arousal

An analysis of variance (ANOVA) was conducted to detect the joint effects of limited-quantity and limited-time on arousal. ANOVA with perceived arousal as the dependent variable revealed the significant effects of the LQS message ($F_{(1,180)} = 41.466$, $p < 0.01$) and the LTS message ($F_{(1,180)} = 34.797$, $p < 0.01$). In general, the high-LQS and -LTS conditions led to higher perceived arousal than the low-LQS and -LTS conditions. Hence, H1 and H2 are supported.

5.4 Results Pertaining to Impulsive Purchase

PLS was used to test the proposed structural model. The measurement model was first assessed by examining (1) individual item reliability, (2) internal consistency, and (3) discriminant validity [36]. The measurement items load generally on their respective constructs, thus demonstrating adequate reliability (Table 1). The high composite reliability and Cronbach's alpha scores shown in Table 2 indicate satisfactory consistency.

The diagonal elements in Table 2 represent the square roots of average variance extracted (AVE) of the latent variables, while the off-diagonal elements represent the correlations among latent variables. For adequate discriminant validity, the square root of the AVE of any latent variable should be greater than the correlation between that particular latent variable and other latent variables [36]. The data presented in Table 2 satisfy this requirement. Moreover, in Table 1, the loadings of indicators on their respective latent variables are higher than the loadings of other indicators on these latent variables, and the loadings of these indicators on other latent variables, thus lending further evidence to discriminant validity.

Bootstrap resampling was performed on the structural model to examine path significance. The results indicate that perceived arousal has a significant and positive effect on impulsive purchase, suggesting H3 is supported. To ensure that our findings are not confounded by other variables, we controlled for the potential effects of gender, age, price consciousness, and online shopping self-efficacy. All control variables have significant influences on the dependent variable.

6   Discussion and Conclusion

6.1   Discussion of Key Findings

The results supported all hypotheses. The degree of scarcity in terms of quantity and time was manipulated within an online environment to investigate the influence of scarcity messages on impulsive purchase. The results show that limited-quantity and limited-time scarcity messages positively influence impulsive purchase. In sum, scarcity messages can maximize impulsive behavior when arousal is stimulated through the provision of scarcity messages in terms of limited-quantity and limited-time.

6.2   Implications

Drawing on the online impulse buying literature and the environmental psychology theory, this study proposes a theoretical model to explain the effect of online scarcity messages. Regardless of the website characteristics, this study suggests that context of website plays an important role in the impulsive purchase process. Promotional discounts are effective and limited-quantity scarcity message (LQS) and limited-time scarcity message (LTS) extremely fuel the enthusiasm for the products, which lead to the special emotion: arousal. The study explains the effectiveness of LQS and LTS appeals, and expects to find that different types of scarcity messages have distinct effects on consumer excited arousal and competitive arousal.

In addition, this study is with practical contributions. First, for product managers interested in creating an excitement and competition around their promotions, scarcity appeal has played a considerable strategic role. Managers can draw on LQS (e.g., releasing a new brand) and LTS (e.g., expanding sales) for generating buyer enthusiasm. Secondly, there is one noteworthy emotion for consumers. Arousal unconsciously manipulated by the retailers by using the scarcity messages and aim at promoting consumption. Being care for controlling arousal for consumers is an effective way to avoid impulsive buying.

6.3 Conclusion

Drawing on the online impulse purchase literature and environmental psychology, we proposed and tested a theoretical model to explain the effects of online scarcity messages in the business market. Regardless of website characteristics, our findings suggest that the online informational environment plays an important role in impulsive purchase. Promotional discounts are effective, and specifically, LQS and LTS are extremely instrumental in fueling the enthusiasm for purchasing products by triggering consumers' arousal. This study provides a foundation for understanding how scarcity messages influence their impulsive purchase behaviors. Our results reveals that the limited-quantity and LTS messages generate arousal, which, in turn, influences consumers' impulsive purchase. These results serve as a basis for future theoretical developments in the area of scarcity message and online impulsive purchase to guide practice.

Appendix A. Measurement Items

Scarcity	[33] (7-point Likert Scale)
Limited quantity	How available do you think the limited-quantity products are? "extremely sufficient" to "extremely insufficient"
Limited time	How available do you think the limited-time products are? "extremely sufficient" to "extremely insufficient"
Arousal	[16] (7-point Likert Scale)
arl1	Relaxed-Stimulated
arl2	Calm-Excited
arl3	Sleepy-Wide awake
arl4	Unaroused-Aroused
Price consciousness	[34] (7-point Likert Scale)
priCon1	I am not willing to go to extra effort to find lower prices
priCon2	I will grocery shop at more than one store to take advantage of low prices
priCon3	The money saved by finding low prices is usually not worth the time and effort
priCon4	I would never shop at more than one store to find low prices
priCon5	The time it takes to find low prices is usually not worth the effort
Online shopping Self-efficacy	[35] (7-point Likert Scale)
onSSE1	I could complete the online shopping if there was no one around to tell me what as I go
onSSE2	I could complete the online shopping if I had never used a shopping website
onSSE3	Wherever an organizational change takes place to a shopping website, I'm sure I can handle it
onSSE4	I could complete the online shopping If I had seen someone else using a shopping website before trying it myself

References

1. Gabler, C.B., Reynolds, K.E.: Buy now or buy later: the effects of scarcity and discounts on purchase decisions. J. Mark. Theory Pract. **21**(4), 441–456 (2013)
2. Jeffrey, S.A., Hodge, R.: Factors influencing impulse buying during an online purchase. Electron. Commer. Res. **7**(3–4), 367–379 (2007)
3. Koo, D.-M., Ju, S.-H.: The interactional effects of atmospherics and perceptual curiosity on emotions and online shopping intention. Comput. Hum. Behav. **26**(3), 377–388 (2010)
4. Verhagen, T., van Dolen, W.: The influence of online store beliefs on consumer online impulse buying: a model and empirical application. Inf. Manage. **48**(8), 320–327 (2011)
5. Piron, F.: Defining impulse purchasing. Adv. Consum. Res. **18**, 509–514 (1991)
6. Rook, D.W.: The buying impulse. J. Consum. Res. **14**(2), 189–199 (1987)
7. Park, C.W., Iyer, E.S., Smith, D.C.: The effects of situational factors on in-store grocery shopping behavior: the role of store environment and time available for shopping. J. Consum. Res. **15**(4), 422–433 (1989)
8. Beatty, S.E., Ferrell, M.E.: Impulse buying: modeling its precursors. J. Retail. **74**(2), 169–191 (1998)
9. Parboteeah, D.V., Valacich, J.S., Wells, J.D.: The influence of website characteristics on a consumer's urge to buy impulsively. Inf. Syst. Res. **20**(1), 60–78 (2009)
10. Xiang, L., et al.: Exploring consumers' impulse buying behavior on social commerce platform: the role of parasocial interaction. Int. J. Inf. Manage. **36**(3), 333–347 (2016)
11. Wells, J.D., Parboteeah, V., Valacich, J.S.: Online impulse buying understanding the interplay between consumer impulsiveness and website quality. J. Assoc. Inf. Syst. **12**(1), 32–56 (2011)
12. Adelaar, T., et al.: Effects of media formats on emotions and impulse buying intent. J. Inf. Technol. **18**(4), 247–266 (2003)
13. Wu, I.-L., Chen, K.-W., Chiu, M.-L.: Defining key drivers of online impulse purchasing: a perspective of both impulse shoppers and system users. Int. J. Inf. Manage. **36**(3), 284–296 (2016)
14. Cialdini, R.B.: Influence: Science and Practice, vol. 4. Pearson Education, Boston (2009)
15. Mehrabian, A., Russell, J.A.: An Approach to Environmental Psychology. The MIT Press, Cambridge (1974)
16. Russell, J.A., Mehrabian, A.: Evidence for a three-factor theory of emotions. J. Res. Pers. **11**(3), 273–294 (1977)
17. Russell, J.A., Pratt, G.: A description of the affective quality attributed to environments. J. Pers. Soc. Psychol. **38**(2), 311 (1980)
18. Donovan, R.J., Rossiter, J.R.: Store atmosphere: an environmental psychology approach. J. Retail. **58**(1), 34–57 (1982)
19. Zhu, M., Ratner, R.K.: Scarcity polarizes preferences: the impact on choice among multiple items in a product class. J. Mark. Res. **52**(1), 13–26 (2015)
20. Bagozzi, R.P., Gopinath, M., Nyer, P.U.: The role of emotions in marketing. J. Acad. Mark. Sci. **27**(2), 184–206 (1999)
21. Wu, C.-S., Cheng, F.-F., Yen, D.C.: The atmospheric factors of online storefront environment design: an empirical experiment in Taiwan. Inf. Manage. **45**(7), 493–498 (2008)
22. Malhotra, D.: The desire to win: the effects of competitive arousal on motivation and behavior. Organ. Behav. Hum. Decis. Process. **111**(2), 139–146 (2010)
23. Ku, G., Malhotra, D., Murnighan, J.K.: Towards a competitive arousal model of decision-making: a study of auction fever in live and Internet auctions. Organ. Behav. Hum. Decis. Process. **96**(2), 89–103 (2005)
24. Pribram, K.H., McGuinness, D.: Arousal, activation, and effort in the control of attention. Psychol. Rev. **82**(2), 116 (1975)

25. Adam, M.T.P., Krämer, J., Müller, M.B.: Auction fever! how time pressure and social competition affect bidders' arousal and bids in retail auctions. J. Retail. **91**(3), 468–485 (2015)
26. Maule, A.J., Hockey, G.R.J., Bdzola, L.: Effects of time-pressure on decision-making under uncertainty, changes in affective state and information prexessing strategy. Acta Psychol. **104**, 283–301 (2000)
27. Barone, M.J., Roy, T.: Does exclusivity always pay off? Exclusive price promotions and consumer response. J. Mark. **74**(2), 121–132 (2010)
28. Garretson, J.A., Burton, S.: Highly coupon and sale prone consumers: benefits beyond price savings. J. Advertising Res. **43**(02), 162–172 (2003)
29. Grappi, S., Montanari, F.: The role of social identification and hedonism in affecting tourist re-patronizing behaviours: the case of an Italian festival. Tourism Manage. **32**(5), 1128–1140 (2011)
30. Aggarwal, P., Jun, S.Y., Huh, J.H.: Scarcity messages. J. Advertising **40**(3), 19–30 (2011)
31. Chang, H.-J., Yan, R.-N., Eckman, M.: Moderating effects of situational characteristics on impulse buying. Int. J. Retail Distrib. Manage. **42**(4), 298–314 (2014)
32. Baker, J., Wakefield, K.L.: How consumer shopping orientation influences perceived crowding, excitement, and stress at the mall. J. Acad. Mark. Sci. **40**(6), 791–806 (2011)
33. Eisend, M.: Explaining the impact of scarcity appeals in advertising: the mediating role of perceptions of susceptibility. J. Advertising **37**(3), 33–40 (2008)
34. Lichtenstein, D.R., Ridgway, N.M., Netemeyer, R.G.: Price perceptions and consumer shopping behavior: a field study. J. Mark. Res. **30**(2), 234–245 (1993)
35. Compeau, D.R., Higgins, C.A.: Computer self-efficacy: development of a measure and initial test. MIS Q. **19**(2), 189–211 (1995)
36. Barclay, D., Higgins, C., Thompson, R.: The partial least squares (PLS) approach to causal modeling: Personal computer adoption and use as an illustration. Technol. Stud. **2**(2), 285–309 (1995)

Gamification in E-Commerce

A Survey Based on the Octalysis Framework

Jovana Karać and Martin Stabauer[✉]

Johannes Kepler University, Linz, Austria
{jovana.karac,martin.stabauer}@jku.at

Abstract. Relying on social connections, online recommendation engines and other enabling technologies, consumers have constantly been increasing expectations and seek experiential value in online shopping. Since customers have more places and ways to shop than ever before, retailers – in order to be successful – must find ways to make online shopping pleasant and enjoyable. They have begun to enhance the online customer experience by incorporating game elements into their business processes, making online shopping not just attractive with innovative products and low prices, but also fun. This concept is known as gamification – a trending topic in both academia and business – and generally defined as the use of game thinking and elements in non-game contexts. In our study, we used a state-of-the-art framework (Octalysis) to analyze a sample of retailers from different industries operating on the European market. Based on an octagonal shape, Octalysis comprises 8 core drives that seek to explain the influence of certain gamification techniques on consumer motivation. Our study focused on determining (a) each retailer's position in the octagon and (b) whether retailers in the same sector target the same core drives. Further, we suggest guidelines for academics and practitioners seeking to convert results into more and better ideas for online shopping.

Keywords: Gamification · E-Commerce · Online retailing · Octalysis · User experience

1 Introduction

Customer experience – strategic focus of many modern companies – continues to evolve as consumers rely on their social connections, online recommendation engines, and other enabling technologies to drive their purchasing decisions. Consumers seek utilitarian and hedonic benefits as well as experiential value in online shopping. Companies want to find ways to provide consumers with enjoyment and positive feelings, and seek to ensure a unique e-commerce experience in order to achieve a competitive advantage. Online experience comprises online functionality, information, emotions, cues, stimuli and products or services [3]. As in many other technological trends (e.g., multi device usage) online communities, social commerce, and online social interaction are becoming increasingly

© Springer International Publishing AG 2017
F.F.-H. Nah and C.-H. Tan (Eds.): HCIBGO 2017, PART II, LNCS 10294, pp. 41–54, 2017.
DOI: 10.1007/978-3-319-58484-3_4

relevant in online shopping. Gamification, although not an entirely new concept, has experienced significant growth in popularity in recent years. In academia, gamification is commonly defined as the adoption of game technology, game design methods and game elements outside the games industry. Gamified systems are game-like and draw inspiration from games, but are not games per se [4]. Since gamification makes shopping more attractive and can change human behavior by increasing motivation, engagement and loyalty, retailers have begun to enhance the online customer experience by implementing game elements and mechanics in online shopping with the aim of increasing customer engagement on their sites [13].

This paper is divided into four sections. The first section introduces the background of the given topic by providing important related work, the methodology and a broader explanation of Octalysis framework. The second section includes the conducted survey and its outcomes, followed by the third section, which analyzes the final results more in depth. Lastly, the fourth section outlines the conclusion of this research and suggests potential future research.

1.1   Related Work

The usage of e-commerce platforms positively influences on user's feeling of excitement, and websites should be fun to use to increase the perceived enjoyment of the client [1]. Online customer experience has become an important success factor in retailing [13], and it manifests as an internal and subjective response of the customer to the e-tailer's website [1]. According to Oliver [16], satisfaction refers to a consumer's psychological state while evaluating the surprise during product acquisition or consumption. Gamification in online retail can help to increase consumer engagement and constitutes a conscious reposition of the shopping experience as a form of entertainment [13]. Many online consumers shop for fun because of experiential shopping motives such as experiential behavior and experiential outcome [25]. They are fun seekers and represent an important customer segment, since they tend to be more impulsive and generate higher sales.

Gamification can produce engaging customer experiences by improving the way customers interact with a company or its brand [18]. Understanding how customer engagement in the online shopping process can be improved is therefore a significant factor in creating a successful digital strategy [13]. The authors of [13] proposed implementing the following retail strategies to maximize the benefits of gamification: Gamification should be (a) optional, (b) used to reduce forms of undesirable consumer behavior and to manage price-comparison behavior, and (c) a source of data to generate insights.

Gamification is defined as the application and integration of game design principles and characteristic game mechanics to change behavior in non-gaming concepts. It is a tool that, if designed and implemented in the right manner, can increase engagement (e.g., [4,5,18]).

On the one hand, multidisciplinary efforts to investigate gamification effects on Human Computer Interaction (HCI) are at an early stage, but on the other hand gamification is considered to be an emerging approach to encouraging user engagement, motivation and enjoyment in a non-gaming but technology-mediated environment [22]. Success in gamification is driven by adequate configuration of gamification dynamics, mechanisms and emotions depending on specific player types [18].

We identified the Octalysis framework (see Sect. 1.3) as the most appropriate gamification framework to be applied in our research. It has previously been employed in research in a variety of contexts. Doumanis and Smith [5] used Octalysis as a module of their framework for evaluating gamified mobile applications. Sanchez-Gordon et al. [19] mapped the Octalysis framework using the ISO 10018 standard and described to which extent the core drives of the Octalysis framework are embedded in this ISO standard. Ewais and Alluhaidan [9] employed the Octalysis framework to explore how gamification is being used in mHealth apps. They investigated the twelve highest rated stress management applications and presented an evaluation based on the Octalysis framework. Economou et al. [6] used the framework to evaluate the effectiveness of serious game platform tools in supporting the creation of motivating and engaging educational simulations.

1.2 Methodology

The survey presented here was conducted from October to December 2016 and followed a qualitative approach in order to evaluate which core drives of the Octalysis framework are prevalent in e-commerce companies of different industries in the European market. This survey had been conducted in several phases. Firstly, researches were searching for potential literature sources in order to identify the most appropriate gamification framework for this type of research. Concerning the industry choice,

Eurostat [8] presented a statistical report that listed the most popular e-commerce industries in the EU in 2016: 61% of all e-buyers bought an item from the category apparel and sporting goods, 52% from travel and holiday accommodation, 44% from household goods and toys, 38% bought tickets for events, 33% purchased books, magazines and newspapers. Within each industry, our analysis includes some of the largest enterprises within the European market, (according to turnover), and selected examples of innovative, technology-driven companies that are gaining in importance. A recent study published by the European Parliament estimated that the collaborative economy has the potential to generate revenues of €575 billion across the EU [10].

1.3 Octalysis

According to Yu-kai Chou [2], pioneer and international keynote speaker on gamification and behavioral design, every successful game appeals to certain core drives and motivates people to make decisions and pursue certain activities. He suggests that the term gamification as adopted by the industry be replaced with "human-focus-design" - a process by which human motivation, and not pure efficiency, shapes the design of the system.

Different types of game motivate differently, for instance through inspiration and empowerment or manipulation and obsession. Based on an octagon (see Fig. 1), Octalysis suggests 8 core drives behind every motivation and desired action such that if no core drive is affected, no behavior is provoked and motivation is zero. Note that a hidden, ninth core drive - Sensation - is not placed in the octagon, because, unlike the other eight core drives, it deals with physical feelings.

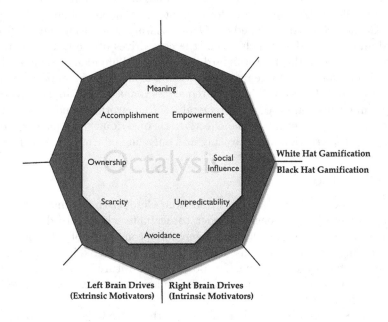

Fig. 1. Octalysis framework based on [2]

We also adopted Chou's general definition of gamification being a combination of game design, game dynamics, motivational psychology, behavioral economics, user experience/user interface, neurobiology, technology platforms and business systems that drive an ROI (Return of Investment). Octalysis defines the following eight core drives [2]:

1. **Epic Meaning and Calling** motivates player by invoking a feeling of doing something on a grand scale, and so s/he devotes a lot of his/her time to creating, maintaining, helping and contributing to project.
2. **Development and Accomplishment** focuses on internal drive and motivation to achieve mastery by making progress, developing various skills and overcoming challenges and involves PBLs (points, badges, leaderboards).
3. **Empowerment of Creativity and Feedback** harnesses users' interest in the process of creating new things and trying different methods and combinations. Players are not only enabled to express their creativity, but also to

see the results of their work in form of the feedback. This is the core drive where the brain simply entertains itself.

4. **Ownership and Possession** motivates users by giving control or ownership of something. Owning and possessing an item motivates consumers to protect or improve it or to collect more.
5. **Social Influence and Relatedness** activities motivate through the influence of others, for instance, by mentorship, social acceptance, competition or envy, companionship and social feedback.
6. **Scarcity and Impatience** involves a commodity that is not immediately or easily obtainable, which increases its desirability.
7. **Unpredictability and Curiosity** is often erroneously thought to be the drive behind points, badges and leaderboards, but refers to being constantly engaged in order to find out what will happen next.
8. **Loss and Avoidance** motivates through the desire to avoid negative effects, consequences or other negative situations.

All core drives, depending on the nature of their motivation, can be viewed either as intrinsic or extrinsic motivators. Extrinsic motivators focus on logic and analytical skills and are shown on the left side of the octagon, while the right side focuses on intrinsic motivators, namely on creativity, self-expression and social dynamics. Self-determination theory distinguishes between two fundamental types of motivation: intrinsic motivation which refers to doing something because it is inherently interesting and enjoyable, and extrinsic motivation, which is doing something in order to achieve a certain outcome [17]. These two types are classified as "Left Brain core drives" and "Right Brain core drives" but the distinction is symbolic and not neurological. This framework further distinguishes between positive (top of the octagon) and negative motivators (bottom of the octagon), which it calls "White Hat" and "Black Hat" gamification, respectively (though the latter is not considered as negative as the name might imply).

2 Survey

This section details the results of our survey, structured according to the industries described in this section. For each industry, we discuss common elements and present company's unique features. Summaries are shown in Figs. 2 and 3, respectively.

2.1 Apparel and Sporting Goods

Fashion is a global business that pushes cultural and social boundaries. Today's growth of the "new economy" affects the structure of the fashion business. This is a fast moving industry where most brands now interact with consumers through their own branded online stores and multi-brand e-tailers. Digital technology gives consumers access to an unprecedented amount of product information. We found that fashion retailers use similar core drives to motivate and engage consumers. **Zalando**[1], for example, has established different channels for different types of customers – Zalando Shop, Zalando Lounge and Zalon – which are particularly good examples of Empowerment and Scarcity. These channels not only let people discover and develop their own styles by connecting them with experienced fashion professionals who choose items from across the range to create individualized styles for everyday or special occasions they also attract customers with exclusive daily offers to which only members have access.

The same elements were found for **Asos**[2], a British retailer that regularly "gamifies" online shopping [13] via fashion bingo, matching celebrities with clothing, and Pinterest competitions to win prizes, which corresponds to both Accomplishment and Empowerment. Aiming to promote positive body images, Asos invites all customers to post images of themselves wearing their purchases under the hashtag #AsSeenOnMe. Using style advice blogs, recommendations, reviews and outfit building, this company encourages its customers to share links to clothes on social media, which falls within the Social Influence and Relatedness core drive. Asos' "Earn While You Shop", three-level reward list available to UK customers only is an example of Unpredictability and Curiosity, while Zalando customers earn e-points, which they can exchange for rewards (available just in United Kingdom and Ireland).

In the cases of single-brand retailers **H&M**[3] and **Marks & Spencer**[4], Social Influence dominates. Aside from offering the Dressing Room application on their official H&M website, where customer can easily select fashion pieces, choose a virtual model and try on the complete outfit before deciding what to buy, H&M also gamifies in other ways: Recall, for example, their well-known campaign featuring David Beckham statues erected in several cities in the USA in which people were able to win prizes by photographing themselves with the statue and sharing them on Instagram. This campaign involved several embedded core drives, such as Accomplishment, Empowerment and Unpredictability. Similar to H&M Dressing Room, Marks & Spencer also has clever tools for making online purchase more interesting: Shapewear Finder, Style Advisor and "Cook with M&S" app. **Zara**[5], the best known brand in the Spanish Inditex group, does not feature strong game elements but makes cautious use of the Social Influence core drive.

2.2 Travel and Holiday Accommodation

The Internet has become a major distribution channel for the hotel industry. Travelers embrace the Internet as their primary means of locating and booking accommodation, making other travel arrangements and learning about making smart online decisions for the best rate possible. Recommender systems are

---

[1] www.zalando.com.
[2] www.asos.com.
[3] www.hm.com.
[4] www.marksandspencer.com.
[5] www.zara.com.

commonly defined as applications which e-commerce sites increasingly exploit to suggest products and provide consumers with information that facilitates their decision-making processes (e.g., [20,21]). New forms of sharing have reached critical mass in recent years, creating new ways of providing goods and services, and opportunities for "connected consumption" and "collaborative consumption" [14].

TripAdvisor[6] is an interactive forum with various game mechanics that motivate travelers to upload reviews and collect not only points and badge, but also votes and compliments from other users who found their reviews useful. This company awards active travelers and businesses with various badges, thereby exploiting the Development and Accomplishment core drive. Further, the Facebook social graph enables users to filter for and read Trip Advisor content created by their Facebook friends only [23]; this functionality is a good example of employing Social Influence and Relatedness. The same core drives are exploited in the case of **Booking.com**[7], where star ratings in combination with reviews can bring a Guest Review award for eligible partners. Inviting customers to submit their favorite summer photos and turning them into animated GIFs was a contest that invoked motivators within the Empowerment and Creativity drives. Prominently displayed "Last chance options" and "time remaining" for bookings motivate travelers through Scarcity to make a purchase and not miss the last chance or best offer.

In the case of **Airbnb**[8], each accommodation is unique, which can be interpreted as an example of exclusivity. This company has gained popularity among researchers and practitioners in recent years, especially viewed through the lens of disruptive innovation theory, sharing economy, and its great impact on the hotel industry (e.g.,[11,26]). It motivates users not only by offering Super-Host badges, travel coupons, priority support and product exclusiveness but also with two-sided reviews as a significant drive for consumer behavior. When users are unsure about the trustworthiness of a provider, they can ask other users for recommendations, which builds trust and reputation among users – an important factor in peer-to-peer systems. Even the presence of the provider's photo has an impact on the decision-making of potential guests [7]. For Airbnb, **Uber**[9] and **BlaBlaCar**[10] building trust is important to success since they do not serve one base of customers alone, but connect buyers and sellers or service providers and customers while ensuring that users have a positive experience. This excellent example of employing Epic Meaning & Calling can be observed in the Airbnb Community Centre, which connects different hosts and inspires people to act, enabling them to help each other, share experiences, ask for advice and above all, feel great while doing this.

---

[6] www.tripadvisor.com.
[7] www.booking.com.
[8] www.airbnb.com.
[9] www.uber.com.
[10] www.blablacar.com.

BlaBlaCar encourages trust-building in its online community by awarding Superhero badges to users who complete their BlaBlaCar profiles, increase their experience levels and leave ratings. In addition to Social Influence and Relatedness, this community also harnesses the Epic Meaning and Calling core drive, as each community member can be "superhero" of trust and contribute not only to company growth and reputation, but, above all, to trust among peers. Every member in the community has an experience level that evolves with time and increasing activity, depending on certain rules. Uber offers different services for different user groups, and has a reward program for active and high-performing drivers: This includes Power Driver Plus awards, congratulations on reaching a specific number of journey or covering specific distances, Six-Star Award contest, in which both drivers and passengers who leave ratings can win.

2.3   Household Items and Toys

Buying furniture involves a complex decision-making process with multiple constraints such as budget, available space and time disposal of currently usable items and fit to existing furniture and lifestyle. The ability for customers to test the physical comfort of an item is essential.

Independent of selling to consumers directly, company websites need to provide information [15]. Ikea[11] has an online showroom that combines music, photography and creativity, and applications such as the Ikea Home Planner let shoppers position virtual Ikea furniture in their homes, so they can see how it looks and fits in the space they have available. This activity emphasises "Play" and therefore falls within the Empowerment core drive. The community photo-sharing website "Share Space" enables users to upload photos of their living space, find and share inspiration comment, and save the photos they like most. Every week Ikea design experts evaluate the photos based on creative usage of design elements, furniture arrangement, innovative ideas and achieving expensive looks on a small budget to select one room as their "Pick of the Week" which is displayed on the Share Space homepage[12], and the user receives a "Pick of the Week" badge.

Additionally, users and their rooms can be acknowledged as Space Sharers, Ikea Fans, Ikea Super Fans, Admired Spaces or Exceptional Spaces, respectively, which reflects several core drives at the same time: Accomplishment, Empowerment and Social Influence. Competitions for children that involves designing and creating toys focus on children's right to play and develop. For every toy, game, book and selected children's furniture sold, the IKEA Foundation donates $1 to support child development, thereby showing strong Epic Meaning and Calling. The Ikea Family loyalty program, in contrast, is an example of Ownership and Unpredictability, as it offers benefits such as free drinks in the restaurant, an extra 10% off sale prices, free product insurance and chance to win Ikea gift cards.

---

[11] www.ikea.com.

[12] www.theshare-space.com.

Danish home retailer **Jysk**[13] gives each member resident in Canada a monthly chance to win CDN$500 gift card, thus motivating via Scarcity and Unpredictability. This company offers prizes in a variety of contests relating to member birthdays, review writing and subscribing to a newsletter.

In the case of the UK-based retailer **Argos**, Scarcity and Impatience are triggered by Argos Clearance, a bargain and sale section of the website, where new and refurbished Argos products are available for a limited time. Likewise, **XXXLutz**[14] has exclusive offers time-limited online. This company uses a 5-star scoring system where customers who are XXXL Community members can evaluate products. It also offers online bargain options and a 3D kitchen planner. The red chair is a trademark of this company but also charity organization committed in helping people and organizations lacking food, medicine and education. Though Epic Meaning and Calling drive lies in challenge of believability, furniture seller **Otto Group**[15] affirms the correctness of its customers' choice by reporting regularly on the importance of sustainable forestry and responsible handling of timber for manufacturing, thus incorporating a global mission into their offerings.

2.4   Books, Magazines, Newspapers; Tickets for Events

In our survey, we combined these two industries. Leading French book retailer **FNAC**[16] and German book store **Thalia**[17] provide their members with advantages and benefits such as special discounts, loyalty bonus, exclusive offers and invitations to cultural events. FNAC offers various themed gift e-cards, for instance, Christmas and Anniversary, and gift e-cards with a range of values. **Relay**[18] provides three levels of subscription packages where customer can choose which digital libraries they want to access. **Eventim**[19], an event and ticket agent, uses ticket alert options for fans and customers and fun-report-like reviews and a star scoring system. Ticket Alarm enables fans to sign up for updates and news on particular artists or events.

Companies in this category motivate mainly through loyalty programs and special discounts. Similar marketing tools were found for all companies listed in this section, and a deeper evaluation revealed that they most closely relate to Ownership and Social Influence. As only a few gamification elements are used in this category, these companies are shown outside the octagon in Fig. 2 and in a very central place of the radar diagram in Fig. 3, respectively. Amazon[20] – the best known company in this category – was not taken into consideration,

---

[13] www.jysk.com.
[14] www.xxxlutz.at.
[15] www.otto.de.
[16] www.fnac.com.
[17] www.thalia.at.
[18] www.relay.com.
[19] www.eventim.de.
[20] www.amazon.com.

since it has already been described in various publications and also been used as an example to explain several core drives of the Octalysis framework [2].

3   Discussion

This paper has identified motivators for online purchase decisions shared within and between a variety of different industries. There are certain similarities between companies within the same industry, but also across different industries. Strong Epic Meaning & Calling is employed in peer-to-peer companies from the travel and accommodation category. Many good business ideas arise when a personal frustration triggers a problem-solving strategy, as in the cases of Airbnb, Uber and BlablaCar.

These companies make heavy use of "storytelling" by connecting, involving and inspiring users to share their personal experience and make them proud of contributing to the community. The best examples of this are community centers, which provide users with a sense of belonging, personal relatedness, feelings of acceptance, and opportunities to share success stories. Companies from the travel and accommodation category mostly rely on motivators within Epic Meaning and Calling, not just in the sense of belonging but also in the sense of increasing trust between users, and connecting actions with environmental sustainability (e.g., Uber and BlablaCar). The same core drive could be found in companies from household and furniture items category. They underline importance of protecting the nature, giving a special attention to charity or supporting children's development and learning. Various Scarcity and Impatience motivators – accommodation in high demand, displaying the number of remaining rooms or people who are currently looking at the same accommodation – encourage users to take up certain offers to avoid missing the last chance. In the case of fashion companies, Scarcity and Impatience motivators are also strongly present but combined with Social Influence. People shop, buy and choose brands because of how it makes them feel. In the fashion industry, purchase decisions involve not only the action of buying garments, but also buying a style. Online fashion shopping therefore essentially relies on buying an image based on a photo. For this reason, e-tailers encourage their customers to share photos on social networks to win prizes. In this industry, the most highly developed motivators belong to the Accomplishment, Empowerment and Social Influence core drives.

In addition to effective filters that help to narrow down searches, fashion sites employ interactive features and encourage online reviews, as they play an important role in purchasing decisions, (see e.g., [12, 24, 27]). One-sided reviews or two-sided reviews on a scale from 1–5 stars are found for each company in our survey. Of course, companies encourage their customers with a variety of approaches to participate in interactive forums, leave reviews, ask questions or rate products. Companies from the travel and accommodation industry motivate users by giving them the opportunity to win badges, awards or special discounts. Ikea also awards interactive customers on its Share Space platform with "kudos" for achievements; for instance when a room has been saved by 5 or 25 people,

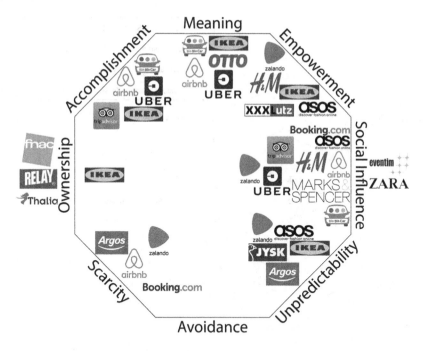

Fig. 2. Results of the survey

users receive the award "Admired Space" and "Exceptional Space", respectively. Bookstore websites do not apply particularly strong game elements to make purchases more entertaining.

Figure 2 summarizes the results: We conclude that most the commonly used motivators are positive, and that the majority of companies uses techniques that employ intrinsic motivators. Although Social Influence has the power of duality when combined with other motivators from the top of the octagon, this drive constitutes a strong positive force, which can be seen in the fashion and travel and accommodation industries. The dominance of the Right-Brain core drives is evident.

In Fig. 3, the surveyed industries and the core drives' distribution across the industries are graphed. The scale from 0 to 5 represents the level of core drive usage in the each industry, where 0 means not presented at all and 5 means high usage. The diagram shows that Ownership, Scarcity, Unpredictability and Avoidance are not commonly used in marked contrast with the other drives in the octagon. For example, Social Influence is rated with 5 points for both the fashion industry and the travel and accommodation industry, whereas Meaning is very heavily used in the travel and accommodation industry and a point less in the household items and toys industry.

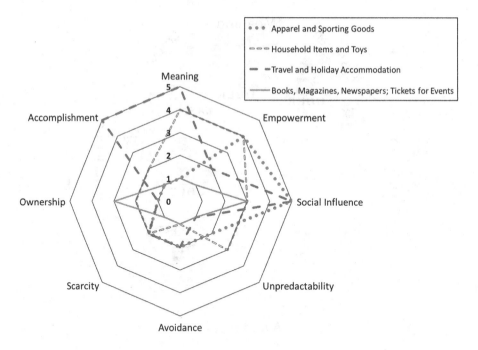

Fig. 3. Classification of industries

4   Conclusions and Future Work

The objective of this work was to investigate how companies from different retail industries use game elements and techniques to motivate and engage their online customers in online purchase. Octalysis was applied as a framework to evaluate and compare existing motivators in a variety of companies and industries. Various core drives were found in the selected companies which demonstrates that Octalysis framework was an adequate and suitable for this task. With the exception of the industries concerned with books, magazines and newspapers and tickets for events, all companies surveyed make strong use of at least one gamification element, thus triggering at least one core drive. Our analysis included 20 companies from 5 different industries; future research could include a greater sample of industries in order to identify similarities and differences among different industrial sectors. Also, a focus on more companies within just one industry could confirm our preliminary results and bring better understanding of the gamified mechanisms and techniques within that industry. Even though some companies use the same core drives, there is a need to highlight the differences in quality (variety of engaging tools and mechanisms) and the power of these drives. One implication for the industry is thus to acquire a deeper understanding of their customers' needs in order to implement game elements as effectively as possible while resisting the temptation to implement a game element because it appears fashionable.

Acknowledgment. This research was funded in part by the Upper Austrian government within the PhD program "Digital Business International", a joint initiative of Johannes Kepler University Linz and the University of Applied Sciences Upper Austria.

References

1. Bilgihan, A., Kandampully, J., (Christina) Zhang, T.: Towards a unified customer experience in online shopping environments: antecedents and outcomes. Int. J. Qual. Serv. Sci. **8**(1), 102–119 (2016)
2. Chou, Y.-K.: Actionable Gamification - Beyond Points, Badges, and Leaderboards. Octalysis Media (2015)
3. Constantinides, E.: Influencing the online consumers's behavior: the Web experience. Internet Res. **14**(2), 111–126 (2004)
4. Deterding, S., Dixon, D., Khaled, R., Nacke, L.: From game design elements to gamefulness: defining "gamification". In: Proceedings of the 15th International Academic MindTrek Conference: Envisioning Future Media Environments, MindTrek 2011, pp. 9–15 (2011)
5. Doumanis, I., Smith, S.: A framework for research in gamified mobile guide applications using embodied conversational agents (ECAs). Int. J. Serious Games **2**(3), 21–40 (2015)
6. Economou, D., Doumanis, I., Pedersen, F., Kathrani, P., Mentzelopoulos, M., Bouki, V.: Evaluation of a dynamic role-playing platform for simulations based on octalysis gamification framework. In: Workshop Proceedings of the 11th International Conference on Intelligent Environments (2015)
7. Ert, E., Fleischer, A., Magen, N.: Trust, reputation in the sharing economy: the role of personal photos in Airbnb. Tourism Manage. **55**, 62–73 (2016)
8. Eurostat: E-commerce statistics for individuals (2016). http://ec.europa.eu/eurostat/statistics-explained/index.php/E-commerce_statistics_for_individuals
9. Ewais, S., Alluhaidan, A.: Classification of stress management mHealth apps based on octalysis framework. In: Twenty-First Americas Conference on Information Systems, Puerto Rico (2015)
10. Goudin, P.: The cost of Non-Europe in the Sharing Economy; Economic. Social and Legal Challenges and Opportunities. Technical report, European Parliamentary Research Service (2016)
11. Guttentag, D.: Airbnb: disruptive innovation and the rise of an informal tourism accommodation sector. Curr. Issues Tourism **18**(12), 1192–1217 (2013)
12. Hu, N., Liu, L., Zhang, J.J.: Do online reviews affect product sales? The role of reviewer characteristics and temporal effects. Inf. Technol. Manage. **9**(3), 201–214 (2008)
13. Insley, V., Nunan, D.: Gamification and the online retail experience. Int. J. Retail Distrib. Manage. **42**, 340–351 (2013)
14. Schor, J.B., Fitzmaurice, C.J.: Collaborating connecting: the emergence of the sharing economy. In: Handbook of Research on Sustainable Consumption. Edward Elgar Publishing Inc. (2015)
15. Oh, H., Yoon, S.-Y., Hawley, J.: What virtual reality can offer to the furniture industry. J. Text. Apparel Technol. Manage. **4**(1), 1–17 (2004)
16. Oliver, R.L.: Emotional expression in the satisfaction response. Satisfaction: A behavioral perspective on the consumer. McGraw-Hill, New York (1997)

17. Rayan, R.M., Deci, E.L.: Self-determination theory and the facilitation of intrinsic motivation, social development and well-being. Am. Psychol. Assoc. **55**, 68–78 (2000)
18. Robson, K., Plangger, K., Kietzmann, J.H., McCarthy, I., Pitt, L.: Game on: engaging customers and employees through gamification. Bus. Horiz. **59**(1), 29–36 (2016)
19. Sanchez-Gordón, M.-L., Colomo-Palacios, R., Herranz, E.: Gamification and human factors in quality management systems: mapping from octalysis framework to ISO 10018. In: Kreiner, C., O'Connor, R.V., Poth, A., Messnarz, R. (eds.) EuroSPI 2016. CCIS, vol. 633, pp. 234–241. Springer, Cham (2016). doi:10.1007/978-3-319-44817-6_19
20. Sarwar, B.M., Karypis, G., Konstan, J.A., Riedl, J.T.: Application of dimensionality reduction in recommender system - a case study. Minnesota University Minneapolis, Department of Computer Science (2000)
21. Schafer, J.B., Konstan, J.A., Riedl, J.: E-commerce recommendation applications. Data Min. Knowl. Disc. **5**, 115–153 (2001)
22. Seaborn, K.: Gamification in theory, action: a survey. Int. J. Hum.-Comput. Stud. **74**, 14–31 (2015)
23. Sigala, M.: The application, impact of gamification funware on trip planning and experiences: the case of TripAdvisor's funware. Electron Markets **25**(3), 189–209 (2015)
24. Sparks, B.A., Browning, V.: The impact of online reviews on hotel booking intentions and perception of trust. Tourism Manage. **32**, 1310–1323 (2010)
25. Wolfinbarger, M., Gilly, M.C.: Shopping online for freedom, control and fun. Calif. Manage. Rev. **43**, 34–55 (2001)
26. Zervas, G., Proserpio, D., Byers, J.W.: The rise of the sharing economy: estimating the impact of airbnb on hotel industry. Technical report, Boston University School of Management (2016)
27. Zhu, F., Zhang, X.M.: Impact of online consumer reviews on sales: the moderating role of product and consumer characteristics. J. Mark. **74**, 133–148 (2010)

Priming and Context Effects of Banner Ads on Consumer Based Brand Equity: A Pilot Study

Harald Kindermann[(✉)]

University of Applied Sciences Upper Austria,
Wehrgrabengasse 1-3, 4400 Steyr, Austria
harald.kindermann@fh-steyr.at

Abstract. Banner advertising is usually placed on suitable, highly frequented websites. The extent to which the brand of a banner ad and the brand of the website influence each other, has not yet been sufficiently investigated. This article provides initial results based on a pilot study which reveals that a positively perceived website can shift a negative banner perception. Furthermore, it is shown that a congruence between banner ad and the website plays an important role. Congruent content supports each other and noncongruent content counteracts the intended advertising effect. Although the study cannot yet be considered as conclusive, the results have the potential to inform entrepreneurial practice on how and where ads should be placed.

Keywords: Context effect · Assimilation and contrast effects · Congruency · Priming · Banner

1 Introduction

Banner advertisements, namely the advertising on websites, are indisputably important and often part of a company's communication mix. The main purpose of display advertising is to deliver general advertisements and brand messages to site visitors. A current study suggests that digital ads have high growth rates if compared with all advertising channels throughout the world. Particularly boosted by the considerable rise of cost efficiency-driven strategies, banner ad expenditures are forecasted to increase by +12.4% in 2016 and +9.6% in 2017 [1]. So, given that banner ad investment will increase, the effectiveness of banner advertising is extremely important for both advertising practitioners and for academics [2]. For example, a recent article focusing on practitioners shows that the recommendations of business consultants are misleading given that they do not adequately capture the effect of banners [3].

In order to evaluate the effectiveness of banner ads, companies usually fall back on click-through rates (CTR). In addition, they may capture constructs like attention, recall, recognition, etc., or/and they measure some long-term communication effects, such as attitude changes [4, 5]. However, research on how banners influence the effectiveness is still in its early stage [2]. At the same time, a number of studies came to controversial empirical results. Some of these are exemplified in the following section.

© Springer International Publishing AG 2017
F.F.-H. Nah and C.-H. Tan (Eds.): HCIBGO 2017, PART II, LNCS 10294, pp. 55–70, 2017.
DOI: 10.1007/978-3-319-58484-3_5

Based on the observation that people searching for specific information on the web tend to ignore even large, colorful banners that are clearly distinguished from other items on a website, a banner blindness view was identified [6]. This tenet is backed inter alia by the observation of Spool et al. [7] that participants in a usability test largely overlooked banners. Even ads which were partly animated were largely ignored by participants. In this context, subjects had obviously learned to ignore banner ads while searching for information. In this vein, if assuming that the CTR is an appropriate measure to capture the effectiveness of banners, everything has to be done to ensure that the visitor's attention is directed towards the banner. Researchers who follow this approach argue that banner ads must be designed with bright colors, they should be animated and should have an impressive size [8, 9]. This view, however, is not supported by Burke et al. and Bayles [10, 11]. Their results demonstrate that such banner attributes do not increase either the recall or the recognition. Rather it was shown that participants had significantly worse memory for the animated banners than for the static ones [10]. On the other hand, some studies provided evidence for a positive advertising effect of animated banners in terms of attention, recall, recognition and CTR. Li and Bukovac (1999) show that animated banner ads resulted in quicker response times and in better recall. Additionally, they found that larger banner ads lead to a better comprehension and a higher CTR in comparison to small banner ads [12]. The study by Schweiger and Reisbeck (1999) also show that the recognition rate of animated banners is higher in comparison to static ads [13].

Research by Pagendarm and Schaumburg (2001) may have the potential to reveal some of these inconsistent findings concerning the effect of animation on banner recognition. They examined whether the user mode - "aimless browsing" versus "goal directed searching" - moderates banner effectiveness. In a recall and recognition test, the aimless browsing subjects performed significantly better than goal directed searching subjects [14]. It is possible to misinterpret the findings as Hamborg [4] did by assuming that banner ads have little or no impact if users are in an information-seeking mode. It is claimed here that this only olds true if the measure of the effectiveness focuses on consciously perceived objects. In a study by Kindermann it was revealed that even unconsciously perceived banners have an effect on consumers [15]. In an empirical study on the impact on banner ads, it was shown that the priming effect triggers already existing attitudes towards the advertised brands. If these attitudes are positive or the advertised brands are unknown, then a banner ad will promote the advertiser's intended impact on purchase intention. If, however, the initial attitudes are negative, then the buying intention will be negatively affected by the banner ad [15]. These results do not depend on whether the banner ad was perceived consciously or completely ignored. Taking all these findings into account, it becomes obvious that many, frequently ignored factors, influence how banners affect a target group. Priming is often a factor that is seriously undervalued [15]. Therefore, it is of utmost importance to take priming and related effects into account to understand the impact of banner ads holistically. One crucial related aspect is the context effect. Basically, a context effect describes the influence of contextual information on one's assessment of a stimulus. The impact of the context effect is considered to be part of top-down evaluation (= existing attitudes) of certain stimuli. This effect can impact our daily lives in many ways in terms of word recognition, learning abilities, memory, and object assessment

[16, 17]. As mentioned before, the assessment of an object is dependent on already existing attitudes, but the variance of attitudes towards objects influence each other. This may happen in such ways that the existing attitudes either converge (= assimilation effect) or diverge (= contrast effect).

Such contrast effects are omnipresent in human perception and largely influence the assessments of objects. An object, for example, appears heavier when compared to a light one, or lighter when it is contrasted with a heavy object. The attractiveness of an alternative can be significantly increased if it is compared to a similar but poorer alternative and vice versa [18]. This contrast effect also holds true for the assessment of physical attractiveness of people [19, 20]. On the other hand, a study by Meyers-Levy et al. demonstrates an assimilation effect [21]. This research shows that the comfort level of the floor that shoppers stand on is crucial. When reviewing products the perception of the product's quality is affected and can either lead to higher perceived quality if the floor is comfortable or lower perceived quality if it is uncomfortable [21].

A further assimilation effect was demonstrated by Sigall and Landy [22], which, when superficially compared to the results of the previously discussed studies by Kenrick and Gutierres, show contradicting results. They showed that the comparison of an averagely attractive person with a highly attractive one leads to an increased perception of attractiveness of the average person. The assimilation of the judgment only occurs when the subjects are perceived as acquainted in some way, for instance if they belong to the same social category. If these examples of different context effects[1] are applied to the effect of banner advertising, then different assumptions can be derived as to how powerful the context effect is. First of all, the banner advertisement and the webpage, where the banner is placed, will influence each other. If an assimilation occurs, a positively perceived banner will positively influence the assessment of the webpage. However, according to Landy and Sigall, this assimilation effect may only occur if the banner and the webpage are perceived in some way as acquainted, i.e. congruent, thus belonging to the same category. In the event of economic products, the question of how a similarity can be established is a pressing one. In the author's opinion, this may be created when the ad product and webpage are of similar product categories. For example, when a banner for drills is displayed on a web shop that offers tools. In such a case, the banner and the website are congruent. But even if congruence can be assumed, the estimation of causality seems unclear. It can be assumed that the opinion of a webpage affects the banner evaluation, or that the banner changes the assessment of the webpage. Both directions are ultimately conceivable. Referring to the social judgment theory [23], the respective involvement of the assessors plays a vital role in the change of attitude. Following this theory, the brand with the high involvement is the independent factor. In this case, the person already as a comparatively stable opinion, and is also ready to defend this opinion. This is described as a high ego involvement [24].

---

[1] The shortly described assimilation effect is a frequently observed bias in evaluating a context stimulus. Hence, the assimilation effect can be considered as a part of the more general context effect. The same holds true for the contrast effect.

In line with this argumentation, the following assumption can be made. Since this is a pilot study, it is not the author's intention to formulate hypotheses.

Assumption 1: If objects - webpages and banners - do not belong to a related category and are not expected to appear together, an assimilation effect will only occur if the banner is integrated into the text of the webpage and not, as expected, on the right hand side. This effect occurs, in particular, on websites that report news (e.g. broadcasting companies).

Another point is the congruency between webpages and banner ads. According to the congruity hypothesis, placing congruent ads improves attitudes and buying intentions [25–28]. A possible explanation for this effect may lie in congruent information which increases the processing fluidity [29, 30]. This ultimately results in a cognitive relief [31, 32]. For further information of the underlying relationships see for instance Furnham et al. (2002), Čech (1989), Lull and Bushman (2015), Moore et al. (2005) [25–28]. If these coherences are applied to the question of congruency, then the above mentioned congruence between the webpage and banner advertising plays a decisive role. In the following a further assumption is formulated:

Assumption 2: If a banner is placed on a product-specific web shop, the perceived congruence between the web-shop and the banner plays a significant role. As an example of congruent advertising, a web shop for tools may be applicable, where banners are placed for drills. In this regard, it may not be congruent if lingerie advertising is placed instead of a drill banner. This non-congruence may then have a negative effect on the banner or/and the brand of the web-shop.

2 Methodology

In order to test these assumptions, a pilot study was conducted. For this purpose, a sufficient number of suitable brands from both, web-pages and banner brands, had to be found. A research project, conducted in 2014, was used in order to be able to make an appropriate selection out of all the possible brands. This project aimed to establish a new measurement approach for the consumer based brand equity [33]. Out of the 250 evaluated brands, those brands were selected which run a webpage or a web-shop, on which banners can be placed (e.g. broadcasting companies) and brands which use banner advertisings. Additionally, those brands were chosen which were judged to be particularly negative or particularly positive. With these selection criteria in mind, the brand selection shown in Table 1 was made.

As can be seen in Table 1, it was impossible to find really positively or negatively judged brands. Hence, to be able to confirm Assumption 1 the following brands were selected: "Der Standard", a brand of an Austrian newspaper with a mean value of 1.61, and the most negatively identified brand "Kotte&Zeller" with a mean value of −1.47, were chosen.

To check Assumption 2, a web-shop for tools ("Zgonc"; mean value = 0.19) and a web-shop for cosmetic products (DM", mean value = 1.33) were selected. Banners

Table 1. The selected brands [Scale: +3 = I like it very much" to "−3 = I don't like it at all]

Brand	Mean	SD	Function
Bosch	1.20	1.32	Banner
Intimissimi	1.42	1.01	Banner
Kotte&Zeller	−1.47	1.68	Banner
Lugner City	−0.92	1.24	Banner
Nivea	1.32	1.38	Banner
der Standard	1.61	1.52	Webpage
DM	1.33	1.34	Web-shop
News	0.03	1.33	Webpage
Zgnoc	0.19	1.42	Web-shop

were placed on the website of these two web-shops as an intervention, once a congruent and once non-congruent banner were placed (see Fig. 2).

3 Empirical Results

Altogether 267 subjects completed the three questionnaires (group1 = 87/group2 = 87/control group = 93). As expected, there was no significant difference in age between these groups (group1 = 25.91/−group2 = 26.28/control group = 26.03; p = 0.932). The same holds true for gender (chi-square test: p = 0.351).

All following results were calculated by means of a one-way between subjects' ANOVA. The spontaneous "liking of a brand" serves as the depended variable. In this respect, the following question was asked: "Please indicate spontaneously how much you like this brand." [Response scale: "+3 = I like it very much" to "−3 = I don't like it at all"]. To reveal any significant differences between all three groups, Fisher's least significant difference (LSD) was calculated post hoc.

3.1 Assumption 1 - Assimilation Effect

Figure 3 in the appendix shows the stimuli used in group 1, group 2, and in the control group in detail. The results of this experimental part (part 1) are summarized in Table 2. It appears that the brand "Kotte&Zeller" benefits from the generally more positively perceived brand "der Standard". The significant difference between the control group and group 2 may be explained by the integration into the webpage, which further strengthens the supposed assimilation effect. Overall, the comparatively bad value of the brand "Kotte&Zeller" is being improved by the positive perception of the website. When it is integrated into the webpage, it was found that the assessment improved significantly.

Experimental part 2 shows the same tendency (see Fig. 4 and the results in Table 3). Here, too, the rather negatively perceived brand "Lugner City" is assimilated by the somewhat positively perceived webpage of "News" and thus more positively judged. One further aspect is still worth mentioning: when the banner is integrated into the webpage, this integration seems to have a negative effect on the perception of the webpage in contrast to part 1 of the experiment. An explanation of this effect could be found in the different ego involvement towards the brands "der Standard" and "News". It can be assumed that this is due to the worse a priori assessment of "News" when comparing it to "der Standard". Although this aspect was taken into account in the survey, it was impossible to gain valid data due to an insufficiently large sample size[2].

3.2   Assumption 2 - Congruency

According to Assumption 2, the perception of a website and a placed banner is reduced if the content of these two brands is not perceived congruently. In order to examine this assumption,

- a banner of a lingerie brand ("Intimissimi") was placed in a web-shop for tools (noncongruent; see Fig. 5) and
- a banner of a drill ("Bosch") was placed in the same web-shop for tools (congruent, see Fig. 6) and
- the same banner of a drill was placed in a web-shop for cosmetics (noncongruent, see Fig. 7) and
- a banner of a hygiene brand ("Nivea") was placed in the same web-shop for cosmetics (congruent; see Fig. 8).

All these versions were presented to and assessed by different groups. In addition, all these mentioned brands were presented to and assessed by a control group for means of comparison.

Once again, the assumed tendency was revealed: If the banner and the webpage are congruent in terms of content, it has a positive effect on the assessment of both brands. If, on the other hand, the brands are noncongruent, then the effect is negative. Even if the results are not significant, the tendency is clearly visible (see Tables 4, 5, 6 and 7). An explanation for this effect can be found in cortical relief.

4   Discussion and Limitations

The focus of this pilot study was to identify the interaction between banner advertising and the perception of the corresponding website. The theoretical foundation can be derived, among other things, from the context effect or the assimilation and contrast theory. The results show a tendency towards the presumed relationship, although most results are not significant. Due to the variety of different stimuli and the consistent tendency, however, it can be assumed that these results are not accidental. Rather, it can be suggested that these preliminary findings are applicable to real-time corporate

---

[2] If from the total number of subjects, those are selected who have a positive opinion of the Brand "News", then only 28 people remain for all three groups. The clear majority (66.1%) have a neutral opinion about this brand. This leads to the assumption that they do not have a high degree of involvement towards this brand.

settings. With a larger sample size, more significant results can be yielded. Further, the influence of ego involvement could not be taken into account. Data show that the subjects have a highly homogeneous involvement towards the selected brands. This aspect could not be investigated as initially planned. It is therefore recommended that these aspects be explored in more detail in future studies.

Yet the following points can be derived even from the small pilot study:

- When placed on a positive website, a negatively perceived banner gains attractiveness. For companies it may therefore be advisable to look for platforms, which are particularly popular.
- Banner ads should be placed in product-specific web-shops only if they are perceived congruently. This finding may also be applicable to conventional advertising media such as print ads or leaflets. Thus, with regard to congruency, advertisements should use stimuli that are as congruent as possible, so that it is congruently perceived. For example, it would not be advisable to place scantily dressed models on advertisements for tools (e.g. Fig. 1). It is also important to ensure that the ad is placed in a congruent medium. For more details, see the study by Lull et al. [27].

Fig. 1. Example – non-congruent ad

Appendix

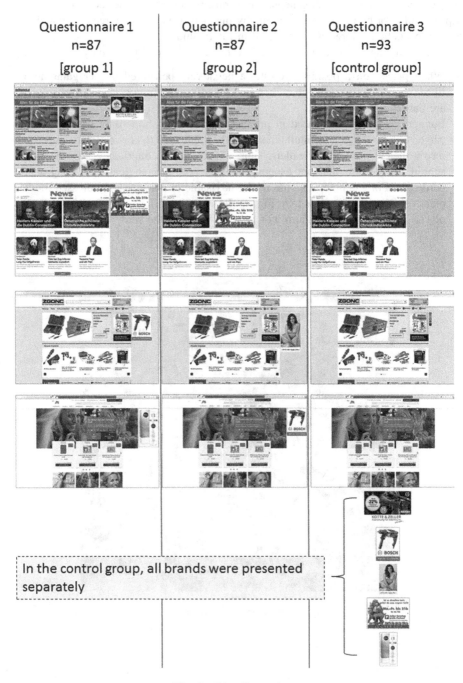

Fig. 2. Stimuli-overview

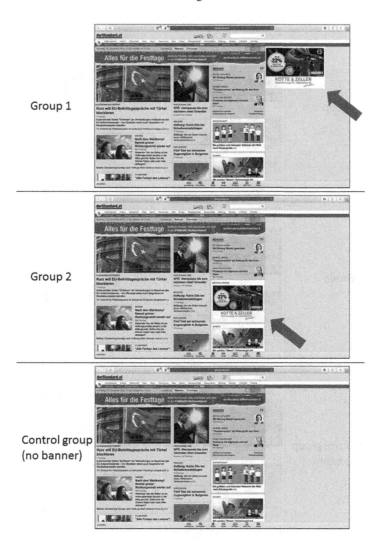

Fig. 3. Assimilation effect – stimuli of part 1 within the experiment

Table 2. Mean values of part 1; Post Hoc: LSD

Brand	Group 1	Control group	p-value	Group 2	Control group	p-value
	n = 87	n = 93		n = 87	n = 93	
Der Standard	1.31	1.38	0.734	1.45	1.38	0.712
Kotte	−1.24	−1.42	0.396	−0.62	−1.42	0.000

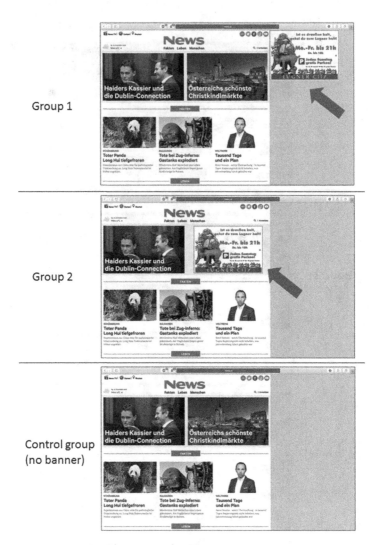

Group 1

Group 2

Control group
(no banner)

Fig. 4. Assimilation effect – stimuli of part 2

Table 3. Mean values of experiment 2; Post Hoc: LSD

Brand	Group 1 n = 87	Control group n = 93	p-value	Group 2 n = 87	Control group n = 93	p-value
News	0.00	−0.10	0.609	−0.39	−0.10	0.121
Lugner City	−1.14	−1.76	0.001	−1.51	−1.76	0.170

Group 2

Control group
(no banner)

Fig. 5. Congruency – stimuli of part 3

Table 4. Mean values of experiment 3; Post Hoc: LSD

Brand	Group 2	Control group	p-value
	n = 87	n = 93	
Zgonc	−0.15	0.10	0.156
Intimissimi	1.05	1.25	0.250

Group 1

Control group
(no banner)

Fig. 6. Congruency – stimuli of part 4

Table 5. Mean values of experiment 4; Post Hoc: LSD

Brand	Group 1	Control group	p-value
	n = 87	n = 93	
Zgonc	0.15	0.10	0.156
Bosch	1.23	1.05	0.001

Group 2

Control group
(no banner)

Fig. 7. Congruency – stimuli of part 5

Table 6. Mean values of experiment 5; Post Hoc: LSD

Brand	Group 2	Control group	p-value
	n = 87	n = 93	
DM	1.63	1.75	0.443
Bosch	0.55	1.05	0.001

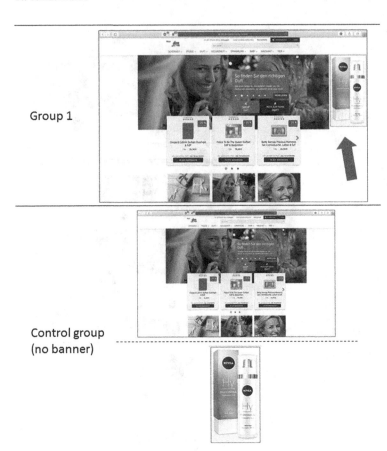

Group 1

Control group
(no banner)

Fig. 8. Congruency – stimuli of part 6

Table 7. Mean values of experiment 6; Post Hoc: LSD

Brand	Group 1	Control group	p-value
	n = 87	n = 93	
DM	1.92	1.75	0.288
Nivea	1.18	1.17	0.952

References

1. Carat: Carat Ad Spend Report (2016)
2. Li, K., Huang, G., Bente, G.: The impacts of banner format and animation speed on banner effectiveness: evidence from eye movements. Comput. Hum. Behav. **54**, 522–530 (2016)
3. Cormann, M.: Multichannel-marketing: Warum der Einzelhandel in der Fashionbranche umdenken muss. Website Boosting, pp. 40–44 (2016)
4. Hamborg, K.-C., Bruns, M., Ollermann, F., Kaspar, K.: The effect of banner animation on fixation behavior and recall performance in search tasks. Comput. Hum. Behav. **28**, 576–582 (2012)
5. Yoo, C.Y.: Unconscious processing of Web advertising: effects on implicit memory, attitude toward the brand, and consideration set. J. Interact. Mark. **22**, 2–18 (2008)
6. Benway, J.P.: Banner blindness: the irony of attention grabbing on the World Wide Web. Proc. Hum. Factors Ergonomics Soc. Annu. Meet. **42**, 463–467 (1998)
7. Spool, J.M.: Web Site Usability: A Designer's Guide. Morgan Kaufmann, San Francisco (1999)
8. Faraday, P.: Visually critiquing web pages. In: Correia, N., Chambel, T., Daven-port, G. (eds.) Multimedia 1999: Proceedings of the Eurographics Workshop in Milano, Italy, 7–8 September 1999, pp. 155–166. Springer, Vienna (2000)
9. Sun, Y., Lim, K.H., Peng, J.Z.: Solving the distinctiveness-blindness debate: a unified model for understanding banner processing. J. Assoc. Inf. Syst. **14**, 49 (2013)
10. Burke, M., Hornof, A., Nilsen, E., Gorman, N.: High-cost banner blindness: Ads increase perceived workload, hinder visual search, and are forgotten. ACM Trans. Comput. Hum. Interact. (TOCHI) **12**, 423–445 (2005)
11. Bayles, M.E.: Designing online banner advertisements: should we animate? In: Proceedings of the SIGCHI Conference on Human Factors in Computing Systems, pp. 363–366 (2002)
12. Li, H., Bukovac, J.L.: Cognitive impact of banner ad characteristics: an experimental study. J. Mass Commun. Q. **76**, 341–353 (1999)
13. Schweiger, W., Reisbeck, M.: Bannerwerbung im Web Zum Einfluß der Faktoren "Animation" und "Platzierung" auf die Selektion. In: Wirth, W., Schweiger, W. (eds.) Selektion im Internet, pp. 221–247. Springer, Wiesbaden (1999)
14. Pagendarm, M., Schaumburg, H.: Why are users banner-blind? The impact of navigation style on the perception of web banners. J. Digit. Inf. [S.l.] 2(1) (2006). ISSN 1368-7506. https://journals.tdl.org/jodi/index.php/jodi/article/view/36/38. Accessed 10 Apr 2017
15. Kindermann, H.: A short-term twofold impact on banner ads. In: International Conference on HCI in Business, Government and Organizations, pp. 417–426 (2016)
16. Brunswik, E.: Perception and the Representative Design of Psychological Experiments. University of California Press, Berkeley (1956)
17. Brunswik, E.: Representative design and probabilistic theory in a functional psychology. Psychol. Rev. **62**, 193 (1955)
18. Bierhoff, H.W.: Sozialpsychologie. Ein Lehrbuch (6., überarbeitete und erweiterte Auflage). Kohlhammer, Stuttgart (2006)
19. Kenrick, D.T., Gutierres, S.E., Goldberg, L.L.: Influence of popular erotica and judgments of strangers and mates. J. Exp. Soc. Psychol. **25**(2), 159–167 (1989)
20. Kenrick, D.T., Gutierres, S.E.: Contrast effects and judgments of physical attractiveness: when beauty becomes a social problem. J. Pers. Soc. Psychol. **38**, 131 (1980)
21. Meyers-Levy, J., Zhu, R., Jiang, L.: Context effects from bodily sensations: examining bodily sensations induced by flooring and the moderating role of product viewing distance. J. Consum. Res. **37**, 1–14 (2010)

22. Sigall, H., Landy, D.: Radiating beauty: Effects of having a physically attractive partner on person perception. J. Pers. Soc. Psychol. **28**, 218 (1973)
23. Sherif, M., Hovland, C.I.: Social Judgment: Assimilation and Contrast Effects in Communication and Attitude Change. Yale University Press, New Haven (1961)
24. Sherif, C.W., Sherif, M.: Attitude, Ego-Involvement and, Change. Wiley, New York (1967)
25. Furnham, A., Gunter, B., Richardson, F.: Effects of product-program congruity and viewer involvement on memory for televised advertisements. J. Appl. Soc. Psychol. **32**, 124–141 (2002)
26. Čech, C.G.: Congruity and the expectancy hypothesis. J. Exp. Psychol. Learn. Mem. Cogn. **15**, 1129 (1989)
27. Lull, R.B., Bushman, B.J.: Do sex and violence sell? A meta-analytic review of the effects of sexual and violent media and ad content on memory, attitudes, and buying intentions. Psychol. Bull. **141**, 1022–1048 (2015)
28. Moore, R.S., Stammerjohan, C.A., Coulter, R.A.: Banner advertiser-web site context congruity and color effects on attention and attitudes. J. Advertising **34**, 71–84 (2005)
29. Reber, R., Schwarz, N., Winkielman, P.: Processing fluency and aesthetic pleasure: Is beauty in the perceiver's processing experience? Pers. Soc. Psychol. Rev. **8**, 364–382 (2004)
30. Reber, R., Schwarz, N.: Effects of perceptual fluency on judgments of truth. Conscious. Cogn. **8**, 338–342 (1999)
31. Kenning, P.: The discovery of cortical relief. Westfälische Wilhelms-Universität Münster (2002)
32. Kenning, P., Plassmann, H., Deppe, M., Kugel, H., Schwindt, W.: Wie eine starke Marke wirkt. Harvard Bus. Manag. **27**, 53–57 (2005)
33. Kindermann, H.: A single-item measure approach to consumer-based brand equity based on evolutionary psychology and neuroscience. J. Mark. Manage. **3**, 76–82 (2015)

Consumers' Trust in Price-Forecasting Recommendation Agents

Eran Rubin[1(✉)], Young Anna Argyris[2], and Izak Benbasat[3]

[1] College of Business Administration, University of Akron, Akron, OH, USA
erubin@uakron.edu
[2] Department of Media and Information, Michigan State University, East Lansing, MI, USA
yelee@msu.edu
[3] Sauder School of Business, University of British Columbia, Vancouver, BC, Canada
izak.benbasat@sauder.ubc.ca

Abstract. With the prevalence of data online, consumers increasingly shop not only for the product that best fits their needs, but also for the best time to purchase the product in order to reduce its cost. In line with this behavior, ecommerce websites often not only offer products, but also provide analytics based statements and recommendations relating to the best time to purchase a perishable product (e.g., air travel). This study examines the effects of such purchase timing statements and recommendations on consumers' trusting beliefs in the recommendation facility. Our theoretical background comes from Toulmin's (1958) argumentation model and the literature related to the role of explanation facilities in enhancing consumers' trust. Results from our pilot study show evidence for the different roles Toulmin elements have, serving as explanation facilities in the context of predictive analytics.

Keywords: Consumer trust · Toulmin's argumentation model · Recommendation agents

1 Introduction

Ecommerce websites often offer not only products, but also advice and arguments related to purchase timing. Most notably, ecommerce sites in the travel industry increasingly provide information intended to affect purchase timing. Sites increasingly show recommendation functionality related to better deal purchasing. Further, the sites provide different statements that relate to the recommendation functionality (See Fig. 1). While the use of such mechanisms in ecommerce websites is becoming increasingly popular, their impact is still not clear. More specifically, do such statements and advice affect the purchase timing? Do the statements increase consumers' trust in the e-commerce site and its recommendation? If so, which statements affect which trusting beliefs?

In this research we examine the effect of purchase timing related statements and advice on trusting beliefs in the site's recommendation facility. In order to analyze statements provided by websites, we refer to Toulmin's [14] model of argumentation, which helps us to categorize statements according to their role in increasing the strength

© Springer International Publishing AG 2017
F.F.-H. Nah and C.-H. Tan (Eds.): HCIBGO 2017, PART II, LNCS 10294, pp. 71–80, 2017.
DOI: 10.1007/978-3-319-58484-3_6

Prices will likely rise within 7 days - BUY

Our model strongly indicates that fares will rise more than $20 during the next 7 days. This forecast is based on analysis of historical price changes and is not a guarantee of future results.

Advice: BUY

go back to your search ↙

7-day low fare prediction

Tip: Wait   There is a high likelihood of at least one major price drop within the next 7 days. Note: Price drops are sporadic and 50% of them do not last longer than 48 hours. Consider your risk tolerance.

To provide the airfare history, we have made more than 175 billion, and counting, airfare observations based on real pricing and availability. Learn more by visiting Our Technology and Data.

Fig. 1. Examples of recommendation and statements from Kayak.com and Farecast.com

of an argument. It has long been shown that well-structured trust assuring arguments can increase consumers' trust in a website and the intention to transact in it [7]. More recent studies have shown that well-structured arguments in the context of health related information are more highly trusted [9], and that the perception about social capital of team members in virtual teams is affected by the quality of the argumentations provided in their profiles [2]. We extend this line of research to analyze how supporting an argument establishes *trusting beliefs* in a recommendation agent driven by *analytics*.

Unlike other domains, analytics based recommendations are derived from highly complex processes and algorithms, which are difficult to grasp by most users. As a result, often only very partial information is provided to the user, and, as shown in the examples above, their evaluation may be difficult, and their implication may be unclear. This is in contrast to other Recommendation Agents (RA), such as product fit RA, in which the logic of recommendation can be more easily conveyed and understood [16]. Therefore, in the context of analytics, the effect of the soundness of the argument is not clear, as information is always very partial. Further, a question that arises is whether partial arguments still effect trust, and if different partial arguments do this in different ways. Arguments associated with analytics about purchase timing are especially interesting, as while generally statements supporting an argument are expected to enhance trust, in the predictive analytics domain they may potentially have adverse effects on trust as well, as they may expose the user to a sense of lack of privacy and surveillance.

By referring to Toulmin's [14] model elements as explanation facilities [16], we theorize on the different effects each individual element of the model can have on trust. The different elements defined by Toulmin are (1) data, the facts and grounds for our recommendation, (2) warrants, the way facts are used to arrive at the recommendation, (3) backings, the justification of why the warrant is valid, and (4) rebuttals and qualifiers, the extent to which the recommendation is sound, as well as the conditions under which it may not hold. We suggest that each one of these can be referred to as an explanation facility, thereby potentially enhancing trust even when brought individually, and potentially in different ways on different trusting beliefs.

Our initial pilot study, shows support for the notion that individual statements can enhance trusting beliefs in the context of predictive business analytics. Backing arguments appear to be mostly associated with benevolence and competence trust. Rebuttals enhance integrity trust. Data enhance all trusting beliefs.

2 Theoretical Background

2.1 Toulmin's Model of Arguments

Toulmin [14] models arguments as composed of different statements to support a claim, or assertion. In the context of our study, the claim referred to is the recommendation provided to the user. According to Toulmin, the core elements of argumentation that come to support a claim are data, warrant, backing and rebuttal. Data relates to facts that helped establish the claim. Warrants relate to the bearing of the claim, or the step made from the data to arrive at the claim. While data are more specific, warrants are general, hypothetical statements, which can act as bridges, and authorize the sort of step to which our particular argument commits. Backings are assurances for the warrant's authority and currency [15]. According to Toulmin's model, as one moves from supporting an argument by providing data alone, to augmenting it also with warrants, backings as rebuttals, the claim is sounder. We suggest that due to the complexity of the predictive analytics domain, and thus the difficulty in providing a sound argument, the use of warrants, backing or rebuttals alone, may still enhance trust. Further we suggest each of the different type of statements may enhance different trusting beliefs.

2.2 Trusting Beliefs

Trusting beliefs refer to the perceptions of the trustee about a trusted entity, with respect to three different dimensions. Namely, these dimensions are competence, benevolence, and integrity [8]. This view of trusting beliefs in the technological artefacts is adopted from the traditional view of trusting beliefs in interpersonal communication [13], since people treat computers as social actors and apply social rules to them [11]. In the context of RA's, competence trust refers a user's perception that the RA has the ability, skills, and expertise to perform effectively in specific domains. Benevolence trust is a user's perception that an RA cares about the user and acts in the user's interest. Integrity trust is the perception that an RA adheres to a set of principles (e.g., honesty and keeping promises) that are generally accepted by consumers [16].

It has been noted that an important distinction exists between competence trust, which is a judgment of ability, and benevolence and integrity trusts, which relate to the morality of the RA [17]. Research suggests that socially, morality related perceptions are given more weight than ability perceptions when people form impressions of others [4]. In the context of ecommerce, evidence for increased satisfaction was found to be associated with increased benevolence trust [17]. It was also found that increased benevolence trust in a seller can explain much of the price premium [10]. Therefore, understanding how such trusting beliefs can be enhanced can potentially have unique practical implications.

2.3 Explanation Facilities

The topic of explanatory capabilities emerged in expert systems, as an attempt to imitate behavior that has been found to be a characteristic of trusted entities such as consultations with human experts [6]. Explanation facilities provide information such as what some terms mean, why certain questions were asked by the system, how conclusions were reached, and why other conclusions were not reached [5]. Different ways have been proposed to classify explanations provided by Knowledge Based Systems and Decision Support Systems [3], and in the context of ecommerce advice, Wang and Benbasat [16] identify 'why', 'how' and 'tradeoff' explanation facilities as potential trust enhancing mechanisms that can reduce agency concerns when shopping online. 'How' explanations reveal the line of reasoning by outlining the logical process involved. 'Why' explanations justify the importance and purpose of the input used by the recommendation facility, in addition to providing justifications for the recommendations provided. 'Tradeoff' explanations provide decisional guidance to enlighten or sway users as they structure and execute their decision-making processes [12, 16]. Wang and Benbasat [16] find that 'how' explanations increases users' competence and benevolence beliefs. They also find that 'why' explanation enhance benevolence beliefs, and 'trade-off' explanations increase integrity beliefs.

3 Hypothesis Development

While each of the how, why, and tradeoff explanation facilities of RAs, refer to a comprehensive explanation, such explanations are largely impractical in the context of analytics based recommendations. The reason is that in analytics recommendations complex algorithms and mathematical computations are involved to processes an excessive amount of data. These are both very challenging to convey by the agent, and to comprehend by the user. To illustrate, consider the explanation facilities provided in the different contexts: 'how' explanations in the context of knowledge based systems refer to showing the entire reasoning tree; in the context of recommendation agents, these explanation provide details about the recommendation rules and priorities[1]. Taken to the context of analytics, explaining to a typical user the algorithm used for the analytical

---

[1] An example provided for a recommendation agent (Wang and Benbasat 2008): if you want a camera that will focus on subjects farther away, the camera with a stronger optical zoom level will have higher priority in my recommendations. Specifically, the four options will determine the following zoom levels: 1. 2X optical zoom and below; 2. Between 2X and 5X optical zoom; 3. 4X optical zoom and above; 4. No minimum requirement in zoom capability.

forecast, is hard to conceive. 'Why' explanations, in both knowledge based systems and recommendation agents, provide full details of how user input may affect the recommendation[2]. However, once again, explaining the effect of specific data points collected on analytics based recommendation, is challenging at best.

Indeed, analytics based recommendations typically do not provide explanation facilities. Rather, as previously pointed out, they often provide short statements of partial information to accompany the recommendation. Essentially these statements come to support a claim (the recommendation); thus, together with the recommendation, these statements help form an argument. While well-formed arguments can help alleviate challenges on claims made (e.g. [7]), it is not clear if partial arguments can help achieve the same or in what way. Further it is not clear how the different components of an argument suggested by Toulmin affect trusting beliefs.

Due to the inherent difficulties in providing explanation facilities in the analytics domain, we suggest that in this domain consumers are receptive to abstract arguments, and that the components of an argument, namely Toulmin's warrant, data, backings, and rebuttals, can be viewed as explanation facilities in this context. Thus, two unique aspects are hypothesized in the analytics based recommendations domain: (1) Since components of an argument may be viewed as explanation facilities, they may enhance the levels of different trusting beliefs; and (2) Since components of an argument are viewed as explanation facilities, even if an argument is not well formed (e.g. includes isolated components, such as only claim and warrant) trusting beliefs may still be enhanced.

We hypothesize about the role of each of the different Toulmin elements in this context, according to our analysis of the correspondence each has to an explanation facility.

Warrants indicate the bearing on the conclusion from the data used. That is, warrants pertain to the nature and justification of the step made taking data to a claim. Warrants are "general, hypothetical statements, which can act as bridges, and authorize the sort of step to which our particular argument commits us and may normally be written very briefly" [15]. Thus, while warrants are provided as part of an argument, and while abstract and brief, we suggest these ideas closely relate to 'how' explanation facilities described in the previous section. Hence, our first hypothesis:

H1: As warrants closely relate to 'how' explanation facilities, the inclusion of warrants in an analytics based recommendation will enhance competence and benevolence trusting beliefs.

Backings come in an argument, to convey the appropriateness of the step made to arrive at the claim. As stated by Toulmin, " 'Is this calculation mathematically impeccable?' may be a very different one from the question 'Is this the relevant calculation?' " [15]. That is, the backing in an argument explains why, in general, the warrant should be accepted as having authority. Backings relate to the more general issue of the

---

[2] An example provided for a Knowledge Based Systems (Dhaliwal and Benbasat 1996): Race of the patient is one of the 5 parameters that identify a patient. It may also be relevant later in the consultation when determining the organisms (other than those seen on cultures or smears) which might be causing the infection.

applicability of a claim. They are assurances, for the authority and currency of the warrants. These ideas closely relate to 'why' explanation facilities described in the previous section. 'Why' explanations are more comprehensive and explain the logic in using the data. Backings help assure that the way the data have been used to arrive at the conclusion is fundamentally valid. Hence, our next hypothesis:

H2: As backings closely relate to 'why' explanation facilities, the inclusion of backings in an analytics based recommendation will enhance benevolence trusting belief.

Rebuttals comment implicitly on the bearing of a warrant. They indicate circumstances in which the general authority of the warrant would have to be set aside. While somewhat different from trade-off explanation facilities, these are very much analogous. While tradeoff explanation elaborate on how a decision between alternatives can be arrived at, rebuttals implicitly imply the consideration of competing alternatives.

H3: As rebuttals closely relate to 'trade-off' explanation facilities, the inclusion of rebuttals in an analytics based recommendation will enhance integrity trusting belief.

Data is the foundation for a claim, or the ground which we produce as support for the assertion. Data are the facts one will present in order to support a claim when it is challenged. Unlike warrants, backings and rebuttals, data does not have an equivalent in an explanation facility. However, data is a fundamental part of an argument. We suggest that data statements have three important aspects that directly relate to trust perceptions. First, they help to close the knowledge gap between the user and the system, or enable the user to "find out easily what the program knows about a particular subject" [1], thus enhancing competence trust; Second, they consists of facts, that are less subject to manipulation, and thus its presentation may enhance integrity trust. Finally, data statements help to show the effort put in the RA design to support objectivity. Thus, potentially enhancing also benevolence trust. Namely, our fourth set of hypotheses:

H4a: Since data statements consists of objective facts, which are less subject to subjective description, data statements enhance integrity trust.

H4b: Since data statements provide information about the knowledge the system has, they help close the knowledge gap between the user and the system and enhance competence trust.

H4c: Since data statements expose the effort put in the RA design to support objectivity they enhance benevolence trust.

4 Pilot Study

4.1 Experiment Design

In a pilot study, 64 subjects were provided a flight purchase scenario for a purchase timing decision task. They were asked to view two recommendations snapshots, which were said to have been provided by two separate recommendation facilities of ecommerce websites. One of the presented recommendations included a Toulmin element of either data, warrant, backing, or rebuttal (Henceforward the Toulmin site), and the other did not (Henceforward the non-Toulmin site). Example of a setting is provided in Fig. 2, a list pertaining to statements of type warrant, backing, rebuttal, and data are provided in Table 1.

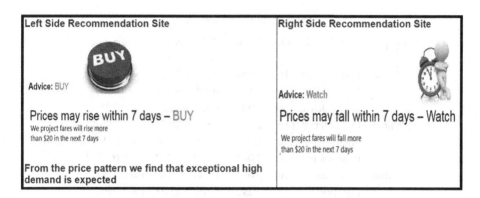

Left Side Recommendation Site	Right Side Recommendation Site
Advice: BUY	Advice: Watch
Prices may rise within 7 days – BUY We project fares will rise more than $20 in the next 7 days	Prices may fall within 7 days – Watch We project fares will fall more than $20 in the next 7 days
From the price pattern we find that exceptional high demand is expected	

Fig. 2. Example of survey for with Toulmin Warrant vs Non-Toulmin

Table 1. Examples of Toulmin elements provided in Toulmin RA

Toulmin element	Example
Data	We used the recent price changes on your flight, as well as more than 2 million past price data points collected on your route
Warrant	From the price pattern we find that exceptional high demand is expected
Backing	In order to learn about processes that are taking place on your route, we matched the recent price pattern on your route and preferred date with past patterns. We found the recent pattern is very indicative of continuous rise in demand for flights on your route and date
	For example, such a pattern was found in the past when a conference was held at your destination
Rebuttal	The prediction may not hold (less than 5% chance it will not hold). For example, in case a special event is scheduled to take place at your destination

The two snapshots presented provided opposing recommendations (i.e. one proposed to buy, and the other to wait, see Fig. 2). To counterbalance differences associated with buy recommendations vs wait recommendations, half of the respondents were provided by the Toulmin site a recommendation to buy, and the other half to wait. The respondents were then asked to decide on whether purchase the flight ticket immediately rather than wait, and then to rate their trusting perception (adopted from Wang and Benbasat [16]) about the two provided sites, comparing between them. Similarly to Kim and Benbasat [7], our measures were on a 15-point scale (i.e., −7 to +7) and respondents were asked to compare the Toulmin site to the non-Toulmin site.

5   Results

Table 2 presents the results with respect to the consumer trusting beliefs, comparing the four types of Toulmin recommendations sites, to the base recommendation site.

Table 2. Experiment results

Group	Trust belief	Obs	Mean	Std. error	Std. dev.	t value
Warrant	Competence	16	−0.813	0.822	3.287	t = −0.9888
	Integrity	16	0.104	0.750	3.001	t = 0.1389
	Benevolence	16	−0.125	0.832	3.329	t = −0.1502
Backing	Competence	16	2.313	0.693	2.771	t = 3.3380**
	Integrity	16	1.646	0.640	2.560	t = 2.5713**
	Benevolence	16	2.083	0.693	2.772	t = 3.0067**
Rebuttal	Competence	16	0.094	0.547	2.189	t = 0.1713
	Integrity	16	1.292	0.655	2.621	t = 1.9709*
	Benevolence	16	0.813	0.552	2.208	t = 1.4722
Data	Competence	16	2.453	0.426	1.703	t = 5.7603**
	Integrity	16	2.396	0.500	2.001	t = 4.7897**
	Benevolence	16	2.333	0.538	2.153	t = 4.3343**

As shown in the table, apparently warrants and how explanation facilities are significantly different. H1 was not supported, suggesting that possibly warrants are too abstract and do not sufficiently reduce the knowledge gap between the recommendation agent and the user.

The table also shows support for H2 that backings enhance benevolence trust. Apparently backings reduce the agency gap between the user and the recommending site. Interestingly, warrants also enhance integrity and competence trust. Still, there is an apparent difference in the levels of trust between the trusting beliefs[3], with integrity beliefs being lower than competence and benevolence. This is in line with our hypothesis as benevolence and competence are known to be correlated: a perception of an entity working in one's favor implies competence of that entity, and the other way around. Similarly, the increased integrity trust can be explained by the idea that if an ecommerce site works for the users' favor rather than only its own, a level of integrity is implied.

With respect to rebuttals, H3 is supported. As expected, rebuttals relate to trade-off explanations and enhance integrity trust. They do not relate to competence of benevolence.

Finally, Hypotheses H4A–H4C are all supported, suggesting the crucial role of data in enhancing trust. These results about data as trust enhancing show an important role of another explanation facility not previously considered. Data as an explanation facility enhances all types of trust, as it reduces the knowledge gap, exposes the efforts made in the RA design, and provides information perceived as unbiased.

6   Summary

In this research we analyze the effect of components of Toulmin's model elements on trusting beliefs in the context of the business analytics domain. Our initial results from

---

[3] The difference between competence and integrity is significant (t = 2.0464).

a pilot study support the notion that Toulmin elements of an argumentation can not only construct an argument and thus enhance the acceptance of a claim. Rather, they can also serve as explanation facilities, and thus may have different roles in enhancing different trusting beliefs. Further, we show the important role of the data element as an explanation facility, enhancing all trusting beliefs. Data is an explanation facility about "how", which may also be perceived as unbiased, as well as reflect on the efforts made in the RA design to support the needs of the user. In the next steps we plan to continue and analyze the role of Toulmin explanation facilities in enhancing different trusting beliefs, by considering interaction effects between Toulmin elements. We are also analyzing further effects of trust enhancement in this domain, such as analyzing propensity for recommendation adoption and propensity to purchase in the e-commerce website. These are a few of our next steps in this project. We believe this research improves our understanding about antecedents of trusting beliefs in the business analytics domain, as well as the role of Toulmin elements as explanation facilities, in this domain, and possibly others as well.

References

1. Buchanan, B.G., Shortliffe, E.H.: Rule-based Expert Systems: The MYCIN Experiments of the Stanford Heuristic Programming Project. Addison-Wesley, Reading (1984)
2. Cummings, J., Dennis, A.: Do SNS impressions matter? Virtual team and impression formation in the era of social technologies. In: 20th Americas Conference on Information Systems, Savannah (2014)
3. Dhaliwal, J.S., Benbasat, I.: The use and effects of knowledge-based system explanations: theoretical foundations and a framework for empirical evaluation. Inf. Syst. Res. 7(3), 342–362 (1996)
4. Goodwin, G.: Moral character is person perception. Current Dir. Psychol. Sci. 24, 38–44 (2015)
5. Gregor, S., Benbasat, I.: Explanations from intelligent systems: theoretical foundations and implications for practice. MIS Q. 23(4), 497–530 (1999)
6. Kidd, A.L.: The consultative role of an expert system. In: Johnson, P., Cook, S. (eds.) People and Computers: Designing the Interface. Cambridge University Press, Cambridge (1998)
7. Kim, D., Benbasat, I.: The effects of trust-assuring arguments on consumer trust in Internet stores: application of Toulmin's model of argumentation. Inf. Syst. Res. 17(3), 286–300 (2006)
8. McKnight, D.H., Choudhury, V., Kacmar, C.: Developing and validating trust measures for e-commerce: an integrative typology. Inf. Syst. Res. 13(3), 334–359 (2002)
9. Mun, Y.Y., Yoon, J.J., Davis, J.M., Lee, T.: Untangling the antecedents of initial trust in web-based health information: the roles of argument quality, source expertise, and user perceptions of information quality and risk. Decis. Support Syst. 55(1), 284–295 (2013)
10. Pavlou, P.A., Dimoka, A.: The nature and role of feedback text comments in online marketplaces: implications for trust building, price premiums, and seller differentiation. Inf. Syst. Res. 17(4), 391–412 (2006)
11. Reeves, B., Nass, C.: The Media Equation: How People Treat Computers, Television, and New Media Like Real People and Places. Cambridge University Press, New York (1996)
12. Silver, M.S.: Decisional guidance for computer-based support. MIS Q. 15(1), 105–122 (1991)
13. Sztompka, P.: Trust: A Sociological Theory. Cambridge University Press, Cambridge (1999)

14. Toulmin, S.E.: The Use of Argument. Cambridge University Press, Cambridge (1958)
15. Toulmin, S.E.: The Uses of Argument. Cambridge University Press, Cambridge (2003)
16. Wang, W., Benbasat, I.: Recommendation agents for electronic commerce: effects of explanation facilities on trusting beliefs. J. Manage. Inf. Syst. **23**(4), 217–246 (2007)
17. Xu, D.J., Cenfetelli, R.T., Aquino, K.: Do different kinds of trust matter? An examination of the three trusting beliefs on satisfaction and purchase behavior in the buyer-seller context. J. Strateg. Inf. Syst. **25**(1), 15–31 (2016)

Mobile Shopping Should be Useful, Convenient and Fun!

Norman Shaw[✉] and Ksenia Sergueeva

Ryerson University, Toronto, Canada
{norman.shaw, sergueeva.ksenia}@ryerson.ca

Abstract. Consumers engage in mobile commerce via their smartphones. They are able to search for product information, compare prices and finalize their purchase without having to enter a physical store. With the choice of many apps, they are motivated by the convenience of shopping any place any time. The Unified Theory of Acceptance and Use of Technology (UTAUT2) is a well-tested theory that explains consumer adoption of a technology innovation. In this study, UTAUT2 is the foundational theory, but instead of specifying the antecedent 'performance expectancy' as reflective, it is specified as formative. In addition, perceived convenience is added and the resultant research model is empirically tested. Using PLS to analyze the data from a questionnaire sent to Canadian owners of smartphones, the results show that performance expectancy, hedonic motivation and perceived convenience are the main significant factors that influence consumers' intention to use an app for mobile commerce.

Keywords: UTAUT2 · Perceived convenience · Hedonic motivation · PLS

1 Introduction

Eight out of ten consumers in North America have engaged in online retailing, with fifteen percent of them making a purchase at least once per week [2]. Seventy seven percent of the population enjoy connectivity 'while on the go' and fifty one percent have used their mobile phone to help them with their purchase [3]. Consumers desire functionality where they can compare prices, receive product advice, follow reviews and make payments. The use of mobile devices for mobile commerce allows consumers the convenience of shopping anywhere at anytime [4, 5].

The capabilities of smartphones are improving each year: screens are larger, app design makes it easy and fun to use and more functionality is packed into an app [6]. Thirty four percent of consumers foresee that their smartphone will be their primary connection for mobile commerce in the future [7]. Recognizing the growing ubiquity of smartphone ownership, various organizations, such as Apple and Google, have developed mobile wallets that enable the smartphone to store payment cards that can then be used in the physical store without the need to produce a plastic card [8, 9]. With consumers having the choice of so many apps, app designers desire to understand what is the motivation to adopt a particular app.

Adoption research has progressed through a number of theories, such as the Theory of Planned Behavior [10], the Theory of Reasoned Action [11] and the Technology

© Springer International Publishing AG 2017
F.F.-H. Nah and C.-H. Tan (Eds.): HCIBGO 2017, PART II, LNCS 10294, pp. 81–94, 2017.
DOI: 10.1007/978-3-319-58484-3_7

Adoption Model (TAM) [12]. In 2003, Venkatesh et al. [13] introduced the Unified Theory of Adoption and Use of Technology, UTAUT, from the synthesis of eight technology models. In 2012, they further extended this theory to UTAUT2 to explain voluntary use [1] which can be applied to consumers, for whom there is no mandate to deploy a specific smartphone app. Adoption is voluntary and UTAUT2 has been applied to, for example, the acceptance of mobile payments [14].

Past studies on technology adoption have empirically shown that perceived usefulness is a key influencing factor on the intention to use an IT artifact [15, 16]. UTAUT and UTAUT2 name this variable 'performance expectancy'. The majority of studies have specified this construct as reflective [17]. Diamantopoulos [18] has argued that the specification between reflective and formative can impact the validity of the theoretical approach. For mobile shopping apps, consumers perceive some features to be more useful than others. The reflective approach of measuring performance expectancy, common in studies of adoption, asks whether the app improves productivity. This tends to ignore the different features within the app. As a simple example, consumers who only wish to use their device to compare prices are using less functionality than those who have activated their mobile wallet. Reflectively, both types of consumers may feel that they are more productive. By specifying the performance expectancy as formative, consumers who deploy more functionality will be measured as more productive. In this study, we specify performance expectancy as a formative construct, where the indicators describe and define the construct, rather than vice versa [19].

Using a smartphone for mobile commerce adds convenience, as it allows the consumer to engage anytime and anyplace [20]. Convenience is not the same as usefulness: the mobile wallet may be perceived as useful, but when it involves opening an app on a smartphone, keying in a security code and attempting to tap it on a payment terminal which may not be tap-enabled, the lack of convenience is a barrier to usefulness. The specification of performance expectancy as a formative construct further ensures that it is differentiated from perceived convenience.

The context of this study is to investigate the factors that influence consumers' intention to use their mobile devices for mobile shopping. Our research question is:

- What factors motivate consumers to adopt a mobile shopping app?

Our supplementary questions are:

- What is the role of hedonic motivation?
- What is the role of perceived convenience?

The contribution of our research is the creation of new theory by extending UTAUT2 with perceived convenience and specifying performance expectancy as a formative construct.

This paper is organized as follows. The next section is the literature review, where we develop our hypotheses and illustrate them with our research model. The third section is the research methods. The fourth section is the analysis of the results. In the fifth section we discus the results and include the limitations of the current research and offer suggestions for future research. We present our conclusions in the final section.

2   Literature Review and Development of Hypotheses

2.1   UTAUT2 as the Foundational Model

Many studies of technology adoption have empirically tested TAM in many contexts [21, 22]. It has been cited 32,977 times (Google Scholar as of 28 January 2017). With its two influencing variables, perceived usefulness (PU) and perceived ease of use (PEOU), its influence and success has been attributed to its parsimony [23]. Many studies added antecedents in order to enrich the findings and in 2003, Venkatesh et al. [13] evaluated the findings of eight common theories of adoption, including TAM, unifying them into UTAUT. PU and PEOU were incorporated into the model, and were named performance expectancy (PE) and effort expectancy (EE) respectively. In addition to PE and EE, there are two other independent variables: social influence (SI) and facilitating conditions (FC).

When TAM was first proposed, systems were deployed in organizations where use was mandatory. With the advent of smaller and cheaper computing devices, innovations became available for consumers whose choice of adoption was voluntary. Venkatesh et al. created UTAUT2 [1] by extending UTAUT with the constructs of habit, price value (PV) and hedonic motivation (HM). UTAUT2 has received wide acceptance [24] and is selected as our theoretical foundation. It has explained behavioral intention with a variance between 56% to 74% [1]. The following paragraphs describe our hypotheses based on the constructs of UTAUT2.

2.2   Performance Expectancy (PE)

Venkatesh et al. [1] empirically tested UTAUT2 in the context of mobile Internet. PE was measured by asking the reflective questions shown in Table 1.

Table 1. Survey items for PE [1]

PE1: I find mobile Internet useful in my daily life
PE2: Using mobile Internet help me accomplish things more quickly
PE3: Using mobile Internet increases my chances of achieving things that are important to me (dropped)
PE4: Using mobile Internet increases my productivity

These questions, like many questions in IT research, are specified as reflective constructs, where any change in the construct changes the indicators [25]. In Table 1, the four items are measuring the concept of usefulness. If a particular respondent were to believe that the app was not useful, then all indicators would be expected to change, as they are each measuring the same thing. The responses are expected to converge. Standard statistical tests, such as Cronbach's alpha [26] are applied. In the study by Venkatesh et al. [1], PE2 had a low correlation coefficient, it was therefore dropped (see Table 1). The indicators are interchangeable and other similar indicators could be added and would be valid so long as they converged.

The concept of a formative construct is different. The composition of the indicators makes up the construct. Each indicator is measuring a different aspect of the latent variable and therefore the indicators are not interchangeable. The resultant score can be considered as an index [27]. Dropping an indicator changes what the construct is measuring. As an example, a stock index, such as the Standard & Poor's 500, is comprised of the value of 500 stocks. Removing even just one of those stocks will certainly change the value of the index, but it also changes the meaning of the index, as we would then have the S&P 499!

In this study, we specify performance expectancy as formative, and measure it in terms of consumers' use of such features as collecting loyalty points, researching products and paying with the mobile wallet.

Hypothesis 1: Performance expectancy, specified as a formative construct, positively influences intention to use apps for mobile shopping.

2.3   Effort Expectancy

Effort Expectancy (EE) is defined as the 'degree of ease associated with the use of the system' [13]. Apps for consumers are aimed, by definition, at large audiences who are able to choose from a large selection. Once an app is downloaded, the expectation is that it will be easy to use with minimal instructions. App designers make use of buttons on the touch screen, colors and sound effects to guide the user. Meta-analysis of the adoption literature has validated the relationship between EE and intention to use (ITU) [28], but the influence of EE has been less conclusive than that between PE and ITU [29]. With the growth of smartphone apps [30], consumers are willing to try new apps, but they must be easy to use. Therefore:

Hypothesis 2: Effort expectancy positively influences the intention to use smartphone apps for mobile commerce.

2.4   Hedonic Motivation

Hedonic motivation is similar to perceived enjoyment, which is defined as 'the extent to which the activity of using the computer system is perceived to be personally enjoyable in its own right' [31]. In the workplace, the primary purpose of the system is to deliver functionality, yet adoption was influenced not only by functionality but by enjoyment too [31]. The purpose of mobile shopping apps is to assist consumers with their shopping needs. Consumers have a large number of apps from which to choose, many of which are offering very similar functionality. They too may be influenced by the enjoyment when using the app.

Hypothesis 3: Hedonic motivation positively influences the intention to use smartphone apps for mobile commerce.

2.5   Social Influence

The Theory of Reasoned Action [11] postulates that users are influenced by 'referent' others who are important to them. Within an organization, a worker is influenced by how his manager perceives his adoption of the system. The worker would also be influenced by his co-workers with whom there is co-dependence. Extant literature has validated this relationship within a mandatory context [28]. In a voluntary setting, 'referent others' would be friends, family and colleagues. They may recommend an app because it is useful or fun. Depending upon the relationship, the individual may decide to use the app based on the influence of 'others'. We propose:

Hypothesis 4: Social influence positively influences the intention to use smartphone apps for mobile commerce.

2.6   Facilitating Conditions

When using a plastic credit card in the store, the infrastructure is in place to ensure that the transaction is completed accurately and securely. In the unlikely event that there are problems, the credit card providers and the retailers have help desks to resolve any issues speedily. These conditions have facilitated the adoption of credit card payments via a physical card. Similar infrastructure and support needs to be in place for mobile shopping apps so that consumers have confidence that the system will work as intended. They need to be assured that facilitating conditions (FC) are in place [32, 33]. Our next hypothesis is:

Hypothesis 5: Facilitating conditions positively influence the intention to use smartphone apps for mobile commerce.

2.7   Habit

Habit is conceptualized as the extent to which people tend to perform behaviors automatically because of learning [1]. Although the sphere of mobile commerce is growing, it is still a fairly new phenomenon specifically in the use of mobile applications to aid the shopping experience. The proportion of consumers using mobile application to make purchases is relatively low with few people accustomed to shopping via mobile applications. Thus, in this paper, the construct habit is dropped.

2.8   Perceived Convenience

We buy from a convenience store because it is typically open longer hours than the supermarket, it is closer to home with less effort required than driving to the shopping centre, and it is fast, because we only buy a few items and there are not many people in the queue in front of us [34]. Similarly we can compare the convenience of mobile shopping. It can decrease the effort required when shopping. For example, prices can be compared across multiple retailers within a few seconds. There is no need to drive to different stores in order to see who has the lowest price. Mobile shopping can eliminate the temporal dimension. Internet sites are open 24/7, such that at any time of the day products can be purchased. And mobile shopping addresses the spatial dimension. Shopping can take place anywhere – at home, at work, or while watching a football game. Mobile shopping is therefore convenient [35] offering the consumer the ability to shop anyplace and at anytime.

Depending upon how they are measured, convenience and usefulness may be confounded. A consumer may perceive that a mobile wallet is useful, but they may perceive it to be inconvenient because the phone has to be available, a security code has to be entered and the payment terminal has to be tap-enabled to accept payment. Although the mobile wallet is useful, it is more convenient to produce the physical card because payment will always function.

Poon [36] suggested that when time and effort are saved, then convenience is being measured. For example, using an app to seek information about a product while in a store is convenient because the app saves the effort of having to find a sales person and saves time because detailed information is readily available over the Internet delivered to the smartphone. The app is also useful because it delivers information about the product, which helps the consumer make a purchasing decision. Convenience can lead to the improvement of productivity by saving time and effort and in order not to confound perceived convenience with performance expectancy, we have specified performance expectancy as a formative construct in this study.

We define perceived convenience (PC) as 'the consumers' belief that the use of the IT artifact will enable them to complete the task in a speedy manner, at a time and place of their choosing' [4]. We therefore propose that:

Hypothesis 6: Perceived convenience positively influences the intention to use smartphone apps for mobile commerce.

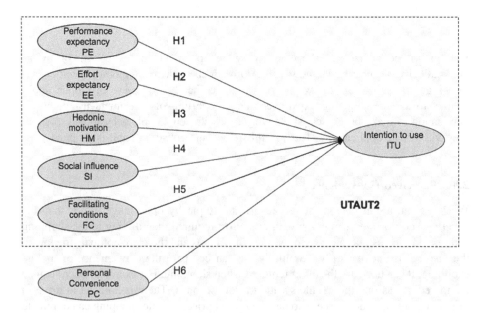

Fig. 1. Research model

2.9　Research Model

The research model is shown in Fig. 1.

3　Research Methods

3.1　Design

The reflective constructs in the model have been used in past questionnaires and their scales were adapted from extant literature. In order to define the formative construct, performance expectancy, subject matter experts were interviewed, with the result that the items to be measured represented the most common features desired by mobile shoppers. See Table 2.

Table 2. Formative indicators of performance expectancy

• Searching information about products
• Comparing prices of products
• Receiving e-coupons
• Buying products over the Internet
• Paying with loyalty points
• Receiving loyalty points
• Receiving digital receipts
• Paying in store with smartphone

The scales were incorporated into a questionnaire. Ten graduate students were recruited to review this questionnaire for clarity. After making some minor modifications, the survey was distributed by a marketing company to a panel of Canadian adults. Returned surveys were checked and those that were incomplete, completed too fast or failed the attention filters built into the questionnaire were discarded. The valid responses were analyzed with Partial Least Squares.

3.2　Data Analysis

The data was analyzed with SmartPLS version 3.2.6 [37]. PLS is suitable for predictive applications and theory building and is also able to handle formative constructs [38]. We followed the methodology set out by Hair et al. [39], first analyzing the validity of the outer model and then evaluating the path relationships of the structural model and their significance. The standard test for the internal consistency of the reflective indicators is the calculation of Cronbach's alpha [40]. Discriminant validity was tested via the Fornell-Larcker criterion [41]. The structural model was analyzed with the PLS algorithm.

4   Results

4.1   Descriptive Statistics

In the sample, there were 189 males (53.7%) and 163 females (46.3%). There were 107 participants aged between 18 to 29, 124 between 30 and 49 and 121 from 50 and older, with the oldest participant being 81. The age and gender are shown in Table 3.

The median length of ownership of smartphones was 4.6 years. The majority of participants had owned a phone for six years or longer. See Table 4.

Table 3. Age groups of sample

Ages	Male	Female	Total
18–29	41	66	107
30–49	73	51	124
50–69	69	41	110
70+	6	5	11
Totals	**189**	**163**	**100%**
Total as %	**53.7%**	**46.3%**	

Table 4. Phone ownership

Years of ownership	No.	%
1	15	0.9%
2	29	3.5%
2	34	6.2%
4	63	15.4%
5	56	17.1%
6+	155	56.8%

4.2   The Measurement Model

The cross loadings of the measurement model were calculated by SmartPLS. The indicators of all reflective constructs were tested for collinearity. The correlation coefficients measuring each construct were greater than 0.708 [42] indicating that they were convergent and reflected the same latent variable. Because performance expectancy was specified as formative, its indicators are not required to converge. Instead its indicators had been selected via interviews with subject matter experts, thereby following recommended practice of content validity [43].

The bootstrap function in SmartPLS was executed with 5,000 samples using the replacement method. The t statistic for each cross loading was calculated and in every case, the significance was $p < 0.001$ validating that the indicators converged and were significant.

Discriminant validity was tested using the Fornell-Larcker score, where the AVE must be greater than the square of the correlations [41]. The results satisfied these

Table 5. Values for Fornell Larcker test

Construct	EE	FC	HM	ITU	PC	PE	SI
Effort expectancy EE	**0.919**						
Facilitating conditions FC	0.486	**0.82**					
Hedonic motivation HM	0.62	0.307	**0.889**				
Intention to use ITU	0.568	0.312	0.707	**0.892**			
Perceived convenience PC	0.55	0.346	0.595	0.611	**0.905**		
Perceived expectancy PE	0.551	0.352	0.687	0.751	0.581		
Social influence SI	0.342	0.243	0.537	0.502	0.442	0.474	**0.951**

Note: the bold value along the diagonal is the square root of the AVE

criteria. Table 5 compares the correlations with the square root of AVE (shown in italic bold along the diagonal). Values for performance expectancy are not calculated as the construct has been specified as formative and therefore the indicators are not expected to be convergent.

The internal consistency of each construct was assessed via Cronbach's alpha [40], where values above 0.8 indicate reliability. The Average Variance Extracted (AVE) for each construct further confirmed the reliability of the model, where the AVE was above the guideline of 0.5 with the exception of the higher order construct, word of mouth. In addition, the Composite Reliability was above the guideline of 0.6 [42].

4.3   The Structural Model

The coefficient of determination R^2 measures the percentage of the response that is explained by our model. SmartPLS calculated R^2 to be 0.660, which is considered moderate [44]. Bootstrapping was conducted with samples of 5,000 in order to test the significance of each path with the model. All hypotheses were supported with $p < 0.001$, with the exception of hypothesis 2. Table 6 summarizes the results. All paths were significant, except for facilitating conditions to intention to use.

Table 6. Path significance

Path	t statistic	p value	Supported
Effort expectancy to ITU	1.992	0.046	$p < 0.05$
Facilitating conditions to ITU	0.692	0.489	
Hedonic motivation to ITU	4.047	0	$p < 0.001$
Perceived convenience to ITU	3.259	0.001	$p < 0.001$
Performance Expectancy to ITU	8.88	0	$p < 0.001$
Social influence to ITU	2.074	0.038	$p < 0.05$

5 Discussion

PE was one of the main factors that influenced consumers' intentions to use smartphone apps for mobile shopping. Meta-analyses of papers of adoption have corroborated that the common influencing factor is usefulness [22, 45], represented by perceived expectancy (PE) in our model. Lee et al. [46] interviewed researchers about TAM and the consensus was that usefulness alone is not enough. Alan Dennis, the Senior Editor of MIS Quarterly at the time, replied that usefulness is self-evident and that the more important question is what makes the innovation useful [46]. In order to answer this question, we followed the suggestion of Cenfetelli [43] and specified PE as a formative construct rather than ask the more general reflective questions about productivity. The significance of the path for PE to intention to use and its relatively large value for its path coefficient suggests that individuals value the usefulness of the formative features measured by the model, features such as searching for information about products, buying products over the Internet and paying in store with their mobile device.

HM was also a significant influencing factor. Davis had found that workers in organizations were more productive when they recognized that the innovation was both useful and enjoyable [31]. Intrinsic motivation was added as a construct to TAM by Venkatesh et al. [47] who investigated determinants of ease of use. Because adoption by consumers is voluntary, UTAUT2 included hedonic motivation to capture intrinsic motivation [1]. The results of our empirical analysis show that HM is significant. In order to engage in mobile shopping, individuals wish to have an enjoyable experience.

Shopping with the help of a mobile app adds convenience. Smartphone owners are able to shop at any time and at any place. They are no longer dependent upon store hours and there is no need to visit the physical store. Browsing to learn about different products and searching for the best price can be conducted from the comfort of home or while on public transportation. When they visit a physical store, consumers can access more detailed product information by scanning the bar code and, at time of payment, their mobile wallet speeds up the payment processing. Our results show that convenience is important to consumers.

Consumers are still influenced by others who they deem to be important. In the workplace, their performance is measured by their manager. In a voluntary situation, there is no manager, but they may perceive that friends and family expect them to use the app. When in a store, they may perceive that the staff anticipates they will have a shopping app. The significance of the relationship between SI and ITU is less than that for PE and HM. An explanation may be that in many instances use of the mobile app may be conducted alone. In such circumstances, social influence is less important.

Many studies have shown that effort expectancy, or ease of use, has less influence than performance expectancy, or usefulness [48]. Our results are similar. Smartphone apps are designed for the small colour screen which is touch enabled. Interfaces are intuitive and there is typically very little learning required. The majority of the participants had owned smartphones for more than six years, so they would be very familiar with apps. When asked if they would find the mobile shopping app easy to use, the majority of them answered yes based on their familiarity with apps in general and their ability to learn new apps with a short learning curve.

The influence of facilitating conditions on intention to use was not significant. Smartphone manufacturers have joined with Internet providers and cell network companies to provide a seamless experience. Today, connectivity is reliable. If something does go wrong, there are support desks operating 24/7. Retail websites have online chat and support. Consequently, facilitating conditions were not significant because of the assumption that the network is reliable.

5.1 Limitations and Future Research

As with all surveys, the sample may not be representative of the general population. We used the services of a marketing company that recruits individuals on to panels. These individuals are rewarded for participation. The survey did include attention filters to ensure that participants were reading the question. In addition, participants who had answered too many questions in a 'straight line' were also eliminated. Nevertheless, the sample consists of a random population from a subset of individuals who are willing to take surveys for a small reward. The survey was only sent to Canadians and therefor their answers about mobile shopping pertain mostly to the Canadian and US marketplace.

Future research could validate the model across other cultures. The theoretical framework lays the foundation for further extension of UTAUT2. Further investigation could test the content validity of the formative specification of performance expectancy.

6 Conclusion

Smartphone ownership continues to grow with more shoppers turning to their smartphone for assistance. Mobile shopping apps allow consumers to search for products from the convenience of their home at a time of their choosing. We have added the construct of perceived convenience to our foundational theory, UTAUT2. In order to ensure that convenience is not confounded with performance expectancy, we have specified PE as a formative construct to ensure that construct specification is consistent with our proposed theory [49].

From a survey of over 300 participants, our results show that hedonic motivation, performance expectancy and perceived convenience are the most significant factors that influence intention to use. PE had a stronger influence than EE, which is consistent with past studies [22, 48]. Because smartphone owners are familiar with many apps, EE has a minor influence on intention to use. Consumers appreciated the convenience of being able to shop at any time and any place, thereby saving time of going to the store.

Our theoretical contribution is the development of a theoretical foundation based on extending UTAUT2. We have added perceived convenience and have differentiated it from performance expectancy by specifying PE as formative, where specific features of mobile shopping have been defined and included in the survey questionnaire. Our results support the theory in the context of mobile shopping. The approach is applicable to the adoption of other technical innovations in other contexts and we suggest that future researchers evaluate the specification of some of their constructs as formative in order to support their theory.

Practitioners should ensure that their app has useful functionality, offers convenience and is engaging. Consumers value the capability to research products, compare prices and purchase via the Internet from their mobile phone. They also value the convenience of using apps in store in order to find more details about a product and to pay with a mobile wallet, obviating the need to carry payment cards. In short, mobile shopping apps should be useful, convenient and fun.

References

1. Venkatesh, V., Thong, J., Xu, X.: Consumer acceptance and use of information technology: extending the unified theory of acceptance and use of technology. MIS Q. **36**(1), 157–178 (2012)
2. Smith, A., Anderson, M.: Online shopping and E-Commerce (2016). http://www.pewinternet.org/2016/12/19/online-shopping-and-e-commerce/
3. Pew Research: Mobile Fact Sheet (2017). http://www.pewinternet.org/fact-sheet/mobile/
4. Kim, C., Mirusmonov, M., Lee, I.: An empirical examination of factors influencing the intention to use mobile payment. Comput. Hum. Behav. **26**(3), 310–322 (2010)
5. Okazaki, S., Mendez, F.: Exploring convenience in mobile commerce: Moderating effects of gender. Comput. Hum. Behav. **29**(3), 1234–1242 (2013)
6. Linder, M.: Online sales will reach $523 billion by 2020 in the U.S. (2016). https://www.internetretailer.com/2016/01/29/online-sales-will-reach-523-billion-2020-us
7. PWC: Total Retail Survey. Online shoppers around the world are fundamentally disrupting retail-again (2016)
8. Liébana-Cabanillas, F., Sánchez-Fernández, J., Muñoz-Leiva, F.: Antecedents of the adoption of the new mobile payment systems: the moderating effect of age. Comput. Hum. Behav. **35**, 464–478 (2014)
9. Euromonitor: Internet Retailing in the US (2016)
10. Ajzen, I.: The theory of planned behavior. Organ. Behav. Hum. Decis. Process. **50**(2), 179 (1991)
11. Fishbein, M., Ajzen, I.: Belief, Attitude, Intention and Behaviour: An Introduction to Theory and Research. Addison-Wesley, Reading (1976)
12. Davis, F.D., Bagozzi, R.P., Warshaw, P.R.: User acceptance of computer technology: a comparison of two theoretical models. Manage. Sci. **35**(8), 982 (1989)
13. Venkatesh, V., et al.: User acceptance of information technology: toward a unified view. MIS Q. **27**(3), 425–478 (2003)
14. Slade, E., Williams, M., Dwivdei, Y.: Extending UTAUT2 To Explore Consumer Adoption of Mobile Payments (2013)
15. Zhang, L., Zhu, J., Liu, Q.: A meta-analysis of mobile commerce adoption and the moderating effect of culture. Comput. Hum. Behav. **28**(5), 1902–1911 (2012)
16. Schepers, J., Wetzels, M.: A meta-analysis of the technology acceptance model: investigating subjective norm and moderation effects. Inf. Manage. **44**(1), 90–103 (2007)
17. Baabdullah, A., Dwivedi, Y., Williams, M.: Adopting an Extended UTAUT2 to Predict Consumer Adoption of M-Technologies in Saudi Arabia (2014)

18. Diamantopoulos, A., Siguaw, J.A.: Formative versus reflective indicators in organizational measure development: a comparison and empirical illustration. Br. J. Manage. **17**(4), 263–282 (2006)
19. Petter, S., Straub, D.W., Rai, A.: Specifying formative constructs in information systems research. MIS Q. **31**(4), 623–656 (2007)
20. Teo, A.-C., et al.: The effects of convenience and speed in m-payment. Ind. Manage. Data Syst. **115**(2), 311–331 (2015)
21. Khechine, H., Lakhal, S., Ndjambou, P.: A meta-analysis of the UTAUT model: eleven years later. Canadian J. Administrative Sci./Revue Canadienne des Sciences de l'Administration. **33**(2), 138–152 (2016)
22. Legris, P., Ingham, J., Collerette, P.: Why do people use information technology? A critical review of the technology acceptance model. Inf. Manage. **40**(3), 191–204 (2003)
23. Benbasat, I., Barki, H.: Quo vadis, TAM? J. Assoc. Inf. Syst. **8**(4), 211–218 (2007)
24. Baptista, G., Oliveira, T.: A weight and a meta-analysis on mobile banking acceptance research. Comput. Hum. Behav. **63**, 480–489 (2016)
25. Jarvis, C.B., MacKenzie, S.B., Podsakoff, P.M.: A critical review of construct indicators and measurement model misspecification in marketing and consumer research. J. Consum. Res. **30**(2), 199–218 (2003)
26. Cronbach, L.J.: Test Validation in Education Measurement. RL Thorndike, Washington (1971)
27. Diamantopoulos, A., Winklhofer, H.M.: Index construction with formative indicators: An alternative to scale development. J. Mark. Res. **38**(2), 269–277 (2001)
28. Dwivedi, Y.K., Rana, N.P., Chen, H., Williams, M.D.: A meta-analysis of the unified theory of acceptance and use of technology (UTAUT). In: Nüttgens, M., Gadatsch, A., Kautz, K., Schirmer, I., Blinn, N. (eds.) TDIT 2011. IAICT, vol. 366, pp. 155–170. Springer, Heidelberg (2011). doi:10.1007/978-3-642-24148-2_10
29. Hess, T.J., McNab, A.L., Basoglu, K.A.: Reliability generalization of perceived ease of use, perceived usefulness, and behavioral intentions. MIS Q. **38**(1), 1–28 (2014)
30. Comscore, The 2015 U.S. Mobile App Report (2015). comScore.com
31. Davis, F.D., Bagozzi, R.P., Warshaw, P.R.: Extrinsic and intrinsic motivation to use computers in the workplace. J. Appl. Soc. Psychol. **22**(14), 1111–1132 (1992)
32. Taylor, S., Todd, P.A.: Understanding information technology usage: a test of competing models. Inf. Syst. Res. **6**(2), 144–176 (1995)
33. Triandis, H.C.: Values, Attitudes, and Interpersonal Behavior. University of Nebraska Press, Lincoln (1979)
34. American Marketing Association: Dictionary (2016). https://www.ama.org/resources/Pages/Dictionary.aspx
35. Yale, L., Venkatesh, A.: Toward the construct of convenience in consumer research. NA Adv. Consum. Res. **13**, 403–408 (1986)
36. Poon, W.-C.: Users' adoption of e-banking services: the Malaysian perspective. J. Bus. Ind. Mark. **23**(1), 59–69 (2008)
37. Ringle, C.M., Wende, S., Becker, J.-M.: SmartPLS3 (2015). http://www.smartpls.com
38. Gefen, D., Straub, D.W., Boudreau, M.C.: Structural equation modeling and regression: guidelines for research practice. Commun. AIS **4**(7), 1–77 (2000)
39. Hair, J.F., et al.: A Primer on Partial Least Squares Structural Equations Modeling (PLS-SEM). SAGE Publications, Thousand Oaks (2014)
40. Cronbach, L.J., Meehl, P.E.: Construct validity in psychological tests. Psychol. Bull. **52**(4), 281–302 (1955)
41. Fornell, C., Larcker, D.F.: Evaluating structural equation models with unobservable variables and measurement error. J. Mark. Res. 39–50 (1981)

42. Henseler, J., Ringle, C.M., Sinkovics, R.R.: The use of partial least squares path modeling in international marketing. Adv. Int. Mark. **20**, 277–319 (2009)
43. Cenfetelli, R.T., Bassellier, G.: Interpretation of formative measurement in information systems research. MIS Q. **33**(4), 689–707 (2009)
44. Hair, J.F., Ringle, C.M., Sarstedt, M.: PLS-SEM: indeed a silver bullet. J. Mark. Theory Pract. **19**(2), 139–152 (2011)
45. Turner, M., et al.: Does the technology acceptance model predict actual use? A systematic literature review. Inf. Softw. Technol. **52**(5), 463–479 (2010)
46. Lee, Y., Kozar, K.A., Larsen, K.R.T.: The technology acceptance model: past, present and future. Commun. AIS **12**, 752–780 (2003)
47. Venkatesh, V.: Determinants of perceived ease of use: Integrating control, intrinsic motivation, and emotion into the technology acceptance model. Inf. Syst. Res. **11**(4), 342–365 (2000)
48. King, W.R., He, J.: A meta-analysis of the technology acceptance model. Inf. Manage. **43**(6), 740–755 (2006)
49. Diamantopoulos, A., Riefler, P., Roth, K.P.: Advancing formative measurement models. J. Bus. Res. **61**(12), 1203–1218 (2008)

Effect of Timing and Source of Online Product Recommendations: An Eye-Tracking Study

Yani Shi[1]([⊠]), Qing Zeng[2], Fiona Fui-Hoon Nah[2], Chuan-Hoo Tan[3],
Choon Ling Sia[4], Keng Siau[2], and Jiaqi Yan[5]

[1] Southeast University, Nanjing, People's Republic of China
yanishi@seu.edu.cn
[2] Missouri University of Science and Technology, Rolla, USA
{qzdg9,nahf,siauk}@mst.edu
[3] National University of Singapore, Singapore, Singapore
tancho@comp.nus.edu.sg
[4] City University of Hong Kong, Kowloon Tong, Hong Kong
iscl@cityu.edu.hk
[5] Nanjing University, Nanjing, People's Republic of China
jiaqiyan@nju.edu.cn

Abstract. Online retail business has become an emerging market for almost all business owners. Online recommender systems provide better service to consumers during their decision making processes. In this study, a controlled lab experiment was conducted to assess the effect of recommendation timing (early, mid, and late) and recommendation source (expert reviews vs. consumer reviews) on online consumers' interest and attention. Eye-tracking data was extracted from the experiment and analyzed. The results suggest that consumers show more interest in recommendation based on consumer reviews than expert reviews. Earlier recommendations do not receive greater attention than later recommendations.

Keywords: Online product recommendation · Eye tracking · Recommendation source · Recommendation timing

1 Introduction

Based on data from the U.S. Census Bureau, U.S. retail e-commerce sales for the first quarter of 2016 has reached $92.8 billion, which accounts for 7.8% of total retail sales (Denale and Weidenhamer 2016). To boost sales, more and more retailers implement recommender systems to support customers' decision making process. However, there are still some recommender systems that are poorly designed or ineffectively implemented. This research explores the effects of the display timing (i.e., early, mid, and late) of the recommendation and the sources of recommendation content (i.e., expert review vs. consumer review). The eye-tracking method is employed in an experiment to study users' attention and interest. We are interested in the differences of pupil dilation and fixation duration in different recommendation timing and recommendation source conditions.

© Springer International Publishing AG 2017
F.F.-H. Nah and C.-H. Tan (Eds.): HCIBGO 2017, PART II, LNCS 10294, pp. 95–104, 2017.
DOI: 10.1007/978-3-319-58484-3_8

This research contributes to the online product recommendation literature by examining the decision process via eye-tracking method. We expect the outcome of this research to be helpful to online retailers in improving their online recommender systems.

2   Literature Review

2.1   Recommendation Timing

Online product recommender systems are widely used to provide consumers with alternatives that they might be interested in. Online retailers rely on recommender systems as a decision aid to the customers to provide better service and to boost sales. According to research conducted by Forrester Research, product recommender systems accounted for 10% to 30% of total sales by a retailer (Schonfeld 2007). Prior studies on product recommender systems mainly focus on the optimization of algorithms to provide more accurate predictions and suggestions to the customers (Hostler et al. 2012).

Timing is a least studied design feature in human-computer interaction research (Zhang et al. 2002). In online production recommendation literature, Ho et al. (2011) studies the timing of web personalization and suggested that an early recommendation is more likely to be accepted than a late recommendation.

2.2   Online Product Review

Two types of online product review are studied as recommendation support in this paper: one is consumer review which is written by product users, and the other is expert review which is written by domain experts. Prior studies examined the different effect of them. Consumer reviews significantly influence participants' evaluation while expert reviews do not in Jacobs et al. (2015)'s study of consumers' evaluation of motion pictures. Consumer recommendations were found to be significantly more trustworthy than expert recommendations (Senecal and Nantel 2004). The results from the study by Utz et al. (2012) also indicated that consumer reviews were the key factor to judge the trustworthiness of online store However, Chiou et al. (2014) found out that online expert reviews have a significantly higher credibility than consumer reviews.

2.3   Eye Tracking Method

The use of eye-tracking devices on information processing tasks has been around for more than a century. With the development of personal computers, researchers start using eye-tracking devices to study and solve problems in human-computer interaction.

Eye fixation is a well-developed predictor of attention. People's attention only focus on the things they need and ignore others that are presumed to be irrelevant (Triesch et al. 2003). Decision makers direct their attention to goal related stimuli (Orquin and Mueller Loose 2013). Cognitive processing during a fixation affects the fixation duration (Rayner 1978). A longer fixation duration on a certain piece of information implies a higher intensity of cognitive processing and higher preference upon choices (Shimojo et al. 2003). Preferences can reinforce people's fixations and enhance their perceptions of attractiveness which in turn influence decision making. Krajbich et al. (2010) suggest that visual fixation process could have a causal effect on people's value comparison process.

Human pupils react not only to the change of environmental luminance, but also to change in cognitive processing (Brisson et al. 2013). Pupil dilation was found to be a consequence of attentional effort (Hoeks and Levelt 1993). According to Laeng et al. (2012), pupil diameter, which is also called "pupillometry", has been used to estimate the intensity of mental activities, change of emotions, change of mental states, and change of attention for more than 50 years. Pupil diameter is very difficult to control voluntarily, which makes pupil dilation a good objective measure.

3 Theoretical Background and Hypotheses

The first factor of this study is the source of recommendations provided by an e-commerce website: expert vs. consumer recommendations. Due to the limited processing capability, consumers cannot process all available information so that they only put their interest in information that are perceived to be relevant to their goals (Bettman et al. 1998). We propose consumer review based recommendation may win over expert review in terms of consumer attention and interest based on the similarity-attraction paradigm (Byrne and Griffitt 1973). The similarity-attraction paradigm posits that people are attracted to people who are similar to them (Byrne and Griffitt 1973). Attraction was found to be positively affected by people with similarities. Also, economic status, simple behavioral acts, and task performance were also found to positively influence perceived attraction among people.

Consumer reviews were written by former consumers who were previously likely to be in or who were facing similar situations with the current customer. Hence, customers can empathize and relate well with consumers who likely had more similarity in goals, experiences, and/or attitudes. Experts, on the other hand, though considered to be a higher authority in certain fields, may not share similarities with current customer. Consequently, consumer recommendations are expected to attract more interest than expert recommendations. Therefore, we propose:

H1: Consumer recommendations will attract greater user interest than expert recommendations.

The second factor refers to timing of recommendations - when the recommendations are offered, i.e., early, middle, or late in the e-commerce shopping process. Galinsky and Mussweiler (2001) found that the first offers served as anchors and were a strong predictor of the final deal in a seller-buyer context. During the buyer's decision making process, his or her judgements rely heavily on the initial anchor. People's judgement are severely biased by uncertainty and anchoring bias can occur (Tversky and Kahneman 1974). As consumers work on shopping tasks, their uncertainty about the outcome will be lower as they carry out the evaluation process. Hence, the initial anchor on a specific product that have gone through the evaluation process can deter attention on subsequent product recommendations offered by the online recommender system.

Based on the anchoring effect and bias, decision makers tend to be more interested in the initial anchor (Adomavicius et al. 2013). In an e-commerce context, after a decision maker is attracted by specific products, they are less likely to attend to other recommendations offered by online recommender systems. Hence, the following hypothesis is proposed:

H2: The earlier a recommendation is offered by online recommender systems, the greater the user attention toward the recommendation.

4 Methodology

A 2 (source) X 3 (timing) X 2 (product type) mixed experimental design was used for his research and the experiment was conducted in a university. The first and second factors are between-subject factors whereas the third factor (product type, laptop & cell phone) is a within-subject factor. Hence, there are 6 (i.e., 2 × 3) experimental conditions in this study. 76 subjects were recruited. They were given extra credits for their class and were provided with souvenirs after the experiment. All subjects have normal eye-sight before or after adjustment. Subjects were randomly assigned to one of the 6 conditions, and the sequence of the two products was also randomly assigned. There was a training session on the use of the experiment shopping website. The subjects need to carry out two shopping tasks: cell phones and laptops. They were asked to complete two shopping tasks: (i) purchase a laptop, and (ii) purchase a cell phone. Both products were chosen because of their popularity among the pilot test subjects. The task sequence was counterbalanced such that some subjects shopped for a cell phone first while others shopped for a laptop first.

The recommendation source was manipulated in two categories: expert review and consumer review. In the experiment, the recommendation source was highlighted on the recommendation pages. The heading used for the recommendation page was either "other consumers recommend this product to you" or "experts recommend this product to you". Several product reviews were provided on each product recommendation page and they were extracted from existing e-commerce websites. On each recommendation page, an image of the recommended product along with specifications of the recommended product were displayed. The recommendation timing was manipulated at three level: right after entering the website (i.e., early recommendation), after clicking "add to shopping cart" for the first chosen product (i.e., mid recommendation), and after clicking "purchase" button (i.e., late recommendation). The shopping website allowed subjects to search using various combination of search criteria to browse product details from the search results. The subjects were allowed to conduct search activities within the product database until decisions were made. Single criteria searches and multiple criteria searches were both supported. There was no time limit given to complete each task.

Three Tobii T60 eye-trackers in three separate lab rooms were used during the experiment. The resolution of the display is 1280 * 1024. The use of three eye-trackers allowed us to conduct three concurrent experimental sessions with the subjects. The moderator (or experimenter) at each of the three stations was given a standardized moderator script to following in conducting the experiment to avoid moderator biases. The luminance of all lab rooms were controlled at the same level.

5 Data Analysis and Results

All data were recorded by Tobii Studio software on Tobii T60 eye-trackers. The corneal reflection based devices computed and recorded the data including time, coordinates of eye movement activities, eye movement activities, and pupil diameter at a sample rate of 60 per second. Several variables were computed by using the video recordings of all subjects. Due to eye-tracking recording failure, 5 out of the 76 data points were excluded from the data set. The manipulations were successful based on results of manipulation check questions in the after-experiment questionnaire. Also, by reviewing the recording footages, we observed that all subjects fixated on the recommendation title which indicated their awareness of the recommendation source.

A data reduction procedure was conducted to convert raw data into cleansed fixation data on the recommendation pages. All data were exported from Tobii Studio in the format of xlsx. Five Excel VBAs were implemented to achieve the following goals: calculating pupil diameter baseline, cleansing data by time, cleansing data by gaze type, removing duplicate fixation entries, and calculating targeted pupil diameters. The pupil diameter baseline was calculated based on the first 100 s of recording during which all subjects were going through the instructions for the experiment.

Fixation durations on the recommendation pages for each subject were calculated. As the total browsing time varied across subjects, we calculated fixation duration per second by dividing total fixation duration by total recommendation browsing time. Pupil dilation was calculated as the percentage of pupil diameter change when browsing the product recommendation page versus the baseline condition (i.e., when reading instructions).

Outlier tests were conducted to detect and remove potential outliers for both dependent variables. 4 outliers were detected and removed for data analysis on pupil dilation. 8 outliers were detected and removed for data analysis on fixation duration per second. Order effects were tested for both dependent variables and no order effects for tasks (i.e., order of product types) were found for pupil dilation or fixation duration per second as dependent variables. ANOVA was conducted using SPSS for each of the dependent variables for the two between-subjects factors: recommendation source and recommendation timing, and one within-subjects factor: product type.

5.1 Data Analysis on Pupil Dilation

The pupil diameter for each task was calculated by averaging the left and right pupil diameters. The average of the pupil diameters was then calculated based on the time stamp of product recommendation page to reveal the target pupil diameter (target PD): diameter of the pupil when looking at the product recommendation page. Pupil dilation was then computed relative to the pupil diameter baseline (PDBL) using following equation.

$$Pupil\, dilation = (target\, PD - PDBL) \div PDBL$$

Pupil dilation reveals the percentage of change on pupil diameter at a given period of time as compared to the baseline. Excluding the outliers, 67 sets of data were used for the analysis. We have an average sample size of 11 for each of the experimental conditions. The descriptive statistics for pupil dilation was shown in Table 1.

Table 1. Descriptive statistics for pupil dilation

	Timing	Source	Mean	# of Subjects
Pupil dilation_cell phone	Early	Expert	−4.04%	12
		Consumer	−0.76%	10
		Total	−2.57%	22
	Mid	Expert	−3.68%	12
		Consumer	−0.29%	11
		Total	−1.78%	23
	Late	Expert	−1.50%	11
		Consumer	0.00%	11
		Total	−0.75	22
	Total	Expert	−3.13%	35
		Consumer	−0.14%	32
		Total	−1.70%	67
Pupil dilation_laptop	Early	Expert	−2.85%	12
		Consumer	0.51%	10
		Total	−1.32%	22
	Mid	Expert	−1.05%	12
		Consumer	1.00%	11
		Total	−0.07%	23
	Late	Expert	−1.84%	11
		Consumer	0.21%	11
		Total	−0.81%	22
	Total	Expert	−1.91%	35
		Consumer	0.58%	32
		Total	−0.72%	67

The results indicate that, recommendation source has a significant effect on pupil dilation there is no significant within-subjects effect (product type) on pupil dilation. However, expert recommendations resulted in an average pupil dilation of −2.5% while consumer recommendations resulted in an average pupil dilation of 0.2%. The difference between them is significant at p value of 0.003 which is less than 0.05. Thus,

H1 is supported, indicating that there was higher interest in consumer recommendations than expert recommendations. The negative value of pupil dilation on expert recommendations indicates that participants have lower interest when browsing expert recommendations.

5.2 Data Analysis on Fixation Duration Per Second

The fixation duration for each task was calculated by adding all fixation time based on the timestamp of product recommendation page. We then calculate the fixation duration per second (FDPS) by dividing the total fixation duration by total browsing time of the recommendation page using following equation.

$$FDPS = Fixation\,Duration \div Total\,browsing\,time$$

We use FDPS to control for different browsing time of the recommendation pages among subjects. For example, a FDPS value of 0.6 indicates that for every 1 s a subject spent on the recommendation page, he/she fixated 0.6 s on the content. This measure revealed the attention levels of the subjects. A higher FDPS indicates a higher level of attention on the recommendation page. 8 sets of data were excluded from the analysis because they were outliers.

Table 2 shows the descriptive statistics for FDPS. The ANOVA results suggest that timing and source do not have significant effects on FDPS. Thus, the second hypothesis is not supported.

6 Discussion and Conclusion

6.1 Discussion

This study used eye-tracking data to explain the effect of recommendation timing and source on user attention and interest during online shopping tasks. The results suggest that pupil dilation varies across sources of recommendations. Trustworthiness of consumer recommendations, which was found to be higher for consumer recommendations by Bettman et al. (1998) and Senecal et al. (2004), may have contributed to the higher interest through larger pupil dilations. This is in line with the similarity-attraction paradigm (Byrne 1973). Former and potential consumers are more similar in terms of experiences, goals, interest, etc. These similarities result in a higher level of attraction between them. The attraction is the foundation of the interest that consumers have on online consumer recommendations. Based on our results, we conclude that using consumer reviews as the source for recommender systems has its advantages in gaining consumers' interest than using expert.

Contrary to our prediction, fixation intensity is not significantly influenced by recommendation timing. Recommendation timing does not have anchoring effect on consumer's attention and interest.

Table 2. Descriptive statistics for FDPS

	Timing	Source	Mean	# of Subjects
FDPS_cell phone	Early	Expert	0.773	12
		Consumer	0.720	11
		Total	0.748	23
	Mid	Expert	0.780	12
		Consumer	0.668	9
		Total	0.732	21
	Late	Expert	0.653	10
		Consumer	0.765	9
		Total	0.706	19
	Total	Expert	0.740	34
		Consumer	0.718	29
		Total	0.730	63
FDPS_laptop	Early	Expert	0.800	12
		Consumer	0.783	11
		Total	0.792	23
	Mid	Expert	0.700	12
		Consumer	0.647	9
		Total	0.677	21
	Late	Expert	0.706	10
		Consumer	0.764	9
		Total	0.733	19
	Total	Expert	0.737	34
		Consumer	0.735	29
		Total	0.736	63

6.2 Limitation

There are some limitations in this study which calls for future work. First, for better experiment control, the recommender system algorithm is not included in the recommender system design in this study. Future research can integrate personalized product recommendation in the experiment design. Second, the subjects are undergraduate students from a university in the United States, which may limit the generalizability of the study. It is possible that their attention to the recommendations varies from those with different demographic and cultural backgrounds.

6.3 Contribution

This research contributes to the understanding of the characteristics of online recommender systems via eye tracking approach. Despite the importance of online recommender systems to online retailers, few guideline exists for online recommender systems on which features of online recommender systems that can help to boost sales.

The findings from this research can help some online retail business owners to increase the effectiveness of their recommender systems in attracting consumers' attention.

The eye tracking method can help open the black box of the decision-making process during online shopping. Eye-trackers are used as a source for objective, non-invasive, continuous, and quantitative data which has the potential to help researchers studying human attention, mental load, cognitive processes, etc.

References

Adomavicius, G., Bockstedt, J., Curley, S., Zhang, J.: Do recommender systems manipulate consumer preferences? A study of anchoring effects. Inf. Syst. Res. **24**(4) 956–975 (2013)

Bettman, J.R., Luce, M.F., Payne, J.W.: Constructive consumer choice processes. J. Consum. Res. **25**(3), 187–217 (1998)

Brisson, J., Mainville, M., Mailloux, D., Beaulieu, C., Serres, J., Sirois, S.: Pupil diameter measurement errors as a function of gaze direction in corneal reflection eyetrackers. Behav. Res. Methods **45**(4), 1322–1331 (2013)

Byrne, D., Griffitt, W.: Interpersonal attraction. Ann. Rev. Psychol. **24**(1), 317–336 (1973)

Chiou, J.-S., Hsiao, C.-C., Su, F.-Y.: Whose online reviews have the most influences on consumers in cultural offerings? Professional vs consumer commentators. Internet Res. **24**(3), 353–368 (2014)

Denale, R., Weidenhamer, D.: Quarterly Retail E-Commerce Sales 1st Quarter (2016)

Galinsky, A.D., Mussweiler, T.: First offers as anchors: the role of perspective-taking and negotiator focus. J. Pers. Soc. Psychol. **81**(4), 657 (2001)

Ho, S.Y., Bodoff, D., Tam, K.Y.: Timing of adaptive web personalization and its effects on online consumer behavior. Inf. Syst. Res. **22**(3), 660–679 (2011)

Hoeks, B., Levelt, W.J.: Pupillary dilation as a measure of attention: a quantitative system analysis. Behav. Res. Methods Instrum. Comput. **25**(1), 16–26 (1993)

Hostler, R.E., Yoon, V.Y., Guimaraes, T.: Recommendation agent impact on consumer online shopping: the Movie Magic case study. Exp. Syst. Appl. **39**(3), 2989–2999 (2012)

Jacobs, R.S., Heuvelman, A., Allouch, S.B., Peters, O.: Everyone's a critic: the power of expert and consumer reviews to shape readers' post-viewing motion picture evaluations. Poetics **52**, 91–103 (2015)

Krajbich, I., Armel, C., Rangel, A.: Visual fixations and the computation and comparison of value in simple choice. Nat. Neurosci. **13**(10), 1292–1298 (2010)

Laeng, B., Sirois, S., Gredebäck, G.: Pupillometry a window to the preconscious? Perspect. Psychol. Sci. **7**(1), 18–27 (2012)

Orquin, J., Mueller Loose, S.: Attention and choice: a review on eye movements in decision making. Acta Psychol. **144**(1), 190–206 (2013)

Rayner, K.: Eye movements in reading and information processing. Psychol. Bull. **85**(3), 618–660 (1978)

Schonfeld, E.: Web sales pitches are getting better, thanks to new programs designed to sell you stuff you didn't even know you wanted (2007)

Senecal, S., Nantel, J.: The influence of online product recommendations on consumers' online choices. J. Retail. **80**(2), 159–169 (2004)

Shimojo, S., Simion, C., Shimojo, E., Scheier, C.: Gaze bias both reflects and influences preference. Nat. Neurosci. **6**(12), 1317–1322 (2003)

Triesch, J., Ballard, D.H., Hayhoe, M.M., Sullivan, B.T.: What you see is what you need. J. Vis. **3**(1), 86–94 (2003)

Tversky, A., Kahneman, D.: Judgment under uncertainty: heuristics and biases. Science **185** (4157), 1124–1131 (1974)

Utz, S., Kerkhof, P., van den Bos, J.: Consumers rule: how consumer reviews influence perceived trustworthiness of online stores. Electron. Commer. Res. Appl. **11**(1), 49–58 (2012)

Zhang, P., Benbasat, I., Carey, J., Davis, F., Galletta, D., Strong, D.: Human-computer interaction research in the MIS discipline. Commun. Assoc. Inf. Syst. **9**, 334–355 (2002)

Optimize the Coupon Face Value
for Online Sellers

Peng Wang$^{(\boxtimes)}$, Rong Du, Yumeng Miao, and Zongming Zhang

School of Economics and Management, Xidian University, Xian 710126, China
15891795977@163.com, durong@mail.xidian.edu.cn,
ymmiao@stu.xidian.edu.cn, zongmingzhang@xidian.edu.cn

Abstract. The impact of online coupons is well recognized, but few studies have attempted to model the optimal coupon face value. This research examines how the online coupon affects the payoff of a seller and analyzes the optimal coupon face value for online seller. We find that both the fixed costs and matching probability play critical roles in whether the seller chooses to offer coupons or not. We also find that, a seller can maximize his/her profit by providing the online coupon with an optimal face value which has been formulated. Finally, we conclude with managerial implications and directions for further studies.

Keywords: Online coupon · Coupon face value · Matching probability · Equilibrium analysis · Online seller

1 Introduction

The phenomenon of online coupons as a means of increasing sales is well-known and widely used in the electronic business. Online sellers choose to offer coupons to shape the potential buyers' attitudes and motivate their purchase. And, there are some sellers who offer the coupons earning lots of money on the online platforms. In contrast, other online venders who do not provide the coupons still make great profits. The difference between the two kinds of sellers raises several questions: In what situation can online sellers benefit from choosing to offer coupons? If a seller offers the coupon, how should he/she optimize the coupon face value to maximize his/her payoff? This paper aims to answer these two questions.

Current research on the online coupons emphasizes the coupon proneness, coupon redemption [1, 2, 14] and online pricing with coupon [10, 11, 18], but few researchers have attempted to model the optimal coupon face value. Ben-Zion [3] has modeled the optimal face value of a discount coupon in traditional economics. But online environment brings some new characteristics, and there is almost no analytic models being developed for online sellers to maximize their profits. This study will fill this gap and sheds some light on the choice of online coupons for sellers.

To do so, we develop a game-theoretic model in which online sellers face choosing to offer coupons or not. We consider an online platform with a group of potential buyers on the one side and a group of potential sellers on the other. We assume the mass of buyers as a fixed value. Besides, the platform offers basic services for free and,

© Springer International Publishing AG 2017
F.F.-H. Nah and C.-H. Tan (Eds.): HCIBGO 2017, PART II, LNCS 10294, pp. 105–113, 2017.
DOI: 10.1007/978-3-319-58484-3_9

meanwhile, sellers have fixed costs to provide products and can choose to offer coupons to increase their exposure. And, each online seller on the basic platform has a unique trading partner and gets the same likelihood noticed by prospective buyers. We define the likelihood as matching probability. For ease of exposition, we simply assume that the trade occurs when the seller is noticed by the trading buyer. Using this framework, we compare the revenues of sellers' payoffs under the two situations in which the sellers offer the coupons or not.

We identify both the matching probability and fixed costs as the key factors in comparing the two situations. Not surprisingly, the matching probability of the seller plays an important role in determining whether to offer the coupon or not. In addition, it is found that when the matching probability is high, the seller with a larger fixed cost can benefit from offering the coupon. Furthermore, we find that a seller can optimize the coupon face value to maximize his/her payoff, and the optimal coupon face value varies according to the matching probability and the fixed costs.

The contribution of this paper is that we identify the circumstances that an online sellers can benefit from offering coupons and optimize coupon face value for the online seller to maximize his/her payoff. And the paper is organized as follows. We give a brief literature review first, and then we formulate a model and make the equilibrium analysis to optimize the coupon face value for online sellers. Finally, we conclude with managerial implications and further research issues.

2 Literature Review

Our study is mainly related to the research about coupons. Firstly, coupon proneness has been widely documented in the literature that buyers with different characteristics, such as age, income, education, brand loyalty, have distinct coupon proneness [9, 17]. Tang and Zhao [22] identified the impact of coupon proneness on mobile coupon sharing in social network sites. Then, the coupon redemption was also studied deeply. Kapil [1] integrated the coupon attraction and coupon proneness as the key factors influencing the coupon redemption. Leone [13] analyzed the impact of coupon face value on the coupon redemption and brand probability. Besides, many scholars associated the coupons with the price discrimination. Narasimhan [18] showed that coupons can be taken as a price discrimination device and be provided to a particular segment of consumers. Moraga-González [16] analyzed different types of coupon under imperfect price information. Furthermore, lots of researchers paid attention to the coupon face value. For instance, Garretson [7] examined the influence of coupon face value on service quality expectations, perceived purchase risks, and purchase intentions in the dental industry. Price [20] modeled the coupon values for ready-to- eat breakfast cereals.

In contrast to the traditional coupons in the offline environment, online environment offers online sellers an opportunity to issue coupons with different face values to potential buyers for immediate online use. Ben-Zion [3] tried to optimize the face value of coupons by analyzing the structure of the market and separating apart the loyal customers. Chiou [6] used panel data to investigate the factors that influence the preference of shoppers for online coupons. Cheng and Dogan [5] emphasized the importance of customer-centric marketing when using Internet coupons. Reichhart [21] compared the effectiveness of e-mail coupons with mobile coupons and the results indicated that e-mail coupons got a higher response rate. Georgia [8] considered the customer loyalty and analyzed the coupon trading. Martín-Herrán [15] combined coupons with the trade deals with on-package coupons and concluded the optimal strategy. Navdeep [19] examined the discount offers can improve the average expenditure, and the coupons can be seen as one type of discount offers. Jiang [10, 11] focused on the online pricing with the discount coupons and modeled to maximize the profits of firms or sellers.

We focus on the coupon face value in the online environment. Garretson [7] and Price [20] analyze the coupon face value in the traditional economics. Ben-Zion [3] optimizes the coupon face value by separating apart the market and still does not refer to the online characteristics. Different from the above research, we consider an online seller facing whether to offer the coupons or not and take the matching probability and fixed costs as the key factors. Then, we optimal the coupon face value for online sellers aiming to maximize their profits.

3 Model

We consider an online two-sided market with multiple sellers and buyers based on a platform. And the platform provides matching between potential sellers and buyers to facilitate transactions. In addition, potential buyers participate in the platform aiming to find their ideal products provided by online venders. We assume that buyers and sellers can participate in the platform without any costs, which is consistent with the popular online platform, Taobao.com, practices. And the platform can make the profit by offering advertising.

We assume that sellers are listed without differentiation which means that each buyer has a unique trading partner on the platform, and each seller will get the same likelihood noticed by buyers. We denote p as the likelihood, also called the matching probability, that the seller's product is noticed by buyers. For ease of exposition, we simply assume that the trading occurs when the seller's product is noticed by the potential buyer, which is often used in the prior literature [4]. So, sellers will try their best to improve the matching probability to increase sales, and they can choose to offer online coupons. Undoubtedly, the coupon face value η, determines the matching probability increased, and we denote p_1 as the matching probability the seller offering the online coupon with value η receives. We easily assume all buyers have coupon proneness.

We assume that each seller in the platform is seen as selling a different product and the competition among sellers is not considered, which is consistent the with exited researches on two-sided markets [4, 12]. Then, each seller will have a fixed cost, k, to provide the product on the platform. We assume that the fixed cost k is distributed on [0, 1]. And the participating buyers and sellers will also obtain profits by occurring transactions. We let s as the expected surplus that a buyer derives from trading and π as the expected revenue that a seller derives. Similarly, we assume $s \leq 1$ and $\pi \leq 1$.

Sellers choose whether to participate in the platform depending on their costs and profits. And we assume a fixed value as the mass of participating sellers which means that the choice of a seller to offer the online coupon will not influence the total mass of participating buyers. The assumption is reasonable because there are vast buyers in online platforms, and a seller' choice can be ignored. Let m be the mass of buyers and n be the mass of sellers participating in the platform. Similarly, we denote n_1 as the mass of participating sellers offering online coupons. As has mentioned above, each buyer has a unique trading partner on the platform, and each seller lists differently. So, the more mass of participating sellers, the more likelihood that a buyer's ideal trading partner is on the platform. And we can assume that the probability that a buyer's trading partner is on the platform is equal to the mass of participating sellers n. Table 1 summarizes the main notations referred above.

Table 1. Summary of Notations

Notation	Definition and Comments
η	coupon face value
k	seller's cost of proving a product
m	mass of participating buyers
n	mass of participating sellers
n_1	mass of participating sellers offering online coupons
p	exposure each participating seller receives, also called "matching probability"
p_1	exposure the participating seller offers the coupon with face value η receives
s	buyer's expected surplus from trading
π	seller's expected revenue from trading

Then, a seller's expected payoff from participating in the platform:

$$mp(\pi - k) \tag{1}$$

Now consider that when a buyer's ideal trading partner offers the online coupon with face value η, the buyer finds the trading partner and will get profit $s + \eta$. And the probability that the buyer can find the partner is p, so her/his profit derived from this trading can be described as $p(s + \eta)$. This transaction can also be interpreted as that the probability that the buyer find the trading partner increases to $p_1(p_1 < 1)$, but the profit still is the expected surplus s, and then the buyer' profit derived from this trading can be described as $p_1 s$. Hence, the buyer' profit derived from this trading can be described as $p(s + \eta)$ and $p_1 s$ simultaneously when $p_1 < 1$. And we can get:

$$p(s + \eta) = p_1 s \quad if \ p_1 < 1 \tag{2}$$

A seller's expected payoff U_s from participating in the platform with offering the online coupon with face value η

$$U_s = \begin{cases} mp_1(\pi - k - \eta) & if \ \eta < \frac{1-p}{p}s \\ m(\pi - k - \eta) & if \ \eta \geq \frac{1-p}{p}s \end{cases} \tag{3}$$

4   Equilibrium Analysis

In this section, we will analyze the participation of sellers. And then, we formulate the coupon face value in order to maximize the profit for the online seller.

Participation of Sellers
We have monotonicity in sellers' participation decisions [4]. In particular, if a seller with a certain cost participates in the platform, the sellers with lower costs also participate in. In addition, if a seller with a certain cost benefits from choosing to offer the online coupon, so does the seller with the lower cost. We denote k_A as the cost of the marginal seller who is indifferent about participating in the platform, k_{A1} as the cost of the marginal participating seller who is indifferent about offering the online coupon with value η, if a seller derives a positive payoff from offering the coupon, her/his payoff from participating in the basic platform service without cost should be positive, which implies $k_{A1} < k_A$. Therefore, the sellers with costs lower than k_A participate in the platform, and the mass of participating sellers is $n = k_A$.

Based on the above denotation and Eq. (2), we can derive the relationship of a marginal seller:

$$mp(\pi - k_A) = 0 \tag{4}$$

And from Eq. (4), we can derive $n = k_A = \pi$

Now we consider the situation that $p_1 < 1$. As the marginal seller offering the coupon with value η, we can derive the relationship based Eqs. (1) and (3):

$$mp_1(\pi - k_{A1} - \eta) = mp(\pi - k_{A1}) \tag{5}$$

From Eqs. (5) and (2), we can get:

$$k_{A1} = \pi - s - \eta \tag{6}$$

When $p_1 \geq 1$. As the marginal seller offering the coupon with value η, we can derive the relationship based on Eqs. (1) and (3):

$$m(\pi - k_{A1} - \eta) = mp(\pi - k_{A1}) \tag{7}$$

From Eqs. (7) and (2), we can get:

$$k_{A1} = \pi - \frac{1}{1-p}\eta \tag{8}$$

From Eqs. (7) and (8), we can get:

$$k_{A1} = \begin{cases} \pi - s - \eta & \text{if } \eta < \frac{1-p}{p}s \text{ and } \eta \leq \pi - s \\ \pi - \frac{1}{1-p}\eta & \text{if } \eta \geq \frac{1-p}{p}s \end{cases}$$

So, we derive that $k_{A1_{\max}} = \pi - s$.

Then, we can conclude the participation of sellers as follows:

Corollary 1. *The sellers who have costs in* $[0, \pi]$ *participate in the platform. And sellers with* $[0, \pi - s]$ *can benefit from offering the online coupons. In addition, when* $p \geq \frac{s}{\pi}$, *the sellers who have costs in* $\left[0, \pi - \frac{s}{p}\right]$ *benefit from offering the coupons with values in* $[0, (1 - p)(\pi - k)]$; *the sellers who have costs in* $(\pi - \frac{s}{p}, \pi - s]$ *benefit from offering coupons with values in* $[0, \pi - s - k]$. *When* $p < \frac{s}{\pi}$, *the sellers who have costs in* $[0, \pi - s]$ *benefit from offering coupons with values in* $[0, \pi - s - k]$.

Proof. All proofs are in the appendix, unless indicated otherwise.

The Optimal Coupon Face Value

The seller maximizes his payoff by choosing the optimal coupon face value $\eta (0 \leq \eta \leq \pi - s)$. Increasing the coupon face value will improve the exposure to the potential buyers. However, increasing the coupon face value also means more costs for the seller. So, the seller' maximum profit is the result of the balance between the coupon face value and the cost followed. And, we also assume the choice of a seller whether to offer the coupon does not influence the mass of participating buyers, that means the mass of buyers, m, is a constant value.

We consider the case that $\eta = 0$ which means the seller does not offer the coupon. From Corollary 1, we can know that the sellers who have the fixed costs in $[\pi - s, \pi]$ will not choose to offer the coupons. So, we can draw the conclusion the seller with cost in $[\pi - s, \pi]$ maximizes his profit by choosing not offering the coupon. Then, we analyze the situation that $0 < \eta \leq \pi - s$. And from Eq. (8), our work becomes how to maximize the Equation:

$$\max U_s = \begin{cases} mp_1(\pi - k - \eta) & \text{if } \eta < \frac{1-p}{p} s \\ m(\pi - k - \eta) & \text{if } \eta \geq \frac{1-p}{p} s \end{cases} \tag{9}$$

From Eq. (9), we can conclude the optimal coupon face value for online sellers:

Proposition 1. *The optimal coupon face value that the seller should offer is:*
When $p > \frac{2s}{\pi + s}$,

$$\eta^* = \begin{cases} \frac{1-p}{p} s & \text{if } k \leq \pi - \frac{2-p}{p} s \\ \frac{\pi - s - k}{2} & \text{if } \pi - \frac{2-p}{p} s < k \leq \pi - s \end{cases}$$

When $p \leq \frac{2s}{\pi + s}$,

$$\eta^* = \frac{\pi - s - k}{2} \quad \text{if } 0 < k \leq \pi - s$$

5   Conclusion

In this paper, we have studied how the choice of offering coupons affects the profits of online sellers. The findings indicate that both the fixed costs and matching probability play essential roles in the choice. We also find that a seller can get profit form providing the online coupon with a face value that depends on the matching probability and fixed cost. Then, we have given the formulation of the optimal coupon face values for online sellers.

Managerial Implications
Our study has several implications. First, we underscore the importance of online sellers to choose the coupon face values according to the matching probability and the fixed costs. This tells online platform managers that matching probability plays a critical role in deciding whether to offer the coupon, and a lower fixed cost always means the seller can offer a higher face value coupon. Second, our analysis indicates that the online seller can maximize his/her payoff by choosing the optimal coupon face value. Moreover, when there is a certain range of choices, a seller with a fixed cost can get profits by providing an online coupon with an optimal face value.

Directions for Further Research
Firstly, in this study we assume that the platform provides the matching services for free, and for further research we can consider the situation when the platform charges a transaction fee. Secondly, this study also assumes all buyers have coupon proneness which is not accurate in the real word, and the various proneness situations should be discussed in the further research. Thirdly, in further studies we can compare online coupons with other promotional services, such as advertisement, and analyze the profits of all participating players.

Acknowledgments. This research is supported by the Shaanxi Humanities and Social Science Talent Plan (HSSTP) through grant ER42015060002. And this research is also supported by National Natural Science Foundation of China (71502132), Natural Science Basic Research Plan in Shaanxi Province of China (2015JQ7274) and the Fundamental Research Funds for the Central Universities (JB150603).

Appendix

Proof of Corollary 1

Proof. From Eq. (4), we can get: $n = k_A = \pi$ which means that the mass of participating sellers is π, and the sellers with $[0, \pi]$ can participate in the platform. And $k_{A1_{max}} = \pi - s$ which means the sellers with $[0, \pi - s]$ can choose offering the coupons. Then, we analyzed the profitable situation.

When $p_1 = \frac{s+\eta}{s} p < 1$, the increased profit of the seller who offers the coupon with value η will be $\sigma U_s = -\frac{1}{s} m p \eta [\eta - (\pi - k - s)]$, and when $\frac{1-p}{p} \leq \pi - s$, that is equal to

$p < \frac{s}{\pi}$, the sellers who have costs in $[0, \pi - s]$ can offer the coupons with values in $[0, \pi - s - k]$.

When $p_1 = \frac{s+\eta}{s} p \geq 1$, the increased profit becomes $\sigma U_s = m[\eta - (1 - p)(\pi - k)]$, and $\eta < \pi - s$, so we can get $p \geq \frac{s}{\pi}$. Then, we discuss the fixed costs, and we can get the sellers who have costs in $\left[0, \pi - \frac{s}{p}\right]$ can offer the coupons with values in $[0, (1 - p)(\pi - k)]$; the sellers who have costs in $(\pi - \frac{s}{p}, \pi - s]$ can offer he coupons with values in $[0, \pi - s - k]$.

Proof of Proposition 1

Proof. Firstly, we do not consider the choice of offering coupons or not and just analyze the Eq. (9). When $\eta < \frac{1-p}{p} s$, the profit of the online seller becomes that $U_s = mp_1(\pi - k - \eta) = m\frac{s+\eta}{s} p(\pi - k - \eta)$. And we can derive that:

$$U_s = -\frac{mp}{s}\eta^2 + \frac{mp}{s}(\pi - k - s)\eta + mp(\pi - k)$$

From the above Equation, we can get that when $\frac{1-p}{p} s < \frac{\pi - k - s}{2}$ which means $p > \frac{2s}{\pi + s}$, the optimal coupon face value is $\eta^* = \frac{1-p}{p} s$.

When $\frac{1-p}{p} s \geq \frac{\pi - k - s}{2}$, the optimal coupon face value becomes: $\eta^* = \frac{\pi - s - k}{2}$.

When $\eta \geq \frac{1-p}{p} s$ which means $p \geq \frac{s}{\pi}$, the profit of the online seller becomes: $U_s = m(\pi - k - \eta)$. We can get that the optimal coupon face value is $\eta^* = \frac{1-p}{p} s$.

Then, we add the condition under which buyers can benefit from offering coupons, and it is also provided by Corollary 1. We can conclude the optimal coupon face value for online sellers as follow:

When $p > \frac{2s}{\pi + s}$, and if $k \leq \pi - \frac{2-p}{p} s$ the optimal coupon face value is $\eta^* = \frac{1-p}{p} s$, and if $\pi - \frac{2-p}{p} s < k \leq \pi - s$, the optimal coupon face value will be $\eta^* = \frac{\pi - s - k}{2}$. When $p \leq \frac{2s}{\pi + s}$ and $0 < k \leq \pi - s$, the optimal coupon face value will be $\eta^* = \frac{\pi - s - k}{2}$.

References

1. Bawa, K., Shoemaker, R.W.: The coupon-prone consumer: some findings based on purchase behavior across product classes. J. Mark. **51**(4), 99 (1987)
2. Bawa, K., Srinivasan, S.S., Srivastava, R.K.: Coupon attractiveness and coupon proneness: a framework for modeling coupon redemption. J. Mark. Res. **34**(4), 517 (1997)
3. Ben-Zion, U., Hibshoosh, A., Spiegel, U.: The optimal face value of a discount coupon. J. Econ. Bus. **51**(2), 159–174 (1999)
4. Chen, J., Fan, M., Li, M.: Advertising versus brokerage model for online trading platforms. MIS Q. **40**(3), 575–596 (2016)
5. Cheng, H.K., Dogan, K.: Customer-centric marketing with Internet coupons. Decis. Support Syst. **44**(3), 606–620 (2008)

6. Chiou-Wei, S.-Z., Inman, J.J.: Do shoppers like electronic coupons? J. Retail. **84**(3), 297–307 (2008)
7. Garretson, J.A., Clow, K.E.: The influence of coupon face value on service quality expectations, risk perceptions and purchase intentions in the dental industry. J. Serv. Mark. **13**(1), 59–72 (1999)
8. Kosmopoulou, G., Liu, Q., Shuai, J.: Customer poaching and coupon trading. J. Econ. **118**, 219–238 (2016)
9. Guimond, L., Kim, C., Laroche, M.: An investigation of coupon-prone consumers. J. Bus. Res. **54**(2), 131–137 (2001)
10. Jiang, Y., Shang, J., Kemerer, C.F., et al.: Optimizing e-tailer profits and customer savings: pricing multistage customized online bundles. Mark. Sci. **30**(4), 737–752 (2011)
11. Jiang, Y., Liu, Y., Wang, H., et al.: Online pricing with bundling and coupon discounts. Int. J. Prod. Res. **11**(3), 1–16 (2015)
12. Jullien, B.: Two-sided markets and electronic intermediaries. CESifo Econ. Stud. **51**(2–3), 233–260 (2006)
13. Leone, R.P., Srinivasan, S.: Coupon face value: it's impact on coupon redemptions, brand sales, and brand profitability. J. Retail. **72**(3), 273–289 (1996)
14. Lichtenstein, D.R., Burton, S.: Distinguishing coupon proneness from value consciousness: an acquisition-transaction utility theory perspective. J. Mark. **54**(3), 54–67 (1990)
15. Martín-Herrán, G., Sigué, S.P.: Trade deals and/or on-package coupons. Eur. J. Oper. Res. **241**(2), 541–554 (2015)
16. Moraga-González, J.L., Petrakis, E.: Coupon advertising under imperfect price information. J. Econ. Manag. Strategy **8**(4), 523–544 (1999)
17. Musalem, A., Bradlow, E.T., Raju, J.S.: Who's got the coupon? Estimating consumer preferences and coupon usage from aggregate information. J. Mark. Res. **45**(6), 715–730 (2013)
18. Narasimhan, C.: A price discrimination theory of coupons. Mark. Sci. **3**(2), 128–147 (1984)
19. Sahni, N.S., Zou, D., Chintagunta, P.K.: Do targeted discount offers serve as advertising? Evidence from 70 field experiments. Manag. Sci., 24 June 2016. Published online
20. Price, G.K., Connor, J.M.: Modeling coupon values for ready-to-eat breakfast cereals. Agribusiness **19**(2), 223–243 (2001)
21. Reichhart, P., Pescher, C., Spann, M.: A comparison of the effectiveness of e-mail coupons and mobile text message coupons for digital products. Electron. Markets **23**(3), 217–222 (2013)
22. Tang, Q., Zhao, X., Liu, S.: The effect of intrinsic and extrinsic motivations on mobile coupon sharing in social network sites. Internet Res. **26**(1), 101–119 (2016)

Acceptance of Personalization in Omnichannel Retailing

Werner Wetzlinger[✉], Andreas Auinger, Harald Kindermann,
and Wolfgang Schönberger

Department for Digital Business, University of Applied Sciences Upper Austria,
Campus Steyr, Wehrgrabengasse 1-3, 4400 Steyr, Austria
{werner.wetzlinger,andreas.auinger,
harald.kindermann}@fh-steyr.at,
w.schoenberger@outlook.com

Abstract. Omnichannel retailing is an approach that enables customers to use multiple online and offline channels of retailers during a customer journey and combine them simultaneously. By embedding digital devices in brick-and-mortar retail stores, retailers are able to better observe customer behavior, to collect customer data, analyze their needs and provide personalized services. This personalization may provide additional value for customers but may also lead to privacy concerns. This paper examines the impact of personalization on privacy concerns and the intention of customers to adopt services in brick-and-mortar retail stores and online shops. The empirical study is based on an online survey that uses a within-subject design including four scenarios that covered the combinations of personalization and non-personalization with the retailing context online shop vs. brick-and-mortar retail store. The subjects had to assess their privacy concerns and their intention to adopt the omnichannel retailing services in these scenarios. 112 subjects participated within this study. Results show that personalized services cause significantly higher privacy concerns than non-personalized services for both contexts. Additionally, consumers expressed higher concerns regarding digital services in the retail store than in the online shop for both personalized and non-personalized services. The intention to adopt the digital services decreased in scenarios with personalized services, both online and offline. However, the intention to adopt personalized services is generally lower in retail stores (with digital elements of omnichannel retailing) than in the online shop. Privacy concerns appeared to have significant negative impact on the intention to adopt in three out of four omnichannel scenarios.

Keywords: E-commerce · Human computer interaction · Omnichannel retail · Personalization · Technology acceptance

1 Introduction

Omnichannel retailing is a cross-channel approach of retailers that provides all channels to customers in an integrated way [1]. In the past, brick-and-mortar retail stores were unique in allowing consumers to touch and feel merchandise and provide instant gratification; Internet retailers (online shop providers), meanwhile, tried to woo

© Springer International Publishing AG 2017
F.F.-H. Nah and C.-H. Tan (Eds.): HCIBGO 2017, PART II, LNCS 10294, pp. 114–129, 2017.
DOI: 10.1007/978-3-319-58484-3_10

shoppers with wide product selection, low prices and content such as product reviews and ratings. As the retailing industry evolves toward a seamless "omnichannel retailing" experience, the distinctions between physical and online will vanish, turning the world into a showroom without walls [2]. Therefore, omnichannel retailing includes all offline, online and mobile channels that enable customers to interact with a retailer in multiple ways. It focuses on a seamless experience across channels, places more emphasis on the interplay between channels and provides services that combine offline and online channels to allow for simultaneous channel usage [3].

This behavior is enabled and supported to a great extent by the omnipresence of smartphones, since they can be used to access (third party) online services while shopping in a brick-and-mortar retail store. Additionally, retailers are implementing and rolling out more and more digital in-store services to improve the customer experience. This includes services that customers can access via personal smartphones as well as dedicated in-store technology [4].

These digital technologies enable retailers to provide personalized services. These tailored services may offer customers additional value, but also require collecting and analyzing data about users and their behaviour to identify customer preferences and needs [5]. This may also lead to privacy concerns of customers and reduce their willingness to use the personalized services.

In the context of online shops this is already widely adopted and users have experienced these services. But the deployment of in-store technologies and omnichannel retailing services also bring more technology-based services to retail stores, providing retailers with the opportunity to collect data in retail stores, too. Consequently, personalized services could also be provided in retail stores. But it is unclear whether privacy concerns and the intention to adopt personalized services in retail stores differ compared to online shops. This is what we examined in this study. We base this study on a study by Sheng/Nah/Siau [6] that investigated the impact of personalization and privacy concerns in a ubiquitous commerce context. We replicated the methodology but altered the context, leading to a replication with a context extension [7].

Structure of the paper. The remaining paper is structured as follows: In Sect. 2 we lay out related work concerning the purchasing context, privacy concerns and the intention to adopt omnichannel retailing services. Section 3 describes the research methodology. Section 4 presents the results of the study. Finally, Sect. 5 discusses the results and draws conclusions.

2 Omnichannel Retailing

In this section we analyze related work of omnichannel retailing aspects that may influence privacy concerns and the intention to adopt omnichannel retailing services to derive hypotheses for the subsequent empirical study.

2.1 Retailing Context

The retailing context defines the conditions that a customer experiences while buying products. For the study two different context categories were chosen:

- Buying in an online shop
- Buying in a retail store

These two alternatives are characterized through different external factors that influence customer behavior.

Online shops are commonly used in developed countries. To access them customers use different devices like desktop PCs, laptops, tablets or smartphones. To customers these shops provide various advantages, e.g. higher product variety, more detailed product information, customer reviews, lower prices, higher price transparency and location - as well as time-independency. To interact with the retailer online shops provide multiple technology based communication services like email, contact form, (video) chat or phone, but do not provide face-to-face interaction with shop assistants [8].

Brick-and-mortar retail stores on the other hand provide the opportunity to obtain personal advice from shop assistants and to experience products, their characteristics and their qualities.

Omnichannel retailing tries to combine online and offline channels and enables customers to even use them simultaneously. Consequently they are able to use online channels to access additional product information or use payment services on smartphones while in a retail store.

For this study we consider the two contexts online shop and retail store as mutually exclusive and compare them in an experimental setting.

2.2 Privacy Concerns

Gathering personal data about customers enables retailers to provide personalized goods and services. In addition, studies show that consumers are willing to disclose such data for personalized services if they provide additional value to the consumer [9]. On the other hand privacy concerns of customers rise. Faced with personalized services, consumers worry about the loss of control over the distribution and use of this data. They may feel profiled and tracked [10]. Expectancy theory claims that users are behaving in a way to maximize positive outcomes while minimizing negative outcomes [11]. Consequently customers would like to obtain personalized products or services, by providing as little information as possible [12, 13]. Additionally the personalization-privacy paradox describes the tendency that consumers who value information transparency are also less likely to participate in personalization [14].

Hence, the result of this risk assessment influences the behavior of consumers. Their willingness to provide data to companies in exchange for services that offset the perceived risks of this disclosure is called privacy calculus [15]. Consequently, depending on the purpose and the context of use the customers' privacy concerns may vary then using certain technologies. Thus, privacy concerns of customers in the context of IS adoption are situation dependent ([16, 17, 18]).

For this study we have to distinguish between the purchasing situations in online shops and retail stores. In both situations customers may have to reveal personal information to a retailer to access personalized services. In the case of retail stores customers also reveal their physical location. Additionally customers are in a public space and using a personalized service may disclose personal preferences to a third person. Consequently they may further lose perceived control over their data which may lead to increased privacy concerns [19].

Thus based on the general tendency of customers to disclose as little information as possible to minimize negative outcomes [11], to create a privacy calculus [20], to abstain from e-commerce transactions when privacy concerns emerge [15] and to prefer situations with high perceived control over personal data [19] we hypothesize that the privacy concerns of personalized services are higher for customers when they are shopping in a retail store than when they are using an online shop.

H1: The privacy concerns triggered by personalized services are higher when customers buy in a retail store than in an online shop.

2.3   Intention to Adopt

Studies have shown that trust, perceived usefulness and perceived ease of use together explain a considerable proportion of variance in intended adoption of online shopping services [21]. Additionally it was found that trust is an important factor for adopting personalized services that require gathering and analyzing personal data of customers [22]. Consequently, for this study we discuss these three factors for personalized services in the contexts of online shops and retails stores:

- **Trust:** It has been shown that in the context of online shops repeat customers trusted e-vendors more than new users [23]. But currently the majority of people have not experienced personalization in retail stores. Additionally, as discussed in Sect. 2.2, the use of personalized services may reveal personal data or preferences which may represent a higher risk in a public space. Consequently we presume trust in personalized services in online shops may be higher than in retail stores.
- **Perceived Usefulness:** Also perceived usefulness was found to be higher in repeat users and the general experience with personalized services in online shops is much higher than in retail stores [23]. The use of technology may also be seen as an additional layer between the customer and the already present products in a retail store. Consequently we presume that perceived usefulness of personalized services in online shops may be higher than in retail stores.
- **Perceived Ease of Use:** Since online shops have already been widely used, users have experience using these systems, and more experience corresponds with higher perceived ease of use ratings in online shops [23]. In-store technologies and systems on the other hand are not very common and may represent an additional layer between the customer and the product, which may be associated with further effort or burden to access products. Thus we argue that perceived ease of use may be higher in online shops.

Consequently, based on [6] we hypothesize that in the context of retail stores the acceptance of personalized services is higher and this leads to a higher intention to adopt them than in online shops.

H2: The intention to adopt a personalized service is higher when customers buy products in an online shop than in a retail store.

2.4 Relation Between Privacy Concerns and Intention to Adopt

A recent study conducted by [24] indicates that privacy concerns are the most important factor for the intention to adopt innovative electronic shopping concepts. Results show that the intention to adopt was reduced when customers feared a possible misuse of personal data generated during the shopping process. Subsequently, concerns about privacy reduce the intention to adopt services based on their expected positive or negative effects.

In the context of this study negative effects are the violation of perceived privacy due to gathering, analyzing and use of personal data. Positive outcomes may be produced by personalized offers, product presentations, vouchers, etc. that are based on user behavior. The consideration of positive effects of personalization due to loss of privacy has to be perceived positively for the user for the decision to use such a service. Hence, if this calculation is negative, the users will not intend to use the service [15]. We therefore hypothesize that there is a similar negative relation between privacy concerns and the intention to adopt personalized services.

H3: Privacy concerns have a negative effect on the intention to adopt services in an omnichannel retailing context.

3 Methodology

In this section we lay out the methodology to test the hypotheses derived in Sect. 2. This is done by conducting an empirical study with a scenario-based online survey. This empirical study is based on a research model that incorporates the three hypotheses and illustrates the way the included factors personalization, context, privacy concerns and intention to adopt influence each other (c.f. Fig. 1):

- **H1:** The privacy concerns triggered by personalized services are higher when customers buy in a retail store than in an online shop.
- **H2:** The intention to adopt a personalized service is higher when customers buy products in an online shop rather than in a retail store.
- **H3:** Privacy concerns have a negative effect on the intention to adopt services in both an online and retail context.

Scenarios. To analyze the influence of personalization and purchasing context we used a scenario-based approach that covered all alternative combinations. Scenarios are usually used in experimental studies to define contexts of a study, to describe user tasks

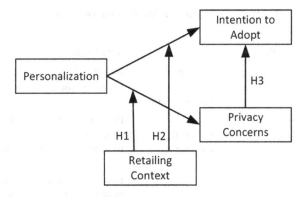

Fig. 1. Research model

or specify certain conditions or variables of a study. Using scenarios enables researchers to analyze phenomena independently from the development stage of needed technologies or functionalities. Consequently, scenario-based approaches can be used to evaluate potential and plausible future situations and to gather information on how people assess them from the present perspective [25].

Consequently, the described research model led to 4 scenarios which are shown in Fig. 2:

	Retailing Context	
	Online Shop	**Retail Store**
Personalization	Scenario 1	Scenario 3
No Personalization	Scenario 2	Scenario 4

Fig. 2. Scenarios for research design

The different scenarios were built by identifying the relevant characteristics of the analyzed phenomenon [25] and therefore describe potential situations which should be thought of by the subject during the online survey.

Retailing context. In the case of omnichannel retailing a study in 2015 [26] revealed that 61% of the subjects were familiar with interactive omnichannel retailing technologies, but only 30% have actually used them actively (mainly self-service terminals). Since only a minority of people have experienced some of these technologies and a comprehensive real world implementation of omnichannel services along the customer journey was not available to us, a scenario-based approach seemed appropriate.

Personalization. The scenarios should also project characteristics of personalization by using technology along multiple stages of a customer journey without being too complex. Additionally, we decided not to include cutting-edge technology to simulate

Table 1. Personalization levels in the two contexts

	Retailing Context			
	Online Shop		Retail Store	
	Scenario 1	Scenario 2	Scenario 3	Scenario 4
	Personalization	No Personalization	Personalization	No Personalization
Welcome Message	Personalized welcome message	Generic welcome message	Push message with personalized welcome message	Push message with generic welcome message
Store navigation	–	–	Push message with store navigation function	No push message for store navigation
Products	Personalized products based on purchase history	Products passed on what other customers bought	Virtual shelf with personalized products based on purchase history and browsing history of the retailer app	Virtual shelf with products that other customers bought
	Inventory in stores nearby based on current position	Inventory in stores nearby when user enters current postal code	–	–
	One-click payment based on saved payment data and preferred payment method	Input of credit card details	Payment with NFC function of retailer app using already saved payment data and method	Payment with debit card using NFC

personalization, because the subjects may not be familiar with it and therefore could struggle to assess it. Hence, the scenarios included technology that we expected the subjects to know about and which were easy to describe, such as virtual shelves and NFC payment (Table 1).

Experimental setting. The study is based on an experimental setting using a within subject design. Thus every subject was exposed to every scenario. To measure privacy concerns and the intention to adopt the omnichannel retail context the subjects had to fill out a survey directly after every scenario without a time limit. The order of the scenarios was randomized.

The survey consisted of the items shown in Table 2.

The items in Table 2 were based on the approved methodology of Sheng/Nah/ Siau [6]. Originally, Sheng/Na/Siau derived the items for privacy concerns (PC1-4)

Table 2. Items to measure privacy concerns and intention to adopt

Privacy Concerns	PC1	When faced with this scenario, it bothers me that the service provider is able to track information about me
	PC2	When faced with this scenario, I am concerned that the service provider has too much information about me
	PC3	When faced with this scenario, it bothers me that the service provider is able to access information about me
	PC4	When faced with this scenario, I am concerned that my information could be used in ways I cannot foresee
Intention to adopt	INT1	When faced with this scenario, I intend to adopt this service
	INT2	When faced with this scenario, I predict I will use this service
	INT3	When faced with this scenario, I plan to use this service

from ([27, 15]) and the items from intention to adopt (INT1-3) ([21, 19]). All items were rated on a 7-point Likert scale from 1 ("strongly disagree") to 7 ("strongly agree"). The order of the items and also the order of the scenarios were randomized for each subject.

Data collection. To conduct this study, non-probability sampling technique was chosen [28], because omnichannel retailing services cannot be considered to be widely implemented and therefore already adopted by a wide population. Consequently, only experienced smartphone users and online shoppers were expected to be potential subjects who have the needed experience with the related technologies, services and personalization issues. Additionally, studies showed that younger people are more likely to adopt new information technologies, while older people are more resistant to using new information technologies. Thus, the subjects were recruited by using social network groups of students in Austria. For our study, students represent a widely homogenous group of subjects with frequent experience in e-commerce, m-commerce and generic smartphone usage.

Survey execution. The online survey was conducted in July 2016 using the survey tool SoSci Survey (www.soscisurvey.de).

4 Results

4.1 Sample and Measurement Model

Overall, 112 questionnaires were finished validly and could be integrated into the sample. All subjects were Austrian students. Demographic details are shown in Table 3.

Before confronting the subjects with the different scenarios their experience with mobile technologies in general and with omnichannel retailing was gathered. All subjects already used smartphones with internet access in general. Explicit experience with retailing services on smartphones was gathered and analyzed based on the number of years smartphones were used (i) with apps from retailers, (ii) if mobile shopping was

Table 3. Demographic information of subjects.

Category		Number of subject	%
Gender	Female	77	69%
	Male	35	31%
Age	19–25	65	58%
	26–30	35	31%
	31–35	8	7%
	>35	4	4%

performed on smartphones, and (iii) if smartphones were used in retail stores to access services (e.g. research for product details, compare prices, mobile payment, location-based services, etc.). The results show that all subjects have experience with using smartphones and a majority of the subjects also have extensive experience using them in a shopping contexts.

Furthermore, the frequency of the usage was collected by using a 6-point Likert scale from never (1) to often (6). For easier readability, the frequency values were cumulated in the three categories rarely, sometimes and frequently in Table 4. The results show that the majority of the subjects not only have extensive experience using smartphones for retailing services, but also use them at least sometimes or frequently. Smartphones are used most intensely not only for mobile shopping activities, but also with retailer apps.

Table 4. Experience and frequency of smartphone usage with retailing services

Smartphone use....	Experience of the subjects in years (%)					Frequency of usage cumulated (%)		
	<2	2–5	5–10	>10	not used	rarely (1–2)	sometimes (3–4)	frequently (5–6)
(i) with retailer apps	24%	39%	5%	0%	32%	47%	24%	29%
(ii) for mobile shopping	38%	30%	5%	0%	27%	41%	32%	27%
(iii) in retail stores	33%	32%	11%	1%	23%	49%	27%	24%

Therefore, we can conclude that the subjects were sufficiently experienced in using smartphones for e-commerce and m-commerce services, which suggests that they are potential omnichannel retailing service users. Additionally, the subjects were relatively young and had a high level of formal education, suggesting they are more likely to adopt new information technology. Although this may limit the generalizability of the study, these subjects are potential customers targeted by omnichannel retailing services and form a homogenous group [6].

Factor Analysis. In order to assess the reliability and validity of the constructs Privacy Concern (PC) and Intention to Adopt (INT) a factor analysis was conducted. All items

Table 5. Factor analysis; rotation method: Oblimin with Kaiser normalization.

	Component	
	Privacy concern	Intention to adopt
PC1	.990	.032
PC2	.974	−.002
PC3	.971	−.018
PC4	.972	−.015
INT1	−.017	.949
INT2	−.014	.937
INT3	.029	.983

Table 6. Variance explained

Factor	Eigen value	Variance explained	Cumulative variance
Privacy concerns	4.608	65.825	65.825
Intention to adopt	1.960	27.998	93.823

were loaded on the constructs they were intended to measure, with non-significant loadings on the other construct, which corresponds to the results of the original study from Sheng/Nah/Siau [6] (Table 5).

Results show items PC1, PC2, PC3 and PC4 load very high on privacy concerns. Items INT1, INT2 and INT3 load very high on intention to adopt.

Cronbach's alpha coefficients for all constructs far exceed the threshold of 0.7 ([29]) and therefore the measurements for privacy concerns and intention to adopt are highly reliable in terms of internal consistency (Table 7).

Table 7. Cronbach's Alpha Coefficients

Construct	Cronbach's Alpha
Privacy concerns	.984
Intention to adopt	.954

4.2 Hypothesis Testing

Hypothesis H1 and H2 claim different effects of personalized services and the purchasing context on privacy concerns and the intention to adopt these services. We used repeated measure ANOVA to analyze this interaction, which can be considered to be an appropriate statistical method in this context.

For examining the relationships between privacy concerns and intention to adopt personalized services (H3) a regression analysis was conducted. Based on the fact that the study is a within-subject design, we tested the relationship between privacy concerns and intention to adopt for each scenario separately in order to guarantee the independence assumption of the regression.

Privacy Concerns. Privacy concers were analyzed using a repeated-measure ANOVA test using the within-subject factors personalization and retailing context as independent variables. Table 8 reports the mean values and standard deviations, Table 9 reports the results of the ANOVA test.

Table 8. Mean and standard deviations for privacy concerns

Within-subject factors		Privacy concerns	
Personalization	Retailing context	Mean	Standard deviation
Personalization	Online shop	4.1473	1.77494
	Retail store	4.7857	1.72908
No Personalization	Online shop	2.9754	1.59000
	Retail store	3.4911	2.00785

Table 9. Results for repeated-measure ANOVA for Privacy Concerns

Factors	F	P-value	Observed power*
Personalization	100.534	.000	1.000
Purchasing Context	27.319	.000	.999
Personalization *Purchasing Context	.472	.494	.105

*calculated with alpha = .05

Figure 3 depicts the interaction effect of personalization and context on privacy concerns. As presented, personalization triggers higher privacy concerns in both online (t = 8.002 p < 0.000) and retail (t = 8.225, p < 0.000) contexts. The difference between customers' privacy concerns for personalized services versus non-personalized services

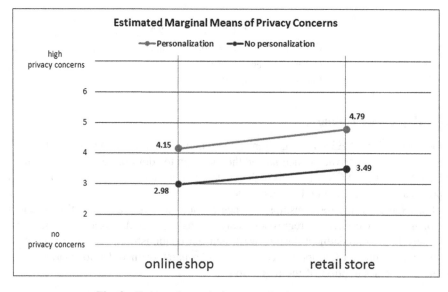

Fig. 3. Estimated marginal means of privacy concerns

is greater in the retail context (mean difference = 1.29) than in the online context (mean difference = 1.17). For non-personalized services, there is a significant difference in privacy concerns between online and retail contexts ($t = 3.167$, $p = 0.002$); for personalized services, the difference between online shop and retail store is nearly the same ($t = 5.428$, $p = 0.000$) and the difference is also significant. Hence, H1 is supported.

Intention to Adopt. The data associated with the intention to adopt was also analyzed using a repeated-measure ANOVA test with the two within-subject factors personalization and purchasing context as independent variables. Table 10 reports the mean values and standard deviations, while Table 11 reports the results of the ANOVA test.

Table 10. Mean and standard deviations for intention to adopt

Within-subject factors		Intention to adopt	
Personalization	Retailing context	Mean	Standard deviation
Personalization	Online shop	4.2738	1.55655
	Retail store	3.4048	1.75098
No Personalization	Online shop	4.5268	1.50982
	Retail store	3.9881	1.73576

Table 11. Results for repeated-measure ANOVA for Intention to Adopt

Factors	F	P-value	Observed power*
Personalization	21.082	0.000	0.995
Purchasing context	14.704	0.000	0.967
Personalization *Purchasing Context	2.353	0.128	0.331

*calculated with alpha = .05

Figure 4 depicts the interaction effect of personalization and context on intention to adopt services. It shows that customers are more willing to adopt personalization services online. Customers' intention to adopt services (personalized or non-personalized) is significantly higher in the online shop than in the retail store context ($t = 5.176$, $p = 0.000$ for personalized services; and $t = 2.629$, $p = 0.010$ for non-personalized services). In online shops, customers tend to be more willing to adopt non-personalized services than personalized services ($t = -1.901$, $p = 0.060$). Also, in the retail store context, customers are more willing to adopt non-personalized services than personalized services ($t = -3.410$, $p = 0.010$). Thus, H2 is supported.

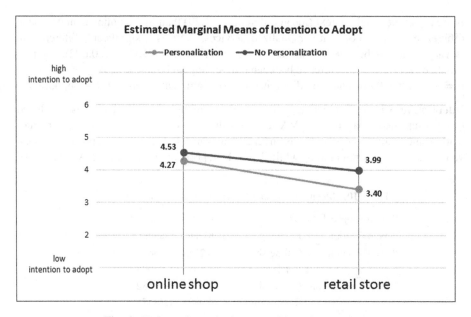

Fig. 4. Estimated marginal means of intention to adopt

Privacy Concerns and Intention to Adopt. We analyzed the relationships between privacy concerns and intention to adopt for each scenario separately. As mentioned earlier, this is needed to satisfy the independence assumption.

In the personalization and online shop scenario, privacy concerns negatively influence intention to adopt (B = −0.286, p = 0.000), as presented in Table 12. This means that if the subjects have privacy concerns, the intention to adopt is lower.

Table 12. Results of regression in personalization in online shop scenario

Results of regression in personalization/online shop					
Model	Unstandardized coefficients		Standardized coefficients	t	Sig.
	B	Std. error	Beta		
Constant	5.460	0.356		15.323	0.000
Personalization/Online	−0.286	0.079	−0.326	−3.618	0.000

In the non-personalization and online shop context, the effect of privacy concerns on intention to adopt is not significant (B = −0.089, P = 0.324), as shown in Table 13.

Table 13. Results of regression in no personalization in online shop scenario

Results of regression in no personalization/online shop

Model	Unstandardized coefficients		Standardized coefficients	t	Sig.
	B	Std. error	Beta		
Constant	4.792	0.304		15.776	0.000
No Personalization/online	−0.089	0.090	−0.094	−0.990	0.324

In the personalization and retail store context, privacy concerns negatively influence intention to adopt (B = 0.416, p = 0.000), as presented in Table 14. This means that privacy concerns also lead to lower intention to adopt in the retail store context.

Table 14. Results of regression in personalization in retail store scenario

Results of regression in personalization/retail store

Model	Unstandardized coefficients		Standardized coefficients	t	Sig.
	B	Std. error	Beta		
Constant	5.395	0.448		12.051	0.000
Personalization/Retail	−0.416	0.088	−0.411	−4.725	0.000

In the non-personalization and retail store context, the effect of privacy concerns on intention to adopt is also significant (B = −0.380, p = 0.000), as shown in Table 15. The privacy concerns of the subjects also have a negative influence on the intention to adopt services in the retail store context, if the services are not personalized.

Table 15. Results of regression in no personalization in retail store scenario

Results of regression in no personalization/retail store

Model	Unstandardized coefficients		Standardized coefficients	t	Sig.
	B	Std. error	Beta		
Constant	5.314	0.298		17.839	0.000
No personalization/retail	−0.380	0.074	−0.439	−5.128	0.000

As presented above, H3 is also supported. The results suggest that privacy concerns have a negative impact on intention to adopt the services.

5 Discussion and Conclusion

This study evaluates the influence of personalization services in an omnichannel retailing context. The conducted study design was derived from an experimental study on the impact of personalization and privacy concerns in a ubiquitous commerce context from Sheng/Nah/Siau [6]. Hence, the context was adapted to two different omnichannel retailing situations in an online shop and in a retail store and four different scenarios for the study were be derived.

Hypothesis H1 and H2 claim that privacy concerns are higher and the intention to adopt personalized services are lower when customers buy in a brick-and-mortar retail store than in an online shop. The results show that both hypotheses could be supported. In addition, personalization of services triggers higher privacy concerns in both, the online shop and retail store context (H1). Data show further that the intention to adopt personalized services is significantly higher in an online shop than in a retail store (H2). Furthermore, it can be stated that in both retailing contexts customers tend to be more willing to adopt non-personalized services than personalized services.

The third hypothesis (H3) analyzed the relationship between privacy concerns and the intention to adopt for each scenario. Results of the regression analysis show that privacy concerns have significant negative effects on the intention to adopt personalized services in online shop and retail store contexts. In the retail store context privacy concerns of the subjects have a significant negative influence on the intention to adopt services even when the services are not personalized. These results indicate that consumers are decidedly more concerned about the influential authority of retailers in a brick-and-mortar in general than in online shops.

Future research could extend this study by examining the moderating effects of demographic features such as age, gender and technology experience. Also the personal trust level and personal attitude to data privacy could be an interesting mediating factor for further studies.

References

1. Beck, N., Rygl, D.: Categorization of multiple channel retailing in multi-, cross-, and omni-channel retailing for retailers and retailing. J. Retail. Consum. Serv. **27**, 170–178 (2015)
2. Brynjolfsson, E., Hu, Y.J., Rahman, M.S.: Competing in the age of omnichannel retailing. MIT Sloan Manage. Rev. **54**, 23–29 (2013)
3. Verhoef, P.C., Kannan, P.K., Inman, J.J.: From multi-channel retailing to omni-channel retailing. J. Retail. **91**, 174–181 (2015)
4. Li, F.C.Y., Dearman, D., Truong, K.N.: Virtual shelves. In: Wilson, A., Guimbretière, F. (eds.) The 22nd Annual ACM Symposium, p. 125
5. Treiblmaier, H., Pollach, I.: The influence of privacy concerns on perceptions of web personalisation. IJWS **1**, 3 (2011)
6. Sheng, H., Nah, F.F.-H., Siau, K.: An experimental study on ubiquitous commerce adoption: impact of personalization and privacy concerns15. J. Assoc. Inf. Syst. **9**, 344–377 (2008)
7. Berthon, P., Pitt, L., Ewing, M., Carr, C.L.: Potential research space in MIS: a framework for envisioning and evaluating research replication, extension, and generation. Inf. Syst. Res. **13**, 416–427 (2002)

8. Rossmann, A., Sonntag, R.: Social commerce – Der Einfluss interaktiver Online-Medien auf das Kaufverhalten der Kunden. In: Deutscher Dialogmarketing Verband e.V. (ed.) Dialogmarketing Perspektiven 2012/2013, pp. 149–178. Springer Fachmedien Wiesbaden, Wiesbaden (2013)
9. Chellappa, R.K., Sin, R.G.: Personalization versus privacy. an empirical examination of the online consumer's dilemma. Inf. Technol. Manage. **6**, 181–202 (2005)
10. Günther, O., Spiekermann, S.: RFID and the perception of control. Commun. ACM **48**, 73 (2005)
11. Vroom, V.H.: Work and Motivation. Wiley, New York (1964)
12. Murthi, B.P.S., Sarkar, S.: The role of the management sciences in research on personalization. Manage. Sci. **49**, 1344–1362 (2003)
13. Adomavicius, G., Tuzhilin, A.: Personalization technologies: a process-oriented perspective. Commun. ACM **48**, 83–90 (2005)
14. Awad, N.F., Krishnan, M.S.: The personalization privacy paradox: an empirical evaluation of information transparency and the willingness to be profiled online for personalization. MIS Q. **30**, 13–28 (2006)
15. Dinev, T., Hart, P.: Internet privacy concerns and their antecedents - measurement validity and a regression model. Behav. Inf. Technol. **23**, 413–422 (2004)
16. Belk, R.: An exploratory assessment of situational effects in buyer behavior. J. Mark. Res. **11**, 156–163 (1974)
17. Cote, J.A., McCullough, J., Reilly, M.: Effects of unexpected situations on behavior-intention differences: a Garbology analysis. J. Consum. Res. **12**, 188–194 (1985)
18. Figge, S.: Situation-dependent services—a challenge for mobile network operators. J. Bus. Res. **57**, 1416–1422 (2004)
19. Xu, H., Teo, H.-H.: Alleviating consumer's privacy concern in location-based services: a psychological control perspective. In: Proceedings of the Twenty-Fifth Annual International Conference on Information Systems (ICIS 2004), pp. 793–806 (2004)
20. Dinev, T., Hart, P.: An extended privacy calculus model for e-commerce transactions. Inf. Syst. Res. **17**, 61–80 (2006)
21. Gefen, D., Karahanna, E., Straub, D.W.: Trust and TAM in online shopping: an integrated model. MIS Q. **27**, 51–90 (2003)
22. Komiak, S.Y.X., Benbasat, I.: The effects of personalization and familiarity on trust and adoption of recommendation agents. MIS Q. **30**, 941–960 (2006)
23. Gefen, D., Karahanna, E., Straub, D.W.: Inexperience and experience with online stores. The importance of tam and trust. IEEE Trans. Eng. Manage. **50**, 307–321 (2003)
24. Zendehdel, M., Paim, L.: Predicting consumer attitude to use on-line shopping: context of Malaysia. Life Sci. J. **10**, 497–501 (2013)
25. Pitkänen, O., Mäntylä, M., Välimäki, M., Kemppinen, J.: Assessing legal challenges on the mobile internet. Int. J. Electron. Commer. **8**, 101–120 (2003)
26. El Azhari, J., Bennett, D.: Omni-channel customer experience: an investigation into the use of digital technology in physical stores and its impact on the consumer's decision-making process. In: XXIV AEDEM International Conference, London, UK (2015)
27. Smith, H.J., Milberg, S.J., Burke, S.J.: Information privacy. measuring individuals' concerns about organizational practices. MIS Q. **20**, 167 (1996)
28. Cooper, D.R., Emory, C.W.: Business Research Methods. Irwin, Chicago (1995)
29. Nunnally, J.C., Bernstein, I.H.: Psychometric theory. McGraw-Hill, New York, London (1994)

Review-Based Screening Interface for Improving Users' Decision Process in E-commerce

Dongning Yan[1,2(✉)] and Li Chen[2]

[1] School of Mechanical Engineering,
Shandong University, Jinan, Shandong, China
yandongning@sdu.edu.cn
[2] Department of Computer Science,
Hong Kong Baptist University, Hong Kong, China
lichen@comp.hkbu.edu.hk

Abstract. Due to the important role of product reviews in e-commerce, some systems have employed different approaches to present reviews on product detail page or comparison page. However, little work has investigated how to present reviews on screening interface for facilitating users to screen out interesting alternatives from a set of options. In this paper, we have developed a novel review-based screening interface in terms of users' behaviors. Concretely, there are two innovations in the interface design: (1) it enables users to eliminate items by sentiment attributes (i.e., the attributes extracted from reviews), and (2) it emphasizes on visualizing the value distribution of each attribute and tradeoffs among attributes. The results of a user study show that our review-based screening interface achieves significantly more positive assessments than traditional screening interface, in terms of users' perceived decision accuracy, cognitive effort, pleasantness and intention to use.

Keywords: Product reviews · Screening interface · Decision making · User study

1 Introduction

With the rapid growth of e-commerce, online users are provided with the access to a greater variety of products and an enormous amount of information about the products. Particularly, product reviews have taken an important role in users' online purchasing process [2, 7, 13, 25]. According to statistics in [14], 84% of Americans have used product reviews to make their online purchasing decisions.

The studies from customer behavior state that people normally go through three stages of decision making in e-commerce: (1) Stage 1-screening out interesting ones for further consideration; (2) Stage 2-evaluating an alternative in details to decide whether to save it as a purchase candidate (the transition between stage 1 and stage 2 is iterative until the user locates a set of candidates); and (3) Stage 3-comparing purchase candidates for the final choice [5]. To help users effectively and efficiently glean information from reviews for making better purchasing decisions, some systems have

© Springer International Publishing AG 2017
F.F.-H. Nah and C.-H. Tan (Eds.): HCIBGO 2017, PART II, LNCS 10294, pp. 130–142, 2017.
DOI: 10.1007/978-3-319-58484-3_11

summarized product reviews by extracting attributes and associated sentiments, and employed different approaches to conveying the attribute-sentiment information mainly at the 2nd and 3rd stages (i.e., showing product reviews at detail page and comparison page) [3, 4, 15, 27]. However, little work has investigated how to present reviews at the 1st stage for facilitating users to screen out interesting alternatives.

Therefore, in this manuscript, we are motivated to develop a novel review-based screening interface. Specifically, in terms of how people utilize reviews to screen out items [26], we made two major innovations in the interface design. Firstly, it supports users to eliminate alternatives by both sentiment attributes (i.e., the attributes extracted from product reviews) and static attributes (i.e., the physical properties of a product). Secondly, to help users effectively determine the cutoff value of an attribute, we visualized the value distribution of each attribute and tradeoffs among attributes. Then, we performed a user study to validate the superiority of our review-based screening interface against traditional screening interface. The results show that people depended highly on sentiment attributes, which points to the benefit of incorporating them in screening interface. Moreover, the novel interface achieves more positive user assessments in terms of perceived decision accuracy, cognitive effort, pleasantness to use, and intention to return.

The remainder content is organized as follows. We first introduce related work in two steams: users' decision-making process during online purchasing and relevant review-based interfaces (Sect. 2). We then describe the details of developing review-based screening interface (Sect. 3). The setup and results of a user study will follow (Sects. 4 and 5). Finally, we conclude the work and discuss our findings' practical implications (Sect. 6).

2 Related Work

2.1 Three-Stage Decision Making Process of Online Purchasing

From the perspective of customers, online purchasing can be viewed as a decision making process, in which the user is required to choose a suitable product among a huge number of options. In classical decision theory, customers are assumed to process all relevant information and explicitly consider trade-offs among attributes to choose an optimal product with the maximum utility [20].

However, some researchers have demonstrated that in complex decision environments (such as choosing an option from a large number of alternatives with a variety of attributes), individuals are often unable to evaluate all available alternatives in great depth for making decisions [1, 8]. Instead, they are inclined to process the information at different stages: (1) the initial screening of available products to determine which ones are worth considering further, and (2) the in-depth comparison of selected products to make the actual purchase decision [10, 18].

In [5], a precise three-stage decision process was proposed: (1) screening out interesting ones that are worth further consideration, (2) reading detailed information about the product selected in the preceding stage and deciding whether to take it as a purchase candidate, and (3) comparing several candidates to make the final choice.

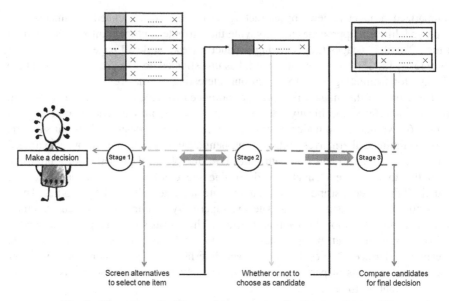

Fig. 1. Three-stage decision-making process of online purchasing [5]

Decision makers basically follow such a linear process, but they cycle between the 1st and 2nd stages until one or more candidates are located (see Fig. 1).

2.2   Review-Based Interface Design

At the detail page of a product (i.e., stage 2), users are inclined to explore the positive/negative sentiments towards one or more attributes. Carenini et al. summarized product reviews in the form of a tree map which visualizes the sentiment and frequency of each attribute via box color and size [3]. In addition, to help users digest reviews in greater detail, Yatani et al. extracted frequently mentioned adjective-noun word pairs from reviews, using the font size and color to represent the occurrence frequency and sentiment [27]. Moreover, Hu et al. and Huang et al. automatically highlighted associated review sentences when users hover over a specific attribute or word pair, to make a balance between reducing information overload and providing original review context [11, 12].

At the comparison interface (i.e., stage 3), users tend to perform a side-by-side and feature-by-feature comparison of product reviews on competing candidates. Liu et al. [15] used bar charts to show positive (above x-axis) and negative (below x-axis) sentiments on the attributes of a camera, with the bar's height representing the number of mentions [15]. Based on Liu et al.'s work, Carenini et al. [4] developed a stacked bar chart to visualize the sentiment of each attribute. Each bar corresponds to a polarity category (from −3 to 3) and its height represents the quantity of that sentiment [4]. Chen et al. [6] developed a comparison interface by combining numerical sentiments (e.g., sentiment score and occurrence frequency) with verbal sentiments (i.e., opinion words/phrases) [6].

To the best of our knowledge, regarding how to present reviews to help users screen out interesting alternatives (i.e., stage 1), few researches have put forward specific design solutions.

3   Review-Based Screening Interface

The studies from consumer decision making state that an effective information display (leading to more accurate decision with less effort) requires an in-depth comprehension of users' decision making behaviors [18]. In [26], we initially did a formative study to empirically investigate how people utilize reviews to make online purchasing decisions. As to the process of screening out interesting alternatives, users' decision making behaviors and design implications are summarized in Table 1.

Table 1. Users' decision making behaviors and design implications at the 1st stage

Users' decision making behaviors	Design implications
To screen out interesting items, people begin with eliminating alternatives with values for an attribute below a cut-off. The process continues with the second attribute, and then the third, until a smaller set of alternatives remains. Specifically, both static attributes and sentiment attributes are utilized in the process	Provide users with the access to eliminating alternatives by both static attributes and sentiment attributes
When determining the cut-off of an attribute, people examine its value distribution to avoid too narrow (few options left) or broad (still many options) results. In addition, cut-offs are also influenced by the tradeoffs among attributes. For example, if the cut-off value of cleanliness is set at 5-stars, the price of the remaining hotels may be beyond the user's acceptable range	Display the value distribution of each attribute and trade-offs among attributes

The review-based screening interface was hence generated to optimize these two design implications. More specifically, the interface generation contains the following three major steps:

Step 1: To develop review-based screening interface, we take online hotel booking as the sample domain for two reasons: (1) it is easier to recruit a sufficient number of target users to test its effectiveness, and (2) we can obtain abundant online hotel reviews from commercial sites. A dataset with 100 B&B (50 in Beijing and 50 in Rome) is used for the experiment; all hotels' specifications and reviews are crawled from Tripadvisor.com in September 2014.

Step 2: In the context of hotel booking, in addition to three static attributes (i.e., district, facility and price), four most frequently mentioned sentiment attributes (i.e., cleanliness, location, value, and service) are incorporated to help users eliminate alternatives. As for "facility" and "district", users tend to specify multiple discrete values (e.g., choosing hotels with wifi, kitchen, and car parking). Therefore, we utilized "press-and stick" toggle buttons as their filters, which support multi-choice and are space-saving [22]. Considering price and sentiment attributes, users are inclined to select data points that are less than a larger number or greater than a smaller number. Hence, their filters are presented in the form of double sliders to facilitate users to adjust the value range (see Fig. 2).

Fig. 2. Screenshot of the review-based screening interface

Step 3: In comparison to pure sliders, we made two major modifications to accommodate presenting the value distribution of each attribute and trade-offs among attributes to help users more effectively determine the cutoff values.

For a slider filter, the value distribution of an attribute can be represented in the form of bar chart (see Fig. 3). The height of a bar is proportional to the number of hotels, which is a good visualization of data because it may reduce learning time and potential misunderstanding [17]. Moreover, the number of hotels with values satisfying the specified range is shown right above bars based on the Gestalt principles of proximity [23].

Because real-time change can effectively reflect the relation of values [16], the trade-offs among attributes are visualized via simultaneous move of slider knobs. For

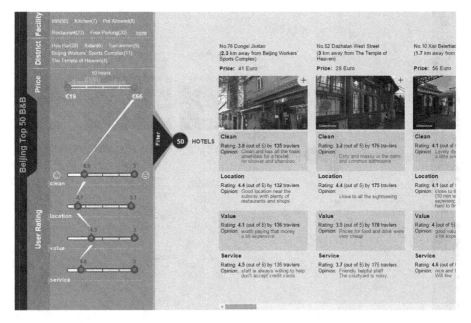

Fig. 3. Screenshot of the review-based screening interface (mouse-over status)

instance, when the user drags the slider knob to reduce price, the slider knobs standing for the maximum values of sentiment attributes will move simultaneously (see Fig. 3). However, users may be inclined to miss the changes because they can only quickly take in information from 1 to 4 degrees of visual angles [24]. With the purpose of clearly expressing the trade-offs among attributes, the corresponding knobs of different sliders are connected with lines, which could be powerful to express relationships [19].

To make critical information prominent and avoid information overload, we employed "details on demand" which shows details "hidden behind" specific points [21]. More specifically, only when users hover over or drag a slider knob, both the bar chart and tapered lines connecting relevant slider knobs are shown up.

4　User Study

4.1　Materials

In this section, we performed a user study to test the effectiveness of our innovative review-based screening interface against the traditional screening interface.

In the traditional screening interface of e-commerce websites, checkbox has been broadly utilized as filter form. Specifically, the filter of each attribute is composed of an array of N checkboxes, each of which represents a value range on the dimension. Users can select products with values within a certain range by clicking corresponding checkbox. For example, the filter of cleanliness is composed of five checkboxes that stand for choosing hotels with 'above 4.5', 'above 4', 'above 3.5', 'above 3' and 'all'

Fig. 4. Screenshot of the traditional screening interface

scores. Every checkbox is followed by the number of products with values within the range (shown in bracket). When a set of products are selected, the number following each checkbox simultaneously changes. Figure 4 provides an example, in which when users click the box labeled 'Restaurant' to select the 23 hotels with restaurant, the distribution of cleanliness scores changes in real-time (e.g., none of the 23 hotels' cleanliness scores are 'above 4.5').

4.2   Evaluation Framework

Given that the objective of the experiment is to identify whether our innovative interface could better support users to screen out interesting alternatives and improve their decision-making process, the measurement was conducted from both objective and subjective perspectives.

Objective measures include users' decision effort and behavior. The decision effort was assessed by users' task completion time. To understand how users actually behaved, we measured the attributes users adopted for narrowing down alternatives.

Except for the above objective measures, users' perception is mainly concerned with interface usability. According to ISO, usability is defined as the extent to which a product can be used by specified users to achieve specified goals with effectiveness, efficiency, and satisfaction in a specified context of use. Grounded in the definition, users' subjective perceptions were assessed by 3 constructs: decision accuracy, cognitive effort and satisfaction. To measure these subjective perceptions, a set of

Table 2. Questions to measure users' subjective perceptions

Constructs	Related questions
Decision accuracy	Q1: I am confident that the hotels I just located by means of filtering are the best for me
Cognitive effort	Q2: I easily obtained and processed relevant information to narrow down options
Satisfaction	Q3: It is pleasant to use the interface to find interesting hotels. (pleasant to use)
	Q4: If possible, I would like to use the interface in the future. (return intention)

Note: Each question was responded on a seven-point Likert scale ranging from 1 'strongly disagree' to 7 'strongly agree'.

questions were pre-designed mostly from existing studies, where they were tested and found to have strong content validity and reliability (see Table 2).

4.3   Within-Subjects Study

We utilized within-subjects method to compare the two interfaces under equal settings, which required all participants to go through both the traditional and innovative interfaces in a random order and finish a randomly assigned task (i.e., *imagine that you will have a trip to Beijing/Rome with your friends in the summer holiday, and need to book a hostel online. The top 50 Beijing/Rome Bed and Breakfast are presented. Please choose interesting one(s) for further consideration*). Compared to between-subjects method, within-subjects method was employed for two reasons [16]. First, fewer participants are needed since each participant is tested on both interfaces. Second, the variability in measurements is more likely due to differences between interfaces than to behavioral differences between participants. To avoid any carryover effect, we developed four (2*2) experiment conditions. The manipulated factors are interfaces' order (innovative interface first or traditional interface first) and tasks' order (locate hotels in Beijing first or in Rome first). Participants were evenly assigned to one of the conditions.

4.4   Procedure and Participants

To collect users' actions and perceptions, we built an online experiment site, including the task description, evaluated interfaces, and questionnaires. All users' actions and answers were automatically recorded in log files. The main procedures of the study can be divided into four steps.

Step 1: Each participant was given a brief introduction to the experiment's objective at the beginning, and then required to fill in his/her personal background and e-commerce experiences.

Step 2: The user was asked to use a randomly assigned interface (traditional interface or innovative interface) to screen out interesting hotels (in Beijing or in Rome). After finishing the task, he/she was automatically led to a page to give his/her opinions on the interface.

Step 3: The user used another interface (e.g., innovative interface if s/he just used traditional interface at step 2) to locate hotels worth further consideration at a new place (e.g., Beijing if s/he just searched for hotels in Rome at step 2). Similarly, when the task was done, s/he was also required to indicate her/his subjective perceptions with the interface he/she just used.

Step 4: After the user went through the two interfaces, s/he was asked to indicate which one s/he prefers and the reasons.

60 participants (28 females) were recruited to take part in the user study. They are university staffs and students pursuing Bachelor, Master or PhD degrees, with different majors, such as Electronics, Engineering, and Architecture. Table 3 gives their demographic profile. In the pre-study questionnaire, they indicated their frequency of Internet use (on average 4.94 'almost daily'), e-shopping experiences (on average 3.63 '1–3 times a month'), and online hotel booking experience (on average 2.60 'a few times every 3 months').

Table 3. Demographic profile of participants in user study

Gender	Female (28), male (32)
Age	21–30 (48), > 30 (12)
Major	Electronics, Engineering, Architecture, etc.
Internet usage	4.94 (daily/almost daily), $st.d. = .42$
E-commerce shopping experience	3.63 (1–3 times a month), $st.d. = .91$
Online hotel booking experience	2.60 (a few times every 3 months), $st.d. = .50$

Note: The scores for 'internet usage', 'e-commerce shopping experience' and 'online hotel booking experience' were given on a 5-point Likert Scale from 1 'least frequent' to 5 'very frequent'.

5 Results

SPSS 22 was used for data analysis. To identify whether the observed differences between the two interfaces are statistically significant, we ran t-test (at 95% confidence level) [9].

5.1 Subjective Measures

We firstly analyzed users' answers to the questionnaires in order to know how they subjectively felt about the two interfaces. Table 4 lists participants' mean response to each question and the significance analysis. We can observe that users gave more positive scores on our innovative screening interface than on the traditional screening interface concerning all 4 questions. The significance analysis further shows that the

Table 4. Comparison on users' subjective perceptions with the two interfaces

Interface	Mean (*st.d.*)	t-test		
		t	*df*	*p*
Q1: Decision accuracy				
Traditional	5.15 (1.09)	−1.94	59	.057
Innovative	5.46 (1.06)			
Q2: Cognitive effort				
Traditional	4.90 (1.35)	−2.49	59	**.016**
Innovative	5.45 (1.29)			
Q3: Pleasant to use				
Traditional	5.17 (1.59)	−2.28	59	**.027**
Innovative	5.63 (1.18)			
Q4: Return intention				
Traditional	5.27 (1.22)	−2.24	59	**.029**
Innovative	5.70 (1.32)			

innovative interface achieves significantly higher scores regarding Q2 "Cognitive effort" (5.46 vs. 5.15 in traditional interface, t = −2.49, p = .016), Q3 "Pleasant to use" (5.63 vs. 5.17 in traditional interface, t = −2.28, p = .027), and Q4 "Return intention" (5.70 vs. 5.27 in traditional interface, t = −2.24, p = .029).

5.2   Objective Measures

Regarding time consumption, users spent more time on narrowing down options with our innovative interface than with the traditional interface, but without significant difference (124.23 vs. 105.38 s, t = −1.89, p = .064). Moreover, we recorded which attributes users adopted in both interfaces (see Fig. 5 (left)). For example, 73% and 51% of participants eliminated alternatives by facility in the traditional interface and innovative interface, respectively. Overall, the average application frequency of the four sentiment attributes (i.e., clean, location, value and service) is slightly higher than that of the three static attributes (i.e., facility, district and price) in both traditional interface (64.8% vs. 60.3%) and innovative interface (56.2% vs. 45%) (see Fig. 5 (right)). The high application frequencies of sentiment attributes indicate the necessity of incorporating them in screening interface to meet individual user's filtering needs.

5.3   User Comments

In the post-study questionnaire, users were asked to choose the interface they preferred. 65% of users (39 out of 60) favored the innovative interface, whereas the other 35% of users liked the traditional checkbox interface. With Chi-square test, the difference is significant (χ^2 = 5.40, p < .05). Further analysis of users' comments made the reasons more explicit as to why the innovative interface was subjectively preferred by the majority of participants.

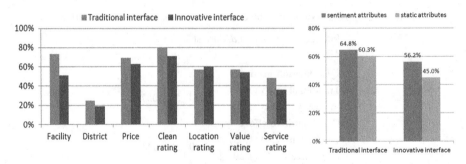

Fig. 5. The frequencies of use of static attributes and sentiment attributes

In total, 47 users gave their comments (34 preferred the innovative interface and 13 preferred the traditional checkbox interface). 19 participants felt the innovative interface is more intuitive, "*The sliders show the filter information directly to me so that I can see all the details without additional click, whereas the checkbox requires more clicks*". The second reason is that the innovative interface supports users to specify more precise cut-off values (18 participants), "*I can choose a more precise cut-off value (e.g., higher than '3.7' for location) with slider compared to the cut-off options (e.g., 'good', 'very good') with checkbox*". Besides, 13 participants felt that it is easier for them to learn the value distribution of an attribute in the innovative interface, "*The bar chat form makes it easier for me to pick up the 'main stream' zone*". The last but not least important reason is that the trade-offs among attributes are more accessible to users in the innovative interface (13 participants), "*The available region of different attributes are related, showing how the change of one preference will affect the others. This eases the procedure of making trade-offs between attributes*".

As to the strong points of the traditional interface, 8/13 users felt that it is more common, "*I am more familiar with the checkbox form, which are broadly employed in commercial websites*". In addition, 6/13 participants indicated that the traditional interface is simpler and easier to understand, while the innovative interface is a little complicated and overladen, "*In checkbox interface the filter is simple and clear, while the 2nd interface contains some distracting visual information*".

6   Discussion

In this paper, we aimed to investigate how to present reviews at the 1ˢᵗ stage for helping users screen out interesting alternatives for further consideration.

Grounded in our prior findings on how users utilize reviews to make online purchasing decisions, we have developed a review-based screening interface as an improvement of the traditional screening interface. Subsequently, we were motivated to conduct a user study to test the effectiveness of our design solution. The results show that our innovative interface performed better than the traditional screening interface, regarding users' perceived decision accuracy, effort and satisfaction. Besides, people actively utilized sentiment attributes to filter products in both interfaces.

As to practical implication, we believe our findings can be suggestive for researchers who are working on developing review-based interfaces. For e-commerce websites, our results provide insights on how to incorporate product reviews into the screening interface to help users screen out interesting alternatives. In fact, the satisfying user experience with our innovative interface suggests that it can be directly employed by the commercial sites to serve their online users.

Acknowledgements. This research is supported by "The Fundamental Research Funds of Shandong University".

References

1. Beach, L.R.: Broadening the definition of decision making: the role of prechoice screening of options. Psychol. Sci. **4**, 215–220 (1993)
2. Bickart, B., Schindler, R.M.: Internet forums as influential sources of consumer information. J. Interact. Mark. **15**, 31–40 (2001)
3. Carenini, G., Ng, R.T., Pauls, A.: Interactive multimedia summaries of evaluative text. In: Proceedings of the 11th International Conference on Intelligent User Interfaces, pp. 124–131 (2006)
4. Carenini, G., Rizoli, L.: A multimedia interface for facilitating comparisons of opinions. In: Proceedings of the 14th International Conference on Intelligent User Interfaces, pp. 325–334 (2009)
5. Chen, L.: Towards three-stage recommender support for online consumers: implications from a user study. In: International Conference on Web Information Systems Engineering, pp. 365–375 (2010)
6. Chen, L., Wang, F., Qi, L., Liang, F.: Experiment on sentiment embedded comparison interface. Knowl. Based Syst. **64**, 44–58 (2014)
7. Chevalier, J.A., Mayzlin, D.: The effect of word of mouth on sales: online book reviews. J. Mark. Res. **43**, 345–354 (2006)
8. Felfernig, A., Friedrich, G., Gula, B., Hitz, M., Kruggel, T., Leitner, G., Melcher, R., Riepan, D., Strauss, S., Teppan, E., et al.: Persuasive recommendation: serial position effects in knowledge-based recommender systems. In: International Conference on Persuasive Technology, pp. 283–294 (2007)
9. Field, A.: Discovering Statistics Using IBM SPSS Statistics. Sage, London (2013)
10. Häubl, G., Trifts, V.: Consumer decision making in online shopping environments: the effects of interactive decision aids. Mark. Sci. **19**, 4–21 (2000)
11. Hu, M., Yang, H., Zhou, M.X., Gou, L., Li, Y., Haber, E.: OpinionBlocks: a crowd-powered, self-improving interactive visual analytic system for understanding opinion text. In: Kotzé, P., Marsden, G., Lindgaard, G., Wesson, J., Winckler, M. (eds.) INTERACT 2013, Part II. LNCS, vol. 8118, pp. 116–134. Springer, Heidelberg (2013). doi:10.1007/978-3-642-40480-1_8
12. Huang, S.-W., Tu, P.-F., Fu, W.-T., Amanzadeh, M.: Leveraging the crowd to improve feature-sentiment analysis of user reviews. In: Proceedings of the 2013 International Conference on Intelligent User Interfaces, pp. 3–14 (2013)
13. Kim, Y., Srivastava, J.: Impact of social influence in e-commerce decision making. In: Proceedings of the Ninth International Conference on Electronic Commerce, pp. 293–302 (2007)

14. Lee, J., Park, D.-H., Han, I.: The different effects of online consumer reviews on consumers' purchase intentions depending on trust in online shopping malls: an advertising perspective. Internet Res. **21**, 187–206 (2011)
15. Liu, B., Hu, M., Cheng, J.: Opinion observer: analyzing and comparing opinions on the web. In: Proceedings of the 14th International Conference on World Wide Web, pp. 342–351 (2005)
16. MacKenzie, I.S.: Human-Computer Interaction: An Empirical Research Perspective. Newnes (2012)
17. McLachlan, P., Munzner, T., Koutsofios, E., North, S.: LiveRAC: interactive visual exploration of system management time-series data. In: Proceedings of the SIGCHI Conference on Human Factors in Computing Systems, pp. 1483–1492 (2008)
18. Payne, J.W., Bettman, J.R., Johnson, E.J.: The Adaptive Decision Maker. Cambridge University Press, Cambridge (1993)
19. Pinker, S.: The Stuff of Thought: Language as a Window into Human Nature. Penguin, London (2007)
20. Salvendy, G.: Handbook of Human Factors and Ergonomics. John Wiley & Sons, Hoboken (2012)
21. Shneiderman, B.: Designing the User Interface: Strategies for Effective Human-Computer Interaction. Pearson Education India (2010)
22. Tidwell, J.: Designing Interfaces. O'Reilly Media, Inc., Sebastopol (2010)
23. Ware, C.: Information Visualization: Perception for Design. Elsevier, Amsterdam (2012)
24. Wickens, C.D., Hollands, J.G., Banbury, S., Parasuraman, R.: Engineering Psychology & Human Performance. Psychology Press (2015)
25. Wu, J., Wu, Y., Sun, J., Yang, Z.: User reviews and uncertainty assessment: a two stage model of consumers' willingness-to-pay in online markets. Decis. Support Syst. **55**, 175–185 (2013)
26. Yan, D., Chen, L.: An empirical study of user decision making behavior in e-commerce. In: Proceedings of the 17th International Conference on HCI, pp. 414–426 (2015)
27. Yatani, K., Novati, M., Trusty, A., Truong, K.N.: Review spotlight: a user interface for summarizing user-generated reviews using adjective-noun word pairs. In: Proceedings of the SIGCHI Conference on Human Factors in Computing Systems, pp. 1541–1550 (2011)

Eye-Tracking Analysis of Gender-Specific Online Information Research and Buying Behavior

Silvia Zaharia[(⊠)], Daniela Kauke, and Ella Hartung

University of Applied Sciences Niederrhein, Krefeld, Germany
silvia.zaharia@hs-niederrhein.de

Abstract. In line with the continuous growth rates in online retailing, the competitive situation for retailers has intensified. In order to strengthen their market position and exploit further potential, online retailers need to address the specific needs of their customers. In this context, a more detailed analysis of gender-specific preferences is expected to be worthwhile, as men and women might have different needs when shopping on the Internet. This study explores in-depth the extent to which the gender-specific design of online shops has an influence on the genders. The aim of this study is to answer the following question: Do women and men exhibit different information research and buying behavior when utilizing online shops designed to appeal to their respective genders? An eye-tracking method was chosen for this study with 80 participants.

The findings illustrate that indeed there are differences between the behavior of men and women. It can be asserted that gender-specific online shop designs have a significant impact on women. Although not backed by strong statistical significance, men nevertheless also tend toward higher average values in the typically feminine shop compared to the masculine one, indicating that also online behavior of men is slightly impacted by gender-specific shop design.

Keywords: Gender commerce · Eye-tracking · Online consumer behavior · Online information research · Online shop design · Web design

1 Introduction

In light of changing online markets, heightened investigation into group-specific needs is an inevitable part of exploiting new potential and staying afloat in the fast-paced online retail world. For this reason, gender marketing, also called gender commerce, has become increasingly important in recent years [1]. Building upon traditional marketing, gender marketing encourages adapting marketing efforts to the unique needs of each gender [2]. Thus, men and women are assigned specific characteristics and stereotypical behavior as a foundation for implementing more targeted marketing activity [2]. With regard to e-commerce, a variety of studies have already been conducted into gender-specific information research and buying behavior [3–28]. However, research has yet to evaluate how women's and men's information research and buying behavior can be influenced by a feminine or masculine online shop-design.

© Springer International Publishing AG 2017
F.F.-H. Nah and C.-H. Tan (Eds.): HCIBGO 2017, PART II, LNCS 10294, pp. 143–159, 2017.
DOI: 10.1007/978-3-319-58484-3_12

Multiple experts have noted that predominately "masculine design thinking" [27] has resulted in the existence of primarily masculine online shops [1]. Meanwhile, the expression "pink it and shrink it" [1, 28], in reference to the feminine optimization of online shops, demonstrates a seriously simplified approach to online gender marketing while strengthening stereotypical assumptions. This research therefore aims to explore the following question: *Do women and men exhibit different information research and buying behavior in online shopping environments depending on the gender-specific design of the online shop?*

2 Conceptual Framework and Hypotheses

2.1 Review of Literature

Regarding research into gender-specific differences in online-shopping, an array of academic work has focused on the constructs of consumer behavior, on the information research and buying process, as well as the online shop-design:

- *Constructs of consumer behavior* covers psychological factors not directly observable [29] (e.g. perceived risk, trust, motives, attitude). The authors come to different conclusions, however. While Chen et al. and Pascual-Miguel et al. determine a connection between gender and perceived risk, [3, 4] Nadeem et al. can confirm no such link [5].
- Studies of the *buying decision process* (including information search and processing, buying decision). According to Rodgers and Harris, women process information more strongly in their left hemispheres, thus absorbing more detail and intricacy from a website than men do. This substantially influences how a product or website is evaluated [23]. Moreover, women absorb information more comprehensively than men do [6, 7, 26] thereby more intensely dealing with the content of the online shop [15]. Male participants, on the other hand, demonstrate holistic and selective information intake [6, 15, 23]. In sum, men behave more functionally in their buying behavior [24]. Bae and Lee indicate that women more highly value the opinions of others. They were able to determine through their research that women are more strongly influenced by online customer reviews in their buying decisions [17].
- Studies focusing on online shop design covers, among others, color, design, usability, images, usually shed light on one element of the online shop (e.g. graphics, reviews, language-style). With regard to gender-specific differences, Mahzari and Ahmadzadeh as well as Ellis und Ficek found women to prefer warm colors and harmonious color schemes [9, 30] while men gravitated toward cool colors and neglected any harmony in the coloring [9, 30, 31]. Dittmar et al. have determined buying environment to have a larger effect on women than on men [24].

In addition to these academic papers, a whole host of non-scientific publications exist on the topic as well. Blog posts and similar articles discuss single elements of online shopping including gender differences in shop design. The authors are unaware, however, of any study looking into the influence that feminine or masculine online shop-design has on men and women's information research and buying behavior.

Scientific studies into gender-specific online information research and buying behavior from recent years focused primarily on surveys (except from the work of Djamasbi et al.) [20]. Since experts point to the necessity of using observations such as eye tracking to examine true behavior, [11, 20] it is of the utmost importance to continue investigating the research question with use of the eye tracking technique.

2.2 Research Object: Online Shops with a Gender-Specific Design

For this study, two online shops were selected. One shop that ranked high on typical female attributes, and one that ranked high on typical masculine attributes. The identification of attributes as well as the selection of these online shops rests on the insights gained from the secondary literature in the previous chapter. Of special interest is the literature on online shop design. The following criteria were used to evaluate the feminine shop design: color scheme, shapes, incorporation of social media, product page, shopping cart/basket, shopping-assistance functionality, trust-building elements, language-style, and sources of inspiration. The masculine shop design was evaluated on functionality, web design, language-style, website construction and product page.

By the end of the screening process, 20 online shops were determined to exhibit gender-typical elements. The first place for feminine design was Zalando, second ABOUT YOU, and third Asos. For the masculine sites, first place was Cyberport, second Amazon and third Conrad.

For the sake of the study, both shops must offer the same type of product, which was, in this case, shoes. After an evaluation, Zalando (www.zalando.de) was selected as the feminine research object. Zalando was originally conceived as a European version of Zappos.com. Amazon (www.amazon.de) was chosen as the typically masculine shop, because the number one, Cyberport, does not offer shoes.

This study did not examine the entirety of both online shops but focused rather on the **product page**. A customer can access the product page from the product overview page. It must be noted that the customer can also arrive at the **product page** via external sources e.g. a search engine, affiliated links or social media platforms.

Overall, the product page has two purposes: (1) to present the customer with enough relevant information on the product so that he or she need not look elsewhere and (2) display the product attractively in order to generate a purchase [32].

2.3 Hypotheses Development

As previously explained in more detail, it is widely understood that there are differences between men and women in their information research and buying behavior on online shops. It can be assumed that an online shop with a feminine design will positively influence the information research and buying behavior of a woman. Similarly, it can be assumed that a masculine online shop design will have a positive effect on a man's information research and buying behavior. The rationale behind these conclusions is that the gender-specific design of the online shop (m/f) better satisfies the needs of each respective gender. This inference, combined with findings in literature, fed the basic hypothesis of this study: *"Women and men exhibit differing information research and buying behaviors when online shops are designed to appeal to their particular gender."*

Deriving Hypothesis 1: It is assumed that female consumers enjoy browsing, often becoming sidetracked during the buying process. In this context, women perceive online shopping as a relaxing experience, opting to take their time in search of inspiration [10, 15]. Studies indicate that men, in comparison, are quicker and more targeted in their approach to online shopping [12, 15, 22, 24]. Kempe also corroborates that men tend to deem online shopping a waste of time and enjoy consumption less than women do. Men are therefore more motivated by efficiency and making a quicker purchase [12]. Contrastingly, women exhibit a more browsing shopping behavior, which can incorporate many diversions [10, 15]. It can therefore be assumed that men require less time than women for the information research process.

Hypothesis 1 (H1): Differences can be seen in men and women's 'dwell time' on online shops depending on the gender-specific design of the shop.

Deriving Hypothesis 2: It is assumed that a gender-specific difference exists regarding the perception and information processing of online shop features (product images, product ratings, recommendations and product descriptions). As a whole, this can be substantiated by the fact that women are more comprehensive information processors while men are more selective [6, 7]. Richard et al. emphasizes that, due to their type of information processing, women are more engaged with a website and even enjoy discovering its content. In comparison, men prefer a more heuristic approach to finding information on a well structured website that enables quick and easy information processing [15]. We predict that these behaviors during online shopping also apply when judging an online shop's various features.

Hypothesis 2 (H2): Differences can be seen in men and women's use and regard of individual features of a product page depending on the gender-specific design of the online shop.

Hypothesis H2 is divided into the following five sub-hypotheses. Doing so guarantees a detailed and more precise assessment of the differences between the gender-specific online shops.

H2a: *Differences can be seen in how men and women regard the **features of the product page as a whole** depending on the gender-specific design of the online shop.*

Regarding how women judge the product image, it could already be determined that they are influenced by the size of the image because women tend to notice details more than men [13]. In the context of the product page, it can therefore be inferred that women contemplate an image longer, in more detail and more often than men do. The corresponding hypothesis is:

H2b: *Differences can be seen in how men and women regard* **product images** *depending on the gender-specific design of the online shop.*

Women more highly value others' opinions [22]. In various surveys, women responded that reviews from other customers are important to their decision process when making purchases [17]. We therefore predict that:

H2c: *Differences can be seen in how men and women regard* **product reviews** *depending on the gender-specific design of the online shop.*

The authors have not been able to find any scientific studies linked to the influence of product recommendations on genders. On the whole, however, women tend to be more susceptible to impulse purchases, [12] so it can rightly be inferred that recommendations (i.e. for other suitable products) have a stronger effect on women.

H2d: *Differences can be seen in how men and women regard* **product recommendations** *depending on the gender-specific design of the online shop.*

Based on the statement that men wish to finalize their purchases quickly and easily, it can be assumed that they more readily look for concise, fact-heavy information and will therefore focus their attention on product descriptions.

H2e: *Differences can be seen in how men and women regard product descriptions depending on the gender-specific design of the online shop.*

3 Methodology

3.1 Design and Participants

The present experiment has a between-subject design [33, 34]. The differences between genders (male/female) are observed as well as the gender-specific design of the online shop (masculine vs. feminine) and the behavior of each gender. This study therefore relies on a two-factorial design with four experimental groups: Gender (male/female) and online shop (masculine design/feminine design).

The experiment is designed to employ an eye-tracker to observe the consumer's behavior [35]. Since the participant is aware that his or her eye movements are being tracked and behavior in the online shop observed, the experiment can be classified as an open observation. However, the participant is not supposed to know the relevance of gender differences for this study as this could have consequences on the authenticity of their behavior [36]. The experiment took place in the research laboratory of the *University of Applied Sciences Niederrhein* in Krefeld and utilized a stationary eye-tracker with a number of adjustable features. As a result, the study is classified as a laboratory experiment [35, 36]. Participants of the study were students (N = 80, 40 women, 40 men, ages 18 to 36). Students were selected at random, which is why they represent different fields of study at the university. There was no direct compensation for the participants.

3.2   Eye-Tracking as an Observational Method

The eye-tracking system RED 250 from SensoMotoric Instruments (SMI) was used throughout the course of the experiment and is based on the cornea-reflectometry or the corneal-reflex method, which is common in modern eye-tracking systems [37, 38]. This system is often preferred over other systems because it neither impairs participants with glasses nor by fixing their chin, therefore leaving the head to move freely [38]. Additionally, it captures a set area on the screen, which simplifies the assessment of gathered data. An initial calibration of the device was crucial for each participant in order to collect optimal measurements. For the calibration procedure, the system measured the test person's eyes. Proper measuring of eye positioning was vital to ensuring the reliability of the data [34].

3.3   Tasks

Duchowski especially highlights the importance of the eye-tracking survey and its function. Eye-tracking surveys are dependent on the tasks given to participants, which is why the assigned task can have a significant influence on the results. Special care should therefore be taken when choosing the task to be carried out [34].

In the present experiment, participants are assigned a task to be accomplished in an online shop. More specifically, the participant is instructed to select one or more items from the online shop and put them in the shopping cart. They are meant to behave as if in a typical online shopping situation. All the while, details are being observed on how the participant reacts to individual features of the (gender-specific) design of the product page. Of interest are the features used – especially by each gender – that therefore influence the buying decision.

The item to be purchased during the experiment was a pair of running shoes. There is a wide selection of running shoes available on both feminine and masculine online shops. They are easy to find in a navigation menu, there is a large quantity of them available, and they are usually accompanied by reviews on the product page. Moreover, the amount of men and women who run recreationally in Germany is at a balanced 53% and 47% respectively [39]. Running is also the second most popular physical activity behind fitness training for ages 18–39 in Germany [40]. Running shoes are available both in the typically masculine online shop (Amazon) and the typically feminine (Zalando).

4   Metrics

The first step will explain how the necessary metrics were extracted using areas of interest (AOIs). The second step will explain which metrics are relevant for this paper.

The AOIs make it possible to analyze selected areas, such as product images, on the online shop. By means of these AOIs, the eye-tracking system determines if and how long the participant examined the relevant area of the screen. The resulting data can then be displayed individually for each subject or as aggregate and median values [37].

For the present study, the product page was divided into four AOIs – product image, product description, recommendations and product rating (see Fig. 1).

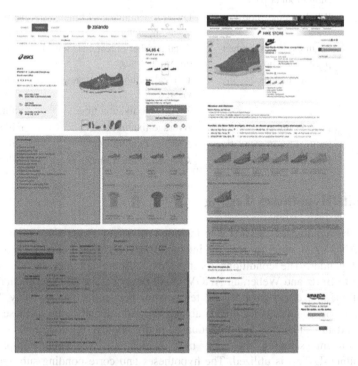

Fig. 1. Areas of interest (AOIs) - product page (This figure shows product pages of www.zalando.de (left side) and www.amazon.de (right side). Please note product pages are only examples. The AOIs vary in size and position.)

In the context of eye-movement measurements, saccades and fixations are the two fundamental types of eye-movement activity. Saccades are fleeting eye "jumps" that move a person's gaze to different points. It has been proven that during saccades, no information is processed as perception is interrupted during the movement [38]. Fixations, on the other hand, are resting periods during which the observer's retinas stabilize and fixate on a point of interest for at least 300 ms [34, 37]. Only during a fixation can information be recognized, analyzed and retained [29, 34, 37, 38].

Due to the established AOIs, other metrics beyond saccades and fixations were collected that both directly and indirectly relate to eye tracking. In this case, other metrics and indicators of interest were those that supplied general insight into information research and buying behavior (e.g. time). Table 1 provides an overview of the areas used in this study and short explanations thereof.

Table 1. Overview eye-tracking metrics

Hypothesis	Features of online shop/Product page	Metric	Unit
H1	Whole online shop	Dwell time/amount of time spent shopping	seconds
H2a	Features of the product page as a whole	Total number of features viewed on product page	count
H2b	Product images	1. Total number of images viewed	count
		2. Average fixation time	milliseconds
H2c	Product reviews	Average fixation time	milliseconds
H2d	Product recommendations	Average fixation time	milliseconds
H2e	Product descriptions	Average fixation time	milliseconds

5 Results/Hypotheses Testing

In testing the hypotheses, the first step included assessing all variables by means of a two-way ANOVA in order to track the interaction and reciprocal effect between online shops and gender. The conditions for the ANOVA are not met for all variables. According to Bortz and Weber, an ANOVA will be robust for all experimental groups that are of equal size and have at least ten persons per group. The two-way ANOVA can therefore be conducted for all variables [41]. Additionally, due to these circumstances, the data will be assessed individually. In this context, the conditions for a t-test for independent samples are not met, which is why the non-parametric Mann-Whitney-U-Test is utilized. The hypotheses and corresponding sub-hypotheses are tested on a 95% significance level. Should the results reach a higher significance level, it will be articulated in the text as well as in figures.

Hypothesis Testing H1: The presented hypothesis is to be tested based on the overall time (in secs.) the participant takes to complete the task (dwell time). Figure 2 shows the dwell time for women and men while shopping on the Zalando or Amazon shops.

The entire ANOVA model exhibits a strong statistically significant result ($F(3.76) = 6.99$, $p = 0.00$). Worth noting is that the effect size of the entire model corresponds to a strong effect of $f = 0.53$, while the main effects and interactions only exhibit a medium effect size.

Main effects and interaction effects can be interpreted in the data. The dwell time is dependent on gender ($F(1.76) = 7.82$, $p = 0.01$): Women exhibit on the whole a longer dwell time (Zalando average $(Avg.) = 199.25$, standard deviation $(SD) = 109.49$; Amazon $Avg. = 114.90$, $SD = 73.35$) than men do (Zalando $Avg. = 116.05$, $SD = 53.63$; Amazon $Avg. = 105.40$, $SD = 41.43$). Furthermore, a significant difference in dwell time can be detected due to the main effect of the online shop ($F(1.76) = 8.21$, $p = 0.01$). The dwell time in the Zalando online-shop is found to be longer in comparison to Amazon. Finally, a significant gender-online shop interaction is present in the results ($F(1.76) = 4.94$, $p = 0.03$). This becomes apparent in that women exhibit an unusually

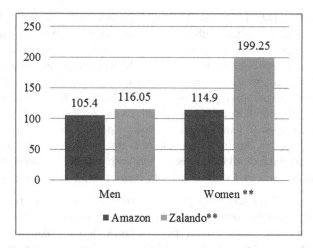

Fig. 2. Dwell time for women and men in the Zalando or Amazon shop (in seconds) (n = 80, **significant at p < .05 level)

high dwell time in combination with the Zalando shop, far beyond what could be expected by virtue of gender and online shops alone.

In an individual review, no significant difference could be determined in comparing the overall dwell time for men on the Zalando and Amazon shops. A significant difference is similarly absent in comparing men and women on the Amazon site. By contrast, women exhibit a high significant difference ($p = 0.01$) in dwell time on Amazon compared to Zalando. Women also spend all together more time in the Zalando online shop.

Beyond this, a p-value of 0.01 proves the existence of a strong significant difference between men and women in the Zalando shop, as women exhibit a significantly longer dwell time. Table 2 provides an overview of the results for the testing of hypothesis H1.

Table 2. Results of hypothesis testing H1 (n = 80, ***significant at p < .01 level, **significant at p < .05 level, *significant at p < .10 level, A = Amazon.de, Z = Zalando.de)

Online shop	Average dwell time (sec.)		Results significance tests	
	Men	Women	ANOVA	Mann-Whitney-U-Test
Amazon	105.40	114.90	Both Main Effects**	Women: A < Z**
Zalando	116.05	199.25	Interaction Effect*	Zalando: Men < Women**

The hypothesis H1 must be partially rejected: the ANOVA demonstrates significant differences. In an individual review of the groups, it can be determined that a significant difference is exclusively seen in women when comparing online shops. Statistically significant differences between men and women are only present in the Zalando shop.

Hypothesis Testing H2: The focus of testing hypothesis H2 rests on the design of the product page features and their effects on the different genders. In sum, it can be ascertained that the findings, resulting from the ANOVA, do not meet the level of significance necessary to confirm the hypothesis. No statistically significant results were recorded for the average fixation time (in ms) on product images, and the average number of viewed images was equally inconclusive. Statistically significant results were seen, however, in the number of features viewed (AOIs), total number of product images viewed, as well as average fixation time (in ms) for product ratings, recommendations and product descriptions. Again, a clear pattern is apparent since significant differences in the Amazon and Zalando shops are seen solely with women. Furthermore, significant differences between men and women are only present in the Zalando shop.

H2a: Total views of product page features. According to the U-Test ($z = -2.63$, $p = 0.01$), a significant difference between Zalando and Amazon is seen exclusively in women. Women view more product page features in the Zalando shop (median (MD) = 3.00) than on Amazon (MD = 1.00). The effect size amounts to $r = 0.42$ thereby corresponding to a medium effect (according to Cohen). There are also significant differences between the genders regarding the number of features viewed in the Zalando shop (according to the U-Test $z = -2.27$, $p = 0.02$). Compared to men, women view significantly more features in the feminine shop (men MD = 2.00, women MD = 3.00), which corresponds to a medium effect according to Cohen ($r = 0.36$).

H2b: Product images. This hypothesis was measured by means of two metrics: (1) total number of images viewed and (2) average fixation time (in ms). For the first metric, the complete model for the total number of images viewed is highly statistically significant $F (3.76) = 4.20$, $p = 0.01$. This also applies to the main effect 'gender' with $F (1.76) = 8.43$, $p = 0.05$. Both significant results indicate a medium to large effect size according to Cohen. The main effect 'online shop' as well as the interaction are not significant, however. Gender, on the other hand, does have an effect on the number of images viewed in the online shop. Women view more images in total (Zalando *Avg.* = 12.55, SD = 10.78; Amazon *Avg.* = 7.45, *SD* = 9.97) compared to men (Zalando *Avg.* = 4.90, *SD* = 4.67; Amazon *Avg.* = 4.85, *SD* = 3.94). In light of these results, the groups were reviewed individually. Only in the Zalando shop a high significant difference was to be seen between the genders ($z = -2.52$, $p = 0.01$). Women viewed more total images in the Zalando shop than men did. For women, it can also be determined that they view on average more total images in the Zalando shop than Amazon, even though the p-value of 0.06 fails to indicate statistical significance in this regard.

For metric two, a significant difference in the average fixation time (in ms) on product images can neither be verified through the ANOVA nor through individual review.

H2c: Product ratings (average fixation time in ms). Regarding the average fixation time on product ratings, the results of the two-way ANOVA show that the complete model, as well as the main effects 'gender' and 'online shop,' are not significant. Only the interaction, with a p-value of 0.04, exhibits a significant result (F $(1.76) = 4.49$, $p = 0.04$). An interaction exists between the main effects 'online shop' and 'gender.' In the (feminine) Zalando shop, women demonstrate medium to high average fixation times (Avg. = 77.19, SD = 92.41) while men demonstrate lower average times

(Avg. = 15.90, SD = 51.55). This distribution flips in the (masculine) Amazon shop, as men exhibit moderate times of 64.53 ms and women lower times of 29.82 ms, although a medium effect of f = 0.25 is present.

In the individual groups, a significant difference (z = −2.37, p = 0.02) in fixation time on product ratings between men and women is solely present in the Zalando online shop. A medium effect size corresponding to r = 0.38 is present here. It can furthermore be determined that women exhibit, on average, a longer view time of product ratings in the Zalando shop than Amazon, even though the p-value of 0.06 fails to prove statistical significance in this regard.

H2d: Recommendations (average fixation time in ms). With regard to average fixation time on recommendations, only one significant difference can be identified. Women fixate on recommendations on the Zalando shop longer (Avg. = 119.33, SD = 137.90) than those on Amazon (Avg. = 57.34, SD = 87.29). The significant difference for this hypothesis is high (z = −2.65, p = 0.01) corresponding to a medium effect size (r = 0.42).

H2e: Product description (average fixation time in ms). By means of the Mann-Whitney U-Test, a significant difference in average fixation times on product descriptions between the Amazon (Avg. = 38.04, SD = 79.39) and Zalando shops (Avg. = 99.46, SD = 120,31) could only be established for women. The corresponding p-value is 0.05, and the effect size according to Cohen is medium (r = 0.32).

Table 3 provides an overview of the results for hypothesis test H2. When considered holistically, H2 must be partially rejected on account of the results of some sub-hypotheses.

Table 3. Results of hypothesis test H2 (n = 80, A = Amazon.de, Z = Zalando.de, M = Men, W = Women, ***significant at p < .01 level, **significant at p < .05 level, *significant at p < .10 level, ns not significant)

Hypothesis	Features of product page & unit	Average		Results significance tests	
		Men	Women	ANOVA	U-Test
H2a	Product page as a whole (count)	A: 2.10	A: 1.85	Interaction*	Women: A < Z**
		Z: 2.00	Z: 2.85		Zalando: M < W*
H2b	Product images (count)	A: 4.85	A: 7.45	Main Effect Gender*	Zalando: M < W*
		Z: 4.90	Z: 12.55		
	Product images (ms)	A: 236.65	A: 253.97	ns	ns
		Z: 253.97	Z: 231.32		
H2c	Product reviews (ms)	A: 64.53	A: 29.82	Interaction*	Zalando: M < W*
		Z: 15.90	Z: 77.19		
H2d	Product recommendations (ms)	A: 79.92	A: 57.34	ns	Women: A < Z**
		Z: 87.97	Z: 119.33		
H2e	Product descriptions (ms)	A: 62.96	A: 38.04	ns	Women: A < Z*
		Z: 93.01	Z: 99.46		

Table 4. Overview of the results for hypothesis test H1 and H2

Hypothesis		Results
H1	Differences can be seen in men's and women's 'dwell time' on online shops depending on the gender-specific design of the shop	Partially reject
H2	Differences can be seen in men's and women's use and regard of features of a product page depending on the gender-specific design of the online shop	Partially reject
	H2a Features of the product page as a whole	Partially reject
	H2b Product images	Reject
	H2c Product reviews	Partially reject
	H2d Product recommendations	Partially reject
	H2e Product descriptions	Partially reject

In summary, significant differences between the Amazon and Zalando shops are only seen in female participants. Differences between male and female participants are apparent only in the Zalando shop. Regarding the ANOVA, significant interactions between 'gender' and 'online shop' can increasingly be seen in both features viewed and product ratings. The main effect 'gender' was significant for product images.

Table 4 provides an overview of the results for hypothesis test H1 and H2.

6   Discussion and Limitations

The discussion of the results will take place on the basis of the hypotheses and sub-hypotheses. Subsequently, the limitations of this study will be dicussed.

6.1   Discussing the Results

It could be observed that for the majority of metrics the female participants' average values were higher in the feminine Zalando shop compared to the masculine shop, Amazon. The male participants exhibited a tendency for higher mean values in the Zalando shop compared to Amazon, however no statistically significant differences can corroborate this. Particularly for total number of viewed features and average fixation time on product ratings, men exhibited lower average values for Zalando than for Amazon.

Product page features. The present experiment demonstrates that women incorporate more features from the product page into their shopping process in online shops with a feminine design. A significant difference is apparent in the total number of features viewed by women in that more were viewed on Zalando than on Amazon. Throughout the study, it has turned out that female participants in particular exhibit strong differences between online shops. This was similarly seen in the number of product page features women viewed compared to men in the Zalando shop. Based on these results, an online shop with a feminine design appears to strengthen or facilitate such behavior. It can therefore be concluded that women utilize significantly more features during their buying process when the shop reflects their needs. In contrast, men don't exhibit any changes in use and viewing behavior regarding the features on the product page.

Product images. There are no significant differences to be seen in average fixation time on product images. This product page feature is of equal importance to both genders. At the same time, it is necessary to recognize that women viewed more images in both shops than men did. Additionally, women's' average value was higher for Zalando than for Amazon, even if the difference cannot technically be deemed significant. Hence, the feminine and masculine online shop designs don't produce the expected effects on participants [42]. One presumption is that online purchasing decisions rely primarily on visuals, especially for clothing and in this case for running shoes. This feature will therefore be viewed and used even when it doesn't entirely reflect or meet the customer's needs.

Product ratings. No unequivocal conclusions could be drawn for this feature from the present experiment. Although the ANOVA points to a significant interaction, no clear results are reflected in the individual reviews by means of the Mann-Whitney U-Test. Though lacking statistical significance, it is apparent that each gender views the product rating longer in their respective gender-specific online shops. A statistically significant difference between men and women is only recognizable in the Zalando shop. It can be inferred that this site's presentation especially appeals to women.

Recommendations. The recommendations are an especially attractive feature for female shoppers to generate impulse purchases [42]. The present experiment shows that both genders trend toward higher average values for recommendation views in the Zalando shop. The significant difference for women between Zalando and Amazon speaks to the positive impact on longer viewing times for women. Zalando, in comparison to Amazon, successfully attracts attention to the recommendation feature by positioning it below the shopping-cart button.

Product description. The experiment shows that women fixate significantly longer on product descriptions for Zalando than for those on Amazon. It can therefore be inferred that superior presentation and organization on the product page support women in their buying process by better supplying them with information. Overall, a significant difference could neither be determined between men and women nor between men shopping on Amazon and Zalando. This speaks to the fact that this feature cannot be exclusively classified as one traditionally used be men during the buying process.

In summary, regarding the initial research question, it can be asserted that gender-specific online shop designs have a significant impact on women only. Although not backed by strong statistical significance, men nevertheless also trend toward higher average values in the typically feminine shop compared to the masculine one.

6.2 Limitations

A number of restrictions arise in conjunction with the research design of the experiment at hand. On account of the chosen design, only two gender-specific online shops were taken into consideration – Amazon for the masculine-design and Zalando for the feminine design.

Furthermore, the experiment only examined the information research and buying behavior as it related to one purchasing object – a pair of running shoes. It would be advisable in future studies to consider purchasing objects that require a higher level of involvement for each respective gender. That way, the influence of the involvement in conjunction with the product could be examined.

Due to the eye-tracking experiment, the corresponding sample size and the selection of experiment participants, the data and results are not representative. The study exclusively examines students, most of who are from the same field of study. Further studies should aim to adjust the circumstances for a more representative sample.

The participants' task for the experiment covers only one aspect of the buying process (the pre-purchase phase). Gender differences can therefore only be uncovered for this one phase. Further studies should take an expanded look at other phases in order to gain insight into the entire buying process. The actual phase of purchase, such as during checkout in online shops, could be especially interesting for future experiments.

The eye-tracker's technical conditions as well as the laboratory environment may indicate further constraints to the experiment.

The parameters of the work presented here, which are constrained by factors such as random sampling, experiment design and location, can be built upon in future studies and complimentary research aiming to map out gender-specific behavior during the buying process.

7 Summary

The purpose of this study was to examine gender-specific online information research and buying behavior in online shopping venues. In this context, the subsequent question should be answered: Do women and men exhibit different information research and buying behavior when utilizing online shops designed to appeal to their respective genders?

The ensuing experiment was organized into three steps. The first step covered available literature and studies relating to gender marketing and online shop design. For a better selection of gender-specific sites, an evaluation of online shops with typically masculine and typically feminine design features was conducted. Building upon the insight gained there, the next step involved developing the research design. Purchasing objects and online shops were selected based on criteria derived from the first step that would best guarantee an answer to the research question. The final step comprised conducting the experiment, for which eighty participants were observed in a laboratory using an eye-tracker. The data secured in step three were used for testing the hypotheses and finally answering the research question.

Regarding gender-specific online shop designs, the experiment shows that this has an impact exclusively on women; men remain comparatively unaffected. It is therefore advised that online shops include more feminine design features when targeting a mixed or predominately female customer base. On account of the study's design, it was able to point to some differences. Nevertheless, further in-depth studies are essential for generating additional insights and optimizing the results at hand.

The experiment was able to show that operators of online shops can better meet the demands of female shoppers by supplying information geared toward a high-quality and varied medial presentation of the product. The buying environment (the online shop) is of special importance for female customers. The general design (e.g. color scheme) more strongly impacts women and their assessment of the online shop.

References

1. Berz, S., Wunsch, A.: Was spricht für geschlechterspezifische E-Shops? http://www.retailtechnology.de/omnichannel/detail/Controller/Article/was-spricht-fuer-geschlechterspezifische-e-shops.html. Retrieved 28 April 2016
2. Kreienkamp, E.: Gender-Marketing, Impulse für Marktforschung, Produkte, Werbung und Personalentwicklung. mi-Fachverlag, Landsberg am Lech (2007)
3. Chen, Y., Yan, X., Fan, W., Gordon, M.: The joint moderating role of trust propensity and gender on consumers' online shopping behaviour. Comput. Hum. Behav. **43**, 272–283 (2015). doi:10.1016/j.chb.2014.10.020
4. Pascual-Miguel, F.J., Agudo-Peregrina, Á.F., Chaparro-Peláez, J.: Influences of gender and product type on online purchasing. J. Bus. Res. **68**, 1550–1556 (2015). doi:10.1016/j.jbusres.2015.01.050
5. Nadeem, W., Andreini, D., Salo, J., Laukkanen, T.: Engaging consumers online through websites and social media: a gender study of Italien Generation Y clothing consumers. Int. J. Inf. Manag. **35**, 432–442 (2015). doi:10.1016/j.ijinfomgt.2015.04.008
6. Zhang, K.Z.K., Cheung, C.M.K., Lee, M.K.O.: Examining the moderating effect of inconsistent reviews and its gender differences on consumers' online shopping decision. Int. J. Inf. Manag. **34**, 89–98 (2014). doi:10.1016/j.ijinfomgt.2013.12.001
7. Tsichla, E., Hatzithomas, L., Boutsouki, C.: Gender differences in the interpretation of web atmospherics: a selectivity hypothesis approach. J. Mark. Commun. **22**(6), 563–586 (2016). doi:10.1080/13527266.2014.903507
8. David, P., Springer, S.: Gender Comments meets Recommendation Engine: Warum Frauen shoppen und Männer einkaufen (2014). https://www.epoq.de/de/gender-commerce-meets-recommendation-engine/. Retrieved 26 May 2016
9. Mahzari, A., Ahmadzadeh, M.: Finding gender preferences in e-commerce website design by an experimental approach. Int. J. Appl. Inf. Syst. (IJAIS) **5**(2), 35–41 (2013)
10. Weinmann, M., Robra-Bissnatz, S.: Die Geschlechter im E-Commerce – Eine empirische Studie über das (Such-) Verhalten und das Erleben von Emotionen am Beispiel der Produktkonfiguration. Herausgeber: Mattfeld, D.C., Robra-Brissant, S. Braunschweig: Multikonferenz Wirtschaftsinformatik 2012 Tagungsband der MKWI 2012 (2012)
11. Jardina, J.R., Phan, M., Nuguyen, D., Chaparro, B.S.: Gender differences in first impressions of web pages: the role of attractiveness, complexity, and brightness on perceived design quality. Hum. Factors Ergon. Soc. **56**, 1604–1608 (2012). doi:10.1037/e572172013-333

12. Kempe, M.: Geschlechtsspezifische Unterschiede beim Online-Shopping, exploratorisch-deskriptiv. Herausgeber: Wagner, Udo; Wiedermann, Klaus-Peter; von der Oelsnitu, Dietrich, vol. 1. Gabler, Wiesbaden (2011). doi:10.1007/978-3-8349-6872-2_15

13. Flavián Blanco, C., Gurrea Sarasa, R., Orús Sanclemente, C.: Gender differences regarding the product's online visual representation: impact on satisfaction and purchase intention. EsicMarket **138**, 145–170 (2011)

14. Ozdemir, E., Kilic, S.: Young consumers' perspectives of website visualization: a gender perspective. Bus. Econ. Res. J. **2**(2), 41–60 (2011)

15. Richard, M.-O., Chebat, J.-C., Yang, Z., Putrevu, S.: A proposed model of online consumer behavior: assessing the role of gender. J. Bus. Res. **63**, 926–934 (2010). doi:10.1016/j. jbusres.2009.02.027

16. Hasan, B.: Exploring gender differences in online shopping attitude. Comput. Hum. Behav. **26**, 597–601 (2010). doi:10.1016/j.chb.2009.12.012

17. Bae, S., Lee, T.: Gender differences in consumers' perception of online consumer reviews. Electron. Commer. Res. **11**, 201–214 (2010). doi:10.1007/s10660-010-9072-y

18. Sebastianelli, R., Tamimi, N., Rajan, M.: Perceived quality of online shopping: does gender make a difference? J. Internet Commer. **7**(4), 445–469 (2008). doi:10.1080/15332860802507164

19. Janda, S.: Does gender moderate the effect of online concerns on purchase likelihood. J. Internet Commer. **7**(3), 339–358 (2008). doi:10.1080/15332860802250401

20. Djamasbi, S., Tullis, T., Hsu, J., Mazuera, E., Osberg, K.: Gender preferences in web design: usability testing through eye tracking. In: Proceedings of the Thirteenth Americas Conference on Information Systems (AMCIS), pp. 1–8 (2007)

21. Sánchez-Franco, M.J.: Exploring the influence of gender on the web usage via partial least squares. Behav. Inf. Technol. **25**(1), 19–36 (2006). doi:10.1080/01449290500124536

22. Chiu, Y., Lin, C., Tang, L.L.: Gender differs: assessing a model of online purchase intentions in e-tail service. Int. J. Serv. Ind. Manag. **16**(5), 416–435 (2005). doi:10.1108/09564230510625741

23. Rodgers, S., Harris, M.A.: Gender and e-commerce: an exploratory study. J. Advertising Res. **43**(3), 322–329 (2003). doi:10.1017/s0021849903030307

24. Dittmar, H., Long, K., Meek, R.: Buying on the internet: gender differences in online and conventional buying motivations. Sex Roles **50**(5/6), 423–440 (2004). doi:10.1023/b:sers. 0000018896.35251.c7

25. Alreck, P., Settle, R.B.: Gender effects on internet, catalogue and store shopping. J. Database Mark. **9**(2), 150–162 (2002). doi:10.1057/palgrave.jdm.3240071

26. Meyers-Levy, J., Maheswaran, D.: Exploring differences in males' and females' processing strategies. J. Consum. Res. **18**, 63–70 (1991). doi:10.1086/209241

27. Kirst, N.: E-Commerce und Gender: Gestaltung von Onlineshops (2015). http://page-online. de/branche-karriere/e-commerce-und-gender-gestaltung-von-onlineshops. Retrieved 28 April 2016

28. Muntschik, V.: Post Gender Marketing (2015). https://www.zukunftsinstitut.de/artikel/tup-digital/01-gendernomics/06-specials/post-gender-marketing/. Retrieved 12 September 2016

29. Kroeber-Riel, W., Gröppel-Klein, A.: Konsumentenverhalten. 10. Auflage. Vahlen, München (2013). doi:10.15358/9783800646197

30. Ellis, L., Ficek, C.: Color preferences according to gender and sexual orientation. Pers. Individ. Differ. **31**, 1375–1379 (2001). doi:10.1016/s0191-8869(00)00231-2

31. Hurlbert, A.C., Ling, Y.: Biological components of sex differences in color preferences. Curr. Biol. **17**(16), 623–626 (2007). doi:10.1016/j.cub.2007.06.022

32. Kollewe, T., Keukert, M.: Praxiswissen E-Commerce. 1. Auflage. O'Reilly, Köln (2014)

33. Falk, J.: Statistik für Wirtschafts- und Sozialwissenschaftler, vol. 1. Wiley-VCH, Weinheim (2015)
34. Duchowski, A.: Eye Tracking Methodology, Theory and Practice, vol. 2. Springer, London (2007). doi:10.1007/978-1-84628-609-4
35. Berekoven, L., Eckert, W., Ellenrieder, P.: Marktforschung - Methodische Grundla-gen und praktische Anwendung, vol. 12. Gabler, Wiesbaden (2009). doi:10.1007/978-3-8349-8267-4
36. Kuß, A., Wildner, R., Kreis, H.: Marktforschung - Grundlagen der Datenerhebung und Datenanalyse, vol. 1. Springer Gabler, Wiesbaden (2014). doi:10.1007/978-3-658-01864-1
37. Schall, A., Romano Bergstrom, J.: Eye Tracking in User Experience Design, vol. 1. Morgan Kaufmann, Waltham (2014). doi:10.1016/c2012-0-06867-6
38. Bente, G.: Erfassung und analyse des blickverhaltens. In: Mangold, R., Vorderer, P., Bente, G. (eds.) Lehrbuch der Medienpsychologie, pp. 297–321. Hogrefe, Göttigen (2004)
39. Statista, Personen in Deutschland, die in der Freizeit (häufig oder ab und zu) Jogging, Wald- oder Geländelauf betreiben, nach Geschlecht im Jahr 2015 (2016). http://de.statista.com/statistik/daten/studie/272408/umfrage/jogger-wald-und-gelaendelaeufer-in-deutschland-nach-geschlecht/. Retrieved 18 May 2016
40. Statista, Umfrage zu den beliebtesten Sportarten in Deutschland nach Alter im Jahr 2016 (Häufigkeitsverteilung) (2016). http://de.statista.com/statistik/daten/studie/539437/umfrage/beliebteste-sportarten-in-deutschland-nach-alter/. Retrieved 18 May 2016
41. Bortz, J., Weber, R.: Statistik für Human- und Sozialwissenschaftler, vol. 6. Springer, Heidelberg (2005). doi:10.1007/b137571
42. Female Commerce, 5 spannende Fakten über das weibliche Kaufverhalten im Netz (2014). http://www.femalecommerce.de/2014/10/28/5-spannende-fakten-%C3%BCber-das-weibliche-kaufverhalten-im-netz/. Retrieved 28 April 2016

Social Media for Business

The Effects of Online Review Message Appeal and Online Review Source Across Two Product Types on Review Credibility, Product Attitude, and Purchase Intention

Ardion Beldad[✉], Fitria Avicenna, and Sjoerd de Vries

University of Twente, Enschede, The Netherlands
{a.d.beldad,s.a.devries}@utwente.nl,
fitria.avicenna@gmail.com

Abstract. The study reported in this paper investigated the effects of online review message appeal and online review source type on review credibility perception, product attitude, and purchase intention across two types of products, namely technical and non-technical. A between-respondent 2 (message appeal: rational vs emotional) × 2 (online review source: experts vs consumers) experiment was implemented with 294 online consumers from Java, Indonesia. Results of analyses indicate that message appeal has a main effect on review credibility (for both technical and non-technical products) and product attitude (for a technical product). However, review source type has no significant effects on all dependent variables. Furthermore, the use of a rational appeal by expert reviewers resulted in higher review credibility perception than the use of a rational appeal by consumers as reviewers; while expert reviews with emotional appeals are regarded less credible than consumer-based reviews with emotional appeals. This interaction effect, however, is present in the non-technical product context only.

Keywords: Expert-written review · Consumer-written reviews · Rational appeal · Emotional appeal · Online review credibility

1 Introduction

People who have no prior experience in using a product or service are more likely to search for relevant product- or service-related information before purchasing it. Nowadays, product- or service-related information comes not only from companies that sell the product or offer the service but also from customers who have already used either of the two or both. Often, pieces of product- or service-related information are contained in online reviews, which also enable customers to effortlessly and uncomplicatedly express their frustration or satisfaction with a product or a service for a wide audience.

In situations involving the decision to purchase high-involvement products or services, primarily characterized by their high prices, consumers will expectedly have high levels of purchase-related risk perceptions and feelings of uncertainty [6, 19].

© Springer International Publishing AG 2017
F.F.-H. Nah and C.-H. Tan (Eds.): HCIBGO 2017, PART II, LNCS 10294, pp. 163–173, 2017.
DOI: 10.1007/978-3-319-58484-3_13

These risk perceptions and feelings of uncertainty would expectedly prompt consumers to consult online reviews as primary sources of the needed information to assuage negative feelings prior to a purchase of a costly product or service [2].

The pivotal role of online reviews in either enhancing or reducing customers' positive attitude towards the review and the product being reviewed and, consequently, their intention to purchase the reviewed product has been echoed in a plethora of research. Specifically, certain online review elements or features such as the review's valence (whether the review is positive or negative about the product or service) [24] and review sidedness (whether or not the review highlights both the product's pros and cons) [22] have been found to shape customers' product attitude and purchase intention.

One aspect of a review message that has not yet received sufficient attention, however, is review message appeal – that is, whether the review message aims at primarily targeting either its readers' rational or emotional bases when making decisions. A study into the use of message appeal strategies in an advertising context [1] shows that the appeal strategies employed in certain messages – either by emphasizing facts or highlighting emotions – have different effects on persuasion and behavioral response.

Product or service reviewers, likewise, could either focus on the relatively objective attributes or features of the commodity being reviewed or on the affective outcomes emerging from the experience of using the commodity. Such a situation triggers the question on whether or not a specific appeal strategy (rational or emotional) employed when writing a review impacts how other customers' perceive the review, in general, and the product being reviewed and, consequently, their willingness to purchase the reviewed product.

Nonetheless, the likelihood that the impact of a specific message appeal strategy would depend on the characteristics of the messenger (the reviewer) should not be discounted. For example, one who possesses in-depth knowledge about a specific commodity's functionalities and qualities might be inclined to employ an objective, matter-of-fact tone when reviewing it. On the contrary, an individual who happens to be either a first-time or a casual product user would be less predisposed to capitalize on objective product-information than on emotions when reviewing a product.

Since online reviews could be written by either a product expert or a non-expert user, the question on whether or not a specific type of online reviewer would shape review credibility perception and purchase intention certainly merits attention, as different types of sources, based on variations in their characteristics, have differential persuasion effects [18]. Besides, message source type might also play a role in moderating the effect of message appeal of certain variables (e.g. review credibility, purchase intention), under the premise that the effectiveness of a certain message appeal might be predicated on the type of message source deploying it.

To test the hypotheses proposed for this research, two studies in either a technical product context or a non-technical product context were implemented using a between-respondent 2 (review message appeal: rational vs emotional) × 2 (review source type: expert vs customer) experiment with consumers in Java, Indonesia.

2 Theoretical Framework

2.1 Online Review Message Appeals

The impact of message appeals on persuasion has been studied in various contexts. Research into message appeals clearly distinguished a rational message appeal from an emotional message appeal. Rational appeal primarily uses objective contents and provides factual and verifiable information about the target of the appeal; while emotional appeal, with the dominance of subjective contents, conveys information that is open to individual interpretation [10].

In advertising research, a rational appeal aims at shaping customers' belief about an advertised commodity by emphasizing its attributes and the benefits of using it [1]. The authors claimed that the use of a rational appeal in a marketing context is supposedly grounded on the belief that customers make rational and logical purchase-related decisions. On the contrary, an emotional appeal is predicated on the emotional and experiential dimension of product consumption and such type of appeal aims at making consumers feel good about a certain product [1].

Given the critical role of online reviews in the process of customer persuasion with their power to influence customers' product attitude and evaluation and, eventually, their purchase intention [9], the use of either rational or emotional appeals or both in online reviews would initially seem obvious. When reviewing products or services, people might focus on either product-related information such as product attributes [14], conceptually equivalent to the rational appeal, or on the emotions that emerged from the experience of using a product or service [13], which are primarily employed in emotional appeals.

While support for the effectiveness of these two types of appeals can be substantially found in several empirical studies, variations in the nature of their effects have also been noted. For instance, in a review of studies into message appeals, Zinn and Manfredo [30] stated that people tend to remember messages with strong emotional appeals than non-emotional messages. However, based on results of a research into appeals in advertisements, a rational appeal results in a more positive attitude towards an advertisement than an emotional appeal [25]. Differences in the impact of the two appeals when used in online reviews have also been noted. Specifically, when reviews pertained to high involvement products, rational appeals are known to result in a more positive brand attitude than emotional appeals [28].

In the current study, as high-involvement products were used for the experimental material, it can also be assumed that the use of a rational appeal, instead of an emotional appeal, in online reviews would also to lead to high levels of review credibility perception and positive product attitude and, eventually, to high levels of purchase intention. Hence, the first research hypothesis is advanced.

Hypothesis 1: The use of a rational appeal in online reviews will result in (a) a higher level of online review credibility perception, (b) a more positive attitude towards the reviewed product, and (c) a higher level of purchase intention than the use of emotional appeal in online reviews.

2.2   Online Review Sources

The fact that online reviews can potentially shape people's purchase behavior could partly explain why they have become prominent persuasion tools in online (or even offline) purchase contexts. An important point accentuated in persuasion research is the indispensability of a message source in amplifying the persuasiveness of a message [5]. Factors such as credibility, likeability, physical attractiveness, and the extent of similarity between the source and the receiver have been found to significantly contribute to a message source's impact on persuasion [18].

Expertise, an important dimension of credibility [20], has been noted to influence how people process and use a persuasive message. Messages coming from expert sources are believed to be more valid or 'correct' than those coming from non-expert sources [4].

Just like any form of recommendation that aims at persuading customers, online reviews could also be written by non-experts or customers who have acquired a certain level of experience with the product or by product experts (e.g. professional editors of a product magazine) [23, 29]. Expert-written reviews come from individuals who are often hired by online vendors, whereas customers reviews are posted by individuals who have already experienced using the product being reviewed [15]. It is argued that consumers are more inclined to trust review sources who are regarded experts in and knowledgeable about the product or service being reviewed [21].

Nonetheless, previous studies have shown that consumer-written reviews tend to result in better outcomes than expert-written reviews. For instance, reviews written by customers are deemed more useful than those written by experts [15]. On the contrary, reviews and ratings from editors as experts resulted in low attraction, on the part of customers, to visit a restaurant's website, as those reviews and ratings may not be regarded as independent consumer ratings but as a form of advertising [29]. Based on these points, the second set of research hypotheses is proposed.

Hypothesis 2: Consumer-written reviews will result in (a) a higher level of online review credibility perception, (b) a more positive attitude towards the reviewed product, and (c) a higher level of purchase intention than expert-written reviews.

2.3   Match Between Online Review Message Appeal and Online Review Source

Using the match-up hypothesis, it has been argued that persuasion occurs when the recipient has internalized the message, and this internalization process requires a degree of congruence between the and his or her message [11]. Previous marketing studies have shown that positive outcomes (e.g. positive product or brand attitude, belief in spokesperson's effectiveness) can be expected when the product endorser matches the product being endorsed [17, 26].

People tend to regard experts to be knowledgeable about products they are evaluating and to be capable of delivering product-related assertions [16], and, hence, they are also likely to expect experts to deliver their messages in a significantly different way compared to their non-expert counterparts. When writing reviews for products or services, for instance, expert reviewers would most likely be expected to use a more objective tone and to sound less emotional than non-experts such as casual product users. On the contrary, casual product users for their lack of in-depth product-related expertise might be expected to rely more on their subjective emotions than on objective facts when reviewing a product. Streaming from these points, hence, are the third and fourth research hypotheses.

Hypothesis 3: The use of a rational appeal in expert-written reviews will result in (a) a higher level of online review credibility perception, (b) a more positive attitude towards the reviewed product, and (c) a higher level of purchase intention than the use of a rational appeal in consumer-written reviews.

Hypothesis 4: The use of an emotional appeal in consumer-written reviews will result in (a) a higher level of online review credibility perception, (b) a more positive attitude towards the reviewed product, and (c) a higher level of purchase intention than the use of an emotional appeal in expert-written reviews.

3   Methods

3.1   Research Design and Procedure

The hypotheses proposed for this study were tested across two types of products to see whether or not the effects of online review message appeal and online review source on review credibility perception, product attitude, and purchase intention would differ between technical and non-technical products. Hence, a between-respondent 2 (online review message appeal: rational vs emotional) × 2 (online review source: expert vs consumer) experiment was conducted with online consumers in Java, Indonesia.

A small-scale survey with 30 respondents was first implemented to systematically identify two items to represent technical and non-technical products. For this preliminary study, respondents were asked to segregate 20 products, which almost had similar prices to ensure that they would all be regarded as high-involvement commodities, into two using a defined set of criteria. For products to be considered as either 'technical' or 'non-technical', the following criteria were used: (a) product requires effort to operate, (b) sufficient time is needed to fully understand how the product works, (c) sufficient time is needed to know the product's functionalities and features, and (d) the product may not be immediately usable after purchase.

Preliminary study participants were instructed to rate the 20 products using the four criteria on a seven-point agreement Likert scale – with 7 representing 'strongly agree' and 1 'strongly disagree' (e.g. when respondents were rating a digital camera, they were most likely to select 'agree' or 'strongly agree' in response to the statement 'sufficient time is needed to fully understand how the product works').

Results show that a smartphone is considered the most technical in the list with a mean score of 5.57 (SD = 1.65), while a pair of sports shoes was considered the less technical with a mean score of 1.93 (SD = 1.62). Hence, the smartphone and the pair of sports shoes were used to represent the technical and non-technical products for the experimental manipulation, respectively.

3.2   Manipulations

The experimental material presented to the participants contained a set of 10 reviews. For the 'rational appeal in online reviews' condition, reviews were written with a rather objective tone in such a way that the emphasis was on the features of the product being reviewed. For the 'emotional appeal in online reviews' condition, reviews were written using emotional expressions, exclamation marks, and adjectives that described the emotional states of reviewers upon using the product being reviewed.

The valence of reviews included for the two message appeal conditions was both positive and negative in an attempt to make the review sets highly realistic. In the actual study, 10 reviews were included for each review appeal type. Based on the finding that a set of reviews with 80% positive reviews would be perceived as more credible than a review set which is 100% positive [7], eight reviews had a positive valence and two reviews had a negative valence.

In manipulating the 'expert reviews' condition, reviews were described to have been written by editors of product magazines or websites and product specialists. Information about expert reviewers' identities (names and profession) was also presented next to their reviews. On the contrary, the 'consumer reviews' condition was manipulated by describing that the reviews were written by individuals who have already used the product. These non-expert reviewers were also identified by indicating their complete names and occupations (e.g. student, teacher).

The manipulations were checked in the main study and were deemed successful, as participants who incorrectly answered the manipulation check questions were excluded from the study. Of the 326 participants who completed the online questionnaire, 32 provided wrong answers to the manipulation check questions. Hence, only the data from 294 participants who correctly answered the manipulation check questions were used for analysis. The exclusion of the 32 participants ensured that all the manipulations were correctly identified by the respondents to whom those manipulations were randomly assigned.

3.3   Participants

Participants for this study were approached using various online social networking sites popular in Indonesia (e.g. Facebook, Line, and Whatsapp). For the first study (technical product context), data from 149 respondents who correctly answered the manipulation questions were subjected to analysis. Out of 149 respondents, 80 were female (46%) and 69 were males (54%).

For the second study (non-technical product context), data from 145 respondents who also answered the manipulation check questions correctly were included for analysis. Of those 145 respondents, 80 (55%) were females and 65 (45%) were males.

3.4   Measurements

The three dependent variables for the study were measured using items derived from previously validated scales. All items that were originally formulated in English were subsequently translated into Bahasa Indonesia for the convenience of research participants.

The first dependent variable 'online review credibility' was measured with five items originally formulated by West [27]. An example of an item for this construct is 'The online review is believable'. The second dependent variable 'product attitude' was measured with four items by Kempf and Smith [12]. An example of an item measuring this construct is 'I feel good about this product'.

The third dependent variable, 'purchase intention' ($\alpha = .89$), was measured with four items by Dodds et al. [8]. An example of an item for this construct is 'I am willing to buy the product after reading reviews about it'.

Presented on Table 1 are the Cronbach's alpha values of the three dependent variables across the two studies.

Table 1. Cronbach's alpha values of the dependent variables across the two studies.

Study 1 (Technical product)			Study 2 (Non-technical product)		
Constructs	# of items	α	Constructs	# of items	α
Online review credibility	5	.91	Online review credibility	5	.91
Product attitude	4	.91	Product attitude	4	.88
Purchase intention	4	.87	Purchase intention	4	.88

4   Results

4.1   Study 1 (Technical Product)

A two-way multivariate analysis of covariance (MANCOVA), by controlling for the effects of product involvement, was performed to test the hypotheses in the technical product context. Results of the analysis based on Pillai's trace show that online review message appeal has statistically significant mains effect on review credibility, product attitude, and purchase intention, $V = 0.22$, $F(3, 142) = 12.99$, $p = .000$.

Results of the univariate analysis of variance, controlling for the effect of product involvement, however, reveal that online review message appeal has significant main effects on review credibility, $F(1, 144) = 34.19$, $p = .000$, and product attitude, $F(1, 144) = 8.71$, $p = .004$. However, the main effect of review message appeal on purchase intention is not significant, $F(1, 144) = .38$, $p = .54$

In particular, review credibility is higher when online reviews used a rational appeal (M = 5.23, SD = .92) than when an emotional appeal is used (M = 4.27, SD = 1.11), hence, hypothesis 1a is supported. Additional, the level of positive product attitude is higher when it is reviewed with a rational appeal (M = 4.85, SD = 1.18) than when it is reviewed with an emotional appeal (M = 4.25, SD = 1.21).

Test for the main effects of online review source type by controlling the effect of product involvement, however, reveals that the second independent does not have a statistically significant effect on the three dependent variables, $V = .02$, $F(3, 142) = 1.08$, $p = .36$. Therefore, hypotheses 2a, 2b, and 2c are not supported.

Furthermore, there are no significant interaction effects for both online review message appeal and online review source type on the three dependent variables, $V = .01$, $F (3, 142) = .34$, $p = .80$. Hypotheses 3a, 3b, 3c, 4a, 4b, and 4c, henceforth, are not supported.

4.2   Study 2 (Non-technical Product)

A two-way multivariate analysis of variance (MANCOVA) was again performed to test the research hypotheses in the non-technical product context. Analysis based on Pillai's trace shows that online review message appeal has a statistically significant effect on the three dependent variables, $V = 0.14$, $F(3, 138) = 7.44$, $p = .000$. Results of the univariate analysis of variance, controlling for the effect of product involvement, however, reveal that online review message appeal has a significant effect on review credibility only, $F(1, 140) = 15.62$, $p = .000$, but not on product attitude, $F(1, 140) = .53$, $p = .47$, and on purchase intention, $F (1, 140) = .25$, $p = .62$.

Specifically, analysis indicates that reviews using a rational appeal (M = 5.27, SD = 1.01) are perceived more credible than reviews using an emotional appeal (M = 4.64, SD = .90). Hence, hypothesis 1a is supported but not hypotheses 1b and 1c.

Additionally, analysis shows that review source type has no significant main effects on the three dependent variables, $V = 0.00$, $F(3, 138) = .20$, $p = .90$. Hence, hypotheses 2a, 2b, and 2c are not supported.

Furthermore, a statistically significant interaction effect between online review message appeal and online review source exists for the three dependent variables, $V = .06$, $F(3, 138) = 3.07$, $p = .03$. However, results of the univariate analysis of variance, controlling for the effect of product involvement, reveal that the interaction effect between source type and review message appeal is statistically significant for review credibility only, $F(1, 140) = 4.40$, $p < .05$, but not for product attitude and purchase intention.

To be more specific, the score for online review credibility is higher in a situation when expert reviewers (M = 5.50, SD = .97) used a rational appeal in their reviews than when non-experts or customers (M = 5.05, SD = 1.01) used it. This result supports hypothesis 3a only.

On the contrary, online reviews written by customers using an emotional appeal (M = 4.77, SD = .73) are perceived more credible than reviews written by experts using an emotional appeal (M = 4.48, SD = 1.05). Again, only hypothesis 4a is supported.

5   Discussion and Future Research Directions

5.1   Discussion of Results

What is clearly emphasized in various research into online reviews is that reviews have the power to shape customers' product attitude and purchase intention, especially when reviews are deemed credible. Previous studies have also noted that certain aspects of online reviews such as valence, sidedness, and argumentation quality [3] can substantially impact how people view online reviews and their disposition to purchase a product or service being reviewed. In this study, the impact of online review message appeal and online review source type on online review credibility, product attitude, and purchase intentions was determined.

The effects of message appeal (rational vs emotional) on attitude and behavioral intention have been researched in various settings, and the results appear to take diverging paths. For instance, while people tend to remember emotional appeals more than rational appeals [30], rational appeals result in a more positive attitude toward the object of the message than emotional appeals [25]. For this study, it was hypothesized that reviews using a rational appeal would result in higher levels of online credibility perception, product attitude, and purchase intention than reviews that used an emotional appeal, based on the finding that a rational appeal has a stronger impact than an emotional appeal when used for high involvement products [28].

Results of the current study, in which two high involvement products were used (a smartphone and a pair of sport shoes from an A+ brand), reveal that, indeed, the use of a rational appeal in online reviews resulted in higher scores for review credibility (for both technical and non-technical products) and for product attitude (only for technical products) than when an emotional appeal was employed.

This particular result has three implications. First, when confronted with reviews of high-involvement products, consumers might be inclined to rely on reviews that contain objective product-related information instead of reviews peppered with subjective and emotive narratives of product-use experience. Second, online reviews that used a rational appeal tend to be perceived as more credible than online reviews that employed an emotional appeal regardless of the type of product being reviewed (technical and non-technical), but especially when the reviews concerned a high involvement product. Third, a certain product, specifically a technical one, would be perceived positively when it is reviewed by emphasizing relevant and objective information about its features and functionalities.

Results of the study show that the source of the online review does not have a bearing on online review credibility, product attitude, and purchase intention. These results somehow suggest that it is not really the messenger that matters but how the message is framed.

Another important point from this study is that the appeal used in online reviews need to match the type of review writers. Specifically, online reviews from experts using a rational appeal are perceived more credible than customer-written reviews that also used the rational appeal. However, this match-up requirement matters for non-technical products only. The result is somehow surprising since one would expect that the match up would be more important when reviews concerned technical products, in which information about their use, features, and/or functionalities could be better understood and be regarded more useful when the information comes from experts who use an appropriate strategy in the design of their information – that is, a rational appeal in the message.

Nonetheless, the result could also be attributed to the nature of the non-technical product. A pair of sports shoes used for the experiment might have been regarded as a commodity that could not be immediately purchased by solely relying on available information about its features. It is highly likely that the product is viewed as an experience product in which objective information about it can only be deemed credible it comes from an appropriate source, and in this context – an expert.

5.2 Future Research Directions

Although the current study has provided some interesting insights into the relevance of online review message appeal and online review source type for high involvement products that are either technical or non-technical, the study is not entirely spared from a number of limitations. However, the general focus and design of the research and its findings have a number of relevant implications for future research.

First, as the study shows that the use of a rational appeal in online reviews results in higher perception of online review credibility compared to the use of an emotional appeal for reviews of high involvement products, one wonders whether or not the type of appeal that will be used in online reviews concerning low-involvement product would still matter. Would a rational appeal still be more impactful than an emotional appeal when used in reviews concerning low-involvement products?

Second, rational appeals are known to be commonly used for products or goods instead of services [1]. As their study did not test the effects of appeal types on review credibility within the contexts of both physical goods and services (and the current study only focused on physical goods), future research could consider testing the impact of these appeal types in relation to the sources (e.g. expert vs non-expert) of online reviews for non-tangible products or services.

References

1. Albers-Miller, N.D., Stafford, M.R.: An international analysis of emotional and rational appeals in services vs goods advertising. J. Consum. Mark. **16**(1), 42–57 (1999)
2. Chen, Y.: Herd behavior in purchasing books online. Comput. Hum. Behav. **24**, 1977–1992 (2008)
3. Cheung, C.M.K., Thadani, D.R.: The impact of electronic word-of-mouth communication: a literature analysis and integrative model. Decis. Support Syst. **54**, 461–470 (2012)
4. Clark, J.K., Wegener, D.T., Habashi, M.M., Evans, A.T.: Source expertise and persuasion: the effects of perceived opposition or support on message scrutiny. Pers. Soc. Psychol. Bull. **38**(1), 90–100 (2012)
5. De Bono, K.G., Klein, C.: Source expertise and persuasion: the moderating role of recipient dogmatism. Pers. Soc. Psychol. Bull. **19**(2), 167–173 (1993)
6. Dholakia, U.M.: A motivational process model of product involvement and consumer risk. Eur. J. Mark. **35**(11/12), 1340–1352 (2001)
7. Doh, S., Hwang, J.: How consumers evaluate eWOM (electronic word-of-mouth) messages. Cyberpsychology Behav. **12**(2), 193–197 (2009)
8. Dodds, W.B., Monroe, K.B., Grewal, D.: Effects of price, brand, and store information on buyers' product evaluations. J. Mark. Res. **28**(3), 307–319 (1991)
9. Duan, W., Gu, B., Whinston, A.B.: Do online reviews matter? — an empirical investigation of panel data. Decis. Support Syst. **45**(4), 1007–1016 (2008)

10. Edell, J.A., Staelin, R.: The information processing of pictures in print advertisements. J. Consum. Res. **10**(1), 45–61 (1983)
11. Kamins, M.A., Gupta, K.: Congruence between spokesperson and product type: a matchup hypotheses perspective. Psychol. Mark. **11**(6), 569–586 (1994)
12. Kempf, D.S., Smith, R.E.: Consumer processing of product trial and the influence of prior advertising: a structural modeling approach. J. Mark. Res. **35**(3), 325–338 (1998)
13. Kim, J., Gupta, P.: Emotional expressions in online user reviews: how they influence consumers' product evaluations. J. Bus. Res. **65**(7), 985–992 (2012)
14. Lee, J., Park, D.H., Han, I.: The effect of negative online consumer reviews on product attitude: an information processing view. Electron. Commer. Res. Appl. **7**(3), 341–352 (2008)
15. Li, M., Huang, L., Tan, C., Wei, K.: Helpfulness of online product reviews as seen by consumers: source and content features. Int. J. Electron. Commer. **17**(4), 101–136 (2013)
16. Lim, B.C., Chung, C.: Word-of-mouth: the use of source expertise in the evaluation of familiar and unfamiliar brands. Asia Pac. J. Mark. Logistics **26**(1), 39–53 (2014)
17. Misra, S., Beatty, S.E.: Celebrity spokesperson and brand congruence. J. Bus. Res. **21**, 159–173 (1990)
18. O'Keefe, D.J.: Persuasion: Theory & Research, 2nd edn. Sage Publications, Thousand Oaks (2001)
19. Pires, G., Stanton, J., Eckford, A.: Influences on the perceived risk of purchasing online. J. Consum. Behav. **4**(2), 118–131 (2004)
20. Pornpitakpan, C.: The persuasiveness of source credibility: a critical review of five decades' evidence. J. Appl. Soc. Psychol. **34**(2), 243–281 (2004)
21. Racherla, P., Friske, W.: Perceived 'usefulness' of online consumer reviews: an exploratory investigation across three services categories. Electron. Commer. Res. Appl. **11**(6), 548–559 (2012)
22. Schlosser, A.: Can including pros and cons increase the helpfulness and persuasiveness of online reviews? The interactive effects of ratings and arguments. J. Consum. Psychol. **21**(3), 226–239 (2011)
23. Smith, D., Menon, S., Sivakumar, K.: Online peer and editorial recommendations, trust, and choice in virtual markets. J. Interact. Mark. **19**(3), 15–37 (2005)
24. Sparks, B.A., Browning, V.: The impact of online reviews on hotel booking intentions and perception of trust. Tourism Manag. **32**(6), 1310–1323 (2011)
25. Stafford, M.R., Day, E.: Retail services advertising: The effects of appeal, medium, and service. J. Advertising **21**(1), 57–71 (1995)
26. Till, B.D., Busler, M.: The match-up hypotheses: physical attractiveness, expertise, and the role of fit on brand attitude, purchase intent, and brand beliefs. J. Advertising **29**(3), 1–13 (2000)
27. West, M.D.: Validating a scale for the measurement of credibility: A covariance structure modelling approach. Journalism Mass Commun. Q. **71**(1), 159–168 (1994)
28. Wu, P.C.S., Wang, Y.C.: The influences of electronic word-of-mouth message appeal and message source credibility on brand attitude. Asia Pac. J. Mark. Logistics **23**(4), 448–472 (2011)
29. Zhang, Z., Ye, Q., Law, R., Li, Y.: The impact of e-word-of-mouth on the online popularity of restaurants: a comparison of consumer reviews and editor reviews. Int. J. Hospitality Manag. **29**(4), 694–700 (2010)
30. Zinn, H.C., Manfredo, M.J.: An experimental test of rational and emotional appeals about a recreation issue. Leisure Sci. **22**(3), 183–194 (2000)

Participation in Collaborative Consumption - A Value Co-creation Perspective

Shun Cai[1], Chee Wei Phang[2(✉)], Xiao Pang[1], and Yicheng Zhang[2]

[1] School of Management, Xiamen University, Xiamen, China
caishun@xmu.edu.cn, 330794000@qq.com
[2] School of Management, Fudan University, Shanghai, China
phangcw@fudan.edu.cn, aniydoris@qq.com

Abstract. In recent years, the phenomenon of sharing economy has emerged in many industries worldwide and businesses leveraging the sharing economy have flourished. Sharing Economy denotes the "collaborative consumption made by the activities of sharing, exchanging, and rental of resources without owning the goods". Value is a central concept in consumer behavior and it directly explains why consumers choose to buy or avoid particular products or services. Therefore, to establish the theoretical linkage between collaborative consumption and consumer value, our study propose a research model to explain why consumers participate in collaborative consumption from a value co-creation perspective. Based prior literature on collaborative consumption and literature on consumer value and value co-creation, we identify five factors as key determinants of attitude towards collaborative consumption, including economic value, social value, entertainment value, convenience value, and trust. A large scale survey was designed and implemented to test our research model. Data analysis results suggested that economic value, social value, entertainment value and trust significantly affect people's attitude towards collaborative consumption. The practical and theoretical contributions of our study are discussed.

Keywords: Sharing economy · Collaborative consumption · Consumer value

1 Introduction

In recent years, the phenomenon of sharing economy has emerged in many industries worldwide and businesses leveraging the sharing economy have flourished [1, 2]. Sharing Economy denotes the "collaborative consumption made by the activities of sharing, exchanging, and rental of resources without owning the goods" [3]. The collaborative consumption is the peer-to-peer-based activity of obtaining, giving, or sharing the access to goods and services, coordinated through community-based online services [1, 2]. Sharing is a phenomenon as old as humankind, while collaborative consumption and the "sharing economy" are phenomena born of the Internet age [1]. With the advancement of Information technology (IT), we have witnessed a flurry of emerging collaborative consumption, including sharing rooms (e.g. AirBnB), sharing cars and bikes (e.g., Relay Rides, Wheelz), and taxi services (e.g. Uber, Didi), etc.

© Springer International Publishing AG 2017
F.F.-H. Nah and C.-H. Tan (Eds.): HCIBGO 2017, PART II, LNCS 10294, pp. 174–189, 2017.
DOI: 10.1007/978-3-319-58484-3_14

Prior research has identified three key drivers of the sharing economy and collaborative consumption, which are changing consumer behavior, social networks and electronic markets, mobile devices and electronic services, which enabled the online interaction among consumers/users and collaborative consumption [4, 5]. Accordingly, existing research on collaborative consumption mainly focus on motivations of participation in the collaborative consumption with an emphasis on factors related to social network, electronic market, mobile devices and services, including trust, reputation of the platform, social capital/social ties [e.g. 6–8]. However, the first driver, i.e., changing consumer behavior has been largely ignored in prior literature, the existing literature on factors related to the first driver, remain insufficient.

Although the importance of collaborative consumption has been widely recognized, a comprehensive, yet theoretically solid framework of motivations to participate in collaborative consumption is still missing in the literature. Value is a central concept in consumer behavior and it directly explains why consumers choose to buy or avoid particular products or services [9–11]. Prior research also suggest that consumer value can be equally important for Internet commerce because it is critical to consumption behavior [12].

Therefore, to establish the theoretical linkage between collaborative consumption and consumer value, our study propose a research model to explain why consumers participate in collaborative consumption from a value co-creation perspective. Based prior literature on collaborative consumption and literature on consumer value and value co-creation, we identify five factors as key determinants of attitude towards collaborative consumption, including economic value, social value, entertainment value, convenience value, and trust.

2 Literature Review and Hypothesis Development

2.1 Collaborative Consumption

Collaborative consumption is not a niche trend anymore [5]. Instead, business leveraging collaborative consumptions has been flourished, for its large scale, large user volume, and profitable trend [6]. Table 1 synthesizes some recent research in collaborative consumption.

While collaborative consumption has previously occurred mostly among close relationships such as family, kin, and friends, the Internet is deemed to engender the opportunity to engage more strangers in this activity [1]. Hence trust has been identified as a key factor in collaborative consumptions. In a study of Airbnb, Ert et al. suggested that the more trustworthy the host is perceived to be from her photo, the higher the price of the listing and the probability of its being chosen [14]. Tussyadiah also highlighted the importance of trust in peer-to-peer accommodation rental services [13].

Economic considerations, such as utility has also been identified in prior literature as a key determinant of consumer participation in various types of collaborative consumptions, such as car sharing [5] and accommodation rental [13]. Lamberton and Rose also showed the relevance of costs and benefits of sharing in promoting commercial sharing [7]. However, participating in collaborative consumption is not simply

Table 1. Summary of selected literature

Dependent variable	Independent variable	Type of collaborative consumption	Major findings	References
Participation in commercial sharing systems	Utility, cost, familiarity, Perceived substitutability of ownership and sharing options, Perceived risk of product scarcity	Car-sharing programs, cellular service, bicycle-sharing plan	1. Show the relevance of costs and benefits of sharing in promoting commercial sharing options; 2. Highlights the explanatory power of perceived product scarcity risk	[7]
Satisfaction with a shared option, likelihood of choosing a sharing option again	Community belonging, cost savings, familiarity, service quality, trust, utility	B2C car sharing service car2go, C2C accommodation sharing service	Satisfaction and the likelihood of choosing a sharing option predominantly explained by determinants serving users' self-benefit. Utility, trust, cost savings, and familiarity were found to be essential, while the effects from service quality and community belonging depends	[5]
Attitude towards CC, behavioral intentions to participate in CC	Sustainability, enjoyment, economic benefits	General	Participation in CC is motivated by sustainability, enjoyment of the activity as well as economic gains	[2]

(*continued*)

Table 1. (*continued*)

Dependent variable	Independent variable	Type of collaborative consumption	Major findings	References
Participation in collaborative consumption	Sustainability, community and economic benefits; Trust, Efficacy, Economic benefits	Peer-to-peer accommodation rental services	Factors deter collaborative consumption include lack of trust, lack of efficacy with regards to technology, and lack of economic benefits. The motivations that drive collaborative consumption include the societal aspects of sustainability and community, as well as economic benefits	[13]
Price, probability of being chosen	Visual-based trust	Airbnb	The more trustworthy the host is perceived to be from her photo, the higher the price of the listing and the probability of its being chosen	[14]

tied to a set of economic aspects of consumption, but also depends on the nature of the functional, social and individual utilities of the certain collaborative consumption. Factors such as sustainability and community have been identified [2, 13]. Nevertheless, research on the social aspect of collaborative consumption has largely been limited.

2.2 A Value Co-creation Framework for Collaborative Consumption

For consumption values which directly explain why consumers choose to buy or avoid particular products [9, 10], different types of values might play their unique roles in shaping consumers' purchase choices. Participating in collaborative consumption is not simply tied to a set of economic aspects of consumption, but also depends on the social aspect in collaborative consumption.

On top of the traditional conceptualization of consumer value, the collaborative consumption in the current sharing economy environment often reflects the nature of value co-creation instead of value delivered largely by the firm themselves. Very often, firms do not create and deliver value to the passive customer, but rather through interaction and dialogue embeds value in the co-creation process between the firm and its active customer [15–17]. This moves the focus to a process of co-creating value through the exchange of resources with other consumers or partners to co-construct unique experiences [17, 18].

A review of the existing literature on collaborative consumption and consumer value shows that in comparison with social aspects, utility orientation dominates collaborative consumption research. Even for the limited social-related research, the positive aspect of social value, often reflected as maintaining interpersonal interconnectivity and social enhancement value [19] is dominated. However, in the offline context, people are particularly prone to avoid interacting with strangers due to "stranger danger" [1] and feelings of anxiety and uneasiness to meet and interact with them [20]. Similarly, not all consumers enjoy interacting with strangers in collaborative consumptions.

Hence, a comprehensive model which includes all relevant dimensions – psychological and functional needs – that constitute the value of collaborative consumption is still lacking. Considering all different aspects that constitute a customer's perception of and willingness to participate in collaborative consumption, it is important to combine a set of value dimensions into one single framework, rather than treating each perceived value separately. Therefore, we propose a value framework in explaining consumer participation in collaborative consumptions, economic value, social value, entertainment value, and convenience value have been identified as key value dimensions. In line with prior literature, trust and perceived personal innovativeness have also been included in the proposed model. The research model and hypotheses are shown in Fig. 1.

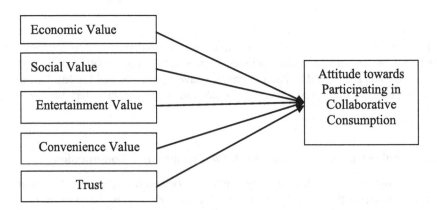

Fig. 1. Research model and hypotheses

Prior literature has identified economic gains as essential in gaining satisfaction and increasing the likelihood of people's choosing collaborative consumption services [2]. Collaborative consumption is perceived as offering more value with less cost [6, 21]. Therefore, we propose that:

H1. Economic value is positively associated with consumer' attitude towards participating in collaborative consumption.

Glind [58] highlighted that the main intrinsic motivation of people using collaborative consumption platforms were social, e.g., 'meeting people' or 'helping out'. In terms of sharing, Prior studies indicate that social interactions and networks have a positive impact on sharing knowledge, i.e., more social interactions lead to a more frequent and intense knowledge exchange behavior [22, 23]. However, in terms of collaborative consumptions with strangers, research in the offline context suggested that people are particularly prone to avoid interacting with nearby strangers due to concerns such as fears of "stranger danger" [1], and feelings of anxiety and uneasiness to meet and interact with them [20]. Such research findings from offline context remind us the possibility that consumers online could behave similarly. Following prior empirical studies in collaborative consumption, we therefore propose that:

H2. Social value is positively associated with consumer' attitude towards participating in collaborative consumption.

Uses and gratifications (U&G) paradigm explains what users can achieve when participating in SNSs from five dimensions, which can be seen as benefit factors attracting SNS users. The five dimensions are purposive value (i.e., informative and instrumental value), self-discovery, maintaining interpersonal connectivity, social enhancement, and entertainment value [19, 24]. Prior research in collaborative consumption also suggested that enjoyment of the activity is essential in gaining satisfaction and increasing the likelihood of people's choosing collaborative consumption services [2, 5]. Accordingly, we propose that:

H3. Entertainment value is positively associated with consumer' attitude towards participating in collaborative consumption.

The value of convenience has long been recognized in marketing and retailing literature [25–27]. For example, Anckar et al. [25] suggested that superior shopping convenience is an essential part of customer value. Szymanski and Hise [27] showed that convenience leads to E-satisfaction in online retailing. Yet few research in collaborative consumption has examined the role of convenience value. Service convenience facilitates the sale of goods and services in collaborative consumption. Because virtually all organizations create value for consumers through performances and because convenience is an important consideration for most consumers [28], we conjecture that convenience value could play an equally important in role collaborative consumption as other consumption situations. Therefore, we propose that:

H4. Convenience value is positively associated with consumer' attitude towards participating in collaborative consumption.

The extant literature shows extensive support for the overall beneficial effect of trust to business transactions and consumptions [29, 30]. Empirical studies report that trust, by bringing about good faith in the intent, reliability, and fairness of partner behaviour [31, 32], reduces the potential for conflict [31]. A large amount of previous research has argued that trust, and relationship commitment, perform vital roles in promoting collaborative relationships [e.g. 33, 34].

Trust can be equally important in collaborative consumptions. Glind [58] high-lighted that lack of trust as the important factors that deter the use of peer-to-peer services such as accommodation. Ert et al. showed that The more trustworthy the host is perceived to be from her photo, the higher the price of the listing and the probability of its being chosen in accommodation sharing [14]. Therefore, we propose that:

H5. Trust is positively associated with consumer' attitude towards participating in collaborative consumption.

3   Research Methods

3.1   Data Collection

To conduct our research, we used a structured survey method. We recruit 278 students who has experience in participating in collaborative consumption from a major university in China for the survey research. A large-scale survey was carried out in December 2016. We send out invitations through the communication platform of Student's Union and about 400 students registered for this survey. Finally, a total of 278 completed surveys were collected. Based on prior literature, it may be appropriate to utilize student subjects if the observation does not include phenomena [23, 35] such as social norms or political views that are structured over time [36, 37]. Finally, we have 278 complete and usable responses for data analysis. Table 2 reports the demographic description of those respondents.

Table 2. Demographic descriptions

	Max.	Min.	Mean
Age	35	18	22
Gender		Male	Female
		104	185
Education		Post-graduate	Graduate
		108	181

We examined the response bias issue with the procedure suggested by Armstrong and Overton [38]. We first compared the participants who registered but not completed the whole research process (either not login the APP, or not complete the final questionnaire) with those who complete the whole process on key demographic variables. The results of the Mann-Whitney tests show no significant differences, suggesting that response bias would not likely affect our findings [38].

Table 3. Constructs and instruments

Construct		Item	Source
Attitude towards collaborative consumption	ATCC1	All things considered, I think collaborative consumption is a positive thing	[2]
	ATCC2	All things considered, I think participating in collaborative consumption is a good thing	
	ATCC3	Overall, sharing goods and services within a collaborative consumption community makes sense	
	ATCC4	I can see myself engaging in collaborative consumption more frequently in the future	
Economic value	ECOG1	I can save money if I participate in collaborative consumption	[39]
	ECOG2	My participation in collaborative consumption benefits me financially	
	ECOG3	My participation in collaborative consumption can improve my economic situation	
Social value	SOVA1	To have something to do with others	[19]
	SOVA2	To stay in touch	
	SOVA3	To impress	
	SOVA4	To feel important	
Entertainment value	ENVA1	I think collaborative consumption is enjoyable	[40]
	ENVA2	I think collaborative consumption is exciting	
	ENVA3	I think collaborative consumption is fun	
	ENVA4	I think collaborative consumption is interesting	
	ENVA5	I think collaborative consumption is pleasant	
Trust	TRUST1	This Platform (store) has the skills and expertise to perform transactions in an expected manner	[41]
	TRUST2	This Platform (store) has access to the information needed to handle transactions appropriately	
	TRUST3	This Platform (store) is fair in its conduct of user (customer) transactions	
	TRUST4	This Platform (store) is fair in its user (customer) service policies following a transaction	
	TRUST5	This Platform(store) makes good-faith efforts to address most user (customer) concerns	
	TRUST6	Overall, this Platform (store) is trustworthy	

(continued)

Table 3. (*continued*)

Construct		Item	Source
Convenience value	CONVE1	It was easy to use collaborative consumption	[28]
	CONVE2	It did not take much time to have collaborative consumption	
	CONVE3	I was able to complete my consumption quickly	
	CONVE4	I did not have to make much of an effort to complete collaborative consumption	
Personal innovativeness	PERIN1	If I heard about a new technology, I would look for ways to experiment with it	[42]
	PERIN2	Among my peers, I am usually the first to try out new information technologies	
	PERIN3*	In general, I am hesitant to try out new information technologies (Reverse)	
	PERIN4	I like to experiment with new information technologies	
Familiarity	FAM1	I once had experience in collaborative consumption	[5]
	FAM2	I was familiar with collaborative consumption	
	FAM3	It was not new for me to participate in collaborative consumption	

3.2 Questionnaire Development

The questionnaire was developed through a two-stage process. We first extensively reviewed the literature to list the candidate constructs and measures that were used in prior research. A draft questionnaire was developed. Each item was measured in a seven-point Likert scale. In the second stage, four researchers reviewed the draft questionnaire, ranked each item according to their content validity, and suggested improvements in wording and the layout of the items. We also include two variables: personal innovativeness and familiarity as control variables in our research model. The instrument for the constructs in our research model and is presented in Table 3.

4 Data Analysis and Discussions

We then conducted data analysis in accordance with a two-stage methodology [43]. The first step in the data analysis is to establish the convergent and discriminant validity of the constructs. We test the measurement model using Principal Components Analysis (PCA) in SPSS (SPSS, Chicago, USA) and Confirmatory Factor Analysis (CFA) in LISREL [44]. In the second step, following Cohen et al. [45]'s recommendations, a hierarchical multiple regression analysis was employed to test our hypotheses using SPSS.

In the first phase, we examine the data using PCA with Varimax rotation. Several items were removed one by one due to cross loadings and after careful examination between the wording of the items and the definitions of the construct. after removing those items, we identify 8 factors with eigen values greater than 1.0. All constructs explain 78.7% of the total variance (EFA results table is available on request).

We conduct the CFA analysis by creating a LISREL path diagram. Using LISREL for confirmatory factor analysis provides a more rigorous assessment of the fit between the collected data and the theoretical factor structure, and satisfies the minimum requirements of assessing the measurement properties of uni-dimensionality, convergent validity, and discriminant validity [46–48].

Uni-dimensionality is the degree to which items load only on their respective constructs without having "parallel correlational pattern(s)" [46, 49]. Uni-dimensionality cannot be assessed using factor analysis or Cronbach's alpha, instead, covariance-based SEM (such as LISREL) provides the ability to compare alternative pre-specified measurement models and examine, through statistical significances and a wide set of the types of fit, which is better supported by the data [48]. A set of criterion has been proposed and adopted in the literature to assess uni-dimensionality, including model fit indices such as GFI, NFI, AGFI, and $\chi2$ to show uni-dimensionality [48]. We apply the following indices and standards to assess model fit: goodness-of-fit index (GFI) and normed fit index (NFI) greater than 0.90, adjusted goodness-of-fit index (AGFI) greater than 0.80 [48], comparative fit index (CFI) greater than 0.90, and root mean square of approximation (RMSEA) lower than 0.08 for a good fit and lower than 0.05 for an excellent fit [50].

We conducted a confirmatory factor analysis (CFA) for the 8 constructs, namely, Attitude towards collaborative consumption (ATCC), Economic Value (ECVA), Social Value (SOVA), Entertainment value (ENVA), Convenience Value (COVA), Trust (TRUST), Personal Innovativeness (PEIN) and Familiarity (FAM). The means and standard deviation of each of the constructs are presented in Table 4.

Table 4. Descriptive statistics and correlations

Variable	FAM	PERIN	ATCC	ECOVA	SOVA	ENVA	TRUST	CONVA
Mean	4.73	4.93	5.65	5.04	4.53	5.2	5.17	4.78
S.D.	1.3	1.05	0.84	1.16	1.11	0.92	0.94	1.17
FAM	**0.84**							
PERIN	0.45	**0.79**						
ATCC	0.44	0.40	**0.88**					
ECOVA	0.16	0.21	0.3	**0.81**				
SOVA	0.1	0.26	0.11	0	**0.83**			
ENVA	0.36	0.43	0.64	0.21	0.43	**0.88**		
TRUST	0.28	0.30	0.52	0.29	0.18	0.52	**0.82**	
CONVA	0.24	0.25	0.19	0.2	0.07	0.3	0.33	**0.89**

Note: Attitude towards collaborative consumption (ATCC), Economic Value (ECVA), Social Value (SOVA), Entertainment Value (ENVA), Convenience Value (COVA), Trust (TRUST), Personal Innovativeness (PEIN) and Familiarity (FAM); The number in parentheses is the square root of AVE. For adequate discriminant validity, the number in parentheses should be greater than the corresponding off-diagonal elements.

The CFA demonstrated good model fit, showing that over half the variance is captured by the latent construct [48, 49, 51].

Convergent validity is assessed using three criteria. First, standardized path loadings, which are indicators of the degree of association between the underlying latent factor and each item, should be greater than 0.7 and statistically significant [48]. Second, composite reliabilities, as well as the Cronbach's alphas, should be larger than 0.7 [52]. Third, the average variance extracted (AVE) for each factor should exceed 0.50 [53]. As shown in Table 5, all path loadings are greater than 0.707 after removing

Table 5. Confirmatory factor analysis results

Construct	Standard loading	t-value	AVE	Composite factor reliability	Cronbach's alpha
Familiarity	0.83	16.23	0.70	0.74	0.871
	0.84	16.57			
	0.84	16.66			
Personal innovativeness	0.82	15.6	0.63	0.68	0.829
	0.74	13.77			
	0.82	15.69			
Attitude towards collaborative consumption	0.91	20.1	0.77	0.79	0.924
	0.96	21.77			
	0.9	19.56			
	0.73	14.37			
Economic value	0.74	13.75	0.65	0.70	0.847
	0.84	16.12			
	0.84	15.99			
Social value	0.7	13.26	0.69	0.73	0.894
	0.81	16.19			
	0.92	19.92			
	0.87	18.08			
Entertainment value	0.83	17.18	0.77	0.79	0.941
	0.81	16.66			
	0.9	19.61			
	0.95	21.61			
	0.88	18.84			
Trust	0.72	13.84	0.68	0.72	0.924
	0.75	14.81			
	0.87	18.24			
	0.9	19.31			
	0.84	17.5			
	0.84	17.22			
Convenience value	0.84	17.12	0.79	0.81	0.916
	0.95	20.84			
	0.88	18.51			

CONVA1 and PERIN4, and all of them are significant. After evaluate the wording of these two items, we decided to keep these two items for further data analysis. The reliability measures are all above 0.7, and the AVEs are all above 0.5. Thus, convergent validity is established.

To test the discriminant validity of each variable, the average variance extracted (AVE) and the inter construct correlation were compared. The results in Table 5 show that all AVEs for the latent variables were greater than the required minimum level of 0.5. Every construct had a larger square root of AVE than its correlations with other constructs. This result indicates that our measurement items have discriminant validity.

As with all self-reported data, there is the potential for the occurrence of common method variance (CMV), i.e., variance that is attributable to the measurement method rather than to the constructs the measures represent [54]. To address this issue, we used several procedural and statistical remedies.

First, we paid careful attention to the wording of the items, and developed our questionnaire carefully to reduce item ambiguity. These procedures would reduce the respondents' evaluation apprehension and make them less likely to edit their responses to be more socially desirable, lenient, acquiescent, and consistent with how they think the researcher wants them to respond when crafting their responses [54, 55]. Second, we performed a Harman's one-factor test via CFA by specifying a hypothesized method factor as an underlying driver of all of the indicators. The results revealed that the fit of the single-factor model was extremely unsatisfactory, indicating the common method variance is not a major source of the variations in the items [56]. Finally, following the literature, we used a marker variable to control for common method bias [57]. We used a statement in political ideology "do you believe that 'from each according to his ability, to each according to his need' is important" as the marker variable, as it was theoretically unrelated to many other variables [54, 57]. All significant correlations remained significant after the partial correlation adjustment. While the results of this analysis do not explicitly preclude the possibility of common method variance, they do suggest that common method variance is not of great concern in this study.

We conducted a 3-step hierarchical multiple regression analysis as recommended by Cohen [45]). According to Cohen et al. [45], hierarchical multiple regression analysis is best suited for identifying causal priority and removing confounding variables. This approach is appropriate when the independent variables need to be ordered in terms of the specific questions that are to be answered by the research study. In this study, after controlling for the possible confounding variables identified through the literature review, we sought to examine the antecedents of attitude towards collaborative consumptions. Through hierarchical multiple regression analysis, we could explore the change in the direct effects of value dimensions and trust when it meets other moderating variables. Therefore, following prior studies, we conducted the 3-step hierarchical multiple regression analysis recommended by Cohen, Cohen [45]). In Model 1 (including control variables only), Model 2 (including both control variables and direct effects), Model 3 (including control variable, direct and moderating effects), the R Square for attitude towards participating in collaborative cons, 0.541, and 0.563, respectively.

Hypothesis 1 that tests the influence of economic value on attitude towards participating in collaborative consumption is consistently significant in Model 2 ($\beta = 0.12$, $p < 0.01$) and Model 3 ($\beta = 0.11$, $p < 0.01$), supporting H1. Hypothesis 2 tests the influence of social value on attitude towards participating in collaborative consumption is consistently significant in Model 2 ($\beta = -0.14$, $p < 0.01$) and Model 3 ($\beta = -0.14$, $p < 0.01$), which is inconsistent with our H2 which hypothesizes a positive influence. The effects from entertainment value (H3) and trust (H5) are also significant. However, the hypothesize effect for convenience value is not significant ($\beta = -0.062$, $p > 0.05$), rejecting H4.

5   Discussions and Conclusions

In conclusion, this research proposes a value framework to key antecedents of consumer attitude towards participating in collaborative consumption.

The first contribution of this article is to establish a systematical framework to analyze the essential factors. Based on consumer value literature, we propose that four types of value, i.e. economic value, social value, entertainment value, together with trust, would affect consumer's attitude towards collaborative consumption. The parsimonious model explains more than 50% variance of consumer's attitude. Second, our results empirically confirm the effects from economic and entertainment value, which are consistent with prior literature. Finally, our results show that the effect from social value may not be always positive across different situations and collaborative consumption types. Although a large number of literature had found the positive effect from social value, the results from our study shows another possibility that social value could be negative in certain circumstances.

References

1. Belk, R.: You are what you can access: sharing and collaborative consumption online. J. Bus. Res. **67**(8), 1595–1600 (2014)
2. Hamari, J., Sjöklint, M., Ukkonen, A.: The sharing economy: why people participate in collaborative consumption. J. Assoc. Inf. Sci. Technol. **67**(9), 2047–2059 (2016)
3. Lessig, L.: Remix: Making Art and Commerce Thrive in the Hybrid Economy. Penguin, New York (2008)
4. Puschmann, T., Alt, R.: Sharing economy. Bus. Inf. Syst. Eng. **58**(1), 93–99 (2016)
5. Möhlmann, M.: Collaborative consumption: determinants of satisfaction and the likelihood of using a sharing economy option again. J. Consum. Behav. **14**(3), 193–207 (2015)
6. Botsman, R., Rogers, R.: What's Mine Is Yours: The Rise of Collaborative Consumption. Harper Business, New York (2010)
7. Lamberton, C.P., Rose, R.L.: When is ours better than mine? A framework for understanding and altering participation in commercial sharing systems. J. Mark. **76**(4), 109–125 (2012)
8. Schor, J.B., Fitzmaurice, C.J.: 26. Collaborating and connecting: the emergence of the sharing economy. In: Handbook of Research on Sustainable Consumption, p. 410 (2015)

9. Sheth, J.N., Parvatiyar, A.: Relationship marketing in consumer markets: antecedents and consequences. J. Acad. Mark. Sci. **23**(4), 255–271 (1995)
10. Sheth, J.N., Newman, B.I., Gross, B.I.: Why we buy what we buy: a theory of consumption values. J. Bus. Res. **22**(1), 159–170 (1991)
11. Zeithaml, V.A.: Consumer perceptions of price, quality, and value: a means-end model and synthesis of evidence. J. Mark. **52**(3), 2–22 (1988)
12. Xu, Y., Cai, S., Kim, H.-W.: Cue consistency and page value perception: implications to Web-based catalog design. Inf. Manag. **50**(1), 33–42 (2013)
13. Tussyadiah, I.: An exploratory on drivers and deterrents of collaborative consumption in travel. In: Tussyadiah, I., Inversini, A. (eds.) Information and Communication Technologies in Tourism. Springer, Cham (2015)
14. Ert, E., Fleischer, A., Magen, N.: Trust and reputation in the sharing economy: the role of personal photos in Airbnb. Tourism Manag. **55**, 62–73 (2016)
15. Payne, A., et al.: Co-creating brands: diagnosing and designing the relationship experience. J. Bus. Res. **62**(3), 379–389 (2009)
16. Prahalad, C.K., Ramaswamy, V.: Co-creation experiences: the next practice in value creation. J. Interact. Mark. **18**(3), 5–14 (2004)
17. Vargo, S.L., Lusch, R.F.: Evolving to a new dominant logic for marketing. J. Mark. **68**(1), 1–17 (2004)
18. Tynan, C., McKechnie, S., Chhuon, C.: Co-creating value for luxury brands. J. Bus. Res. **63** (11), 1156–1163 (2010)
19. Dholakia, U.M., Bagozzi, R.P., Pearo, L.K.: A social influence model of consumer participation in network- and small-group-based virtual communities. Int. J. Res. Mark. **21** (3), 241–263 (2004)
20. Gudykunst, W.B., Nishida, T.: Anxiety, uncertainty, and perceived effectiveness of communication across relationships and cultures. Int. J. Intercultural Relat. **25**(1), 55–71 (2001)
21. Gansky, L.: The Mesh: Why the Future of Business is Sharing. Portfolio Penguin, New York (2010)
22. Tsai, W., Ghoshal, S.: Social capital and value creation: the role of intrafirm networks. Acad. Manag. J. **41**(4), 464–476 (1998)
23. Chai, S., Das, S., Rao, H.R.: Factors affecting bloggers' knowledge sharing: an investigation across gender. J. Manag. Inf. Syst. **28**(3), 309–341 (2011)
24. Cheung, C.M.K., Chiu, P.-Y., Lee, M.K.O.: Online social networks: why do students use facebook? Comput. Hum. Behav. **27**(4), 1337–1343 (2011)
25. Anckar, B., Walden, P., Jelassi, T.: Creating customer value in online grocery shopping. Int. J. Retail. Distrib. Manag. **30**(4), 211–220 (2002)
26. Srinivasan, S.S., Anderson, R., Ponnavolu, K.: Customer loyalty in e-Commerce: an exploration of its antecedents and consequences. J. Retail. **78**(1), 41–50 (2002)
27. Szymanski, D.M., Hise, R.T.: E-satisfaction: an initial examination. J. Retail. **76**(3), 309–322 (2000)
28. Berry, L.L., Seiders, K., Grewal, D.: Understanding service convenience. J. Mark. **66**(3), 1–17 (2002)
29. Shin, H., Collier, D.A., Wilson, D.D.: Supply management orientation and supplier/buyer performance. J. Oper. Manag. **18**(3), 317–333 (2000)
30. Cai, S., et al.: Knowledge sharing in collaborative supply chains: twin effects of trust and power. Int. J. Prod. Res. **51**(7), 2060–2076 (2013)
31. Zaheer, A., McEvily, B., Perrone, V.: Does trust matter? Exploring the effects of interorganizational and interpersonal trust on performance. Organ. Sci. **9**(2), 141–159 (1998)

32. Krishnan, R., Martin, X., Noorderhaven, N.G.: When does trust matter to alliance performance? Acad. Manag. J. **49**(5), 894–917 (2006)
33. Kumar, N., Scheer, L.K., Steenkamp, J.-B.E.M.: The effects of perceived interdependence on dealer attitudes. J. Mark. Res. **32**(3), 348–356 (1995)
34. Ring, P.S., Van de Ven, A.H.: Developmental processes of cooperative interorganizational relationships. Acad. Manag. Rev. **19**(1), 90–118 (1994)
35. Agarwal, R., Karahanna, E.: Time flies when you're having fun: cognitive absorption and beliefs about information technology usage. MIS Q. **24**(4), 665–694 (2010)
36. Ahuja, M.K., Thatcher, J.B.: Moving beyond intentions and toward the theory of trying: effects of work environment and gender on post-adoption information technology use. MIS Q. **29**(3), 427–459 (2005)
37. Sears, D.O.: College sophomores in the laboratory: influences of a narrow data base on social psychology's view of human nature. J. Pers. Soc. Psychol. **51**(3), 515–530 (1986)
38. Armstrong, J.S., Overton, T.S.: Estimating nonresponse bias in mail surveys. J. Mark. Res. **14**(3), 396–402 (1977)
39. Bock, G.-W., et al.: Behavioral intention formation in knowledge sharing: examining the roles of extrinsic motivators, social-psychological forces, and organizational climate. MIS Q. **29**(1), 87–111 (2005)
40. van der Heijden, H.: User acceptance of hedonic information systems. MIS Q. **28**(4), 695–704 (2004)
41. Bhattacherjee, A.: Individual trust in online firms: scale development and initial test. J. Manag. Inf. Syst. **19**(1), 211–241 (2002)
42. Agarwal, R., Prasad, J.: A conceptual and operational definition of personal innovativeness in the domain of information technology. Inf. Syst. Res. **9**(2), 204–215 (1998)
43. Anderson, J.C., Gerbing, D.W.: Structural equation modelling in practice: a review and recommended two-step approach. Psychol. Bull. **103**(3), 411–423 (1988)
44. Jöreskog, K.G., Sörbom, D.: LISREL for Windows. Scientific Software International, Inc., Lincolnwood (2006)
45. Cohen, J., et al.: Applied Multiple Regression/Correlation Analysis for the Behavioral Sciences, 3rd edn. Lawrence Erlbaum Associates, Hillsdale (2003)
46. Bagozzi, R.P., Fornell, C.: Theoretical concepts, measurement, and meaning. In: Fornell, C. (ed.) A Second Generation of Multivariate Analysis. Praeger Publishers, Westport (1982)
47. Teo, H.H., Wei, K.K., Benbasat, I.: Predicting intention to adopt interorganizational linkages: an institutional perspective. MIS Q. **27**(1), 19–49 (2003)
48. Gefen, D., Straub, D.W., Boudreau, M.: Structural equation modelling and regression: guidelines for research practice. Commun. AIS **4**(7), 2–76 (2000)
49. Segars, A.H.: Assessing the unidimensionality of measurement: a paradigm and illustration within the context of information systems research. Omega **25**(1), 107–121 (1997)
50. McKnight, D.H., Choudhury, V., Kacmar, C.: Developing and validating trust measures for e-commerce: an integrative typology. Inf. Syst. Res. **13**(3), 334–359 (2002)
51. Hair, J.F., et al.: Multivariate Data Analysis. Prentice Hall, Upper Saddle River (1998)
52. Nunally, J.C.: Psychometric Theory. McGraw-Hill, New York (1978)
53. Fornell, C., Larcker, D.: Evaluating structural equation models with unobservable variables and measurement error. J. Mark. Res. **18**(3), 39–50 (1981)
54. Podsakoff, P.M., et al.: Common method biases in behavioral research: a critical review of the literature and recommended remedies. J. Appl. Psychol. **88**(5), 879–903 (2003)
55. Tourangeau, R., Rips, L.J., Rasinski, K.: The Psychology of Survey Response. Cambridge University Press, Cambridge (2000)

56. Malhotra, N.K., Kim, S.S., Patil, A.: Common method variance in IS research: a comparison of alternative approaches and a reanalysis of past research. Manag. Sci. **52**(12), 1865–1883 (2006)
57. Lindell, M.K., Whitney, D.J.: Accounting for common method variance in cross-sectional design. J. Appl. Psychol. **86**(1), 114–121 (2001)
58. Glind, P.B.: The consumer potential of Collaborative Consumption: Identifying the motives of Dutch Collaborative Consumers & Measuring the consumer potential of Collaborative Consumption within the municipality of Amsterdam. Master thesis, Faculty of Geosciences, Utrecht University, The Netherlands (2013)

How to Get Endorsements? Predicting Facebook Likes Using Post Content and User Engagement

Wei-Fan Chen[✉], Yi-Pei Chen, and Lun-Wei Ku

Institute of Information Science, Academia Sinica, Taipei, Taiwan
{viericwf,ypc82,lwku}@iis.sinica.edu.tw

Abstract. We view the prediction of Facebook likes as a content suggestion problem and show that likes can be much better predicted considered post content or user engagement. Experiments presented are based on a dataset of over 4 million likes collected from over seventy thousands of users in fan pages. The proposed model adopts the similarity metric to appraise how a user may like a document given his or her liked documents, as well as the Restricted Boltzmann Machine (RBM) to estimate whether a user would like a document given the like records of all users. The model achieves a precision of 5–10% and a recall of 2–55%. The commonly used label propagation model is implemented and tested as a baseline. Different models and settings are compared and results show superiority of the proposed model.

Keywords: Recommendation system · RBM · BLEU · Facebook

1 Introduction

It has been shown that Facebook likes, as a kind of easily accessible digital records of behavior, can be used to automatically and accurately predict a range of highly sensitive factoid and opinioned personal attributes, including age, gender, parental separation and political views, stance, happiness, respectively [1]. However, literature shows that most researches use real likes instead of predicting them [2], which makes the information of a large quantity of new documents difficult to be utilized.

Predicting Facebook likes is to predict "who will read and like the current document enough to push the like button". It is similar to the product recommendation problem, which predicts "who will view and like the product enough to purchase it". However, there are still several differences between them, and the major difference is the degree of willingness. For the product recommendation research, there are usually view records and purchase records showing two different degrees of willing for utilization. View records indicates the relevance and slight preference, while purchase records show the strong preference (to the degree of willing to spend their money). Instead in Facebook, we have only like records, whose degree of willing is between view and purchase records. It costs some effort to push the like button, but the effort is little compared to the purchase. The difference in degrees of willing leads to different challenges.

In Facebook, social network should help a lot in predicting likes. However, the privacy issue has become crucial for all social media and the social network, e.g., friend

© Springer International Publishing AG 2017
F.F.-H. Nah and C.-H. Tan (Eds.): HCIBGO 2017, PART II, LNCS 10294, pp. 190–202, 2017.
DOI: 10.1007/978-3-319-58484-3_15

information is not easily accessible anymore. Many researches ask volunteers to access their social network, but this is not feasible in real applications.

In this paper, we solve the Facebook like prediction problem with only the public information: the document content and the user engagement to the document. Therefore, we divide our research problem into two sub-problems: predicting likes by document content and predicting likes by user engagement. The former is realized by calculating similarities between documents with the intuition that users should like to read similar documents, i.e., documents of preferred topics or viewpoints. The latter is realized by a Restricted Boltzmann Machine (RBM) as it is shown to have good prediction power with enough known records [3]. Then we conquer this problem with a weighted function considering these two sub-models. Through the prediction of likes, we hope to provide valuable reference for the government and the companies to get more endorsements by their documents.

2 Related Work

The recommendation problem has been widely studied for decades [3]. It is known as collaborative filtering (CF) and researchers divide them into item-based, user-based and hybrid according to their recommendation strategy.

For item-based CF, it recommends items that similar to user's previous liked items or purchased products [4, 5], some of them has been adopted on business like Amazon [4]. The key point of item-based CF is presenting each item as a vector and then performing an item-to-item similarity matrix. For example, the item vector in Linden's work is an M dimensional vector, where each dimension correspond to a customer [4]. Also, there are ways to compute the similarity between items, e.g., cosine similarity, *Pearson-r* correlation, or the adjust cosine similarity where the values in each dimension of the vector are normalized firstly [5]. Besides product recommendation, document recommendation is similar to our work. For example, PRES (Personalized REcommender System) used TF-IDF of each word as a document vector and utilized cosine similarity to recommend web posts based on content [6]. The major difference between PRES and our work is that we focus on predicting the "like" behavior on Facebook but PRES aimed at retrieving relevant (judged by user feedback) hyperlinks to users.

For user-based CF, items that liked by similar users will be recommended. It can be performed using the same ideology in item-based CF: presenting a user as a vector according to her liked/purchased record and then computing a user-to-user similarity matrix. However, the shortage of using user vectors instead of item vectors is the sparsity of the user vectors because the size of users is significant larger than the size of items. To deal with this problem, researchers added more information on how to compute the similarity between users, e.g., social relationship [7], similar interests [8] or similar video viewing records [9]. Researches using user-based CF have shown that user information benefits the recommendation for product [7], document [8, 10, 11], and even video [9]. Besides, some researches in social network domain use belief propagation for marketing [12, 13], which can be considered as a variation of user-based CF to utilize the user information.

As for hybrid model, it combines item-based and user-based information to recommend [14, 15]. However, the problem turns to the combination of two information as Melville addressed [14]. In this paper, we propose a late-fusion approach, which combines two information via a weighted function.

3 Method

As mentioned, we propose a hybrid model that incorporates probabilities from the item-based model and the user-based model. Given a set of users and a set of documents, the likes form a matrix $L \in R^{|U| \times |D|}$, where one column indicates one user and one column indicates one document. The matrix L is a sparse matrix where the elements $l_{i,j}$ in L equals to one if user u_i liked the document d_j in the dataset. In fact, the like prediction is to estimate the "unknown" elements in L, where the user u_i did not click like to document d_j. In our paper we aim at estimating the $l_{i,j}$ using item-based method and user-based method. Assuming that they can be independently estimated, formally we write,

$$p(l_{i,j}) = w \cdot p_{user}(l_{i,j}) + (1 - w) \cdot p_{item}(l_{i,j}) \tag{1}$$

where $p(l_{i,j})$ is the estimated value of $l_{i,j}$, $p_{user}(l_{i,j})$ and $p_{item}(l_{i,j})$ denote the probability estimated by the user-based and item-based model, respectively, and w is used to control the weights of the two models.

In the following, we will detail how we compute two probabilities based on different features.

3.1 Item-Based Model: BLEU

As for item-based model, we recommend documents that similar to the documents that the user liked. There are two assumptions used in our item-based model. First, users have no preference among documents, that is, users equally liked them. Second, we have very long term liking history that logs likings of the user and thus all kinds of liked documents were known, then we can model the liking probability via similarities. With this in mind, given a document d_j, we compare d_j with what user liked before, and choose the highest similarities among all comparisons as the estimated probability. Formally,

$$p(l_{i,j}) \cong \max(sim(d_j, d_m)), \forall d_m \in D_i \tag{2}$$

where d_j is the target document, D_i is the documents that user u_i liked, d_m is one of document in D_i, and $sim(.)$ is the similarity function. In this paper, we approach the similarity function by the BLEU score.

BLEU is a modified form of precision which compares the candidate translation against multiple reference translations. It is a commonly used measurement for the quality of bilingual machine translation considering the similarity of n-grams between the candidate translation and the reference translations [16]. To predict whether a user u_i will like the current document d_j, we view it as the candidate translation of the reference translation set D_i, which includes all kinds of documents this user has ever liked in the whole dataset. That is, the document d_j is an alternative way to express the same content of one document in D_i. As a result, if the translation quality is high enough to indicate that d_j can be derived from D_i, user u_i would like document d_j with the estimated probability. To calculate BLEU scores, documents are tokenized into words and all punctuations are removed. However, unlike machine translation, the topics of the reference documents may vary. Therefore, we calculate BLEU scores between d_j and each reference document d_m, and report the BLEU score by maximizing these BLEU scores.

Then for each user u_i, we sort the probabilities among the documents not in D_i and recommend the top n documents to the user.

3.2 User-Based Model: RBM

For user-based model, we recommend documents liked by other users that similar to the target user. The main challenge in presenting a user as a vector is the sparsity of the like pattern of a user, where a like pattern is a high dimensional vector and there are only a few of ones but most of the values are zero. In our paper, we use a simple deep learning model – Restricted Boltzmann Machine (RBM) to encode a like pattern into a low-dimensional and dense vector as shown in Fig. 1 [11].

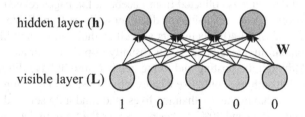

Fig. 1. A sample RBM network

Formally, for each user, the like pattern is a binary vector $\mathbf{L}_i = \{l_{i,1}, l_{i,2}, \ldots l_{i,j}, \ldots l_{i,|D|}\}$, where $l_{i,j} = 1$ if the user like the document d_j, and $|D|$ is the number of documents in our dataset. Then the RBM aims to optimize the parameters that maximize the observed probability $p(\mathbf{L}_i)$, shown in Eq. 3.

$$\theta = \underset{\theta = \{\mathbf{W}, \mathbf{b}_L, \mathbf{b}_h\}}{\arg\max} \ \ln p(\mathbf{L}_i) \tag{3}$$

where $\mathbf{W}$, $\mathbf{b}_L$ and $\mathbf{b}_h$ are weights, bias for visible layer and bias for hidden layer, respectively. Then the RBM model optimizes the joint probability of the visible layer $\mathbf{L}_i$ and the hidden layer $\mathbf{h}$ in Eq. 4, where the energy function is defined in Eq. 5.

$$p(\mathbf{L}_i, \mathbf{h}) = \frac{1}{\mathbf{Z}(\theta)} e^{-\mathrm{E}(\mathbf{L}_i, \mathbf{h})} \tag{4}$$

$$E(\mathbf{L}_i, \mathbf{h}) = -\sum_{l_{i,j} \in \mathbf{L}_i, h_k \in \mathbf{h}} l_{i,j} h_k W_{j,k} - \sum_{l_{i,j} \in \mathbf{L}_i} l_{i,j} b_{l_k} - \sum_{h_k \in \mathbf{h}} h_k b_{h_k} \qquad (5)$$

After the training process, we used the parameters θ to predict likes. The one step Gibbs sampling was adopt to approximate the probability of a user to like the document as in Eqs. 6 and 7, suggested in [11].

$$\theta = \underset{\theta = \{\mathbf{W}, \mathbf{b_L}, \mathbf{b_h}\}}{\arg\max} \ \ln p(\mathbf{L}_i) \qquad (6)$$

$$p(l_{i,j} = 1 | \hat{p}_i) = \sigma(b_{l_j} + \sum_{\hat{p}_k \in \hat{p}_i} \hat{p}_k W_{j,k}) \qquad (7)$$

where $\hat{p}_k \in \hat{p}_i$ is the probability of the hidden layer given the visible layer, and $p(l_{i,j} = 1 | \hat{p}_i)$ is the like probability for the document d_j of the user given the hidden layer. We then use the probability in Eq. 7 to recommend the top n documents for the user.

4   Experiments

4.1   Dataset

The experimental dataset was collected from Facebook fan pages related a same topic —— nuclear power. The posting time of documents spans from September 2013 to August 2014. A total of 34,402 documents as well as their author and liker IDs were recorded. For content-duplicated documents (usually re-posts), their authors and likers were merged. Although the posting and liking behavior might have different implications, we default that authors should like whatever they posted. In addition, we removed users and documents having fewer than ten likes, and randomly selected 10% of likes per user as the testing data and 90% of likes per user as the training data. Table 1 shows the result after removing these users and documents.

Table 1. Like statistic

#documents	#users	#likes/doc	#likes/user	#likes (training)	#likes (testing)
34,402	77,416	123.48	54.87	3,821,359	426,609

4.2   Baselines

We use label propagation as a baseline to find potential likes. Given the like matrix $\mathbf{L}$, a transition matrix $\mathbf{T}$ that defines the label transition probability from document to document, the goal of label propagation is to update $\mathbf{L}$ given $\mathbf{T}$. Formally,

$$\mathbf{L}' = \alpha \cdot \mathbf{L}^0 + (1 - \alpha) \cdot \mathbf{T} \cdot \mathbf{L} \qquad (8)$$

where L^0, L and L' are the prior label, the label from previous iteration and the updated label; T is the transition matrix, and α is the prior parameter that determines the initial label priority. Note that the label here denotes whether the user likes the document. We repeatedly compute Eq. (8) to update L and predict new likes. Different factors are considered in building the transition matrix T: co-liker, semantic similarity using BLEU score or n-gram vector. That is to say, a higher probability to be liked by a certain user are assigned to two documents that are liked by similar users or use similar words. Co-like T_L is calculated by the *Jaccard* coefficient where $U(d)$ is liker set of document d:

$$T_L(i,j) = \frac{\left| U(d_i) \cap U(d_j) \right|}{\left| U(d_i) \cup U(d_j) \right|} \tag{9}$$

For semantic similarity using BLEU score T_B, we use the BLEU score calculated in the Sect. 3.1. On the other hand, for semantic similarity using n-gram T_g, we first present a document with a binary vector $v(d) \in R^{|V|}$ using n-gram features, where $|V|$ is the size of n-grams in our dataset, including uni-gram, bi-gram and tri-gram. Then for any two documents, we compute the cosine similarity using their n-gram vectors to form the transition matrix.

4.3 Evaluation Metric

For each user u_i, assuming a set of documents D_i was liked by u_i in the testing data, we recommend top n documents D_n for the user (likes in the training data will not be recommended). The precision is given by $|D_i \cap D_n|/|D_n|$, and the recall is given by $|D_i \cap D_n|/|D_i|$. In the results section, we report the user average precision and the user average recall on top n *documents*. We plot the ROC curves (Receiver Operating Characteristic) and the PRT curves (Precision-Recall-Threshold) for further discussion.

5   Predicting Facebook Likes

We first demonstrate the performance of prediction of the item-based model and the user-based model. Then, the result of the hybrid probability model is reported.

5.1   Item-Based Model

For item-based model, documents that have similar content would be recommended to be liked by the same set of users. The PRT curve in Fig. 2 shows the precision and recall when recommending different numbers of documents per user. The limitation of item-based model on Facebook data can be found from Fig. 2. Recalls are lower than 5% and precisions are lower than 0.5%. Owing to the fact that the documents in our dataset are all related to a same topic, the recommendation system based on semantic features is hard to predict like. Even though some documents are semantically similar to what a user liked before, the documents that hold opposite opinion might not interest the user.

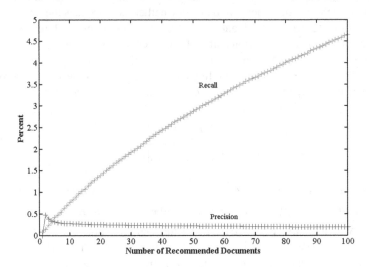

Fig. 2. PRT for item-based model

5.2   User-Based Model

In the user-based model, we generate the probability for each document and user pair. The same set of documents would be recommended to users having similar like- records. The PRT curve in Fig. 3 shows that user-based model has higher recall but lower precision. This tendency can also be found in the related work, where the user-based model has precision in the range of 2–10% while recall in the range of 3–16%. However, our

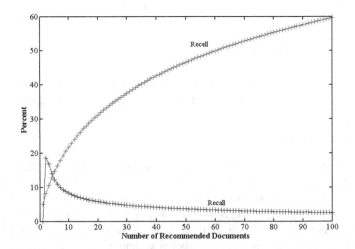

Fig. 3. PRT for user-based model

user-based model using RBM achieves higher precision (in the range of 5–10%) and recall (in the range of 2–55%). Comparing with item-based model, the performance of user-based model is significantly better. It suggests that user-based model successfully captures the taste of users and predicts the interesting documents to the target audiences.

5.3 Hybrid Model

For the hybrid model, we joint the item-based model and the user-based model, setting w as 0.5 (which means item-based and user-based model are equally important). The PRT curve is shown in Fig. 4. We find that the worse results of item-based model propagate noise to the hybrid model. It suggests that our late-fusion method using weighted function would be seriously harmed by noisy components.

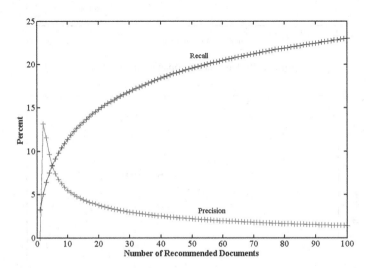

Fig. 4. PRT for hybrid model

5.4 Discussion

For comparison, we implement the label propagation, which has been widely used in classification [17] or recommendation problems [9]. Figure 5 shows the PRT curves of label propagation with co-liker feature and Fig. 6 shows the ROC curves of label propagation with co-liker feature and our user-based model using RBM. Comparing with RBM model, the label propagation is based on the same information but the results in Fig. 6 show that the proposed model successfully utilizes the visible units of RBM, and largely improves the performance. The label propagation does not perform well on the like prediction problem especially because of the sparsity of the like matrix. However, the user-based model using RBM can encode the user information into a dense vector and decode it to generate the like prediction.

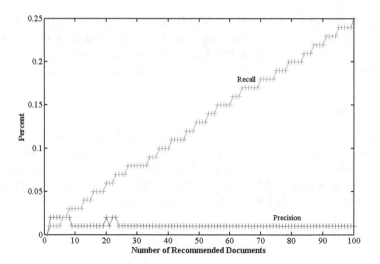

Fig. 5. PRT for label propagation (co-liker)

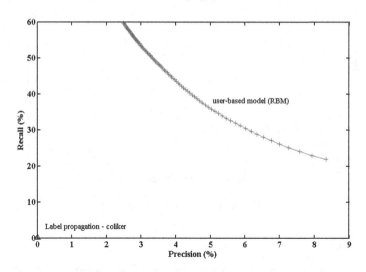

Fig. 6. ROC for RBM and label propagation with co-liker

Figures 7 and 8 show the PRT curves of label propagation with the *n*-gram vector similarity and the BLEU score, respectively. Figure 9 shows the ROC curves of above label propagation models and our item-based model. From Figs. 7 and 8, we can tell that the like prediction methods using semantic features are limited. Besides, the BLEU score is slightly better than simple cosine similarity of *n*-gram vectors.

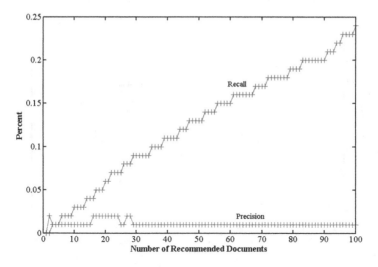

Fig. 7. PRT for label propagation (*n*-gram vector)

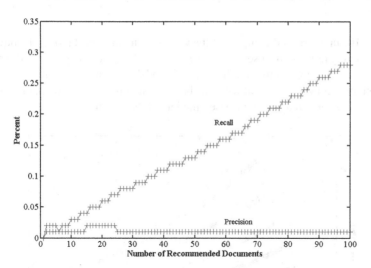

Fig. 8. PRT for label propagation (BLEU score)

Figure 9 shows that the strategy to find documents which are similar to the liked documents is better than propagate like information among a semantic similarity matrix. Receiving the like information from the most similar documents would be better than receiving the information from all documents. This phenomenon can be found in some related work where they suggested finding and propagating information to the nearest neighbors (four nearest neighbors in their paper) [18].

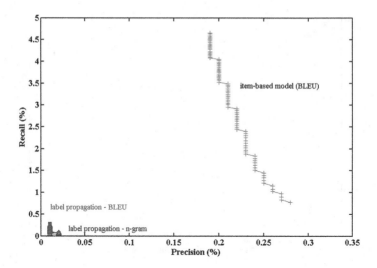

Fig. 9. ROC for item-based model, label propagation with n-gram vector, and label propagation with BLEU score

Figure 10 summarizes the impact of the weight w in our hybrid model. It shows that the model purely relies on the user-based model ($w = 1.0$) achieves the best performance. Though the results suggest that the item-based model has limited performance on like prediction problem when we deal with the dataset contains only one topic, the results in Figs. 7, 8 and 9 show that the item-based model still has its merit.

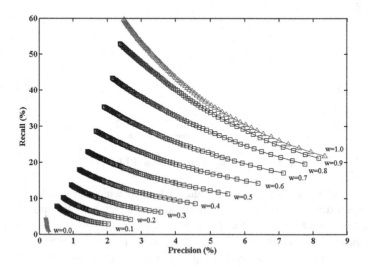

Fig. 10. ROC for different weights

6 Conclusion

In this paper, we have proposed different recommendation models based on the document content or the user engagement. The proposed models successfully utilize the similarity between documents and the probabilities from the visible units of RBM. We have shown that the proposed model outperforms the commonly adopted label propagation model. Moreover, we show that item-based model relying on semantic features cannot achieve satisfied results than user-based model. In the future, we will test more similar models and methods to integrate the user-based and item-based information to improve the probability approximation for new upcoming documents.

Acknowledgements. Research of this paper was partially supported by Ministry of Science and Technology, Taiwan, under the contract MOST 104-2221-E-001-024-MY2.

References

1. Kosinski, M., Stillwell, D., Graepel, T.: Private traits and attributes are predictable from digital records of human behavior. Proc. Nat. Acad. Sci. **110**(15), 5802–5805 (2013)
2. Bachrach, Y., Kosinski, M., Graepel, T., Kohli, P., Stillwell, D.: Personality and patterns of Facebook usage. In: Proceedings of the 4th Annual ACM Web Science Conference, pp. 24–32. ACM (2012)
3. Su, X., Khoshgoftaar, T.M.: A survey of collaborative filtering techniques. Adv. Artif. Intell. **2009**, 4 (2009)
4. Linden, G., Smith, B., York, J.: Amazon.com recommendations: item-to-item collaborative filtering. IEEE Internet Comput. **7**(1), 76–80 (2003)
5. Sarwar, B., Karypis, G., Konstan, J., Riedl, J.: Item-based collaborative filtering recommendation algorithms. In: Proceedings of the 10th International Conference on World Wide Web, pp. 285–295. ACM (2001)
6. Van Meteren, R., Van Someren, M.: Using content-based filtering for recommendation. In: Proceedings of the Machine Learning in the New Information Age: MLnet/ECML2000 Workshop, pp. 47–56 (2000)
7. Guy, I., et al.: Personalized recommendation of social software items based on social relations. In: Proceedings of the Third ACM Conference on Recommender Systems, pp. 53–60. ACM (2009)
8. Carmel, D., et al.: Personalized social search based on the user's social network. In: Proceedings of the 18th ACM Conference on Information and Knowledge Management, pp. 1227–1236. ACM (2009)
9. Baluja, S., et al.: Video suggestion and discovery for youtube: taking random walks through the view graph. In: Proceedings of the 17th International Conference on World Wide Web, pp. 895–904. ACM (2008)
10. Guy, I., Jacovi, M., Shahar, E., Meshulam, N., Soroka, V., Farrell, S.: Harvesting with SONAR: the value of aggregating social network information. In: Proceedings of the SIGCHI Conference on Human Factors in Computing Systems, pp. 1017–1026. ACM (2008)
11. Salakhutdinov, R., Mnih, A., Hinton, G.: Restricted Boltzmann machines for collaborative filtering. In: Proceedings of the 24th International Conference on Machine Learning, pp. 791–798. ACM (2007)

12. Chen, W., et al.: Influence maximization in social networks when negative opinions may emerge and propagate. In: SDM 2011, vol. 11, pp. 379–390. SIAM (2011)
13. Ayday, E., Zou, J., Einolghozati, A., Fekri, F.: A recommender system based on belief propagation over pairwise Markov random fields. In: 2012 50th Annual Allerton Conference on Communication, Control, and Computing (Allerton), pp. 703–707. IEEE (2012)
14. Melville, P., Mooney, R.J., Nagarajan, R.: Content-boosted collaborative filtering for improved recommendations. In: Eighteenth National Conference on Artificial Intelligence, pp. 187–192. American Association for Artificial Intelligence (2002)
15. Barragáns-Martínez, A.B., Costa-Montenegro, E., Burguillo, J.C., Rey-López, M., Mikic-Fonte, F.A., Peleteiro, A.: A hybrid content-based and item-based collaborative filtering approach to recommend TV programs enhanced with singular value decomposition. Inf. Sci. **180**(22), 4290–4311 (2010)
16. Papineni, K., Roukos, S., Ward, T., Zhu, W.-J.: BLEU: a method for automatic evaluation of machine translation. In: Proceedings of the 40th Annual Meeting on Association For Computational Linguistics, pp. 311–318: Association for Computational Linguistics (2002)
17. Baluja, S., Ravichandran, D., Sivakumar, D.: Text classification through time-efficient label propagation in time-based graphs. In: KDIR 2009, pp. 174–182 (2009)
18. Wang, F., Zhang, C.: Label propagation through linear neighborhoods. IEEE Trans. Knowl. Data Eng. **20**(1), 55–67 (2008)

Dueling for Trust in the Online Fantasy Sports Industry: Fame, Fortune, and Pride for the Winners

Craig C. Claybaugh[1(✉)], Peter Haried[2], Langtao Chen[1], and Nathan Twyman[1]

[1] Missouri University of Science and Technology, Rolla, USA
{claybaughc,chenla,nathantwyman}@mst.edu
[2] University of Wisconsin–La Crosse, La Crosse, USA
pharied@uwlax.edu

Abstract. Trust is a necessary condition for many industries. However, trust may not be the most important factor driving participation in online fantasy sports gambling. In this research we examine how different classifications of gamblers (i.e., passive gamblers, problem gamblers, and pathological gamblers) perceive their participation in fantasy sports. We argue that trust is not commonly a primary consideration and that trust does not need to be present in these types of online transactions. To prove this relationship, a trust model is proposed to be tested in the context of online fantasy sports with a focus on the market leader in the industry: fanduel.com.

Keywords: Trust · Online gambling · Fantasy sports · Personal motivation

1 Introduction

Gambling and its associated behaviors and motivations have a rich history of study [1]. The legalization of gambling has only made the subject more of a pressing need for society to understand. The problems associated with gambling have only intensified with the advent of online gambling [2]. Ease of access and the ability to find many forms of gambling is online has removed significant barriers to participation, and popularity has soared [3]. The traditional sports book has been transformed through technology into a new industry of fantasy sports [4].

One form of gambling experiencing significant growth due to internet developments is the fantasy sports industry. Fueled by technology and easy accessibility, fantasy sports have enjoyed incredible growth and unprecedented popularity in the twenty-first century [5]. Fantasy sports have grown to become a global business with billions of dollars in revenue each year with participation in almost every major market in the world. The evolution of offering daily sports betting action online to anyone in any country has increased the appeal of participation [6, 7].

Yet participation is still not universal and little has been done in the literature to study the demographics of this emerging market and the drivers of people to participate. Are the participants of fantasy sports the same as those who sit in casinos all over the world or are they unique? Do they have the same motivations to participate in betting as those who favor a roulette wheel? Drawing on past literature on trust and pathological

© Springer International Publishing AG 2017
F.F.-H. Nah and C.-H. Tan (Eds.): HCIBGO 2017, PART II, LNCS 10294, pp. 203–212, 2017.
DOI: 10.1007/978-3-319-58484-3_16

gambling, the authors question the notion that trust plays a defining role in influencing participation in daily online fantasy sports. This study proposes a model of gambling intention more focused on intrinsic motivation (pride among peers) as a bigger determination of participation as opposed to other motivations seen in past studies. To validate this proposed model of gambling intention, a survey instrument will be developed and tested.

1.1 Online Fantasy Sports and Fanduel

Sports gambling as an industry, both legal and illegal, has existed for more than 100 years [7]. Online sports gambling promises to revolutionize the way people gamble because it opens up the possibility of immediate, individual, 24-hour access to gambling in every home with Internet or mobile access [8, 9]. This is especially true of online fantasy sports. In a traditional fantasy football league for example a participant acted as a "make believe" general manager who selected real Major League Baseball (MLB) or National Football League (NFL) players for his or her fantasy roster, made trades and other roster moves during the season, determined success from the input statistics generated by real MLB or NFL players in real games, and competed for pride and relatively small cash prizes awarded on a one-time basis at the end of the season.

However a new model of fantasy sports has emerged fueled by technology and demand in the industry: daily sports gambling. This type of gambling has been widely available in sports books at many casinos but required a physical presence in Nevada to operate. Now these are available online to anyone with internet access. The proliferation of daily fantasy sports has been categorized as a game of skill [10] and has such the web sites supporting the industry have grown. An online daily sports league involves selecting players and receiving a payout or winnings at the end of just one day of sports action [5]. Unlike the traditional fantasy sports model of delayed payout these leagues offer daily market action.

One of the most popular of these sports betting sites is Fanduel.com. Founded in 2009, Fanduel is a web-based sports fantasy game [11]. Fanduel offers various types of sports betting action ranging from traditional season based sports leagues to daily, weekly or monthly games of skill. This proposed study seeks to look at how participants in Fanduel approach their justification in participating in the "action" to test their skills.

2 Proposed Model of Gambling Intention

The conceptual background in this paper draws on the theory of reasoned action (TRA) [12]. This study seeks to extend trust formation and integrate the theory of reasoned action (TRA) in the context of participation in online fantasy sports. The proposed model of gambling intention can be found in Fig. 1 below. The concepts of gambling involvement, trust formation, and personal motivations are used to form the research model which seeks to examine how participants are motivated to use fantasy sports gambling systems such as Fanduel.com.

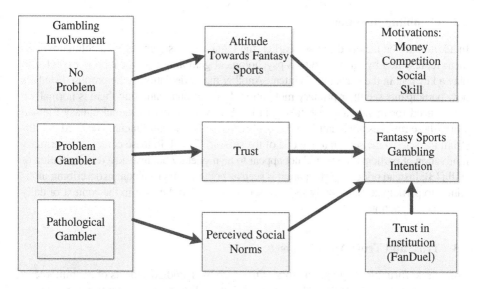

Fig. 1. Proposed model of gambling intention–fantasy sports

2.1 Gambling Involvement

Prior studies suggest that online gamblers, relative to others, are much more likely to be problem or pathological gamblers [13–15]. Factors driving the intention of these pathological gamblers may differ from more responsible gamblers. Many people gamble from time to time in their lives without any problems. However, some people exhibit what is called excessive gambling, i.e., problem or pathological gambling behavior which negatively influences their lives and the lives of significant others and creates major health costs for the community [16, 17]. The essential feature of pathological gambling is persistent and recurrent maladaptive gambling behavior that disrupts personal, family or vocational pursuits [16]. Problem gambling is often considered to be a less severe form of pathological gambling [18]. In this study we will consider problem and pathological gambling as two distinct categories of increasing severity. The study also seeks to look at how non-problem gamblers also are motivated to participate in fantasy sports.

Online gambling research has tended to focus on attempting to explain the motives and demographics behind online gambling. The primary reasons given for people engaging in Internet gambling include: (a) the relative convenience, comfort, and ease of Internet gambling; (b) an aversion to the atmosphere and clientele of land-based venues; (c) a preference for the pace and nature of online game-play; and (d) the potential for higher wins and lower overall expenditures when gambling online [15]. Research also has demonstrated that past gambling participation has a strong relationship with individual's attitude formation and future behavioral intentions [10]. In particular, past success and use of online gambling influences attitude formation and modification towards the habit. This study is in line with past attitude and trust research and examines how different gamblers perceive their participation in online fantasy sports.

2.2   Gambling Intention

In addition to the factors discussed earlier, the fantasy sports gambler's gambling involvement represented by an individual's psychological gambling classification is expected to play a key role in the participant's intent. Another major deviation in the proposed study is how participants see their primary motivation. In traditional gambling there is normally a strong need for money and risk taking [13]. However, in the traditional fantasy football world these rewards are small (hundreds of dollars) and the fulfillment is delayed months (from the start of the season to the end of the season) [7, 10]. In these contexts the primary motivation of participation would not appear to be monetary but instead a demonstration of skill [13]. Instead pride of participation is seen as being more prominent in describing motivation to participate. This study seeks to see if this is also the case in the context of daily sports betting action.

2.3   Trust and Trust Antecedents

Trust, trust formation, and precursors of trust are well studied aspects of ecommerce in general in the IS field [19, 20]. TRA suggests that one's behavioral intention is a function of an individual's attitude towards the behavior and the individual's subjective norms [12]. In our research, we will incorporate the personal gambling involvement of the individual, where gambling involvement represents the online gambler's pathological gambling habits, to investigate what role an online gambler's pathological classification plays in the factors behind his/her online gambling intention. As online consumers begin to question the trustworthiness of online gambling, the usage statistics and apparent growth of the online gambling industry suggests that consumers are continuing to engage in online gambling at an increasing rate. This would appear contradictory to the traditional view that trust and e-commerce usage are critically linked to one another [21]. Thus, the online gamblers' trust in online sports gambling may not be a critical factor for online sports gambling usage and therefore requires further investigation.

An individual's attitude is represented by the degree to which the individual likes or dislikes an object in the context of fantasy sports [12]. In TRA research "object" typically represents a human behavior. The theory suggests that an individual's attitude towards a behavior involves the individual's belief that a particular behavior will lead to certain outcomes and the individual's evaluation of those outcomes. If the individual believes that the behavior's outcome will be relatively beneficial compared to alternatives, the individual is more likely to perform or intend to perform the behavior [22]. In this study we focus on an individual's intention to participate in online fantasy sports. Thus, the expected would be:

Hypothesis 1: Attitude toward fantasy sports is positively related to the intention to participate in fantasy sports online for all online gambler involvement classifications.

2.4   Subjective Norms

Subjective norms are an individual's beliefs about whether the people who are important to the individual will approve of a particular behavior under consideration [23].

Thus, when deciding whether to execute a particular behavior, people consider the normative expectations of others they view as important. People important to the individual typically include those in their social circle and peers. Examples include friends, coworkers and schoolmates. When a participant in fantasy sports thinks their peers are OK with participation they are more inclined to intend to participate. Similar to prior e-commerce findings the study expects that:

Hypothesis 2: Subjective norms are positively related to the intention to participate in fantasy sports online for all online gambler involvement classifications.

2.5 Trust and Gambling Involvement

Trust has been shown to play a significant role in website usage, particularly under uncertain conditions where high risk is involved [19]. Fantasy sports participants are considered similar to e-commerce consumers studied in past research. Research also shows that the growing popularity of online shopping comes with additional risk factors such as fear of fraud, security concerns, privacy and lack of trust that have dissuaded consumers to purchase online [24, 25]. Consumers are assumed to be vulnerable because they are dependent on the appropriate use of information by the website (Fanduel) when they participate in fantasy sports. In our research, the trustee will be represented by the online fantasy sports website and the trustor is the gambler participating online.

Participation in online fantasy sports involves a number of trusting behaviors. Fantasy sports participants provide personal information, such as a name, address and possibly a social security number when they register. As the fantasy sports participants attempt to gain real money online they have to believe that the games they play are not rigged against them. This context shows there are no face to face assurances to demonstrate the other competitors are real.

Online gambling and its related behaviors are fundamentally different from other forms of risk. General online gambling has increased in popularity even though the gamblers have not trusted the sites they patronize [26]. Online gamblers continue to hand over large sums of money to the online casinos even when they report not trusting online gambling. Given the past relationship with trust and general online gambling it would seem that trust would not play a key role in the fantasy sports gambling context. As such the following is proposed:

Hypothesis 3: Trust in Fanduel is not related to the intention to participate in fantasy sports online for all online gambler involvement classifications.

Participants in online fantasy sports are expected to follow similar demographic patterns of gambling involvement as past studies. Each of the classifications of gamblers represents a different way in which a participant become a problem gambler. This is similar to how other website adoption patterns vary by demographic profiles [27]. Those with no problem at all still participate in fantasy sports. Given the perception that fantasy sports are a skill game it is expected that a gambling involvement classifications will be involved in fantasy sports. Moreover, the different involvement profiles of the gamblers are expected to moderate the trust they have in the website and influence their future intention to participate in online fantasy sports. Given that the classifications are psychological it is expected that each of them will impact all measures of perception in the study. As such the following is proposed:

Hypothesis 4a: Gambler involvement classification will influence a participant's attitude towards the online fantasy sports website.

Hypothesis 4b: Gambler involvement classification will influence a participant's perception of trust in the online fantasy sports website.

Hypothesis 4c: Gambler involvement classification will influence a participant's perception of social norms in the online fantasy sports website.

2.6 Institutional Trust

Institution based trust refers to the belief that the needed structural conditions are present in an institution, in this context Fanduel, to enhance the probability of achieving a successful outcome [19]. Perceptions of the structural characteristics of assurance in Fandule, such as safety and security guarantees, can influence the trusting beliefs towards the website [28]. A participant may not trust Fanduel as a company, but he/she may trust the control systems that monitor its performance or other assurances provided by the site [29]. Participants of online fantasy sports with a high sense of trust in the Fanduel website would believe that the legal and technological security safeguards would protect one from loss when engaging in their gambling activity. These arguments suggest that:

Hypothesis 5: Institution based trust is positively related to the intention to participate in fantasy sports.

2.7 Gambling Individual Motivations

Specialized websites such as Fanduel should show differences in participation based on different user characteristics [30]. Given the probability that different fantasy sports games exhibit different payment outcomes this should attract persons to practice this "skill" based on a diverse set of motivations. Profiling the disparate characteristics of participants, both for no problem and pathological gamblers, will assist in understand how these individuals pursues their fantasy sports participation without reporting significant difficulty as a result [31]. A number of motivations to participate in fantasy sports are possible beyond money [32]. These other motivations include the desire to dominate a competitive event, a means to interact with friends or family, or a need to demonstrate a skill or strategy. The individual motivations are expected to influence perceptions of other aspects of the fantasy sports website.

Hypothesis 6: Individual motivations to participate in gambling will vary for the gambler involvement classifications and influence their intention to participate in fantasy sports.

3   Method

A survey will be conducted to evaluate the role of trust and psychological factors in explaining the online gambler's intent. Although our sample is expected to be large (N = 100+) and diverse, the sample is also self-selected to a degree. Thus, it is not possible to ensure that it is representative of the broader population of Internet gamblers. During the survey participants will be required to complete a profile questionnaire in order to control for the user's web experience, prior knowledge or use of online gambling. Participants will be given a definition of gambling ("Gambling is any activity that you play in which you are putting money, or something of monetary value, at risk since winning and/or losing is based at least partly on chance"), to keep in mind when responding to the instrument.

3.1   Subjects and Procedure

Subjects for this study will be focused on a single fantasy sports website: Fanduel.com. Online gambling message boards will be used to target potential participants, since the message board participants will have experience gambling online and are expected to be participating in online gambling.

3.2   Measures

The potential measures and their sources are shown in the appendix. These measures are consistent with how past studies have measured and analyzed both trust and online gambling.

4   Expected Contributions and Discussion

This study has the potential to validate how individuals approach the world of online fantasy sports. By systematically investigating fantasy sports participation we will extend the theoretical boundaries of the TRA with a focus on attitude formation in this domain. Each of the three classifications of gamblers - no problem, problem, or pathological - will each participate for different reasons. Moreover, trust is not expected to play a central part in the formation of their attitude towards participation. Trust is also not expected to influence the gambler types to continue to use Fanduel. Instead, each of the classifications will find other reasons to continue to use Fanduel. Some will continue to use Fanduel as a way to test their skills while others will be focused on fame and fortune.

Of course there is no single way for a person to justify how they choose to participate in fantasy sports. One of the keys to the long term success of the industry is to change their approach to marketing themselves and position the fantasy sports website to appeal to a large audience made up of different customer segments. This study seeks to support the assumption that the different gambler classifications each approach the participation decision uniquely. Understanding how each customer type approaches this decision will be a key part of how Fanduel approaches the way they interact with each of them.

A future study might expand this work and look at how participants approach specific types of fantasy sports. For example, fantasy football or fantasy baseball both might vary in how participants are induced to participate. Another study might look at comparing online and direct (i.e. at a sports book in a casino) fantasy sports participation. Online versions of traditional gambling options are here to stay, but adoption on these games is not guaranteed to supplant the traditional ones. Another study might also look to compare the two biggest competitors in the fantasy sports market: Fanduel and Draftkings.

Appendix: Measurement Items

Pathological Gambling Diagnostic Criteria - Five (or more) of the following [33]:

1. Is preoccupied with gambling (e.g., preoccupation with reliving past gambling experiences, handicapping or planning the next venture, or thinking of ways to get money with which to gamble.
2. Needs to gamble with increasing amounts of money in order to achieve the desired excitement.
3. Has repeated unsuccessful efforts to control, cut back, or stop gambling.
4. Is restless or irritable when attempting to cut down or stop gambling.
5. Gambles as a way of escaping from problems or of relieving a dysphoric mood (e.g., feelings of helplessness, guilt, anxiety, depression).
6. After losing money gambling, often returns another day to get even ("chasing" one's losses).
7. Lies to family members, therapist, or others to conceal the extent of involvement with gambling.
8. Has committed illegal acts such as forgery, fraud, theft, or embezzlement to finance gambling.
9. Has jeopardized or lost a significant relationship, job, or educational or career opportunity because of gambling.
10. Relies on others to provide money to relieve a desperate financial situation caused by gambling.

Behavioral intention to use Fanduel [34]

I intend to use Fanduel in the next month.
I predict I would use Fanduel in the next month.
I plan to use Fanduel in the next months.

Attitude toward fantasy sports [34]

Using Fanduel to participate in fantasy sports is a bad/good idea.
Using Fanduel to participate in fantasy sports makes me happy.
I like using Fanduel to participate in fantasy sports.

Subjective Norm [34]

The person's perception that most people who are important to him think he should or should not perform the behavior in question.

People who influence my behavior think that I should use Fanduel.
People who are important to me think that I should use Fanduel.

Trust [35]

Fanduel is trustworthy.
Fanduel is one that keeps promises and commitments.
I trust Fanduel because they keep my best interests in mind.

Individual Motivations [32]

Extent to which the subject agrees with the following statements.

Money. I participate in fantasy sports to make or win money.
Competition. I participate in fantasy sports to compete with others and beat them.
Social. I participate in fantasy sports as a means of interacting with friends or family, or to meet new people.
Skill. I participate in fantasy sports to develop and demonstrate my fantasy skills.

References

1. Dielman, T.E.: Gambling: a social problem? J. Soc. Issues **35**(3), 36–42 (1979)
2. Quilty, L.C., Lobo, D.S., Zack, M., Crewe-Brown, C., Blaszczynski, A.: Hitting the jackpot: the influence of monetary payout on gambling behaviour. Int. Gambl. Stud. **16**(3), 481–499 (2016)
3. Hancock, G.T.: Upstaging US gaming law: the potential fantasy sports quagmire and the reality of US gaming law. T. Jefferson L. Rev. **31**, 317 (2008)
4. Paul, R.J., Weinbach, A.P.: Does sportsbook.com set pointspreads to maximize profits? J. Prediction Markets **1**(3), 209–218 (2012)
5. Braig, K., Polesovsky, A., D'Angelo, L.A., Irwin, K.: Unsure bet: the future of daily fantasy exchange wagering. Gaming Law Rev. Econ. **17**(7), 499–505 (2013)
6. Haried, P.: Customer loyalty in the online gambling industry: are problem gamblers loyal customers? In: American Society of Business and Behavioral Sciences Conference Proceedings (2014)
7. Kaburakis, A., Rodenberg, R.M., Holden, J.T.: Inevitable: sports gambling, state regulation, and the pursuit of revenue. Harvard Bus. Law Rev. Online **5**, 27–38 (2015)
8. Keller, B.: The game's the same: why gambling in cyberspace violates federal law. Yale Law J. **108**(7), 1569–1609 (1999)
9. Kish, S.A.: Betting on the net: an analysis of the government's role in addressing internet gambling. Fed. Commun. Law J. **51**(2), 449–466 (1999)
10. Rose, I.N.: Are daily fantasy sports legal? Gaming Law Rev. Econ. **19**(5), 346–349 (2015)
11. Fanduel. https://www.fanduel.com/about, Accessed 22 Feb 2017
12. Fishbein, M., Ajzen, I.: Belief, Attitude, Intention and Behavior: An Introduction to Theory and Research. Addison-Wesley, MA (1975)
13. Griffiths, M., Parke, A., Wood, R., Parke, J.: Internet gambling: an overview of psychosocial impacts. UNLV Gaming Res. Rev. J. **10**(1), 27–39 (2006)

14. Ladd, G.T., Petry, N.M.: Disordered gambling among university-based medical and dental patients: a focus on internet gambling. Psychol. Addict. Behav. **16**, 76–79 (2002)
15. Wood, R.T., Williams, R.J.: Problem gambling on the internet: implications for internet gambling policy in North America. New Media Soc. **9**(3), 520–542 (2007)
16. Shaffer, H.J., LaBrie, R., LaPlante, D., Nelson, S.E., Stanton, M.V.: The road less traveled: moving from distribution to determinants in the study of gambling epidemiology. Can. J. Psychiat. **49**(8), 504–516 (2004)
17. Raylu, N., Oei, T.P.: Pathological gambling: a comprehensive review. Clin. Psychol. Rev. **22**(7), 1009–1061 (2002)
18. Volberg, R.A.: The future of gambling in the United Kingdom: increasing access creates more problem gamblers. BMJ **320**, 1556 (2000)
19. McKnight, D.H., Choudhury, V., Kacmar, C.: Developing and validating trust measures for e-commerce: an integrative typology. Inf. Syst. Res. **13**(3), 334–359 (2002)
20. Claybaugh, C.C., Haseman, W.D.: Understanding professional connections in Linkedin - a question of trust. J. Comput. Inf. Syst. **54**(1), 94–105 (2013)
21. Wu, J., Liu, D.: The effects of trust and enjoyment on intention to play online games. J. Electron. Commer. Res. **8**(2), 128–140 (2007)
22. Sheppard, B.H., Hartwick, J., Warshaw, P.R.: The theory of reasoned action: a meta-analysis of past research with recommendations for modifications and future research. J. Consum. Res. **14**(3), 325–343 (1988)
23. Franzoi, S.L.: Social Psychology. McGraw-Hill, New York (2003)
24. Gefen, D., Karahanna, E., Straub, D.W.: Trust and TAM in online shopping: an integrated model. MIS Q. **27**(1), 51–90 (2003)
25. Suh, B., Han, I.: The impact of customer trust and perception of security control on the acceptance of electronic commerce. Int. J. Electron. Commer. **7**(3), 135–161 (2003)
26. Landes, R.S.: Layovers and cargo ships: the prohibition of internet gambling and a proposed system of regulation. New York Univ. Law Rev. **82**, 1–34 (2007)
27. Claybaugh, C.C., Haried, P., Yu, W.B.: Diffusion of a professional social network: business school graduates in focus. Int. J. Hum. Capital Inf. Technol. Prof. (IJHCITP) **6**(4), 80–96 (2015)
28. Keen, P., Ballance, G., Chan, S., Schrump, S.: Electronic Commerce Relationships: Trust by Design. Prentice Hall PTR, New Jersey (1999)
29. Tan, Y.H., Thoen, W.: Formal aspects of a generic model of trust for electronic commerce. Decis. Support Syst. **33**(3), 233–246 (2002)
30. Claybaugh, C.C., Haried, P.: Professional social network participation of business school graduates: effects of university, degree type, and gender. Int. J. Inf. Syst. Soc. Change (IJISSC) **5**(1), 1–15 (2014)
31. Smith, M.D., Rousu, M.C., Dion, P.: Internet poker: examining motivations, behaviors, outcomes, and player traits using structural equations analysis. J. Gambl. Issues **27**, 1–23 (2012)
32. Neighbors, C., Lostutter, T.W., Cronce, J.M., Larimer, M.E.: Exploring college student gambling motivation. J. Gambl. Stud. **18**(4), 361–370 (2002)
33. Winters, K.C., Specker, S., Stinchfield, R.S.: Measuring pathological gambling with the diagnostic interview for gambling severity (DIGS). In: Marotta, J.J., Cornelius, J.A., Eadington, W.R. (eds.) The Downside: Problem and Pathological Gambling, pp. 143–148. University of Nevada, Reno (2002)
34. Venkatesh, V., Morris, M.G., Davis, G.B., Davis, F.D.: User acceptance of information technology: toward a unified view. MIS Q. **27**(3), 425–478 (2003)
35. Pavlou, P.A.: Consumer acceptance of electronic commerce: integrating trust and risk with the technology acceptance model. Int. J. Electron. Commer. **7**(3), 101–134 (2003)

Internet Use and Happiness:
A Longitudinal Analysis

Richard H. Hall[(⊠)]

Department of Business and Information Technology,
Missouri University of Science and Technology, Rolla, MO, USA
rhall@mst.edu

Abstract. This is an extension of a previous study, which explored the relationship between happiness and Internet use [1]. An Internet Use Scale (IUS), developed in the previous study, was administered to college students along with the Flourishing Scale [2] and the Satisfaction with Life Scale [3]; and three new open-ended questions. We compared changes in the relationship between these measures, and their mean values, across the two samples, and carried out qualitative analyses of the open-ended questions. Results indicated that those who reported spending less time on the internet, less time expressing emotions, and more time checking facts, scored higher on measures of happiness. Further, participants found negative affective expression on the Internet particularly aversive. Finally, those with lower happiness scores were more likely to report playing on-line games; and those with higher happiness scores were more likely to identify Internet disinformation as aversive.

Keywords: Happiness · Internet

1 Why Study Happiness and the Internet?

Following the dawn of the new millennium, research on happiness increased dramatically, largely spurred on by the fact that people increasingly rate happiness as a major life goal. For example, recent surveys have indicated that the strong majority of people across many countries rate happiness as more important than income [2]. Lyubomirsky [3] sums this research up, "…in almost every culture examined by researchers, people rank the pursuit of happiness as one of their most cherished goals in life" (p. 239).

In addition, there is a large body of evidence that suggests situational factors, in particular wealth, play a surprisingly small role in determining happiness. Some suggest that this may be the result of society moving into a post-materialistic phase, where basic needs have been largely met for many in industrialized countries, so pursuit of self fulfillment becomes more important [3].

Finally, there are number of studies that indicate that happy people, in general, have a positive effect on society. For example, there is evidence that happier people are more successful and socially engaged [4].

F.F.-H. Nah and C.-H. Tan (Eds.): HCIBGO 2017, PART II, LNCS 10294, pp. 213–222, 2017.
DOI: 10.1007/978-3-319-58484-3_17

2   What Is Happiness?

For the most part, researchers agree that happiness is inherently subjective, In fact, the term is often used interchangeably with "subjective well-being" (SWB) [5]. David Myers [6], one of the leading researchers in the area, stated that happiness is "… whatever people mean when describing their lives as happy." (p. 57). Despite the potential for ambiguity with such a definition, there is considerable agreement, at least across Western culture, as to what happiness means [7]. Most people equate happiness with experiences of joy, contentment, and positive well being; as well as a feeling that life is good, meaningful, and worthwhile [8].

As a consequence, self-report measures have served as the primary measure of happiness. Examples include the Satisfaction with Life Scale (SLS), the Subjective Happiness Scale (SHS), and the Steen Happiness Index (SHI). Psychometric studies of these self-report measures indicate that they are, by and large, reliable over time, despite changing circumstances; they correlate strongly with friends and family ratings of happiness; and they are statistically reliable. Sonja Lyubomirsky [8] sums this up, "A great deal of research has shown that the majority of these measures have adequate to excellent psychometric properties and that the association between happiness and other variables usually cannot be accounted for by transient mood" (p. 239). These psychometric studies illustrate the general agreement among people as to what constitutes happiness.

One other interesting point, regarding the definition of happiness and its measurement, is that mean happiness is consistently above a mid-line point in most populations sampled [5]. For example, three in ten Americans say they are "very happy", only 1 in ten report that they are "not too happy", and 6 in 10 say they are "pretty happy" [6]. Therefore, there appears to be a positive set point, where most people appear to be moderately happy, and this is independent of age and gender [7].

3   Individual Difference and Happiness

Happiness is surprisingly stable over time [8] even with major changes in life circumstances [9], and there appears to be no time in life that is most satisfying [10]. These findings are consistent with research that indicates some individual difference traits are predictive of happiness. Further, happiness may also be strongly tied to genetic predisposition. We now turn to a discussion of this research.

Twin studies indicate that there is a strong genetic component in happiness [11, 12]. For example, Lykken and Tellegen [12] assessed the well being of twins at ages 20 and 30. They correlated the happiness scores between monozygotic twins at stage 1 with the score for their twin at stage 2 (cross time/cross twin) and found a correlation of .4, while the test-retest correlation where each twin's score was correlated with himself/herself was only .5. Further the cross twin/cross time correlation for dizygotic twins was only .07. Therefore, heritability appears to account for a large part of the stability in happiness.

As mentioned, some other individual difference measures have been found to consistently correlate with happiness, in particular extroversion. For example, in a cross-cultural study Lucas and colleagues found that extraversion correlated with positive affect in virtually all 40 nations they examine [14]. Extroversion, as a predictor of happiness, is strongly related to the literature to be discussed, which relates social interaction with happiness, in that there is a clear relationship between the number and quality of social relationships and happiness. One would expect that an extrovert would be more likely to seek out and form these types of relationships.

Religiosity is another variable that has been found to consistently predict happiness [6]. In addition, those who report higher levels of religiosity tend to recover greater happiness after suffering from negative life events [14]. This finding has been found for peoples' self reports of their degree of religiosity, and for behavioral measures such as Church attendance [6]. As with extroversion, the impact of religiosity may be, at least partly, explained by the importance of social interaction in determining happiness, in that those who attend Church regularly, and interact with others in a positive social environment, are more likely to be happy [16]. Further, people often derive meaning and purpose from religious practices, which is another important correlate of happiness [6].

In addition to behavioral tendencies, with respect to individual differences, the research of Lyubomirsky and colleagues provides substantial evidence that there are consistent differences between happy and unhappy people in the ways they process ("construe") information. For example, studies from Lyubomirsky's laboratory have found that happy people are less sensitive to social comparisons [17], tended to feel more positive about decisions after they were made [18], construed events more positively [18], and are less inclined to self-reflect and dwell on themselves [17]. This difference in information processing dispositions in happy vs. unhappy people is presumably one reason why the effects of circumstantial factors are relatively minimal.

Another individual difference factor, which has been identified as important in predicting happiness, is the autoletic personality, which refers to people who tend to regularly experience "flow" [19]. Flow refers to a kind of experience that is engrossing and enjoyable to such a degree that it becomes "autoletic" – worth doing for its own sake [19]. The autoletic personality and the flow concept are consistent with the views of happiness researchers who have suggested that engagement is a fundamental component of a happy life [20].

4   Happiness and the Internet

Studies that have examined the relationship between the Internet and happiness have been conducted at least since the relatively early days of the World Wide Web. Most of these have focused on communication/collaborative activities and the Internet. As we mentioned, these types of activities have been found in non-internet studies to be strongly related to happiness.

4.1   The Internet Paradox

In 1998 Kraut and colleagues reported the results of a reasonably extensive study of early World Wide Web users where they followed the activity of mostly first time

Internet users over a period of years. Researchers administered periodic questionnaires and server logs indicating participant activity on the web. (Participants were provided with free computers and internet connections) [21].

Over all, the results showed that the Internet had a largely negative impact on social activity, in that those who used the Internet more communicated with family and friends less. They also reported higher levels of loneliness. Interestingly, they also found that email, a communication activity, constituted the participants main use of the Internet. The researchers coined the term "internet paradox" to describe this situation in which a social technology reduced social involvement.

These researchers speculated that this negative social effect was due to a type of displacement, in which their time spent online displaced face-to-face social involvement. Although they note that users spent a great deal of time using email, they suggest that this constitutes a low quality social activity and this is why they did not see positive effects on well being [21]. They find further support for this supposition in a study reported in 2002, where they found that business professionals who used email found it less effective than face-to-face communication or the telephone in sustaining close social relationships [22].

Since the time that this Internet paradox was identified, a number of studies over the next twelve years have found, fairly consistently, results that contradict the Kraut et al. results. More recent studies have indicated the potential positive social effects of the Internet and their relationship to well being. Further, the effect appears to be getting stronger as the Internet and the users mature.

In fact, one of the first challenges to this Internet paradox was provided by Kraut himself when he published follow up results for participants in the original Internet-paradox study, including data for additional participants. In this paper, "Internet Paradox Revisited," researchers report that the negative social impact on the original sample had dissipated over time and, for those in their new sample, the Internet had positive effects on communication, social involvement, and well being [23]. Therefore, it appears that the results of the original Kraut et al. study were largely due to the participants' inexperience with the Internet. Within just a few years, American society's experience with the Internet had increased exponentially. Further, the Kraut studies concentrated on email, whereas there are many other social communication tools available on the modern web.

4.2   Displacement Versus Stimulation Hypothesis

More recently, researchers have examined the relationship between on-line communication and users' over all social networks, explicitly addressing the question of whether or not on-line communication "displaces" higher quality communication, or "stimulates" it. Presumably, the former would negatively affect well being, while the latter would enhance it [24].

In one large scale study, over 1000 Dutch teenagers were surveyed regarding the nature of their on line communication activities, the number and quality of friendships, and their well being.

They found strong support for the stimulation hypothesis. More specifically, these researchers developed a causal model, which indicated that instant messaging lead to more contact with friends, which lead to more meaningful social relationships, which, in turn, predicted well being. Interestingly, they did not find this same effect for chat in a public chat room. They attributed this finding to the fact that participants reported that they interacted more with strangers in the chat room as compared to their interaction with friends with instant messaging [24].

4.3   The Internet and Social Connectedness

Despite studies, such as the one just mentioned, which have found a relationship between internet use and positive outcomes, there is still a great deal of press suggesting that the internet can effect users negatively, causing social isolation, and shrinking of social networks. This is purported to be especially true for adolescents [25].

Researchers with the Pew Internet and Daily Life Project set out to examine this concern directly in one of the most comprehensive studies of the effect of the Internet on social interaction, reported in 2009 [25]. Contrary to fears, they found that:

- A variety of Internet activities were associated with larger and more diverse core discussion networks.
- Those who participated most actively with social media were more likely to interact with those from diverse backgrounds, including race and political view.
- Internet users are just as likely as others to visit a neighbor in person, and they are more likely to belong to a local voluntary organization.
- Internet use is often associated with local activity in community spaces such as parks and restaurants, and Internet connections are more and more common in such venues.

Although these outcomes did not explicitly include happiness, they do support the contention that Internet activities can enhance the amount and quality of social relationships, which has been implicated in a number of studies as a strong and consistent predictor of happiness.

5   Research Overview

This study is a replication and extension of one conducted in 2016 [1] which also explored the relationship between internet activities and happiness. An internet-use-scale (IUS) was developed and subjected to initial psychometric analyses, and modified accordingly, resulting in a 13 item scale, representing three categories of internet use: Affective expression, Information Gathering, and Total Time (spent on the internet). Results indicated that both happiness measures were negatively related to the Time category, and one happiness measure was positively related to the information gathering factor. The current research extends this through the administration of the revised IUS and the same two happiness measures: Flourishing Scale [2] and the

Satisfaction with Life [3] scale, with a larger sample. Further we collected responses to three new open-ended questions, which we analyzed quantitatively, by breaking student's comments into individual Internet activities and classifying these into use categories. Finally, we explored differences in these comments/categories as a function of students' scores on the happiness measures.

6 Questions

6.1 Internet Use and Happiness

What is the relationship between internet use and happiness?

6.2 Internet Use and Happiness Over Time

How does the relationship between happiness and internet use, and the mean happiness and use scores differ between the 2016 and 2017 sample?

6.3 Internet Activities

Based on open-ended self report: (1) What are the prime types of activities people engage in on the internet; (2) What activities do they enjoy; (3) What activities are aversive; and (4) How do these differ as a function of happiness scores.

7 Research Method

7.1 Participants

Thirty-four students enrolled in an undergraduate course in digital media at a small Midwestern technological research University in the spring of 2017 served as the participants in this study.

7.2 Measures

The Internet use scale (IUS) [1] was administered to assess internet use. The 13 item scale represents three internet use categories: Affective Expression, Information Gathering, and Time Spent on the Internet. The Flourishing Scale (FS) [2], and the Satisfaction with Life Scale (SWLS) [3] were administered to represent happiness. In addition, participants were required to respond to three open-ended questions: "Describe the ways in which you most commonly interact with the Internet."; "Describe the activities that you enjoy most when interacting with the internet.; and "Describe the activities that you enjoy least when interacting with the internet."

7.3   Procedure

Participants completed the survey on-line, which consisted of the measures delineated above.

8   Results

8.1   Relationship Between Internet Usage and Happiness

In order to assess the relationship between happiness and internet use measures, and to compare the two samples (2016 & 2017), a series of zero-order correlations were computed among the happiness and internet use measures. These results appear in Table 1.

Table 1. Correlation between internet use and happiness as a function of year

Happiness	Factor					
	Affective expression		Info gathering		Time	
	2016	2017	2016	2017	2016	2017
Flourishing	−.087	−.35*	.46*	.53**	−.54**	−.54**
SWLS	−.312	−.15	−.18	.18	−.58**	−.30(*)

(*)p < .10; *p < .05; **p < .01

8.2   Internet Use, and Happiness as a Function of Time

In order to compare the two samples on their internet use and happiness, a series of one-way analyses were computed with the three internet usage factors, and two happiness scores as the dependent measures and time (2016 vs 2017) as the independent variable. Note that these scores were computed as means of the items such that the internet usage scores could range from −7 to +7 with higher scores representing more affective expression, information gathering, and time spent on the internet. Scores on both happiness scales ranged from 1–7 with greater scores representing higher levels of happiness. These results are presented in Table 2.

Table 2. Internet usage and happiness as a function of sample year

Measure	2016	2017
Affective expression*	.36	−.50
Info gathering	5.64	5.67
Time*	.26	−.431
Flourishing	5.31	5.57
SWLS*	4.33	4.90

*p < .05

8.3   Qualitative Analyses

All student responses to the three open-ended items were first broken into individual statements, such that each statement referred to one Internet activity. These were then classified into categories. These statements/categories were then further broken down into two groups: High Happiness (those scoring above the median on the mean of the two happiness scales); and Low Happiness (those scoring below the median).

With respect to the first question: "Describe the ways in which you most commonly interact with the Internet." four categories emerged. These categories were "Passive Uses", including reading and watching; "Communication", including things like social media and email; "Gaming", including on-line gaming; and "Work" which consisted of school work and general fact checking. These categories were consistent across the high- and low-happiness groups, with the exception that those in the Low happiness group were more than twice as likely to mention on-line gaming as a primary activity.

For the second question: "Describe the activities that you enjoy most when inter-acting with the Internet." The categories remained the same, with the exception that the "work" category disappeared and, again, those in the low-happiness group mentioned on-line gaming as an enjoyable activity twice as much as those in the high-happiness group.

For the third question: "Describe the activities that you enjoy least when interacting with the internet", the categories changed significantly, and was not as consistent across the two happiness groups. "Negative Affective Expression" was clearly the main cat-egory for both groups. Some representative comments: "I dislike negativity on the Internet, whether it's people arguing or complaining about something or someone."; "… seeing others hate on one another"; and "… when people are jerks." A second category that emerged for both groups was, not surprisingly, "work", including homework, research, etc.

For those in the high-happiness group there was a clear third category that immerged regarding dis-information with comments such as "Fake News Reports", "I worry about the accuracy of information …"; and "… reading posts on social media that have no factual backing". On the other hand, those in the low-happiness group did not mention this as an aversive Internet phenomenon. Interestingly, there were also some in the high-happiness group who mentioned on-line gaming as a negative experience, contrasting markedly with the low-happiness group, where on-line gaming was a primary category representing enjoyment of the internet.

9   Conclusions

Taken together, the results paint a picture of the happy versus unhappy Internet user. First, those who spend more time on the Internet are less happy. This was demonstrated in the 2016 sample [1] and replicated in the 2017 sample. Further, the qualitative analysis indicated that those who scored lower in happiness were much more likely to report spending time playing and enjoying video games, while there were some in the high-happiness who even reported this as a negative experience. This may very likely be related to the time-on-the-internet finding, since, an often sited negative consequence of on-line video gaming is the amount of time it takes away from other important life activities [26].

Second, when interacting with the Internet, those who report spending more time gathering information and carrying out research score higher on happiness measures. There was a strong relationship between this usage factor and the flourishing scale in both the 2016 and 2017 sample. Note that this usage factor refers to the degree to which someone is likely to spend time checking facts on the internet, but also the degree to which one is aware of the potential inaccuracy of information. One item scored positively on this sub-scale is "I'm skeptical of the accuracy of information I find on the internet". This was further supported by the qualitative analysis where a number of those in the high-happiness group reported that they found factual inaccuracy on the Internet as a major negative; while those in the low-happiness group did not mention it. As one of those in the high-happiness group described this, "I worry about the accuracy of information I find and often check several different websites for information."

Third, those who use the Internet as a method for negative affective expression are less happy. Although this relationship was statistically significant with only one happiness measure in the 2017 sample; it's certainly true that people are in general agreement that those who participate in negative affective expression are causing unhappiness for others. By far, the most common theme that emerged with respect to the open-ended question on what people like least about the Internet, was the aversion people have for negative-affective expression. Across both happiness groups users found it aversive when "people are jerks", as on participant put it.

Finally, we carried out some analyses to compare changes in the participants' views between the 2016 and 2017 sample, with respect to their happiness and Internet usage scores. The good news, in terms of what we've learned about the Internet and happiness, is that those in the 2017 sample report spending significantly less time online than the 2016 sample; when online are significantly less likely to participate in affective expression; and, perhaps consequently, scored significantly higher on the satisfaction with life scores.

References

1. Hall, R.H.: Internet use and happiness. In: Nah, F.F.-H., Tan, C.-H. (eds.) HCIBGO 2016. LNCS, vol. 9751, pp. 37–45. Springer, Cham (2016). doi:10.1007/978-3-319-39396-4_4
2. Diener, E., Wirtz, D., Tov, W., Kim-Prieto, C., Choi, D., Oishi, S., Biswas-Diener, R.: New measures of well-being: flourishing and positive and negative feelings. Soc. Indic. Res. **39**, 247–266 (2009)
3. Diener, E., Emmons, R.A., Larsen, R.J., Griffin, S.: The satisfaction with life scale. J. Pers. Assess. **49**, 71–75 (1985)
4. Lyubomirsky, S., King, L., Diener, E.: The benifits of frequent positive affect: does happiness lead to success. Psychol. Bull. **6**, 803–855 (2005)
5. Diener, E.: Subjective well-being: the science of happiness and a proposal for a national index. Am. Psychol. **55**, 34–43 (2000)
6. Myers, D.G.: The funds, friends, and faith of happy people. Am. Psychol. **55**, 56–67 (2000)

7. Freedman, J.: Happy people: what happiness is, who has it, and why? Harcourt Brace Jovanovich, New York (1978)
8. Magnus, K., Diener, E.: A longitudinal analysis of personality, life events, and subjective well-being. In: Annual Meeting of the Midwestern Psychological Association, Chicago, IL (1991)
9. Costa, P.T., McCrae, R.R., Zonderman, A.B.: Environmental and dispositional influences on well-being: longitudinal follow-up of an American national sample. Br. J. Psychol. **78**, 299–306 (1987)
10. Myers, D.G., Diener, E.: Who is happy? Psychol. Sci. **6**, 10–19 (1995)
11. Lykken, D.T., Tellegen, A.: Happiness is a stochastic phenomenon. Psychol. Sci. **7**, 186–189 (1996)
12. Tellegen, A., et al.: Personality similarity in twins reared apart and together. J. Pers. Soc. Psychol. **54**, 1031–1039 (1988)
13. Lucas, R.E., et al.: Cross-cultural evidence for the fundamental features of extraversion. J. Pers. Soc. Psychol. **79**, 452–468 (2000)
14. McIntosh, D.N., Silver, R.C., Wortman, C.B.: Religion's role in adjustment to a negative life event: coping with the loss of a child. J. Pers. Soc. Psychol. **65**, 812–821 (1993)
15. Ellison, C.G., Gay, D.A., Glass, T.A.: Does religious commitment contribute to individual life satisfaction. Soc. Forces **68**, 100–123 (1989)
16. Lyubomirsky, S., Ross, L.: Hedonic consequences of social comparison: a contrast of happy and unhappy people. J. Pers. Soc. Psychol. **73**, 1141–1157 (1997)
17. Lyubomirsky, S., Ross, L.: Changes in atractiveness of elected, rejected, and precluded alternatives: a comparison of happy and unhappy individuals. J. Pers. Soc. Psychol. **76**, 988–1007 (1999)
18. Lyubomirsky, S., Tucker, K.L.: Implications of individual differences in subjective happiness for perceiving interpreting and thinking about life events. Motiv. Emot. **22**, 155–186 (1998)
19. Csikszentmihalyi, M.: If we are so rich, why aren't we happy? Am. Psychol. **54**(10), 821–827 (1999)
20. Seligman, E.P., et al.: Positive psychology progress: empirical validation of interventions. Am. Psychol. **60**(5), 410–421 (2005)
21. Kraut, R., et al.: Internet paradox: a social technology that reduces social involvement and psychological well-being? Am. Psychol. **53**(9), 1017–1031 (1998)
22. Cummings, J., Butler, B., Kraut, R.: The quality of online social relationships. Commun. ACM **45**, 103–108 (2002)
23. Kraut, R., Kiesler, S., Boneva, B., Cummings, J., Helgeson, V.: Internet paradox revisited. J. Soc. Issues **58**, 49–74 (2002)
24. Valkenburg, P.M., Peter, J.: Online communication and adolescent well-being: testing the stimulation versus the displacement hypothesis. J. Comput.-Mediated Commun. **12**, 1169–1182 (2007)
25. Hampton, K.N., Sessions-Goulet, L., Her E.J., Rainie, L.: Social Isolation and New Technology. Report of the Pew Internet and American Life Project (2009). www.pewinternet.org/2009/11/04/social-isolation-and-new-technology
26. Kuss, D.J., Griffiths, D.: Internet gaming addiction: a systematic review of empirical research. Int. J. Ment. Health Addict. **10**, 278–296 (2011)

A Theoretical Model of Incorporating Gamification Design into On-line Marketing

Hsiu Ching Laura Hsieh[(⊠)] and Chiao Yu Hwang

Department of Creative Design, National Yunlin University of Science
and Technology, 123 Section 3, University Road, Douliou, Yunlin, Taiwan
laurarun@gmail.com

Abstract. Applying gamification design to websites for promoting users' experiences is a vital issue at present and in the future that in-depth discussions are necessary. This study intend to discuss experience from the aspects of human-computer interaction design, psychology, marketing, and communication to develop a "model applying gamification to networks for promoting marketing" with interdisciplinary knowledge and in-depth experiences and to treat it as the new possibility to effectively create users' experiences. The objectives of this study contain 1. to enhance online marketing and users' experiences with gamification design and 2. to construct a "model applying gamification to networks for promoting marketing", which could enhance users' experiences, by incorporating interdisciplinary theories.

Keywords: Game · Gamification · On-line marketing

1 Research Background and Objective

The idea of gamification has been emphasized in many fields [14, 16]. Gartner, the globally famous technology research and advisory company, listed gamification as a primary technology in 2011 [4]. "Gamification" refers to utilize the human nature of being fond of playing around and the characteristics of games being able to inspire people for transforming dull things into fascinating playing processes. The idea is also applied to education to enhance learning motivation, and a lot of enterprises start to apply it to crowdsourcing [15, 21] or staff training [10]. Akito [1] also indicated that gamification was not simply the fad or trend; the power of games was existed, but current information environment provided proper space & time approach and media for actualizing the creativity of gamification as well as resulted in great changes in life, thinking, and marketing. Accordingly, design researchers should face the importance of gamification design, incorporate interdisciplinary theoretical knowledge for further explanations, deepen the understanding and application of the operation mechanics, and master in the application of gamification to networks. The objectives of this study contain 1. to enhance online marketing and users' experiences with gamification design and 2. to construct a "model applying gamification to networks for promoting marketing", which could enhance users' experiences, by incorporating interdisciplinary theories.

F.F.-H. Nah and C.-H. Tan (Eds.): HCIBGO 2017, PART II, LNCS 10294, pp. 223–233, 2017.
DOI: 10.1007/978-3-319-58484-3_18

2   Game and Gamification

The literature review in this study is cut in from the aspects of games and gamification to analyze the gamification design from the aspect of marketing, to analyze the audience pleasure model of gamification users from the aspect of communication studies, and to analyze users' experiences and gamification design from the aspect of human-computer interaction design.

According to McCormick [16], the prototype idea of gamification existed in 1980s. Although the word "gamification" was not used then, cases to apply game elements and game mechanics to educational learning had appeared, but did not induce too much attention. It was emphasized after the popularity of Foursquare in 2010. The commonly accepted definitions of "gamification" include "attracting users engaging in it and solving problems through game thinking processes and game mechanics" [23] and "enhancing users' experiences and engagement with computer game elements in non-game situational contexts" [6]. Apparently, games are not the purpose of gamification, but to bring interesting and fascinating experiences, with game elements and game mechanics in non-game situational contexts, to provide motivation and attract users' active engagement so as to achieve the preset goal. Zichermann and Cunningham [25] regarded "game elements" as the basic elements to construct games as well as the basis to guide the entire gaming process and "game mechanics" as the design to optimize and reinforce game elements. Hunicke, Leblanc, and Zubek [9] proposed MDA architecture to divide games into mechanics, dynamics, and aesthetics. The "mechanics" referred to the algorithm guiding the entire game processing and consisted of game rules and goals through various mechanics, "dynamics" was the interactive behavior derived from game mechanics, and "aesthetics" was players' perception and experiences in the process as well as the fun of games. Werbach and Hunter [22] proposed DMC system, where "mechanics" referred to the basic process to promote the game schedule and players' participation, including challenge, opportunity, feedback, and winning state, and "components" was used for describing the specific elements of mechanics, containing badges, points, and billboard. Although different words were used, the statements were covered in the MDA architecture. In short, "game elements" proposed by Zichermann and Cunningham [25] and "mechanics" mentioned by Werbach and Hunter [22] are the basic compositions to guide the game processing, including the design of game rules, goals, definitions of victory or defeat, and game state feedback.

"Mechanics" might contain specific elements to construct or reinforce such mechanics, as "components" described by Werbach and Hunter [22], e.g. points, badges, levels, and billboard. "Game mechanics" indicated by Zichermann and Cunningham are actually such specific components. Components are not the fundamental elements of games that lack of such components would not affect the operation or integrity of the entire game; however, they could have the games be more diversified and become more attractive, such as inducing players with billboard or badges or opening hidden special tasks by enhancing levels. Creatively selecting and combining various game components would design more delicate and complicated game processes and enhance the novelty and charms of games. "Mechanics" is the core of entire games, and the application of various game components could make game mechanics more complicated.

Game players would generate game dynamics in the interactive process, when participating in games, to further form the aesthetic experiences of games. The attractive and inductive entertainment experiences of games are the so-called game aesthetics.

What are the differences between "gamification" and "game"? Deterding et al. [6] regarded the boundary between games and gamification being fine and fuzzy and presenting experiential and social characteristics. "Game" is the "play form" with rules and goals [3], aiming to offer entertainment. "Gamification", on the other hand, is a kind of "design strategy" to apply game elements and mechanics [6] for promoting participation motivation with gaming fun. Gamification is the flexible combination and utilizes game mechanics and various components to enhance the playfulness; in other words, it is not necessary to design complete games for gamification [1]. Referring to the metaphor of Deterding et al. [6], various game elements in gamification could be regarded as separately bricks, which could be freely combined and applied according to objectives and needs that the more game elements would approach to a complete game. Gamification presents flexibility, and the use of game elements and mechanics might appear various combinations and changes, might design a completely mature game with rich game elements and complicated mechanics to achieve the gamification objective, and might create the gaming fun and achieve the gamification effect by simply using few game elements and mechanics.

Wu [23] pointed out gamification as a kind of design strategy that, compared to the final design result, the objective of the activity design should be the important discrimination condition. In other words, the discrimination of game and gamification should be judged with the real goal behind the activity. Accordingly, gamification might be presented with the complicated and complete form of game or simply involved in some game mechanics. In this case, could the use of some game components in the activity be called gamification, or is it gamification to include playful properties for people enjoying the participation? Barr [3] pointed out the discrimination between "game" and "play" that there were definite rules and goals in games, with which the best and worst performance was defined; players pursuing the better state and exploring and performing under preset rules were the aesthetic perception of playfulness, challenge, and sense of accomplishment in games [11]. Consequently, gamification is not randomly developed playfulness to create entertainment experiences, but applies game components and mechanics to set definite participation rules and goals for the gaming fun. By reviewing the previous gamification cases, they contained certain rules and goals. For example, Starbucks used the mechanics of checking in Foursquare for exchanging badges as the game rule, and had the goal of exchanging collected badges with preference. In this case, regardless the simple or complicated activity or the number of game components or mechanics, definite game rules and goals were the basic conditions to achieve gamification. Yeh [24] pointed out three major differences between game and gamification. First, "game" was essentially a kind of playfulness, while "gamification" was a design strategy. Second, the development of games aimed to provide entertainment value, while the entertainment value of "gamification" was to increase motivation and have activities without gaming goals become more attractive. Third, gamification created fun by flexible combination and various game components and mechanics, rather than designing a game with complete structure. Nevertheless, definite rules and goals were the lowest standards to construct gamification.

3   Analyzing Gamification Design from the Marketing Dimension

Gamification design is further analyzed with Akito [1] research theory of enhancing marketing, as following. (1) Right sense of challenge: With the picture or stage design, the game level design has the players unconsciously learn the behaviors in games. The users perceive that they have their own choices; indeed, those are specific actions arranged in games. The picture design of Mario is the best example. Regarding automatic adjustment of levels, too difficult or too simple games would tire players that games with moderate difficulty should be designed. (2) Faster and more definite message response: Instant message should be responded in short time. The clarification of message responses and the response elements of badges, levels, and status should clearly remind the players. (3) Diversity of message response: Same stimulations would tire people. Difficult and simple game structures should be designed, and the changes of music and images could be added so that the players are not tired of seeing the same pictures and hearing the same sound. Besides, a game without definite ending time would tire players that special activities could be regularly held. (4) Adjustment of structure: The "strategy", which is merely presented in the game, needs to be specially introduced to the game to enhance the gaming fun. The stop of strategies and the balance of game adjustment could prevent the non-default functions in the game from being the tricky tool for players. Other skills like the design of interface, the structure of game introduction, and the design of exchange are also important. Foursquare is the most famous and successful gamification case of "incentives drive". The users check in the platform for badges (or points) and might possibly become "mayor", who could enjoy free coffee (Prince, 2013). In order to have the users understand Dropbox and carefully browse the website and message board, Dropbox designed Dropbox Quest in May 2014, in which the one who beat the game the most rapidly, could acquire more space or gifts [10]. Nike + Running allowed joggers uploading the mileage to FB; it was the gamification case to accumulate sense of accomplishment, create sports motivation, and acquire the sense of conquest.

Kapp [13] revealed that games offered alternative experiences to simulate real learning opportunities. "Accepting failure" is an element of gamification. In most learning environments, it is considered that failure should be avoided. It explains that it is not encouraged to try error learning in traditional environments. Learners could not realize the reasons for wrong answers or incorrect results and possible way to make improvement, but are simply informed the failure. Failure should be accepted, which is an important part of gamification design [13]. Another element is interest curve, which is the process or sequence of events in the gaming process, could help players continuously engage in games, and master the players' interests in different parts of the game. The third element is storytelling, which allows users engaging in the story to achieve the goal of educational entertainment. The last element is feedback, which should be rapid and instant. Feedback is a primary element in learning processes. Feedback with high frequency and targets could assist in efficient learning [13]. The common application of gamification is the scoring system, e.g. points, levels, and achievement, and then education or working situations [17]. Such mechanics could enhance users' use of services and change of behaviors because of external rewards [25]. As there is the word "game" in gamification that it is often misunderstood as playing; as a matter of fact, the application is just a minimum element in games, i.e. scoring system, and there are goals behind games [17].

Akito [1] pointed out the innovation principles of gamification design. (1) Reinforcing relationship: The major strength of gamification is to reinforce the relationship with customers and continuously offer services for customers. In order to reinforce the relationship with customers, what customer behaviors need to be changed? Such a thought might be combined with the creativity of gamification. In addition to retail stores and restaurants, language cram schools, beauty parlors, and clinics could reinforce the relationship with customers through gamification to change certain business models. (2) Visibility of message response: Are there any actions to have message responses be more definite? Could message responses be automatically responded through computer systems? Could it be measured with quantitative data? For instance, Denkimmter successfully changed electricity meters into power message responses for players. In other words, the faster and more definite message responses would better excite players. (3) Analysis of addictive action: A lot of people addicted to certain affairs, e.g. fishing, fashion trend, or making dished, are similar to addicted to games. Any addictive things could be analyzed. In such action processes, are there any prompts or clues? Trying to decompose each element in the process must have certain "addictive" motivation. Such "motivation" could be gamified for people to experience. (4) Paying attention to the change of technology: Low costs and high popularity of new sensors, convenience of smart phones, and the expansion of gamification resulted from technology innovation are predictable. For example, when "smart meters", which present the function of telecommunication, are popular and could be used for producing low-cost games. Moreover, when electric vehicles are popular, the game of reducing the emission of carbon dioxide would attract more people to join in. (5) Improvement of game rules: Foursquare and Level UP (developed by SCVNGR) are user positioning games developed via the locations of restaurants, but present distinct game rules. Foursquare allows people gaining badges or points by walking in and checking in the shops, while Level UP, added in missions and exploratory game elements, allows gaining points by walking in the stores and checking out that it is a game architecture with double rules. It is also a good idea to seek for feelings or clues, as making a new game, when intending to improve game rules. (6) Incorporating game rules: For example, there are various game rules for the games of calling, raising money, sending e-mail in "My Obama", aiming to have Obama win the president election. Reviewing the history of games, there are multi-directional rules in games dividing labors and incorporating with each other. (7) Considering from business model: The pioneer game enterprises successfully construct business models in new fields, but there are some failure examples. Are there any ways to acquire new users? Where are the profits? How to change the method to raise money? Reconsidering the improvement from such existing business models is also a good method. By using certain service games, the more trial users show the more business opportunities.

4   Analyzing Gamification Users' Audience Pleasure Model from the Aspect of Communication Studies

From the aspect of communication studies, Chang [5] mentioned four characters of gaming behaviors, including "non-utilitarian", "autonomy", "rule-based", and "quantitative result", so that the pleasure essence is hidden in the gaming behaviors. The consumption behaviors in games are the autonomy of users' self-willingness, which is purely the viewpoint to experience gaming behaviors and non-real interests (non-utilitarian). Moreover, definite rule reference and actual behavioral outcomes (quantitative results) have the gaming behaviors full of intrinsic pleasure. Online-game audience (users) pleasure model contains the following four types. (1) Controllability pleasure, which is affected by complexity and players' interaction. (2) Sociability pleasure, including sense of belonging, intimacy, and sense of control. (3) Narrativity pleasure, which is influenced by story aesthetics and stories. (4) Performance pleasure, the imagination to extend and reinforce the real world. Among such four types of pleasure, controllability pleasure and sociability pleasure are the most common and the most important, while narrativity pleasure and performance pleasure are not the common experiences of each user. Narrativity pleasure is related to the aesthetic presentation of texts and the story structure, has to cross over the threshold to generate controllability pleasure, and can move around the game world. Performance pleasure, on the other hand, is related to the extension of daily life experiences, is users' presentation different from the real identity position and another ideal ego, often complements the shortcomings in the real world, and reinforces and practices the inner desires and imagination. Similar to narrativity pleasure, users' experience descriptions of performance pleasure are obviously less than controllability pleasure and sociability pleasure. Such four types of media pleasure are not single and exclusive media experiences; they often appear with "compound" and interlock with each other to commonly reinforce the audience's pleasure. The most common and the strongest interlocking model is the compound of controllability pleasure and sociability pleasure [5].

5   Analyzing the Application of Gamification to Websites from the User-Centered Human-Computer Interaction

Gamification aims to have players engage in tasks and encourage desirable behaviors [17]. Zichermann and Cunningham [25] defined gamification as the thinking process in games and the utilization of game mechanics allowing users engaging in and solving problems. Based on the above definition, Nicholson [17] proposed three application theories to construct user-centered meaningful gamification and to have users perceive the fun of tasks and really establish internalized experiences. These could be explained aiming at the possible effect of external motivation induced by reward mechanics.

1. Universal design for learning: Universal design for learning came from education, aiming to have designers develop the curriculum contents suitable for diverse learning groups. Various methods could be utilized for learning, rather than examinations or oral reports [21].

2. Organismic integration theory: Organismic integration theory explained how external motivation integrated activity into personal self-perception. Having users identify the goal being meaningful could better generate the autonomous behaviors, such as connecting users' goals and value. Too much external motivation might have users appear negative perception. To avoid such a situation, it was necessary to have a user appear meanings on the game contents.

3. Situational relevance and situated motivational affordance: Situational relevance expected to involve in users. Situated motivational affordance [6] came from the motivation affordability theory. Merely when a user's background and points of view conformed to the system could the user be induced the motivation by the system to satisfy the motivation need, like ability, autonomy, and relatedness.

4. Player-generated content: The idea of user-generated contents was from the game research, "Gaming 2.0". "Second life" was the game to achieve the idea. The players constructed more than one game, i.e. developing a system, which allowed users modifying the game at any time and developing the content. Such an approach could better have users set the goals.

Jensen [11] also proposed to design meaningful games, which had users' experiences in priority, related achievement with individuals, applied narrative power, and stressed on users being "playing", i.e. related to users' situations. It is important to incorporate situational contexts in gamification design. Deterding [6] indicated that it was a blind point in gamification design to ignore situations. Prince [18] also revealed that it was not interesting to remove game elements and be in non-gaming situations. Readers might separate from daily life when they were forced to play, but were not really playing. Considering that users' situational contexts could present players' autonomy, autonomy is one of motivation needs. Ability presentation is another motivation; and, social is the last motivation. Wikipedia is the example applying such motivation needs.

6 Relevant Models Applying Gamification to Websites

From the aspect of psychology, Przybylski, Rigby, and Ryan [19] constructed the game-participation motivation model, which discussed the relationship between users' motivation and satisfaction. They compared satisfaction elements (competence, autonomy, relatedness) with motivation elements (sense of accomplishment, social sense, immersion), trying to find out the factors in the achievement of user behaviors. The economic model constructed by Hamari and Eranti [8] defined sense of accomplishment as symbolic, completely logic, and rewarding. From the aspect of business service, Aparicio et al., [2] constructed four procedures for the recyclable gamification process and defined major objectives, minor objectives, selection of game mechanics, and analysis of efficiency. Gamification MDA (mechanics-dynamics-aesthetics) model [10] was constructed based on the relationship between users' experiences and designers' intention and was the mix of rules, systems, and pleasure, where the pleasure perception was associated with the perception of aesthetics. A game-participation motivation model was constructed from the aspect of psychology [19] to discuss the relationship between users' motivation and satisfaction. The research compared satisfaction elements (Competence, autonomy, Relatedness) with motivation elements (sense of accomplishment, social sense, immersion), intending to find out the factors in the achievement of user behaviors. From the aspect of economy, Hamari and Eranti [8] constructed the economic model and defined sense of accomplishment as symbolic, completely logic, and rewarding. Nonetheless, from above gamification-related literatures, user experience design has not been used as the core to discuss whether the application of gamification can enhance the interdisciplinary model with effective marketing. Accordingly, a "model applying gamification to networks for promoting marketing" is constructed in this study to enhance users' experiences.

7   Construction of a Theoretical Model

The application of users' experiences in human-computer interaction, theory of communication studies, and theory of experience aesthetics could possibly improve and reinforce the application of gamification design to website experience design. From above literature review, it is found that pleasure experiential modules in communication studies correspond to users' experiences in human-computer interaction and it is possible to promote experiences to pleasure, satisfaction, sociability, and learnability. From the research on human-computer interaction, users' experiences cover users' objective (usability) and subjective psychological perception, and the application of pleasure experiential modules in communication studies to network interaction could generate aesthetic experiences, meaningful experiences, and emotional experiences

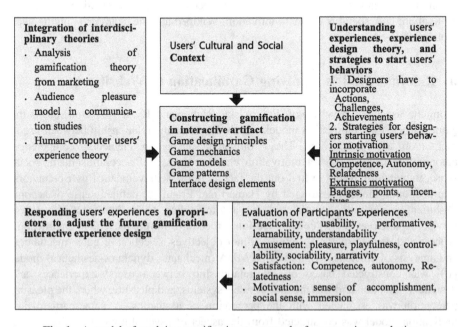

Fig. 1. A model of applying gamification to networks for promoting marketing

(controlled pleasure experience, sociable pleasure experience, narrative pleasure experience, performative pleasure experience). It is found in this study that the integration of gamification design, marketing knowledge, users' experiences in human-computer interaction, and theory of communication studies could improve and reinforce online marketing efficiency and promote users' experiences. For this reason, the core procedures for the model applying gamification to online marketing are organized, according to literature review. Step 1: Focusing on users' cultural and social context. Step 2: Understanding users' experiences and experience design theory and starting the strategy of user behaviors. Step 3: Constructing interactive artifact. Step 4: Applying gamification to networks for enhancing the evaluation of marketing efficiency. The detailed explanations are shown in Fig. 1.

8 Conclusion

1. Users' Cultural and Social Context

User-centered design has gradually been emphasized in past years. Antin [7] mentioned that the design of gamification systems or platforms could consider users' social and psychological needs and the background context, the meanings of games to them, and individual differences. When such considerations are taken into account for gamification design, a satisfactory and popular system, which could better have users engage in and feel being supported, could be developed.

2. Understanding users' experiences, experience design theory, and strategies to start users' behaviors

- Integration of designers: actions, challenges, achievements.
- Strategies for designers starting users' behavioral motivation

  Intrinsic motivation: competence, autonomy, relatedness.
  Extrinsic motivation: badges, points, incentives.

3. Constructing gamification in interactive artifact

Game design principles, Game mechanics, Game models, Game patterns, Interface design elements.

4. Evaluation of Participants' Experiences

- Theory of human-computer interaction could be applied to practicality: e.g. usability, performatives, learnability, understandability.
- Aesthetic experiences and theory of communication studies could be applied to amusement: e.g. pleasure, playfulness, controllability, sociability, narrativity.
- Theory of psychological motivation could be applied to satisfaction: e.g. competence, autonomy, relatedness.
- Theory of psychological motivation could be applied to motivation: sense of accomplishment, social sense, immersion.

A theoretical "model applying gamification to networks for promoting marketing" is constructed in this study. The following dimensions are taken into account for constructing such a model, including culture and social context, motivation model from the aspect of psychology to discuss user satisfaction elements (competence, autonomy, relatedness) and motivation elements (sense of accomplishment, social sense, immersion), "theory of pleasure experiential modules" in communication studies, "users' experiences" in human-computer interaction, and theory of experience design, to construct the interactive design entity, further practice users' real experiences, responses, and evaluation, and respond users' experiences to the proprietor for adjusting the future gamification interactive experience design entity. It is a recyclable process. The constructed model is a phase study in the entire research. There are successive experimental steps (expert interview, user survey, questionnaire interview) to collect data and validate the practicability of this model. The expected benefits of this research are to incorporate gamification design into online marketing communicated proprietors, researchers, and designers for effective design suggestions and to offer users with pleasant use experiences.

References

1. Akito, I.: Playing games from thinking, design to marketing: gamification time. China Times, Taipei City (2013)
2. Aparicio, A.F., Vela, F.L.G., Sánchez, J.L.G., Montes, J.L.I.: Analysis and application of gamification. Proc. Interaccion **12**, 1–2 (2012)
3. Barr, P.: Video game values: play as human-computer interaction. Doctoral Dissertatio. Victoria University of Wellington (2008)
4. Brockmeier, J.: Gartner Adds Big Data, Gamification, and Internet of Things to Its Hype Cycle (2011). http://www.readwriteweb.com/enterprise/2011/08/gartner-adds-big-data
5. Chang, Y.: Experiential pleasure of online gamers. Chin. J. Commun. Res. **19**, 61–95 (2011)
6. Deterding, S., Dixon, D., Khaled, R., Nacke, L.: Gamification: toward a definition. CHI 2011, Vancouver, BC, Canada (2011)
7. Deterding, S.: Gamification: designing for motivation. Interaction **19**(4), 14–17 (2012)
8. Hamari, J., Eranti, V.: Framework for designing and evaluating game achievements. In: DiGRA 2011: Think Design Play, pp. 1–20 (2011)
9. Hamari, J., Koivisto, J., Sarsa, H.: Does gamification work?: a literature review of empirical studies on gamification. In: Proceedings of the 47th Hawaii International Conference on System Sciences, Waikoloa, HI, USA (2014)
10. Huling, R.: Gamification: Turning work into play. H+ Magazine (2010). http://hplusmagazine.com/gamification-turning-work-play/
11. Hunicke, R., LeBlanc, M., Zubek, R.: MDA: a formal approach to game design and game research. In: Proceedings of the AAAI Workshop on Challenges in Game AI, p. 4 (2004)
12. Jensen, M.: Engaging the learner: gamification strives to keep the users interest. T + D **66** (1), 40–44 (2012)
13. Kapp, K.M.: Games, gamification, and the quest for learner engagement. T + D **66**(6), 64–68 (2012)
14. Marczewski, A.: Gamification: A Simple Introduction & a Bit More. Amazon ebook (2012)
15. Markoff, J.: In a Video Game, Tackling the Complexities of Protein Folding. The New York Times (2010). http://www.nytimes.com/science/05protein.html
16. McCormick, T.: Anthropology of an idea gamification. Foreign Policy **201**, 26–27 (2013)

17. Nicholson, S: A user-centered theoretical framework for meaningful gamification. In: Games + Learning + Society 8.0, Madison, WI (2012)
18. Prince, J.D.: Gamification. J. Electron. Resour. Med. Libr. **10**(3), 162–169 (2013)
19. Przybylski, A.K., Rigby, C.S., Ryan, R.M.: A motivational model of video game engagement. Rev. Gen. Psychol. **14**(2), 154–166 (2010)
20. Raymer, R.: Gamification: using game mechanics to enhance elearning. eLearn Mag. (2011). http://elearnmag.acm.org/archive.cfm?aid=2031772
21. Rose, D.H., Meyer, A.: Teaching every student in the digital age: universal design for learning (2002)
22. Werbach, K., Hunter, D.: For the Win: How Game Thinking can Revolutionize your Business. Wharton Digital Press, Philadelphia (2012)
23. Wu, D.: From game to gamification: preliminary research of gamification marketing theory. Mass Commun. Res. **124**, 215–251 (2015)
24. Yeh, N.: To establish meaningful gamification in library services. J. Libr. Inf. Sci. **40**(2), 67–76 (2015)
25. Zichermann, G., Cunningham, C.: Gamification by Design: Implementing Game Mechanics in Web and Mobile Apps. O'Reilly Media, Sebastopol (2011)

Extracting Important Knowledge from Multiple Markets Using Transfer Learning

Tokuhiro Kujiraoka[✉], Fumiaki Saitoh, and Syohei Ishizu

Aoyama Gakuin University, 5-10-1 Fuchinobe, Shagamihara,
Kanagawa 252-5258, Japan
c5616177@aoyama.jp, {saitoh,ishizu}@ise.aoyama.ac.jp

Abstract. The aim of this study is to extract a customer's needs from their reviews of an electronic commerce (EC) site using transfer learning. Transfer learning involves retaining and applying the knowledge learned from one or more tasks to efficiently develop an effective hypothesis for a new task. Recently, with the spread of EC sites, customer reviews have become a beneficial information source, as they include customers' opinions or product reputations, and can attract attention. However, this information is too huge to browse conveniently. Moreover, to develop new products with a competitive advantage, it is necessary to incorporate customers' opinions. Therefore, it is necessary to extract the customers' opinions from the enormous amount of customer reviews.

In this research, we focus on markets where multiple products compete. With the spread of smartphones, multiple products, e.g., cameras, compete in the same market. We want to understand customers' needs efficiently by extracting com-mon requests by consumers from the information about these multiple products. Hence, we propose a method of extracting customers' needs using transfer learning to comprehensively handle multiple products' information for this market.

Keywords: Transfer learning · Random forest · Ensemble learning · Text mining · Customer review

1 Introduction

Recently, online shopping, which allows people to purchase products from the inter-net, has been spreading widely. The market size for electronic commerce (EC) sites has been increasing. The average growth rate for the past 10 years is as much as 7.3% and the sales from online shopping in Japan exceeded 58 billion dollars in 2014. Therefore, the market for EC sites has been expanding and is expected to in-crease in the future. In addition, through customer review services, purchasers can freely describe their evaluations, impressions, opinions, and satisfaction with the products. Online shoppers often use customer reviews when making a purchasing decision. Since these are a valuable information source, as they contain personal voices, re-searchers have been trying to analyze the relevance of EC sites to marketing.

© Springer International Publishing AG 2017
F.F.-H. Nah and C.-H. Tan (Eds.): HCIBGO 2017, PART II, LNCS 10294, pp. 234–245, 2017.
DOI: 10.1007/978-3-319-58484-3_19

How-ever, these are huge quantities of information, which require considerable time and effort to review. To effectively utilize this enormous review data, researchers have investigated extracting only the necessary information and classifying the customer reviews by some criteria. In this research, the aim is to efficiently process huge amounts of customer reviews and extract customer needs. In this paper, we focus on smartphone reviews posted in customer reviews of EC sites. Smartphones are spreading quickly and their ownership rate exceeded 70% in 2016 in Japan. However, some markets are shrinking due to the spread of smartphones. This is because products with multiple functions, e.g., smart phones, and products with single functions, e.g., digital cameras, coexist in the same market. Products with multiple functions infringe on the market share of single-function products. As an example of this situation, we chose the market around the smartphone. Since smartphones can fulfill multiple functions, consumer demand is different for each product or function. Therefore, it is effective to extract the customer's needs for each smartphone function and demand. Thus, it is necessary to consider not only smartphone information but also information on competing products. Transfer learning is a comprehensive method for handling extensive information. It utilizes knowledge obtained from different resources to efficiently solve a given task. We consider that customer needs can be efficiently extracted using competing product information about smartphones. Extracting the knowledge creates new value by transferring the knowledge learned about one product to another. In this study, we use the Random Forest (RF) classifier, which is an ensemble-learning method. RF uses the voting of multiple decision trees to predict or identify data. These trees are generated by bootstrap random sampling and are not allowed to overlap; thus, the risk of overfitting is reduced. Although RF can also be applied to high dimensional data, it cannot be applied to sparse data containing many zeroes. In this research, we use the text from customer reviews to create a word-frequency matrix. This matrix is likely to be large and sparse. The Random Forest method does not learn well with this matrix. Thus, it is necessary to convert the sparse matrix to a dense matrix, using non-negative matrix factorization (NMF). This method is often used for text data and can easily extract topics.

2 Background and Related Works

2.1 Customer Reviews

There are several papers directly in the customer's review. There are many studies on customer reviews, because customers' opinions are directly reflected in customer reviews and it is a useful source of information. Studies of customer review include research that extracts only necessary information and research that classifies reviews. Both studies are being studied to efficiently process enormous amounts of review data in order to grasp the needs of customers. We introduce some research. Okada et al. [3] use SVM for automatic review of documents for review of travel sites. Firstly, they define evaluation sentence pattern using sentence patterns of Japanese, and the effectiveness of classification when using it was investigated experimentally. As a result, it was found that it is difficult to improve classification accuracy simply by incorporating evaluation expressions. Přichystal [1] measures the quality of products and services from reviews. The author considers that the evaluation is based on human emotions. However, handling a large amount of data is almost impossible to process manually, it takes time to read all product reviews. They aim to automatically find human emotions hidden in customer reviews.

2.2   NMF(Non-negative Matrix Factorization)

In this research, since we used NMF when contracting the dimension of text data, so its effectiveness is shown from related research. SAWADA [5] proves that NMF is valid for document data. NMF is a method of analyzing a matrix composed of positive values including many zeros, and the result obtained by NMF utilizes a feature in which data elements are clustered based on the frequent pattern of the data. As a result of the experiment, it became possible to cluster news articles. Kimura et al. [12] proposes transfer learning by NMF. Kimura et al. pro-posed a transfer learning method based on conservativity of feature space based on the metastatic hypothesis that the feature space used for approximate expression between domains is similar. The proposed method is applied to transfer learning in document clustering and shows the effect of the proposed method. It is known that the proposed method has a wide applicability because it has an advantage that it does not require a label for data given as the original domain.

2.3   Machine Learning(Random Forest and Transfer Learning)

We introduce the research related to RF adopted in this research and the research related to metastasis learning. Transfer learning is used for a fairly wide range of machine learning frameworks, and the definite definitions cannot be said clearly. This idea is widely used that in order to efficiently find an effective hypothesis of a new task, it is necessary to obtain knowledge learned by one or more different tasks and to apply it [14]. In other words, it is to solve the problem efficiently by utilizing knowledge learned from different information source for a problem to be solved. Currently, as more data is available due to the spread of the Internet, it is required to use these information efficiently and effectively. There is transfer learning as a means for that. Fukumoto et al. [15] classifies documents using random forests. We proposed a method to generate co-occurrence matrix to extract useful information from large-scale document data, and document classification using the result. Compared with SVM and Bagging, it indicates that RF has high classification accuracy. A related study in transfer learning is TrBagg by Kamishima et al. [8]. TrBagg is a technique applied Bagging to transfer learning. Dai et al. [16] proposes TrAdaBoost applying AdaBoost to transfer learning. We explain the two studies that are the basis of our research. Kamishima et al. [8] proposes transfer learning using Bagging which is a type of ensemble learning. The algorithm is simple, and the transfer learning of this research is based on this method. Based on the idea that a weak learner that reduces the prediction error is not used. Kumagae et al. [10] proposes an algorithm (OptTrBagg) that points out and solves the problem of transfer learning proposed by Kamishima [8]. The authors use proposal method to predict the purchase of products using information on multiple EC sites. Experimental results showed that this proposed method is effective. Since the proposed method has no fixed framework, several proposed methods have been proposed.

3 Method

In this research, we extract the customer's reviews from a market where multiple products compete, using transfer learning by random forest. First, we applied a text mining technique to the collected data. Many languages, including English, are generally divided between word and word by space. However, in the case of Japanese, since between word and word are not divided by space, it is necessary to separate the words using a morphological analysis. We then create a word-frequency matrix; i.e., a matrix expressing the word-appearance frequency for one review.

In this research, since we deal with approximately 3000 customer reviews, the created frequency matrix is likely to be sparse. RF does not work well on sparse matrices, so they need to be converted to dense matrices. Therefore, we per-form non-negative matrix factorization, which transforms the sparse matrix into a dense matrix and reduces the dimension. We perform transfer learning by RF on the reduced data and extract common knowledge. Next, we describe a non-negative matrix factorization and RF outline for transforming a large-frequency sparse matrix to a dense matrix. We subsequently describe transfer learning as the process of the proposed method.

3.1 Non-negative Matrix Factorization

A decision tree is difficult to create if the target data is a large sparse matrix. Therefore, RF does not work well. Document data, e.g., customer reviews, are most likely to be sparse, because the documents are not very long; however, we deal with a vast number of reviews and many words appear. To avoid this, we use non-negative matrix factorization (NMF). If we use NMF, we can transfer from a sparse matrix to a dense matrix and reduce the dimensions without losing information.

NMF is a method of decomposing one non-negative matrix into two non-negative matrices and approximating them. The dimension can be reduced without losing the latent meaning of the original matrix. NMF is often used for document, sound, and image data. Several frequent patterns are obtained by implementing NMF. That is, highly similar variables are reduced to synthetic variables. Moreover, since similar words affect common latent variables, it is relatively easy to determine the meaning of the reduced variables. From this property, we can expect that the analysis accuracy will be improved and the interpretation can be expanded in the knowledge extracted from the data.

A schematic diagram of the non-negative matrix factorization is shown in Fig. 1. NMF can approximate the original data matrix X ($I \times J$ matrix) as the product of two

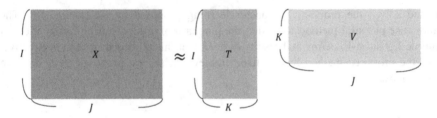

Fig. 1. NMF schematic

matrices $(X \simeq TV)$. K is the basis and indicates the number of dimensions we want to reduce. In this algorithm, each element t_{ik}, v_{kj} of the matrix T, V is first initialized with a non-negative random number. The specified number of updates is determined using Eqs. (1) and (2).

$$t_{ik} \leftarrow t_{ik} \frac{\sum_j x_{ij} v_{kj}}{\sum_j \hat{x}_{ij} v_{ik}} \tag{1}$$

$$v_{kj} \leftarrow w_{kj} \frac{\sum_i x_{ij} v_{ik}}{\sum_i \hat{x}_{ij} v_{ik}} \tag{2}$$

NMF has already been proven to be able to extract document topics from text data []. In this research, the knowledge is extracted learning a matrix T by RF

3.2   Random Forest (RF)

In this research, we use a RF which is one of machine learning methods to learn product information. RF is one of ensemble learning methods, and a transition learning method in bagging, which is a type of ensemble learning, has al-ready been proposed. Transfer learning using a random forest has also been pro-posed, but if the number of data is proven to improve accuracy when the number of target data is few, it is not effective when the number of data is many.

Decision Tree
Since the Random Forest is ensemble learning with the decision tree as a weak learner, we first outline the decision tree. Decision tree analysis is a data-mining method that uses classification and prediction. As shown in Fig. 2, it has a tree structure and a directed graph that is not closed. A leaf (color) represents a classification, and a branch (no color) is a tree structure representing a collection of features up to that classification. Various algorithms have been proposed for constructing decision trees. In the Random Forest, learning by the most representative Classification and Regression Tree (CART) analysis is used.

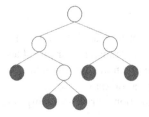

Fig. 2. Decision tree schematic

Random Forest

Random Forest is a machine-learning algorithm proposed by Leo Breiman in 2001. Its advantage is that it can cope with high dimensional data, while reducing the risk of over-learning. On the other hand, the disadvantage is that when the data is a sparse matrix, it cannot be implemented well. We construct multiple decision trees using samples generated with ensemble learning, and a random sampling overlap by boot-strap sampling, and perform identification, regression, and clustering using the results.

In the identification case, the data is classified into the class with the majority decision of the output class of the decision tree. In the regression case, the value is determined by the average value of the output of the decision tree. Compared to other machine-learning methods, e.g., support vector machines and neural networks, the calculation speed is high and it is said to be highly accurate. A schematic diagram of a Random Forest is shown in Fig. 3. The Random Forest algorithm is shown below.

STEP 1   Extract bootstrap specimens that allow random duplication
STEP 2   Build decision tree from bootstrap specimen
             –Randomly extracted feature quantities without allowing duplication
STEP 3   Construct a repetition model with STEP 1, STEP 2 specified times
STEP 4   Identify by the majority vote of the constructed decision tree

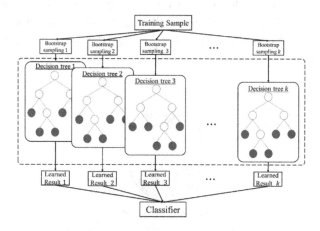

Fig. 3. Random Forest Schematic

3.3   Transfer Learning

In this section, we explain about transfer learning and the proposed transfer learning method using Random Forest. Transfer learning has not established much of a defini-tion but it is a learning method that efficiently solves for a certain task using knowledge learned from information on related or similar tasks. We call the domain to be predicted the transfer destination (target domain), and the data the transfer source (source domain).

In this research, we consider the problem of using the data about smartphones to gain knowledge about cameras. The desired knowledge is the common colored knowledge between product A and products B, C, or D. Product A is the target do-main (smart-phone) and products B, C, and D (cameras, etc.) are the source domains; we extract the specialized needs by transferring the knowledge of the competing camera products.

First, we summarize the symbols to be handled in this research. $\mathcal{D}_T$ is the target domain that we want to predict, or improve the accuracy of the knowledge transfer. The source domain that transfers knowledge is $\mathcal{D}_S$. In this paper, the smartphone infor-mation is $\mathcal{D}_T$ and the camera information is $\mathcal{D}_S$. $\mathcal{D}$ is the combined data of $\mathcal{D}_T$ and $\mathcal{D}_S$.

When RF is learning, a parameter should be defined that determines the size of the forest. If a model is built from the target domain by setting the parameter to B, when the model is built from the combined target and source domain data, the parameter will be B'.

3.4   Proposed Method

The transition learning implemented in this paper refers to TrBagg, and a similar algorithm is implemented by Random Forest instead of Bagging. Transfer learning using Random Forest consists of two algorithms for learning and selecting the available decision trees. First of all, in the learning part, we obtain a set $\mathcal{F}_{T+S}$ of decision trees learned by combining the target domain and source domain, and a set $\mathcal{F}_T$ of decision trees learned from the target domain. In the filtering part, we combine the decision trees obtained by Algorithm 1, and arrange them in ascending order according to the pre-diction error for the target domain. Let e be the prediction error of the rearranged decision tree $\hat{f}_1$, and we add $\hat{f}_1$ to $\mathcal{F}'$ and $\mathcal{F}^*$. We repeat this $(B + B')$ times to predict by majority vote using a decision tree by adding a target domain $\mathcal{F}'$ in order from $\hat{f}_2$. At

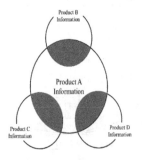

Fig. 4. Common knowledge that can be extracted from transfer learning

this time, if a decision tree is added that improves the prediction error for the target domain, it is added to $\mathcal{F}^*$, and e is updated to the error e' at that time. Figure 5, Algorithms 1 and 2 show transfer learning using RF. (Figure 4)

Algorithm1 *Transfer Learning by Random Forest*

1: **INPUT** $\mathcal{D}_T, \mathcal{D}_S, B, B'$
2: $\mathcal{D}_{T+S} = \mathcal{D}_T \cup \mathcal{D}_S$ (union)
3: $\mathcal{F} = \{\emptyset\}, \mathcal{F}_T = \{\emptyset\}$
4: **for all** t = 1 to B **do**
5:     $\mathcal{D}'_{T+S} \leftarrow$ Bootstrap sample from $\mathcal{D}_{T+S}$
6:     $\hat{f}_t \leftarrow$ Clasiifire learnd from $\mathcal{D}'_{T+S}$
7:     $\mathcal{F}_{T+S} = \mathcal{F} \cup \hat{f}_t$
8: **for all** t = 1 to B' **do**
9:     $\mathcal{D}'_t \leftarrow$ Bootstrap sample from $\mathcal{D}_T$
10:     $\hat{f}_t \leftarrow$ Clasiifire learnd from $\mathcal{D}'_t$
11:     $\mathcal{F}_T = \mathcal{F}_T \cup \hat{f}_t$
12: **end for**
13: $\mathcal{F}^* = Filtering(\mathcal{F}, \mathcal{F}_T)$
14: **OUTPUT** $\mathcal{F}^*: \{\hat{f}_1, \hat{f}_2, \cdots, \hat{f}_n\}$

Algorithm2 *Filtering*

1: function Filtering
2: **INPUT** $\mathcal{F}: \{\hat{f}_1, \hat{f}_2, \cdots, \hat{f}_B\}, \mathcal{F}_T: \{\hat{f}_{T_1}, \cdots, \hat{f}_{T_{B'}}\}$
3: $\mathcal{F} = \mathcal{F} \cup \mathcal{F}_T$
4: $\{\hat{f}_1, \cdots, \hat{f}_{B+B'}\}$: Sort $\mathcal{F}$ prediction error for $\mathcal{D}_T$(ascending)
5: $\mathcal{F}' = \{\emptyset\}; \mathcal{F}' \cup \hat{f}_1$
6: $\mathcal{F}^* = \{\emptyset\}; \mathcal{F}^* \cup \hat{f}_1$
7: $e \leftarrow$ Prediction error to $\mathcal{D}_T$ by $\hat{f}_1$
8: **for all** $t = 1$ to $B + B'$ **do**
9:     $\mathcal{F}' = \mathcal{F}' \cup \hat{f}_t$
10:     $e' \leftarrow$ Prediction error to $\mathcal{D}_T$ by $\mathcal{F}'$
11:     **if** $e' \leqq e$ **then**
12:         $\mathcal{F}^* = \mathcal{F}^* \cup \mathcal{F}'$
13:         $e = e'$
14:     **end if**
15: **end for**
16: **OUTPUT** $\mathcal{F}^* = \{\hat{f}_1, \hat{f}_2, \cdots, \hat{f}_n\}$

In this section explain the proposed method. The proposed method is divided into 4 stages and it is as following.

STEP 1   Collect customer reviews and perform morphological analysis to create frequency matrix
STEP 2   Since the random forest does not function when it is a sparse matrix, it converts to a dense matrix and reduces the dimensions using nonnegative matrix factorization (NMF)

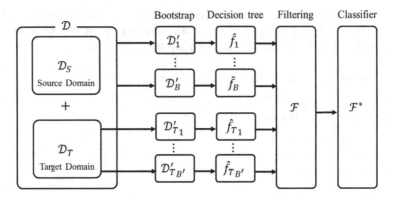

Fig. 5. Schematic transfer learning by RF

STEP 3   Learns the feature amount of the reduced data in chapter 2, class label as "good" or "bad" evaluation for products. Construct model by Transfer learning using random forest

STEP 4   Classify the review of smartphone with the constructed model and extract customer needs

4   Experiment and Result

4.1   Experiment Condition

We gathered 1324 reviews on smartphones and 1912 reviews on digital cameras, totaling 3236 reviews from review data provided by Rakuten, Inc. and are the subject of investigation. We performed morphological analysis on text data, created frequency matrix, and reduced dimensions using non-negative matrix factorization.

The number of decision trees in the random forest was 500. We summarized data and parameter using this experiment as following table

4.2   Result

We summarize the results predicted with the constructed model. For comparison, we summarize the results of the following experiments (Tables 4, 5 and 6):

(1)   Predicting the target domain with the model generated by the RF from the target domain,

(2)   Predicting when smartphone is transferred by transfer learning, and

(3)   Prediction when smartphone is target domain by transfer learning

Needs specialized for highly evaluated camera function

- I ordered it for my husband, it was unused and in a beautiful state and charged a little, it was very good. Shipping was also fast. The camera function is superior to

Table 1. Number of data

	Good (4 ~ 5)	Bad (1 ~ 3)	Total
Smart phone	643	681	1324
Camera	947	965	1912

Table 2. Parameter of NMF

Base	50
Number of update	100

Table 3. Parameter of RF

Number of decision tree	B	50
	B'	100
Number of selected feature		14

Table 4. Accuracy and prediction Table 1

(1)	Good	Bad
good	526	92
bad	39	464
	Accuracy	88.31%

Table 5. Accuracy and prediction Table 2

(2)	Good	Bad
good	512	87
Bad	131	391
	Accuracy	80.6%

Table 6. Accuracy and prediction Table 3

(2)	Good	Bad
good	405	206
Bad	223	287
	Accuracy	61.74%

my cell phone, the shutter is quickly turned off and the image is also good, so I wanted my part as well.

- I ordered it for easy tomorrow free, gift wrapping, but I am satisfied with the arrival of goods as desired. Calls and e-mails are main, so the items here are enough. Also, since the number of pixels of the camera is quite poor in the model before this item, I made it to this model. The opponent who gave it is also pleased.
- I received it in two days after placing an order. I could use it as soon as I inserted the SIM card (^ - ^). The camera is also beautiful and the motion is crisp and comfortable. Good shopping was done!

Needs specialized for lowly evaluated camera function

- The camera is really nice. Especially, I think that shooting at night cannot be imitated by other mobile phones. However, other than that, the touch panel is particularly bad.
- There are some difficulties to use such as not being able to directly write the photos taken with the camera application on the SD card, but was it a place that ordinary smartphone was said?

5 Discussion

We compared the model based on the Random Forest generated from the target domain, and the model using transition learning using two of the transfer targets and the source domain. The results showed that the accuracy decreased. However, since our aim is to extract camera-specific reviews from high-rated smartphone reviews, we can predict that the prediction accuracy will drop. We consider that classification using other product information may result in reviews closer to the needs of the camera. Looking at the actually extracted review, it can be seen from the review of the smartphone that the customer's voice with respect to the camera function is included. From this result, it can be said that the need for the camera function against that from the smartphone review can be extracted.

6 Conclusion

In our paper, we extracted the customers' needs from the smartphone reviews. Due to the diversity of smartphone demands, we tried to subdivide the needs by transferring competing product information. Through this experiment, we classified reviews specialized for cameras by selecting camera-review information from smartphone re-views and extracting customers' needs. We can extract camera function needs for smartphones from the classified reviews. However, since the method has not been verified, this paper was simply a proposal of the extraction method. The obtained results leave much room for verification, and we must also verify other products. Moreover, the suggested transfer learning with RF is simple, and we should consider a more sophisticated method in the future.

Acknowledgements. In this research, we used Rakuten market review data provided by Rakuten, Inc. Ltd. and the National Institute of Informatics. The authors would like to thank them.

References

1. Přichystal, J.: Mobile application for customers' reviews opinion mining. In: 19th International Conference Enterprise and Competitive Environment 2016, vol. 220, pp. 373–381 (2016)
2. Review decision about the documents by the ratio of a review sentence by classifier a sentence review. Inf. Process. Soc. Jpn. **2012-NL-205**(2), 1–5 (2012)

3. Okada, M., Takeuchi, K., Hashimoto, K.: An investigation of an effectiveness of estimation sentence patterns for a classification of customer reviews considering their conditions. In: The 28th Annual Conference of the Japanese Society for Artificial Intelligence, vol. 28, pp. 1–3 (2014)
4. Kobayashi, T., Saitoh, F., Ishizu, S.: Important quality element and preference rule extraction in the case of competition among different types of products. In: The Japan Society for Management Information Autumn National Research Competition, pp. 331–334 (2015)
5. Sawada, H.: Nonnegative matrix factorization and its applications to data/signal analysis. Inst. Electron. Inf. Commun. Eng. **95**(9), 829–833 (2012)
6. Lee, D.D., Sebastian Seung, H.: Learning the parts of objects with nonnegative matrix factorization. Nature **401**, 788–791 (1999)
7. Takaya, N., Kumagae, Y., Ichikawa, Y., Sawada, H.: Adopting transfer learning towards item purchase prediction on web marketing. Int. J. Inform. Soc. **7**(1), 19–27 (2015)
8. Kamishima, T., Hamasaki, M., Akaho, S.: TrBagg: a simple transfer learning method and its application to personalization in collaborative tagging. In: Proceeding of the 9th IEEE International Conference on Data Mining, pp. 219–228 (2009)
9. Medhat, W., Hassan, A., Korashy, H.: Sentiment analysis algorithms and application: a survey. Ain Shams Eng. **5**, 1093–1113 (2014)
10. Kumagae, Y., Murata, M., Takaya, N., Uchiyama, T.: Transfer leaning for prediction of purchase items using multiple e-commerce sites' information. In: DEIM Forum 2012, C8–6 (2012)
11. Kotani, N.: Knowledge selection based on value in transfer learning. Inst. Syst. Control Inf. Eng. **28**(6), 275–283 (2015)
12. Kimura, K., Yoshida, T.: Topic graph based transfer learning via generalized KL divergence based NMF. Inf. Process. Soc. Jpn **2011-MPS-85**(3) (2011)
13. Asoh, H., Kobayashi, M., Kobayashi, I.: Transfer learning of language models based on combinatorial structure of topics. In: The 28th Annual Conference of the Japanese Society for Artificial Intelligence (2014)
14. Kamishima, T.: Transfer learning. Jpn. Soc. Artif. Intell. **25**(4), 1–9 (2010)
15. Fukumoto, S., Futcida, T.: Document classification by machine learning based on co-occurrence relations of words. Inf. Process. Soc. Jpn. **2014-DBS-160**(28) (2014)
16. Dai, W., Yang, Q., Xue, G.-R., Yu, Y.: Boosting for transfer learning. In: Proceedings of the 24th International Conference on Machine Learning, ICML 2007, pp. 193–200 (2007)

Numbers Speak Where Words Fail: Exploring the Effect of Online Consumer Reviews on Consumer Decision Making

Fei Liu[(⊠)]

Department of IT Management, Copenhagen Business School,
Copenhagen, Denmark
afl.itm@cbs.dk

Abstract. Consumers are increasingly relying on online consumer reviews (OCRs) to facilitate their decision making process as a credible source of information. This study seeks to explicate why consumers deem OCRs as helpful and how they make use of OCRs in their decision making process. By drawing on Simon's decision making model, this study posits that the two forms of OCRs (i.e., numerical ratings and opinionated reviews) facilitate consumers' decisional processes in terms of the effectiveness of constructing consideration sets and the efficiency of arriving at a final decision. Consumers' performance in decisional process in turn determines the justifiability of and the confidence in their decisional outcomes. To empirically test all the hypotheses proposed in this study, a field survey was conducted on users of a custom-developed online restaurant review website equipped with OCR curation features and populated with real restaurant review data. Except for two unexpected findings, all hypotheses were supported by the data analysis results. It is worth noting that, *numerical rating* exerts stronger positive influence on decisional process efficiency comparing to *opinionated review*. Furthermore, decisional outcome justifiability mediates the positive effects of both *decisional process effectiveness* and *decisional process efficiency* on *decisional outcome confidence*. This study contributes to both research and practice by offering a more in depth explanation to consumers' reliance on OCRs through the lens of bounded rationality and providing excitable guidelines for enhancing the benefits of OCRs via curation features.

Keywords: Online consumer review · Bounded rationality · Decisional process · Decisional outcome · Curation design

1 Introduction

Consumers are increasingly relying on online consumer reviews (OCRs) to facilitate their decision making process [4, 33]. According to Mudambi and Schuff [25], OCRs refer to comments generated by peer consumers on the basis of their evaluation on a pertinent product or service. Recognizing the salient role played by OCRs in steering consumers' purchase decision [29, 40], leading e-commerce sites, such as Amazon, have leveraged on OCRs to assist consumers' product evaluation [20] and to in turn

© Springer International Publishing AG 2017
F.F.-H. Nah and C.-H. Tan (Eds.): HCIBGO 2017, PART II, LNCS 10294, pp. 246–263, 2017.
DOI: 10.1007/978-3-319-58484-3_20

elicit consumers' trust in the sites [37]. The strength of OCRs resides in two aspects. First, OCRs supply timely and cost-free information regarding peer-consumers' experience with a product or service [11, 17, 38]. Consequently, approximately 92% of consumers seek advice from OCRs prior to making purchase decisions [5]. Second, OCRs are deemed more reliable and trustworthy compared to firm-generated information [15]. eMarketer [10] reported that more than 92% of consumers trust ORCs more than the product description provided by the manufacturers.

Prior literature has corroborated consumers' reliance on OCRs when making purchase intention by substantiating the connection between OCRs and product sales [6, 8, 41]. For instance, Chevalier and Mayzlin [6] uncovered that both *review volume* and *average review rating* contribute to boosting book sales. According to Clemons et al. [8], the valence of salient reviews is influential in promoting the sales of newly launched beers. Lastly, Yang and Mai's [41] work revealed that *review volume* drives up sales of video games due to consumers' tendency to adopt *review volume* as a heuristic for assessing the quality of a pertinent game. Intrigued by consumers' reliance on OCRs, more recent studies attempted to unravel the underlining characteristics of OCRs that evoke consumers' perceived *review helpfulness* [25]. Mudambi and Schuff's [25] seminal work gave impetus for this stream of research by exploring how product type moderates the influences of *review extremity* and *review depth* on *review helpfulness*. Subsequent studies extended the range of antecedents of review fullness by incorporating source-relevant characteristics, such as *reviewer credibility* and *reviewer expertise*, [19, 31, 43] in addition to the content-relevant characteristics accentuated by Mudambi and Schuff's [25]. The abovementioned findings are insightful in terms of distinguishing between more helpful OCRs and less helpful ones, yet are insufficient for explicating how OCRs are helpful in consumers' decision making process. This study hence aims to tackle this research gap by elucidating the role of OCRS in consumers' decisional process.

To achieve this research objective, this study subscribes to *Simon's bounded rationality* paradigm and adopts *Simon's decision making model* as a theoretical scaffold [35]. *Bounded rationality* posits that few human decision makers can live up to the *substantive rationality* assumed by the classical economic model of decision making [26]. Instead of insisting on obtaining the optimal decisional outcome, human decision makers rely on their decisional processes to establish their confidence in their decisional outcomes. This *procedural rationality* is a compromise made by human decision makers to cope with the constraints posed by their limited time, information, and cognitive capacities [26]. The prominent role of decision justifiability is further corroborated by *decision justification theory* [9], as justification helps to deter individuals from regretting their decisions. By integrating the paradigm of *bounded rationality* in the underexplored role of OCRS in consumer decisional process, the following two research questions emerge:

- How do consumers rely on OCRs in their decisional process?
- How do consumers justify their decisional outcomes on the basis of their decisional processes?

To better answer the abovementioned research questions, this study is situated in the context of online service selection (i.e., online restaurant selection) despite the predominant focus on online product selection in prior literature [42]. Unlike product, service is perishable and its intangible process is experiential in nature [16]. Consequently, the selection process is more complex, contains more ambiguity, and hence renders *bounded rationality* more salient. This study hence seeks to explicate how *bounded rationality* manifests in consumers' dependency on OCRs in online service selection process. Guided by *Simon's decision making model* [35], this study delineates between *numerical rating* and *opinionated review* of OCRs as two distinct information sources at the *intelligence* stage [21, 25]. Subsequently, this study articulates the roles of both forms of OCRs in facilitating the *effectiveness* of generating alternatives at the *design* stage and the *efficiency* of deciding on the most desirable alternative at the *choice* stage [35]. Last but not least, this study explains the impact of the decisional process on consumers' *justifiability* of and *confidence* in their decisional outcome [35].

2 Bounded Rationality and Decision Making Model

Simon proposed the paradigm of *bounded rationality* with the recognition that it is unrealistic to assume *substantive rationality* for human decision makers [26]. Decision making in the real world setting often involves uncertainties due to missing information [26]. Even with perfect information, limited time and cognitive capacities tend to prevent decision makers from exhausting all possible alternatives and seeking out the optimal outcomes [36]. Instead, human decision makers are governed by *procedural rationality*, meaning they justify the adequacy of their decisional outcome by their decisional process [26]. Munier et al. [26] applied computer simulations to prove that incorporating *bounded rationality* in their algorithm can lead to improved decision making performance in terms of accuracy and efficiency when missing information was involved.

With this premise, Simon put forward a model of decision making that consists of three distinct stages: *intelligence*, *design*, and *choice* [35]. At the *intelligence* stage, decision makers collect information to identify and formulate problems. The *design* stage resembles the process, in which decision makers devise and evaluate possible solutions to address the problems produced in the *intelligence* stage. Finally, decision makers arrive at a most satisfactory solution by comparing all possible alternatives against each other in the *choice* stage. This study subscribes to *Simon's decision making model* and puts forth a research model that describes how consumers take advantage of OCRs in their decisional processes. This research mode also articulates how consumers leverage on their decisional process to justify their decisional outcomes.

3 OCRs and Decisional Process

Numerical rating and *opinionated review* are two major constituent forms of OCRs [21, 25]. *Numerical rating* is an ordinal representation of a reviewer's attitude towards a product or service. Due to its concise nature, it allows consumers to make swift judgement [12] by facilitating categorical thinking [22]. *Opinionated review* takes the form of written comments that offer background information and logical reasoning behind a reviewer's assessment. It is cognitively more demanding and leaves room for personal interpretation [29, 30]. Thereby, on the basis of their examination of a piece of *opinionated review*, consumers may arrive at a conclusion that differs from the reviewer's opinion. Both *numerical rating* and *opinionated review* function as the key information sources in the *intelligence* stage that convey reviewers' experiences and judgements to consumers [35].

Both forms of OCRs are expected to facilitate consumers' decisional processes in the *design* stage [35]. The two-stage model of choice making corroborates that decision makers tend to include a sufficient amount of viable alternatives into their consideration set at the *design* stage before selecting the most satisficing alternative at the *choice* stage [3]. *Decisional process effectiveness* refers to the extent to which the decisional process is effective for consumers in evaluating a sufficient number of alternatives. *Decisional process effectiveness* hence corresponds to the adequacy of a consumer's consideration set at the *design* stage. On the other hand, *decisional process efficiency* represents the extent to which consumers are able to economize time and efforts in the decisional process to arrive at the final decision. Therefore, *decisional process efficiency* is an indicator of the speed with which consumers arrive at the most promising option from their consideration sets in the *choice* stage.

3.1 Decisional Process Effectiveness

The provision of *numerical rating* and *opinionated review* can heighten *decisional process effectiveness* since they allow consumers to identify viable alternatives to be included into their consideration sets. However, because *numerical rating* is devoid of qualitative attributes, consumers often steer away from viable alternatives due to mediocre ratings without considering the potential fit of their attributes. In contrast, *opinionated review* contains ample information about various attributes of each alternative, thus encouraging consumers to uncover alternatives that fit their own preferences [29, 30]. Accordingly, *opinionated review,* in comparison to *numerical rating,* is more conducive to expanding the variety and coverage of the pool of alternatives [3]. As a result, *opinionated review* is more beneficial than *numerical rating* in elevating *decisional process effectiveness* in the *design* stage. This study hence hypothesizes:

- **Hypothesis 1:** The provision of numerical rating positively influences consumers' perceived decisional process effectiveness.
- **Hypothesis 2:** The provision of opinionated review positively influences consumers' perceived decisional process effectiveness.
- **Hypothesis 3:** The provision opinionated review exerts a stronger positive influence on consumers' perceived decisional process effectiveness as compared to the provision of numerical rating.

3.2 Decisional Process Efficiency

Consumers' *decisional process efficiency* in the *choice* stage can be facilitated by the provision of *numerical rating* and *opinionated review*. Both forms of OCRs allow consumers to leverage on reviewers' judgments in order to expedite their comparisons among alternatives. The concise nature of *numerical rating* is especially suitable for discriminating among alternatives in an efficient manner [12, 25]. In comparison, relying on *opinionated review* to isolate the most desirable alternative is not as efficient. Specifically, evaluating the rich information available in *opinionated review* is more cognitively demanding. The increased complexity of considering multiple attributes renders the most desirable option less apparent, thus impeding the facilitating effect of *opinionated review* on *decisional process efficiency* in the *choice* stage. This study hence hypothesizes:

- **Hypothesis 4:** The provision of numerical rating positively influences consumers' perceived decisional process efficiency.
- **Hypothesis 5:** The provision of opinionated review positively influences consumers' perceived decisional process efficiency.
- **Hypothesis 6:** The provision numerical rating exerts a stronger positive influence on consumers' perceived decisional process efficiency as compared to the provision of opinionated review.

4 Decisional Process and Decisional Outcome

Consumers' performance in their decisional processes plays a pivotal role in the justification of their decisional outcomes. In accordance with *decision justification theory*, consumers have to overcome two obstacles to prevent regretting their decisions [9]. In particular, consumers justify their decisions with cognitive evaluations against certain criteria and establish confidence to counter the affective feeling of self-blame [9]. Guided by the *bounded rationality* paradigm, this study contends that *decisional process effectiveness* and *decisional process efficiency* contribute to countering the cognitive and affective components of decisional regret respectively.

4.1 Decisional Outcome Justifiability

Decisional outcome justifiability is defined as consumers' awareness of the thoughtful and comprehensive process through which they arrive at their decisions [32]. Prior studies attest to the connection between a carefully conducted decisional process and the *decisional outcome justifiability* [9, 32]. Conceivably, it is likely for *decisional process effectiveness* and *decisional process efficiency* to enhance *decisional outcome justifiability*. Specifically, *decisional process effectiveness* helps to bolster the evidential support to the comprehensiveness and accountability of the consideration set. Furthermore, *decisional process effectiveness* increases the number of counterfactuals that help to legitimize the final choice [32]. On the other hand, *decisional process efficiency* facilitates consumers' recollection of their heuristics and reasoning for arriving at the final choices, thus increasing the likelihood for consumers to regard their selections as intuitive and reasonable. This study hence hypothesizes:

- **Hypothesis 7:** Consumers' perceived decisional process effectiveness positively influences their perceived decisional outcome justifiability.
- **Hypothesis 8:** Consumers' perceived decisional process efficiency positively influences their perceived decisional outcome justifiability.

4.2 Decisional Outcome Confidence

Decisional outcome confidence captures consumers' feeling that their decisions are correct. The feeling of confidence suppresses the feeling of self-blame, which resembles the affective dimension of decisional regret [9]. Both *decisional process effectiveness* and *decisional process efficiency* are expected to strengthen consumers' *decisional outcome confidence*. For instance, since consumers often draw confidence in their final choices from the size and coverage of their consideration sets, *decisional process effectiveness* is expected to enhance consumers' *decisional outcome confidence*. In contrast, *decisional process efficiency* helps to evoke an impression that the process of arriving at the final decision was simple and straightforward. The resulting underestimation of the complexity of deciding on the most desirable choice can inflate consumers' confidence in their final decisions. This study hence hypothesizes:

- **Hypothesis 9:** Consumers' perceived decisional process effectiveness positively influences their perceived decisional outcome confidence.
- **Hypothesis 10:** Consumers' perceived decisional process efficiency positively influences their perceived decisional outcome confidence.

By conducting four consecutive experiments, Reb and Connelly [32] confirmed that *decisional outcome justifiability* can preemptively mitigate the likelihood of decision makers to regret their decisions. Along the same vein, *decisional outcome justifiability* can help to relieve consumers from the anxiety of being responsible for making undesirable decisions. Consequently, it is more likely for consumers to feel confident about their decisions when perceiving higher *decisional outcome justifiability*. This study hence hypothesizes:

- **Hypothesis 11:** Consumers' perceived decisional outcome justifiability positively influences their perceived decisional outcome confidence.

5 Methodology

To empirically validate the hypotheses proposed by this study, a field survey was conducted on a custom-developed online restaurant review site. To ensure the realism of this custom-developed site, its design was emulated after that of a leading online restaurant review sites, it is also populated with a real dataset that contains detailed descriptions of 1,079 restaurants in the San Francisco region together with about

268,000 reviews for these restaurants written by roughly 91,000 diners. Two OCR curation features are implemented for each restaurant to display both *numerical ratings* and *opinionated reviews*. The *numerical rating* curation feature depicts a histogram of the distribution of ratings as well as a trend line for the variation of average rating throughout the time. The *opinionated review* curation feature resembles a word cloud that summarizes the most prominent keywords in reviewers' written comments. This custom-developed site encourages participants to employ both forms of OCRs in their decisional processes and to facilitate the recollection of their decision making experience when answering the questionnaire.

5.1   Development of Survey Measures

Measurement items for *numerical rating, opinionated review, decisional process effectiveness*, and *decisional process efficiency* were newly developed in accordance with established psychometric procedures [24]. The measures for *decisional outcome justifiability* and *decisional outcome confidence* were developed by extending existing instruments [32]. Table 1 summarizes all measurement instruments developed for this study.

5.2   Field Survey Administration

At the beginning of each survey session, respondents were asked to report their demographic backgrounds. They were then directed to the online review website and instructed to conduct two restaurant selection tasks. The first task is goal-oriented and respondents were offered well-structured criteria for the targeted restaurants whereas the second task is exploratory hence granting respondents the freedom to select a restaurant according to their own preference [2, 27]. The scenarios of both tasks are presented in Table 2. Respondents were asked to make their decisions basing on the *numerical ratings* and *opinionated reviews* curated for each restaurant. Upon the completion of both tasks, respondents were brought back to an online survey questionnaire that measures their dispositions pertaining to the provision of *numerical rating* and *opinionated review*, the effectiveness and efficiency of their decisional processes, as well as the justifiability of and confidence in their decisional outcomes. 170 undergraduate students from a large university in the United States were recruited for this field survey. The demographics of this sample are presented in Table 3.

5.3   Model Testing

This study evaluated both the measurement model and the structural model by employing Partial Least Square (SmartPLS 2.0 M3) [7]. Partial least squares (PLS) analysis is more preferable than other analytical methods since this study seeks to simultaneously analyze the psychometric properties of the measures (i.e., the measurement model) as well as the coefficients of the hypothesized nomological network (i.e., the structural model) [39].

Table 1. Instrument and measurement properties for reflective measures [Sample N = 170]

Construct	Definition	Reflective measures [7-point Likert scale]	Mean (S.D.)	Item loading
Numerical Rating (NR)	Extent to which a consumer believes that numerical ratings are provided for each product or service featured on the online review website	The online review website provides **numerical ratings** assigned by other consumers for each restaurant featured on the site	5.65 (1.27)	0.82
		The online review website provides **numerical scores** assigned by other consumers for each restaurant featured on the site	5.26 (1.44)	0.92
		The online review website provides **numerical values** assigned by other consumers for each restaurant featured on the site	5.20 (1.45)	0.87
Opinionated Review (OR)	Extent to which a consumer believes that opinionated reviews are provided for each product or service featured on the online review website	The online review website provides **other consumers' comments** for each restaurant featured on the site	6.02 (1.16)	0.85
		The online review website provides **other consumers' feedback** for each restaurant featured on the site	5.93 (1.10)	0.86
		The online review website provides **other consumers' impressions** for each restaurant featured on the site	5.95 (1.10)	0.90
		The online review website provides **other consumers' opinions** for each restaurant featured on the site	5.90 (1.15)	0.93
		The online review website provides **other consumers' views** for each restaurant featured on the site	5.92 (1.12)	0.90
Decisional Process Effectiveness (PE)	Extent to which the decisional process is effective for consumers in evaluating a sufficient number of alternatives	Reviews provided via the online review website allow me to assess an **acceptable number of restaurants** when deciding on which restaurant to visit	5.56 (1.21)	0.96
		Reviews provided via the online review website allow me to **evaluate an**	5.48 (1.18)	0.95

(*continued*)

Table 1. (*continued*)

Construct	Definition	Reflective measures [7-point Likert scale]	Mean (S.D.)	Item loading
		appropriate number of restaurants when deciding on which restaurant to visit		
		Reviews provided via the online review website allow me to **go through a reasonable number of restaurants** when deciding on which restaurant to visit	5.54 (1.17)	0.95
Decisional Process Efficiency (PI)	Extent to which consumers expend less time and efforts in the decisional process to arrive at the final decision	The **process of deciding** on which restaurant to visit is **efficient** based on reviews provided via the online review website	5.32 (1.36)	0.88
		The **process of deciding** on which restaurant to visit is **fast** based on reviews provided via the online review website	5.12 (1.49)	0.94
		The **process of deciding** on which restaurant to visit is **free of hassle** based on reviews provided via the online review website	4.94 (1.50)	0.91
		The **process of deciding** on which restaurant to visit is **effortless** based on reviews provided via the online review website	4.75 (1.50)	0.91
Decisional Outcome Justifiability (OJ)	Extent to which consumers are aware of the thoughtful and comprehensive process through which they arrive at their decisions	I am **clear about how** I arrive at my decision about which restaurant to visit based on reviews provided via the online review website	5.60 (1.14)	0.92
		I can **explain to others how** I arrive at my decision about which restaurant to visit based on reviews provided via the online review website	5.55 (1.32)	0.94
		I can **justify to others** how I arrive at my decision about which restaurant to visit based on reviews provided via the online review website	5.59 (1.20)	0.95

(*continued*)

Table 1. (*continued*)

Construct	Definition	Reflective measures [7-point Likert scale]	Mean (S.D.)	Item loading
		I can **understand how** I arrive at my decision about which restaurant to visit based on reviews provided via the online review website	5.65 (1.21)	0.95
Decisional Outcome Confidence (OC)	Extent to which consumers feel that their decisions are correct	I am **certain** that I have made the **right decision** about which restaurant to visit based on reviews provided via the online review website	5.04 (1.40)	0.94
		I am **confident** that I have made the **right decision** about which restaurant to visit based on reviews provided via the online review website	5.04 (1.42)	0.97
		I am **sure** that I have made the **right decision** about which restaurant to visit based on reviews provided via the online review website	4.96 (1.43)	0.96

Measurement Model. This study assessed the measurement model by evaluating internal consistency, as well as the convergent and discriminant validity of all focal constructs in our survey instrument. To ensure internal consistency, the reliability of each individual measurement item was examined by its loading on the corresponding construct. As shown in Table 1, all loadings exceed 0.7, indicating good item reliability. Additionally, construct reliability indexes, including Cronbach's alpha, composite

Table 2. Restaurant selection tasks

Task 1: Find a restaurant for your friend's birthday dinner

Scenario: You are planning to visit your best friend, Peter, who lives in the Russian Hill area of San Francisco and likes New American food, next Saturday. Peter will be having his birthday on the same day. You plan to surprise Peter during your visit by bringing him to a nice New American restaurant to celebrate his birthday.

Because you are unfamiliar with the area around Russian Hill, you decide to turn to TasteSF, a newly set up online review website for restaurants in San Francisco, to choose an American (NEW) restaurant in the Russian Hill area.

Task 2: Find a restaurant for yourself

You are taking a trip to San Francisco next Saturday. You would like to enjoy a meal alone in a nice restaurant. Because you are unfamiliar with San Francisco, you decide to turn to TasteSF, a newly set up online review website for restaurants in San Francisco, to choose a restaurant you prefer.

Table 3. Sample demographics [Sample N = 170]

Demographic		No. Respondents	Percentage
Gender	Male	88	51.8%
	Female	82	48.2%
Age	Age 12 to 18	3	1.8%
	Age 19 to 29	153	90.0%
	Age 30 to 49	13	7.6%
	Age 60+	1	0.6%
Education	Less than college education	20	11.8%
	College education or higher	149	87.6%
	Unwilling to disclose	1	0.6%
Income	$0 to $30,000	140	82.4%
	$30,000+ to $50,000	9	5.3%
	$50,000+ to $75,000	4	2.4%
	$75,000+	2	1.2%
	Unwilling to disclose	15	8.8%

reliability and the Average Variance Extracted (AVE) were assessed [13, 28]. Results illustrated in Table 4 indicate that all aforementioned indictors exceed suggested thresholds, suggesting good internal consistency. Subsequently, the square root of AVE of every construct in the measurement model was found to be greater than the correlations of each construct with other constructs (see Table 4). Furthermore, according to the loading and cross-loading matrix depicted in Table 5, no measurement item loads higher on a construct than on the one it intends to measure. Therefore, the results presented above resemble strong evidences of convergent validity and discriminate validity.

Structural Model. The nomological network of the structure model is illustrated in Fig. 1. The estimated coefficients substantiate the positive relationships between *numerical rating* ($\beta_1 = 0.220$, $t = 4.866$) as well as *opinionated review* ($\beta_2 = 0.210$, $t = 4.582$) and *decisional process effectiveness*, hence supporting Hypothesis 1 and 2. Likewise, the positive influences induced by *numerical rating* ($\beta_4 = 0.354$, $t = 6.489$) and *opinionated review* ($\beta_5 = 0.156$, $t = 3.094$) are validated, thus supporting Hypothesis 4 and 5. Hypothesis 7 and 8 are supported because both *decisional process effectiveness* ($\beta_7 = 0.220$, $t = 3.513$) and *decisional process efficiency* ($\beta_8 = 0.466$, $t = 7.449$) pose positive effects on *decisional outcome justifiability*. *Decisional process efficiency* ($\beta_{10} = 0.473$, $t = 9.025$) also exerts positive influence on *decisional outcome confidence* whereas *decisional process effectiveness* ($\beta_9 = 0.003$, $t = 0.096$) does not, therefore only supporting Hypothesis 10. Lastly, Hypothesis 11 is supported by the

Table 4. Internal consistencies and inter-construct correlation matrix [Sample N = 170]

Construct	Cronbach's α [> 0.70]	CR [> 0.70]	AVE [>0.50]	NR	OR	PE	PI	OJ	OC
Numerical Rating (NR)	0.84	0.90	0.76	**0.87**					
Opinionated Review (OR)	0.93	0.95	0.79	0.44	**0.89**				
Decisional Process Effectiveness (PE)	0.95	0.97	0.91	0.31	0.31	**0.95**			
Decisional Process Efficiency (PI)	0.93	0.95	0.83	0.42	0.31	0.64	**0.91**		
Decisional Outcome Justifiability (OJ)	0.96	0.97	0.88	0.22	0.37	0.52	0.61	**0.94**	
Decisional Outcome Confidence (OC)	0.96	0.97	0.92	0.28	0.23	0.50	0.70	0.66	**0.96**

Table 5. Loading and cross-loading matrix [Sample N = 170]

Items	NR	OR	DPE	DPI	DOJ	DOC
NR1	**0.82**	0.49	0.35	0.36	0.25	0.23
NR2	**0.92**	0.32	0.25	0.34	0.15	0.27
NR3	**0.87**	0.32	0.20	0.40	0.16	0.22
OR1	0.45	**0.85**	0.25	0.22	0.25	0.16
OR2	0.39	**0.86**	0.23	0.27	0.28	0.17
OR3	0.39	**0.90**	0.27	0.27	0.35	0.21
OR4	0.36	**0.93**	0.29	0.29	0.38	0.23
OR5	0.38	**0.90**	0.31	0.33	0.37	0.23
DPE1	0.35	0.29	**0.96**	0.64	0.48	0.48
DPE2	0.27	0.30	**0.95**	0.61	0.51	0.51
DPE3	0.28	0.29	**0.95**	0.59	0.50	0.44
DPI1	0.38	0.31	0.66	**0.88**	0.60	0.61
DPI2	0.39	0.32	0.62	**0.94**	0.61	0.65
DPI3	0.36	0.27	0.56	**0.91**	0.49	0.65
DPI4	0.42	0.23	0.50	**0.90**	0.50	0.64
DOJ1	0.25	0.35	0.54	0.63	**0.92**	0.65
DOJ2	0.19	0.32	0.44	0.57	**0.94**	0.61
DOJ3	0.20	0.35	0.49	0.54	**0.95**	0.61
DOJ4	0.19	0.38	0.48	0.54	**0.95**	0.61
DOC1	0.28	0.21	0.46	0.65	0.59	**0.94**
DOC2	0.27	0.23	0.49	0.68	0.65	**0.97**
DOC3	0.25	0.21	0.49	0.69	0.66	**0.96**

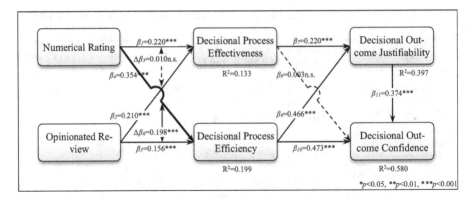

Fig. 1. The resulting structural model [N = 170]

significant positive relationship between decisional outcome justifiability and decisional outcome confidence (β_{11} = 0.374, t = 6.993). The unsupported Hypothesis 9 implies that eliciting a sufficient number of alternatives in the consideration set does not ensure consumers' confidence in their final choices.

With regard to the comparative hypotheses, Hypothesis 3 is not supported since the path coefficient between *numerical rating* and *decisional process effectiveness* does not differ significantly from that between *opinionated review* and *decisional process effectiveness* ($\Delta\beta3$ = 0.010, t = 0.227). Surprisingly, *numerical rating* contributes equally to boosting decisional process effectiveness probably because it helps consumers to exclude undesirable alternatives from their consideration sets [18, 37]. Nonetheless, Hypothesis 6 is supported by the significant difference between the positive effect imposed by numerical rating and that imposed by opinionated review on decisional process efficiency ($\Delta\beta6$ = 0.198, t = 3.841).

Because the dataset in this study was collected via a single survey questionnaire, common method bias could be a potential threat to the internal validity of this study. To mitigate the concern for common method bias, this study conducted the one-factor extraction test [14] by performing exploratory factor analysis (EFA) on 22 variables. Five salient components with eigenvalues greater than 1.00 were extracted with no single factor accounting for more than 50% of the total variance explained [34], suggesting that it is unlikely for common method bias to erode the validity of data analysis results in this study.

Mediation Analysis. Following standard guidelines [1], mediation analysis was performed to evaluate all mediating effects existing in the nomological network. Table 6 summarizes the results of mediation analysis. For a mediating effect to hold, coefficients in the independent paths column must be significant. Moreover, when the path from IV to the mediator as well as the path from the mediator to the dependent variable (DV) are controlled, the path coefficient from IV to DV should decrease in both magnitude and significance [1]. If the path coefficient from IV to DV becomes non-significant, the mediating effect can be interpreted as a full mediation. Otherwise, it should be interpreted as a partial mediation. The results in Table 6 illustrate that both *decisional process effectiveness* and *decisional process efficiency* fully mediate the positive influence of *numerical rating* but partially mediate that of *opinionated review* on *decisional outcome justifiability*. The unexpected direct impact of *opinionated review* on *decisional outcome justifiability* can be explained by the reasoning and logics available in written comments, which offer extra means for consumers to justify their final selections. *Decisional process efficiency* fully mediates the positive effects induced by both numerical rating and opinionated review on *decisional outcome confidence*. Finally, *decisional outcome justifiability* fully mediates the positive relationship between *decisional process effectiveness* and *decisional outcome confidence*.

Table 6. Results of mediation analysis

Relationship	IV: NR		Relationship	IV: OR	
	Independent Paths	Full Model		Independent Paths	Full Model
NR → PE	0.220***	0.220***	OR → PE	0.210***	0.210***
PE → OJ	0.220***	0.223***	PE → OJ	0.220***	0.187***
NR → OJ	0.220***	-0.057 n.s.	OR → OJ	0.377***	0.183***
Full Mediation			**Partial Mediation**		
PE → OC	0.003 n.s.	0.003 n.s.	PE → OC	0.003 n.s.	0.011 n.s.
NR → OC	0.280***	-0.005 n.s.	OR → OC	0.229***	-0.072 n.s.
No Mediation			**No Mediation**		
NR → PI	0.354***	0.353***	OR → PI	0.156***	0.157***
PI → OJ	0.466***	0.488***	PI → OJ	0.466***	0.430***
NR → OJ	0.220***	-0.057 n.s.	OR → OJ	0.377***	0.183***
Full Mediation			**Partial Mediation**		
PI → OC	0.473***	0.475***	PI → OC	0.473***	0.478***
NR → OC	0.280***	-0.005 n.s.	OR → OC	0.229***	-0.072 n.s.
Full Mediation			**Full Mediation**		
Relationship	IV: PE		Note: IV: Independent Variable, NR: Numerical Rating, OR: Opinionated Review, PE: Decisional Process Effectiveness, PI: Decisional Process Efficiency, OJ: Decisional Outcome Justifiability, OC: Decisional Outcome Confidence.		
	Independent Paths	Full Model			
PE → OJ	0.216***	0.220***			
OJ → OC	0.374***	0.374***			
PE → OC	0.501***	0.003 n.s.			
Full Mediation					

6 Discussion

Adhering to the *bounded rationality* paradigm and *Simon's decision making model* [35], this study advances a research model to explicate how consumers take advantage of OCRs in their decision making process. Empirical evidence proves that curating both numerical and textual components of OCRs can improve both the *effectiveness* regarding eliciting an adequate consideration set and the *efficiency* in terms of deciding on the most desirable option of consumers' decisional processes. Moreover, results show that both *decisional process effectiveness* and *decisional process efficiency* help consumers to justify their decisional outcomes which in turn strengthens the consumers' confidence in their own decisions. Results did not establish a connection between *decisional process efficiency* and *decisional outcome confidence*. This study hence identifies consumers' *procedural rationality* as the key to their reliance on OCRs when evaluating and selecting services online [26].

6.1 Implications for Research

This study seeks to contribute to extant literature in OCRs on multiple fronts. First, this study is among the first that examines consumers' reliance on OCRs from the perspective of *Simon's decision making model* [35]. This theoretical lens compels this study to unravel the role played by OCRs in facilitating consumers' decision making process, and to help them in justifying the adequacy of the decisional outcome. Second, this study delineates between the *numerical rating* and *opinionated review* of OCRs and uncovers their distinct effects on consumers' decision making process. In particular, *numerical rating* prevents consumers from including undesirable alternatives into their consideration sets [18, 37] whereas *opinionated review* allows users to extend the size and diversity of their consideration sets by supplying rich information. Additionally, *numerical rating,* as compared to *opinioned review*, is more effective in expediting the process of arriving at the most desirable option in the pool of viable alternatives while the latter can pose direct impact on consumers' decisional outcome justifiability by exposing them to reviewers' reasoning and arguments. Third, this study helps to decipher how consumers depend on their decisional process to justify their decisional outcomes and to develop confidence in their decisions. Governed by *procedure rationality,* consumers would justify their decisional outcomes by drawing upon *decisional process effectiveness,* which indicates whether a sufficient amount of alternatives was included in the consideration set, and *decisional process efficiency,* which reflects whether the process of making the final choice was intuitive and reasonable. In line with *decision justification theory* [9], consumers derive confidence in their decisional outcomes from *decisional outcome justifiability*. However, the positive relationship between *decisional process efficiency* and *decisional outcome confidence* implies that consumers are likely to perceive a decision to be less difficult and are thus more confident in their decisions, if the decision making process was quick and effortless.

6.2 Implications for Practice

Practitioners who seek to make use of OCRs can also derive implications from the findings of this study. First, this study helps to draw practitioners' attention to one of the main values of OCRs, which is to help consumers justify their decisions. Consequently, this study encourages practitioners to better utilize OCRs to reassure consumers of their decisions. Second, this study can serve as an example in the employment of curation features to boost the benefits of OCRs with the objective of facilitating consumers' decision making process. For instance, *numerical rating curation features* can be implemented to highlight the underlining patterns in reviewers' ratings in the forms of histograms and trend lines. In addition, *opinionated review curation features* can be designed to extract recurring themes and sentiments from reviewers' written comments and present them in the form of review highlights or word clouds. This study further suggests that practitioners should prioritize curating *numerical ratings* over *opinionated reviews* as the former is more effective, as compared to the latter, in heightening *decisional process efficiency* while offering comparable utility in facilitating *decisional process effectiveness*.

6.3 Limitations and Future Research Directions

This study faces a number of limitations. First, the empirical investigation of this study was situated in the context of an online service selection. Due to the prevalent uncertainty in online service evaluation, such a context is more preferable for investigating consumer' *bounded rationality*. Nonetheless, caution should be exercised when generalizing the findings in this study to the context of online product selection. Second, the sample of this study comprises largely of undergraduate students. Although student sample is adequate for studying phenomena pertaining to the use of OCRs [23], future studies can bolster their external validity by utilizing a more diverse sample. Third, spurious causality inferences may exist due to the cross-sectional nature of field survey, which is the main research method of this study.

References

1. Baron, R.M., Kenny, D.A.: The moderator–mediator variable distinction in social psychological research: conceptual, strategic, and statistical considerations. J. Pers. Soc. Psychol. **51**(6), 1173–1182 (1986)
2. Browne, G.J., et al.: Cognitive stopping rules for terminating information search in online tasks. MIS Q. **31**(1), 89–104 (2007)
3. Browne, G.J., Pitts, M.G.: Stopping rule use during information search in design problems. Organ. Behav. Hum. Decis. Process. **95**(2), 208–224 (2004)
4. Cao, Q., et al.: Exploring determinants of voting for the "helpfulness" of online user reviews: A text mining approach. Decis. Support Syst. **50**(2), 511–521 (2011)
5. ChannelAdvisor: Through the Eyes of the Consumer: 2010 Consumer Shopping Habits Survey (2010)

6. Chevalier, J.A., Mayzlin, D.: The effect of word of mouth on sales: Online book reviews. J. Mark. Res. **43**(3), 345–354 (2006)
7. Chin, W.W.: Commentary: Issues and opinion on structural equation modeling. MIS Q. **22**(1), vii–xvi (1998)
8. Clemons, E.K., et al.: When online reviews meet hyperdifferentiation: A study of the craft beer industry. J. Manag. Inf. Syst. **23**(2), 149–171 (2006)
9. Connolly, T., Zeelenberg, M.: Regret in decision making. Curr. Dir. Psychol. Sci. **11**(6), 212–216 (2002)
10. eMarketer: Moms Place Trust in Other Consumers. http://www.emarketer.com/Article/Moms-Place-Trust-Other-Consumers/1007509
11. Ertimur, B., Gilly, M.C.: So whaddya think? Consumers create ads and other consumers critique them. J. Interact. Mark. **26**(3), 115–130 (2012)
12. Fiske, S.T., Taylor, S.E.: Social Cognition: From Brains to Culture. Sage, Los Angeles (2013)
13. Fornell, C., Larcker, D.F.: Evaluating structural equation models with unobservable variables and measurement error. J. Mark. Res. **18**(1), 39–50 (1981)
14. Harman, H.H.: Modern Factor Analysis. University of Chicago Press, Chicago (1976)
15. Jabr, W., Zheng, E.: Know yourself and know your enemy: An analysis of firm recommendations and consumer reviews in a competitive environment. MIS Q. **38**(3), 635–654 (2014)
16. Kahn, B.K., et al.: Information quality benchmarks: Product and service performance. Commun. ACM **45**(4), 184–192 (2002)
17. Lawrence, B., et al.: When companies don't make the Ad: A multi-method inquiry into the differential effectiveness of consumer-generated advertising. J. Advert. **42**(4), 292–307 (2013)
18. Lee, M., et al.: Effects of valence and extremity of eWOM on attitude toward the brand and website. J. Curr. Issues Res. Advert. **31**(2), 1–11 (2009)
19. Li, M., et al.: Helpfulness of online product reviews as seen by consumers: Source and content features. Int. J. Electron. Commer. **17**(4), 101–136 (2013)
20. Lim, B.C., Chung, C.M.Y.: The impact of word-of-mouth communication on attribute evaluation. J. Bus. Res. **64**(1), 18–23 (2011)
21. Liu, F. et al.: Deciphering individuals' preference for user generated content: effects of personality on users' processing of online review information. In: Proceedings of the 36th International Conference on Information Systems (ICIS 2015), Fort Worth, Texas, 13–16 December (2015)
22. Macrae, C.N., Bodenhausen, G.V.: Social cognition: Categorical person perception. Br. J. Psychol. **92**(1), 239–255 (2001)
23. McKnight, D.H., et al.: Developing and validating trust measures for e-commerce: an integrative typology. Inf. Syst. Res. **13**(3), 334–359 (2002)
24. Moore, G., Benbasat, I.: Development of an instrument to measure the perceptions of adopting an information technology innovation. Inf. Syst. Res. **2**(3), 192–222 (1991)
25. Mudambi, S.M., Schuff, D.: What makes a helpful online review? a study of customer reviews on amazon.com. MIS Q. **34**(1), 185–200 (2010)
26. Munier, B., et al.: Bounded rationality modeling. Mark. Lett. **10**(3), 233–248 (1999)
27. Nadkarni, S., Gupta, R.: A task-based model of web site complexity. MIS Q. **31**(3), 501–524 (2007)
28. Nunnally, J.C., Bernstein, I.H.: Psychometric Theory. McGraw-Hill, New York (1994)
29. Park, D.H., Kim, S.: The effects of consumer knowledge on message processing of electronic word-of-mouth via online consumer reviews. Electron. Commer. Res. Appl. **7**(4), 399–410 (2008)

30. Park, D.H., Lee, J.: eWOM overload and its effect on consumer behavioral intention depending on consumer involvement. Electron. Commer. Res. Appl. **7**(4), 386–398 (2008)
31. Racherla, P., et al.: Factors affecting consumers' trust in online product reviews. J. Consum. Behav. **11**(2), 94–104 (2012)
32. Reb, J., Connolly, T.: The effects of action, normality, and decision carefulness on anticipated regret: Evidence for a broad mediating role of decision justifiability. Cogn. Emot. **24**(8), 1405–1420 (2010)
33. Salehan, M., Kim, D.J.: Predicting the performance of online consumer reviews: A sentiment mining approach to big data analytics. Decis. Support Syst. **81**, 30–40 (2016)
34. Schriesheim, C.A.: The similarity of individual directed and group directed leader behavior descriptions. Acad. Manag. J. **22**(2), 345–355 (1979)
35. Simon, H.A.: Rational decision making in business organizations. Am. Econ. Rev. **69**, 493–513 (1979)
36. Simon, H.A.: The information-processing theory of mind. Am. Psychol. **50**(7), 507–508 (1995)
37. Sparks, B.A., Browning, V.: The impact of online reviews on hotel booking intentions and perception of trust. Tour. Manag. **32**(6), 1310–1323 (2011)
38. Thompson, D.V., Malaviya, P.: Consumer-generated Ads: Does awareness of advertising co-creation help or hurt persuasion? J. Mark. **77**(3), 33–47 (2013)
39. Wixom, B.B.H., Watson, H.J.: An empirical investigation of the factors affecting data warehousing success. MIS Q. **25**(1), 17–41 (2001)
40. Xia, L., Bechwati, N.N.: Word of mouse: The role of cognitive personalization in online consumer reviews. J. Interact. Advert. **9**(1), 3–13 (2008)
41. Yang, J., Mai, E.S.: Experiential goods with network externalities effects: An empirical study of online rating system. J. Bus. Res. **63**(9), 1050–1057 (2010)
42. Zadeh, L.A. et al.: Fuzzy sets and their applications to cognitive and decision processes. In: Proceedings of the US–Japan Seminar on Fuzzy Sets and Their Applications, Held at the University of California, Berkeley, California, 1–4 July 1974. Academic Press (2014)
43. Zhu, L., et al.: Is this opinion leader's review useful? Peripheral cues for online review helpfulness. J. Electron. Commer. Res. **15**(4), 267–280 (2014)

Social Presence and Dishonesty: Perceptions from Security Guards

Susan Siebenaler[1], Andrea Szymkowiak[1(✉)], Paul Robertson[1],
Graham Johnson[2], and Jan Law[1]

[1] Abertay University, Dundee, UK
{0804355, a.szymkowiak, p.robertson,
j.law}@abertay.ac.uk
[2] NCR, Dundee, UK
graham.johnson@ncr.com

Abstract. Self-service technologies within retail enable customers to scan, bag and pay for their items independent from staff involvement. The use of self-service, due to its nature of reducing social interaction between customers and staff, has been implicated in creating opportunities for thefts to occur. However, the perception of social presence, such as induced by surveillance, induces customers to show more prosocial behavior. As security personnel are at the forefront to deal with dishonest customers, we conducted semi-structured interviews with security guards in two major supermarkets in the UK to assess factors surrounding theft, with a view to identify operational or technological opportunities to address theft. Our findings show that the perceived motivational and situational factors contributing to theft are complex. We conclude that surveillance in its current form does not appear to provide a sufficient social presence to prevent potential theft at self-service checkouts (SCOs). Future research could focus on additional surveillance measures to induce social presence, such as technological implementations in the SCO itself.

Keywords: Self-service · Social presence · Surveillance · Retail

1 Introduction

Self-service technologies have been increasingly adopted over the past two decades, and include self-service kiosks within airports, hotels, retailers, cinemas and, more recently, fast-food restaurants. The main driver for this is to offer speed and convenience to the consumer. Within retail, self-service checkouts (SCOs, see Fig. 1) enable customers to scan, bag and pay for their items, often without assistance from staff. For convenience, SCOs are usually located near to the shop exit, as their use typically represents the completion of a customer's shopping.

Retail staff involvement at the SCO area is limited to assisting customers, for example, to approve the purchase of age restricted items, such as alcohol, or to help with any technological issues. The effects of this overall lack of interaction with a member of staff (social presence) at SCOs is of growing interest to criminology and consumer behavior researchers, as it opens new avenues of conduct for customers [7, 17].

© Springer International Publishing AG 2017
F.F.-H. Nah and C.-H. Tan (Eds.): HCIBGO 2017, PART II, LNCS 10294, pp. 264–281, 2017.
DOI: 10.1007/978-3-319-58484-3_21

Leading theories from social psychology have previously influenced the social setting within a retail environment from opportunities of interaction with staff to awareness of security to the proximity to other customers [20, 29, 34, 36, 38]. However, the introduction of technology to the retail sector has been implicated as creating opportunities for theft [7]. Nevertheless, there is little research available regarding the prevalence of theft or shrinkage in stores who adopt self-service compared to those that do not [9], and many companies do not share their findings [7, 9]. However, a recent survey [23] has shown that stores that use SCO are more likely to experience theft than those that do not. Given the increase in the use of self-service technology globally, the benefits of self-service far outweigh its costs. At the same time, and for the benefit of retailers, there is a need to understand potentially novel forms of dishonest behavior arising from the use of new technology.

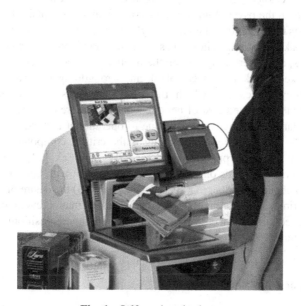

Fig. 1. Self-service checkout

The aim of the current study was to explore the current scenarios of dishonest retail customer behaviors at self-service, and to identify opportunities that may arise from these scenarios to address shrinkage. As it was not feasible within our field study to interview dishonest customers in relation to thefts at SCO, store security guards were interviewed with regard to their perceptions of customer dishonesty at SCOs. As security guards have the means (and role) to monitor dishonest customer behavior in detail, either in person or via closed-circuit television (CCTV), their perceptions and insights can provide valuable information on the factors surrounding theft at SCOs, with a view to identifying approaches to combat customer dishonesty. In the following sections, we will briefly review the research on customer dishonesty, the effects of surveillance and social presence, followed by a description of our study.

1.1 Customer Theft

Recent estimates suggest that customer theft accounts for 35% and internal theft for 33% of shrinkage, with process failures and inter-company fraud making up the remaining 32% [7]. The figures appear favorable or even stable, compared with earlier estimates reported in 2004 [4] of 48% (Europe) and 31% (US) shrinkage attributed to customers, and 40% in 2002 [21] and 1984 [6], respectively. Figures may vary across the years and more widely by country [4], however, it appears reasonable to suggest that shrinkage has been and continues to be an ongoing challenge for retailers. This is also reflected in the earlier estimate that as many as 60% of customers have said that they have shoplifted at some point in their lives [25, 26]. There is an ongoing need to investigate and address underlying factors for shrinkage, and explanations may be sought from theories in criminology.

The Rational Choice perspective [14] focuses on contextual factors and decision making, rather than the psychological profiles of offenders to explain the motivation of crime. It suggests that potential offenders weigh up the costs and benefits of committing a crime, and make a rational choice based on the dominance of one factor. In the context of SCOs, customers weighing up the likelihood of being detected stealing may be inclined to take the risk, as they can blame any wrongdoing as a fault of the machine or process if they are caught, which Beck [7] defines as the "self-scan defence" (p. 212). Thus, the perceived cost of being caught may be reduced as the system may potentially be blamed for any 'mistakes' due to operational factors.

Extending the idea that decision making is the critical component in committing crime, the Crime Triangle put forward by Clarke and Eck [13] suggests that the occurrence of a crime depends on three factors: (1) a target with opportunity available, (2) the ability to obtain a product in a specific place, and (3) the desire of the offender to complete the crime. Eliminating one of these factors may prevent the crime. For example, increased surveillance, security tags, and employee positioning can address available opportunity.

1.2 Surveillance and Social Presence

There has been an increasing number of surveillance measures to reduce crime within retail over the past few decades [37], indicating that theft continues to be an ongoing issue. Historically, counteracting theft in retail has been addressed by introducing a social presence in a variety of ways including formal surveillance, e.g., CCTV, the presence of security guards and staff, or informal surveillance, such as mirrors or lights, to maximize visibility and encourage positive social interaction [31]. The importance of surveillance is also evidenced by the finding that shoplifters themselves perceive formal surveillance as one of the biggest deterrents for stealing [12].

Social presence

The presence of others influences our behavior in everyday activities. Social presence has been defined as the perception of another real or imagined being or psychological involvement with something or someone in mediated communication [11, 32], but definitions vary [28]. In the context of this study we use the definition of social presence in the widest sense as the perception of another. Social presence induces individuals to alter their behavior to give a positive impression [31] or increases self-awareness linked with prosocial behaviors [30]. The presence of others, such as other customers, even if we do not interact with them, may still influence our behavior [2, 19] and may influence decision making in a retail context [1]. Social presence can also be introduced by virtual characters or embodied agents (as co-presence) [e.g., 3] affecting human behavior. Thus, we would expect that the perception of a social presence on the part of a customer – even in the absence of direct interaction with staff - would increase the likelihood of honest behaviors to some extent.

Social presence - or its absence - may be relevant from two perspectives for the current study. Firstly, to the extent that customers may perceive a reduced social presence at a SCO itself due to limited staff interactions, the likelihood for prosocial behavior may decrease, resulting in a higher likelihood of dishonest behaviors.

Second, as already mentioned, historically, social presence has also been induced by the introduction of formal surveillance, such as CCT and security guards, which may affect customer behavior. However, research finding are often inconclusive with respect to the effectiveness of formal surveillance to affect crime [15].

CCTV

Formal surveillance, such as represented by CCTV and store security guards, have been popular methods used to deter thefts for many years and are seen to be effective by managers [24]. However, Beck and Willis [10] argued that customers may have become inured [8] to traditional CCTV and it may no longer be an effective measure of theft prevention, although it may still be useful for confirmation of a suspected theft. As intentional shoplifters perceive formal surveillance as a major deterrent, they are highly intent on avoiding it [12], giving credence to its effectiveness; if CCTV can be avoided though, its efficiency as a deterrent will naturally be impaired.

Security guards

Security guards are the most widespread and recognizable form of surveillance to prevent crime in public places [33]. Kajalo and Lindblom [24] reported that security managers perceive the use of store security guards to be the most effective formal surveillance method.

The effectiveness of the use of security guards as a social presence in crime prevention has been explored in previous research [37], however, their effectiveness after the implementation of self-service technologies has not yet been fully evaluated.

As security guards are a vital element of store security, this research considers their perceptions of customers and their role in relation to customer theft at self-service checkouts. We were particularly interested in how security guards perceive customer behavior surrounding theft, how supported security guards feel in their ability to supervise checkouts, and their thoughts on technological implementations to support their role. The findings from the research may enhance knowledge of the nature of dishonest behavior at SCOs, and inform technological or operational opportunities. This knowledge may ultimately lead to the identification of measures that can support security and store staff in their role and reduce shrinkage for retailers.

2 Method

2.1 Participants

Six security guards (five males and one female) from two major UK supermarkets participating in the study were interviewed on the store premises. Four of the security guards were located at one store and two at the other. Their experience in security ranged from 12 months to 21 years and their ages varied between 23 and 46 years.

2.2 Setting

Both stores were of moderate to large size for the UK, with a size of 45,000 square feet and 67,000 square feet, respectively, and located in urban shopping centers. One store had one self-service checkout area containing ten SCOs located near the main door (67,000 sq. ft.). The other store had two separate SCO areas containing six SCOs in each (i.e. a total of twelve within the store), with one area positioned at the main door and the other nearer the back end of the store (45,000 sq. ft.). In each of the stores, security guards were typically placed near the entrance of the main door, with a view of the SCO machines.

2.3 Procedure

Interviews with security guards took place either during work or break time in private staff rooms within the work premises with permission of the store. The security guards had been provided with information on the study, i.e., to explore aspects of customer behavior at SCOs, by the store managers, and prior to the actual interview. All six security guards volunteered to take part in the research. All staff agreed for their interviews to be recorded and a typical interview lasted about 20 min. Participants were debriefed on the nature of the study at the end of the interview.

2.4 Results

Semi-structured interviews allowed for security guards' (SGs) opinions and attitudes to surface, which provided cues for further prompting and discussion that formed the basis of the following analysis. Responses were transcribed and then coded using NVivo software to identify occurring themes. In order to assess the reliability of the coding, two coders performed the analysis. Inter-rater reliability for the key themes was confirmed as the average Cohen's Kappa, $\kappa = .882$, $p < 0.01$, which indicated a very good overall agreement between the two coders [27].

These themes were then grouped into higher-order categories, i.e., antecedents of theft, factors surrounding committed theft, after the (suspected) theft, thus preserving a logical order of activities related to theft, as well as staffing roles and measures as to how to address theft.

1. Antecedents of theft.

In line with their job description, all SGs stated that monitoring, i.e. "watching" was one of the most important parts of being a security guard, to identify suspicious behavior and thefts, and meet store policy guidelines for stopping someone suspected of theft. A typical day in the life of a security guard may include a variety of security activities, including store and alarm checks, making random patrols, and monitoring CCTVs and customer activity.

1.1 *Customer characteristics.* SGs reported that many customers who are caught stealing usually act alone, however, many customers act in a group, with one customer trying to distract a staff member.

> *"Either/or but on the whole – individuals. One person will walk and distract, but majority have been alone."* (SG3)

With respect to monitoring activity at SCO, most SGs perceived that the intention of theft could be identified from a customer's behavior.

> *"If watching, you can see it* [the intent to steal], *they* [the customers] *usually look around themselves, always looking for the position of the person in charge of the self-service checkouts."* (SG1)

> *"[The customers] look around a bit nervous, they make mistakes, maybe testing the water."* (SG3)

However, at the same time, all SGs pointed out that there is no 'stereotypical thief' as far as the demographic of the customer is concerned.

> *"It can be anyone."* (SG5)

> *"[There are] all different types [of] people you would never expect."* (SG4)

> *"[There is] not a stereotype, such as your average drug user. Everyone has this perception, but it's not."* (SG3)

More specifically, SGs identified a variety of customers types that may steal, ranging from school kids to the elderly to affluent customers, as and if the opportunity presents itself.

> *"Opportunistic thieves at different time of the day. School kids before and after school."* (SG3)

> *"Banned a granny from store* [for stealing]."* (SG4)

> *"Folk walk out at the chance opportunity regardless* [of] *whether they have plenty of money to pay for it. Nine times out of ten it's just opportunity and it's someone that's 'well to do'."* (SG2)

The motivations of customers that steal were not perceived to be uniform, but could be categorized in three different motivations, the first arising from financial hardship and need, and the second being attributed to financial gain.

> *"People are needy and desperate, stealing for their kids. Or you get ones stealing [...] like, whisky to resell."* (SG2)

A third motivation for theft SGs identified appears to be less associated with a premeditated intent to be dishonest, but rather a consequence of situational factors that may occur, for example, when customers need staff assistance, but staff are busy helping other customers:

"They [the customers] *wouldn't steal otherwise if the wee lassie* [staff] *wasn't busy. I think they just get irate that they are waiting a length of time* [...] *and they are needing help. Frustration is a big part of it."* (SG2)

"People may steal through frustration." (SG3)

To the extent that frustration is associated with lack of technological assistance or staff, which thereby provides an opportunity to be dishonest, addressing both of these factors could be an important dimension in theft prevention.

The association between opportunism and dishonesty is discussed in more detail in the next section as a separate category.

1.2 *Busyness, opportunism and staff.* Opportunism seems a major factor in relation to thefts at SCO, be it associated with intent or with frustration. Unsurprisingly, all SGs stated that more thefts occur at SCOs when the store is busy.

"It [theft] *tends to happen at busier times of the day because there are a lot more people for the one cashier to deal with, so they see the opportunity and take it."* (SG6)

"Busier days [are] *easier for a thief, as* [there is] *more for the one cashier* [means SCO staff] *to deal with. If quiet, it's one on one, they won't do it. If busy, greater risk* [of theft occurring]*."* (SG3)

"It's a lot easier to steal at self-scan than from [traditional staffed] *checkouts because there is one person - 5/6/4 machines - they* [staff] *cannot see everything."* (SG1)

The next comment is also noteworthy, as most SGs reported that more thefts occur at SCOs compared to staffed checkouts:

"Yes, [theft] *more prone through SCO than manned. Because they are manned there's a personal interaction. Do get the odd one at manned* [checkout], *nesting, push through or walk through. SCO gives option of saying 'it's not my fault, it didn't scan', and* [customers] *can try to deceive camera by looking as if they are making payment, and worker is fooled as they are watching over six checkouts as opposed to one, so customer interaction is less; therefore* [there is] *more opportunity for an opportunistic thief before realisation sets in."* (SG3)

SGs clearly perceive SCO staff members struggling to supervise multiple SCOs. And also expressed sympathy with the SCO staff, as they are seemingly put in a difficult situation of having to juggle many customers at busy times:

"Speaking from experience things happen; people walk away, abandon them [the SCOs], *they won't scan something, put it in bag. It's a bit much to ask to have attention on all eight* [SCOs] *and you often find they* [staff] *get the blame. I have covered it and it's a hard job. One on one with a cashier - if there's chance of error then the person* [staff member at cashier checkout] *is more responsible than SCO* [staff member]*."* (SG4)

The comments also hint at the responsibility SGs ascribe to SCO staff. While a traditional staffed checkout (cashier) has the sole responsibility for the purchasing transaction with the customer, SCO staff are responsible for multiple interactions at the same time, which appears to induce a dilution of perceived responsibility for the SCO staff due to perceived pressure. This is also illustrated by the following quote:

> *"A weight mismatch comes up on SCO - if girls* [SCO staff] *are busy they just clear it; they don't look in the bag so there is pressure on the staff."* (SG5)

Having discussed customer characteristics and the busyness at SCOs associated with lack of staff assistance (social presence) providing opportunities for theft, SCO layout was also identified as a factor associated with dishonest behavior, and presents the final theme in this category.

1.3 *Layout of SCOs.* SGs identified the layout or design of the SCO as a component that could be relevant in addressing thefts. Stores where the SCOs are arranged in two parallel rows with customers and staff located in between those rows are particularly troublesome since when a staff member helps one customer, s/he has his/her back to half of the other checkouts, which means that the other SCOs are not monitored. This arrangement makes it easier for thefts to occur, since social presence or the effect of watching is reduced.

Many SCOs are also situated at the entrance to the shop making it easy for a quick escape for thieves.

> *"Fact that it's near the door.* [Thieves] *will always go to bottom one coz they are right next to the door. Common sense - by the time they get to me at the door the lassie* [SCO staff] *could have shouted for me to stop them, but they are straight out the door; the nearer they are the door the better. Better having one bank or two banks up the top. It's a quick exit."* (SG1)

2. Factors surrounding committed theft.

2.1 *Methods of theft.* SGs noted that SCO is easy to trick. Customers are perceived to adopt a variety of methods to shoplift, such as concealing items, swapping bar codes or leaving the store without paying, which clearly shows intent on part of the customer.

> *"*[It is] *quite easy to deceive the machine."* (SG3)

> *"Walking off without paying."* (SG6)

> *"Concealment of the item. Ticket swapping. Scan cheaper. Make-up easy to conceal."* (SG4)

> *"Two weeks ago we had a girl scanning one thing with two things in hands, so* [she] *scanned one thing, put the other one behind and both in the bag".*

> *"Ticket swapping with reduction stickers."* (SG5)

> *"Scanning bananas for £1 and putting down steaks."* (SG2)

Concealing items, and swapping bar codes are methods shoplifters may adopt irrespective of which method of shopping they adopt, i.e., these methods are not exclusively linked to the use of SCOs. Indeed, these actions may most likely occur while the customer is still in the middle of the store. However, there are unique types of theft associated with SCO, such as scanning cheaper items instead of expensive one, or simultaneous scanning of two items, as expressed in the last comment. Due to the control the customer has SGs perceive there are more opportunities for theft to occur compared to traditional checkouts.

> *"More chances and opportunities;* [the customers] *can make it look like they are paying or not paying for some. Can't get away with that at a cashier unless you conceal it before the till or if the cashier was in on it."* (SG4)

This last comment hints at the possibility of a staff member being complicit in dishonest behavior, i.e., 'sweethearting'. Historically, sweethearting occurs when a staff member facilitates friends, family or colleagues to steal by not scanning their goods or by providing illegitimate discounts and it has been associated with shrinkage [7]. Sweethearting was not flagged up as a major factor associated with SCO use by the SGs we interviewed, but it is not possible to exclude this as a method of theft, just as it would occur with traditional staffed checkouts.

2.2 *Type and value of stolen items.* SGs stated that they have seen an increase in thefts of high value items such as electrical items and make-up and everyday items such as fresh produce and expensive meat.

> *"Expensive electrical items and expensive alcohol and clothing."* (SG4)

> *"Usually it's just their daily shop; it can be milk and bread and stuff."* (SG1)

Customers tend to use the 'scan & bag' method of theft where they scan a cheap item and bag an expensive one, or they will weigh the item and select loose veg/fruit when it should be a steak.

2.3 *Types of excuses/customer accountability.* SGs noted that customers that have been caught stealing indicate it was a mistake, however, this appears to be similar irrespective of how customers shop, i.e. irrespective of SCO use.

> *"We always get that story* [i.e., that customers indicate it is a 'mistake' when they get caught] *whether they have been through checkout or not. They turn it around to be our fault, but that's their guilt; makes them more guilty."* (SG5)

> *"The smarter dressed will say it's a mistake."* (SG4)

However, SGs recognized that there may be a 'grey area' where customers may indeed accidentally make a mistake.

> *"A lot of times it* [mistake] *can happen, aye. Most the times they are chancing their arm."* (SG5)

In this case, the role of CCTV becomes important to confirm whether a customer has intent to steal, or whether indeed the customer merely made a mistake.

> *"Yes, they* [customers] *do* [make mistakes]. *Until I check back the CCTV I can't actually comment on that."* (SG2)

"Case dependent. CCTV can see if it's been a genuine mistake or not." (SG3)

In this case, the formal surveillance measure, which has historically been seen to deter theft, is mostly used for confirmation of dishonest intent. The role of surveillance is discussed in the next category.

3. After the (suspected) theft.

As SGs noted, some thieves may be professional, but some may be opportunistic. Once a customer is suspected of theft, SGs will look at the CCTV footage to assess a suspect's body language/behavior throughout the store to create a clearer picture whether they have acted in a suspicious manner prior to a theft, such as looking to where the member of staff is before concealing an item (see also *1.1 Customer characteristics in* **1**. Antecedents of theft).

3.1 *CCTV.* CCTV can be very useful in helping see whether a theft appeared to be on purpose or not and can be used as evidence for prosecution. However, thefts tend to be over and done with quickly and the perpetrator has left by the time a member of staff is able to alert security and the CCTV can be analyzed.

> *"By the time they have seen that there has been a walk off we will look at* [CCTV] *footage but that person is long gone."* (SG5)

CCTV in store does not always allow SGs to view entire interactions with SCOs due to their positioning. SGs are in the uncomfortable position that, with a short distance between a SCO and store exit, any alarms regarding potential theft may be raised too late by a member of staff.

3.2 *Police involvement.* SGs generally felt that not much will happen to those who face prosecution after having been caught for alleged stealing. SGs state that thieves who have planned on stealing at the SCOs are unlikely to pay fines that they receive, and police involvement may not be an effective deterrent for them. Opportunists will make excuses regarding the technology of the SCOs, as they will either pay for their items or say they will be back to pay for them and then never return. This then makes managers reluctant to contact police for every theft that occurs at SCOs.

> *"Manager doesn't usually want to pursue it; if you bring the manager down then they don't want to do anything about it"* (SG1)

Thus, security guards are put in a difficult position, having to balance their perceived duties with store policies.

3.3 *Store policy and accountability.* To stop a customer suspected of theft, SGs have to follow a particular policy involving store management. SGs feel that the policy can restrict their ability to deal with thefts efficiently.

> *"Would I go and stop myself without a member of staff ... not with* [store name] *policies, because we would be penalised regardless of whether we were right or wrong."* (SG2)

It seems that SGs at times may not feel supported by the store policy in their perceived role. Associated with this, SGs state they are made heavily aware of the repercussions of falsely stopping someone, as it can lead to newspaper articles and ultimately give bad press for the store which they feel could impact on their job.

"Have to think about reputation and false arrest. False arrest can lead to local papers and can be a bad thing." (SG1)

SGs appeared to be very aware of their store policy and how false arrests may lead to negative repercussions for them personally. This appeared to leave SGs feeling torn between fulfilling their job role and protecting their job. Clearer guidelines for the role and rights of SGs may address this issue. With new technology, for example, by the introduction of random checks before customers reach the exit (as is done for 'scan while you shop technologies' via 'random basket checks') may allow them to be more confident in their role. However, random product checks may be difficult to accept by customers.

4. Staffing roles

Customers ask SGs for assistance in removing clothing tags etc. which takes away from their role as a security guard, meaning thefts may be more likely to occur as they are impaired in the ability to monitor for criminal activity.

"Sometimes by yourself at the door operating cameras and still have to check all keys and door seals. Fire exit doors with security seals, key checks for locked areas given out then given back at end of day" (SG4)

"Problems dealing with alarm goes off at front door, because of tags being left on [items]*"* (SG6)

SGs state that they can become frustrated with SCO staff if they feel they are not vigilant enough to detect thefts. SGs also stated that manned checkout staff who do not correctly remove security tags can waste a lot of the security guards' time as this leads to door alarms going off and unnecessary checks needing to be made. Clearer guidelines for job roles and expectations of staff members may reduce these issues occurring and disrupting the role of the SG.

5. How to address theft

SGs offered some suggestions to reducing thefts at self-service checkouts. All stated that more vigilance would reduce thefts at self-service checkouts. Better technology was also stated as being likely to reduce thefts at self-service checkouts as they were too easy to trick. Also the SCOs positioning in the store was described as providing a quick exit (i.e. when the SCO is close to the exit) and making it easier for thieves to get away and difficult for security guards to stop them.

As a concluding question, the interviewer explored SGs' thoughts on whether technological implementations on the SCO itself may affect thefts, such as screen cameras. Security guards felt that CCTV on a SCO could be effective if perceived by the customer.

"I think if customers could see it [camera at SCO] *and were more aware they were being watched it definitely would."* (SG4)

However, there was also a realization that shoplifting is an ongoing problem, with measures to counteract it lagging behind.

> "[...] *in general thieves are always adapting and evolving, whether it be a trolley pusher – it doesn't matter what it is.* [Thieves are] *always going to find ways round it. If they get caught one way, they will share information and find a new way to do it."* (SG1)

> "*They* [thieves] *are always one step ahead. You are catching up with them all the time because they just think of something new."* (SG5)

3 Discussion

This study explored factors around customer dishonesty at SCOs from the perception of security guards (SGs), with a view to identify possible opportunities to address shrinkage in retail. SGs' responses were grouped into five main categories, antecedents of theft, factors surrounding committed theft, what happens after the (suspected) theft, staffing roles, and how to address theft, which we discuss in turn.

Antecedents of theft. SGs provided a number of responses with respect to the type of customer committing theft. SGs suggested that there is no 'stereotypical' thief, in that shoplifters vary in age demographics and apparent wealth, which is in line with the inconsistent findings regarding shoplifter demographics others have noted [18]. Potential offenders reveal themselves rather by their body language than their demographic [18], e.g. by scanning the store for staff or other surveillance, which was also noted by SGs in the current study, who reported potential thieves can be spotted by the way they monitor where store staff are positioned at SCO.

There was an overall agreement from SGs that there were more thefts at SCOs when the store was busy and that there were more thefts at SCOs overall, compared to traditional manned checkouts. All security guards stated that it was easier to steal using SCOs due to only one member of SCO staff being generally present. These findings are consistent with those of Creighton et al. [16] who found that SCO staff reported feeling under pressure when SCOs are busy, as they are impaired in their ability to watch for thefts and assist customers at SCOs. Store staff also felt this increased the risk of thefts occurring [16], which in turn mirrors the perceptions of security staff in the current study.

The findings suggest that the implementation of a social presence, for example, via cameras within the SCO area, or indeed on/at the SCO itself [16], or strategically placed staff within the SCO area, could provide an opportunity to increase surveillance perceived by the customer, especially when the shop is busy. As an alternative, camera systems that could automatically monitor a customer's behavior to flag up suspicious customer activity to staff would represent a technical solution to spot potential suspect behavior, and is in line with, for example, biometric technology implementations.

SGs perceived that some consumers may steal because of frustration, for example, when they have to wait for staff because staff are assisting customers elsewhere. Frustration has been implicated in theft at SCO [35] in a recent study and is noteworthy as a motivator, as it can be speculated that frustrated consumers may not be habitual shoplifters. The blurry line between initial intent and theft happening through frustration is interesting to the extent that frustration may increase the desire to steal, which represents one aspect of the Crime Triangle [13]. This would suggest that addressing frustration may be the critical factor for customers in this category, as it could be expected that customers were not initially intent on stealing, yet were somehow tempted into it.

Frustration experienced at SCO may also be addressed by, for example, training staff to deal with frustrated customers effectively, or indeed, providing more staff at SCO for customer assistance. In addition, the implementation of technology that could flag up if a customer is likely to be frustrated may be helpful in this instance, for example, when a SCO process may take too long. Interface design may also address some of the user frustrations, for example, by introducing anthropomorphic agents or indeed real staff in an image area on the screen to induce social presence to deal with customer frustration.

Finally, the layout of the store was flagged up as critical for committing thefts, as SGs pointed out that more thefts occur at SCOs near 'the doors'. This suggests modifying SCO layout, by, e.g., increasing the distance between SCOs and the exit.

Furthermore, social presence when exiting the store could be enhanced by introducing mirrors [31], embodied agents or indeed robots [22] or cameras [16] displaying the customer's footage in the SCO area.

Factors surrounding committed theft. SGs noted that SCOs are easy to trick and that customers use a number of methods to steal, including concealing items by simultaneously scanning two items, with one item being concealed, or scanning cheaper instead of more expensive items (e.g. bananas for steaks). The responses are consistent with recent findings by Taylor [35], reporting many techniques of theft, such as selecting items that are less expensive than the loose items being weighed, or selecting cheap cooking tomatoes instead of expensive vine tomatoes, etc. The methods of theft are creative and SGs noted that they are always trying to 'catch up'.

With respect to the type of item stolen, SGs noted an increase in thefts of high value items (electrical, make-up, clothing) but also everyday items. Typically, customers scan a cheap item and bag an expensive one. While bar codes can be swapped in the store, before a customer even proceeds to a staffed or SCO checkout, the difference in price between cheap and expensive items is probably bigger at SCO than at staffed checkouts. At staffed checkouts, staff may actually notice the difference if the price for an expensive item is too low. However, at SCOs swapped price tags may go unnoticed until a SCO staff member actually checks the prices and receipts.

Our findings are consistent with a study by Bamfield [4], who also noted that items that were reported stolen were typically of high value, a relatively small size, and often designer brands or in great or regular demand by the public. Those findings point again to a wider demographic of customer, refuting the idea of a 'stereotypical' thief motivated by financial need as outlined above.

SGs pointed out that most thieves caught stealing, irrespective of whether they use SCOs or not, tend to indicate that it was a 'mistake', however, they also acknowledged that honest mistakes could have been made by customers. SGs state that the majority of people who are suspected of theft at SCOs will blame the technology as there are grey areas of security that allow for this to happen, which means it can be difficult to prove customer intent. This is consistent with research from Beck [7] who calls this the self-scan defence. With respect to the thief with intention to steal, others [35] have noted that a large majority of thieves admit that they stole initially by accident, but that shoplifting became a routine after that, especially when it was easy to do the first time. Here, staff vigilance, but also increased tagging of items or technological implementations at SCO, such as item recognition, may be useful means to address the first experience of a successful theft.

After the (suspected) theft. SG stated that, once a customer is suspected of theft, the role of CCTV is to confirm that a theft has occurred. The finding that CCTV in its current form is not effective in deterring thefts is noteworthy, given that shop-lifters perceive the presence of formal surveillance effective as a deterrent [12]. This points to the implementation of more effective ways of inducing perceived surveillance – and staff assistance – for customers at SCO to prevent theft. For example, adaptions such as onscreen cameras may increase a sense of social presence and reduce the likelihood of such behaviors occurring [30], especially if this camera surveillance cannot be avoided by the customer using the SCO.

The findings also suggest that SGs are under many pressures from store policies and other expectancies of their role, as they have to abide by store policies once a customer is suspected of theft. Having to perform their role as Security Guards effectively has to be balanced with the potential damage to the store's reputation, if a false arrest is made. Some expressed feeling demoralized by the lack of authority they have when someone is caught and a suspect is not further prosecuted. That this may be a valid perception is supported by findings from recent research [5] showing that only a small proportion of shoplifters are apprehended and prosecuted, and is consistent with an earlier study [21] which noted only 24% of all apprehended shoplifters being prosecuted.

SCOs may increase the number of instances of 'walking' off with goods that have not been paid for [5] and SGs in the current study commented on this too. Clear position of the SCO could assist security guards and members of staff in reducing thefts occurring, as they would have more time to evaluate and act on suspected 'walkers' or thieves in general. Taylor [35] also highlights the matter of reduced staff presence at SCOs as a factor that can influence thefts, suggesting that implementations that induce presence may reduce thefts, in line with what was earlier discussed regarding the store layout above. However, Hoffman et al. [22] state that initial effects of a social presence may reduce if customers learn that the risk of repercussions is limited.

Staffing roles. SGs can become frustrated with SCO staff if they perceive staff are not vigilant enough to detect thefts. SG also stated that staff who do not correctly remove security tags can waste a lot of the security guards' time, as this leads to door alarms going off and unnecessary checks needing to be made. This is impacting on their task to monitor for criminal activity. There was an overall agreement among SGs that SCO staff were under pressure when SCOs were busy and they could not 'do everything' or be held responsible for thefts when the SCO area was busy, however, there was also the perception that this impacted on their own role too. This suggests that clear guidelines should assist both SCO staff and security guards, in particular, when the store is busy, as it appears that both staff groups are distracted from being an effective social presence at this time [16], and this may be affecting their working relationships. The findings suggest that security implementations within a SCO could assist both SCO staff and SGs, perhaps allowing customers to de-tag items after valid payments have been made.

How to address theft. SGs stated a number of factors to address theft, ranging from better vigilance, to better technology at SCOs and story layout with respect to SCO positioning further away from the door. The theme of 'watching' was alluded to multiple times. Clearly, SGs perceive surveillance as effective in deterring thefts, and so do shoplifters [12], with store managers [24] perceiving security guards to be the most effective surveillance method. However, given that an increasing number of formal surveillance measures are implemented to address crime [39], it is questionable to which extent these are indeed successful, given the shoplifting figures generally, and the absence of exact figures of theft at SCOs [Taylor 16].

It should be noted that SGs commented positively on the implementation of cameras on SCOs, provided the customers were aware of this type of surveillance. As sho-plifters tend to avoid cameras (if they are aware of them), implementing them where customers cannot avoid them, i.e. at the SCO itself, may be useful, as noted above. The perception of a social presence has been linked to more positive behavior via an enhanced self-awareness [30, 31] and should be considered. Given that customers have to direct their attention to the SCO while conducting their transactions, a highly visible camera on the SCO screen may not go unnoticed, and thus, may raise their awareness of social presence.

4 Conclusions

The thoughts and views of security guards are important in understanding perceived customer motivations and behaviors surrounding theft at SCO. The research presented clearly suggests that security guards feel security measures for reducing thefts at SCOs could be improved.

Thefts may occur for multiple reasons and involving self-service in customer transactions may create a complex situation, with many factors at play. Customers may over- or undercharge themselves, and they may or may not be aware of it. The control that customers experience at SCO may create situations where theft can occur by accident. However, theft that can be conducted easily, whether intentional or non-intentional, may predispose individuals to repeat this behavior [35], and thus should be avoided. Factors that bring about theft, such as the busyness of the store combined with opportunity for stealing at SCO, should be recognized and could be addressed by, for example, enhancing surveillance temporarily during busy times. Others have noted that the implementation of social presence has a positive effect on human behavior [30, 31], and this should also be the case with regard to reducing theft, be it via enhancing staff presence or other, technological implementations at SCO (cameras, mirrors, embodied agents etc.).

Given that we interviewed staff on their work premises, the cooperation of staff and the stores was paramount to conducting the study. This research is part of a larger research project focused on the effects that a social presence may have within a retail environment, and in particular, theft. One limitation of our study was the relatively small sample, thus, findings may not be generalizable to different cohorts of security guards or indeed, different countries or types of stores. However, the interviews allowed us to get a comprehensive, in-depth view of the perceptions of security guards in relation to theft, which was valuable in understanding the factors that may be addressed to prevent theft. Given that our findings were also consistent with the work of others hints at the validity of the discussed findings.

SGs considered surveillance as one of the most important factors to address theft. However, our study indicated that a constant social presence is difficult to achieve consistently and effectively. Given that social presence has been shown to be effective in modifying people's behavior [e.g., 1, 2, 19, 30, 31] it would be reasonable to suggest that future research should consider variations on how social presence is implemented in retail. Methods could include the implementation of technology within SCOs or varying social presence over a period of time to avoid habituation effects. With technological advances within the retail sector there is great potential to address theft to ultimately benefit businesses and customers, and their experiences, and also support the staff working in retail.

Acknowledgments. We would like to thank the stores and security guards for their participation in this study. We would also like to thank NCR for supporting this project.

References

1. Ahmad, S.N.: The role of social facilitation theory on consumer decision making: A conceptual framework. Am. J. Manag. **16**, 80–89 (2016)
2. Argo, J., Dahl, D., Manchanda, R.: The influence of a mere social presence in a retail context. J. Consum. Res. **32**, 207–212 (2005)
3. Bailenson, J.N., Swinth, K., Hoyt, C., Persky, S., Dimov, A., Blascovich, J.: The independent and interactive effects of embodied-agent appearance and behavior on self-report, cognitive, and behavioral markers of copresence in immersive virtual environments. Presence Teleoperators Virtual Environ. **14**, 379–393 (2005)
4. Bamfield, J.: Shrinkage, shoplifting and the cost of retail crime in Europe: a cross-sectional analysis of major retailers in 16 European countries. Int. J. Retail Distrib. Manag. **32**, 235–241 (2004)
5. Bamfield, J.: Shopping and Crime. Palgrave Macmillan, Basingstoke (2012)
6. Baumer, T., Rosenbaum, D.: Combating Retail Theft: Programs and Strategies. Butterworth, Stoneham (1984)
7. Beck, A.: Self-scan checkouts and retail loss: Understanding the risk and minimising the threat. Secur. J. **24**, 199–215 (2011)
8. Beck, A.: Developments in Retail Mobile Scanning Technologies: Understanding the Potential Impact on Shrinkage Loss Prevention. ESRC, Leicester (2015)
9. Beck, A., Hopkins, M.: Scan and rob! Convenience shopping, crime opportunity and corporate social responsibility in a mobile world. Secur. J. (2016). doi:10.1057/sj.2016.6
10. Beck, A., Willis, A.: Context-specific measures of CCTV effectiveness in the retail sector. In: Surveillance of Public Space: CCTV, Street Lighting and Crime Prevention. Crime Prevention Studies Series 10, pp. 251–269 (1999)

11. Biocca, F., Harms, C., Gregg, J.: The Networked Minds measure of social presence Pilot test of the factor structure and concurrent validity. Paper presented at the 4th Annual International Workshop on Presence 2001 USA, Philadelphia (2001)
12. Carmel-Gilfilen, C.: Bridging security and good design: Understanding perceptions of expert and novice shoplifters. Secur. J. **26**, 80–105 (2013)
13. Clarke, R., Eck, J.E.: Become a Problem-Solving Crime Analyst. Routledge, London (2014)
14. Cornish, D.B., Clarke, R.V. (eds.): The Reasoning Criminal: Rational Choice Perspectives on Offending. Transaction Publishers, London (2014)
15. Cozens, P.M., Saville, G., Hillier, D.: Crime prevention through environmental design (CPTED): A review and modern bibliography. Property Manag. **23**, 328–356 (2005)
16. Creighton, S., Johnson, G., Robertson, P., Law, J., Szymkowiak, A.: Dishonest behavior at self-service checkouts. In: Nah, F.F.-H., Tan, C.-H. (eds.) HCIB 2015. LNCS, vol. 9191, pp. 267–278. Springer, Cham (2015). doi:10.1007/978-3-319-20895-4_25
17. Dabholkar, P.A., Bagozzi, R.P.: An attitudinal model of technology-based self-service: moderating effects of consumer traits and situational factors. J. Acad. Mark. Sci. **30**, 184–201 (2002)
18. Dabney, D.A., Hollinger, R.C., Dugan, L.: Who actually steals? A study of covertly observed shoplifters. Justice Q. **21**, 693–728 (2004)
19. Dahl, D., Manchanda, R., Argo, J.: Embarrassment in consumer purchase: The roles of social presence and purchase familiarity. J. Consum. Res. **28**, 472–481 (2001)
20. Harrell, G.D., Hutt, M.D., Anderson, J.C.: Path analysis of buyer behavior under conditions of crowding. J. Mark. Res. **17**, 45–51 (1980)
21. Hollinger, R.C., Davis, J.L.: 2002 National Retail Security Survey: Final Report. University of Florida, Gainesville (2002)
22. Hoffman, G., Forlizzi, J., Ayal, S., Steinfeld, A., Antanitis, J., Hochman, G., Finkenaur, J.: Robot presence and human honesty: Experimental evidence. In: Proceedings of the Tenth Annual ACM/IEEE International Conference on Human-Robot Interaction, pp. 181–188. ACM, Portland (2015)
23. Home Office: Crime against Businesses: Findings from the 2014 Commercial Victimisation Survey. Home Office, London (2015)
24. Kajalo, S., Lindblom, A.: The perceived effectiveness of surveillance in reducing crime at shopping centers in Finland. Property Manag. **28**, 47–59 (2010)
25. Klemke, L.W.: Exploring adolescent shoplifting. Sociol. Soc. Res. **67**, 59–75 (1982)
26. Kraut, R.E.: Deterrent and definitional influences on shoplifting. Soc. Probl. **25**, 358–368 (1976)
27. Landis, J.R., Koch, G.G.: The measurement of observer agreement for categorical data. Biometrics **33**, 159–174 (1977)
28. Lowenthal, P.: The evolution and influence of social presence theory on online learning. In: Kidd, T.T. (ed.) Online Education and Adult Learning: New Frontiers for Teaching Practices, pp. 124–139. IGI Global, Hershey (2009)
29. Nicholson, M., Clarke, I., Blakemore, M.: Multichannel consumer behaviour in the retail fashion sector: Toward a longitudinal ethnography. Paper presented at the 11th International Conference on Research in the Distributive Trades, vol 1. EIM Business Policy Research, Tilburg (2001)
30. Pfattheicher, S., Keller, J.: The watching eyes phenomenon: The role of a sense of being seen and public self-awareness. Eur. J. Soc. Psychol. **45**, 560–566 (2015)
31. Reynald, D.M., Elffers, H.: The future of Newman's defensible space theory linking defensible space and the routine activities of place. Eur. J. Criminol. **6**, 25–46 (2009)
32. Short, J., Williams, E., Christie, B.: The Social Psychology of Telecommunications. Wiley, London (1976)

33. Sklansky, D.A.: Not your father's police department: Making sense of the new demographics of law enforcement. J. Crim. Law Criminol. **96**, 1209–1243 (2006)
34. Stoltman, J.J., Morgan, F.W., Anglin, L.K.: An investigation of retail shopping situations. Int. J. Retail Distrib. Manag. **27**, 145–153 (1999)
35. Taylor, E.: Supermarket self-checkouts and retail theft: The curious case of the SWIPERS. Criminol. Crim. Justice **16**, 552–567 (2016)
36. Uzzell, D.L.: The myth of the indoor city. J. Environ. Psychol. **15**, 299–310 (1995)
37. Welsh, B.C., Farrington, D.P., O'Dell, S.J.: Effectiveness of public areas surveillance for crime prevention: Security guards, place managers and defensible space. Swedish National Council for Crime Prevention, Stockholm (2010)
38. Willis, P.: Common Culture. Open University, Milton Keynes (1990)
39. Yaniv, G.: Shoplifting, monitoring and price determination. J. Socio Econ. **38**, 608–610 (2009)

The Duality of Envy in Online Social Information Consumption: An Exploratory Study

Yi Wu[1], Ben C.F. Choi[2(✉)], and Annie Tran[2]

[1] College of Management and Economics, Tianjin University, Tianjin, China
yiwu@tju.edu.cn
[2] School of Information Systems and Technology Management,
UNSW Business School, Sydney, Australia
chun.choi@unsw.edu.au, annietran8@hotmail.com

Abstract. This study investigates the duality of envy in online social information consumption. By drawing on the Social Comparison Theory, this study identifies three key aspects of social information consumption, namely social exhibition, network attention strength, and network attention valence, to be important determinants of positive and negative envy emotions induced by such consumption. More importantly, this research elucidates better understanding of individuals' response strategies pertinent to the online social networking environment. To do so, this research investigates the multiplex perspective of online social network usage to determine the behavioral responses of online social network users in regards to online social information consumption. Subsequently, this research empirically examines the impacts of social information consumption have on users' envy emotions and motivations specific to usage of social networking platforms. The research model was tested using an experiment. Contributions are discussed.

Keywords: Online social information consumption · Social Comparison Theory · Benign envy affects · Malicious envy affects · Behavioral responses · Appreciative usage · Derogatory usage

1 Introduction

Envy emotions, which are often caused by social comparison, have become increasingly common over the years as individuals increasingly rely on online social networks to develop, maintain, and communicate with friends. While envy emotions are often triggered by upward social comparison in traditional settings, envy emotions could be invoked by both upward social comparison and downward social comparison in online social networks. Indeed, studies show that Facebook users are often depressed by their friends' social activities and updates on Facebook [1]. Interestingly, increasingly studies reveal that online social network users could also be motivated by social information to engage self-enhancement behaviors. For instance, Gonzales and Hancock's study shows that Facebook users are motivated by their friends' social updates making Facebook a "unique awareness-enhancing stimuli" [2].

F.F.-H. Nah and C.-H. Tan (Eds.): HCIBGO 2017, PART II, LNCS 10294, pp. 282–297, 2017.
DOI: 10.1007/978-3-319-58484-3_22

The issue of envy triggered by social information consumption has recently drawn substantial attention from Information Systems (IS) scholars [3]. In online social networking environment, the information dissemination and content synthesizes mechanisms greatly enable users the ability to easily retrieve and view content generated by friends [4]. Thus, the online social networking environment represent a major platform of social information consumption [5]. Furthermore, the effects of social information consumption in online social networks could be much more impactful than that in offline settings [6]. This is because individuals could be exposed to a vastly larger pool of content in social media, while their exposure could be limited by physical and temporal limitations [7]. Moreover, the re-dissemination mechanisms might facilitate recurring exposure to social information, which could lead to elevated impact through repeated consumption [8]. These unique aspects of online social information consumption warrant careful investigation. Hence, our first research question is, what are the key types of social information consumption in the online social networking environment?

Although social comparison often induces negative envy emotions in offline settings, such negative implication might not be the sole effects in online social networks, which typically consist of divergent and heterogeneous social circles. As a result, individuals are not likely to expose to a monolithic type of social information consumption. The IS literature has substantially broadened understanding of envy emotions associated with technology usage [9]. Krasnova et al. [3], for instance, noted that social information consumption would lead to envy on SNS. While most of these studies have focused on examining the negative aspect of envy emotions, the envy literature has uncovered the positive aspect of envy emotions. Whereas negative envy emotions subsume individuals' negative sentiment towards socialization and interactions with others, positive envy emotions are characterized by positive sentiment towards social interactions and enhancement to interpersonal bonding [10]. For example, Toma and Hancock [11] investigated motivations to use Facebook and found that consumption of online social networking services could allow individuals to achieve self-affirmation, which helps them uphold their perceptions of self-worth. Hence, the second research question is, what are the positive envy emotion and negative envy emotion induced by online social information consumption?

Finally, extant IS literature has demonstrated that individuals take on behavioral strategies to recover from the emotions triggered by online social information consumption [3]. Past research examining envy responses suggest that individuals could performance a rich spectrum of behavioral responses to address the emotions provoked by envy. Although enriching understanding of behavioral response to envy emotions, there is a lack of research into individuals' response in the context of online social information consumption. Thus, to better understand individuals' response strategies pertinent to the online social networking environment, the final research question is, what are the behavioral responses to positive envy emotion and negative envy emotion in online social networks? Specifically, this study proposes and examines a multiplex perspective of online social network usage.

To answer the questions, we develop a research model of the two types of online social information consumption, which incorporates factors specific to online social networks. We propose to test the proposed model through a laboratory experiment. By developing and validating this model, our work is expected to contribute to both research and practice in this area.

2 Literature Review

2.1 Social Comparison Theory

Online social network users do not only generate and disseminate content but also consume content generated by their friends [4, 12]. Past studies suggest that while the generation and dissemination of self-relevant content might help users present and manage their desired identities in the online environment [e.g., 7, 13], emerging research reveals that the consumption of social updates could cause some unforeseen consequences, such as depression and envy [e.g., 1, 3, 14]. For this reason, users' psychological responses to social updates cannot be fully understood without investigating how users consume social update. The Social Comparison Theory is especially useful for studying the impact of social updates on individuals [15]. Social comparison is the process of thinking about information about one or more other people in relation to the self [16, pp. 520–521]. This theory has been applied widely to explain various phenomena including interpersonal comparisons [17], leader-member relationships [18], peer pressure [19], and appearance evaluation [20]. The theory has also been used as a conceptual tool for explaining individuals' behavior to social information consumption on online social networks [e.g., 21, 22].

The Social Comparison Theory posits that individuals compare oneself with others in order to evaluate or to enhance some aspects of the self [23]. According to the theory, by evaluating others, individuals develop perceptions of relative standing, which could have substantial impact on their self-concept, level of aspiration, and feelings of well-being. In his seminal work, Festinger [15] postulated that others who are similar to an individual are especially useful to that individual in generating accurate evaluations of his or her abilities and opinions. Indeed, a rich body of literature based on social comparisons suggests that an individual's social standing relative to referents influences attitudes, aspirations, and behaviors.

The social comparison literature has revealed that individuals typically perform self-evaluations by focusing on two types of social information, namely upward social comparison information and downward social comparison information. More importantly, recent research examining social media usage suggests that the consumption of social information is an important determinant of envy affects, which are important drivers of a rich spectrum of online social networking behaviors.

2.2 Upward Comparison and Downward Comparison

Festinger [15] postulates that there is a "unidirectional drive upward" in which individuals make ability comparisons, in particular with "similar others" who are marginally better than themselves. This upward comparison process is generally a good drive for self-improvements [24]. For instance, in an academic context, Blanton et al. [25] revealed that upward comparison, which was comparing lower grade performers with higher grade performers, produced improved subsequent academic results. Collectively, past research suggests that upward comparison could powerfully drive individuals' motivations to achieve self-enhancement.

Yet past research has revealed that at times individuals could be forced to make upward comparison. For instance, in a study examining the effects of advertisements on social comparisons, Richins [26] found that consumers compared themselves with models in the advertisement when the physical attractiveness of the models was emphasized. Indeed, evidence suggests that individuals could find themselves worse off by performing upward comparisons.

When applied to social information consumption in online social networks, social comparison can be realized through the consumption of social information among interconnected users [27]. Recent IS research suggests that social information consumption could lead to unexpected psychological impact on users. For instance, Krasnova et al. [3] found that social information consumption on SNS could elevate individuals' perceptions of envy, which could have detrimental impacts on their cognitive well-being and affective well-being. Accordingly, this study draws on the social comparison theory to focus on two key types of social information consumption, namely self-enhancing consumption and self-depreciating consumption. Self-enhancing consumption refers to the extent to which users pay attention to social updates that help strengthen their self-esteem. For example, users could be most interested to follow the updates generated by friends who are less well-off academically. By observing others' struggling in completing course assignments, users could feel somewhat better off. Self-depreciating consumption refers to the extent to which users pursue social updates that damage their self-esteem. For instance, users could be tempted to follow friends who frequently publicize their luxurious lifestyle, such as posting photos about them attending classy dinner events, showing off branded products, and visiting exotic places. In essence, whereas self-enhancing consumption corresponds to downward comparison in self-evaluations, self-depreciating consumption corresponds to upward comparison.

2.3 The Duality of Envy

Envy is an emotion that occurs as a result of social comparison with another person who is either superior or inferior in terms of a valued possession, characteristic, or achievement. While past research has mainly focused on elucidating the negative implications of envy, increasing evidence suggests that envy could have positive implications on individuals. In terms of the negative implications, envy is often considered an undesirable and maladaptive emotion. Indeed, envy is typically associated with an array of undesirable consequences, such as depression, feelings of inferiority, anxiety, and reduced happiness. In terms of the positive implications, envy could help alert individuals to being outperformed by others and hence motivating individuals to level these differences or even surpass competitors. Indeed, recent research suggests that the envy emotions could spur individuals to mitigate the damaging effects of threatening social comparisons on their self-esteem [28].

In general, envy emotions can be categorized into two types, namely benign envy affects and malicious envy affects. Benign envy affects are characterized by positive regard of others, desire for superior fortune and the action tendency to improve one's own position by moving upward [10]. Benign envy affects emerge if an individual appraises others' advantage as deserved and personal control as high. Past research suggests that benign envy affects activate goals to level oneself up, such as increasing willingness to pay, inducing impulsive desire for coveted consumer products [29], and improving upward persistence and performance. Collectively, benign envy affects helps individual perform self-evaluation, which is the central motivate for comparing with upward standards.

Malicious envy affects are characterized by hostile feelings toward others and action tendencies intended to damage their superior positions. This type of envy affects often emerge if an individual appraises others' advantage as undeserved and personal control as low. The negative impact of malicious envy affects have been well established [30]. For instance, in a study on malicious envy responses, Zizzo and Oswald [31] found that malicious envy affects could motivate individuals to destroy some of their own money in exchange for the destruction of even more money from the person they envied. More importantly, the envy literature suggests that malicious envy affects could induce an array of envy-coping strategies, which are typically self-defensive, with the ultimate aim of overcoming or responding to invidious emotions.

In essence, the consumption of social information is a key source of envy emotions, which can be largely classified into benign envy affects and malicious envy affects. It is important to note that the two types envy emotions are distinct and dualistic in traditional studies. Yet, in the online social networking environment, social information can be concurrently made available from a highly divergent and heterogeneous social network. As a result, individuals could simultaneously consume both types of social information and hence concurrently develop the two types of envy emotions.

3   Research Model and Hypotheses

The research model is presented in Fig. 1.

3.1   Determinants of Envy Affects

When applying the concept of social exhibition in an online social networking context, social comparison can be realized and becomes highly evident through the consumption of such social information among interconnected users [27]. Specifically, SNS provides a medium for users to curate and consume information from their social networks in the form of positive social exhibition and negative social exhibition. Recent IS research on information consumption and social networks have categorically suggested the prevalence of positive social exhibition on self-depreciating consumption in online social networks [3]. As such, compared with negative social exhibition, positive social exhibition of information for consumption enables upward social comparison through the evaluation of individuals that are better off than oneself.

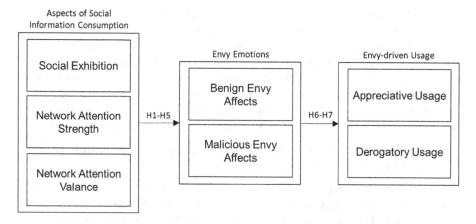

Fig. 1. Research Model

Supporting this, a study conducted by Chou and Edge [32] revealed that SNS users are more likely to concur that others online are much "happier" and have "better lives". Therefore,

H1a: Compared to negative social exhibition, positive social exhibition will lead to weaker benign envy affects.

In terms of social networking sites like Facebook, both network attention strength and network attention valence are highly evident as a means of measuring how users respond and interact with their social networks online. Past research have found that SNS like Facebook have affected the lives of SNS users and the way they interact with their social networks online [33]. Content consumption on SNS does not only positively affect individuals. For example, particularly given the large dissemination channel and network attention SNS provides; individuals can be exposed to negative implications of content consumption online such as emotions of jealousy and envy as well as their self-esteem [29]. Network attention strength is largely represented based on the amount of explicit responses and peer attention harnessed from an online social network toward a user's social update – this is in the form of popularity [34]. As such, these explicit responses are often made by the user's social network as an indication of their awareness and acknowledgement of the social information being exhibited [35]. Therefore, compared with low network attention strength, high network attention suggests that the social information exhibited is of great popularity due to its wide dissemination and acknowledgment by other users [36]. As such, individuals might develop a sense of malevolence as one receives high network attention leading to weakened benign envy affects. Hence,

H1b: Compared to low network attention strength, high network attention strength will lead to weaker benign envy affects.

More so, depending on the type of information exhibited, the valence of attention can be interpreted differently. As SNS users continue to curate and exhibit social updates online, the valence of attention from their networks (other SNS users) would vary. Past research suggests that individuals receiving positive network attention valence have attracted sympathy and are well-supported (psychological support) by their social networks online, projecting a greater sense of achievement to others [37]. As such, compared to the exposure and consumption of social exhibition with negative network attention valence, positive network attention valence suggests that individuals would find themselves experiencing substantial damaging social comparisons. Therefore, individuals are more likely to experience weaker benign envy affects. Hence,

H1c: Compared to negative network attention valence, positive network attention valence will lead to weaker benign envy affects.

Extant research around the envious emotions online have highlighted the importance of social network attention on SNS user behavior [10]. A recent study conducted by Tandoc et al. [1] have demonstrated that individuals are highly influenced by the amount of attention they anticipate to receive and actually receive. In instances where the network attention strength is low, individuals begins to question and compare themselves to better others [11]. In the case of negative network attention valence, the effect of network attention strength on benign envy is more likely to be strengthened. As a result, individuals might develop a greater sense of benevolence or superiority as one receives multiple negative network attention. As supported by Greitemeyer [38], individuals' self-esteem heightens as others receive negative responses from their social networks. Consequently, in the case of positive network attention valence, the effect of network attention strength on benign envy affects is likely to be low (weakened). As individuals are likely to develop a sense of resentment and hostility as one receives multiple positive network attention. Therefore, the strength of benign envy affects associated with network attention strength would not be as effective when faced with a positive network attention condition. Therefore,

H2a: In the negative network attention valence condition, compared to low network attention strength, high network attention strength will lead to stronger benign envy affects.

H2b: In the positive network attention valence condition, compared to low network attention strength, high network attention strength will lead to weaker benign envy affects.

Furthermore, extant research studies around social networks and user behavioral responses have indicated that the types of social information and content one exhibits online to their social networks are crucial measures of attention, which are key drivers of examining SNS usage patterns and experiences. More so, past research have found that SNS like Facebook have affected the lives its users specially around the way they interact and react online [33]. For example, Krasnova et al. [3] found that the consumption of social information on SNS can not only have positive effects on SNS users, but can also have negative effects such as psychological distress leading to emotions of envy. Through the consumption of positive social exhibition, the likelihood of individuals experiencing self-depreciation and envy becomes apparent [38]. As such, in the case of positive social exhibition, the negative influence of network attention valence will influence the network attention strength. Therefore, compared to negative social exhibition, positive social exhibition will result in the increased likelihood of attracting negative network attention as individuals develop stronger emotions of hostility when making comparative judgments online. This will weaken benign envy affects. Hence,

H3: Compared to negative social exhibition, positive social exhibition will strengthen the negative moderation influence of network attention valence on the impact of network attention strength on benign envy affects.

The SNS environment and the subsequent social exhibition of information in which users interact with, have shown to actively trigger social comparative judgments (i.e. social comparisons). This includes the negative effects on users as they perform evaluations of self. Compared to negative social exhibition, ample evidence suggests that with positive social exhibition, individuals could find themselves worse off (e.g. decreasing prosocial behaviors and interactions with others) by performing upward comparisons [3]. More so, recent research have acknowledged the prevailing existence of negative effects on individuals with exposure to and consumption of positive social exhibition [38]. For instance, Tandoc et al. [1] found individuals are more likely to become depressed and envious through the consumption of positively exhibited information on social networks. To further support this, Chou and Edge [32] study demonstrated that upon viewing social updates made by their social networks, the SNS users were more likely to agree that others online have "better lives" and are more successful than themselves. Undeniably, this provokes the SNS experience of users and consumers of positive social exhibition leading to stronger experiences of malicious envy affects online. Therefore,

H4a: Compared to negative social exhibition, positive social exhibition will lead to stronger malicious envy affects.

Extant research suggests that network attention strength is a pivotal aspect of social information consumption. In the context of social networking the amount of attention and responses social updates or information yielded, reflects it exposure levels [36]. Compared to low network attention strength, a high network attention strength suggests that the social update exhibited for consumption has been exposed to a large proportion of poster's social network and have been acknowledged via responses. Supporting this, in the context of SNS, network attention strength is determined by the total number of immediate responses and peer attention harnessed – this is measured through the responses selected (such "likes" and "sads" on Facebook) [7]. Given the strong network attention strength, individuals who consume the social exhibition with strong network attention strength from others online might develop a greater sense of malevolence as attention is focused on the one individual. Furthermore, ample evidence has revealed the negative impact of intensive exposure and attention to self-depreciating social information. For instance, Kross et al. [39] examined the impact of online social networking on emotional wellness and found that the audience size and intensity of responses would expose individuals to substantial damaging social comparisons in cases where individuals are perceived to be more inferior than others. This could result in notable deterrence in their subjective well-being, which strengthens the malicious envy affects. Hence,

H4b: Compared to low network attention strength, high network attention strength will lead to stronger malicious envy affects.

It is indeed understood that the valence of network attention varies based on the type of social exhibition curated. According to past research, individuals hold a greater sense of self-achievement and support when they receive positive network attention valence over negative network attention valence [24]. For example, Gonzales and Hancock [2] study revealed that the presence of self-presentation and social exhibition of one's accomplishment online, makes it difficult for others consuming the exhibition to avoid feeling envious. This is supported by recent research where individuals would find themselves enforced to benchmark against the mass of relevant "achievements" reported by others [40]. Therefore, as these achievements yield upon support and positive network attention valence, individuals will find themselves being exposed to considerable negative social comparisons (when performing upward comparison) [3]. Hence, individuals are more likely to experience stronger malicious envy affects. Hence,

H4c: Compared to negative network attention valence, positive network attention valence will lead to stronger malicious envy affects.

Recent studies have examined the emotional impacts of social information consumption on SNS users [3]. In examining the emotional impacts on SNS users being exposed to different social exhibition and attention responses, Tandoc et al. [1] have found that the amount of attention individuals have received significantly influences SNS users' response behavior and emotions of envy. More so, the magnitude of network attention is important as its suggests that a social update exhibited for consumption has reached a large audience and is well-supported [36]. Therefore, the more positive attention or support responding to a social update along with high (strong) network attention would result in other individuals to perform comparative judgments of oneself against the recognized achievements and social acknowledgements of others [34]. For example, Crusius and Mussweiler [29] revealed that individuals' envious desires impulses when they do not have what others have online. This includes the amount of network attention and social readership one does not receive in comparison to others online. Comparatively, in the case of negative network attention, the effect of network attention strength on malicious envy affects is likely to be weakened. As individuals might develop a sense of benevolence as one receives numerous negative network attention. Therefore, the strength of malicious envy affects associated with network attention strength would not be as effective when faced with a negative network attention valence condition. Hence,

H5a: The effect of network attention strength on malicious envy affects is stronger in the positive network attention valence condition than in the negative network attention valence condition.

Recent research examining social media usage advocates that the consumption of social information exhibited is a key determinant of network attention on envy affects, which are important drivers of a rich spectrum of online social networking behavior. Past IS research have revealed that individuals observing others' positive exhibition of their high achievement online could find themselves feeling inspired or motivated to follow friends who publicize their success. However, Krasnova et al. [3] found that the consumption of positively exhibited information lead to harmful damages to online social network users' affective well-being. This is further supported by a study conducted by Steers et al. [41], on Facebook usage and emotional impacts of individuals when they are presented with positive content. As such, individuals reaction to social exhibition varies based on social comparisons and other aspects of social information (such as the strength and valence of network attention) [36]. As such, when the positive moderation influence of network attention valence is weakened, the affiliated responses from individuals online (e.g. through expressions and reactions of "likes" and "sads" on Facebook) will strengthen the malicious envy affects. Therefore, compared to negative social exhibition, positive social exhibition will result in the increased likelihood of attracting negative network attention valence as individuals foster greater emotions of inferiority when making comparative judgment online. Hence,

H5b: Compared to negative social exhibition, positive social exhibition will weaken the positive moderation influence of network attention valence on the impact of network attention strength on malicious envy affects.

3.2 Behavioral Responses to Envy Emotions

The social comparison theory contends that individuals' envy emotions are vital in shaping their behaviors in social interactions [15]. While past research has identified an array of envy-coping strategies, Krasnova et al. [3] suggest that these coping strategies can be classified based on two key objectives, namely self-enhancement and self-defense. Through self-enhancement, individuals attempt to re-establish and enhance their evaluation of self. Following Krasnova et al. [3], this study examines appreciative usage, which refers to SNS usage activities an individual actions with the focus to show gratitude to others online (i.e. on social networks). Benign envy affects help individuals recognize their self-worth, which is important in motivating further self-improvement. More importantly, benign envy reinforces individuals' belief on their efficacy and capability, which is expected to propel them to taken on self-enhancing behavior.

Through self-defense, individuals attempt to overcome or respond to invidious emotions by inflicting reciprocal damages. To this end, this study focuses on derogatory usage, which refers to SNS usage activities an individual actions with the focus to demean others online. Given that the sources of benign envy do not pose any substantial threat to individuals' self-worth, it is unlikely that they would be motivated to perform derogatory actions against those who have posted benign-inducing social information. Therefore,

H6a: Benign envy affects will increase appreciative usage.
H6b: Malicious envy affects will reduce appreciative usage.

Furthermore, past research examining envy suggests that malicious envy affects could be transmuted into a variety of intense emotions, which might invoke aggressive behavior responses [42]. For example, Van de Ven et al. [10] found that individuals who experienced negative envy were often associated with undesirable emotional outburst, such as renting of frustration, public expression of resentment, and active demonstration of mood disturbance. More importantly, malicious envy affects are found to trigger strong impulses, which could override individuals' rationality and provoke socially damage behavior. Accordingly, when individuals experience malicious envy affect, they are expected to perform less appreciative SNS usage, which tends to generate a distal positive effect on their self-worth, but engage immediate responses through derogatory SNS usage. Therefore,

H7a: Benign envy affects will reduce derogatory usage.
H7b: Malicious envy affects will increase derogatory usage.

4   Research Methodology

A 2 (Social Exhibition: Negative vs. Positive) × 2 (Network Attention Strength: Low vs. High) × 2 (Network Attention Valence: Negative vs. Positive) factorial design laboratory experiment was conducted. Eight experimental condition scenarios were created by manipulating social exhibition, network attention strength and network attention valence. These scenarios were modelled based on the actual Facebook environment and layout.

Social exhibition was manipulated by presenting participants with either a positive or negative scenario in the form of a Facebook social update that is exhibited for information consumption by a poster (i.e. Person X). Based on the social exhibition of the positive and negative information scenarios, network attention strength and valence were also manipulated. Network attention strength was manipulated by changing the total number (i.e. the count) of attention in the form of Facebook reactions (i.e. likes, hahas, sads, angries) as "low" or "high" regarding the social exhibition. Recent research has reported that a Facebook user has an average of 338 friends. Therefore, low network attention strength is represented with 15 responses from the poster's social network – i.e. approximately 5% of an average Facebook user's online friends. Whereas, respectively, high network attention strength is represented with 65 responses – i.e. approximately 20% of an average Facebook user's online friends. Network attention valence was manipulated by categorizing the type of positive and negative network attention that can received based on the social exhibition. As such, the type of social reactions are manipulated to represent network attention valence. Negative network attention valence was represented by "sads" and "angries" reactions, whereas positive network attention valence was represented by "likes" and "hahas" reactions.

Before the main experiment, a pilot test was employed to evaluate the quality of the experimental design and to assess the appropriateness of the experimental stimuli. From the pilot test, the suitable positive social information scenario and negative social information scenario were identified.

A total of 213 participants were recruited to participate in the experiment to ensure sufficient power (0.8) with a medium effect size (where $f = 0.25$) for both the main effects and interaction effects.

5   Data Analysis and Results

5.1   Respondent Demographics and Background Analysis

Among the 213 participants, 107 were male and 106 were females. The age of the participants ranged from 18 to 27. The average time a participant spent on completing the entire experiment was 24.58 min. No Significant differences were found among participants randomly assigned to each of the eight experimental conditions with respect to age and gender, indicating that subjects' demographics were quite homogeneous across different conditions.

5.2   Results on Benign Envy Affects

ANOVA with benign envy affects as dependent variable reveals the significant effects of social exhibition (F (1, 213) = 14.99, p < 0.01), network attention strength (F (1, 213) = 5.09, p < 0.05), and network attention valence (F (1, 213) = 47.69, p < 0.01).

Hence, H1a, H1b, and H1c are supported. The result of ANOVA also revealed that the interactions are significant. In particular, the interaction between network attention strength and network attention valence is significant (F (1, 213) = 16.87, p < 0.01). Hence, H2a and H2b is supported. Additionally, the 3-way interaction is significant (F (1, 213) = 28.52, p < 0.01). To understand the 3-way interaction effect, a simple mean comparison was conducted.

Results of the simple effect analysis show that when social exhibition is negative, the effect of network attention strength on benign envy affects is significant (F (1, 106) = 1246.98, p < 0.01). The effect of network attention valence on benign envy affects is significant (F (1,106) = 17.24, p < 0.05). However, the interaction between network attention strength and network attention valence on benign envy affects is not significant (F (1, 106) = 1.12, p = 0.82).

When social exhibition is positive, the effect of network attention strength on benign envy affects is significant (F (1, 106) = 0.13, p < 0.05). The effect of network attention valence on benign envy affects is significant (F (1,106) = 0.57, p < 0.05). The interaction between network attention strength and network attention valence on benign envy affects is significant (F (1, 106) = 33.61, p < 0.01). Overall, the result supports H3.

5.3   Results on Malicious Envy Affects

ANOVA with malicious envy affects as dependent variable reveals the significant effects of social exhibition (F (1, 213) = 47.19, p < 0.01), network attention strength (F (1, 213) = 34.93, p < 0.05), and network attention valence (F (1, 213) = 145.10, p < 0.01). Hence, H4a, H4b, and H4c are supported. Furthermore, the result of ANOVA also reveals that the interactions are significant. In particular, the interaction between network attention strength and network attention valence is significant (F (1, 213) = 5.17, p < 0.05). Hence H5a is supported. Additionally, the 3-way interaction is significant (F (1, 213) = 16.58, p < 0.01).

To understand the interaction effect, a series of simple mean comparisons was conducted for benign envy affects and malicious envy affects. Results of the simple effect analysis show that when social exhibition is negative, the effect of network attention strength on malicious envy affects is significant (F (1, 106) = 41.99, p < 0.01). The effect of network attention valence on malicious benign envy affects is significant (F (1, 106) = 37.24, p < 0.01). The interaction between network attention strength and network attention valence on malicious envy affects is significant (F (1, 106) = 25.03, p < 0.01).

When social exhibition is positive, the effect of network attention strength on malicious envy affects is significant (F (1, 106) = 5.40, p < 0.05). The effect of network attention valence on malicious envy affects is significant (F (1, 106) = 111.37, p < 0.01). The interaction between network attention strength and network attention valence on malicious envy affects is not significant (F (1, 106) = 1.35, p = 0.248). Therefore, H5b is supported.

5.4   Determinants of Appreciative Usage and Derogatory Usage

To investigate how appreciative usage can be influenced, a regression was performed using benign envy affect and malicious envy affect as the independent factors. Additionally, perceived closeness, self-esteem, Facebook usage experience, gender, and age were considered as control variables. The adjusted R-Square is 0.27. The standardized coefficient of benign envy affect is 0.43 (p < .01) and malicious envy affect is –0.06 (p = .22). Therefore, H6a is supported, but not H6b.

To investigate how derogatory usage can be influenced, a regression was performed using benign envy affect and malicious envy affect as the independent factors. Additionally, perceived closeness, self-esteem, Facebook usage experience, gender, and age were considered as control variables. The adjusted R-Square is 0.20. The standardized coefficient of benign envy affect is –0.49 (p < .01) and malicious envy affect is .028 (p < .01). Therefore, H7a and H7b are supported.

6   Contributions

This study contributes to user psychology and IS literature as a whole, in numerous aspects. By drawing on the Social Comparison Theory, this study offers several key theoretical contributions to the research community. The first theoretical contribution this study makes, is that it is one of the first attempts to investigate the unique role of envy – to extend on current IS and psychology literatures' understanding on both positive and negative implications of envy emotions specific to online social information consumption and technology usage. A general understanding in the literature is that envy is typically an undesirable emotion, which could cause substantial negative implications in social interactions. While the envy literature has largely focused on explaining the negative implications of envy, emerging research has revealed the prevalence of its positive implications. Yet extant research studies have mostly focused on the negatives of envy. As such, the issue of envy triggered by social information consumption and comparison is relatively new and has recently drawn substantial attention from IS researchers [3]. Whilst IS literature has considerably broadened understanding of envy as an emotion associated with technology usage. For example, Chen and Lee [34] research was conducted around users' emotions as they were exposed to different aspects of Facebook. More so, Krasnova et al. [3] research also noted that social information consumption would lead to envy on SNS. Extant research studies are still limited to how envy on SNS mediates the relationship between social information consumption and users' affective and cognitive well-being, base-lining on the negative implications of envy.

The second theoretical contribution is that prior studies have failed to recognize that "benign envy affects" and "malicious envy affects" may exercise different influences. Extant research studies have instead subsumed these two constructs into one construct (i.e. "envy") [10], and subsequently, many researchers have failed to acknowledge the possible differences. Individuals can indeed embrace positive envy (i.e. benign envy) towards others – and at the same time, others may experience negative envy (i.e. malicious envy), and vice versa. As such, benign envy affects are particularly evident when individuals perform downward social comparisons i.e. when individuals are perceived to be better off than others or when individuals' belief on their efficacy and capability are reinforced. Whereas, malicious envy affects are especially evident when individuals unavoidably enforce themselves to benchmark against the successes and achievements of their social networks. As such, this may enable individuals to perform upward social comparison – however, individuals may not necessarily embrace malicious envy as a direct result of upward comparison as individuals can experience malicious envy affects by simply being exposed to the social exhibitions with high network attention. Therefore, the "benign" and "malicious" perspectives of envy affects have profound differences in online social networks. Hence, this research study enriches IS literature by providing empirical evidence which recognizes that benign envy affects and malicious envy affects are two independent, separate constructs.

The third theoretical contribution is that past research studies have predominately emphasized on information disclosure in online social network [4]. As such, to add to current research, this study examines the impact of social information consumption in online social networks by drawing on the concurrent performance of upward social comparison and downward social comparison. Furthermore, the key elements of social information consumption are identified and the respective envy-driven behavioral responses of users are testified through the execution of a laboratory experiment with hypothetical scenarios. As such, this research study contributes to current literature through the exploration of an area of online social networks that has been lightly tapped by extant research. Therefore, this study extends on IS literature through the provision of granular understanding on the impact of social information consumption – particularly, social exhibition, network attention strength and network attention valence in online social networks.

References

1. Tandoc, E.C., Ferrucci, P., Duffy, M.: Facebook use, envy, and depression among college students: Is Facebooking depressing? Comput. Hum. Behav. **43**, 139–146 (2015)
2. Gonzales, A.L., Hancock, J.T.: Mirror, mirror on my Facebook wall: Effects of exposure to Facebook on self-esteem. Cyberpsychology Behav. Soc. Networking **14**(1–2), 79–83 (2011)
3. Krasnova, H., et al.: Research note—why following friends can hurt you: an exploratory investigation of the effects of envy on social networking sites among college-age users. Inf. Syst. Res. **26**(3), 585–605 (2015)
4. Choi, B.C., et al.: Embarrassing exposures in online social networks: An integrated perspective of privacy invasion and relationship bonding. Inf. Syst. Res. **26**(4), 675–694 (2015)
5. Kim, Y., Sohn, D., Choi, S.M.: Cultural difference in motivations for using social network sites: A comparative study of American and Korean college students. Comput. Hum. Behav. **27**(1), 365–372 (2011)
6. Yan, L., Tan, Y.: Feeling blue? Go online: an empirical study of social support among patients. Inf. Syst. Res. **25**(4), 690–709 (2014)
7. Zeng, X., Wei, L.: Social ties and user content generation: Evidence from Flickr. Inf. Syst. Res. **24**(1), 71–87 (2013)
8. MacKinnon, R.: China's "networked authoritarianism". J. Democracy **22**(2), 32–46 (2011)
9. Anderson, C.L., Agarwal, R.: The digitization of healthcare: boundary risks, emotion, and consumer willingness to disclose personal health information. Inf. Syst. Res. **22**(3), 469–490 (2011)
10. Van de Ven, N., Zeelenberg, M., Pieters, R.: Appraisal patterns of envy and related emotions. Motiv. Emot. **36**(2), 195–204 (2012)
11. Toma, C.L., Hancock, J.T.: Self-affirmation underlies Facebook use. Pers. Soc. Psychol. Bull. **39**(3), 321–331 (2013)
12. Kane, G.C. et al.: What's different about social media networks? A framework and research agenda. MIS Q. (2012). Forthcoming
13. Ellison, N.B., Steinfield, C., Lampe, C.: The benefits of Facebook "friends": Social capital and college students' use of online social network sites. J. Comput. Mediated Commun. **12**(4), 1143–1168 (2007)
14. Rosen, L.D., et al.: Is Facebook creating "iDisorders"? The link between clinical symptoms of psychiatric disorders and technology use, attitudes and anxiety. Comput. Hum. Behav. **29**(3), 1243–1254 (2013)
15. Festinger, L.: A theory of social comparison processes. Hum. Relat. **7**(2), 117–140 (1954)
16. Wood, J.V.: What is social comparison and how should we study it? Pers. Soc. Psychol. Bull. **22**(5), 520–537 (1996)
17. Brewer, M.B., Weber, J.G.: Self-evaluation effects of interpersonal versus intergroup social comparison. J. Pers. Soc. Psychol. **66**(2), 268–275 (1994)
18. Huang, J., et al.: Leader–member exchange social comparison and employee deviant behavior: Evidence from a Chinese context. Soc. Behav. Pers. Int. J. **43**(8), 1273–1286 (2015)
19. Roels, G., Su, X.: Optimal design of social comparison effects: Setting reference groups and reference points. Manage. Sci. **60**(3), 606–627 (2013)
20. Nabi, R.L., Keblusek, L.: Inspired by hope, motivated by envy: Comparing the effects of discrete emotions in the process of social comparison to media figures. Media Psychol. **17**(2), 208–234 (2014)
21. Burke, M., Marlow, C., Lento, T.: Feed me: motivating newcomer contribution in social network sites. In: Proceedings of the SIGCHI Conference on Human Factors in Computing Systems. ACM (2009)

22. Kamal, N., Fels, S., Ho, K.: Online social networks for personal informatics to promote positive health behavior. In: Proceedings of Second ACM SIGMM Workshop on Social Media. ACM (2010)
23. Wood, J.V.: Theory and research concerning social comparisons of personal attributes. Psychol. Bull. **106**(2), 231–248 (1989)
24. Breines, J.G., Chen, S.: Self-compassion increases self-improvement motivation. Pers. Soc. Psychol. Bull. **38**(9), 1133–1143 (2012)
25. Blanton, H., et al.: When better-than-others compare upward: Choice of comparison and comparative evaluation as independent predictors of academic performance. J. Pers. Soc. Psychol. **76**(3), 420 (1999)
26. Richins, M.L.: Social comparison and the idealized images of advertising. J. Consum. Res. **18**(1), 71–83 (1991)
27. Sundararajan, A., et al.: Research commentary—information in digital, economic, and social networks. Inf. Syst. Res. **24**(4), 883–905 (2013)
28. Johnson, C.: Behavioral responses to threatening social comparisons: From dastardly deeds to rising above. Soc. Pers. Psychol. Compass **6**(7), 515–524 (2012)
29. Crusius, J., Mussweiler, T.: When people want what others have: the impulsive side of envious desire. Emotion **12**(1), 142 (2012)
30. Hoelzl, E., Loewenstein, G.: Wearing out your shoes to prevent someone else from stepping into them: Anticipated regret and social takeover in sequential decisions. Organ. Behav. Hum. Decis. Process. **98**(1), 15–27 (2005)
31. Zizzo, D.J., Oswald, A.J.: Are people willing to pay to reduce others' incomes? Ann. d'Economie et de Stat., 39–65 (2001)
32. Chou, H.-T.G., Edge, N.: "They are happier and having better lives than I am": the impact of using Facebook on perceptions of others' lives. Cyberpsychol. Behav. Soc. Netw. **15**(2), 117–121 (2012)
33. Madge, C., et al.: Facebook, social integration and informal learning at university: 'It is more for socialising and talking to friends about work than for actually doing work'. Learn. Media Technol. **34**(2), 141–155 (2009)
34. Chen, W., Lee, K.-H.: Sharing, liking, commenting, and distressed? The pathway between Facebook interaction and psychological distress. Cyberpsychol. Behav. Soc. Netw. **16**(10), 728–734 (2013)
35. Laidlaw, K.E., et al.: Potential social interactions are important to social attention. Proc. Natl. Acad. Sci. **108**(14), 5548–5553 (2011)
36. Lee, S.Y.: How do people compare themselves with others on social network sites?: The case of Facebook. Comput. Hum. Behav. **32**, 253–260 (2014)
37. Kingstone, A.: Taking a real look at social attention. Curr. Opin. Neurobiol. **19**(1), 52–56 (2009)
38. Greitemeyer, T.: Facebook and people's state self-esteem: The impact of the number of other users' Facebook friends. Comput. Hum. Behav. **59**, 182–186 (2016)
39. Kross, E., et al.: Facebook use predicts declines in subjective well-being in young adults. PLoS ONE **8**(8), e69841 (2013)
40. Oldmeadow, J.A., Quinn, S., Kowert, R.: Attachment style, social skills, and Facebook use amongst adults. Comput. Hum. Behav. **29**(3), 1142–1149 (2013)
41. Steers, M.-L.N., Wickham, R.E., Acitelli, L.K.: Seeing everyone else's highlight reels: How Facebook usage is linked to depressive symptoms. J. Soc. Clin. Psychol. **33**(8), 701–731 (2014)
42. Smith, R.H., Kim, S.H.: Comprehending envy. Psychol. Bull. **133**(1), 46 (2007)

Context Sensitive Digital Marketing - A Conceptual Framework Based on the Service Dominant Logic Approach

Konrad Zerr[✉], Rudolf Albert, and Anja Forster

Business School University of Applied Science, Tiefenbronner Straße 65, 75175 Pforzheim, Germany
{konrad.zerr,anja.forster}@hs-pforzheim.de,
rudolf.albert@gmail.com

Abstract. The "Service Dominant Logic" (SDL) approach suggests that value for the consumer is generated only while using a product (value in use). Extending this perspective, the concept "value in context" considers the impact of the specific usage situation. We shall develop a classification of context dimensions with respect to their relevance in influencing the value for the customer.

While technology today provides innumerous systems to measure context factors, it is highly important to develop suitable algorithms to transform data into knowledge allowing real time reactions as there are presentation of information, automated execution of functions and services and tagging of customer data for future use. While presentation of information is already used in smart online marketing we see a lot of potential for innovations in context-sensitive online services and will provide some ideas in this paper.

We will focus on two key challenges for digital brand management: brand integration and customer integration into the context of the usage situation. To this end we introduce the term "brand viscosity" describing the capability of the brand to adjust to a specific context situation. E.g. it should be possible to select and combine context-relevant brand attributes out a set of predefined brand-specific symbols, language styles and stories and digitally display those that promise the highest value in context. In such way, the brand substance, the brand image and its relationship with the customer, who is considered as "value (co) creator", are designed so that they can adapt to the specific context conditions without losing its basic identity.

This paper is addressed to marketers by giving guidelines for the design of a context-sensitive digital marketing approach as well as to researchers by providing a framework to link the theoretical concepts of SDL, digital brand management and the concept of context-sensitivity.

1 Introduction

Already in 2000, Kenny and Marshall claimed the need for Contextual Marketing. They challenged companies "…to use the power and reach of the internet to deliver tailored messages and information to customers at the point of need." [1] Compared to

© Springer International Publishing AG 2017
F.F.-H. Nah and C.-H. Tan (Eds.): HCIBGO 2017, PART II, LNCS 10294, pp. 298–312, 2017.
DOI: 10.1007/978-3-319-58484-3_23

then, technology today provides numerous possibilities for measuring context and delivering not only tailored information but also other context specific marketing reactions. Sensors, embedded systems, wearables, visual and audio recording – all enlarge the scope of digitally visible context parameters. Highly important, however, are suitable algorithms to transform data into knowledge allowing real time reaction. To develop such algorithms for real-time contextual marketing, models are required that can capture the interdependencies between three factors: the context situation, the value generated while using a digital service or product and the marketing reactions influencing the situation. The objective of this paper is to design a conceptual framework for context sensitive digital marketing. For that purpose, we will classify relevant context dimensions and describe theoretical models as a basis for the development of an algorithmic processing context sensitive to real-time marketing reactions. We shall group possible marketing reactions and generate some ideas for innovations in context sensitive online services. Finally, we will draft the challenges on digital brand management within a context sensitive real time world. The guiding principle for these concepts is the "Service Dominant Logic" (SDL) approach.

2 Contextual Digital Marketing Based on the Service Dominant Logic Approach

2.1 "Value in Context" as a Paradigm of Digital Marketing

Marketing must offer benefits, that is, promote value-creation not just for the company, but especially for its customers and target groups. Such values may be informational ("information value"), entertaining ("experience value"), or supporting ("service value") [2, 3]. An information value can arise, for example, from algorithmically generated, individual product recommendations, such as are provided by Amazon Prime or Netflix. An experience value arises for example through entertaining content or usability that is appropriate to the target group. A comfortable search function within Netflix can provide a service value.

Customer values are always context-dependent which fact justifies the service dominant logic approach (SDL approach). It suggests that value for the customer is generated only while using a product or service ("value in context") [4–6]. It is not the provider who creates value, but the customers themselves who are "value producers" by integrating their resources into an interactive usage process characterized by specific context factors. The supplier offers only value potentials. Condensation of this process is a cognitive and emotional customer experience, from which future expectations of benefit arise.

For providers of digital services, the task is to support this "production process" on the customer side as well as possible. It is this value in context perspective that makes the SDL approach ideal as a conceptual framework for digital marketing. It helps the automated identification of both the resources entered by the customer in an interaction situation and the specific context factors that characterize it. The classification of these two aspects and the diagnosis of their influence on the value in context is a prerequisite to be able to react algorithmically and automatically along with the usage situation.

2.2   Definition of "Context" and "Context Sensitive Digital Marketing"

The term context is used in different scientific disciplines and is correspondingly complex. In the linguistic and literary sciences, context denotes analyzing and understanding of verbal expressions or texts that are created under specific circumstances. In psychology and sociology, context is considered to be an influencing factor on human behavior and the shaping of social network relationships [7]. In computer science, on the other hand, context plays an important role in the development of so-called "context-sensitive" systems within the framework of "pervasive computing", "context aware computing" [8, 9], "ubiquitous" or "embedded computing" concepts.

Dey provides a frequently cited definition from the point of view of "context aware computing": "Context is any information that can be used to characterize the situation of an entity. An entity is a person, place, or object that is considered relevant to the interaction between a user and an application, including the user and applications themselves" [10]. Therefore, situational aspects are only contextual if they are closely related to the interacting person or the object. Context thus includes a valuation of a situational aspect about its relevance for a concrete action [11]. Out the perspective of pervasive computing, Ferscha concretizes the concept of context sensitivity as a "... system behavior that considers the present and possibly expected future situation of an artefact or the user and acts in a correspondingly plan-based (intelligently) manner." [12][1]

In linking these two perspectives, we define context-sensitive digital marketing as plan-based, automated marketing reactions based on the identification and interpretation of the relevant circumstances - relevant to the respective interaction situation and the related purpose. The identification and interpretation of the context as well as the marketing reactions derived from it are usually automated and real-time. One of the challenges of digital marketing is therefore to filter out the most relevant factors for customer-oriented value generation from the multiplicity of situational factors surrounding an interaction situation in real-time [13].

2.3   Classification of "Context"

Context classifications support the identification of value-relevant factors by providing a "search frame" orientation. With marketing aspects, the linking of the sociological-psychological and the information-technological perspective appears promising. However, we see three broad deficits in the approaches discussed so far in the literature. These are usually enumerative, barely link the mentioned perspectives, or they do not adequately consider the new possibilities arising from developments in sensor technology.

Therefore, we have developed a two-dimensional model for context classification. Each context factor can accordingly be described using two dimensions:

- Dimension 1: Inner and outer context factors [13].
- Dimension 2: Latent and acute context factors.

---

[1] Original text: "...Systemverhalten, das die gegenwärtige und ggf. auch erwartete zukünftige Situation eines Artefaktes oder des Benutzers berücksichtigt und entsprechend planbasiert (intelligent) handelt."

Dimension 1 establishes the reference of the context factor to the user. With the **"inner context"** we refer to context factors of the usage situation, which are directly connected to the person generating the benefit. This includes the psychological and demographic characteristics of the user, his or her personality as well as cultural character and the associated long-term values. Other context factors in this class may be the belonging to a specific customer segment, a social group or a social milieu. We also consider here the utilization history or intensity and the duration of the relationship with the service provider. Particularly relevant are the motivation and the intention, as well as the current emotional mood that determines the interaction situation. Precisely such factors can be quite different depending on the usage situation even regarding an identical object of action.

Outer context factors are the aspects directly surrounding the acting individual, which are usually consciously perceived and which shape the contact situation. These factors interact with the inner context and influence the intentional, motivational and emotional processes in the contact situation. Outer context factors include the technical, temporal, spatial, social and climatic context within which an interaction takes place. To illustrate: there are experimental studies showing that purchasing behavior, perceived value, and price stability are influenced by the device used **(technical context)** [14, 15]. **The spatial environment**, e.g. private or public space [16] influences the emotional condition of the user, the usage behavior and thus the perceived value [17]. Similarly, the **temporal** or **climatic** context may also act as a value-influencing factor in a usage situation. Other aspects which indirectly affect the use situation and exert an influence on their experience are, for example, the geographic space within which the usage situation is located (for example, during a holiday trip) and the associated **cultural environment** of use.

Dimension 2 describes the relationship between the depicted outer or inner context factors and the concrete usage situation. We distinguish between "acute" and "latent" context. The **latent context** includes those influencing factors that have an indirect value-influencing effect in a concrete usage situation. These are rather static compared with the acute use situation. They exert an influence on the specific interaction situation but are not strongly influenced by it (for example, stable psychographic or demographic characteristics, cultural characteristics, climatic conditions, etc.). Even if they are stable in a largely unchanged manner over several use situations, their influence on the respective value generation may differ due to interactions with other factors.

The **acute context** refers to influencing factors that define the individual moment in a unique way with respect to a specific usage situation. These can, on the one hand, be distinguished by their degree of variability during the interaction. A supplier could record these in a real-time situation and to influence them through interaction-specific value propositions. These factors include, for example, the acute emotional condition of a user that can be weakened or strengthened by specific digital marketing reactions or the concrete motive behind a usage situation, which can be changed by dynamic reactions. Different from these very volatile context factors, on the other hand, are those which are unique in terms of the value-generating interaction situation (for example, persons present, temperature of the room, public or private interaction site) but that cannot be changed from the supplier's point of view.

Table 1. Two-dimensional context classification and example assignment of context factors.

Context factors	Latent (static)	Acute (dynamic)
Inner *(Person-related and can* *be influenced by provider* *real-time or longer-term)*	milieu personality type demographic features cultural impact recoveries interaction history etc. ...	emotional condition action motive/intention interaction behavior etc. ....
Outer *(Related to the usage* *situation and considered* *by the provider as a* *framework)*	climate zone season place of residence social networking etc.	cultural environment social environment/people present location of interaction weather, temperature, time intermediate medium used etc.....

In Table 1 the two-dimensional classification of context factors will be summarized by means of examples.

The acute context factors must be identified, classified and converted into automated marketing reactions based on real-time data. The latent context factors, on the other hand, can be allocated based on historical data and linked to the real-time data. The combination of context factors of different types allows the definition of diverse contextual scenarios on the basis of which automated, digital marketing reactions can be defined in a real-time plan-based manner.

3   Identification of the Context in the Digital Usage Situation as the Base of Context-Sensitive Digital Marketing

3.1   Necessary Algorithms and Models for Contextual Digital Marketing

In the field of computer science, there are different, in some cases overlapping, research areas that offer approaches for the development of context-sensitive systems. Examples include "pervasive computing", "context aware computing", "ambient intelligence", "ubiquitous" or "embedded computing" [18, 19]. What is common to all is ultimately the question of how information technology can ubiquitously support people discretely in reaching their goals and intentions while considering situational aspects.

The technical possibilities to find answers to this question have grown enormously in recent years. The advancement of sensor technology is at the forefront of capturing context-oriented data. Ever smaller, more powerful sensors, embedded in everyday objects (embedded systems) offer theoretically almost unlimited possibilities to understand the contextual situations in which people are acting. These sensors often do not work independently, but are networked, communicate with each other, and transmit their data to central servers or data warehouses in the cloud ("internet of things"). Data generated from different sources can be aggregated into "big data" pools, which, using appropriate analysis processes and instruments (real time processing), allow a realistic and comprehensive picture of the current context and context-appropriate reactions [20].

Smart phones, but also smart TV, wearables, such as smart watches or smart textiles, smart meters, connected, autonomous vehicles – all these systems include sensor technologies and embedded analysis algorithms for detecting the user context. Smart TV, for example, already offers the option of switching regional adapted TV advertising based on geographic data. If the smart TV is within the same Wi-Fi as the smartphone, tablet or notebook of a user, then the usage data collected there can theoretically be combined with those of the Smart TV. This allows a deep understanding of interests, preferences and moods of a user. The smart phones like those developed as part of Google's "Tango Project" can actively detect their environment and display it in real-time. Outer and inner context factors become comprehensible in the usage situation. Machines which "see" or understand language provide possibilities for automated cognitive performance in the assessment of context situations, also situations involving emotional or social interactions [12, 21].

The data provided by sensor technology and other sources require algorithms – i.e. unique, automated executable action rules – for dealing with the data collected to give it meaning relevant to the solution of a specific problem.

Depending on their contribution to solving the problem, three different types of algorithms can be distinguished:

- Algorithms that provide action-guiding information; E.g. Information about the shopping history and the product interests of an online buyer.
- Algorithms that also link information to knowledge and, on this basis, provide automated recommendations for action; E.g. Information about product interests of an online customer linked to the actual buying behavior of similar customers and resulting purchase recommendations.
- Algorithms that automatically decide and trigger context-dependent actions as well as independent actions for task fulfillment. E.g. An automatic braking operation of a collision protection system in a car or bots which independently pre-configure the goods baskets or order products upon reaching certain price thresholds.

The development of such algorithms should be based on sound theory and empirically verifiable models. From our point of view, three model types are necessary to implement a context-sensitive digital marketing approach to increasing the value in context during digital interaction situations (see Fig. 1):

- Models that attribute the context to data: E.g. the emotional dimension "relaxed" can be attributed to usage time (evening), used device (tablet) and tiredness (slow control activity).
- Models describing the effect of the context: These help to identify the relevant context dimensions for a specific usage situation, as well as to determine the direction and magnitude of its influence on the value in context [22].
- Marketing response models: These models show what marketing reactions under specific context conditions are suitable to optimize the customer experience during the interaction and thus the value in context. This requires modeling of the relationship between value proposition, contextual situation and value creation (value in context).

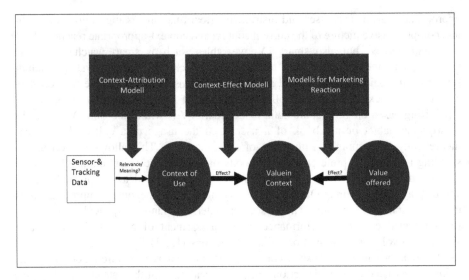

Fig. 1. Necessary models for developing digital marketing algorithm.

For the development of algorithms of the relations formulated in these models, computer science and statistics provide a variety of concepts and tools. Most recently, there have been significant advances in both the so-called symbolic and sub-symbolic procedures of artificial intelligence[2]. Taxonomies, ontologies, or neural networks help in the definition of context situations and the systematization of possible value propositions. Logic, rule-based closing, or "case based reasoning" considering historical data, enable the implementation of self-optimizing, learning-capable marketing reaction models. This also applies to non-directional or directed correlations between contextual situations and value propositions [22]. Correlation or similarity measures provide the statistical basis for collaborative or content-based filtering. Netflix, for example, uses this to automatically display product recommendations [23]. Simple or Bayesian probability calculations can help determine the relevance of different context dimensions for the value in context. Causal relations between the context situation and value in context can also be recognized by multivariate statistical methods or data mining techniques.

3.2   The Reaction Possibilities of Contextual Digital Marketing

According to Dey & Abowd context sensitive software systems allow basically three possible responses [10, 20]:

- Presentation of context-oriented information or functions
- (Automated) Execution of functions or services
- Tagging: enhancement of data with context information for subsequent marketing activities

---

[2] For a critical discussion of appropriate methods see [24], p. 127–142.

The first aspect is already an important part of a professional online marketing. As part of the Real-Time Bidding and Advertising, Programmatic Marketing or Targeting online marketing actions are controlled depending on different contextual factors.

We see potential for innovations in the offer of context-sensitive, value adding online services. Amazon and Netflix for example show that well-crafted, intelligent recommendation systems deliver valuable information on context-appropriate consumption options. This could be further developed in the future into automated "curated shopping" systems that provide situation-specific, useful and individual recommendations in real time. Further potential for increasing the value in context results from context-sensitive assistance and support systems. "real-time pricing" or "dynamic pricing" models may establish individual and context specific prices depending on the customer-specific payment readiness that has been algorithmically determined in the specific context.

The contextual information of a usage situation need not necessarily always act as trigger for real-time based digital marketing responses. It may be also useful to archive them first and use them later. For this purpose, it is usually necessary to link the manifold of incoming context-based information with data from other sources by using methods like record linkage, data matching and/or data fusion [25]. This creates valuable "big data" pools, which can be exploited by methods of data mining.

4 Challenges for the Digital Brand Management

4.1 The Digital Brand Management Frame

It has been shown that new technological possibilities, created by sensor technologies and the connected internet of things, create almost unlimited options for a data-based, real-time-based digital marketing. Previous approaches, e.g. the already mentioned real-time bidding, targeting or programmatic marketing or the use of the currently strongly discussed "bots" in the marketing communication fall short however. They are by no means sufficient to exploit the available technological tools for identifying relevant context factors and for deriving automated marketing reactions. In addition, their field of application is limited to a comparatively small task of brand management. Brand management overall, however, faces the challenge of exploiting the many new possibilities.

To this end, a rethink or paradigm shift of traditional brand management appears necessary. In the literature, the context-oriented design of the brand appearance is often assigned to the "operational perspective" [26]. This point of view ignores the value in context as the driver of the customer-oriented brand value in a digital real-time world. The value in context perceived by the customer in an interaction situation is essentially determined by the value contribution a brand can achieve, considering in particular the acute context factors.

Therefore, real-life situations should not be dismissed as an operational task, but rather planned strategically. This means putting more focus on the contribution a brand can deliver to the value in context, considering the acute context factors in a specific interaction. Bonchek and France formulate aptly: *"A brand is not something you manage over time. It's something you deliver in the moment"* [27]. Rigid positioning models need to be made dynamic without diluting the brand identity. Keller claims in this regard *"..provide them (consumers, the author) with a highly customized and tailored brand experience.."* [28] and he warns against the risk of dilution of the brand [28, 29]. For these reasons, other authors demand that the brand's **"responsiveness"** and **"interactivity"** be improved in the digital environment [30, 31].

In the real-time digital world, we see a central task of context-sensitive brand management in the re-alignment of the tension field between brand continuity and brand adaptation. We refer to this adjustment as the **"brand viscosity"**, that is, the ability to adapt and integrate the brand in a specific interaction situation. The brand viscosity must be determined in such a way that an optimal balance is found between the respective value in context on the one hand and the customer-oriented brand value on the other. The illustrated models for context attribution, effect and reaction require a distinctive, brand adequate operationalization. Based on this, algorithms can be developed that realize a defined viscosity of the brand in concrete situations. It is necessary to identify the relevant context factors for the brand, to interpret them in their interactions, to anticipate contextual scenarios and to develop strategy-compliant reaction patterns for the digital interaction.

If one follows the idea of the service dominant logic approach, the generation of value in context is dependent not only on the value offered by the brand, but also on the customer's responses to specific context factors. Merrilees therefore sees a paradigm shift from a "customer-centric" to a "customer-driving" marketing [31]. The value in context is influenced by the context-dependent behavior and feeling of the customer himself. The customer becomes the "value (co-) creator". His or her ability and willingness to be involved in the generation of values in the acute use situation is also dependent on, or interacts with, personal emotions and experiences. These, in turn, are ultimately value-creating or determine the value in context of the customer [29, 32].

A further central task of context-sensitive brand management is therefore twofold: First, to positively influence the customer's context-dependent willingness to integrate into the process of value generation; second, to influence the customer's experiences with the process during the interaction. To this end, based on the models presented, systems are to be developed that can be addressed to customers in real-time in a context-oriented manner that promote customers' willingness to integrate. The aim is to increase the brand experience, the associated value in context and ultimately the "customer based brand value".

Figure 2 summarizes these ideas. It illustrates that the value in context is, on the one hand, influenced by the brand viscosity, i.e. the adaptability of the brand to the specific context of the interaction situation. On the other hand, it is influenced by the customer's context-dependent willingness to integrate. The value in context, determined by brand viscosity and customer integration, then forms the basis for the creation of a customer-oriented brand value as the central goal of the brand management [33].

4.2   Brand Viscosity as Challenge for the Digital Brand Management

Figure 2 shows, on the left, the basic design elements for determining the brand viscosity [34]:

- The brand substance, i.e. the functional, emotional, aesthetic and social brand performance in the sense of the offered value potential.
- The brand image, i.e. the associations and perceptions associated with the brand, caused by the communication of the value potential by means of brand-specific symbolism, language and stories.
- The brand relations, i.e. the definition of the roles and responsibilities between supplier and customer in the context of an interaction situation [27].

With respect to the brand substance, this means for example that the functional, emotional, aesthetic and social performance of the brand is carefully enriched with contextual components. A successful example of this is the context-dependent, event-oriented design of the emotional-aesthetic brand performance of Google's signature in the form of Google doodles.

Further possibilities include the augmentation of the core performance of a brand by context-dependent additional services. For example, the automotive industry already offers its customers, in a variety of ways, context-sensitive, digital "smart services". They help to increase the value contribution of the brand to the customer in a specific usage situation. The potential, derived from consideration of, in particular, acute context factors, seems far from being exhausted.

The brand substance forms the basis for the creation of a credible, authentic **brand image**. This can also be outlined in a context-dependent manner and in real-time. Thus, it is conceivable and technically possible, depending on the context situation, to select

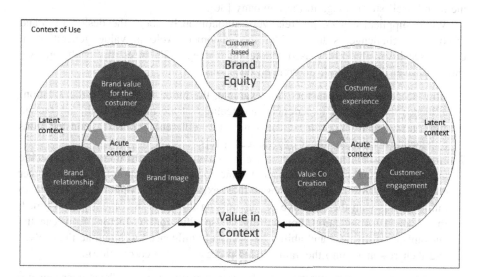

Fig. 2. Brand viscosity and customer integration as the central challenges of context-oriented brand management.

from a set of brand attributes predefined within the framework of the positioning strategy those which are specifically relevant to the context, and to emphasize them in communications with the customer. From a predefined set of brand-specific symbols, language styles and stories, it should be possible to select, combine, and digitally display those that promise the highest value in context. To that end, the mentioned elements that enrich the brand with meaning should be modularized, then a suitable combination of those modules should be assigned to context scenarios within the context effect model and integrated into the marketing reaction model.

Finally, it is also necessary to shape **brand relationships** with customers in a context-specific manner. Depending on the context, the roles between the provider and the customer can be defined differently within the framework of the interaction, and role-specific information or services can be offered in real-time. For example, depending on the proficiency of a viewer, Netflix could assign different roles (for example expert or layman) and use it for corresponding recommendations or information.

4.3   Customer Integration as Challenge for the Digital Brand Management

Within the SDL approach, the customer's engagement during the interaction situation, his or her willingness to provide resources in the moment, and the resulting experiences become central for the value creation. The principles developed there can be guidelines for brand management in the digital real-world. Especially in the world of social networks, customers are active co-creators of the brand, of its identity and of the value-generating experiences that relate to it [35]. The importance of the customers in shaping the brand has grown so far that the question is increasingly raised as to whether the brand itself still belongs to the company [36].

While suppliers can decide relatively autonomously about the design of brand viscosity, a challenge is to consider the customer's role in value generation in context-sensitive, algorithm-based marketing concepts. To meet this challenge, we should answer three central, interrelated questions:

1. How do acute context factors (for example, the mood of a user or the location) influence the customer experiences and feelings at the moment of the interaction and how can algorithms respond to different context constellations (interaction-related customer experiences) [31]?
2. How strong is the involvement and engagement of the customer in the specific interaction situation with respect to the brand (interaction-related customer engagement) [28, 31] and what possibilities exist from the supplier's perspective to influence this with the objective of maximizing the value in context in real time?
3. In the acute use situation, considering the specific context factors, how can the customers' willingness and ability be positively influenced to integrate themselves and their resources into the value-added process? (value co-creation)

In the comprehensive literature, the "customer experience" and "customer engagement" concepts are usually considered in the role they play in the long-term customer relationship over several interaction phases [37, 38]. From our point of view, this focus must be supplemented in a real-time world by the insights gained from the acute, interaction-related perspective. At the core of context-sensitive brand management is, above all, the dynamics that arise between the supplier and the user at the moment of use of the brand, considering the specific contextual factors in the immediate situation. The context-dependent possibilities of influence in the moment of value creation are to be considered more intensively in the light of the now diverse technological possibilities, while considering the strategic objectives of the brand management.

In particular, Merrilees models the relationship between interactive "brand experiences", customer engagement and value co-creation [31]. He clarifies that the brand-specific sensations and experiences generated in the interaction situation substantially influence the customer's commitment and willingness to participate in the use situation. He also assumes that the willingness to value co-creation differs significantly because of different interactive experiences with "hedonic brands" and "functional brands". While Merrilees assumes a moderate willingness to participate in functional brands due to the dominant cognitive processes, the emotional experiences of hedonic brands lead to a strong willingness to participate in the generation of value [28, 31]. Therefore, comparable context constellations for the same customer are to be interpreted differently from the point of view of brand management, depending on the type of brand, meaning they are to be addressed with different marketing reactions.

But Merrilees hardly considers the significance of acute context factors for the value in context. The concept of brand management needs to formulate "customer experience" as more than experience and sensation related to the moment of the interaction. Experiences are more than "long-term experiences" with the brand. Hence, the need arises to provide value-generating experiences in their dependence on acute contextual factors, e.g. the acute emotional mood of the user, the existing social environment or the location of the use.

For example, Netflix could design its product recommendations very differently depending on whether a user is sad or euphoric, lonely or together with a partner or in a group of friends seeking relaxation. In the same way, the cognitive, emotional or behavior-oriented commitment of the customer should also be considered as context-dependent and possibly open to influence from the marketing strategy. After a long working day, a tired, overworked user will have a different "psychological or physical investment… in that brand" [39] than in a relaxed holiday situation. Finally, the willingness and ability of a customer to bring resources (for example, knowledge, personal data, time, etc. [40]) into the process of value creation must also be viewed and controlled in a context-dependent manner. Digital brand management should better understand customers as a resource of value creation in the usage situation and develop algorithms to influence customer integration depending on the contextual factors characterizing the situation.

5 Summary

In this article, a concept is developed and presented based on the Service-Dominant Logic Approach. The concept can serve as an orientation in the design of context-sensitive digital marketing approaches. It was shown that in a real-world environment, the "utilization moment" and the factors influencing it are central in the creation of a value in context. This is at the same time the driver of the customer-oriented brand value. Brand management in the digital real-time world becomes more complex as brand perception and brand use are context-dependent, changeable and more difficult to influence at any time. To overcome this complexity, it is necessary to formulate brand-specific models for context allocation, context effect and marketing reaction. A central task of brand management in the digital real-time world is to formulate context scenarios and to define possible marketing reactions. For this purpose, it is important to understand which context dimensions are relevant for the brand and how they function in the value creation process. At the same time, to ensure the integrity of brand management, it is imperative to prevent unintended contextual scenarios in digital usage situations. Even in a real-world environment, the importance of the brand is retained: strong brands shape the context. Weak brands are formed by the context!

References

1. Kenny, D., Marshall, J.F.: Contextual marketing – the real business of the internet. Harvard Bus. Rev. **78**, 119–125 (2000)
2. Holbrook, M.: Special session summary customer value – a framework for analysis and research. Adv. Consum. Res. **23**, 138–142 (1996)
3. Edvardsson, B., et al.: Why is service-dominant logic based service system better? Int. J. Qual. Serv. Sci. **5**(2), 171–190 (2013)
4. Sandström, S., et al.: Value in use through service experience. Manag. Serv. Qual. **18**(2), 112–126 (2008)
5. Vargo, S.L., et al.: On value and value co-creation: a service systems and service logic perspective. Eur. Manage. J. **26**, 145–152 (2008)
6. Vargo, S.L., Lusch, R.F.: Evolving to a new dominant logic for marketing. J. Mark. **68**, 1–17 (2004)
7. Chandler, J.D., Vargo, S.L.: Contextualization and value in context: how context frames exchange. Mark. Theor. **11**(1), 35–49 (2011)
8. Dey, A.K.: Understanding and using context. Pers. Ubiquit. Comput. **5**, 4–7 (2001)
9. Schilit, B.N., Adams, N., Want, R.: Context aware computing applications. In: IEE Workshop on Mobile Computing Systems and Applications, 8–9 December 1994. http://csis.pace.edu/~marchese/CS396x/L3/wmc-94-schilit.pdf. Accessed 21 Dec 2016
10. Dey, A.K., Abowd, G.D.: Towards a better understanding of context and context-awareness. Graphics, Visualization and Usability Center and College of Computing. Georgia Institute of Technology, Atlanta/Georgia 8 July 1999. ftp://ftp.cc.gatech.edu/pub/gvu/tr/1999/99-22.pdf. Accessed 20 Jul 2016
11. Winograd, T.: Architectures for context. J. Hum. Comput. Interact. **16**(2–3), 401–419 (2001)

12. Ferscha, A.: Pervasive computing: connected > aware > smart. In: Mattern, F. (Hrsg.): Die Informatisierung des Alltags – Leben in smarten Umgebungen, S. 3–10. Springer, Heidelberg (2007)

13. Zerr/Linxweiler/Forster, Kontextorientiertes Marketing zur Steigerung des "value in context". In: Theobald E. (Ed.), Brand Evolution – Moderne Markenführung im digitalen Zeitalter, 2. Aufl., Wiesbaden, pp. 167–195 (2017)

14. Brasel, S.A., Gips, J.: Tablets, touchscreens, and touchpads: how varying touch interfaces trigger psychological ownership and endowment. J. Consum. Psychol. **24**(2), 226–233 (2014)

15. Hildebrand, C., Der Tablet-Effekt – Wie (und warum) Multi-Touch Geräte ihre Produkte erlebbar machen, Lecture at the 9th NeuroMarketing Congress, München, 21 April 2016. www.neuromarketing-wissen.de, http://neuromarketing-wissen.de/wp-content/uploads/2016/04/Hildebrand_Handout_NMK2016.pdf. Accessed 05 Jul 2016

16. Nagel, W., Fischer V.: Multiscreen Experience Design: Prinzipien, Muster und Faktoren für die Strategieentwicklung und Konzeption digitaler Services für verschiedene Endgeräte, Schwäbisch Gmünd (2013)

17. Mau, G.: Die Bedeutung der Emotionen beim Besuch von Online-Shops. Determinanten und Wirkungen. Wiesbaden, Messung (2009)

18. Hong, J.-Y., et al.: Context-aware systems: a literature review and classification. Expert Syst. Appl. **36**, 8509–8522 (2009)

19. Musumba, G.W., Nyongesa, H.O.: Context awareness in mobile computing: a review. Int. J. Machine Learn Appl. **2**(1), Art. #5, 10 pages (2013). http://dx.doi.org/10.4102/ ijmla.v2i1.5

20. Perera, C. et al.: A survey on internet of things from industrial market perspective. IEEE Access J. (2015). https://arxiv.org/pdf/1502.00164.pdf, www.arxiv.org. Accessed 18 Jul 2016

21. Chitkara, R.: Mobile innovation forecasts – Phase II Wrap-up: context as a driving force for mobile innovation, PwC – Innovation Institute (Editor), p. 6 (2014). http://www.pwc.com/gx/en/technology/mobile-innovation/assets/pwc-context-as-driving-force.pdf Accessed 20 Jul 2016

22. Ziegler, J., Lohmann, S., Kaltz, W.: Kontextmodellierung für adaptive webbasierte Systeme. In: Stay, C. (Hrsg.): Mensch & Computer 2005: Kunst und Wissenschaft – Grenzüberschreitungen der interaktiven ART, München, pp. 181–189 (2005)

23. Drösser, C.: Total Berechenbar? – Wenn Algorithmen für uns entscheiden. München (2016)

24. Hofstetter, Y.: Sie wissen alles - wie intelligente Maschinen in unser Leben eindringen und warum wir für unsere Freiheit kämpfen müssen. München (2014)

25. Cielebak, J., Rässler, S.: DataFusion, Record Linkage und Data Mining. In: Bauer N., Blasius J. (Hrsg.): Handbuch Methoden der empirischen Sozialforschung, Wiesbaden, pp. 367–382 (2014)

26. Esch, F.R., Köhler, I.: Brand Engagement – Wie Marken versuchen enge Kundenbeziehungen zu generieren. Transf. Werbeforschung Prax. **62**(4), 20–28 (2016)

27. Bonchek, M., France, C.: Build your brand as a relationship. Harvard Bus. Rev. 09 May 2016. https://hbr.org/2016/05/build-your-brand-as-a-relationship. Accessed 04 Jan 2017

28. Keller, K.L.: Reflections on customer-based brand equity: perspectives, progress, and priorities. Acad. Mark. Sci. Rev. **6**, 1–16 (2016). Published online 20 May 2016

29. Swaminathan, V.: Branding in the digital era: new directions for research on customer-based brand equity. Acad. Mark. Sci. Rev. **6**, 33–38 (2016). Published online 20 May 2016

30. Gürhan-Canli, Z., Hayran, C., Sarial-Abi, G.: Customer-based brand equity in a technologically fast-paced, connected, and constrained environment. Acad. Mark. Sci. Rev. **6**, 23–32 (2016). Published online 20 May 2016

31. Merrilees, B.: Interactive brand experience pathways to customer-brand engagement and value co-creation. J. Prod. Brand Manage. **25**(5), 402–408 (2016)
32. Grönross, C., Voima, P.J.: Making sense of value and value-co-creation in service logic. In: Working Paper 559. Hanken School of Economics (2011)
33. Keller, K.L.: Conceptualizing, measuring, and managing customer-based brand equity. J. Mark. **57**(1), 1–22 (1993)
34. Zerr, K., Eberling G.: Kommunikationscontrolling in Dienstleistungsunternehmen. In: Esch, F.-R., Langner, T., Bruhn, M. (Hrsg.), Wiesbaden, pp. 629–658 (2016)
35. Hajli, N., Shanmugam, M., Papagiannidis, S., Zahay, D., Richard, M.O.: Branding co-creation with members of online brand communizies. J. Bus. Res. **70**, 136–144 (2017)
36. Black, I., Veloutsou, C.: Working consumers: Co-creation of brand identity, consumer identity and brand community identity. J. Bus. Res. **70**, 416–429 (2017)
37. Brodie, R.J., Hollebeek, L.D., Juric, B., Ilic, A.: Customer engagement: conceptual domain, fundamental propositions, and implications for research. J. Serv. Res. **14**(3), 252–271 (2011)
38. Doorn, J., et al.: Customer engagement behavior: theoretical foundations and research directions. J. Serv. Res. **13**(3), 253–266 (2010)
39. Zhang, M., Guo, L., Hu, M., Liu, W.: Influence of customer engagement with company social networks on stickiness: Mediating effect of customer value creation. Int. J. Inf. Manage. (2016). Article in press
40. Ple, L.: Studying customers' resource integration by service employees in interactional value co-creation. J. Serv. Mark. **30**(2), 152–164 (2016)

Encouraging the Participation in Mobile Collaborative Consumption Using Gamification Design

Yicheng Zhang[1(✉)], Chee Wei Phang[1], Shun Cai[2], and Chenghong Zhang[1]

[1] Fudan University, Shanghai, China
yichengzhang14@fudan.edu.cn
[2] Xiamen University, Xiamen, China

Abstract. Mobile technologies may facilitate collaborative consumption among strangers that can help merchants "attract customers through customers" beyond close relational boundary. To leverage on this opportunity, it is important to understand what may motivate consumers to participate in such collaborative consumptions when they do not know each other, given that embarrassment of interacting with strangers may inhibit one from doing so. In this study, we propose that the use of a gamification strategy can increase consumer response to a mobile collaborative consumption offer. Through conducting a field experiment, we show that when asked to invite a nearby stranger to enjoy a group discount together, a gamification design whereby the group discount is randomly split between participants can promote the consumer likelihood to do so, compared to the typical design of equal splitting of the discount (pure economic gains). Similarly, the acceptance rate of invitation from a stranger was also enhanced with a gamification design.

Keywords: Mobile technology · Collaborative consumption · Gamification · Mobile app

1 Introduction

The Internet has brought about novel forms of sharing and consumption practices including collaborative consumption [1, 2]. Collaborative consumption refers to peer -to-peer-based activity of obtaining, giving, or sharing the access to goods and services [3]. Through collaborative consumption, consumers share information and resources with each other to attain mutual consumption benefits. Examples of collaborative consumption today include Airbnb, Zipcar, and group deals [2].

Conventionally collaborative consumption has occurred within a small contact boundary involving close relationships such as family, kin, and friends [4]. An example being a consumer inviting him/her friends to buy a larger volume of a product together to enjoy deeper discounts. With the advancements in information technologies (IT), the cost of connection and communication among people becomes much lower [3]. Mobile technologies further enable consumers to act on a collaborative consumption opportunity instantly at the actual consumption place via mobile technologies [5]. The implication is that consumers may now easily engage strangers who happen to be nearby to

© Springer International Publishing AG 2017
F.F.-H. Nah and C.-H. Tan (Eds.): HCIBGO 2017, PART II, LNCS 10294, pp. 313–322, 2017.
DOI: 10.1007/978-3-319-58484-3_24

participate in the collaborative consumption together, thus increasing the likelihood of enjoying the mutual consumption benefits. For instance, a merchant may send a group discount to its customer appearing nearby via a mobile app (such as a social networking or instant messaging tool), which requires him/her to invite another person in order to enjoy the discount. Upon receiving the offer, the consumer may invite his/her friend to enjoy the deal together. Yet, friends or close relationships may not be always within close proximities. In this case, the consumer may consider inviting another user of the app who is also near the merchant, thus solving the problem of close relationships' absence. Mobile apps make this possible and viable with the GPS location information and social functions that allow users to know each other's presence and make invitation to a nearby user to participate in a collaborative consumption. The flexibility afforded for collaborative consumption among strangers is of significance to enlarge the scale and impact of this emerging consumption practice.

However, even facilitated by mobile technologies, people tend to avoid interacting with strangers [2]. In the online context, prior studies have indicated that people are more at ease interacting with strangers due to anonymity and a sense of feeling that others are "distant" away [6, 7]. In contrast, in the offline context, people are inclined to avoid meeting or interacting with strangers in person due to a feeling of anxiety [8] or fear of potential "stranger danger" [2]. Thus, it is important to understand how we can stimulate people's tendency to interact with strangers when presented with a mobile collaborative consumption opportunity, such as a group discount.

In addition to economic gains, prior studies have identified fun or enjoyment as a crucial factor that increases people's likelihood of adopting collaborative consumption services [3, 9]. Concomitantly, in recent years, gamification emerges as a popular strategy employed by firms to engage consumers and promote their consumption behaviors [10]. In this study, through conducting a randomized field experiment, we compare the use of pure economic gains and gamification design in inducing consumers to participate in a mobile collaborative consumption offer. In particular, we self-developed a mobile app and collaborated with a chained dessert shop to conduct the experiment. We created a salient collaborative consumption context – a message sent to consumers via our self-developed app to highlight a chance to enjoy the promoted product (milk tea) at an attractive discount by inviting another consumer. We manipulated pure economic gains by offering discounts to both parties (inviter and invitee) at equal amount, and gamification through a random draw design whereby the amount of discount enjoyable by both parties is randomly distributed thus adding a fun element. We then investigate whether using the gamification design can increase people's inclination to invite a stranger (we also included the scenarios of inviting a friend for comparison purpose) to participate in the collaborative consumption compared to offering pure economic gains.

A total of 322 participants recruited from a public university were randomly assigned into 5 groups including 4 treatment groups (a 2×2 full factorial design: pure economic gains vs. gamification, inviting a stranger vs. a friend) and 1 control group, each receiving a single promotional message with request to invite a stranger or a friend. Participants could respond to the message directly from the mobile app, and made decision on whether to participate by inviting others to enjoy the group deal together.

The remainder of this paper is organized as follows. Section 2 discusses the conceptual background of our study, Sect. 3 describes the research method employed, i.e., field experiment, followed by Sect. 4 that presents the data analysis results. Finally, we conclude in Sect. 5.

2   Conceptual Background

2.1   Collaborative Consumption

In collaborative consumption, both the contribution and use of resources are intertwined through peer-to-peer networks enabled by technologies [2, 3]. This new form of consumption has the potential to transform businesses, consumerism, and the way people live with its economic and societal benefits [11, 12]. Trough collaborative consumption, people share and obtain access to rooms (AirBnB, Roomorama), tools (SnapGoods), cars and bikes (RelayRides, Wheelz), and ad hoc taxi services (Uber, Lyft).

Prior research on collaborative consumption has investigated factors that motivate consumer participation in collaborative consumption. Economic gains, enjoyment of the activity, and societal aspect of sustainability and community were identified as key factors in improving satisfaction and increasing people's tendency to choose collaborative consumption services [8, 9].

In our context of offering collaborative group deals, in addition to economic gains that are essential to such deals, we also consider enjoyment as a salient factor motivating people to participate in this form of collaborative consumption. Specifically, we attempt to provide the enjoyment factor through a gamification strategy, which we will discuss next. We expect when people feel that participating in a group deal is fun and enjoyable, they are more likely to invite others to obtain the group discount together.

2.2   Gamification

Gamification, or the idea of using game design elements in non-game contexts, has been a trending practice in interaction design and digital marketing to motivate and increase user engagement and retention [14]. Numerous applications now involve the idea of gamification– ranging across productivity, finance, health, education, sustainability, as well as news and entertainment media. Many software vendors now offer "gamification" as a software service layer of reward and reputation systems with points, badges, levels and leader boards.

The heightened interest in gamification is also reflected in the growing number of papers published on gamification. Several studies have investigated the psychological outcomes of gamification [10]. Although gamification elements vary in different contexts, positive experiences such as enjoyment and engagement from gamification were consistently recognized [15–17].

Accordingly, as a popular means to enhance the enjoyment felt by users, we are interested in whether incorporating a gamification design can motivate the engagement in collaborative consumption. In addition, with the huge investments being made into gamification-related efforts, we hope to also contribute to the understanding of the effectiveness of gamification using a field experiment approach.

3   Research Method

In this study, we developed a mobile app that allows merchants to send group deal promotional messages to consumers who are near their shop. To enjoy the group deal, receivers are to invite another consumer via the mobile app interface, which randomly displays one surrounding (less than 500 m) user (friend or stranger) whom they can invite.

Based on the app, we conducted a randomized field experiment with the cooperation of a chained dessert shop in the campus of a large public university in China. We create a salient collaborative consumption context – a message sent to consumers highlighting a chance to enjoy a promoted product (milk tea) at an attractive discount (50% off normal price with an additional 5-yuan[1] discount), conditional on inviting another consumer to purchase the product together.

We manipulated (1) motivational appeal (economic gains vs. gamification) and (2) target subject to invite (stranger vs. friend) via the promotional message and the function of the app. In terms of the motivational appeal of participating in the group deal, we manipulated (1) economic gains by giving pure monetary discount to the inviter and invitee (equal amount); (2) gamification by pooling the additional 5-yuan discount from both the inviter and invitee (i.e., total 10-yuan), and split it to both parties through a random draw[2]. Through the promotional message in the app, we displayed a randomly selected target whom the participant was to invite to enjoy the group deal together; the target was either a stranger or a friend of the participant (known through a survey conducted prior to the experiment that assessed the relationships among the participants). Thus, together with a control group (no additional discount), our experiment was a 5-group between-subject design. A total of 322 participants were recruited from the university campus and randomly assigned into the 5 groups with similar size (64 or 65 in each group). We tested if there was a difference in the demographics of participants in the different groups; no significant difference was found. Randomization was achieved by using SAS software's random number generator and running the RANUNI function, which returns a random value from a uniform distribution [18].

Since the mobile app was new to the participants, we provided a short demo to them when they came to sign up before the experiment began. We told the participants that they were to help assess a new mobile app as a test user (to prevent guessing of the experiment purpose), and that the app would deliver a piece of information every day at a specific time during the course of the experiment (4 days). They were told that the information they receive via the app would consist of those related to their everyday living on the campus.

---

[1] Equivalent to approximately USD 0.70; the price is the milk tea is around USD3.

[2] One of the participants of the inviter-invitee pair would draw a random amount from a box (which might be 1- to 9-yuan); the rest will be automatically given to the other participant.

To obtain incentive at the end of the experiment (about USD 11), the participants were to check in the app every day, read the information received in the app (a button is provided for the participants to click to indicate they have read it), and decide whether to respond if applicable.

Before the experiment, the participants had to fill in a preliminary survey designed to capture the following information. First, we obtained the participants' demographic characteristics, such as gender and age. Second, we obtained users' mobile usage experience including their years of using mobile (mobile year) and the number of apps installed on the mobile (app amount). We used these covariates to control for the potential alternative explanations for our results due to different users' mobile usage experience. For example, it is possible that users with more apps installed might be more likely to respond to the mobile deal received because they are more familiar with such mobile commercial information. Finally, the participants were asked to indicate their friends from the list of all participants (pre-collected when the participants registered online). According to their selection, we added them as friends in the database in advance, which then enabled us to manipulate the target invitee to be a friend or a stranger when presenting the participants with the group deal offer.

The experiment lasted 4 days: the promotion message was sent on the third day of the experiment (unknown to the participants); on other days the participants received non-experiment related messages such as campus news. Every time a message was delivered to the app there would be a notification and the participants needed to check in and indicated they have read it. Therefore, we were able to monitor the participants' usage of app and remove those who did not read the promotion message via the check-in information during the study. To control for possible time effects, every participant was ensured to receive a message at the same time on each experiment day. The promotion message was sent at 2:00 pm and expired 6 h after the message was sent. The six-hour time frame was given to ensure the participants have enough time to coordinate the collaborative consumption, as will be explained shortly. As the shop we collaborated is located within the university campus from where the participants were recruited, travel distance was not an issue if the participants decided to go purchase the designated product.

Once received the message, participants would decide whether to participate in the group deal. If he/she decided to participate, he/she would click on the "invite" button in the app to invite the displayed user to enjoy the group deal together. For the invitee, they would decide whether to accept, reject or ignore the invitation. For those who reached the agreement of participation (i.e., the invitee agreed to participate with the inviter), they would go to the store and make purchase of the discounted item.

4   Data Analysis Results

The research design with randomized field experiment can control for consumers' unobservable heterogeneity and thus avoid the endogeneity and causality biases that might confound estimation results [19–21].

Our experiment focuses on the dependent variables: Invitation and Acceptance. Invitation is a dummy variable which identifies whether a focal participant made an invitation to the given subject. If the focal participant made the invitation, the variable of *Invitation* equals to 1, 0 otherwise. *Acceptance* is a dummy variable which is conditional on *Invitation*. If the invitee accepted the invitation, the variable *acceptance* equals to 1, 0 otherwise.

The independent variables are stranger and gamification. Both stranger and gamification are dummy variables to identify the treatment effects. If a participant was assigned to invite a stranger, stranger is set to 1, 0 otherwise. If a participant received a message with a gamification discount design (vis-à-vis pure economic gains), gamification was set to 1, 0 otherwise. To account for differences between individual participants, we included control variables related to individual characteristics, i.e., gender, age, mobile year (years of using mobile), and app amount (number of apps installed). These variables were collected in the survey prior to the field experiment. In addition, for acceptance, since an invitee may more likely accept when receiving multiple invitations from the inviter (the inviter could send multiple invitations), we include invite times (number of invitations per participant) as a control variable as well. Among the participants, 22 did not read the promotion message through the mobile app and thus were removed from the sample. The descriptive statistics of all the variables are listed in Table 1.

Table 1. Definitions and descriptive statistics of variables

Variable	Definition	Obs.	Mean	S.D.	Min.	Max.
Invitation	Whether to send the invitation	300	0.34	0.47	0	1
Acceptance	Whether the invitation was accepted by the invitee	102	0.42	0.50	0	1
Stranger	0 for stranger, 1 for friend	300	0.52	0.50	0	1
Gamification	0 for pure economic gains, 1 for gamification discount design	300	0.40	0.49	0	1
Gender	1 for female, 0 for male	300	0.63	0.48	0	1
Age	Year old	300	23.15	2.66	19	36
Mobile year	Years of using mobile	300	4.06	1.07	1	5
App amount	Number of apps installed on mobile phone	300	3.11	1.15	1	5
Invite times	Number of times a participant sent out invitation	300	0.50	0.89	0	6

Prior to statistical tests, we descriptively compared the responses of the participants in different groups. Table 2 shows the descriptive statistics of Invitation and Table 3 shows the descriptive statistics of Acceptance. As shown in Table 2, compared to those who were to invite a friend, the invitations of strangers was much lower (mean = 0.508 > 0.355; mean = 0.323 > 0.263, for respectively the gamification and economic gains conditions), which is not surprising given the likely psychological barriers that prevent people from inviting strangers.

Table 2. Comparison of descriptive statistics for *Invitation*

	Gamification design			Pure economic gains design			Control
	Stranger (n = 62)	Friend (n = 59)	Total (n = 121)	Stranger (n = 57)	Friend (n = 62)	Total (n = 119)	Total (n = 60)
Invitation	0.355 (0.482)	0.508 (0.504)	0.430 (0.497)	0.263 (0.444)	0.323 (0.471)	0.294 (0.455)	0.250 (0.437)

Notes: n indicates the total number of observations. There are some differences in the observation number between the groups because not all the participants read the promotion message through the mobile app.

Table 3. Comparison of descriptive statistics for *Acceptance*

	Gamification design			Pure economic gains design			Control
	Stranger (m = 31)	Friend (m = 42)	Total (m = 73)	Stranger (m = 29)	Friend (m = 24)	Total (m = 53)	Total (m = 25)
Acceptation	0.387 (0.495)	0.357 (0.485)	0.370 (0.486)	0.173 (0.384)	0.583 (0.504)	0.359 (0.484)	0.320 (0.476)

Notes: m indicates the total number of invitation times within the group. For example, in the group with gamification design and with potential invitee to be a friend, the total number of invitations were 42.

Compared to the control group, the invitation percentage with additional discount given was higher in general (mean = 0.430 > 0.250; mean = 0.294 > 0.250, for respectively the gamification and economic gains conditions). Furthermore, for the two motivational appeal types, the gamification discount design (mean = 0.430) was more likely to motivate invitation than the pure economic gains (mean = 0.294). Regardless of whether a friend or a stranger was to be invited, the invitation percentage was higher when the discount design is made in a gamification way than in a pure economic gains way (mean = 0.508 > 0.323; mean = 0.355 > 0.263). These provide initial descriptive evidences that gamification can encourage more participation in collaborative consumption.

As shown in Table 3, the number of invitations is higher for groups with gamification design than the ones with pure economic gains (m = 73 > 53), which is consistent with the statistics in Table 2. In addition, the acceptance percentage was slightly higher with gamification discount design than the pure economic gains design (mean = 0.370 > 0.359). For the groups with strangers as target invitee, the gamification discount design motivated higher acceptance of invitation than the pure economic gains design (mean = 0.387 > 0.173), while the situation for the groups with friends as target invitee was exactly the opposite (mean = 0.357 < 0.583). These statistics suggest that gamification not only can encourage more invitations but also can motivate greater likelihood of accepting invitations, particularly for strangers.

To comprehensively assess the effect of gamification on Invitation and Acceptance, we conducted logistic regression for all treatment groups (n = 240, m = 126). For Invitation, the results of model (1, 2) in Table 4 show that the coefficient of gamification in the regression of all treatment groups was positively significant (b = 0.597, $p < 0.05$), indicating groups with gamification design had significant higher invitations. Also when the target invitee was a stranger, people were less likely to make invitation than when the target invitee was a friend (b = −0.451, $p < 0.1$). In addition, the moderating effect of gamification on the stranger groups was not significant (b = −0.313, p > 0.1). For Acceptance, the results of model (3) indicate the main effects of gamification and stranger were not significant alone (b = −0.0166, P > 0.1; b = −0.155, P > 0.1). However, they may combined to affect the Acceptance. As the results indicated in model (4), for the groups involving strangers, the acceptation percentage was significantly lower than the groups involving friends (b = −0.726, p < 0.1). In addition, gamification actually had a moderating effect on the stranger groups for accepting invitations, i.e., strangers were more likely to accept invitation with the gamification design (b = 1.579, p < 0.1).

Table 4. Analysis of *Invitation* and *Acceptance* (logistic regression modeling)

Dependent variables	(1)	(2)	(3)	(4)
	Invitation	Invitation	Acceptance	Acceptance
Core independent variables				
Gamification	0.608**	0.597**	−0.166	−0.0689
	(0.277)	(0.278)	(0.419)	(0.435)
Stranger	−0.463*	−0.451*	−0.515	−0.846*
	(0.277)	(0.277)	(0.414)	(0.465)
Gamification * Stranger		−0.313		1.579*
		(0.555)		(0.867)
Control variables				
Gender	−0.00552	−0.00166	−0.161	−0.0922
	(0.292)	(0.292)	(0.421)	(0.428)
Age	0.0271	0.0253	−0.0598	−0.0503
	(0.0535)	(0.0536)	(0.0723)	(0.0743)
Mobile year	0.0108	0.0184	0.236	0.202
	(0.143)	(0.143)	(0.236)	(0.241)
App amount	−0.127	−0.124	−0.161	−0.177
	(0.121)	(0.121)	(0.182)	(0.186)
Invite times			−1.421***	−1.388***
			(0.462)	(0.472)
Constant	−0.944	−0.937	2.656	2.567
	(1.305)	(1.306)	(1.912)	(1.958)
Observations	240	240	126	126

Note: 1. The variable Gamification * Stranger has been centered.
2. Standard errors in parentheses
3. *** p < 0.01, ** p < 0.05, * p < 0.1

5 Conclusion

To enlarge the scale and impact of collaborative consumption, it is important to motivate people to engage others in exchanging and sharing resources, be them friends or strangers; otherwise, it may be constrained by limited social contact boundary. Mobile technologies may facilitate this ends by making it easier for people to connect and communicate with each other ad hoc and "micro-coordinate" with each other any place, any time. Yet, psychological barriers are likely to prevail that prevent people from doing so, especially when the other party to engage in collaborative consumption is a stranger.

Via a field experiment, our study highlights gamification as a promising way to encourage people to participate in collaborative consumption. Besides providing economic gains, enhancing the enjoyment of the activity via gamification design can be effective as well. The results show that regardless of whether friends or strangers are concerned, a gamification discount design works better in motivating invitation to others than a pure economic gains design. Furthermore, when receiving an invitation from a stranger, gamification could enhance one's likelihood to accept the invitation.

Overall, these findings may contribute to the literature on mobile ecommerce, collaborative consumption, and gamification. We hope our study can motivate further research along this promising direction.

Acknowledgments. This work was supported by the National Natural Science Foundation of China (grant #71471044 and #71490721).

References

1. Belk, R.: Sharing. J. Consum. Res. **36**(5), 715–734 (2010)
2. Belk, R.: You are what you can access: sharing and collaborative consumption online. J. Bus. Res. **67**(8), 1595–1600 (2014)
3. Hamari, J., Sjöklint, M., Ukkonen, A.: The sharing economy: why people participate in collaborative consumption. J. Assoc. Inf. Sci. Technol. **67**(9), 2047–2059 (2016)
4. Rusbult, C.E., Agnew, C.R.: Prosocial motivation and behavior in close relationships. In: Prosocial Motives, Emotions, and Behavior: The Better Angels of Our Nature, pp. 327–345 (2010)
5. Chen, H., Phang, C.W., Zhang, C.: Inviting strangers to participate in collaborative consumption through mobile app (2016)
6. Davenport, D.: Anonymity on the Internet: why the price may be too high. Commun. ACM **45**(4), 33–35 (2002)
7. Kang, R., Dabbish, L., Sutton, K.: Strangers on your phone: why people use anonymous communication applications. In: Proceedings of the 19th ACM Conference on Computer-Supported Cooperative Work & Social Computing, pp. 359–370. ACM, February 2016
8. Gudykunst, W.B., Nishida, T.: Anxiety, uncertainty, and perceived effectiveness of communication across relationships and cultures. Int. J. Intercultural Relat. **25**(1), 55–71 (2001)
9. Möhlmann, M.: Collaborative consumption: determinants of satisfaction and the likelihood of using a sharing economy option again. J. Consum. Behav. **14**(3), 193–207 (2015)

10. Hamari, J., Koivisto, J., Sarsa, H.: Does gamification work? – a literature review of empirical studies on gamification. In: The Hawaii International Conference on System Sciences, pp. 3025–3034 (2014)
11. Botsman, R., Rogers, R.: What's Mine is Yours: How Collaborative Consumption is Changing the Way We Live. Collins, London (2011)
12. Cardona, J.C., Stanojevic, R., Laoutaris, N.: Collaborative consumption for mobile broadband: a quantitative study. In: Proceedings of the 10th ACM International on Conference on Emerging Networking Experiments and Technologies, pp. 307–318. ACM, December 2014
13. Malhotra, A., Van Alstyne, M.: The dark side of the sharing economy... and how to lighten it. Commun. ACM 57(11), 24–27 (2014)
14. Deterding, S., Dixon, D., Khaled, R., Nacke, L.: From game design elements to gamefulness: defining "gamification". In: International Academic Mindtrek Conference: Envisioning Future Media Environments, pp. 9–15 (2011)
15. Montola, M., Nummenmaa, T., Lucero, A., Boberg, M., Korhonen, H.: Applying game achievement systems to enhance user experience in a photo sharing service. In: International Mindtrek Conference: Everyday Life in the Ubiquitous Era, pp. 94–97. ACM (2009)
16. Dong, T., Dontcheva, M., Joseph, D., Karahalios, K., Newman, M., Ackerman, M.: Discovery-based games for learning software, pp. 2083–2086 (2012)
17. Li, W., Grossman, T., Fitzmaurice, G.: GamiCAD: a gamified tutorial system for first time autocad users. In: ACM Symposium on User Interface Software and Technology, vol. 44, pp. 103–112. ACM (2012)
18. Deng, C., Graz, J.: Generating randomization schedules using SAS programming. In: Proceedings of the 27th Annual SAS Users Group International Conference, pp. 267–270. SAS Institute, Cary (2002)
19. Gneezy, A., Gneezy, U., Nelson, L.D., Brown, A.: Shared social responsibility: a field experiment in pay-what-you-want pricing and charitable giving. Science 329(5989), 325–327 (2010)
20. Goldfarb, A., Tucker, C.: Online display advertising: targeting and obtrusiveness. Market. Sci. 30(3), 389–404 (2011)
21. Aral, S., Walker, D.: Tie strength, embeddedness, and social influence: a large-scale networked experiment. Manag. Sci. 60(6), 1352–1370 (2014)

Analytics, Visualization and Decision Support

Development of an Online Checklist for the Assessment of Alarm Systems and Alarm Management in Process Control

Martina Bockelmann[✉], Peter Nickel, and Friedhelm Nachreiner

Gesellschaft für Arbeits-, Wirtschafts- und Organisationspsychologische
Forschung e.V. (GAWO), Oldenburg, Germany
martina.bockelmann@gawo-ev.de

Abstract. In the past, poorly designed alarm systems and inadequate alarm management contributed to the emergence of critical events with partially serious consequences. Based on the experience gained from these incidents, guidelines were created with recommendations for the design of alarm systems and alarm management. A comprehensive checklist has been developed to analyze the current design quality of alarm systems and alarm management and has been used in various control rooms across different branches of industry in Germany. Using the checklist, design deficiencies can be identified and action needs can be derived. So far, the results also show systematic differences in the application of the checklist between individual assessors and between groups of assessors.

Keywords: Alarm system · Alarm management · Ergonomic design · Checklist · Process control · Industrial safety

1 Introduction

Investigation reports from the 1970s until today inform about critical events, with some disclosing serious consequences for employees, companies, the environment and the public. Details convey that poorly designed alarm systems and alarm management jointly contributed to incidents such as at Three Mile Island nuclear power plant (1979), in the oil refineries of Texaco (1994) and BP (2005) and on the oil rig Deepwater Horizon (2010). As causal factors, reports present issues like non-response of alarms, high alarm rates, poor prioritization of alarms, non-ergonomic and inappropriate design of displays and controls and the lack of systematic training of the control room operators in dealing with critical situations, to name but a few [e.g. 1–3].

Parallel to and as a consequence of the events, several guidelines and standards have been evolved presenting requirements for an ergonomic design of alarm systems and alarm management [e.g. 4–8]. In addition, the events triggered research into safety and human factors and also lessons learnt from experience in the field (best practice) resulting in publications with available findings and recommendations [9–11].

Well-designed alarm systems and adequate alarm management, which fulfil ergonomic requirements, should therefore have an impact on system availability, system

© Springer International Publishing AG 2017
F.F.-H. Nah and C.-H. Tan (Eds.): HCIBGO 2017, PART II, LNCS 10294, pp. 325–332, 2017.
DOI: 10.1007/978-3-319-58484-3_25

reliability and operational safety – especially in the case of critical process trends and process conditions.

However, it is unclear to what extent these design requirements and recommendations have been applied in operational practice. Therefore, a research project has been conducted to address the following questions:

1. How can the ergonomic design quality of alarm systems and alarm management be easily, consistently and reliably assessed?
2. What is the current quality of the design in control rooms in process industries? [not covered by this paper]
3. What are important ergonomic recommendations to further improve existing and future alarm systems and alarm management? [not covered by this paper]

For this purpose, a checklist has been developed in order

1. to analyze and evaluate the design quality of alarm systems and alarm management in different control rooms and within various sectors of industry and
2. to derive hints for potential improvements or needs for action to implement design requirements and recommendations where appropriate.

2   Methods

2.1   Checklist Development

The design of the computerized checklist was based on the results of a feasibility study carried out in 2008/2009 in six control rooms from three chemical companies [12, 13].

For the present study, an extended knowledge base has been further established based on a systematic review of individual design requirements from relevant ergonomics literature as well as relevant guidelines, normative provisions and specifications [e.g. 2, 5–8, 14, 15]. Potentially relevant design requirements were collated, summarized and structured into thematic areas, such as design of alarm systems (e.g. prioritization), design of operator requirements (e.g. operator performance limits) and design of alarm management (e.g. performance monitoring and improvements).

A complete evaluation of all potentially relevant characteristics for an alarm system was not possible for technical, temporal and financial reasons; an operationalization of all existing requirements is further impossible due to the singularities of each control system and the process under control. Therefore, a sample of prominent and substantial characteristics from the knowledge base was selected by expert reviewers in a multi-staged process and transferred into easily usable items. All items were transferred into questions and were supplemented by examples and notes. The answer categories in the checklist were either pass/fail decisions (yes/no) or decisions for traffic light categories ('Green' = good design, requirement fulfilled, 'Yellow' = design basically OK, but better solutions would be conceivable, 'Red' = unsatisfactory design solution calling for improvement).

The computerized checklist was implemented as (1) an offline version using a portable computer and (2) an online version provided by a browser via internet.

2.2 Checklist Suitability

The usability of the checklist was tested in a multi-step procedure. A draft version of the checklist was presented to experts in ergonomics and human factors. The review resulted in a final draft version with several amendments (e.g. new and deleted items, rephrasing of questions and examples).

This final draft of the checklist was tested for usability in operational use by a senior member of staff from a chemical company and by two human factors and ergonomics experts (HF/E experts). The senior staff member was asked to go through the checklist, read each checklist characteristic carefully and write a comment in the event of ambiguities, misleading wording, doubling etc. The HF/E experts were required to apply the checklist in a typical control room within the chemical industry under realistic investigation conditions and comment about structure, content and checklist design.

Comments and suggestions for improvement by both parties were subsequently discussed by the above mentioned expert group. Final adjustments (e.g. reduced ambiguity of questions through rephrasing, refining and supplementing examples) resulted in the final version for the presented study.

The final version of the checklist contains 148 items, assigned to the following design areas:

1. Alarm generation/alerting
2. Alarm presentation
3. Alarm prioritization
4. Alarm system functionalities and technical measures
5. Operator performance limits
6. Action guidelines and system interactions
7. Control and feedback
8. Alarm culture and alarm philosophy
9. Continuous improvement
10. Documentation
11. Training

2.3 Checklist Application

Application of the checklist in control rooms required several methods of data collection, such as observation, visual inspection, interviews with control room operators and supervisors, physical measurements and document analyses.

In total, alarm systems have been investigated at 15 workplaces in different control rooms in 12 companies from three industrial sectors, i.e. electrical power generation and distribution, food industry and chemical industry.

Each alarm system was evaluated by two HF/E experts and – where possible – by two experienced practitioners (e.g. technicians, system engineers, safety experts etc.) from participating companies independently on different days, thus providing for different kinds of expertise. This allows tests of different aspects of the usability of the checklist, e.g. by users with different educational background and know-how, as well as a verification of rater effects, e.g. status effects (HF/E experts vs. experienced practitioners) and effects of individual raters within these groups.

An alarm system investigation carried out by HF/E experts lasted between 7 and 10 hours and varied according to the complexity of the process under control, the process control system under investigation, the type and extent of the alarm management activities and the events specific to the days of assessment. A shift change was intentionally included, if possible, in order to be able to observe different operators in interaction with the alarm system and by doing so, to reduce operator-specific variance. No information is available about the time required for investigations carried out by the engineering staff of participating companies.

2.4 Statistical Analysis

After a first descriptive analysis of the data, observer agreement was determined in order to find out whether the raters had assessed the items of the checklist identically or at least similarly in the assessment of the systems. Cohen's kappa (κ) and, in addition, weighted kappa (κ_w, only for polytomous system of answer categories, traffic light categories, n = 123) were used as (rough) indices of observer agreement.

The advantage of weighted kappa is that the extent of disagreement in non-identical judgements is taken into account in the calculation of the index [16, 17]. In the present investigation, this means that differing judgements in the form of "good design" (= 'Green') and "unsatisfactory design solution" (= 'Red') would achieve a higher weight than a deviation between "good design" (= 'Green') and "design basically OK" (= 'Yellow').

If two practitioners – in addition to two HF/E experts – are also available for the assessment of each alarm system, six kappa coefficients can be calculated for each system. For 15 investigated systems, it results in a maximum of 90 indexes.

The classification of Landis and Koch [18] was used to classify the kappa coefficients (see Tables 1 and 2).

Kappa or weighted kappa can, however, only be considered as a first, global measure of observer (dis)agreement, since no conclusions can be made as to the possible causes of the variability or disagreement in the ratings [19]. On the other hand, it provides some first impressions on the level of agreement in using the checklist and thus, its usability for the purpose intended. Since not all data have been collected in the present study, some considerations will be given about potential reasons for relatively higher or lower levels of agreement.

3   Results

At present, 30 assessments done by the two HF/E experts and 21 assessments done by experienced practitioners are available, i.e. nine ratings by practitioners are still missing.

Based on the data available at the time of submitting this report, the results obviously identify differences in design quality of alarm systems and alarm management as well as requirements for design improvement (e.g. in the area of design of human-machine-interface, prioritization of alarms, alarm management and concerning operator training in alarm systems and the handling of alarms).

Table 1. Distribution of kappa coefficients (classification according to Landis & Koch, 1977 [18])

	"slight" (0,00–0,20)	"fair" (0,21–0,40)	"moderate" (0,41–0,60)	"substantial" (0,61–0,80)	"(almost) perfect" (0,81–1,00)
HF/E expert – HF/E expert			5	**10**	
HF/E expert – Practitioner	3	**23**	16		
Practitioner – Practitioner		**4**	4		1

(modes in bold)

In general, the HF/E experts tended to rate the systems more strictly than the practitioners from the companies, as shown in the example in Fig. 1. In this example, the assessments of the HF/E experts agree quite well. In comparison to the HF/E experts, the experienced practitioners judged much milder – especially assessor EP1; i.e. they classified design aspects more often as "good design". Moreover, the assessments of the practitioners also differ from each other.

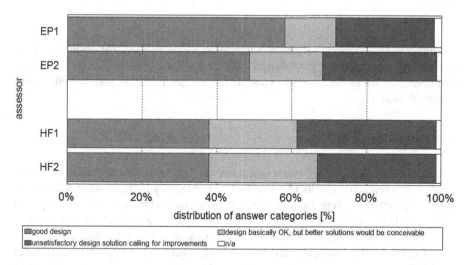

Fig. 1. Relative frequencies of answer categories per assessor at workplace 1 (Color figure online)

Regarding the inter-rater agreement, 66 out of a maximum of 90 possible kappa coefficients have been calculated so far, since the system assessments by nine practitioners are not yet available.

The kappa coefficients within the HF/E experts group range from moderate to good agreement, which is higher than in the other two groups (see Table 1). In particular, the kappa coefficients between HF/E experts and experienced practitioners show a wide range (slight to moderate) and are generally rather low. The values within the practioners group are between fair to moderate, with one exception (almost perfect). However, here some doubts can be raised, since both raters shared a room, filled in and finished their checklists at nearly the same time and wrote similar comments, so that they might have discussed their assessments.

The weighted kappa coefficients show a somewhat higher level (see Table 2). With one exception, the inter-rater agreements between the HF/E experts are substantial to almost perfect. The inter-rater agreements of the comparisons between HF/E experts and practitioners are significantly lower. The spectrum ranges from fair to substantial agreement. The weighted kappa coefficients between experienced practitioners are widely distributed, ranging from fair to almost perfect.

Table 2. Distribution of weighted kappa coefficients (classification according to Landis & Koch, 1977 [18])

	"slight" (0,00–0,20)	"fair" (0,21–0,40)	"moderate" (0,41–0,60)	"substantial" (0,61–0,80)	"(almost) perfect" (0,81–1,00)
HF/E expert – HF/E expert			1	**11**	3
HF/E expert – Practitioner		10	**24**	8	
Practitioner – Practitioner		1	**4**	3	1

(modes in bold)

Higher weighted kappa values, as compared to kappa, suggest that deviations in the form of one scale unit (e.g. "good design" and "design basically OK") are more frequent than discrepancies in the form of two scale units ("good design" and "unsatisfactory design solution").

4   Discussions

The calculation of kappa coefficients (κ/κ_w) already indicate some patterns of agreement and disagreement. The results of these analyses obviously indicate some differences, and most probably systematic differences between individual assessors and types of assessors (HF/E experts vs. experienced practitioners) in using the checklist and its assessment criteria. There can be several different reasons for such a result.

For example, the concepts used in the checklist were not clear to the practitioners (the HF/E experts were engaged in the description of the concepts, so they should be aware of their content, which is supported by their higher agreement), which would be supported by the disagreement between the groups of raters. This would have to be addressed by a reformulation of the concepts, basic training in using the checklist and the concepts behind the items or additional information material (e.g. examples) to explain the item content.

A further reason for deviation in evaluation could be the fact that the raters observed different situations leading to differences between the investigation objects. It was not unusual that the practitioners carried out or finished their assessments weeks or months later than the HF/E experts for company reasons. Meanwhile, the design quality of the alarm system and alarm management could have changed.

On the other hand, there could be difficulties with individual items and their scaling. This cannot be analyzed satisfactorily by using kappa coefficients. However, Generalizability Theory [G-theory; 20, 21] can provide the relevant information about the (absolute and relative) contribution of several systematic error terms (rater, group of raters, item, control system under inspection and their interactions) to the error of measurements. This can be done by performing an analysis of variance and estimating the size and proportion of all variance components indicating error of measurement (i.e. the systematic error components plus random error) simultaneously. Such a statistical analysis is in progress, but can only be finished after the data collection and processing have been completed. The assessment of the psychometric properties [according to ISO 10075-3; 22] of the checklist using a G-theoretical approach is still in progress.

With a view to the severe consequences which may be associated with poorly designed alarm systems and inadequate alarm management, the importance of well-designed and well-managed systems becomes particularly apparent. Therefore, a systematic and continuous alarm system and alarm management analysis is an important element in the safety concept of a company to ensure the functionality of an alarm system and the requirements for continuously monitoring, maintaining or improving its performance and, finally, to keep a plant in a safe state [e.g. 11, 14].

For this purpose, an objective, reliable, valid, sensitive, diagnostic and easy-to-use instrument would be desirable, with which the design state of alarm systems, including the alarm management, can be evaluated in order to identify potential design deficiencies and to implement appropriate work-design measures if necessary.

Acknowledgements. The research for the study was partly funded by the Forschungsgesellschaft für angewandte Systemsicherheit und Arbeitsmedizin e.V. (FSA) [http://www.fsa.de/en/home/].

References

1. Kemeny, J.G., Babbitt, B., Haggerty, P.E., et al.: Report of The President's Commission on the Accident at Three Mile Island (1979). http://www.threemileisland.org/downloads/188.pdf. 20 December 2016
2. Health & Safety Executive (HSE): HSE Information Sheet, Chemicals Sheet No. 6. Better alarm handling (2000). http://www.hse.gov.uk/pubns/chis6.pdf. 20 December 2016
3. U.S. Chemical Safety and Hazard Investigation Board (CSB): Investigation Report: Refinery Explosion and Fire (15 Killed, 180 Injured). BP, Texas City, Texas; March 23, 2005. Report No. 2005-04-I-TX, March 2007 (2007). http://www.csb.gov/bp-america-refinery-explosion. 20 December 2016
4. ANSI/ISA 18.2: Management of Alarm Systems for the Process Industries. ISA, Research Triangle Park (2009)
5. DIN EN 62682: Alarmmanagement in der Prozessindustrie. Beuth, Berlin (2013, 2016)
6. EEMUA 191: Alarm systems. A guide to design, management and procurement. EEMUA, London (2013)
7. NA 102: Alarmmanagement. NAMUR, Leverkusen (2008)

8. YA-711: Principles for alarm system design. Norwegian Petroleum Directorate, Stavanger (2001)
9. Bransby, M.L., Jenkinson, J.: The Management of Alarm Systems. HSE Books, Sudbury (1998)
10. Ivergård, T., Hunt, B. (eds.): Handbook of Control Room Design and Ergonomics: A Perspective for the Future. CRC Press, Boca Raton (2009)
11. Hollifield, B.R., Habibi, E.: Das Alarm-Management Handbuch. Ein umfassender Ratgeber. Nino Druck GmbH, Neustadt (2012)
12. Bockelmann, M.: Entwicklung und Überprüfung eines Prototyps eines Instrumentes zur Beurteilung und Optimierung des Gestaltungszustandes von Alarmsystemen – eine Machbarkeitsstudie (unpublished diploma thesis). Carl von Ossietzky Universität, Oldenburg (2009)
13. Bockelmann, M., Schütte, M., Nachreiner, F.: Entwicklung und Überprüfung eines Prototyps eines Instrumentes zur Beurteilung und Optimierung des Gestaltungszustandes von Alarmsystemen – Ergebnisse einer Machbarkeitsstudie. In: Gesellschaft für Arbeitswissenschaft (ed.) Neue Arbeits- und Lebenswelten gestalten, pp. 905–908. GfA-Press, Dortmund (2010)
14. Health & Safety Executive (HSE). Human Factors Briefing Note No. 9. Alarm Handling (n.d.).http://www.hse.gov.uk/humanfactors/topics/09alarms.pdf. 20 December 2016
15. VDI/VDE 3699-5: Prozessführung mit Bildschirmen – Alarme/Meldungen. Beuth, Berlin (2014)
16. Bortz, J., Lienert, G.A., Boehnke, K.: Verteilungsfreie Methoden in der Biostatistik. Springer, Berlin (2000)
17. Bortz, J.: Statistik für Human- und Sozialwissenschaftler. Springer Medizin, Heidelberg (2005)
18. Landis, J.R., Koch, G.G.: The measurement of observer agreement for categorical data. Biometrics 33, 159–174 (1977)
19. Schütte, M.: Reliabilitätsbestimmung arbeitsanalytischer Verfahren. In: Nickel, P., Hänecke, K., Schütte, M., Grzech-Šukalo, H. (eds.) Aspekte der Arbeitspsychologie in Wissenschaft und Praxis, pp. 79–102. Pabst, Lengerich (2004)
20. Cronbach, L.J., Gleser, G.C., Nanda, H., Rajaratnam, N.: The Dependability of Behavioral Measurements. Theory of Generalizability for Scores and Profiles. Wiley, New York (1972)
21. Brennan, R.L.: Generalizability Theory. Springer, New York (2001)
22. ISO 10075-3: Ergonomic principles related to mental workload – Part 3: Principles and requirements concerning methods for measuring and assessing mental workload. ISO, Geneva (2004)

How Correct and Defect Decision Support Systems Influence Trust, Compliance, and Performance in Supply Chain and Quality Management

A Behavioral Study Using Business Simulation Games

Philipp Brauner[1,2(✉)], André Calero Valdez[1,2], Ralf Philipsen[1,2], and Martina Ziefle[1,2]

[1] Human-Computer Interaction Center at RWTH Aachen University, Aachen, Germany
[2] Chair of Communication Science, RWTH Aachen University, Aachen, Germany
{brauner,calero-valdez,philipsen,ziefle}@comm.rwth-aachen.de

Abstract. Supply Chains and production networks are complex sociotechnical cyber-physical systems whose performance is determined by system, interface, and human factors. While the influence of system factors (e.g., variances in delivery times and amount, queuing strategies) is well understood, the influence of interface and human factors on supply chain performance is currently insufficiently explored. In this article, we analyze how performance is determined by the correctness of Decision Support Systems and specifically, how correct and defect systems influence subjective and objective performance, subjective and objective compliance with the system, as well as trust in the system. We present a behavioral study with 50 participants and a business simulation game with a market driven supply chain. Results show that performance (−21%), compliance (−35%), and trust (−25%) is shaped by the correctness of the system. However, this effect is only substantial in later stages of the game and occluded at the beginning. Also, people's subjective evaluations and the objective measures from the simulation are in congruence. The article concludes with open research questions regarding trust and compliance in Decision Support Systems as well as actionable knowledge on how Decision Support Systems can mitigate supply chain disruptions.

Keywords: Compliance · Trust · Decision support system · Supply chain management · Enterprise resource planning · Human factors · Business simulation game · Sociotechnical Cyber-Physical systems · Internet of production

1 Introduction

Global sourcing, increased competition, shorter innovation cycles, increased customers' demand on product variety and quality, and shorter ramp-up processes challenge the effectiveness of increasingly complex and globally dispersed cross-company supply chains [1–4]. Manufacturing companies therefore seek for methods to understand and manage their operation's stability, performance, and overall resilience [5]. We consider supply chains (SC) as complex socio-technical cyber-physical systems whose resilience, performance, and stability

© Springer International Publishing AG 2017
F.F.-H. Nah and C.-H. Tan (Eds.): HCIBGO 2017, PART II, LNCS 10294, pp. 333–348, 2017.
DOI: 10.1007/978-3-319-58484-3_26

is determined by system factors (e.g., delivery times or economic stability), human factors (e.g., ability to cope with variances in processes, understanding of the underlying system), and interface factors (e.g., data presentation, Decision Support Systems). Considerable efforts have been invested in understanding and reducing the complexity that arises from the system factors, such as Lean Manufacturing, shortening the length of the SC, or the reduction of the SC's complexity [1, 2, 6, 7]. However, the influences from interface and human factors on supply chain performance is currently insufficiently explored and therefore neither adequately addressed in teaching and vocational training, in the strategic design of supply chains, and the design and evaluation of enterprise resource planning systems.

Therefore, the following article presents a behavioral experiment that investigates the influence of the interface, namely of correct and defect Decision Support System (DSS), on compliance with the system, trust, decision efficacy, and overall supply chain performance.

In the remainder of this article Sect. 2 presents the related work on Supply Chain Disruptions, Decision Support Systems, and Business Simulations and Business Simulation Games. Section 3 describes our research model and operationalizes the investigated variables. Section 4 then presents the results of our empirical study. Section 5 concludes that adequate Decision Support Systems can mitigate the effect of supply chain disruptions and can therefore strengthen the resilience of the production network. The final Sect. 6 outlines the limitations of the study and a future research agenda.

2   Related Work

This section of related work presents the causes of supply chain disruptions in Sect. 2.1, Decision Support Systems in Sect. 2.2, and Business Simulation games in Sect. 2.3.

2.1   Supply Chain Disruptions

Supply chain disruptions can be triggered by a variety of causes ranging from unexpected demand spikes, industrial accidents, strikes, terror attacks, wars, or natural disasters. A systematic review of causes for supply chain disruptions can be found in Snyder et al. [1]. A prominent example for a disruption is the *bullwhip effect* or *Forrester effect* [8]: A singular variance in the customer's order in combination with insufficient communication upstream the supply chain is amplified at each tier and yields in stock level graphs that look like a bullwhip. Although identified and formalized over 50 years ago, this effect is still frequently discussed [4, 9, 10].

Methods for mitigating supply chain disruptions are manifold, but most focus on organizational aspects of the production network. Examples are the *postponement strategy* that increases the sourcing potential by increasing compatibility with other suppliers, the term *strategic stocks* refers to the concept of additional safety stock inventories to compensate demand fluctuations, or changes to the *pricing strategy* and other methods to redirect demand to products less affected by disruptions [6].

Blackhurst et al. identified that research on supply chain disruptions provides many high level, but only limited practical information on preventing and handling disruptions. Using semi-structured interviews and focus groups they studied the source for supply chain disruptions and focused on the three areas of *disruption discovery, disruption recovery*, and *supply chain redesign* [5]. A key finding is the importance of visibility and predictive analysis of potential supply chain disruptions by operatives. Specifically, they state that human operators have limited abilities to process the enormous amount of information available today and are therefore limited in their ability to detect upcoming disruptions. They suggest an automated supply chain intelligence that triggers human intervention after certain thresholds have been reached. This relates to the idea of Decision Support Systems presented in the next section.

2.2 Decision Support Systems

Precursors of Decision Support Systems (DSS) have been developed since the 1950's and 1960's and they aim at harnessing the computational power and storage abilities of computers to automate the programmable part of operational, tactical, or strategic decision problems [11, 12]. This part is usually routine, repetitive, structured and therefore easily solved by computers. The systems encode knowledge, models, and decision rules in a computable form and provide support through querying systems, reports, or visualizations to decision makers. These can integrate the results into the non-programmable part of the decision problem, which is often new, creative, ill-structured, or difficult to solve. Data warehouses [12], OLAP [13], and data-mining [14] are modern forms of DSSs and artificial intelligence is gaining importance due to its ability to facilitate processing of a large amount of fuzzy information [15]. Summarizing, adequately designed DSS are a necessity to enable decision makers to handle the growing amount of information and complexity and to facilitate the success of the Industrial Internet and Industry 4.0 [16, 17].

Ben-Zvi used a business simulation game to engage students in the development and use of Decision Support Systems in an educational setting and investigated their perceived usefulness and their relationship to performance [18, 19]. The study found that perceived benefits of using a DSS, user satisfaction, and performance of the simulated company are strongly related. Also, support systems with higher complexity yielded in higher company performance. Although situated in an entrepreneurial context, neither the influence of supply chain effects, nor the influence of deliberately defect DSS's were investigated.

Brauner et al. investigated the influence of a correct and defective DSS compared to no DSS (baseline) in regard to decision efficiency (speed) and effectivity (correctness) in a table reading task of limited complexity [20]. As expected, a correct DSS increased speed and accuracy of the task compared to the baseline experiment. In contrast, a defective DSS had a devastating effect on task accuracy, whereas the speed was only mildly affected. Thus, the defective support system annihilates the subjects' task accuracy, despite knowing about its defectiveness. Strikingly, the devastating effect only emerged for more complex tasks, whereas it could be compensated in easier settings. This study is the basis for the experiment presented in this article.

2.3 Business Simulation Games

Simulated business and supply chains are an established method to identify and quantify supply chain disruptions, to convey knowledge and expertise about supply chain management and material disposition, as well as to study human decision making in controlled experimental, although sufficiently complex scenarios [21]. An early example are behavioral studies on the Beer Distribution Game by Sterman [22]. They found that a singular increase in customer's demand is amplified upstream the supply chain, yielding in the well-known bullwhip effect described above. Later, Lee et al. [4] identified the processing of demand signals, rationing of the inventory, order batching, as well as price fluctuations as the key causes for the emergence of the bullwhip effect. Furthermore, Wu and Katok investigate the influence of learning and communication on the bullwhip effect and found that experience alone is not sufficient for reducing the effect, but that collaboration and communication in combination with expertise reduces the order amplification [23]. Sarkar and Kumar investigated the effect of upstream (i.e., from the retailer) and downstream (i.e., from the supplier) disruptions and weather sharing knowledge about the disruption mitigates its effect in a behavioral experiment [24]. For upstream events (i.e., disruptions at the manufacturer) sharing information lead to a reduction in variances and overall supply chain costs, whereas limited effects were found for sharing information about downstream disruptions (e.g., at the retailer).

We developed the *"Quality Intelligence Game"*, a sophisticated simulation model embedded in a turn-based business game rooted in Forrester's Beer Distribution Game [8] (focus on multi-echelon effects) and Goldratt's game (focus on quality variances along the supply chain) [25]. Players are part of market driven supply chain and must invest in the internal production quality, the incoming goods inspection, and the procurement of supplies. They must infer the current state of the production from the presented data and then need to find an optimal tradeoff between these three measures. Neglecting at least one of the measures yields in poor performance, as delivery bottlenecks or poor product quality are punished by the customer.

The underlying supply chain simulation model and the game's user interface can be experimentally controlled to investigate the influence of supply chain disruptions, unexpected changes to supplier's quality, or to the presentation of the company's various metrics, such as stock level, costs for quality inspection, and customers' complaints, or other KPIs. The average product quality or the attainted performance can then serve as a benchmark for evaluating learning interventions, the influence of system complexity, or changes to the user interface.

3 Research Design

To understand the influence of the correctness of the decision support system on trust, compliance respectively use of the system, and overall performance, we applied a three-stage experimental design (Fig. 1 illustrates the research design):

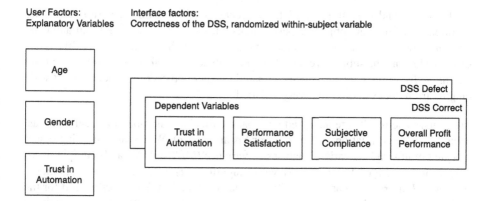

Fig. 1. Visualization of the experimental plan.

First, a pre-questionnaire captures the subjects' demographic data, trust in automation using a generic scenario (i.e., an app that suggests the number of beverages to buy for a party). Second, the participants played two rounds of the "Quality Intelligence Game" business simulation game—16 turns each—described above (without artificially induced supply chain disruptions) and log files capture company, interaction, and performance metrics. Third, a final questionnaire measures the subjects' evaluation of the perceived game performance, the trust towards the DSS, as well as the perceived compliance with the system for each of the two rounds. Unless otherwise noted, all subjective measures are captured on 6-point Likert scales from 0 to 5 (max.) and are rescaled to 0% to 100%.

Explanatory user factors: *Trust in Automation* (TiA) is captured on the scale by Jian et al. [26]. To measure the individuals' generic trust towards a support system we let them evaluate a fictitious app for planning the number of beverages to buy for a party. Despite the scenario based approach, the scale achieved an excellent internal reliability ($\alpha = .804$, 12 items).

Within-subject factors: The *Correctness* of the Decision Support System is the within-subject factor and the players randomly started either with a *defect* or a *correct* DSS in the first round of the game. In the *correct* condition, the DSS suggested very good, although not perfect orders for all turns of the game. In the *defect* condition, the suggestions of the DSS were about 50% below the value of the correct condition (easy to perceive as the suggestion is way below the customer's order and the penalties skyrocket in the following turns). To give the participants a false sense of security, the DSS always started with correct suggestions for the first five turns; then it switched to *defect* mode until the end of the game. In contrast to previous studies on this game, no disruptions were investigated as within-subject factors (cf., [27]).

Dependent variables: The trust in the DSS was captured after each round with the *Trust in Automation* scale from above [26]. The participants' compliance with the DSS is captured using a *subjective compliance* Likert scale ranging from 0% to 100%.

To understand the influence of the correctness of the DSS on performance, we captured subjective and objective performance measures. Based on Goldratt and Cox, the *company profit* is calculated as the cumulated net profit for each round of the game [25]. In addition, the subjects reported on their subjective *performance satisfaction* and the *subjective relative performance* compared to other players on a 6-point Likert scale ranging from "not satisfied" to "very satisfied".

Methods: The results are analyzed with parametrical and non-parametrical methods, using bivariate correlations (Pearon's r or Spearman's ρ), Wilcoxon tests, single, and repeated multi- and univariate analyses of variance (M/ANOVA), and multiple linear regressions. The type I error rate (level of significance) is set to $\alpha = .05$ (findings . $05 < p < .1$ are reported as marginally significant). Pillai's value is considered for the multivariate tests and effect sizes are reported as η^2. If the assumption of sphericity is not met, Greenhouse-Geisser–corrected values are used, but uncorrected dfs are reported for legibility. As the performance from the simulation model is not normally distributed ($KS\text{-}Z_{round1} = 1.946$, $KS\text{-}Z_{round2} = 2.054$, $p < .001$) analyses of this model are performed with non-parametrical tests. Whiskers in diagrams represent the standard error (SE), arithmetic means are reported with standard deviations (denoted $\pm$).

3.1   Description of the Sample

40 people (23 male, 17 female) aged 20–56 ($M = 28.5 \pm 8.6$) years participated voluntarily in the web-based study and completed both rounds of the game (from 54 participants in the first round 25% did not completed second round). The initial Trust in Automation (TiA) had an average score of $73.0 \pm 13.9\%$ (0–100% max.) and it was neither related to age, nor gender.

4   Results

The results section is structured as follows: First, the link between objective measures from the simulation model and the participant's subjective responses is established. Second, as the experimental setup taints the effect of practice and learnability with the effect of the correctness of the decision support system, the effect of correctness is discussed for each of the two consecutive rounds individually (between-subject). Third, a brief evaluation of the influence of practice and the communalities between both rounds is presented. Forth, the effect of correctness of the DSS is analyzed for both rounds combined (within-subject).

4.1   Preface: Congruency of System and Subjective Measures

The results show a strong relationship between the measures captured in the simulation game and the participant's subjective responses. Thus, users are able to estimate how well they have performed.

Most importantly, the data shows a strong relationship between the performance measured in the simulation model and the performance satisfaction in the first ($\rho_{n=57} = .669$, $p < .001$) and second round of the game ($\rho_{n=44} = .300$, $p = .048 < .05$), as well as the perceived relative performance in the first ($\rho_{n=54} = .460$, $p < .001$) and second round ($\rho_{n=40} = .609$, $p = <.001$). Hence, player's that reported a high performance and high satisfaction were actually good in the game.

Correspondingly, the number of order changes in the game's user interface is also strongly *negatively* related to the subjective compliance in the first ($\rho_{n=54} = -.721$, $p < .001$) and second round of the game ($\rho_{n=37} = -.755$, $p < .001$). Hence, participants who followed the suggestions of the DSS made less changes to the orders and reported a higher compliance with the system. On average, the number of order changes in the first round is 9.2 ± 6.1 and 9.8 ± 6.6 in the second round of the game compared to a maximum of 18 possible changes. The reported compliance is at $37.0 \pm 28.1\%$ respectively $45.7 \pm 30.5\%$ and thus in the same range as the measured compliance.

As subjective and objective measures behave similarly, the following sections focus on the subjective measures reported by the participants of the study. This facilitates the use of the more powerful parametrical methods for analyzing the study, despite the non-parametrical measurements from the simulation model.

4.2   Independent Evaluation of Both Rounds

This section illuminates the effect of the DSS' correctness independently for the first and second round of the game (i.e., neglecting influences of repetition).

In the first round, participants with a correct DSS achieved a higher *overall profit* ($Md = 11075$), higher *performance satisfaction* ($61.4 \pm 30.3\%$), and higher *relative performance* ($52.6 \pm 21.6\%$) than participants with a defective DSS ($Md = -29825$, $51.0 \pm 33.6\%$, $46.7 \pm 22.9\%$). Likewise, the reported and measured *compliance* with the system is higher for the correct system ($41.8 \pm 30.1\%$, $Md = 9.5$) compared to the defective system ($32.5 \pm 28.8\%$, $Md = 10.5$). The *Trust in Automation* score is also higher for the correct system ($66.2 \pm 15.9\%$) than for the defective system ($56.9 \pm 20.5\%$). However, despite all measures tending towards a positive effect of a correctly working DSS, the effect is merely significant for the *overall profit* (see Table 1 and Fig. 2, left).

Table 1. Effect of a Decision Support System's correctness in the first round of the game.

Overall profit	Order changes	Subjective compliance	Performance satisfaction	Relative performance	Trust in automation
Defect DSS:					
Md = −29825 M = −20708 ± 34644	Md = 10.5 M = 10.1 ± 5.5	32.5 ± 25.8%	51.0 ± 33.6%	46.7 ± 22.9%	59.9 ± 20.5%
Correct DSS:					
Md = 11075 M = 3274 ± 16627	Md = 9.5 M = 9.2 ± 6.7	41.8 ± 30.1%	61.4 ± 30.3%	52.6 ± 21.6%	66.2 ± 15.9%
U = 508.5 p = .027 < .05*	MW-U = 681.5 p = .673 > .05	F = 1.492 p = .227 > .05	F = 1.501 p = .226 > .05	F = .959 p = .332 > .05	F = 3.574 p = .064 > .05

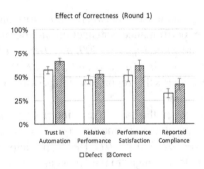
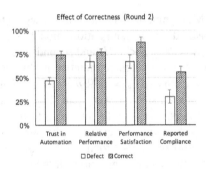

Fig. 2. Effect of a correct and defect DSS on *Trust in Automation, Performance Satisfaction, Subjective Relative Performance*, and *Subjective Compliance* for the first and second round of the game (whiskers indicate the SE).

In the second round, the effect of the correctness of the DSS are much clearer. Even though the difference is not significant, the *overall profit* is higher ($Md = 11675$) for the correct DSS than for the defective DSS ($Md = -10150$). Likewise, the measured and reported *compliance* with the correct DSS is higher ($56.0 \pm 28.6\%, Md = 7$) than for the defect DSS ($30.0 \pm 26.9\%, Md = 14$).

The correct DSS is also positively influencing the *performance satisfaction*, which is significantly higher for the correct system ($87.8 \pm 24.7\%$) than for the defect system ($67.3 \pm 33.5\%$). Although the difference is not significant, a similar—though smaller—effect seems to emerge for the subjective *relative performance* ($77.1 \pm 17.1\%$ vs. $67.0 \pm 28.5\%$). Consequently, the *Trust in Automation* is also significantly higher for the correct system ($74.3 \pm 20.7\%$) than for the defect system ($47.2 \pm 15.7\%$). Table 2 and Fig. 2, right shows these effects.

4.3   Effect of Repetition and Learnability

On average, the *overall performance* of the first and second round of the game were strongly related ($\rho = .751, p < .001$), but without a significant increase in attained performance ($Z = -.132, p = .895 > .05$). This suggests two conclusions: First, that some participants consistently play good, whereas others play bad. Second, that the

Table 2. Effect of a Decision Support System's correctness in the second round of the game.

Overall profit	Order changes	Subjective compliance	Performance satisfaction	Relative performance	Trust in automation
Defect DSS:					
Md = −10150	Md = 14.0	30.0 ± 26.9%	67.3 ± 33.5%	67.0 ± 28.5%	47.2 ± 15.7%
M = −12928 ± 32007	M = 10.9 ± 7.0				
Correct DSS:					
Md = 11675	Md = 7.0	56.0 ± 28.6%	87.8 ± 24.7%	77.1 ± 17.1%	74.3 ± 20.7%
M = 6059 ± 11284	M = 8.7 ± 6.1				
MW-U = 309.0	MW-U = 364.5	F = 7.807	F = 5.516	F = 1.934	F = 23.494
p = .056 > .05	p = .283 > .05	p = .008 < .05*	p = .024 < .05*	p = .172 > .05	p < .001**

influence of the DSS's correctness is rather strong and diminishes the influence of practice or learnability identified in earlier work [28].

Furthermore, the *order changes* in the first and second round of the game are positively related ($\rho_{n=49} = .557, p < .001$), which again indicates that some participants are more likely to adjust the order levels suggested by the DSS than others.

A RM-MANOVA with the *game* (round 1 and round 2) as within-subject factor and *Trust in Automation, Relative Performance, Performance Satisfaction*, and *Compliance* as dependent variables revealed on overall significant effect ($F_{2,29} = 12.267, V = .629, p < .001$). Neither *Trust* ($F_{1,32} = .077, p = .784 > .05$) nor the reported *Compliance* ($F_{1,32} = 1.007, p = .323 > .05$) are significantly different after the first and second round of the game. Yet, significant effects emerge for *relative performance* ($F_{1,32} = 39.871, p < .001$), as well as for the *performance satisfaction* ($F_{1,32} = 13.444, p = .001$). *Relative performance* increases from 49.6% to 72.2% and *performance satisfaction* increases from 56.1% to 77.8%. Figure 2 left illustrates the influence of repetition.

4.4 Influence of the Defect Decision Support System

In addition to the findings present in Sect. 4.2 this section now analyses the influence of the DSS with a focus on the within-subject factor correctness (neglecting a possible influence of practice).

On average, the attained *performance* with a correctly working DSS was higher (4479 ± 14523) than with a defect DSS (-17275 ± 33486) and this difference is significant ($Z = -2.647, p = .008 < .05$). Also, the number of order changes for the correct DSS is slightly lower (9.0 ± 6.4) than for the defect DSS (10.4 ± 6.1). Yet, this difference is only marginally significant ($Z = -1.893, p = .058 < .1$).

Based on the congruence of the objective measures from the simulation model and the subjective measures established in Sect. 4.1, the following sections investigate the subjective measures using parametrical methods.

A RM-MANOVA with *Correctness* as within-subject variable and *Trust in Automation, Compliance, Performance Satisfaction,* and *Subjective Relative Performance* as dependent variables revealed a strong and significant overall effect ($V = .471, F_{4,29} = 6.455, p < .001, \eta^2 = .471$). *Correctness* significantly influences all four considered dependent variables, namely *Trust in Automation* ($F_{1,32} = 21.670, p < .001, \eta^2 = .404$), *Compliance* ($F_{1,32} = 4.643, p = .039 < .05, \eta^2 = .127$), *Performance Satisfaction* ($F_{1,32} = 8.274, p = .007 < .05, \eta^2 = .205$) and *Subj. Relative Performance* ($F_{1,32} = 7.386, p = .011 < .05, \eta^2 = .188$).

Specifically, the reported *Trust* in the correct DSS ($69.8 \pm 2.6\%$) was sig. higher than the reported *Trust* in the defect system ($52.6 \pm 2.7\%$). Accordingly, the reported *compliance* was also higher for the correctly working system ($48.4 \pm 4.3\%$) compared to the lower *compliance* with the defective system ($31.6 \pm 4.0\%$). Likewise, a correct DSS yields in higher perceived *relative performance* ($63.3 \pm 3.3\%$) and higher *performance satisfaction* ($73.3 \pm 4.3\%$) compared to the defect system ($55.3 \pm 4.0\%$, resp. $58.0 \pm 4.8\%$). Figure 3 shows these significant effects.

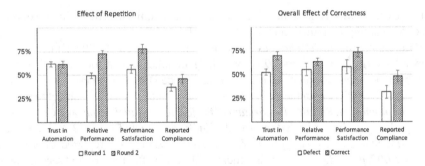

Fig. 3. Effect of practice (round 1 vs. round 2) and overall correctness (round 1 + 2) on *Trust in Automation, Relative Performance, Performance Satisfaction,* and *Subjective Compliance* (whiskers indicate the SE).

To understand if *Trust, performance, compliance,* and *profit overall* are interrelated and if this interrelationship is influenced by the correctness of the system, the following paragraphs present a correlation analysis of these four measures.

Correct DSS: For the correct Decision Support System, there are strong and significant relationships between the *Trust* in the system and the reported *compliance* ($\rho_{n=48} = .343, p = .017 < .05$), *relative performance* ($\rho_{n=47} = .550, p < .001$), and *performance satisfaction* ($\rho_{n=50} = .519, p < .001$). As expected, the relationship between subjective *relative performance* and *performance satisfaction* is also very high ($\rho_{n=48} = .716, p < .001$). However, the reported *compliance* is unrelated to *relative performance* ($\rho_{n=45} = .164, p = .281 > .05$) and *performance satisfaction* ($\rho_{n=48} = .042, p = .777 > .05$). Figure 4 (left) illustrates these relationships.

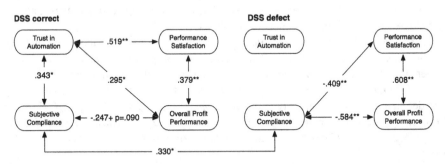

Fig. 4. Spearman's ρ correlations between *Trust in Automation, Performance Satisfaction, Subjective Compliance* and attained *Overall Profit* for the *correct* and the *defect* DSS.

Defect DSS: For the defect Decision Support System, the reported *Trust* is neither related to the reported *compliance* ($\rho_{n=41} = .177, p = .268 > .05$), the *relative performance* ($\rho_{n=44} = -.170, p = .271 > .05$), nor the *performance satisfaction* ($\rho_{n=48} = -.109, p = .462 > .05$). The reported *compliance* is negatively associated with *relative performance* ($\rho_{n=40} = -.317, p = .047 < .05$) and the *performance satisfaction* ($\rho_{n=43} = -.409,$

$p = .006 < .05$). Again, subjective *relative performance* is strongly related with *performance satisfaction* ($\rho_{n=47} = .777, p < .002$). Figure 4 (right) presents the interrelationships for the defect Decision Support System.

Surprisingly, the generic *Trust in Automation* is neither related to the *Trust* in the correct system ($r = .173, p = .246 > .05$), nor to the *Trust* in the defect system ($r = .089, p = .567 > .05$), nor are the *Trust* in the correct and the defect system related ($r = .254, p = .100 > .05$). Also, neither subjective *relative performance* ($\rho_{n=40} = .193, p = .233 > .05$), nor *performance satisfaction* ($\rho_{n=44} = .016, p = .918 > .05$) are associated across both rounds. However, the reported *compliances* for both DSSs (defect, correct) are positively related ($\rho_{n=46} = .330, p = .046 < .05$).

5 Discussion

Our study provides some valuable insights regarding the positive influence of correctly working Decision Support Systems on performance, compliance, and trust, the harmful effects of defective DSS, as well as some methodological tidbits that may guide future research on business simulation games, Decision Support Systems, and human-factors in complex sociotechnical cyber-physical systems.

5.1 Benefits of Decision Support Systems

The study show that correctly working Decision Support System have an apparent positive influence on trust in a support system, compliance with the system, thus also on overall perceived and actual performance. Compared to the defective systems, the participants reported higher trust levels, a higher compliance, as well as higher performance satisfaction and most importantly, they also realized higher cumulated company profits. In summary, correctly working support systems are a valuable tool to relieve workers from repetitive or difficult tasks and increase their overall efficiency, as well as the overall efficiency of the manufacturing company.

5.2 Risks of Decision Support Systems

While the finding that a correct Decision Support System yields in a higher company profit seams trivial, the reverse perspective deserves attention: Although the subjects of the presented study must have noticed the defect of the DSS (the suggested orders were *clearly* below the customer's demand and the penalties increased), they still have followed the suggestion of the system to some extent, which has diminished the overall profit of the company, as well as the subjective performance.

This finding relates well to a study published earlier that illuminated the influence of corrected and defective DSSs in less complex table reading tasks [20]. However, the previous study concluded that the negative influence of defective DSSs on effectivity emerges only for more complex tasks, as defectiveness can easily be compensated for simple tasks. In contrast, this study investigated the influence of correctness in context and in a complex environment, but without an experimental consideration of task complexity. Consequently, future work must address how correctness and defectiveness of Decision Support Systems influences efficiency, effectivity, and trust in relationship to complexity of the simulated environment.

In summary, defective support systems have an overall negative effect on work's efficiency, and thus a negative effect on the overall performance of companies and cross-company supply chains as complex sociotechnical cyber-physical systems.

5.3   Correct vs. Defect Decision Support Systems

For the case of a correct DSS, the study identified a higher trust in the automated system, as well as a positive relationship between trust and the compliance with the system, the satisfaction with the attained performance, as well with the actual performance. On the contrary, if the DSS is defect, trust is significantly lower and trust is independent to the compliance, satisfaction with the attained performance, as well as the actual company profit.

Surprisingly, there is a moderate negative association between the compliance with the system and the performance satisfaction in the case of a defect support system. Meaning that the participants complying with the system have noticed the defectiveness and their poor performance (hence the lower performance satisfaction and lower overall profit). Still, it is unclear why they followed the system's orders and under which conditions and when they would have started to neglect the system's suggestions. Interestingly, there was no relationship between compliance and performance satisfaction for the case of a correct Decision Support System. We conclude that people complying with a correct system do not feel the same level of accomplishment as people and may attribute their performance to the support system and not to their own individual abilities. Future work should therefore more closely address the role of attribution and Attribution Theory (cf. [29]) in regard to compliance with Decision Support Systems, performance satisfaction, as well as attained performance.

Interestingly, the reported compliance levels for the defect and the correct DSS are moderately related. This indicates that some subjects are more inclined to comply with the system and obey its orders than others. This raises the questions which and why operators in cyber-physical production systems are more likely to abdicate orders of the DSS than others, how operators can be trained to detect and disobey defective systems, and how trust in the system can be reestablished after such an incident.

A remarkable trifle of the study is the negative association of compliance with the system and the attained overall profit for both, the correct (although not significant) and the defect system. We assume that this relationship is caused by people focusing solely on the decisions support system and neglected other parts of the business simulation game. For the case of the defective system, compliance with the faulty suggestions obviously has a devastating effect. For the case of the correct system, focusing solely on the support system and thereby neglecting other parts of the simulated company also yields in lower profits, as managing the order levels was just one of three tasks in the game (for an isolated perspective of a single task see [20]).

5.4 Methodological Contributions

From the methodological perspective, the study revealed that objective measures from the simulation model are in accordance with the subjective measures reported by the participants, that the subjective measures require calibration through training, and that we identified a possible lower barrier for the applied trust scale.

Methodologically, the study established a strong relationship between the various perceived measures of the study (e.g., performance and compliance) and the objective measures captured in the underlying simulation of business game. As most objective efficiency and effectivity measures from simulations or actual production environments do not follow parametrical distributions, their statistical analysis—especially if combined with elements from psychometrical measures as in this study—is impeded. However, due to this strong relationship of objective and subjective measures, future studies can build on the analyses of the parametrical subjective measures which extends the methodological portfolio by more sophisticated statistical methods.

Apparently, a correctly working Decision Support System has a profound positive influence on objective and subjective *company profit*, objective and subjective *compliance*, as well as in *trust* in the system. Still, these effects are only discernible, yet not significant, for the first round of the game. Only in the second round of the game, these effects gain in power and yield in statistically significant results. We assume, that this is caused by a missing internal calibration and anchoring of the respective measures for first round of the game. In the subsequent round, a reference frame is established and yields in more separated measures, lower spreads, and clearer results. Therefore, future research addressing Trust, compliance, or perceived performance must ensure that an adequate reference frame or anchoring is established by providing training sessions or repeated measurements.

An additional trifle is a step towards the calibration of psychometric trust scales. Due to our empirical methodology with the induced malfunction of the DSS, we have measured the lower barrier of the trust scale by Jian et al. [26]. Due to the defectiveness of the DSS, it is rather unlikely that avg. trust scores will fall below the value of 52.6% on this scale. However, our approach is unsuitable to identify an upper barrier of this scale, as the current rating is not only affected by the correctness of the DSS, but probably also tainted by the effect of the underlying simulation model and the individual's abilities to cope with the supply chain's complexity. Future work will therefore have to address methods to empirically determine the scale's upper barrier.

In contrast to the compliance with the system and despite its high internal reliability, the three measurements of *Trust in Automation* were not related. This indicates that Trust in Automation—as least as captured in this study—is not an individual personal trait, but rather a state that is heavily influenced by the automated system and the reliability of this automation.

5.5 Summary

The study has shown that correctly working Decision Support Systems do have a positive influence on the effectivity of the simulated cross-company supply chain. We therefore conclude that adequately designed Decision Support Systems can mitigate supply chain disruptions and that DSSs are one fundamental pillar to strengthen the resilience of manufacturing companies and likely other complex sociotechnical cyber-physical systems. Yet, defective Decision Support System can have a devastating effect on the performance, which was also identified for different settings in previous research [20]. Consequently, future research must identify how supply chain operators and workers in material disposition can be trained to notice defective Decision Support Systems, disobey their orders, and act successfully despite the lack of decision support.

Concluding, by empowering operators to harness the benefits of correctly working decision support and to mitigate the drawbacks of defective support systems, the overall performance of cross-company supply chains can be increased, their resilience can be strengthened, and their overall viability be established.

6 Outlook

In the current experiment the effect of the correctness of the Decision Support System is not clearly separated from and thereby tainted by the effect of repeating several rounds of the game (e.g., practice, fatigue, motivational change) discovered in earlier studies (e.g., [27]). Consequently, a follow up study with a significantly larger sample size should investigate this effect and must separate, identify, and quantify the influence of these factors.

Furthermore, the negative influence of a defective DSS has been shown in an abstract experimental setting and in this study with the business simulation game. Future studies must therefore investigate the influence of defective support systems in more complex or realistic settings. Hereto, the business simulation game's adjustable complexity might be used to help to increase the understanding of the interaction of interface and system complexity.

Finally, strategies and trainings must be identified, developed, and evaluated that enable operators to recognize defective or deflective support systems and therefore prevent blind obedience of these systems.

Acknowledgements. We thank all participants for their willingness to contribute to our research and our colleagues Sebastian Stiller, Marco Fuhrmann, Hao Ngo, Robert Schmitt, for support and in-depth discussions on this work. Furthermore, we like to thank Sabrina Schulte for her research support. The German Research Foundation (DFG) founded this project within the Cluster of Excellence „Integrative Production Technology for High-Wage Countries" (EXC 128) and the integrated cluster domain ICD-D1 [30].

References

1. Snyder, L.V., Atan, Z., Peng, P., Rong, Y., Schmitt, A.J., Sinsoysal, B.: OR/MS models for supply chain disruptions: a review. IIE Trans. **48**, 89–109 (2016)
2. Trent, R.J., Monczka, R.M.: Pursuing competitive advantage through integrated global sourcing. Acad. Manage. Executive **16**, 66–80 (2002)

3. Brauner, P., Philipsen, R., Fels, A., Fuhrmann, M., Ngo, H., Stiller, S., Schmitt, R., Ziefle, M.: A game-based approach to meet the challenges of decision processes in ramp-up management. Qual. Manage. J. **23**, 55–69 (2016)
4. Lee, H.L., Padmanabhan, V., Whang, S.: Information distortion in a supply chain: the bullwhip effect. Manage. Sci. **43**, 546–558 (1997)
5. Blackhurst, J., Craighead, C.W., Elkins, D., Handfield, R.B.: An empirically derived agenda of critical research issues for managing supply-chain disruptions. Int. J. Prod. Res. **43**, 4067–4081 (2005)
6. Tang, C.: Robust strategies for mitigating supply chain disruptions. Int. J. Logistics **9**, 33–45 (2006)
7. Blum, M., Runge, S., Groten, M., Stiller, S.: Interrelationships between product quality and different demand cases in ramp-up scenarios. Procedia CIRP **20**, 81–84 (2014)
8. Forrester, J.W.: Industrial Dynamics. MIT Press, Cambridge (1961)
9. Sarkar, S., Kumar, S.: Demonstrating the effect of supply chain disruptions through an online beer distribution game *. Decis. Sci. J. Innovative Educ. **14**, 25–35 (2016)
10. Brauner, P., Runge, S., Groten, M., Schuh, G., Ziefle, M.: Human factors in supply chain management – decision making in complex logistic scenarios. In: Yamamoto, S. (ed.) HIMI 2013. LNCS, vol. 8018, pp. 423–432. Springer, Heidelberg (2013). doi:10.1007/978-3-642-39226-9_46
11. Gorry, G.A., Morton, M.S.S.: A framework for management information systems. Sloan Manage. Rev. **13**, 50–70 (1971)
12. Kimball, R., Ross, M.: The data warehouse toolkit: the complete guide to dimensional modelling. Wiley, New York (1996)
13. Codd, E., Codd, S., Salley, C.: Providing OLAP to User-Analysts: An IT Mandate (1993)
14. Bra, A., Lungu, I.: Improving decision support systems with data mining techniques. In: Advances in Data Mining Knowledge Discovery and Applications. InTech (2012)
15. Phillips-Wren, G.: AI tools in decision making support systems: a review. Int. J. Artif. Intell. Tools **21** (2012)
16. Brauner, P., Ziefle, M.: Human factors in production systems – motives, methods and beyond. In: Brecher, C. (ed.) Advances in Production Technology. LNPE, pp. 187–199. Springer, Cham (2015). doi:10.1007/978-3-319-12304-2_14
17. Calero Valdez, A., Brauner, P., Schaar, A.K., Holzinger, A., Ziefle, M.: Reducing complexity with simplicity - usability methods for industry 4.0. In: 19th Triennial Congress of the International Ergonomics Association (IEA 2015), Melbourne, Australia (2015)
18. Ben-Zvi, T.: The efficacy of business simulation games in creating Decision Support Systems: an experimental investigation. Decis. Support Syst. **49**, 61–69 (2010)
19. Ben-Zvi, T.: Measuring the perceived effectiveness of decision support systems and their impact on performance. Decis. Support Syst. **54**, 248–256 (2012)
20. Brauner, P., Calero Valdez, A., Philipsen, R., Ziefle, M.: Defective still deflective – how correctness of decision support systems influences user's performance in production environments. In: Nah, F.F.-H., Tan, C.-H. (eds.) HCIBGO 2016. LNCS, vol. 9752, pp. 16–27. Springer, Cham (2016). doi:10.1007/978-3-319-39399-5_2
21. Brauner, P., Ziefle, M.: How to train employees, identify task-relevant human factors, and improve software systems with business simulation games. In: Dimitrov, D., Oosthuizen, T. (eds.) Proceedings of the 6th International Conference on Competitive Manufacturing 2016 (COMA 2016), pp. 541–546. CIRP, Stellenbosch (2016)
22. Sterman, J.D.: Modeling managerial behavior: misperceptions of feedback in a dynamic decision making experiment. Manage. Sci. **35**, 321–339 (1989)
23. Wu, D.Y., Katok, E.: Learning, communication, and the bullwhip effect. J. Oper. Manage. **24**, 839–850 (2006)

24. Sarkar, S., Kumar, S.: A behavioral experiment on inventory management with supply chain disruption. Int. J. Prod. Econ. **169**, 169–178 (2015)
25. Goldratt, E.M., Cox, J.: The goal: a process of ongoing improvement. North River Press, Great Barrington (1992)
26. Jian, J.-Y., Bisantz, A.M., Drury, C.G.: Foundations for an empirically determined scale of trust in automated system. Int. J. Cogn. Ergon. **4**, 53–71 (2000)
27. Philipsen, R., Brauner, P., Stiller, S., Ziefle, M., Schmitt, R.: Understanding and supporting decision makers in quality management of production networks. In: Advances in the Ergonomics in Manufacturing. Managing the Enterprise of the Future 2014: Proceedings of the 5th International Conference on Applied Human Factors and Ergonomics, AHFE 2014, pp. 94–105. CRC Press, Boca Raton (2014)
28. Stiller, S., Falk, B., Philipsen, R., Brauner, P., Schmitt, R., Ziefle, M.: A game-based approach to understand human factors in supply chains and quality management. Procedia CIRP **20**, 67–73 (2014)
29. Niels, A., Guczka, S.R., Janneck, M.: The impact of causal attribution s on system evaluation in usability tests. In: Proceedings of the SIGCHI Conference on Human Factors in Computing Systems, pp. 3115–3125 (2016)
30. Schlick, C., Stich, V., Schmitt, R., Schuh, G., Ziefle, M., Brecher, C., Blum, M., Mertens, A., Faber, M., Kuz, S., Petruck, H., Fuhrmann, M., Luckert, M., Brambring, F., Reuter, C., Hering, N., Groten, M., Korall, S., Pause, D., Brauner, P., Herfs, W., Odenbusch, M., Wein, S., Stiller, S., Berthold, M.: Cognition-enhanced, self-optimizing production networks. In: Brecher, C., Özdemir, D. (eds.) Integrative Production Technology - Theory and Applications, pp. 645–743. Springer International Publishing, Heidelberg (2017)

Impact of Mobile IT Consumerization on Organizations – An Empirical Study on the Adoption of BYOD Practices

Christian Meske[1(✉)], Stefan Stieglitz[1], Tobias Brockmann[2], and Björn Ross[1]

[1] University of Duisburg-Essen, Duisburg, Germany
{christian.meske,stefan.stieglitz,bjoern.ross}@uni-due.de
[2] innoscale AG, Berlin, Germany
brockmann@innoscale.de

Abstract. The last few years have seen more and more employees using their personal mobile devices for work-related tasks. This phenomenon is part of a broader trend known as IT consumerization. Enterprises and employees have recognized that they might profit from these developments and implemented "Bring Your Own Device" (BYOD) policies, but they also have to face new challenges. This study investigates which types of employees adopt BYOD and how they benefit from it. To address these questions, the authors conducted a survey with 219 participants. Participants were classified into adopter types based on the Diffusion of Innovation Theory. The results indicate that early adopters and the early majority use their personal smartphones more often for work-related tasks than laggards, and that innovators and early adopters more often receive work-related email on their personal smartphones than other adopter types. It is concluded that DOI can successfully be applied to explain BYOD adoption behavior. Differentiated management strategies have to be applied in order to address the whole workforce.

Keywords: BYOD · Mobile · Diffusion of innovation theory · IT consumerization · Adoption

1 Introduction

In recent years, mobile devices have invaded both private and business life [1–3]. This phenomenon is part of a digital transformation process in many societies, of which, for instance, the diffusion of social network sites like Facebook is also part [4].

Employees increasingly use their own devices in a business context [1]. Particularly since 2012, the press and the web community have termed this development 'Bring Your Own Device' (BYOD) [5–7]. In academic research this phenomenon has been discussed for many years under the name IT consumerization [8]. IT consumerization describes the usage of consumer IT resources for business purposes [9]. From the point of view of the employees, their personal devices are often easier to use than those provided by their employer, for example because they are more familiar with the operating system. Accordingly, employees claim to be more productive when using their own devices [10, 11].

© Springer International Publishing AG 2017
F.F.-H. Nah and C.-H. Tan (Eds.): HCIBGO 2017, PART II, LNCS 10294, pp. 349–363, 2017.
DOI: 10.1007/978-3-319-58484-3_27

Thanks to the accelerating diffusion of smartphones and the increase in mobile applications, employees can easily use their own devices for work-related tasks [12].

Enterprises need to be aware of the adoption of mobile services by their workforce, because it might influence employees' productivity, work-life balance, and communication behavior [12]. They often deal with these issues by providing BYOD policies directed at the employees or by implementing 'mobile device management' (MDM) software in order to maintain a high level of security and to create a homogeneous software landscape [13].

Some recent studies, such as those by Gartner and the German management magazine "CIO", reflect on BYOD from a critical perspective. They observe that the willingness of employees to adopt BYOD is not as strong as press reports suggest [5, 14]. In our research, we draw on Rogers' Diffusion of Innovation (DOI) theory [15] to explain this phenomenon. DOI theory predicts that certain types of technology users are more open to adopting the BYOD mindset than others. A major goal of this research is therefore to identify which types of employees, following the DOI theory, adopt the Bring Your Own Device philosophy. The differences between adopter groups are also examined.

Our research concentrates on smartphones. Until now, little research has investigated the adoption of BYOD practices regarding smartphones by employees. In contrast to traditional mobile devices like laptop computers, smartphones are wearable computers [16, 17]. Therefore, they differ with regard to frequency of usage, types of tasks and willingness to use one's own device for work-related tasks [18]. However, empirical data on this phenomenon are scarce. In order to address the research questions and contribute to this research area, we provide empirical data on smartphone usage and BYOD adoption collected in a large-scale survey.

The remainder of this paper is structured as follows. Section 2 provides a comprehensive literature review in the field of IT consumerization and mobile IT management. Section 3 introduces the diffusion of innovation theory and argues that IT consumerization in an innovation in this sense. In Sect. 4 the methodology and propositions of our empirical study are presented. Section 5 presents and discusses the results. The final section draws conclusions and provides an outlook for further research.

2   Related Work

2.1   IT Consumerization

The diffusion of mobile devices, such as feature phones and Personal Digital Assistants (PDAs), started in the early 1990 s and increased quickly in the following decades [19]. The Apple iPhone, launched in 2007, popularized the concept of mobile applications (apps), leading to new potentials for smartphones. Additionally, the growing coverage of the mobile broadband infrastructure accelerated the dispersion of smartphones [20]. Research in the field of mobile devices today covers a multiplicity of research areas such as the security of mobile applications and devices and the design and development of mobile applications. Furthermore, some studies have specifically evaluated the use of mobile technologies for business purposes [21–24].

The accelerating diffusion of mobile devices, especially of smartphones, has massively influenced business as well as private life [12, 25, 26], offering several challenges and opportunities for organizations as well as for employees [8, 27]. Such professional use of technologies that are already applied in private contexts can also be observed with the introduction of social software in organizations [see e.g. 28–32].

Organizations need to manage their transformation into a so-called mobile enterprise [33, 34]. The term 'mobile enterprise' describes a corporation or large organization that supports business processes by using mobile applications via wireless mobile devices such as smartphones [35]. Harris et al. [8] define IT consumerization as 'the adoption of consumer applications, tools and devices on the workplace'. As organizations integrate enterprise mobility into their business strategy to benefit from increased flexibility and productivity advantages, they face the challenge of dealing with a large variety of employee-owned mobile devices [36–40].

Nevertheless, BYOD offers the potential to increase organizational performance [34]. Miller et al. [39] identified several positive aspects like reduced acquisition and training cost and a high speed of adoption. Despite the advantages of BYOD, the relaxation of IT restrictions that a BYOD policy engenders leads to several new operational challenges for IT management, such as the rollout of updates and the proper management of IT services according to the job responsibilities arising [41].

BYOD is a new phenomenon and there is still little scientific research available [42]. The bulk of the literature consists of studies executed by consulting firms and it mostly offers descriptions of the phenomenon as well as normative advice for executives [43]. Researchers have recognized, however, that IT consumerization is driven by employees [6, 37, 39]. To the knowledge of the authors, no research has been conducted to investigate the adoption of BYOD with a strong focus on smartphones from an organizational perspective.

2.2 Mobile IT Management

A major goal of organizations is to ensure maximal performance in terms of productivity and profitability, inventory, competitive advantages, and costs [44]. Organizational performance can be increased by using mobile IT effectively. A well-designed company-wide strategy needs to be established. The strategy should address both technical (e.g. choice of devices and functionality support) and organizational issues [34]. Three processes (cf. Fig. 1) need to be managed successfully for maximal organizational performance through mobile devices: the mobile IT conversion process, the mobile IT use process, and the competitive process.

Not every enterprise is able to convert its IT investments into IT assets effectively and efficiently. The mobile IT conversion process, for example, is influenced by the number of supported business activities, the level of integrated management and the level of technical and business knowledge. Traditionally, IT management has been responsible for all of a company's IT expenditures and for converting these investments into assets. Allowing IT consumerization by implementing a BYOD policy introduces privately owned mobile IT assets into the company [34]. Expenses incurred privately create enterprise assets. The benefits from a management point of view are evident. At

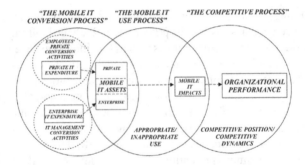

Fig. 1. Model for mobile IT organizational performance [28]

the same time, employees experience higher satisfaction and feel more productive because they are allowed to use a device with which they are familiar. They are more independent and have a higher degree of freedom in their choice of applications and functions. On the other hand, IT management is confronted with several challenges. They are confronted with a loss of control over the devices. Managing these devices is more complex and usually needs special mobile device management software and higher support. Still, IT assets accrued through employees' smartphones may result in positive IT impact (e.g. new services, redesigned business processes) when used appropriately for work activities. For an effective 'mobile IT use process' as regards IT consumerization, user skills as well as existing business processes need to be taken into account. Finally, an effective competitive process is needed for an enterprise to transform its IT impacts into greater organizational performance — i.e. to achieve competitive advantages relative to its competitors [45]. However, managing successful IT consumerization requires the input of employees. They are the main driver for IT consumerization and responsible for the benefits gained in the end. Hence, this research concentrates on the behavior of employees and their adoption of smartphones in enterprises.

3   Theoretical Background

3.1   Diffusion of Innovation Theory

Rogers [15] developed the DOI theory to explain a variety of innovations ranging from agricultural tools to organizational innovations [15, 46]. The theory is based on four key elements: innovation, communication channels, time and the social system. According to Rogers [15], innovations may be concepts, ideas, practices, technologies or objects — anything an individual, organization or other unit of adoption considers new. Communication channels describe the way in which information about the innovation is transmitted from one individual to another. Time, as an element of innovation diffusion, refers specifically to the period it takes for an innovation to pass through the innovation-decision process, from first knowledge of the innovation to the final decision to adopt or not. Finally, the social system in which the innovation is diffusing, and its structure are important elements to consider. The members of the social system can be classified according to their innovativeness into five categories: innovators, early adopters, the early and late majority, and laggards [15]. Empirical data suggests that the number of members adopting an innovation approximately resembles a normal, bell-shaped curve. Accordingly, the cumulative distribution — the fraction of people who have adopted the innovation over time — is an s-shaped curve.

Rogers [15, p. 287–292] reviews several decades of research on adopter categories to identify characteristics associated with innovativeness and, hence, early adoption of innovations. Innovativeness is highly correlated with socioeconomic characteristics such as a high level of education and a high social status (indicated by variables such as income and wealth). Personality variables related to innovativeness include a positive attitude towards change, an ability to cope with uncertainty, and a favorable attitude towards science. Finally, innovativeness is also related to communication behavior. Early adopters end to be highly connected, have a great deal of knowledge and are valued by their peers, taking the role of opinion leaders.

The diffusion of an innovation follows a five-step process [15, p. 169]. The process occurs over a certain time and uses different communication channels. The five stages of the process — knowledge, persuasion, decision, implementation and confirmation. During the knowledge stage, an individual is first confronted with an innovation, but lacks information. This is followed by the persuasion stage, in which the individual tries to gather more detailed information about the innovation. The decision stage describes a weighting of innovation advantages and disadvantages. At the end of this stage, the individual decides whether to adopt the innovation or not. The person later implements the innovation in the implementation stage, evaluates the innovation and seeks more information. The last stage is the confirmation stage, in which the decision and the usage are finalized.

Moore and Benbasat [47] applied the DOI theory in the Information Systems (IS) domain to study IT innovations in organizations. Since then it has been an important foundation of the adoption models used in IS research for more than two decades [48–50]. Prescott and Conger [51] reviewed ten years of DOI research by information technology researchers and classified studies according to their locus of impact. They found that DOI theory is applicable to explain the diffusion of technological innovations in an intra-organizational context.

In recent years, researchers have also begun to use the DOI theory to explain inter-organizational and societal topics, particularly in research on mobile IS [52]. Monchak and Kim [53] conducted a meta-analysis of diffusion of innovations in Information Systems for the years 2003 to 2011 based on publications in the top eight IS journals. The authors found that the application of DOI theory in Information Systems research is primarily divided into eight categories: perceived attributes of innovations, types of innovation decisions, communication channels, the nature of social science, the extent of change agents' promotion efforts, adopter categories, the stages of adoption and the stages of an innovation process in an organization [53]. However, DOI theory has always also been the object of some criticism. The theory is based on agricultural methods and medical practice. Rogers [15] categorizes the criticisms of diffusion research into four categories: its pro-innovation bias (the "implication that an innovation should be diffused" [15, p. 106]), its individual-blame bias (the "tendency to side with the change agencies … rather than with the individuals" [15, p. 118]), the recall problem (survey respondents being "asked to look back in time in order to reconstruct their past history of innovation experiences" [15, p. 127]), and the issue of equality (e.g. the widening of the socioeconomic gap [15, p. 130]).

3.2 IT Consumerization as an Innovation

In this article the DOI theory is used as a theoretical foundation to explain the progress of the BYOD mindset regarding smartphones in enterprises. How does IT consumerization match the definition of innovation according to Rogers [15]? Recall that Rogers defines an innovation as a concept, idea, practice, technology or objects perceived as new. BYOD, of course, is not a technology per se, because technology refers to the making, modification, usage and knowledge of tools, machines or techniques. It is instead a mindset regarding the use of technology in a social system. Similarly, IT consumerization describes an enterprise-wide tendency to use consumer IT devices. BYOD and IT consumerization can therefore be classified as 'practices' in the sense of Rogers' [15] definition.

The diffusion of these practices, however, is not altogether different from the diffusion of a technology. Analogous to the adoption of e.g. a new software system, the permission of and support for BYOD have extensively influenced IT management and enabled new values and challenges [54]. Its diffusion is based on extensive communication in social systems. The relationships and characteristics between different adopters and adopter categories therefore need to be examined to understand the progress of this innovation. In our study, DOI is used as a basis for gathering retrospective information about the diffusion progress of the BYOD mindset.

4   Empirical Study

4.1   Survey

As a first step in investigating employees' attitudes towards BYOD, we developed a questionnaire. The survey captures the current BYOD attitudes of employees in enterprises and shows whether different adopter types exhibit different attitudes towards BYOD. We decided to ask employees instead of IT managers or CIOs, as our goal is to examine end-user attitude and behavior.

We focused our survey on employees who actually use smartphones in their daily business life. The study is limited to smartphone users as we assumed that the phenomenon of IT consumerization is much more relevant for smartphones than for laptops or other devices (e.g. because smartphones are cheaper, are frequently used in private life and users are often emotionally attached to their smartphones, etc.). Furthermore, from the perspective of organizations, it is especially challenging to integrate consumer smartphones in business IT.

The online survey was carried out between October 29 and November 12, 2012, using the online survey tool LimeSurvey. It was directed at German employees. The questionnaire comprised 30 questions consisting of dichotomous items (yes/no), multiple-choice items and five-point Likert scale items. It was spread through social media: On LinkedIn, a call for participation was posted to two user groups related to the topic 'mobile' and 47 private messages were sent to personal contacts. On XING, a large German business SNS, a call for participation was posted to three user groups on the topic 'mobile' and 42 private messages were sent to personal contacts. Additionally, a call for participation was published in a large German online blog on mobile topics.

The questionnaire consisted of three sections, each focusing on a specific point of interest. The first section gathered demographic data. The second section was designed to investigate the participants' attitudes towards BYOD. The questions included whether participants receive work-related email on their personal smartphone, and to what extent they use their own phone for business purposes. Finally, the third section was designed to gather the data necessary to classify participants into adopter categories according to the DOI theory.

4.2 Identification of Adopter Categories

To investigate which adopter types were represented in the sample, the questionnaire included items that could be linked to the characteristics typical for the different adopter categories. These characteristics are based on Rogers' [15] review of innovation diffusion research. Rogers describes early adopters as venturesome individuals with cosmopolite social relationships and substantial financial resources who are willing to take risks. Laggards tend to be isolates in their social systems, limited in their resources, and suspicious of innovations. The other adopter categories occupy a position on the continuum between these two extremes. Table 1 presents the seven criteria we used to

Table 1. Adopter classification cheme

Characteristic	Question(s)	Adopter categories	
		Innovators	Laggards
Age	Age	Youngest	Oldest
Social status	Income	Highest income	Smallest income
	Expected financial support	No expectations	Expect all costs to be paid for
Knowledge of innovations	Number of used operating systems (OSs)	High number of used OSs	Used at most 1 OS
	Use of mobile social networking sites (SNSs)	Highest SNS activity	Lowest SNS activity
Opinion leadership	Frequency of contacts from persons for tech questions	Very frequent	Never been asked
Ability to cope with uncertainty, fatalism	Use of security mechanisms on smartphones (e.g. access control)	Insecure devices	Secured devices

assign participants to adopter categories. For example, the knowledge of (IT-related) innovations was measured by asking for the number of operating systems used and the amount of social networking site activity. Opinion leadership was measured using the frequency of contacts from peers containing questions about technology, e.g. how to configure a smartphone to access corporate email or how to access the enterprise network on one's personal smartphone. Age was also used to allocate participants to adopter categories. While Rogers [15] concluded that age is not directly related to innovativeness, this conclusion is based on empirical studies from a variety of domains such as agriculture. In technology adoption research, age has been shown to play a prominent role [55]. For example, older workers are less likely to be knowledgeable about technology and are more anxious about using it. This anxiety is naturally likely to extend to technology-related practices such as BYOD.

Together, these criteria represent each of the three types of characteristics associated with innovativeness according to Rogers [14]: socioeconomic characteristics, personality variables, and communication behavior. Participants who could not be unambiguously assigned to an adopter category because of their apparently conflicting characteristics were removed from the sample.

4.3 Propositions

In order to investigate the current state of adoption of the BYOD mindset, and the relationship between the adopter categories according to DOI theory and employees who have a favorable opinion of BYOD, we formulate three propositions. The analysis was conducted by first allocating the participants to the adopter categories. Then, for each adopter category, the propositions were examined.

P01: Innovators, early adopters and the early majority use their personal smartphones more often for work-related tasks than laggards and the late majority.

The proposition P01 posits a positive relationship between a tendency to adopt innovations early in the sense of DOI and the frequency of personal smartphone use for work-related tasks. If DOI can be used to explain BYOD adoption, the early adopter types (innovators, early adopters and early majority) will have a more positive attitude towards BYOD and will be more likely to use personal smartphones for work.

P02: Innovators and early adopters more often receive work-related email on their personal smartphones than other adopter types.

Individuals who choose to receive work-related email on their personal smartphone regularly are generally more likely to have a positive attitude towards BYOD. In summary, if DOI explains the adoption of BYOD, the survey results should support these propositions.

5 Results and Discussion

5.1 Results

We received a total of 219 completed questionnaires. 151 respondents (69%) own a smartphone and are employed. In order to answer the research question only those participants owning a smartphone are relevant. Therefore, all further evaluation is based on this group (n = 151). Table 2 summarizes the demographic data collected.

Table 2. Demographic data of participants (n = 151)

Age[a]	16–30 years: 42% 31–45 years: 46% 46–60 years: 12%	Income	0€–1.500€: 14% 1.501€–3.000€: 22% 3.001€–4.500€: 30% >4.500€: 34%
Gender	Male: 81% Female: 19%	Married	Yes: 38% No: 62%
Responsibility for employees	Yes: 36% No: 64%	Children	Yes: 33% No: 67%
Industry	Internet/IT: 40% Education/NGO: 8% Finance: 6% Media: 5% Automotive: 4% Other: 37%[b]	Division/Departments	Marketing: 13% IT/Org: 39% Management: 18% Purchasing/Sales: 8% Production: 4% Other: 18%[c]

[a] There were no participants under 16 or over 61 years.

[b] The category "Other" consists of industries accounting for less than 4% of responses

[c] The category "Other" consists of departments accounting for less than 4% of responses

The following section collected data on the use of smartphones. 64% of respondents have used their smartphones for at least two years (15% for one year, 12% for more than three years). This is not surprising, as it is common practice in Germany to provide customers with a new device when they sign a new mobile phone contract, which usually runs for two years. 55% of the participants have been equipped with a smartphone for professional use by their employer.

53% of participants retrieve their company email with a personal device, while 47% do not do so, preferring to keep business and private life separate. This split among the surveyed employees illustrates that BYOD is a practice in the process of being adopted. 47% of the participants who use their personal device to retrieve company email do so with the explicit permission of their employer, while only 2% do so in clear violation of the employer's policy. As a side note, all of the participants in this last group have an alternative smartphone provided by their employer. However, their desire to use their personal device seems to be particularly high. Moreover, 22% of those employees who do not receive emails on their personal device accept the company's ban on the retrieval of email and 15% do not see any added value in it. Interestingly, 81% of all respondents have already sent email with business content to their personal email accounts to be able to access it from anywhere.

Only 3% of the participants do not respond to professional communication in their leisure time at all. The boundary between job and private life is already seems to be heavily blurred, which is also a positive signal to BYOD. The presence of children or the participants' marital status does not appear to be related to their attitude on BYOD.

However, people who work away from the office on at least one day per week use their private smartphone to a higher percentage for business (14% vs. 19%).

The final part of the survey was used to classify participants into adopter categories. 16% of the employees who never use their private smartphone for business purposes state that they would expect 100% of the initial costs to be compensated for by the employer, were they to use it for work. In contrast, merely 7% of those already using their smartphones between 50% and 100% of the time for business purposes expect their employer to cover any of the costs at all. This observation suggests that expectations regarding the coverage of expenses are a major factor preventing more employees from adopting a favorable view of BYOD.

Most of the respondents apply access protection mechanisms on their smartphone (80%) and need to authenticate themselves in order to get access to enterprise data (57%). The participants are relatively experienced with different mobile operating systems. 78% have already used a different operating system apart from the current one. This goes hand in hand with the question whether a change of the operating system would be difficult, to which 31% replied yes.

5.2   Discussion of Propositions

The participants were divided into the adopter categories. Overall, 44% of the 151 respondents (67) could be clearly assigned to an adopter category by applying the classification scheme described in Sect. 4.1. The remaining 84 (56%) of the participants could not be unambiguously classified. Rogers [15, p. 281] provides reference values for the size of the adopter categories. Compared with these values, it can be stated that the innovators are slightly overrepresented in our sample (9% compared to the reference value of 2.5%). The group of early adopters nearly fits the expected size of 13.5%. In the sample, there is an imbalance between the early majority (42%) and the late majority (27%) in contrast to the reference values of 34% each. Laggards are underrepresented with 6% compared to the 16% reference value. In summary, the s-shaped curve in this sample is shifted left and has a steeper incline. Based on the sample and their attitude towards BYOD, the outcome of the analysis is shown in the representation of adopter categories.

P01: Innovators, early adopters and the early majority use their personal smartphones more often for work-related tasks than laggards and the late majority.

Table 3. Usage of personal smartphones for work

Adopter category	% of respondents in category
Innovators	83% more than 50% work-related usage time
Early adopters	90% more than 50% work-related usage time
Early majority	82% more than 50% work-related usage time
Late majority	48% more than 50% work-related usage time
Laggards	34% more than 50% work-related usage time

Table 3 summarizes the results regarding P03. In our data set, 83% of the innovators use their smartphone more than 50% of the time for business purposes. In contrast, only 48% of the late majority and only 34% of the laggards use their smartphones more than 50% of the time for business purposes. This underlines that the participants in these adopter groups seem to prefer BYOD.

Another fact could also be observed. There is a descending trend from innovators to laggards as regards employees who are equipped with smartphones by their employer. Whereas innovators and early adopters are not provided with devices, the late majority and laggards are offered devices. Furthermore, more than 48% of the late majority and 34% of the laggards use their personal smartphones more than 50% of the time for work-related tasks, even if they are equipped with a company smartphone. However, this leads to the assumption that just providing employees with mobile devices does not prevent BYOD. Enterprises are obliged to a greater extent to ensure successful BYOD management. They have to develop policies, choose the right devices and consider different employee types and their preferences.

P02: Innovators and early adopters more often receive work-related email on their personal smartphones than other adopter types.

Given the results of the survey (see Table 4), we can verify the proposition since all of the participants classified as innovators receive emails on personal phones and 81% of the early adopters do so as well. In comparison with the laggards, only 34% of the respondents receive work-related emails on their personal smartphones. With respect to our data, it can be argued that innovators and early adopters and at least the early majority use their personal devices regularly to receive work-related email. Moreover, these groups have usually sent work-related email to their personal email account in order to have the content available on their personal smartphone while they are on the move.

Table 4. Usage of personal smartphones to receive work-related email

Adopter category	% of respondents in category
Innovators	100% "yes, regularly"
Early adopters	81% "yes, regularly"
Early majority	67% "yes, regularly"
Late majority	48% "yes, regularly"
Laggards	34% "yes, regularly"

Summing up, the adopter categories *innovators*, *early adopters* and *early majority* have a positive attitude towards BYOD. While innovators and early adopters are usually the most instrumental to triggering critical mass, the results of the survey suggest that BYOD has already reached the early majority group. However, the attitude towards BYOD of the late majority and laggards is already more positive than expected.

6 Conclusion

In this article, we discussed the BYOD mindset regarding smartphones as a certain type of IT consumerization, and an innovation in the sense of Rogers' Diffusion of Innovation theory. The results of our survey indicate that in fact BYOD has been adopted by innovators, early adopters and the early majority. The results of the survey suggest that it is not sufficient for enterprises to develop a generic BYOD strategy for smartphones. The personnel structure is usually heterogeneous and the employees have different attitudes. Therefore, a differentiated BYOD strategy is necessary. Innovators will rarely change their behavior to comply with company policy and will instead always want to give new gadgets a chance, even at their workplace. As our results indicate, prohibiting BYOD may not be a suitable instrument, since 2% of participants still act in defiance of the employer's policies and retrieve their emails with a personal device. Managers should keep this in mind and attempt to accommodate the needs of these groups. The late majority and laggards need more structure. They are supposed to be equipped with devices, policies and training. Thus, these findings contribute knowledge that is of interest to practitioners. Moreover, the diffusion and attitude of employees towards BYOD have been examined, which is highly relevant from an academic perspective. We suggest that DOI theory could be used to explain the adoption of IT consumerization, particularly BYOD adoption in different domains.

We are aware that this study has some limitations. On the one hand, the participants recruited were, to a large extent, employees with an IT background from Germany. Consequently, it can be assumed that the participants are generally technology-savvy, and are thus perhaps more innovative and have a more positive attitude towards BYOD than the general population or employees in other fields.

For further research a survey with a more clearly defined target group, for example based on a single enterprise, may be appropriate. A comparison of different industries and cultural influences might also provide deeper insights for research. Additionally, we plan to start a series of interviews with employees in order to better understand their behavior regarding BYOD.

References

1. Aquino, C., Radwanick, S.: Mobile Future in Focus 2012 (2012). http://www.comscore.com/Insights/Presentations_and_Whitepapers/2012/2012_Mobile_Future_in_Focus
2. Mohr, N., Sauthoff-Bloch, A.K.: Mobile Web Watch 2011 (2012). http://www.accenture.com/SiteCollectionDocuments/Local_Germany/PDF/Accenture-Studie-Mobile-Web-Watch-2011.pdf
3. Sammer, T.: Why is there variation in the nature of organizational mobile IT adoption? an empirical study of the influence of organizational culture on organizational mobile IT adoption. In: 12th International Conference on Mobile Business, Berlin, pp. 1–12 (2013)
4. Larosiliere, G., Meske, C., Carter, L.: Determinants of social network adoption: a country-level analysis (nominated for the best paper award). In: Proceedings of the 48th Hawaii International Conference on System Sciences (HICSS), pp. 3424–3433 (2015). doi:10.1109/HICSS.2015.412

5. Dobe, B.: BYOD vor dem Absturz (2012). http://www.cio.de/bring-your-own-device/2896418/
6. Harris, M.A., Patten, K., Regan, E., Fjermestad, J.: Mobile and connected device security considerations: a dilemma for small and medium enterprise business mobility? In: Proceedings of the 18th Americas Conference on Information Systems, Seattle, pp. 1677–1683 (2012)
7. Hopkins, N., Sylvester, A., Tate, M.: Motivations for BYOD: an investigation of the contents of a 21st century school bag. In: Proceedings of the 21st European Conference on Information Systems, Utrecht (2013)
8. Harris, J.G., Ives, B., Junglas, I.: IT consumerization: when gadgets turn into enterprise IT tools. MIS Q. Executive 11, 99–112 (2012)
9. Köffer, S., Ortbach, K.C., Niehaves, B.: Exploring the relationship between IT consumerization and job performance: a theoretical framework for future research. Commun. Assoc. Inf. Syst. 35, 261–283 (2014)
10. Moore, G.: Systems of Engagement and The Future of Enterprise IT. AIIM, p. 14 (2011)
11. Stieglitz, S., Lattemann, C., Brockmann, T.: Mobile applications for knowledge workers and field workers. Mobile Inf. Syst. 2015, 1–8 (2015). doi:10.1155/2015/372315
12. Ahuja, M.K., Chudoba, K.M., Kacmar, C.J., Mcknight, D.H., George, J.F.: IT road warriors: balancing work-family conflict, job autonomy, and work overload to mitigate turnover intentions. MIS Q. 31, 1–17 (2007)
13. Rhee, K., Jeon, W., Won, D.: Security requirements of a mobile device management system. Int. J. Secur. Appl. 6, 353–358 (2012)
14. Gartner. Gartner's 2012 Hype Cycle for Emerging Technologies Identifies 'Tipping Point' Technologies That Will Unlock Long-Awaited Technology Scenarios 2012 (2012). https://www.gartner.com/newsroom/id/2124315
15. Rogers, E.M.: Diffusion of Innovations, 5th edn. The Free Press, New York (2003)
16. Cheikh-Ammar, M., Barki, H.: Technology desirability. In: Proceedings of the 33rd International Conference on Information Systems, Orlando (2012)
17. Ruegge, I.: Mobile Solutions - Einsatzpotenziale, Nutzungsprobleme und Lösungsansätze, Mobile Solutions - Einsatzpotenziale, Nutzungsprobleme und Lösungsansätze, Teubner Research (2007)
18. Amft, O., Lukowicz, P.: From backpacks to smartphones: past, present, and future of wearable computers. IEEE Pervasive Comput. 8, 8–13 (2009). doi:10.1109/MPRV.2009.44
19. Wiredu, G.O.: User appropriation of mobile technologies: Motives, conditions and design properties. Inf. Organ. 17, 110–129 (2007). doi:10.1016/j.infoandorg.2007.03.002
20. Ladd, D.A., Datta, A., Sarker, S., Yu, Y.: Trends in mobile computing within the IS discipline: a ten-year retrospective. Commun. Assoc. Inf. Syst. 27, 285–316 (2010)
21. Chandra, S.S., Srivastava, S.C., Theng, Y.L.: Evaluating the role of trust in consumer adoption of mobile payment systems: an empirical analysis. Commun. Assoc. Inf. Syst. 27, 561–588 (2010)
22. Markova, M., Aula, A., Vainio, T., Wigelius, H., Kulju, M.: MoBiS-Q: a tool for evaluating the success of mobile business services. In: Proceedings of the 9th International Conference on Human Computer Interaction with Mobile Devices and Services, Singapore, pp. 238–245 (2007). doi:10.1145/1377999.1378013
23. Penttinen, E., Rossi, M., Tuunainen, V.K.: Mobile games: Analyzing the needs and values of the consumers. J. Inf. Technol. Theory Appl. 11, 5–22 (2010)
24. Steele, R., Tao, W.: MobiPass: a passport for mobile business. Pers. Ubiquit. Comput. 11, 157–169 (2006). doi:10.1007/s00779-006-0100-9
25. Schadler, T., McCarthy, J.: Mobile is the New Face of Engagement-CIOs Must Plan Now for New Systems of Engagement. Forrester Research (2012)

26. Willis, D.A.: Bring Your Own Device: New Opportunities. New Challenges, Gartner (2012)
27. Golden, A.G., Geisler, C.: Work-life boundary management and the personal digital assistant. Hum. Relat. **60**, 519–551 (2007). doi:10.1177/0018726707076698
28. Stieglitz, S., Schallenmüller, S., Meske, C.: Adoption of social media for internal usage in a global enterprise. In: Proceedings of the IEEE 27th International Conference on Advanced Information Networking and Applications, pp. 1483–1488 (2013). doi:10.1099/WAINA. 2013.212
29. Stieglitz, S., Riemer, K., Meske, C.: Hierarchy or activity? the role of formal and informal influence in eliciting responses from enterprise social networks. In: Proceedings of the 22nd European Conference on Information Systems (2014)
30. Riemer, K., Stieglitz, S., Meske, C.: From top to bottom: investigating the changing role of hierarchy in enterprise social networks. Bus. Inf. Syst. Eng. **57**, 197–212 (2015). doi:10.1007/ s12599-015-0375-3
31. Stieglitz, S., Meske, C.: Maßnahmen für die Einführung und den Betrieb unternehmensinterner Social Media. HMD – Praxis der Wirtschaftsinformatik, pp. 36–43 (2012). doi:10.1007/BF03340735
32. Meske, C., Brockmann, T., Wilms, K., Stieglitz, S.: Social collaboration and gamification. In: Stieglitz, S., Lattemann, C., Robra-Bissantz, S., Zarnekow, R., Brockmann, T. (eds.) Gamification - Using Game Elements in Serious Contexts, pp. 93–109. Springer, Berlin (2016). doi:10.1007/978-3-319-45557-0_7
33. Dery, K., MacCormick, J.: Managing mobile technology: The shift from mobility to connectivity. MIS Q. Executive **11**, 159–173 (2012)
34. Stieglitz, S., Brockmann, T.: Increasing organizational performance by transforming into a mobile enterprise. MIS Q. Executive **11**, 189–204 (2012)
35. Basole, R.C.: The emergence of the mobile enterprise: a value-driven perspective. In: Proceedings of the 6th International Conference on the Management of Mobile Business, ICMB 2007, p. 41 (2007). doi:10.1109/ICMB.2007.63
36. Davis, G.B.: Anytime/anyplace computing and the future of knowledge work. Commun. ACM **45**, 67–73 (2002). doi:10.1145/585597.585617
37. Johnson, N.: The pathway to enterprise mobile readiness: analysis of perceptions, pressures, preparedness, and progression. In: Proceedings of the 18th Americas Conference on Information Systems, Seattle, pp. 2517–2524 (2012)
38. LaBarre, O.: Banks may not be able to resist 'bring your own device'. Bank Syst. + Technol. – Online **49**, 16–18 (2012)
39. Miller, K.W., Springfield, I., Voas, J., Fellow, I., Hurlburt, G.F., Index, C.: BYOD: security and privacy considerations. IT Prof. **14**, 53–55 (2012)
40. Perry, M., O'Hara, K., Sellen, A., Brown, B., Harper, R.: Dealing with mobility: understanding access anytime, anywhere. ACM Trans. Comput.-Hum. Interact. **8**, 323–347 (2001). doi:10.1145/504704.504707
41. Bergstein, B.: IBM Faces the Perils of "Bring Your Own Device" (2012). http:// www.technologyreview.com/business/40324/
42. Sawyer, S., Winter, S.J.: Special issue on futures for research on information systems: Prometheus unbound. J. Inf. Technol. **26**, 95–98 (2011). doi:10.1057/jit.2011.7
43. Niehaves, B., Köffer, S., Ortbach, K.: IT consumerization – a theory and practice review. In: Proceedings of the 18th Americas Conference on Information Systems, Seattle (2012)
44. Melville, N., Kraemer, K., Gurbaxani, V.: Review: information technology and organizational performance: an integrative model of IT business value. MIS Q. **28**, 283–322 (2004)
45. Sambamurthy, V., Zmud, R.: IT Management Competency Assessment: A Tool for Creating Business Value Through IT. Financial Executives Research Foundation, Morristown (1994)

46. Tornatzky, L., Klein, K.: Innovation characteristics and innovation adoption-implementation: A meta-analysis of findings. IEEE Trans. Eng. Manage. **29**, 28–43 (1982). doi:10.1109/TEM. 1982.6447463

47. Moore, G.C., Benbasat, I.: Development of an instrument to measure the perceptions of adopting an information technology innovation. Inst. Manage. Sci. **2**, 192–222 (1991). doi:10.1287/isre.2.3.192

48. Agarwal, R., Prasad, J.: The role of innovation characteristics and perceived voluntariness in the acceptance of information technologies. Decis. Sci. **28**, 557–582 (1997). doi:10.1111/j. 1540-5915.1997.tb01322.x

49. Plouffe, C.R., Hulland, J.S., Vandenbosch, M.: Research report: richness versus parsimony in modeling technology adoption decisions - understanding merchant adoption of a smart card-based payment system. Inf. Syst. Res. **12**, 208–222 (2001)

50. Venkatesh, V., Morris, M.G., Davis, G.B., Davis, F.D.: User acceptance of information technology: toward a unified view. MIS Q. **27**, 425–478 (2003)

51. Prescott, M.B., Conger, S.A.: Information technology innovations: a classification by IT locus of impact and research approach. Innovation **26**, 20–41 (1995). doi:10.1145/217278.217284

52. Kim, Y., Seoh, H., Lee, S., Lee, B.G.: Analysing user's intention and innovation diffusion of smartphones. In: Proceedings of the 5th International Conference on Ubiquitous Information Technologies and Applications, Sanya, pp. 1–6 (2010). doi:10.1109/ICUT.2010.5677850

53. Monchak, A., Kim, D.J.: Examining trends of technology diffusion theories in information systems. In: Proceedings of the 32nd International Conference on Information Systems, Shanghai, pp. 1318–1329 (2011)

54. Weiß, F., Leimeister, J.M.: Consumerization. IT-Innovationen aus dem Konsumentenumfeld als Herausforderung für die Unternehmens-IT. Wirtschaftsinformatik **54**, 351–354 (2012). doi:10.1007/s11576-012-0338-y

55. Morris, M.G., Venkatesh, V.: Age differences in technology adoption decisions: Implications for a changing work force. Pers. Psychol. **53**, 375–403 (2000)

A Review on Neuropsychophysiological Correlates of Flow

Fiona Fui-Hoon Nah$^{(\boxtimes)}$, Tejaswini Yelamanchili, and Keng Siau

Missouri University of Science and Technology, Rolla, MO, USA
{nahf, tyybf, siauk}@mst.edu

Abstract. Games are captivating from a human-computer interaction point of view. They can induce an intensely involving and engaging experience termed flow, which refers to the optimal state of experience when one is fully immersed in an activity. This paper provides a review of the neural and psychophysiological correlates of flow as well as some directions for future research.

Keywords: Neural correlates · Psychophysiological correlates · Brain imaging · Electroencephalogram · Functional magnetic resonance imaging · Flow

1 Introduction

Gaming has become a realizable form of entertainment for players of all ages and background [1]. Video games can evoke strong feelings due to their simulated environments, and such feelings are characterized by activations of the temporal, parietal, and dorsolateral areas [2–5]. Some studies have linked brain activities to video game play. An example of such studies is the use of a content-based event-related analysis for investigating the neural correlates of circumscribed gameplay events [6]. In this review paper, we identify the neural and psychophysiological correlates of the state of flow.

Flow is an optimal experience where people are so involved in an activity that they lose track of time and nothing else seems to matter. It is a subjective experience of effortless attention, reduced self-awareness, and enjoyment that typically occurs during optimal task performance [7]. Flow can occur when the challenge posed by a task matches the skill of the individual carrying out the task [7–9]. However, it is still not known what exactly happens in the brain when the flow state is achieved.

The human brain acts as a duty director for the human nervous system. It is composed of many interconnected neurons that form a complex system, from which thought, behavior, and creativity emerge. It receives information from the sensory organs and delivers output to the muscles. The cerebrum is largely responsible for the execution of cognitive functions. The frontal lobes of the cerebrum are responsible for executive control actions [10]. The frontal lobes are a large brain region representing 30% of the cortical surface. Brain activities can differ from one state to another; EEG is a technique/tool that can be used to record such activities using waveforms [11]. Research has shown that during the state of flow, the cortical activity is reduced [12].

© Springer International Publishing AG 2017
F.F.-H. Nah and C.-H. Tan (Eds.): HCIBGO 2017, PART II, LNCS 10294, pp. 364–372, 2017.
DOI: 10.1007/978-3-319-58484-3_28

2   Literature Review

Flow represents a psychological state where people are completely absorbed or engaged in an activity and are performing on the edge of their ability [13]. Flow has been conceptualized to comprise the following nine components [7]:

1. Balance of challenge and skill: A key aspect of the state of flow is that the skill of the individual and the challenge of the activity need to be in balance with each other. If the challenge is less than the skill, boredom occurs. If the challenge is substantially higher than the skill, anxiety can arise.
2. Clear goals: The goals/objectives of the task or activity must be clear and unambiguous.
3. Immediate feedback: The performance feedback on the task or activity should be clear, immediate, and unambiguous.
4. Paradox of control: The individual perceives control of his/her actions and the environment.
5. Loss of self-consciousness: Because of the pre-occupied activity, the individual "loses" oneself and experiences a sense of separation from the world around him/her.
6. Concentration on task at hand: The individual focuses or pays complete attention on the task or activity, such that all other distractions are blocked from his/her awareness.
7. Transformation of time: Time no longer seems to pass the way it normally does. The individual loses track of time and the perception of time is distorted.
8. Merging of action and awareness: The individual is so involved in the activity that his/her actions become spontaneous, just like automatic responses.
9. Autotelic nature: The activity that consumes the individual is intrinsically rewarding and motivating to him/her.

The relationship between skill and challenge lays the foundation for the psychological state or concept of flow [14]. An opportunity to perform an action is considered as challenge, and the capability to perform that action is known as skill. In the state of flow, attention is effortless [9]. When one is in flow, "one is given over to the activity so thoroughly that action and attention seem effortless" [15, p. 1].

3   Neuropsychophysiological Correlates of Flow

This review focuses on synthesizing the literature on neuropsychophysiological correlates of flow. The following databases have been utilized for identifying relevant published articles: ACM Digital Library, Scopus, PsycINFO, ABI/Inform, and IEEE. We have used various combinations of search keywords: 'neural', 'physiological', 'psychophysiological', 'correlates', 'flow', 'brain activity', 'cortex activity', 'gaming', 'electroencephalogram (EEG)', 'brain imaging'. The set of articles included in the review is comprised of a combination of conceptual and empirical papers. The findings are presented in Table 1.

Table 1. Summary of findings

Reference	Concept	Findings	Measurement	Paper type
Hamilton et al. [16]	Physiological aspects of flow experience	Flow as a personality trait in daily activities Subjects scored high on IES: the increased attention led to decreased effort measured using EEG, EP	Intrinsic Enjoyment Scale (IES); Electroencephalogram (EEG); Evoked Potentials (EP)	Empirical study
Gusnard et al. [17]	Neural correlates of flow	In the state of flow, the Dorsomedial Prefrontal Cortex (DPC) is expected to have very minimal or no activity DPC deals with self-related emotions and in the flow state, self-related emotions are eliminated	Functional Magnetic Resonance Imaging (fMRI)	Empirical study
Marr [18]	Synthetic theory; Biobehavioral theory of flow; Neurophysiological and cognitive explanations for flow phenomenon	Reduction in brain mechanism when participant experienced flow Dopamine (neurotransmitter) could be a neurophysiological correlate of flow		Conceptual study
Dietrich [19]	Neurophysiological theory of flow experience; Theory of hypofrontality	Flow results from down-regulation of prefrontal activity in the brain During flow state, the activities are performed without interference of conscious control system, making the process efficient and fast		Conceptual study
Sanchez-Vives and Slater [20]	Virtual reality	Modern video games evoke strong feelings The sensory motor network is activated during flow state Flow influences midbrain reward structures	Functional Magnetic Resonance Imaging (fMRI)	Empirical study
Goldberg et al. [12]	Global resource allocation network	Activity decreases in Medial Prefrontal Cortex (mPFC) during flow state mPFC contributes to self-referential mental activity Since flow is a highly focused state of task engagement leading to shut down of self-referential activities, it causes a decrease in mPFC	Functional Magnetic Resonance Imaging (fMRI)	Empirical study
Kivikangas [21]	Psychophysiology of flow experience	Flow is associated with increased positive valence and decreased negative valence Flow is negatively associated with corrugators supercilli (CS, frowning muscle) and found no effect on zygomaticus major (ZM, smiling muscle) and orbicularis oculi (OO, "eyelid muscles")	Electromyography (EMG) Electrodermal (EDA) Activity Flow State Scale (36 item questionnaire)	Empirical study

(continued)

Table 1. (*continued*)

Reference	Concept	Findings	Measurement	Paper type
		Increased electrodermal activity (high arousal indication) with an experimental flow condition		
Mandryk and Atkins [22]	Skin Conductance	EDA can be used to assess flow, which is associated with emotional arousal	Electrodermal Activity (EDA)	Empirical study
Nacke and Lindsey [23]	Psychophysiology of flow experience	Increased activity of zygomaticus major (ZM, smiling muscle) and orbicularis oculi (OO, "eyelid muscles") and an increase in electrodermal activity (EDA) to be associated with the experimentally induced flow condition	Electrodermal Activity (EDA) Electromyography (EMG)	Empirical study
De Manzano et al. [24]	Physiological aspects of flow	High flow values associated with activation of zygomaticus major (ZM, smiling muscle) and sympathetic activation. Flow is also associated with deep breathing. Found no relation between corrugators supercilli (CS, frowning muscle) and flow	Electromyography (EMG) Electrodermal Activity (EDA)	Empirical study
Keller et al. [25]	Flow	Flow experience is associated with elevated cortisol levels, reduced heart rate variability, a stressful state of increased workload. All of the above lead to questioning the current, exclusively positive, picture of the flow phenomenon	Electrocardiogram (ECG/EKG) Kubios HRV Analysis	Empirical study
Klasen et al. [26]	Flow experience	Correlation between game pleasure and motor activity to demanding game situation. Decrease in cortical activity during the flow state	Functional Magnetic Resonance Imaging (fMRI)	Empirical study
Bavelier et al. [27]	Neural circuitry: fronto-parietal network	The fronto-parietal network recruitment was low ($\sim$ no significant action in frontal areas). Parietal activation was restricted to a smaller region, inferior and superior parietal lobules	Functional Magnetic Resonance Imaging (fMRI)	Empirical study
Peifer [4]	Psychophysiological correlates of flow experience	Flow has an inverted u-shaped relation with hypothalamic-pituitary-adrenal (HPA) axis activation and sympathetic arousal	Questionnaire; Electrocardiography (ECG/EKG); Cortisol	Empirical study
Berta et al. [28]	Physiological signal analysis for flow. Subdivision of brain frequency bands.	EEG alpha – attenuates in a video game play. EEG low beta – discriminates among gaming conditions	Electroencephalogram (EEG)	Empirical study

(*continued*)

Table 1. (*continued*)

Reference	Concept	Findings	Measurement	Paper type
		Alpha, low-beta, and mid-beta bands show greatest differences between flow, boredom, and anxiety		
Leger et al. [29]	Neural activity	During flow, the activity in the cortical regions, particularly the frontal and parietal regions, is decreased. EEG alpha, EEG beta, electrodermal activity, heart rate, and heart rate variability can explain cognitive absorption, which is closely related to flow	Electroencephalogram (EEG); Electrodermal Activity (EDA); Electrocardiogram (ECG/EKG)	Empirical study
Li et al. [30]	Neural activity	Reduction in density of theta oscillations from the left side of the dorsolateral prefrontal cortex (DLPFC) represents an increase in game engagement	Electroencephalogram (EEG)	Empirical study

The nervous system is the core component of the brain, and neurons are the core components of the nervous system. Neurons operate on electrical impulses and chemical signals [12]. The human brain can be generally divided into three parts: (1) Forebrain (2) Midbrain (3) Hindbrain [10]. The cerebrum is responsible for most cognitive functions. The cerebrum, or cortex, is channeled into four lobes: frontal, parietal, occipital, and temporal. Each lobe has its specific predefined set of functions to perform. The functions of the lobes are: frontal – planning, motor/physical movement, emotion, problem solving; parietal – perception of stimuli, associated with movement and recognition; occipital – visual processing; temporal – memory, speech, perception and recognition of auditory stimuli. The largest portion of the brain is the cerebrum, which is widely channeled into two parts, the left and right hemispheres [10].

The frontal lobe functions are related to central executive processes [31]. Some research studies have shown that executive actions do not depend on frontal cortical activation but rely on the frontal-parietal network [32]. Prefrontal Cortex (PFC) in the front lobe of the brain is responsible for the execution of cognitive functions [32]. Most of the user-game engagement brain activities occur in Dorsolateral Prefrontal Cortex (DLPFC), which is the prefrontal cortex of the brain [26]. Previous research has shown that DLPFC is responsible for executive functions such as cognitive flexibility, planning, inhibition, and reasoning [32–34]. Medial prefrontal cortex (mPFC) plays a role in the integration of emotional and cognitive processes by incorporating emotional biasing signals or markers into the decision-making process [18]. EEG recordings are converted into spectral band frequencies (delta, theta, beta, alpha, and gamma) [35].

The alpha, low-beta, and mid-beta bands show greatest differences between three states of user experience, namely, flow, boredom, and anxiety. The frontal and parietal regions have low activity when one is in flow [28]. In addition, the alpha band is positively correlated with flow, whereas the beta band is negatively correlated with flow. The theta oscillations from the left side of the DLPFC can explain engagement [29].

EEG oscillations resemble the synchronized activities in the neuronal population in the brain [36]. These oscillations represent a subset of the brain's electrical activities at a point in time. We can record these activities on the surface of the scalp with the help of electrodes (EEG headset). Many neurons will need to be synchronously active to detect oscillations of an activity at the scalp level [35]. Researchers have estimated that tens of thousands of synchronously activated pyramidal cortical neurons are involved for an EEG oscillation to emerge [37, 38]. In EEG research, the oscillations are classified into low-frequency oscillations and high-frequency oscillations. Delta and theta waves are considered low frequency, whereas beta, alpha, and gamma waves are considered high frequency.

Delta waves (1–4 Hz) are primarily associated with deep sleep (sometimes coma) but can also be present in the waking state. The power of the theta oscillations increases when information is retrieved from working memory [39, 40] because theta is related to memory performance [33, 41]. Theta waves (4–8 Hz) are associated with creative inspiration and deep meditation, and they arise when consciousness slips. An increase in game engagement implies a reduction in the density of theta oscillations [42].

Alpha (8–12 Hz) usually appears over the occipital region (posterior regions). Alpha represents relaxed awareness. Alpha waves are produced with the eyes closed and they signal a scanning or waiting pattern [43]. Alpha waves are reduced or eliminated by opening the eyes, by hearing unfamiliar sounds, or by anxiety [44]. Alpha oscillations are also considered indicators of the notion of happiness. Alpha oscillations increase with focus or concentration [45]. The upper alpha oscillations are associated mainly with long-term memory processes [12]. For the upper alpha band, the connectivity decreases in a condition with higher executive demands [46].

Beta (12–30 Hz) primarily deals with active thinking, active attention, focus on the outside world, and solving concrete problems. A very high beta represents a person's panic state, and is found in frontal and central regions. Gamma (30–32 Hz) represent arousal. The rate of gamma wave occurrence is very low [35].

In summary, brain activity in the cortical regions, especially in frontal and parietal lobes, decreases during the state of flow. The alpha band is positively correlated with flow, the beta band tends to be negatively correlated with flow, and the theta oscillations from the left side of the DLPFC correlate with flow.

4 Conclusion and Future Research

In our ongoing and future research, we are interested to assess the neuropsychophysiological correlates of different states of user experience including flow, boredom, and anxiety, as well as the degree to which user states can be explained by or assessed using their neuropsychophysiological correlates. We plan to use time frequency decomposition and machine learning techniques to address the above questions. One of the main goals of our research is to improve the assessment and evaluation of user experience in human-computer interaction research. We are also interested to utilize both the questionnaire approach and the neuropsychophysiological correlates of flow to test and assess a theoretical framework for flow in gaming developed by Nah and her colleagues [47]. Another implication of this research is to contribute to improving brain-computer interfaces of smart devices by having computers respond to users based on the users' states of experience.

References

1. Hartmann, T., Klimmt, C.: Gender and computer games: exploring females' dislikes. J. Comput. Mediated Commun. 11(4), 910–931 (2006)
2. Baumgartner, T., Speck, D., Wettstein, D., Masnari, O., Beeli, G., Jäncke, L.: Feeling present in arousing virtual reality worlds: prefrontal brain regions differentially orchestrate presence experience in adults and children. Front. Hum. Neurosci. 2(8), 1–12 (2008)
3. Fairclough, S.H.: Psychophysiological inference and physiological computer games. In: Brain-Computer Interfaces and Games Workshop at Advances in Computer Entertainment, p. 19 (2007)
4. Peifer, C.: Psychophysiological correlates of flow-experience. In: Engeser, S. (ed.) Advances in Flow Research, pp. 139–164. Springer, New York (2012)
5. Rani, P., Sarkar, N., Liu, C.: Maintaining optimal challenge in computer games through real-time physiological feedback. In: Proceedings of the 11th International Conference on Human Computer Interaction, vol. 58, pp. 22–27, July 2005
6. Weber, R., Ritterfeld, U., Mathiak, K.: Does playing violent video games induce aggression? Empirical evidence of a functional magnetic resonance imaging study. Media Psychol. 8(1), 39–60 (2006)
7. Csikszentmihalyi, M.: Flow: The Psychology of Optimal Experience. Harper & Row, New York (1990)
8. Anshel, M.H.: Sport Psychology: From Theory to Practice. Pearson, San Francisco (2011)
9. Csikszentmihalyi, M.: Finding Flow: The Psychology of Engagement with Everyday Life. Basic Books, New York (1997)
10. Miller, B.L., Cummings, J.L.: The Human Frontal Lobes: Functions and Disorders. Guilford Press, New York (2007)
11. Libenson, M.H.: Practical approach to electroencephalography. Elsevier Health Sciences, Philadelphia (2012)
12. Goldberg, I.I., Harel, M., Malach, R.: When the brain loses its self: prefrontal inactivation during sensorimotor processing. Neuron 50(2), 329–339 (2006)
13. Csikszentmihalyi, M., Csikszentmihalyi, I.S.: Optimal Experience: Psychological Studies of Flow in Consciousness. Cambridge University Press, Cambridge (1992)
14. Nah, F., Eschenbrenner, B., DeWester, D., Park, S.: Impact of flow and brand equity in 3D virtual worlds. J. Database Manag. 21(3), 69–89 (2010)
15. Kahneman, D.: Attention and Effort. Prentice-Hall, Englewood Cliffs (1973)
16. Hamilton, J.A., Haier, R.J., Buchsbaum, M.S.: Intrinsic enjoyment and boredom coping scales: validation with personality, evoked potential and attention measures. Pers. Individ. Differ. 5(2), 183–193 (1984)
17. Gusnard, D.A., Akbudak, E., Shulman, G.L., Raichle, M.E.: Medial prefrontal cortex and self-referential mental activity: relation to a default mode of brain function. Proc. Nat. Acad. Sci. 98(7), 4259–4264 (2001)
18. Marr, A.J.: In the zone: a biobehavioral theory of the flow experience. Athletic Insight Online J. Sport Psychol. 3(1) (2001). http://www.athleticinsight.com/Vol3Iss1/Commentary.htm

19. Dietrich, A.: Neurocognitive mechanisms underlying the experience of flow. Conscious. Cogn. **13**(4), 746–761 (2004)
20. Sanchez-Vives, M.V., Slater, M.: From presence to consciousness through virtual reality. Nat. Rev. Neurosci. **6**(4), 332–339 (2005)
21. Kivikangas, J.M.: Psychophysiology of flow experience: an explorative study, Master's thesis, University of Helsinki (2006)
22. Mandryk, R.L., Atkins, M.S.: A fuzzy physiological approach for continuously modeling emotion during interaction with play technologies. Int. J. Hum Comput Stud. **65**(4), 329–347 (2007)
23. Nacke, L., Lindley, C.A.: Affective ludology, flow and immersion in a first-person shooter: measurement of player experience. J. Can. Game Stud. Assoc. **3**(5), 1–22 (2009)
24. De Manzano, Ö., Theorell, T., Harmat, L., Ullén, F.: The psychophysiology of flow during piano playing. Emotion **10**(3), 301–311 (2010)
25. Keller, J., Bless, H., Blomann, F., Kleinböhl, D.: Physiological aspects of flow experiences: skills-demand-compatibility effects on heart rate variability and salivary cortisol. J. Exp. Soc. Psychol. **47**(4), 849–852 (2011)
26. Klasen, M., Weber, R., Kircher, T.T., Mathiak, K.A., Mathiak, K.: Neural contributions to flow experience during video game playing. Soc. Cogn. Affect. Neurosci. **7**(4), 485–495 (2012)
27. Bavelier, D., Achtman, R.L., Mani, M., Focker, J.: Neural bases of selective attention in action video game players. Vis. Res. **61**, 132–143 (2012)
28. Berta, R., Bellotti, F., De Gloria, A., Pranantha, D., Schatten, C.: Electroencephalogram and physiological signal analysis for assessing flow in games. IEEE Trans. Comput. Intell. AI Games **5**(2), 164–175 (2013)
29. Léger, P.M., Davis, F.D., Cronan, T.P., Perret, J.: Neurophysiological correlates of cognitive absorption in an enactive training context. Comput. Hum. Behav. **34**, 273–283 (2014)
30. Li, M., Jiang, Q., Tan, C.H., Wei, K.K.: Enhancing user-game engagement through software gaming elements. J. Manag. Inf. Syst. **30**(4), 115–150 (2014)
31. Sanei, S., Chambers, J.A.: EEG Signal Processing. John Wiley & Sons, Chichester (2013)
32. Collette, F., Vander, L.M.: Brain imaging of the central executive component of working memory. Neurosci. Biobehav. Rev. **26**(2), 105–125 (2002)
33. Babiloni, C., Babiloni, F., Carducci, F., Cappa, S.F., Cincotti, F., Del Percio, C., Miniussi, C., Vito Moretti, D., Rossi, S., Sosta, K., Rossini, P.M.: Human cortical rhythms during visual delayed choice reaction time tasks: a high-resolution EEG study on normal aging. Behav. Brain Res. **153**(1), 261–271 (2004)
34. Brann, D.W., Dhandapani, K., Wakade, C., Mahesh, V.B., Khan, M.M.: Neurotrophic and neuroprotective actions of estrogen: basic mechanisms and clinical implications. Steroids **72** (5), 381–405 (2007)
35. Müller-Putz, G.R., Riedl, R., Wriessnegger, S.C.: Electroencephalography (EEG) as a research tool in the information systems discipline: foundations, measurement, and applications. Commun. Assoc. Inf. Syst. **37**(1), 1–46 (2015)
36. Okada, Y.: Empirical bases for constraints in current-imaging algorithms. Brain Topogr. **5** (4), 373–377 (1993)
37. Baillet, S., Mosher, J.C., Leahy, R.M.: Electromagnetic brain mapping. IEEE Signal Process. Mag. **18**(6), 14–30 (2001)
38. Pizzagalli, D.A.: Electroencephalography and high-density electrophysiological source localization. Handb. Psychophysiol. **3**, 56–84 (2007)

39. Speckmann, E.J., Elger, C.E., Gorji, A.: Neurophysiological basis of EEG and DC potentials. In: Schomer, D.L., da Silva, F.L. (eds.) Niedermeyer's Electroencephalography: Basic Principles, Clinical Applications, and Related Fields, pp. 17–32. Lippincott Williams & Wilkins, Philadelphia (2011)

40. Jensen, O., Tesche, C.D.: Frontal theta activity in humans increases with memory load in a working memory task. Eur. J. Neurosci. **15**(8), 1395–1399 (2002)

41. Klimesch, W., Schimke, H., Schwaiger, J.: Episodic and semantic memory: an analysis in the EEG theta and alpha band. Electroencephalogr. Clin. Neurophysiology **91**(6), 428–441 (1994)

42. Klimesch, W., Doppelmayr, M., Russegger, H., Pachinger, T.: Theta band power in the human scalp EEG and the encoding of new information. NeuroReport **7**(7), 1235–1240 (1996)

43. Horne, J.A.: Why We Sleep: The Functions of Sleep in Humans and Other Animals. Oxford University Press, Oxford (1988)

44. Da Silva, F.L.: Neural mechanisms underlying brain waves: from neural membranes to networks. Electroencephalogr. Clin. Neurophysiol. **79**(2), 81–93 (1991)

45. Pfurtscheller, G., Stancak, A., Neuper, C.: Event-related synchronization (ERS) in the alpha band—an electrophysiological correlate of cortical idling: a review. Int. J. Psychophysiol. **24** (1), 39–46 (1996)

46. Sauseng, P., Klimesch, W., Schabus, M., Doppelmayr, M.: Fronto-parietal EEG coherence in theta and upper alpha reflect central executive functions of working memory. Int. J. Psychophysiol. **57**(2), 97–103 (2005)

47. Nah, F., Eschenbrenner, B., Zeng, Q., Telaprolu, V., Sepehr, S.: Flow in gaming: literature synthesis and framework development. Int. J. Inf. Syst. Manag. **1**(1/2), 83–124 (2014)

Information Visualizations Used to Avoid the Problem of Overfitting in Supervised Machine Learning

Robbie T. Nakatsu[✉]

Loyola Marymount University, Los Angeles, CA, USA
rnakatsu@lmu.edu

Abstract. This paper will look at what types of information graphics and visualizations can support supervised Machine Learning tasks: in essence, how to support the problem of model validation and model overfitting. In particular, I look, graphically, at model performance as a function of model complexity. With an appropriate information graphic, we can visualize at what point the model becomes too complex and starts to deteriorate in performance because of model overfitting. I will look at two actual case studies—the first, a regression task using polynomial regression and the second, a classification problem using neural networks. I create information graphics, in particular fitting graphs, to support the end-user in visualizing which model is the best choice.

Keywords: Information visualizations · Machine learning · Data science · Data analytics · Overfitting · Regression tasks · Classification tasks · Data-driven decision making · Regression · Neural networks · Cross validation · Fitting graphs

1 Introduction

Data Science is defined as "a set of fundamental principles that guide the extraction of knowledge from data" [1, p. 2]. In recent years, the discipline has gained prominence as vast amounts of data in almost every industry have become available. Increasingly, businesses and organizations today view data as a strategic asset that can be mined to help them make better decisions. In marketing, for instance, data-mining techniques may be used to better understand target markets, cross-sell to current customers, or otherwise provide better and more-tailored customer service. In general, many organizations today are looking for ways to enable data-driven decision-making in which decisions are based on the analysis of data, rather than intuition alone.

One important area in data science that has garnered attention is **Machine Learning**, a subfield of AI (Artificial Intelligence) that gives computers the ability to learn without being explicitly programmed [2]. Machine Learning involves building predictive models based on the experience of seeing many data examples. In this paper I will look at two types of Machine Learning that involve the prediction of future outcomes: (1) **Regression** problems predict a *continuous-valued* outcome from a large set of data (e.g., predicting future sales of a customer based on historical purchases, and

© Springer International Publishing AG 2017
F.F.-H. Nah and C.-H. Tan (Eds.): HCIBGO 2017, PART II, LNCS 10294, pp. 373–385, 2017.
DOI: 10.1007/978-3-319-58484-3_29

customer characteristics). (2) **Classification** problems predict a *discrete-valued* outcome, or class, from a large historical dataset (e.g., predicting whether an email is spam or not based on seeing an historical dataset of past emails). Both types of tasks are known as **supervised** learning tasks, because they involve training methods in which the targeted outcome is known in advance—hence, the training algorithms are "supervised" or fed the right answer [3].

The difficulty of Machine Learning algorithms is that they are sometimes difficult to understand and use. First, there are a wide variety of techniques such as linear regression, logistic regression, discriminant analysis, decision trees, neural networks, and support vector machines—just to name some of the more popular techniques in use today. Although there exist many "canned" routines in R, and other statistical packages, that are easy to run and use (see e.g., [4]), many users have a difficult time understanding how the algorithms work, let alone whether they are even appropriate for a given task at hand. Many of the algorithms, such as neural networks and support vector machines, are especially problematic because they are black boxes that don't provide an easy-to-understand model on how they work—hence, it is difficult to see how accurate their predictions are.

Second, a central problem in Data Science and Machine Learning is the problem of model overfitting. This refers to "finding chance occurrences in data that look like interesting patterns, but which do not generalize to unseen data" [1, p. 111]. By training a dataset using a Machine Learning algorithm, the data scientist may develop a model that fits well to a current set of data, but does not fit well to future, unseen cases. The solution to this problem is to validate your model on a test dataset, also known as the holdout dataset, because it has been set aside and not used to train the Machine Learning algorithm. I explain the procedure in more detail in Sect. 3.1 of the paper.

In this paper, I illustrate how the model validation task can be supported with information visualizations. The Fitting Graph, notably, is an important information graphic that can be used to visualize model underfit and overfit. I demonstrate the procedure with two tasks: a regression task that predicts the value of a home in the Boston area (Sect. 5), and a classification task that predicts whether a breast tumor is benign or malignant (Sect. 6).

2   A Taxonomy of Supervised Machine Learning Algorithms

Machine Learning algorithms fall into two main categories: (1) supervised and (2) non-supervised. Supervised learning algorithms are the more powerful of the two types because they enable you to predict a target, or outcome variable, from other variables called predictors or features. Hence, I focus this paper on these types of tasks and how well they can predict future cases. Non-supervised learning algorithms can be useful too but not for prediction. One example is clustering (sometimes referred to as segmentation analysis), which attempts to cluster a dataset into homogeneous groups. For example, a marketer may want to identify customers with similar purchasing, or demographic characteristics, so that advertising campaigns can more effectively target these groups.

Within the supervised category, we may distinguish between two types of tasks: (1) regression and (2) classification. While regression attempts to estimate or predict the numeric value of some variable, classification attempts to predict which of a set of classes an individual case belongs to. In both cases predictive accuracy is the benchmark on how well the Machine Learning algorithm is performing. Inference tasks, by contrast, focus on understanding how Y changes as a function of the feature variables (X's). The goal of such tasks is not predictive accuracy, but how well we understand the relationships between the variables—hence, they are sometimes referred to as descriptive rather than predictive. In such cases, model interpretability and simplicity may be a more important criteria for model selection. I do not address inference tasks in this paper.

A central challenge in Machine Learning is choosing the algorithm, or method, for a given application. The choice is not so simple to make. Table 1 shows that there are many different algorithms and techniques at a data scientist's disposal in making the choice. The first point to note is that most of the algorithms work either for regression tasks or classification tasks, but not both—the exceptions in the table are neural networks and support vector machines, which can be used for both task types. Each of the algorithms has relative advantages and disadvantages, but it may be difficult for the data scientist to determine which is the best approach, especially at the outset, when little is known about the nature of the dataset. Furthermore, the field continues to evolve with new and improved learning algorithms, making it difficult to keep track of all the approaches, much less understand which is the best approach.

Table 1. Machine learning algorithms for supervised tasks (regression and classification)

Regression tasks	Classification tasks
Linear regression	Logistic regression
• Ridge regression	Nearest neighbor
• The Lasso	Linear discriminant analysis
Regression splines	Quadratic discriminant analysis
Regression trees	Naïve Bayes
Model trees	Decision trees
Neural networks[a]	Neural networks[a]
Support vector machines[a]	Support vector machines[a]

[a] Denotes Dual Use Algorithms.

Fortunately, for the data scientist, two computing trends have helped with the selection process. The first trend is the dramatic increases in computational power over the last decades, which has made running computationally intensive Machine Learning algorithms more possible. Many more people and organizations have become eager to use Machine Learning techniques, because now they can easily be run on inexpensive computers. Early on, in the 1970s, most of the Machine Learning techniques were linear methods, because fitting non-linear relationships was thought to be computationally infeasible. Today, with the rapid increases in computational power, fitting non-linear models, such as with neural networks, support vector machines, and polynomial regression, has become much more routine and commonplace [4]. As a result, the data scientist has many more choices in his/her toolkit. Furthermore, cross-validation techniques are no longer computationally prohibitive—in the past, it was infeasible for problems with large n (number of rows in the dataset) and/or large p (number of predictors). The second trend is the development of easy-to-use, canned routines that even the non-technical person, who may lack a sophisticated mathematical or AI background, can master and use. Significantly, R is emerging as the language of choice for the data science community, with new routines and approaches becoming widely available for free. An active community of Machine Learning specialists and R programmers continue to contribute new and improved R routines on Machine Learning and information visualization (see e.g., [5]).

3   The Central Problem of Overfitting

If we develop more and more complex models, we are likely to find patterns in our data. Unfortunately, these patterns may simply be chance occurrences in the data that will not generalize well to unseen cases. The data scientist's end goal, however, should be to develop models that will predict well for cases that have not yet been observed. Finding patterns in your training dataset that do not generalize to unseen cases is broadly known as **overfitting.**

The problem of overfitting is graphically illustrated in Fig. 1 above. I randomly generated a set of x values from a normal distribution with mean 5 and SD = 10. I then calculated y (by applying the quadratic function (y = x2–5x + error), with the error term also randomly generated from a normal distribution with mean 0, SD = 5. Hence, the correct fit for this set of data is quadratic and known in advance. The resulting x–y plot is shown in Fig. 1.

I fitted the data with four different functions using regression:

$$y = \beta_0 + \beta_1 x \, (\text{linear model}) \tag{1}$$

$$y = \beta_0 + \beta_1 x + \beta_2 x^2 \, (\text{quadratic model}) \tag{2}$$

$$y = \beta_0 + \beta_1 x + \beta_2 x^2 + \beta_3 x^3 \ldots + \beta_{10} x^{10} \, (\text{polynomial of degree 10}) \tag{3}$$

$$y = \beta_0 + \beta_1 x + \beta_2 x^2 + \beta_3 x^3 \ldots + \beta_{15} x^{15} \, (\text{polynomial of degree 15}) \tag{4}$$

As can be seen in Fig. 1, Model (1), the linear model, underfits the data because it does not model the curvature in the data. The linear model is too simple and results in a poor fit ($R^2 = 0.269$). Model (2) is the correct fit when a quadratic term is added to the regression model, resulting in a smooth curve. The model fit increases dramatically as a result ($R^2 = 0.938$). Models (3) and (4) overfit the data. Both models chase after the noise in the data, as can be seen in Fig. 1, and result in more erratic curves. When a polynomial of degree 15 is fit to the data, the curve becomes extremely erratic. The R^2 increases slightly to 0.945 and 0.954, respectively for Models (3) and (4), but these

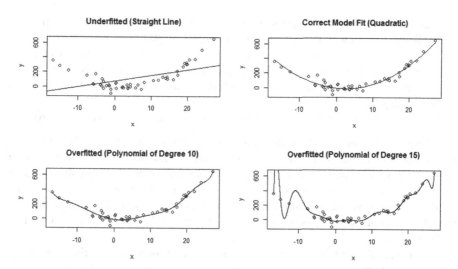

Fig. 1. Four regression models fitted on the same set of data. On the upper left, a simple linear regression underfits the data ($R^2 = 0.269$). On the upper right, the correct quadratic model is fitted ($R^2 = 0.938$). The bottom row shows two overfitted models: on the bottom left, a polynomial of degree 10 is fitted ($R^2 = 0.945$) and on the bottom left a polynomial of degree 15 is fitted ($R^2 = 0.954$).

increases are erroneous and misleading, because they are modeling a better fit in the training data only.

It is easy enough to generate information graphics (in two dimensions) on how a given predictor X influences Y. The non-linearity in the data is apparent in Fig. 1. Furthermore, the overfitting models seem to chase after random noise, also apparent in the bottom two graphs in Fig. 1. However, the determination of model underfitting and overfitting for more complex models involving multiple variables cannot be easily visualized.

3.1 Model Validation: Holdout Evaluation and K-Fold Cross-Validation

This simple example illustrates a central problem in Machine Learning: it is easy to generate more complex models that fit the training data well, but at some point, too much complexity will result in poor performance on data not yet seen. To avoid the problem of overfitting, the model must be validated on a test dataset (or holdout data) that has not been used to train the Machine Learning algorithm.

The procedure for holdout evaluation is simple:

1. Divide your dataset into two samples: a training dataset and a test dataset (an 80/20 split is commonplace in which 80% of the data is the train the model and the remaining 20% is used to validate it).
2. Build separate models on different complexity levels using your training dataset.

3. Validate each model using the test dataset. Test each model, created in step 2, for predictive accuracy on the test dataset. For regression problems, predictive accuracy is defined as the lowest mean error–either mean squared error (MSE) or mean absolute error (MAE). For classification problems, predictive accuracy refers to how well your classifier chooses the right class—or lowest % of misclassified cases (error rate).
4. Choose the model with the highest predictive accuracy—i.e., lowest test error.

There are a few problems with the holdout evaluation method described above. First, even though the test dataset will give us an estimate of predictive accuracy, it is just a single estimate. The single estimate (especially when the sample size is small) may have been a particularly lucky, or unlucky, split between training and test datasets [1]. Second, because we are splitting the data sample into two sets, we are building the model on a smaller set of cases, so we may not generate the best model without use of all of the data.

To address the first issue, a procedure known as **k-fold cross-validation** makes better use of a limited dataset. K-fold cross validation begins by randomly splitting a dataset into k partitions called folds (a typical choice for k is five or ten). K-fold cross validation then iterates k times. In each iteration, a different fold is chosen as the test dataset, while the other k−1 folds are combined to form the training dataset. After iterating k times in this way, an average of the k test errors is calculated so that a more accurate estimate of test error is obtained [1, 3, 4]. Addressing the second issue, once the best model is selected—the one having the lowest average test error—the model can then be re-trained on the entire dataset.

4 Information Visualizations of Overfitting: The Fitting Graph

By visualization, we mean a process by which numerical data and information are converted into meaningful images. A formal definition is given by Spence [6]: "the process of forming a mental model of data, thereby gaining insight into the data."

A fitting graph is an information visualization that illustrates model underfit and overfit. Figure 2 is an example of a typical fitting graph. This figure contains two curves: the top curve represents the test error, and the bottom curve represents the training error. Both curves show how error changes as a function of model complexity. By model complexity, we are referring to the complexity of the predictive model, as specified by the Machine Learning algorithm. The definition of model complexity differs depending on the Machine Learning algorithm used. Here are some examples of how a model can be made more complex in three different Machine Learning contexts:

Regression: adding more X terms, or features, to the model; adding higher-order polynomial terms; adding interaction terms.
Neural Networks: adding more features, or inputs; adding more layers; adding more nodes.
Decision Trees: adding more features, or inputs; having more branches on your decision tree.

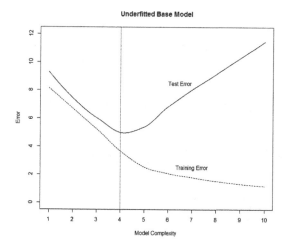

Fig. 2. A fitting graph. The base model (model complexity = 1) is underfitted

Most Machine Learning algorithms are prone to overfitting, so it is important to look at the fitting graph to determine whether the model is overfitted or not. Figure 2 illustrates three key characteristics that apply to all types of fitting graphs. (I use these three characteristics as a check on whether my Machine Learning algorithm is performing as it should, and whether it has been correctly set up):

- The training error curve is always lower than the test error curve for all levels of model complexity.
- The training error curve will decrease as you increase model complexity.
- The test error curve displays a typical "u-shape" in which it decreases first for lower levels of model complexity, and, then, at some point, increases for higher levels of model complexity.

(Note that for the second and third bullet points, the decreases and increases may not occur monotonically due to random fluctuations in your data, as well as way that you are defining "model complexity". In particular, model complexity may not be defined uniformly).

In Fig. 2, the point on the test error curve that represents the minimum test error represents the best model. The vertical line on Fig. 2 indicates where the minimum occurs (model complexity = 4). All models to the left side of the vertical line represent underfitted models, while all models to the right side represent overfitted models.

Figure 3 is an example of another fitting graph. The difference with this graph is that the base model (model complexity = 1) is the correct fit. As evidenced by Fig. 3 the test error starts out at a minimum, and then increases (or remains the same) for higher levels of model complexity. An example is when a simple linear regression, without higher order terms, is the correct fitting model: the data is best fit by a straight line; hence, higher order terms will not decrease the test error.

Finally, Fig. 4 illustrates how a test error curve can plateau, or flatten out, on a portion of the curve. When this happens, the model at the left end of plateau,

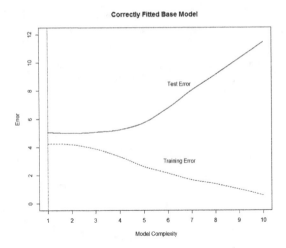

Fig. 3. A fitting graph. The base model (model complexity = 1) is correctly fitted

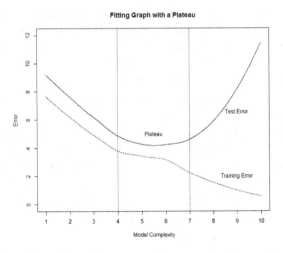

Fig. 4. Fitting graph with a plateau. Between model complexity 4 and 7, the test error doesn't change that much.

representing lower model complexity, may be selected, even if it is not the minimum test error. In Fig. 4, for example, model complexity = 4, may be the selected model, even though complexity levels 5 and 6 result in a lower test error. Simpler, less complex models that are easier to understand may be desired, when more complex models result in only marginal improvements in predictive accuracy. Hence, we may use the fitting graph to assess the tradeoff between test error and model simplicity—plateaus on a test error curve allow us to visualize this.

5   Case I: Regression Task Using Polynomial Regression

For this first example, I used the Boston housing dataset, which is part of the MASS library in R. The dataset contains data on 506 neighborhoods around Boston, Massachusetts. Using polynomial regression, I sought to predict medv (median house values in 000's) from the following five predictors:

1. lstat: percent of households with low socioeconomic status)
2. age: average age of houses
3. rm: (average number of rooms per house)
4. ptratio: pupil/teacher ratio
5. dis: mean distance to five Boston employment centers

The actual datasets contains 13 predictors, but only these five were selected for the analysis. For more information on the Boston dataset, see [7, 8].

To create regression models of varying degrees of complexity, I ran the regression ten times, ranging from a linear fit (polynomial of degree 1) all the way up to a 10th order polynomial fit. For example, the cubic fit (polynomial of degree 3) would include the following predictors in the regression model:

$$y = \beta_0 + \beta_{11}\text{lstat} + \beta_{21}\text{age} + \beta_{31}\text{rm} + \beta_{41}\text{ptratio} + \beta_{51}\text{dis}$$
$$+ \beta_{12}\text{lstat}^2 + \beta_{22}\text{age}^2 + \beta_{32}\text{rm}^2 + \beta_{42}\text{ptratio}^2 + \beta_{52}\text{dis}^2$$
$$+ \beta_{13}\text{lstat}^3 + \beta_{23}\text{age}^3 + \beta_{33}\text{rm}^3 + \beta_{43}\text{ptratio}^3 + \beta_{53}\text{dis}^3$$

Each of the ten models was trained and validated on a training/set split of 406 training records and 100 test records. To avoid the unreliability inherent in a single estimate of test error, as discussed in Sect. 3.1 above, I randomly generated 10 training/test splits and calculated the average training and test set errors. The **mean absolute error**—or the average absolute difference between the predicted value and the actual value—was calculated and averaged over the 10 randomly generated test samples The results are given in Table 2 and graphically illustrated in Fig. 5.

Table 2. Training error and test error for different levels of model complexity. Model complexity represents degree of polynomial used to fit the regression model.

Model complexity	Training error	Test error
1	3.55	3.63
2	3.00	3.01
3	2.98	3.06
4	2.82	**2.94***
5	2.75	2.94
6	2.69	2.99
7	2.66	3.55
8	2.54	4.18
9	2.48	4.47
10	2.46	9.22

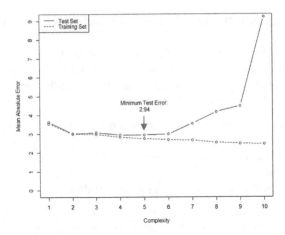

Fig. 5. Fitting graph for regression problem

From the analysis, it appears that a polynomial of degree 4 yields the regression model with the highest predictive accuracy. However, there appears to be a plateau between complexity levels 2 and 6 (the test errors range from 2.94 to 3.01, all equal from a practical standpoint). Hence, the quadratic model (polynomial of degree 2) might be the best choice in terms of balancing model simplicity and predictive accuracy.

6   Case II: Classification Task Using Neural Networks

In the second example, I used the Wisconsin Breast Cancer Diagnostic dataset from the UCI Machine Learning Laboratory [9] to model a classification task, which predicts whether a breast cancer tumor is malignant or benign. The breast cancer dataset includes 569 cases of cancer biopsies with 32 predictors. The diagnosis column has been recoded so that 1 represents a malignant tumor and 0 represents a benign one. To simplify the analysis, I have included only the first ten predictors contained in the dataset, namely, the means of the following biopsy features: radius, texture, perimeter, area, smoothness, compactness, concavity, points, symmetry, and dimension. For more information about this dataset, see [10].

To create neural networks of varying degrees of complexity, I ran the neural network algorithm seven times, varying the number of nodes from one to seven in the hidden layer (the middle layer in Fig. 6). Compare the simple one-node hidden layer model (Fig. 6, left side) to the complex seven-node hidden layer model (Fig. 6, right side).

Each of the seven neural network models was trained and validated on a training/set split of 469 training records and 100 test records. Again, to avoid the unreliability inherent in a single estimate of test error, I randomly generated 10 training/test splits and calculated the average training and test set errors. The errors were calculated as a percent of cases that were misclassified by the neural network. The results are provided in Table 3 and graphically illustrated in Fig. 7.

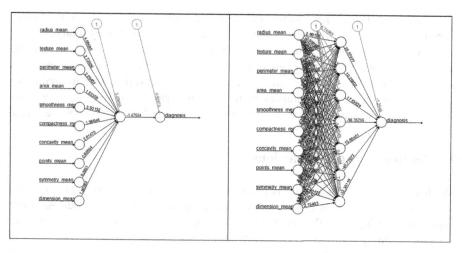

Fig. 6. Two neural networks: the left side has one node in the hidden layer, and the right side has seven nodes in the hidden layer.

Table 3. Training error and test error for different levels of model complexity. Model complexity represents number of nodes in the hidden layer of the neural network.

Model complexity	Training error	Test error
1	8.19%	9.70%
2	1.71%	7.33%
3	1.17%	5.90%
4	1.00%	5.50%
5	0.85%	*4.80%
6	0.85%	5.70%
7	0.77%	6.00%

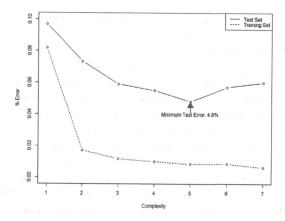

Fig. 7. Fitting graph for classification problem

From the analysis, it appears that the neural network with five nodes in the hidden layer is the best-performing model in terms of accuracy in predicting malignancy of breast tumors. It is interesting to note how the neural network model is able to generate error rates less that 1% on the training data. This points to how prone neural networks are to overfitting. Given enough complexity, the neural network is able to predict the malignancy of breast cancer tumors with close to perfect accuracy on the training dataset. The real test, however, is how well the neural network performs on the test data.

7 Discussion and Conclusions

The future of Machine Learning is promising and exciting. In recent years, we have witnessed an explosion of interest in the field, as more and more methods and techniques are developed by the Machine Learning community. In the era of Big Data, Machine Learning will play a central role in how we gain insights and make sense of complex and massive datasets.

The validation techniques described in the paper are applicable to a wide range of supervised Machine Learning algorithms. What this means is that one can try out a great many types of algorithms, and choose the one that has the highest predictive accuracy on a test dataset. This is especially useful for the end-user who may not have a sophisticated understanding of the mathematics underlying these techniques, but certainly can learn how to apply these cross-validation techniques.

Information visualizations can greatly aid the data scientist in the task of "right-fitting" a model: neither one that is underfit (too simple) nor one that is overfit (too complex). Information graphics like the fitting graph are especially useful in understanding how predictive accuracy varies as a function of model complexity. With an information graphic, we are able to more quickly form a mental model of our data: we are able to visualize how quickly test errors are increasing or decreasing as a function of model complexity. It may happen very quickly, or very slowly—as in Fig. 4, when the test error curve flattens out. The graphic enables us to see this relationship more easily, and assess, for example, trade-offs between model simplicity and model performance.

In this paper, I have simplified the discussion and presented model complexity as a one-dimensional construct. In the regression problem, I represented model complexity by varying the degree of the regression equation: I varied it from 1 (linear regression equation) to 10 (a polynomial regression equation of degree 10). In fact there are other ways of increasing model complexity other than increasing the degree of the polynomial regression equation–namely, the addition of interaction terms, or the addition of more predictors (or Xs). Likewise, the example on neural networks has been simplified. Here, model complexity is represented by the number of nodes in the hidden layer, but I could also have added additional layers to the model, as well as additional input features. The purpose of this simplification was to plot the fitting graph on a single axis of model complexity, and illustrate the relationship between model complexity and predictive accuracy (or error). Without the representation of model complexity as monotonically increasing on the x-axis, it would have been difficult to discern the general patterns in the fitting graph.

References

1. Provost, F., Fawcett, T.: Data Science for Business. O'Reilly Media Inc., Sebastopol (2013)
2. Samuel, A.L.: Some studies in machine learning using the game of checkers. IBM J. Res. Dev. **3**(3), 210–229 (1959)
3. Lantz, B.: Machine Learning in R, 2nd edn. Packt Publishing Ltd., Birmingham (2015)
4. James, G., Witten, D., Hastie, T., Tibshirani, R.: An Introduction to Statistical Learning with Applications in R. Springer, New York (2013)
5. Wickham, H., Grolemund, G.: R for Data Science: Import, Tidy, Transform, Visualize, and Model Data. O'Reilly Media Inc., Sebastopol (2017)
6. Spence, R.: Information Visualization, vol. 1. Addison-Wesley, New York (2001)
7. Harrison, D., Rubinfeld, D.L.: Hedonic prices and the demand for clean air. J. Environ. Econ. Manag. **5**, 81–102 (1978)
8. Belsey, D.A., Kuh, E., Welsch, R.E.: Regression Diagnostics. Identifying Influential Data and Sources of Collinearity. Wiley, New York (1980)
9. http://archive.ics.uci.edu/ml
10. Mangasarian, O.L., Street, W.N., Wolberg, W.H.: Breast cancer diagnosis and prognosis via linear programming. Oper. Res. **43**, 570–577 (1995)

Evaluation of Total Quality Management Using CSR Company Reports

Shu Ochikubo[✉], Fumiaki Saitoh, and Syohei Ishizu

Aoyama Gakuin University, Shibuya, Japan
occc.shhh@outlook.jp,
{saitoh,ishizu}@ise.aoyama.ac.jp

Abstract. In recent years, serious quality accidents and quality troubles such as recalls have occurred frequently, and Total Quality Management (TQM) is important as effective management to prevent quality troubles beforehand. There is also a Quality Management Level Research [6] (TQM research) that is jointly implemented by the Union of Japanese Scientists and Engineers and the Nikkei. In the TQM survey, the rankings on the six criteria of quality management and comprehensive rankings have been announced. However, concrete TQM activities have not been announced. Meanwhile, Corporate Social Responsibility (CSR) report has published abundant descriptions about the role of customers, employees, society and management who are stakeholders of companies. In this research, we aim to evaluate and extract the characteristics of the company's quality management activities according to the six criteria of the TQM survey using corporate CSR reports.

Keywords: TQM · PLSA · MDS · Word colud

1 Introduction

Serious quality problems have occurred in recent years: complaints about products and services and product recalls may in fact pose a critical risk to the sustainability of affected companies. Total Quality Management (TQM) is important for preventing this problem and refers to "a process, an organization, a person, and a system being combined organically, and company management being conducted from the viewpoint of customers." Because quality problems are ultimately caused by problems with the company systems, TQM is important for their prevention and is also relevant in the context of corporate social responsibility. A research of the extent to which TQM is employed by Japanese companies was jointly administered by the Union of Japanese Scientists and Engineers and the Nikkei. The evaluation of the research was based on responses related to the six criteria shown in Table 1.

Using the TQM research, a ranking of companies according to these six criteria was published, revealing which companies are excellent in each criterion. The research responses were not published, however, and we had difficulty understanding the beneficial practices of the highly ranked companies based on the results. Furthermore, many studies on TQM concern the introduction of TQM to a company, such as Kamio [1], while there are few studies of concrete TQM plans already in use at companies.

© Springer International Publishing AG 2017
F.F.-H. Nah and C.-H. Tan (Eds.): HCIBGO 2017, PART II, LNCS 10294, pp. 386–399, 2017.
DOI: 10.1007/978-3-319-58484-3_30

Table 1. Six criteria evaluated in the research

Customer orientation	Establishment and compliance of the processes
Top management commitment	Personnel training for TQM
Management of relief, safety and trust	Utilization and deployment power of the systems

On the other hand, most companies publish Corporate Social Responsibility (CSR) reports in order to fulfill their accountability to stakeholders. These CSR reports usually present significant efforts on the part of companies to the stakeholders. The aims of CSR and TQM are different, but their scopes are closely related. Good practices of companies within the scope of TQM may therefore be discovered by making use of this relationship. In this study, we thus use text data from CSR reports that contain information about the quality management of companies and analyze the data according to the TQM criteria in order to identify best TQM practices for each criterion. We use dimension reduction techniques, such as Probabilistic Latent Semantic Analysis (PLSA), which is effective for such hyperspace data.

Focusing on references that companies make to stakeholders, Kitora [5] investigates how each company influences CSR efforts. Many prior studies attempt to quantify corporate characteristics that affect corporate information disclosure. By directly performing text mining, corporate orientation to stakeholders can be grasped directly, and thus qualitative corporate characteristics can also be discerned. Clarifying the influence on information disclosure using regression is advantageous. However, although it is possible to extract the word of the factor influencing the problem, it is impossible to extract the document can be mentioned.

In the research of Saitoh [3], a large sparse matrix can be translated to a small dense matrix using PLSA of a customer review. After this conversion, the arrangement of review sentences is visualized by making a self-organizing map. Because a large sparse matrix can be converted to a small dense matrix using PLSA as in Saitoh's research, it is considered to be very effective for analysis of text in high dimensional data. For nonlinear data, such as a frequency matrix, when visualization is performed by principal component analysis or correspondence analysis and when the cumulative contribution rate to the number of dimensions is low, a lot of information is lost, and only a small amount remains. Although it is necessary to explain the data with information, PLSA, which can approximate the high dimensional semantic space of the original data with a few dimensions, can be effective for the visualization of text data.

2   Analysis Procedure

The overall analysis procedure will first be explained to provide an outline. The Steps 1 to 4 correspond to the interested companies selection, and Steps 5 to 7 correspond to the TQM information extraction.

Step 1.   Data collection
> From the company ranking produced by the TQM research evaluation, we selected the top ten companies (first to tenth place) and the ten companies in

the 89th to 98th places. Also the CSR reports contain varying amounts of documents, they are divided into two groups according to the quantity of documents. The results of this are shown in Table 1.

Step 2.   PLSA

PLSA is effective as a technology for extracting useful knowledge from big data and is often used as a method for high dimensional text data. In this study, this method is used for document evaluation and document extraction.

Step 3.   Calculation of company similarity by Cosine similarity and Visualization of similarity using Multi-dimensional Scaling (MDS)

We calculate the cosine similarity to visually grasp similarity in the PLSA results of Step 2. We also visualize similarity with MDS using the result of the cosine similarity.

Step 4.   Company evaluation and selecting companies of interest

We evaluate companies from the results of Steps 1 to 3 and select companies of interest.

Step 5.   Data collection

We subdivide CSR reports of the companies of interest for specific TQM activity extraction. In order to facilitate the TQM activity extraction, we prepare a frequency table of nouns by adding the six criteria from the research to the data.

Step 6.   PLSA

As in Step 2, PLSA is performed on the frequency table of nouns created in Step 5.

Step 7.   TQM activity extraction

We extract TQM activity of companies from the results of Step 6.

3   Analysis Method

3.1   Probabilistic Latent Semantic Analysis (PLSA)

PLSA is an effective method for extracting useful knowledge from big data and is also used as a clustering method. It is an effective method for high dimensional text data. In thinking of PLSA, it is assumed that there is a latent class z that becomes a common topic between the document d and the word w appearing therein. This latent class is generated probabilistically. The concept of PLSA can be illustrated with the graphical model in Fig. 1. It can be represented by three kinds of random variables, and as shown in Eq. 1, the number of words w included in document d is $n(d, w)$. We maximize i Eq. 1 by taking the log-likelihood. A document d belongs to the document set D, and a word w belongs to the word set W.

$$L = \sum_{d \in D} \sum_{w \in W} n(d, w) \log P(d, w) \tag{1}$$

We use the Expectation Maximization (EM) algorithm to maximize Eq. 1. The EM algorithm is a learning algorithm for incomplete data that can be used for parameter

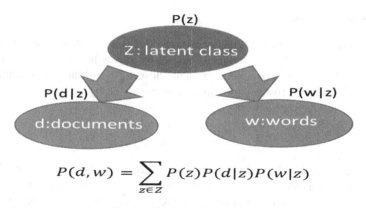

$$P(d, w) = \sum_{z \in Z} P(z)P(d|z)P(w|z)$$

Fig. 1. PLSA graphical model

estimation of a mixed distribution model. It is a method that approaches the optimal solution by successively improving the solution, and it converges quickly in the initial stage. In the E step, the expected value of the log-likelihood function is obtained according to the current parameter value. In the M step, the parameter is updated so as to maximize the expected value of the log-likelihood obtained in the E step. The E step is shown in Eq. 2, and the M step is shown in Eqs. 3 to 5.

E-step

$$P(z|d, w) = \frac{P(z)P(d|z)P(w|z)}{\sum_{z \in Z} P(z)P(d|z)P(w|z)} \qquad (2)$$

M-step

$$P(w|z) = \frac{\sum_d n(d, w)P(z|d, w)}{\sum_{d,w'} n(d, w')P(z|d, w')} \qquad (3)$$

$$P(d|z) = \frac{\sum_w n(d, w)P(z|d, w)}{\sum_{d'',w} n(d'', w)P(z|d'', w)} \qquad (4)$$

$$P(z) = \frac{\sum_{d,w} n(d, w)P(z|d, w)}{\sum_{d,w} n(d, w)} \qquad (5)$$

3.2   Word Cloud

We extracted meaning by visualizing topics generated by PLSA with a word cloud. It is possible to select a plurality of frequently occurring words in the document and impress the contents of the method also sentence using size to correspond to the frequency. In this study, the probability that a word belongs to a topic, rather than the word's frequency, is expressed by the size of the letters.

3.3   Cosine Similarity

Cosine similarity is a similarity calculation method that is used to compare documents in a vector space model. It expresses similarity by angles between vectors. A value close to 1 indicates similarity, while a value close to 0 indicates dissimilarity. The calculation formula for cosine similarity can be expressed by Eq. 6

$$\cos(a,b) = \frac{\sum a_i b_i}{\|a\| \cdot \|b\|} \tag{6}$$

where a_i and b_i are the ith elements of a and b, respectively, the numerator on the right side is the inner product of a and b, and the denominator is the product of the lengths of the two vectors. The closer the cosine is to 1, the more similar to vectors are considered to be. In this research, because the similarity calculated in Eq. 6 is treated as a distance, we convert similarity to distance using Eq. 7.

$$\cos(a,b) = d = 1 - \cos(a,b) \tag{7}$$

3.4   Multi-dimensional Scaling (MDS)

MDS is a method of multivariate analysis and is a way of placing novel data between individuals in two- or three-dimensional space in the vicinity and other things in the distant place. A matrix $D_{m \times m}$ is as shown in Fig. 2 below. The distance can be freely defined, but it must satisfy the distance axioms of Eqs. 8 to 10. In this research, the content of the data is the distance found using the cosine similarity as shown in Eq. 7. The distance d in Eq. 7 is data satisfying the axioms of distance.

$$d_{ij} \geq 0 \tag{8}$$

$$d_{ij} = d_{ji} \tag{9}$$

$$d_{ij} + d_{jk} \geq d_{jk} \tag{10}$$

$$D_{m \times m} = \begin{bmatrix} & \text{data 1} & \text{data 2} & \cdots & \text{data } j & \cdots & \text{data } m & \\ & 0 & d_{12} & \cdots & d_{1j} & \cdots & d_{1m} & \text{data 1} \\ & d_{21} & 0 & \cdots & d_{2j} & \cdots & d_{2m} & \text{data 2} \\ & \cdots & \cdots & \cdots & \cdots & \cdots & \cdots & \cdots \\ & d_{i1} & d_{i2} & \cdots & d_{ij} & \cdots & d_{im} & \text{data } i \\ & \cdots & \cdots & \cdots & \cdots & \cdots & \cdots & \cdots \\ & d_{m1} & d_{m2} & \cdots & d_{mj} & \cdots & 0 & \text{data } m \end{bmatrix}$$

Fig. 2. Matrices handled by MDS

By converting the distance matrix $D_{m \times m}$ obtained in Fig. 2 as shown in Eq. 11, the eigenvector of the matrix $Z_{m \times m}$ is taken as the coordinate value of the point.

$$z_{ij} = -\frac{1}{2}(d_{ij}^2 - \sum_{i=1}^{m} \frac{d_{ij}^2}{m} - \sum_{j=1}^{m} \frac{d_{ij}^2}{m} + \sum_{i=1}^{m} \sum_{j=1}^{m} \frac{d_{ij}^2}{m^2}) \tag{11}$$

4 Result of Analysis

We first present the analysis results of the interested company selection STEP.

4.1 Data Collection

We obtained CSR reports from the companies shown in Table 2 and created a noun frequency table for each group.

Table 2. Grouping by document quantity

Companies with large document volume	Word count	Companies with low document volume	Word count
Sony	177,000	GC	47,000
Casio	169,000	AMADA	44,000
Toshiba	165,000	SAPPORO	43,000
FUJIFILM	121,000	Konica Minolta	43,000
Fujitsu	104,000	DNP	40,000
SHARP	100,000	Canon	37,000
Kubota	76,500	Asahi	35,000
SHOWA DENKO	70,000	TOKAI RIKA	35,000
LIXIL	65,000	SHIMADZU	35,000
		NISSHIN OilliO	26,000
		Nomura Research Institute	12,000

4.2 Introduction of PLSA

In the noun frequency tables, PLSA was used to generate ten topics and a visualization of the top 40 words with a high probability of belonging to each topic in the word cloud to illustrate the meaning of each topic. We determine the meaning of each topic using the word cloud and then decide which company to focus on. Figure 3 shows a word cloud for Topic 4 of Companies with low document volume. Figure 4 presents a diagram showing the affiliation probability of a company to Topic 4.

In Topic 4, it seems that information about stakeholders is described because it contains words such as "customer," "product," "employee," and "production." Konica Minolta is a company with a higher probability of being affiliated with subjects in

Fig. 3. A word cloud of Topic 4 for companies with low document volume

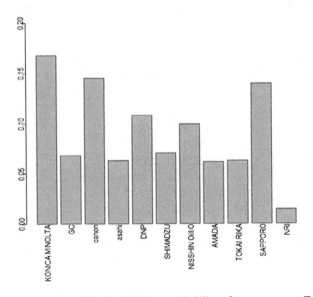

Fig. 4. Diagram showing the affiliation probability of a company to Topic 4

Topic 4. In this way, a meaning for each topic is posited. Table 3 summarizes topics of companies with a high document volume, and Table 4 summarizes topics of companies with a low document volume.

4.3 Calculation of Company Similarity with Cosine Similarity and Visualization of Similarity with MDS

By using each company's probability of affiliation to each topic, we calculate the similarity of the company using cosine similarity as shown in Eq. 6 in Sect. 4, and

Table 3. Topic summary of companies with high document volume

Topic1	Thought to describe projects related to the environment.
Topic2	Thought to describe the emission of environmental substances
Topic3	Thought to concern customer-oriented information, human resource development, etc.
Topic4	Thought to describe environmental activities and services.
Topic5	Thought to describe chemical emissions and employees.
Topic6	Thought to contain information about safety management at the time of trading and product development.
Topic7	Thought to describe environmental activities and conservation
Topic8	Thought to describe safety management of products and transactions in the supply chain.
Topic9	Thought to describe corporate social activities
Topic10	Thought to describe each stakeholder.

Table 4. Topic summary of companies with low document volume

Topic1	Thought to describe the company's tasks and activities.
Topic2	Thought to contain information about the environment and social contributions.
Topic3	Thought to contain information about safety management, improvement and so on for production in the supply chain.
Topic4	Thought to describe each stakeholder.
Topic5	Thought to describe the company's environmental activities.
Topic6	Thought to describe efforts to achieve customer satisfaction.
Topic7	Thought to describe environmental and social activities.
Topic8	Thought to describe efforts related the global environment, such as energy conservation.
Topic9	Thought to mainly describe the company's products.
Topic10	Thought to describe employee health management.

following the distance axiom in Eq. 7, we recalculate the distance. Each company's affiliation probability to a topic was converted to similarity, but it was converted for 10 topics (10 dimensions), making visualization in a single figure difficult. Visualization is therefore performed with MDS, which can be used to arrange multidimensional information in a two-dimensional or three-dimensional space. Figures 5 and 6 contain visualizations of the relationship between companies with a high document volume and companies with a low document volume. (Red letters denote the top 10 companies; blue letters denote the lower 10 companies.)

In Fig. 5, the grouping takes a relatively near form, with the top ten companies tending to shift toward the positive side of the y-axis, while the lower ten companies tend to shift towards the negative side. In contrast, the lower ten companies showed relatively greater variability in Fig. 6. The reason for this is that in Fig. 5, the document volume is large and the contents of the document are comparatively similar, whereas

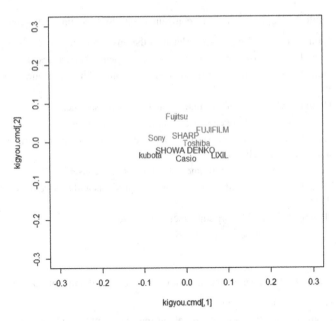

Fig. 5. Visualization of the relationship between companies with high document volume (Color figure online)

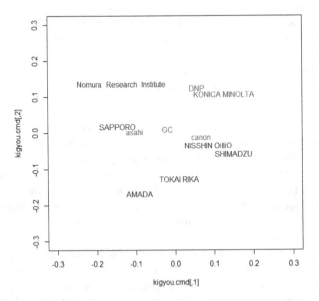

Fig. 6. Visualization of the relationship between companies with low document volume (Color figure online)

Table 5. Companies of interest

Highly ranked companies that have a high probability of affiliation to TQM topics	Konica Minolta GC Toshiba
Low ranked companies with a low probability of affiliation to TQM topics	Kubota
Low ranked companies with higher affiliation probability to environmental topics	Sapporo

the document volume is small in Fig. 6 meaning that the content may depend on the company.

Based on these analyses, companies of interest were selected. The selected companies and the reasons for their selection are summarized in Table 5.

5   TQM Information Extraction Step

Because the TQM information extraction step is similar to the step for selecting companies of interest mentioned in Sect. 5, we only describe differences between the extraction procedure and the evaluation procedure in this section. To make this easier to understand, we focus in particular on Konica Minolta in the explanation.

5.1   Data Collection

The target of the data is five companies, "Toshiba," "GC," "Konica Minolta," "Sapporo," and "Kubota," listed in Table 5. For the extraction of quality management information in this section, we use Evaluation and Difference to evaluate concrete TQM, finely divide each company's CSR reports, and obtain frequency matrices of nouns. The TQM is evaluated according to the six criteria of the TQM research described in Table 1. When considering the meaning of the topic, the quality management information contains many duplicate words and similar words. We therefore add items related to each criteria of the TQM research as data. Table 6 shows the question items of the TQM research.

5.2   Introduction of PLSA

We first focus on Konica Minolta as an example and to derive topic meanings (Fig. 7).

In word cloud for Topic 3 in Fig. 8, words related to quality management such as "people," "employees," "quality management," "president" can be seen, so we connect this to "human resource development to achieve quality management," "individual commitment" and the like. In the diagram of probability of affiliation to "manager's commitment" and "personnel training for quality management" is also high. We posit the meaning of topics for the other four companies in this same way.

Table 6. Question items of the TQM research

Customer intention	Do you conduct a customer satisfaction research?
Manager commitment	How do you position and disseminate the concept of quality emphasis, such as being "customer-oriented" and "putting quality first," in the corporate philosophy and management philosophy?
Personnel training for TQM	Do you create a mid- to long-term plan for quality management education throughout the company?
Management of relief, security, and trust	Do you conduct employee satisfaction researchs?
Establishment, observance of the process	Do you clarify the roles and processes of each organization in manufacturing so as to ensure and improve the quality of products to be offered to customers?
Utilization, development power of the systems	Do you investigate what kind of products customers want and reflect this in new products in a timely way?

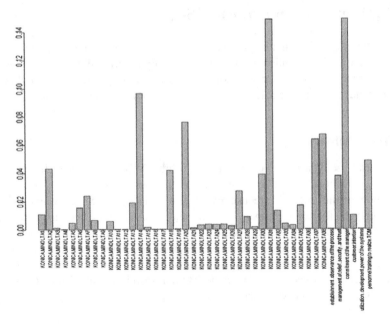

Fig. 7. Affiliation probability of Topic 3

5.3 TQM Activity Extraction

TQM activity is extracted based on the meaning of the topics derived in Step 6. Tables 7 and 8 display which information from the CSR report topics relate to TQM information.

A large portion of the TQM information obtained from the CSR reports, as shown in Tables 7 and 8, was found to be "manager commitment," "customer intention," and

Fig. 8. Word cloud for Topic 3

Table 7. Konica Minolta topics and TQM criteria

Konica Minolta	Establishment, observance of the process	Management of relief, security, and trust	Personnel training for TQM	Utilization, development power of the systems	Customer intention	Manager commitment
Topic1			○			
Topic2						
Topic3		○	○			○
Topic4	○			○	○	
Topic5						○
Topic6		○	○			
Topic7					○	
Topic8						
Topic9					○	○
Topic10				○		

Table 8. GC topics and TQM criteria

GC	Establishment, observance of the process	Management of relief, security, and trust	Personnel training for TQM	Utilization, development power of the systems	Customer intention	Manager commitment
Topic1			○			○
Topic2						
Topic3						
Topic4						
Topic5			○			
Topic6						
Topic7	○			○		○
Topic8			○		○	
Topic9			○		○	○
Topic10					○	○

Table 9. TQM information extraction result

Konica Minorta	TQM information includes descriptions of executive personnel education, top management topics for human resource development of employees, and training of business leaders
GC	TQM information includes a description of the management philosophy and quality management, a concrete statement that the president has confirmed to what extent company policy has been implemented by going to the site
Toushiba	TQM information includes descriptions of management's commitment, such as measures for risk compliance management
Sapporo	TQM information includes information about human resource development, establishment of a group quality assurance system, compliance, and information on the six criteria is mixed
Kubota	TQM information includes descriptions of specific measures such as securing of quality and training of human resources to expand production bases and improve customer satisfaction

Table 10. CSR report contents for each company based on analysis of main contents

Konica Minorta	Contained information about "environment," "effort for customers," and "human resource development"
GC	Contained information about "environment," "management commitment," and "human resource development"
Toushiba	Contained information about "environment," "effort for customers," and "management structure"
Sapporo	Contained information about "environment," "social contribution," and "management structure"
Kubota	Contained information about "environment" and "social contribution"

"personnel training for TQM." The criterion for placement of the circles in these tables is shown in Eq. 12.

$$\left\{ \frac{100}{\text{Number of documents} + 6} \right\} \times 2 \tag{12}$$

The number of documents in Expression 12 refers to the number of CSR reports of each company as a subdivision, and the 6 in the denominator represents the six criteria. The value obtained in Eq. 12 is rounded off to the third decimal place, and the probability of exceeding Eq. 12 is judged to be high for topics. Table 9 shows the TQM information extracted for each company.

6 Discussion

In this study, we evaluated TQM and extracted TQM information using corporate CSR reports. We selected companies of interest using the analysis result of PLSA. Companies with a high probability in the topic on quality management were "Konica

Minolta," "GC," and "Toshiba." Conversely, "Kubota" was a company with a low probability of topics related to TQM, while "Sapporo" had a high probability of topics on environmental information. Based on these results, we selected these five companies to focus on. In the MDS results (Figs. 5 and 6), companies with high document volume were located relatively close together. The reason for this is the large amount of documents and their contents are not biased. Because many of the top companies are electrical manufacturers, their CSR reports are considered to be similar. We subsequently extracted each company's TQM information. The results of extraction indicate that most of the TQM information included in the CSR report is related to "manager commitment," "customer intention," and "personnel training for TQM." Table 10 summarizes the main contents described in each company's CSR report.

7 Conclusions

In this study, using the text data of the corporate CSR reports, we used PLSA to probabilistically classify and evaluate the company's CSR reports. The extent to which each company disclosed TQM information to customers was extracted. In the corporate evaluation, we analyzed contents using PLSA and posited topic meanings with word clouds so that we could focus our attention on companies with a high probability of affiliation to topics related to quality management. By classifying the CSR report of the companies of interest and adding the six criteria from the TQM level research to the data, classification of documents related to quality management was facilitated. Finally, we were able to obtain information on TQM activities of companies from Table 9.

References

1. Kamio, M.: A study of management in the aspect of human-being. Prod. Manage. **3**(1), 30–33 (1996). (In Japanese)
2. Shibayama, N., Nakagawa, H.: Introducing off-diagonal elements to singular value matrix in probabilistic latent semantic indexing. Trans. Japan. Soc. Artif. Intell. **26**(1), 262–272 (2011). (In Japanese)
3. Saitoh, F.: Visualization of online customer reviews and evaluations based on Self-organizing Map. In: Proceedings of 2014 IEEE International Conference on Systems, Man and Cybernetics (SMC), pp. 182–187
4. Hofmann, T.: Probabilistic latent semantic analysis. In: Proceedings of Uncertainty in Artificial Intelligence, pp. 289–296 (1999)
5. Kitora, Y.: Relationship between the corporate stance toward stakeholders and disclosures on corporate websites. Environ. Conserv. Eng. **39**(2), 103–111 (2010). (In Japanese)
6. Union of Japanese Scientists and Engineers: The result of the 9th JUSE Quality Management Level Research announced. JUSE 10, March 2016. (Online)

Contract Visualisation: Sketches for Generic Interfaces

Lei Shi[(⊠)] and Daniela Alina Plewe

University Scholars Program, National University of Singapore,
18 College Avenue West, Singapore 138593, Singapore
{danielaplewe, shi.lei}@nus.edu.sg

Abstract. Our aim is to develop general heuristics for the visualization of contracts, which may serve as guidelines for interface developments of legal technology software. We introduce three approaches to interactive contract visualisations and discuss their strengths and weaknesses. They all address the negotiation phase preceding an agreement. We believe the nature of contracts is to capture and organise potential future events and therefore introduce the concept of "possibility spaces" as a starting point for the first two visualizations. Focusing on the "modalities" of contracts seems to us the most promising approach and is explored in the third example. From a methodological point of view, we develop visualisations through abstraction and focus on the common characteristics of all contracts. In that sense, we do not "illustrate" contracts. Through these visualisations we hope to make contracts easier to understand, be it on paper or via legal technology.

Keywords: Contract visualisation · Contract simplification · Proactive law · Modalities of contracts · Computable contracts · Communication design · Applied ergonomics

1 Introduction

Contract visualisation has become a vivid area of innovation engaging lawyers, researchers, designers, and practitioners alike. The different motivations for so-called "contract simplification" gravitate around the aim to enhance understandability and transparency of contracts. As elaborated in previous research [1, 2] we believe, that there exists oftentimes during the process of contracting a gap between the legal representation of an agreement and the goals and intentions of the negotiators.

Helena Haapio [3], an academic and lawyer herself spearheading the proactive law initiative states that "Proactive lawyering is not about applying legal rules to facts that happened in the past, but about applying sound legal practices to create future facts and to plan a future course of conduct", ideally preventing litigation. An important aspect of preventive law is to enhance the understanding of a legal setting before and during the negotiation, before signing a contract (therefore understanding its implications) and after in case of violations of the agreement.

With this paper, we aim to develop a general visual approach supporting the various stages relevant to contracting. We will start with a short overview of current

© Springer International Publishing AG 2017
F.F.-H. Nah and C.-H. Tan (Eds.): HCIBGO 2017, PART II, LNCS 10294, pp. 400–411, 2017.
DOI: 10.1007/978-3-319-58484-3_31

practices in the area of "contract simplification". These include i.e. abstract visual languages and icons [4] which may need to be learnt, narratives like "comics contracts" [5] which may underrepresent the intended complexities of an agreement, but could work well with illiterate legal partners (e.g. in developing countries). The approach to illustrate specific situations relevant to the contractual content may prove inflexible (and therefore potentially unsalable) if they need to be created for each context from scratch. Inspired by the existing approaches to visual contract simplification, we aim to develop a visual language which combines abstract and specific elements.

We develop three models of representing legal contracts. We introduce the concept of "possibility space" (model one and two) to display counterfactual "states of the worlds" [7] which contracts aim to organize. For the last model, we assume that contracts can be reduced to core modal categories, such as obligations, prohibitions, permissions and the concept of options ("no obligation") [6]. These rather high level abstractions are the core entities relating to the parties involved.

2 Current Practices of Contract Simplification

Under the concept of "proactive law" [3] legal academics, practitioners, and policy-makers have identified and described increasingly the deficiencies in current legal practice and the opportunities for innovation. One main concern is the lack of transparency of legal documents and the focus on technicalities rather than on the actual deal-design of an agreement.

Under the concept of "contract simplification" a range of ideas and approaches have surfaced ranging from linguistic simplifications (natural language), reductions to code (if law equals somehow computer code) and approaches for simplifications via visualisations and graphical means.

2.1 From Language to Code

There are different kinds of linguistic representations for contracts [8], see Fig. 1.

Prose Contracts	Standard English Contracts	Auditable Contracts	Term-Generated Contracts	Machine-Readable Contracts	Machine-Coded Contracts
Contracts drafted in an unrestricted style	Contracts drafted in everyday language and simple sentence forms	Contracts capable of computer analysis to assess their principal characteristics	Contracts assembled from a term sheet	Contracts drafted in a high-level computer language, comprehensible by non-programmers	Contracts drafted in computer code

Fig. 1. Natural language progression

In Fig. 1, Martin describes a natural progression of language goes from prose language in contracts to Standard English (formal language) contracts to auditable language meaning language that could be analysed by computers. From there we progress to the formation of contracts using high-level machine readable languages. In the next step, contracts are coded by machines. To achieve full automation of the legal process, regulatory and enforceability issues across legislations need to be resolved.

Due to the blockchain technology and the Ethereum project [9] built upon that technology, the time for the real automation in contracts might arrive soon. The vision behind the Ethereum platform is to facilitate building software on the "blockchain". The blockchain technology is a chain" that is a distributed ledger in the form of databases, whereby the distribution prevents fraudulent changes within this digital record. Blockchains can be public, but don't have to be. For the vision of "smart contracts" as proposed by Nick Szabo [10] all information is public and therefore transparent for all members of society. Szabo (and others, such as Meng Wong [11] from Legalese) view contracts as a set of "if-then rules", which therefore are prone to be represented via code (computer code and programming languages) and not natural language or legal lingo.

Through this technology contracts can become self-executing – similar to all software: once the premise of a rule if fulfilled, the consequence can be triggered automatically. The vision of smart contracts as self-automated contracts for the better of society preventing human errors and flaws [10] have been widely discussed and serious concerns have been raised. One of these is of course transparency and control of such software programs.

Coming back to the role of contract simplification and the role visualisation may play: smart contracts – provided they are meant to serve humans will need to be controlled and understood in their complexities. We believe there is huge potential even for less radical approaches to self-executing software in the form of smart contracts.

2.2   From Language to Visualization

Images and visualizations [12] can convey complex problems in a simpler way and increase understandability [1]. Hence, it seems beneficial that if we could find out of way to visualize contracts, it would benefit all the parties as they are now easily comprehended with all their consequences. This also brings us back to the idea of "proactive law" [3], instead of focusing on the technicalities of contracts and minimising damages in situation of violation, better understanding of the contracts arguably helps the design of deals and mitigates the possibility of violation in the first place.

Visualization of contracts can have been discussed in different forms. In "Next Generation Deal Design", Haapio, Plewe and De Rooy [5] discuss different forms of visualizations. Namely, visualization as contracts, visualization for contracts, visualization in contracts and visualization about contracts. They all serve different purposes and some might be arguably more practical in real life. Furthermore, under visualization as contracts, the idea of using comic illustrations as contracts are brought about. However, we believe that the practicality of visualizations and their creation is an important point and therefore favour approaches where the visualisation is somehow automated [3] as well as simple to understand.

3 Existing Approaches

Recent research explores various categories of visualizing contracts. Haapio, Plewe, De Rooy [5] introduce at least four ways: visualization *as* contracts, visualization *for* contracts, visualization *in* contracts and visualization *about* contracts.

Mahler points out that there is no single icon that can be understood universally [6]. Hence, educational cost of helping people to understand all the icons tend to be high. For example, the concept of authority is common in contracts, but there is not a universal icon that every potential user could understand. We would think of using the icon of a crown to symbolize "authority", but not only the crown icon is different throughout the world, not everyone understands what a crown is.

De Rooy proposes to convey the contractual dialogue between parties via the combination of text and visuals in the form of contracts. [5] He uses comic drawings to represent possible scenarios in the case of an employee agreement. Most possible job requirements and consequences are captured using those drawings, however, the comic contracts have a challenge: hard to automate and therefore commercially hard to scale. Hence, it may have limited use cases, unless there is a way to translate text into comic-images in an automated way. Considering the current state of AI this seems hard to realize in the near-term future. However, comic contract once generated can have tremendous social impact and help to empower illiterate segments of the population.

Most of the existing proposed solutions rely on categorizations and conventional symbols. Potential limitations of such strategies are that Icon families are oftentimes not systematic oftentimes and can't be easily extended and are therefore potentially inflexible. Another approach is introduced by Passera et al. [4] where she enriches contracts with automated visualization mostly representing quantitative data, for example, she illustrates in an interactive chart a payment clause with its penalties in case of the violation of the agreement.

4 Models of Visualization

For our first two visualisations we introduce the concept of "possibility space" By possibility space we mean the "possible worlds" which if-then rules are describing. This understanding is inspired by David Lewis Possible World semantics [13]. We use his modal semantics as a kind of metaphor to craft a visualisations, which can express contracts the way they organize the future states of the world.

One obvious approach is to organize the possibilities of the future along in a chronological fashion with a timeline and some branching universes. Visualising Lewis Possible worlds would probably look like this: he aims to define the semantics of modal logics via various possible worlds with so-called "accessibility relations" between them. So, for example, if in a world, A x is possible, then from world A can be accessed a world B in which x is true. From world A is also accessible a world C, in which x is not true. And – depending what degree of granularity one's underlying logic allows for, any degree between true, no true- such as not known, the opposite is not known etc. We will use this kind of "accessibility- relation" between "Zustaende der Welt" ("states of the world") [7] to describe the various scenarios in a branching time universe a contract aims to cover. However, this approach at least in theory suffers from the combinatorial explosion and therefore may only be useful when small possibility spaces are sufficient to show.

Since contracts have always an element of time to them, we will experiment with various other ways to capture time. Interactive media and its origin in the concept of "hypertexts" [14] supports this kind of thinking naturally, we believe. However, this approach may provide a false sense of security and may not capture the eventualities of the future as efficient as language can. We may be reminded through these sketches, that language as means of simplification (mostly through the power of abstraction) may be considered the most expressive and efficient medium – a reason, why contracts are probably till today conveyed in text.

Nevertheless, we will also explore a hybrid approach of combining text and spatial position of text (concept clustering) to reduce complexities. This approach will be based on representing the parties and their obligations, permissions and prohibitions and in that sense at least make the contract and the actionable components clear to all parties. We may conclude through our research that visualising the varieties of possibilities is perhaps not necessary and efficient (i.e. aesthetically elegant).

4.1   Model 1: Road Progression Model

This models puts emphasis on a timeline, analogically model the progress of a contract to the progress on the timeline. It conveys how one decision may have far reaching consequences. Three key component is represented in the road progression model, they are the representation of concepts, the key milestones as well as the end of the contract.

At the beginning of modelling, we define the icons used for modelling contracts, then we represent the contract with those icons, lastly, we explore what may cause the termination of the contracts. Here we use tenancy agreement to model the contract.

As shown in Fig. 2 a definition section where all the icons are defined upfront to avoid confusion in the future. Today's contracts are complex and their meaning is not always clear to those who are impacted. What is presented above is a way to make contracts more engaging with icons replacing words.

As shown above in Figs. 3 and 4, this model focuses on the importance of timeline, every contract has its life time. In the case of a public housing tenancy contract, 5 year can be a critical time as it is the time when the tenant can start renting out the house. This condition is represented through the middle block. If tenants choose to rent it out, the contract continues, else a new contract is required.

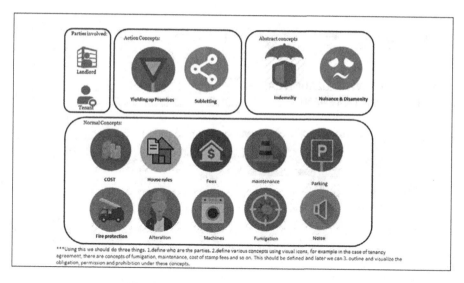

Fig. 2. Road progression model interface 1

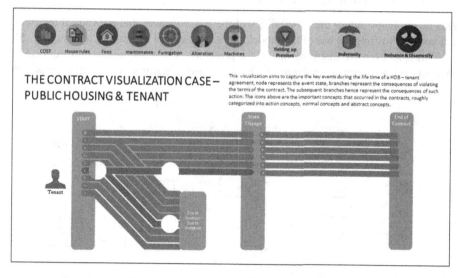

Fig. 3. Road progression model interface 2

Furthermore, by making the interface interactive shown in the Fig. 4 the user may be able to click on a change of event to know the consequences of his actions. For example, if the tenant illegally sublets the house, this would lead to a premature termination of the contract and certain penalties may apply.

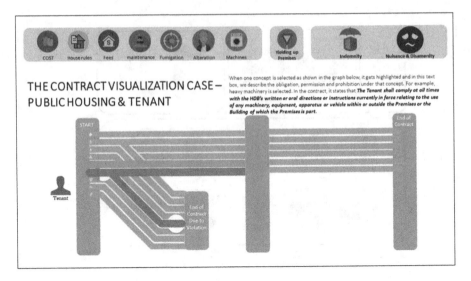

Fig. 4. Road progression model interface 3

4.2 Model 2: Spanning Tree Model

This model maps out all the possibilities of the consequences that are caused by users' actions. To illustrate the use of the model, our example is an insurance contract (Fig. 5):

This is an example mapping out all the possibilities that may occur in the course of contracts. It leads from general terms to the more specific terms, covering all aspects both

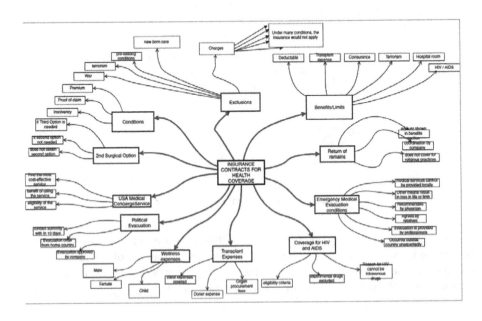

Fig. 5. Spanning tree model interface

parties need to know about the contract. However, if one takes a look at the exclusion terms one may realize that in many possible ways, the contract would be void and the insured person would not get paid. If we start tracing the conditions to different terms, we would run into an explosion of possibilities branching out from one scenario to another.

Since insurance policies are usually based on a timeline, multiple scenarios might happen along the timeline and events happened before hand might affect the events happened after. In this particular example, the insurance policy states that it only insures up to four persons from the same family, hence, in the case of political evacuation, it means only four of the family members' evacuation fees will be covered. On the visual representation, this requires more layers. Hence, more events would lead to a combinatorial explosion which is counter intuitive to the purpose of visualization as its aim is to simplify the contract. Nevertheless, this model maps out the possibility space and helps to navigate the contracts which is valuable for the understanding of the contracts.

4.3   Model 3: Modalities Model

Inspired by Lewis's [13] Possible World Semantics to model modal logics and Mahler [6] work on visualising modalities, we will now introduce a visualisation based on high-level abstractions such as the four modalities "permission", "prohibition",

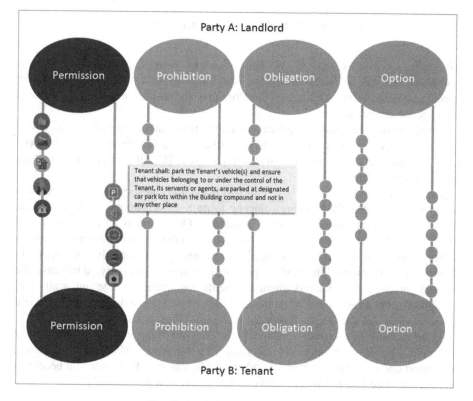

Fig. 6. Modalities model interface 1

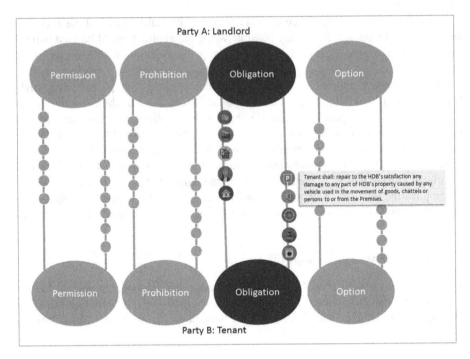

Fig. 7. Modalities model interface 2

"obligation" as well as "option". We believe that by visualising abstractions such as modalities, we can avoid some of the drawbacks of other visualisations, which oftentimes tend to be too specific and therefore may not lead towards a universal visual language for contracts.

Similar to our previously proposed negotiation platform, in this concept, users first list the participating parties and a kind of market or negotiation space [15] between them. For each party, there is a "corridor of negotiation" [16] allowing for actions along the various modalities.

All terms in the contract can be categorised in the four categories above. Permission is the action of officially allowing someone to do a thing; consent or authorization. Prohibition is the action of forbidding something. Obligation is an act or course of action to which a person is morally or legally bound; a duty or commitment and option is the defined as no obligation for example the U turn sign, you are given the option to U turn. Top and bottom of the model represents both sides of the party, in this case, the landlord and the tenant. Each dot/item represents one action that a tenant is allowed, prohibited or obligated to do. When the user click on one dot, a floating sticker would appear to show the specific term that dot represents (Figs. 6 and 7).

In the example of a tenancy agreement - for each party the various items are defined and could – provided an interactive interface – be unfolded, looked upon, discussed, and agreed upon etc. by each party. In other worlds, this visualisation would become a strategic interface (Plewe) to facilitate also the negotiation process [15].

5 Comparison

We would evaluation the usefulness of these three models based on the criteria we have identified:

1. Supporting a visual language for contracting - reusable and universally applicable organizational principles or building blocks (e.g. diagram parts) usually describe best practice structures or concepts of specific domains which can be adapted and used in various contexts.
2. Capture the chronological nature of the possibility space – if necessary
3. Increasing understandability – before contracting and negotiation, during contract drafting and after the contract is signed, i.e. understand the implications within the possibility space
4. Facilitating users in different roles (e.g. managers, laypersons, software engineers or lawyers) often use a law or contract for different purposes. It is important for a legislator, contract designer or law-interpreting person to know the rationale behind a certain norm, contract or law.

The road progression model qualifies for the first three factors. Specific maps would be generated for specific group of people. In the case for Tenancy agreement, there would be two maps generated. One for tenant, one for landlord. As the landlord is the one with power, it is understandable that in the contract constructed, there would be fewer disadvantaged terms for him. However, in Singapore, the government does have terms that protects the rights of the tenant for example and does not allow short term renting. This should be considered in the landlord map. It is important that the model is modularised so that its interface can be used by code. Furthermore, this model is excellent at showing the change of event in time, this is modelled by the concept of 'road' where violations of certain terms would lead to different consequences. However, one disadvantage of this model is the categorization which cannot be standardised. It changes with the focus of the contracts which makes the automation of this model difficult.

Like the model above, the spanning trees model is good at the first three points. It is more intuitive than the Road Progression model as it aims to include all possible scenarios in its representation. However, actions that could be taken in sequence and this would lead to a combinatorial explosion that implies too many possibilities and makes it practically infeasible to visualize the whole possibility space.

The road progression model and the spanning tree model are both visualizing modalities implicitly. However, a major disadvantage is that they are not easily automated. There are hardly a standardised ways to exhaust all the possible concepts that could appear in one contract. This implies, all possible cases would need to be represented in the software before determining their interconnections. In the last model, modalities are being expressed explicitly, making it possible for the system to exhaust all terms of contracts.

The modalities model has a great advantage that is its clarity of representation. For both model above, they are categorised based on the terms that are used in the contract. They change when the focus of contract changes. But with deontic modalities, all the terms under this model are categorised by the nature of the action. This simplifies and consolidates the terms in a contract and makes the interface more logical. It would work well with code too. Its Drawback is, that users do have to learn the abstractions used as explained in Mahler's paper [6] – but hopefully the modalities are intuitively to grasp.

6 Conclusion

On a philosophical note, all forms of representations are forms of reductions of complexity and suffer to some degree from inadequacies. This remains a challenge for any documentation of an agreement, be it as code, text or a combination of those aiming to anticipate future events.

The emergence of new legal technologies provide opportunities and also demand new and interactive solutions to facilitate and capture agreements between humans. Visualisations will become increasingly important to support not only human-human interactions but also computer-human interactions. Any constellation is imaginable, e.g. lawyers among each other, lawyers and deal-makers, laymen negotiating, peer to peer online contracting and any users of legal software.

Generic modality based interfaces as the here proposed model 3 could be promising candidates to support technology based contracting. It seems desirable, if interfaces cater independently from the domain to a variety of contracts without introducing specific visual elements (e.g. illustrations), icons (leading to rather inflexible visual language which might be difficult to extend/adapt ad hoc) or particular conventions (which may have to be "learnt").

In the context of the blockchain enabled platform Ethereum modalities based interfaces such a model 3 could be implemented. When contracts can be read and analysed automatically, and the particular modalities, such as obligations, permissions and prohibitions can be identified automatically – then this approach could enable the automation of the visualizations within such a modal visual framework. We will explore such frameworks in further research.

References

1. Plewe, D.A.: A visual interface for deal making. In: O'Grady, Michael J., Vahdat-Nejad, H., Wolf, K.-H., Dragone, M., Ye, J., Röcker, C., O'Hare, G. (eds.) AmI 2013. CCIS, vol. 413, pp. 205–212. Springer, Cham (2013). doi:10.1007/978-3-319-04406-4_20
2. Plewe, D., de Rooy, R.: Integrative deal-design: cascading from goal-hierarchies to negotiations and contracting. J. Strateg. Contracting Negot. (JSCAN) (2016)
3. Haapio, H.: Introduction to proactive law: a business lawyer's view. Scand. Stud. Law **49**, 21–34 (2006)
4. Passera, S., Haapio, H., Curtotti, M.: Making the meaning of contracts visible – automating contract visualization. In: Schweighofer, E., et al. (eds.) Transparency. Proceedings of the 17th International Legal Informatics, Symposium IRIS 2014, pp. 443–450. Österreichische Computer Gesellschaft OCG, Wien (2014)

5. Haapio, H., Plewe, D., de Rooy, R.: Next generation deal design: comics and visual platforms for contracting. In: Internationales Rechtsinformatik Symposion (IRIS), Salzburg, p. 8 (2016)
6. Mahler, T.: A graphical user interface for legal texts? In: Svantesson, D.H.B., Greenstein, S. (eds.) Internationalisation of Law in the Digital Information Society. Nordic Yearbook of Law and Informatics 2010–2012, pp. 311–327. Ex Tuto Publishing, Copenhagen (2013)
7. Wittgenstein, L.: Tractatus Logico-Philosophicus. Harcourt, Brace, New York (1922)
8. Martin, K.: Auditable Contracts: Moving from Literary Prose to Machine Code. http://legalexecutiveinstitute.com/auditable-contracts-moving-from-literary-prose-to-machine-code/. Accessed 2016
9. Ethereum Project: Ethereum. https://www.ethereum.org
10. Szabo, N.: Nick Szabo – the idea of smart contracts. In: Nick Szabo's Papers and Concise Tutorials. http://szabo.best.vwh.net/smart_contracts_idea.htm. Accessed 1997
11. Wong, M.W., Haapio, H., Deckers, S., Dhir, S.: Computational contract collaboration and construction. In: Schweighofer, E., et al. (eds.) Proceedings of the 18th International Legal Informatics Symposium IRIS 2015, pp. 505–512. Österreichische Computer Gesellschaft OCG, Wien, Vienna (2015)
12. Passera, S.: Enhancing contract usability and user experience through visualization - an experimental evaluation. In: Proceedings of the 16th International Conference on Information Visualisation, IV 2012, Montpellier (2012)
13. Lewis, D.: Counterfactuals and comparative possibility. J. Philos. Logic 2(4), 418 (1973)
14. Nelson, T.: Complex information processing: a file structure for the complex, the changing and the indeterminate. In: ACM/CSC-ER Proceedings of the 1965 20th National Conference (1965)
15. Plewe, D.A., Lee, H.: Simulating the outcomes of contracts: a visual interface supporting start-up financing. In: Kantola, J.I., Barath, T., Nazir, S., Andre, T. (eds.) Advances in Human Factors, Business Management, Training and Education. AISC, vol. 498, pp. 823–831. Springer, Cham (2017). doi:10.1007/978-3-319-42070-7_76
16. Lax, D., Sebenius, J.: 3-D negotiation: powerful tools to change the game in your most important deals (2006)

Understanding Color Risk Appropriateness: Influence of Color on a User's Decision to Comply with the IT Security Policy—Evidence from the U.S. and India

Mario Silic[1(✉)], Mato Njavro[1], and Goran Oblakovic[2]

[1] University of St. Gallen, St. Gallen, Switzerland
mario.silic@unisg.ch, mato.njavro@unisgh.ch
[2] Zagreb School of Economics and Management, Zagreb, Croatia
goblakov@zsem.hr

Abstract. Color is a complex visual and design element that can produce various emotional, psychological and physical outcomes that can be expressed through religious, cultural, political or social meanings. Past studies have confirmed that culture is an important and integral part of the decision-making process in which color appeal is a salient antecedent to behavioral intentions in culturally distinct countries. However, in the context of computer warning messages, we are lacking clear evidence of how color risk appropriateness (CRA) affects users' decision-making processes. Supported by the color-in-context theory, our research investigates the color risk appropriateness impact on the perceived risk in two different cultures. We found that different colors behave differently in the specific warning banner context in which CRA is an important antecedent to users' compliance. Overall, we advance current theoretical understanding on the color-risk dimension and its importance for the user's decision-making processes.

Keywords: Psychology of color · Warning banner message · User compliance

1 Introduction

Color is a complex visual and design element that can produce various emotional, psychological and physical outcomes that can be expressed through religious, cultural, political or social meanings. As such, color can play an important role in making informed decisions in which color meaning is associated with the cultural or real-world situations. Numerous studies confirmed this relationship showing that, for example, the impact of color on marketing drives product sales [1]. Interestingly, it was found that color has to "fit" or be "appropriate" to the product that it represents [2]. This suggests that people have some personal expectations about how the color environment should look, and, consequently, they try to find the best match between the expectations and the suggested color scheme. How to predict the color risk appropriateness (CRA) that would predict one's reaction [3] is an important aspect that has received little attention in the context of IT security.

© Springer International Publishing AG 2017
F.F.-H. Nah and C.-H. Tan (Eds.): HCIBGO 2017, PART II, LNCS 10294, pp. 412–423, 2017.
DOI: 10.1007/978-3-319-58484-3_32

The majority of the past studies [e.g., 4–7] investigated the role of color on eCommerce shopping behaviors, providing clear evidence that color drives consumer attitudes and behaviors towards purchasing. More recently, several studies have confirmed that culture is an important and integral part of the decision-making process in which color appeal (the degree to which colors are defined as pleasing and appealing) [4] is a salient antecedent to behavioral intentions in culturally distinct countries [8], but also that color has different arousal effects [9–12]. However, in the context of computer warning messages, we are lacking clear evidence of how color risk appropriateness affects users' decision-making processes. A computer warning message represents the communication designed to prevent users from hurting themselves or others [13] and, as such, are rather effective in assisting users throughout the decision-making process [14–16]. However, warning messages suffer from several shortcomings in which ignorance of the warning message seems to be the most important one [11, 17–19]. Although this ignorance can be explained by habituation, in reality, the number of studies that investigated the relationship between color risk appropriateness and users' cognitive decision-making processes is still relatively low. In other words, understanding how color fits in with culture-risk dimension (color risk appropriateness) that drives behavioral intentions when it comes to deciding whether to be compliant or not with IT security policy, in the presence of the warning message, can be an important factor influencing a user's security decisions.

In this research paper, we investigated the role of CRA, the Color Appeal and information fit-to-task on the behavioral intentions to be compliant with warning messages. More precisely, supported by the color-in-context theory, as suggested by Elliot and Maier [20], we intend to understand how CRA influences a user's decision-making process among cultural groups in the U.S. and China.

In the following sections, we present the theoretical background and propose our research model. Next, we describe the methodology and present the results. We conclude by discussing the results, implications and limitations of our study.

2 Theoretical Framework

2.1 Color-in-Context Theory

In the human decision-making process, the color red has various meanings: (1) danger or caution (e.g., red ink used for grading students [21]), (2) anger cue (e.g., person becomes red [22]), or (3) sex and romance (e.g., facilitates approaching potential mates [23]). Overall, the color red in humans can be associated with different situations in different contexts.

Recently, color-in-context theory [20] has been suggested to explain the relationship between color and psychological functioning. This theory explains that the influence of color on affect, cognition and behavior is a function of the psychological context in which the color is situated [24]. In other words, it could be that the red color will have a different arousal effect depending on the context or culture in which it is used. In other words, it could be that the color red is not the most appropriate in certain cultures in which red does not have the same meaning. Table 1 shows the color-culture chart for India and the U.S.

We can see that the color red has the same meaning associated with danger and caution in both cultures and that the color yellow has quite a different meaning among the U.S. and Indian cultures. Theory draws on social learning and biology in which we can expect to see responses to color stimuli based on the learning process in which we associate color with a particular message (0, in the driving context, humans, by default, associate red with danger and the word "STOP"). However, through the social learning process, we can often have different interpretations. For example, the color blue on a ribbon can be a positive sign that indicates a winning situation, while blue on a piece of meat has a negative connotation as it suggests that the meat is rotten [25].

Table 1. Color-Culture Chart for India and U.S.

Color	India	United States
Red	Color of purity, fertility, love, beauty, wealth, opulence and power, fear and fire	Danger, stop
Black	Evil, negativity, darkness, lack of appeal	Funerals, death, mourning
Yellow	Sacred and auspicious	Cowardice, temporary, happiness, joy, caution, warning of hazards and hazardous substances
White	Unhappiness, symbol of sorrow in death of family member, funerals, peace and purity	Purity

At its core, the color-in-context theory suggests that color can carry meaning that provides an explanation of psychological functioning that is context-specific and automatic. Overall, the theory argues that color does not contain the "feeling" component only, but is much more dynamic and can actively participate in the psychological reasoning and decision-making process.

Theory further explains that, in order to understand which meanings are associated with which colors, one has to go through the learning process in which associations have to be established. Human beings are constantly exposed to this learning process in which they are reminded about these associations (e.g., red warning stop sign).

However, one issue with this learning association process, in the warning message context, is that these associations are imposed on a global level and, as such, may not be the most effective in culturally distinct countries.

In this context, the question of the red color risk appropriateness can play an important role in the decision-making process when the user is confronted with the warning banner message. In the computer setting, it seems that most of the implementations of the user interfaces were simply copied from other areas where red is universally used as the color of danger [12]. Hence, what is expected is that the red color will motivate a protective behavior in which an individual confronted with a red warning message will trigger an avoidance motivation [26] leading to risk-averse behaviors [12].

2.2   Color, Decision-Making and Culture

The relationship among color, decision-making and culture is still in the early research stages in the IT security field. Although past research has already established a clear link between color and the decision-making processes [12] in the computer digital realm, we are still missing empirical validation regarding which colors are appropriate for the warning message context. Indeed, a study done by Silic, Cyr, Back and Holzer [8] found that color appeal is a significant predictor of the perceived risk and behavioral intentions to comply with the warning message content. The study revealed that color applications (red, yellow and green) are producing different effects in different cultures. For instance, red is the most appealing color in U.S. culture but not in the Indian culture. This is quite an interesting finding as it suggests that color plays a different role in a different cultural setup. However, one limitation of this study is that it does not identify which color is then the most appropriate to the risk situation that is represented by the warning message. Indeed, as highlighted in the study: "this indicates that another color application should be tested to understand if, for example, white is the most efficient color for the warning message context in Indian culture" [8, page 533].

As the warning message represents a risk-taking task in which the user is expected to make a binary decision (continue or exit), we can expect to see, similar to other contexts, behaviors that would trigger avoidance motivation or eventually contradictory effects in which color will cause risk-averse situations. Moreover, according to Wogalter, Conzola and Smith-Jackson [27], "warning components that are effective in one culture may not be effective in others, it is important to do cross-cultural testing of warnings whenever appropriate and possible."

Overall, we aim to understand the following research question: which color applications are the most appropriate to the specific cultural setting in the specific warning message context?

3   Hypothesis Development

Relationships between Color Risk Appropriateness, Color Appeal, Information fit-to-task and Perceived Risk (PR)

Color risk appropriateness is the degree to which color reflects its fit to culture regarding the level of the risk perception. It is about how much the color application effectively transmits the risk associated with certain actions and if it adequately meets the cultural risk perceptions. For example, if red represents danger in a particular cultural environment, then we can expect that the red color will have a higher degree of CRA and will consequently be associated with danger or a risky situation. As PR is measuring the degree of putting one's information, data or computer at risk (Johnston & Warkentin, 2010), then we can expect that CRA will positively influence the perceived risk. Hence, we hypothesize:

H1: Color risk appropriateness will have a positive impact on perceived risk.

Further, if the warning message itself, in which color represents an important design element, is visually pleasing, appealing and has a design that meets viewers' expectations, then we can expect that the risk of being non-compliant with the action proposed by the warning message will be affected in such a way that higher color appeal will be positively related to PR. Also, as CRA reflects the fit-to-culture dimension, we argue that higher CRA will lead to higher color appeal. As PR brings the situation of uncertainty about negative consequences and usually leads to losses [28], in the warning message content, this loss would be represented by clicking on the continue button, which would suggest that the user may incur possible negative consequences (e.g., being affected by malicious software) as result of his/her action. This would suggest that, for example, if the yellow color in Indian culture is an appropriate color to signal the risk, then we would expect to see a positive impact on the perceived risk level in the Indian culture. Clearly, in different cultural contexts, we can expect to see different user reactions based on their color preferences when it comes to the right level of CRA [29–31]. Hence, we argue that color appeal will positively influence risk appropriateness. Therefore, we hypothesize:

H2: Color appeal will have a positive impact on color risk appropriateness.

One issue with warning message content is that it may contain words or phrases that can be difficult to understand by the typical user with limited IT knowledge. That is, many users may not know what "SSL" or "malware" keywords mean, which can cause some content interpretation issues. In that situation, users may not be able to decide which action to take (continue or exit), based on the content of the warning message, as they cannot fully understand it. This is why the understanding of the warning content can be of high importance. This would mean that the warning information is effective and provides enough information to make the right decision. Information-fit-to-task represents the level of understanding of the warning content and if the warning, as such, is effective in transmitting the right information [32]. Here, color is also part of the "information" system together with the message content. Hence, we hypothesize:

H3: Information-fit-to-task will have a positive impact on CRA.

The Relationship between Perceived Risk and Behavior Intention (BI)
Past research has already demonstrated that, in the warning message context, we can expect to see positive relationships between PR and BI [8]. Behavior intention refers to paying attention to the security risks by exercising caution and terminating actions that may lead to potentially dangerous and risky situations [33]. Overall, PR is influencing the user's decisions [34], where the risk of putting one's information and data is associated with the behavioral intentions in such a way that the user will either try to avoid the risky behavior (leading to abandonment of his/her actions) or will, on the contrary, continue his/her actions despite the possible negative consequences. We argue that, in the warning message content, similar to past studies [e.g. 35], PR will be positively associated with BI. Hence, we hypothesize:

H4: Perceived risk will have a positive impact on behavioral intention.

The Relationship between Culture and Color Risk Appropriateness
According to the cultural relativism, color perception is driven [36, 37] by different associations and the learning process in which user expectations have to be met. For

example, Google translated its search engine website into most of the local languages as this was the expectation of its users and something that facilitates the learning and adoption processes. This cultural component seems to be an important criterion that is influencing the psychological reasoning, as suggested by the color-in-context theory. Consequently, in a different cultural context, we can expect to have a different influence on the relationship between CRA and PR. Moreover, taking into account the existing issue of habituation with warning messages, we can expect that some standard colors (e.g., red) will not be positively associated with PR. In addition, supported by the color-in-context theory, we argue that some colors (e.g., yellow) may have quite a different impact on the risk perception in the U.S. and Indian cultures. Hence, we hypothesize:

H5: The influence of CRA on PR will be influenced by cultural dimension with a different impact depending on the color application (black, red, yellow or red).

Our research model is depicted on Fig. 1.

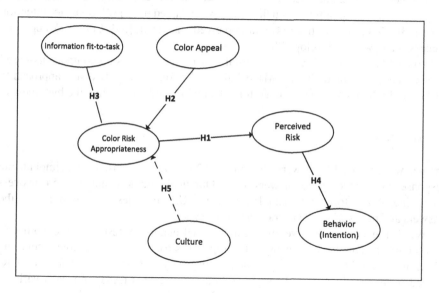

Fig. 1. Research model

4 Research Design

4.1 Participants, Measures and Procedures

To test our research model, we used participants recruited from Amazon Mechanical Turk. Each participant had to visit a web link in which, after a few seconds, a warning message was displayed, represented by one of four different color applications (black, red, white or yellow). A standard warning message from Google Chrome (Fig. 2) was used. After acknowledging the warning message, participants were taken to an online survey in which they had to provide answers to the questions related to the warning message they saw. The choice of the four color applications is based on the color-culture chart as proposed by [38], but also on the past studies that have found these colors to be the most appealing in the U.S. and Indian cultures [e.g., 8–10, 12].

Fig. 2. Warning message displayed (adapted from Google Chrome version 46)

All measures were adapted from past studies, wherever possible, and measured on a 7-point Likert scale. Information fit-to-task was adapted from [32], Behavior Intention from [33], Color Appeal from [4] and Perceived Risk from [39]. Color risk appropriateness is a new item developed for this study.

To analyze our model, we used Partial Least Squares (PLS), a components-based structural equation modeling (SEM) technique. We followed the two-step approach to SEM [40] by first assessing the overall model quality and then testing the hypotheses.

5   Results

In total, we received 382 answers. We removed 28 for various reasons (e.g., implausible response times, incomplete answers, etc.). Our final sample contained 354 answers consisting of 193 from India and 161 from the U.S. Females comprised 133 of the answers and males 221. The average age was 38.4.

We then examined the overall research model quality by testing the reliability of measurement items for each construct (Cronbach's α), and checking convergent and discriminant validity using principal components analysis. Composite reliabilities (CR) ranged from 0.8027 to 0.9562. Average variance extracted (AVE) for each variable construct was higher than the recommended 0.5 [41]. To establish discriminant validity, we calculated the square root of the reflective construct's AVE and checked that the AVE of each latent construct was higher than the construct's highest-squared correlation. As the calculations did not reveal any lower AVE, we concluded that the discriminant validity test had been established. We also calculated variance inflation factors (VIFs) and found, as per [42, 43] recommendation, no value higher than 5. Hence, this provided evidence that we do not have multicollinearity issue. Finally, we checked for cross-loadings by making sure that the construct's loading was higher than any other cross-loading of the indicator with other constructs. All constructs were higher than the suggested 0.7 value.

At the end, we wanted to be sure that we did not have any issue with the common method bias as we collected answers from single respondents. We used two procedures:

Harman's single-factor test [44, 45] and the statistical approach developed by [46]. Both tests showed that the common method bias is not an issue for this study.

5.1 Analysis of Models

In Table 2 below, we report the results from the full model and results per each country for all four color applications:

Table 2. Model analysis

		IFT->CRA	CA->CRA	CRA->PR	PR->BI
Full sample(n=355)					
	Path coefficient	0.215	0.588	0.292	0.486
	t-Value	4.252	9.658	5.651	10.793
	R^2	0.532	0.532	0.085	0.237
India					
Black N=46	Path coefficient	0.225	0.582	0.528	0.463
	t-Value	1.461	3.762	4.664	4.697
White N=51	Path coefficient	0.065	0.730	0.319	0.538
	t-Value	0.549	6.671	2.044	5.347
Red N=56	Path coefficient	0.370	0.363	0.210	0.543
	t-Value	2.888	1.831	1.702	6.479
Yellow N=40	Path coefficient	0.567	0.115	0.260	0.478
	t-Value	2.659	0.472	1.245	3.948
US					
Black N=42	Path coefficient	0.043	0.786	-0.026	0.543
	t-Value	0.319	8.001	0.181	2.986
White N=43	Path coefficient	0.040	0.759	0.604	0.533
	t-Value	0.269	7.365	5.724	3.233
Red N=40	Path coefficient	0.369	0.554	0.250	0.587
	t-Value	3.191	5.612	1.845	5.883
Yellow N=36	Path coefficient	0.383	0.579	0.553	0.481
	t-Value	3.176	4.484	4.332	3.529

Note: significant paths are indicated in the grey color

From the results, we observed that the full model is supported across all relationships with all path coefficients being positive. The corresponding t-values for each relationship were statistically significant. When it comes to country model testing, we saw different results. Comparing India's black color application to the U.S., we could see that the black CA->CRA and CRA->PR relationships were positive and significant in the India sample, while, for the U.S., CRA->PR was not significant (t-value = 0.181), while color seemed to produce the same effects for both countries with all relationships being positive and significant except for IFT->CRA, which is not supported. Interestingly, the color red was not significant for CA->CRA and CRA->PR in the India sample and for CRA->PR in the U.S. sample. Finally, the color yellow was not significant for CA->CRA and CRA->PR in India's case but fully supported and positive in the U.S. sample. Further, we can observe that, for the Indian culture, CRA->PR is supported for black and white colors, and, for the U.S. culture, CRA->PR is supported for white and yellow.

Overall, from the results presented in Table 2, we concluded that H1, H2, H3 and H4 are supported. Also, H5 is supported as we found different color applications to have a different effect on the relationship between CRA->PR.

6   Discussion, Limitations and Future Studies

Supported by the color-in-context theory, our research was aimed at analyzing the impact of CRA on PR and consequently on the behavioral intentions to comply with the warning banner message. In the next sections, we derive theoretical and practical implications of our study.

We found that all of our hypothesized relationships are supported. In particular, we found that CRA is positively associated with PR. This is an interesting finding as it suggests that the right choice of the color is an important factor in the user's decision-making process. Indeed, if a higher degree of the color appeal is achieved, higher color appropriateness to the risk dimension will be obtained. Consequently, these relationships will positively influence the degree of the CRA on PR, which in turn, will influence the intention to be compliant with the warning message suggestion.

Past research has introduced the color appeal construct [4], which provided an initial understanding of the appeal of the warning message, but, in our research, we offer a more advanced view of the color-risk dimension through the new construct of CRA. This is an important insight for future theorizing as we uniquely positioned the color-in-context theory in the warning message context demonstrating that color plays an important role in the user's decision-making process. Further, we found that culture plays a vital role in defining the right choice of the color design element being an integral part of the warning message.

In that context, some unexpected findings were revealed. To start, we did not find any support for our hypothesis for the CRA to PR relationship in the U.S. sample. This suggests that the red color is not efficient. This can be explained by the habituation effect, which is most likely causing this insignificant effect of the red color. This is even more pronounced in the Indian sample in which red is neither appealing nor appropriate to transmit the risk. Conversely, the white color is appealing and appropriate in Indian and U.S. cultures, suggesting that white is less influenced by the habituation effect. However, this finding has to be taken with precaution as it could be that users were simply surprised to see an unexpected color (e.g., white as opposed to red), and, consequently, they reacted with more precaution, stopping their behavior. The other two colors (black and yellow) received mixed attention from users. While yellow was found to be appealing and an efficient color to transmit risk in the U.S., yellow was fully ignored in the Indian culture. Finally, black was found to be a good risk color in Indian culture but not in U.S. culture (even having a negative relationship with the perceived risk).

Overall, these insights are important in order to better understand how risk-color dimension behaves in the unique warning message context. Indeed, by better understanding how different cultures react to different colors in a specific context, it would also be possible to better predict users' behaviors when it comes to their decision-making processes.

These findings suggest that user interface designers should take into account the importance of the cultural dimension and adapt the look and feel of the warning message. One recent example of such an action is the introduction of the yellow warning message in Google Chrome. However, this would most likely work only in the U.S. culture and could be less efficient in other cultures. Clearly, software programmers need to be more cautious during the product design phase since there is currently only one way to approach the topic of the warning messages in different cultures, which does not seem to be efficient in preventing hazards from occurring.

Future research should include more cultures in order to fully validate our findings. Also, it would be interesting to see more color-based research in other security contexts, such as anti-virus or other warning base contexts, to understand users' behaviors and expectations. Our research also has several limitations. We did not use the "deception" approach but relied on the answers from participants, which could reduce the accuracy of the study. Also, we did not test which colors are the most efficient to be used in a given culture but rather focused on the risk appropriateness of the color.

7 Conclusion

Supported by the color-in-context theory, our research investigates the color risk appropriateness impact on the perceived risk in two different cultures. We found that different colors behave differently in the specific warning banner context in which CRA is an important antecedent to users' compliance. Overall, we advance current theoretical understanding on the color-risk dimension and its importance for the user's decision-making processes.

References

1. Singh, S.: Impact of color on marketing. Manag. Decis. **44**, 783–789 (2006)
2. Bottomley, P.A., Doyle, J.R.: The interactive effects of colors and products on perceptions of brand logo appropriateness. Mark. Theory **6**, 63–83 (2006)
3. Fernández-vázquez, R., Stinco, C.M., Meléndez-martínez, A.J., Heredia, F.J., Vicario, I.M.: Visual and instrumental evaluation of orange juice color: a consumers'preference study. J. Sens. Stud. **26**, 436–444 (2011)
4. Cyr, D., Head, M., Larios, H.: Colour appeal in website design within and across cultures: a multi-method evaluation. Int. J. Hum Comput Stud. **68**, 1–21 (2010)
5. Sokolik, K., Magee, R.G., Ivory, J.D.: Red-hot and ice-cold web ads: the influence of web ads' warm and cool colors on click-through rates. J. Interact. Advertising **14**, 31–37 (2014)

6. Bagchi, R., Cheema, A.: The effect of red background color on willingness-to-pay: the moderating role of selling mechanism. J. Consum. Res. **39**, 947–960 (2013)

7. Conway, C.M., Pelet, J.-E., Papadopoulou, P., Limayem, M.: Coloring in the lines: using color to change the perception of quality in e-commerce sites. In: ICIS, p. 224 (2010)

8. Silic, M., Cyr, D., Back, A., Holzer, A.: Effects of color appeal, perceived risk and culture on user's decision in presence of warning banner message. In: Proceedings of the 50th Hawaii International Conference on System Sciences (2017)

9. Silic, M.: Understanding colour impact on warning messages: evidence from us and India. In: Proceedings of the 2016 CHI Conference Extended Abstracts on Human Factors in Computing Systems, pp. 2954–2960. ACM (2016)

10. Silic, M., Cyr, D.: Colour arousal effect on users' decision-making processes in the warning message context. In: Nah, F.F.-H.F.-H., Tan, C.-H. (eds.) HCIBGO 2016. LNCS, vol. 9752, pp. 99–109. Springer, Cham (2016). doi:10.1007/978-3-319-39399-5_10

11. Silic, M., Barlow, J., Ormond, D.: Warning! a comprehensive model of the effects of digital information security warning messages. In: The 2015 Dewald Roode Workshop on Information Systems Security Research, pp. 1–32. IFIP (2015)

12. Silic, M., Silic, D., Oblakovic, G.: The effects of colour on users'compliance with warning banner messages across cultures. In: ECIS. ECIS (2016)

13. Wogalter, M.S.: Purposes and scope of warnings. In: Handbook of Warnings, pp. 3–9. Lawrence Erlbaum Associates, Mahwah (2006)

14. Coleman, S.: The Minnesota income tax compliance experiment: replication of the social norms experiment. SSRN 1393292 (2007)

15. Goldstein, N.J., Cialdini, R.B., Griskevicius, V.: A room with a viewpoint: using social norms to motivate environmental conservation in hotels. J. Consum. Res. **35**, 472–482 (2008)

16. Schultz, P., Tabanico, J.J.: Criminal beware: a social norms perspective on posting public warning signs*. Criminology **47**, 1201–1222 (2009)

17. Akhawe, D., Felt, A.P.: Alice in Warningland: a large-scale field study of browser security warning effectiveness. In: Usenix Security, pp. 257–272 (2013)

18. Sunshine, J., Egelman, S., Almuhimedi, H., Atri, N., Cranor, L.F.: Crying wolf: an empirical study of SSL warning effectiveness. In: USENIX Security Symposium, pp. 399–416 (2009)

19. Silic, M., Back, A.: Deterrent effects of warnings on user's behavior in preventing malicious software use. In: Proceedings of the 50th Hawaii International Conference on System Sciences, Hawaii (2017)

20. Elliot, A.J., Maier, M.A.: Color-in-context theory. Adv. Exp. Soc. Psychol. **45**, 61–125 (2012)

21. Elliot, A.J., Maier, M.A., Moller, A.C., Friedman, R., Meinhardt, J.: Color and psychological functioning: the effect of red on performance attainment. J. Exp. Psychol. Gen. **136**, 154 (2007)

22. Fetterman, A.K., Robinson, M.D., Gordon, R.D., Elliot, A.J.: Anger as seeing red: Perceptual sources of evidence. Soc. Psychol. Pers. Sci. **2**(3), 311–316 (2010). doi: 10.1177/1948550610390051

23. Bielert, C., Girolami, L., Jowell, S.: An experimental examination of the colour component in visually mediated sexual arousal of the male chacma baboon (Papio ursinus). J. Zool. **219**, 569–579 (1989)

24. Meier, B.P., D'agostino, P.R., Elliot, A.J., Maier, M.A., Wilkowski, B.M.: Color in context: psychological context moderates the influence of red on approach-and avoidance-motivated behavior. PLoS ONE **7**, e40333 (2012)

25. Elliot, A.J.: Color and psychological functioning: a review of theoretical and empirical work. Front. Psychol. **6**, 368 (2015)

26. Maier, M.A., Elliot, A.J., Lichtenfeld, S.: Mediation of the negative effect of red on intellectual performance. Pers. Soc. Psychol. Bull. **34**(11), 1530–1540 (2008)

27. Wogalter, M.S., Conzola, V.C., Smith-Jackson, T.L.: Research-based guidelines for warning design and evaluation. Appl. Ergonomics **33**, 219–230 (2002)
28. Cunningham, S.M.: The major dimensions of perceived risk. In: Risk Taking and Information Handling in Consumer Behavior, pp. 82–108 (1967)
29. McKnight, D.H., Choudhury, V., Kacmar, C.: Developing and validating trust measures for e-commerce: an integrative typology. Inf. Syst. Res. **13**, 334–359 (2002)
30. Singh, N., Zhao, H., Hu, X.: Cultural adaptation on the web: a study of American companies' domestic and Chinese websites. J. Global Inf. Manage. (JGIM) **11**, 63–80 (2003)
31. Lin, C.S., Wu, S., Tsai, R.J.: Integrating perceived playfulness into expectation-confirmation model for web portal context. Inf. Manag. **42**, 683–693 (2005)
32. Loiacono, E.T., Watson, R.T., Goodhue, D.L.: WebQual: an instrument for consumer evaluation of web sites. Int. J. Electron. Commer. **11**, 51–87 (2007)
33. Ng, B.-Y., Kankanhalli, A., Xu, Y.C.: Studying users' computer security behavior: a health belief perspective. Decis. Support Syst. **46**, 815–825 (2009)
34. Antony, S., Lin, Z., Xu, B.: Determinants of escrow service adoption in consumer-to-consumer online auction market: an experimental study. Decis. Support Syst. **42**, 1889–1900 (2006)
35. Gewald, H., Dibbern, J.: Risks and benefits of business process outsourcing: a study of transaction services in the German banking industry. Inf. Manag. **46**, 249–257 (2009)
36. Berlin, B., Kay, P.: Basic Color Terms: Their Universality and Evolution. University of California Press, Los Angeles (1991)
37. Kay, P., Berlin, B., Merrifield, W.: Biocultural implications of systems of color naming. J. Linguist. Anthropol. **1**, 12–25 (1991)
38. Russo, P., Boor, S.: How fluent is your interface? Designing for international users. In: Proceedings of the INTERACT 1993 and CHI 1993 Conference on Human Factors in Computing Systems, pp. 342–347. ACM (1993)
39. Johnston, A.C., Warkentin, M.: Fear appeals and information security behaviors: an empirical study. MIS Q. **34**(3), 549–566 (2010)
40. Anderson, J.C., Gerbing, D.W.: Structural equation modeling in practice: a review and recommended two-step approach. Psychol. Bull. **103**, 411 (1988)
41. Fornell, C., Larcker, D.F.: Evaluating structural equation models with unobservable variables and measurement error. J. Mark. Res. (JMR) **18**, 39–50 (1981)
42. Hair, J.F.: Multivariate Data Analysis. Prentice Hall, Upper Saddle River (2009)
43. Kline, R.B.: Principles and Practice of Structural Equation Modeling. Guilford Press, New York (2011)
44. Podsakoff, P.M., MacKenzie, S.B., Lee, J.-Y., Podsakoff, N.P.: Common method biases in behavioral research: a critical review of the literature and recommended remedies. J. Appl. Psychol. **88**, 879 (2003)
45. Podsakoff, P.M., Organ, D.W.: Self-reports in organizational research: problems and prospects. J. Manag. **12**, 531–544 (1986)
46. Liang, H., Saraf, N., Hu, Q., Xue, Y.: Assimilation of enterprise systems: the effect of institutional pressures and the mediating role of top management. MIS Q. **31**, 59–87 (2007)

Not All Books in the User Profile Are Created Equal: Measuring the Preference "Representativeness" of Books in aNobii Online Bookshelves

Muh-Chyun Tang[⊠], Tzu-Kun Hsiao, and I-An Ou

Department of Library and Information Science, National Taiwan University,
No. 1, Section 4, Roosevelt Road, Taipei 10617, Taiwan
muhchyun@gmail.com, c9118061@gmail.com

Abstract. The study proposes a novel construct of "representativeness" that aims to measure the degree to which a book in the user's online bookshelf is able to represent his/her reading preference, based on the assumption that not all books are equally important when it comes to constructing individual users' preference profiles. Thirty-five online bookshelf aNobii users were recruited, who were asked to perform a judgment task involving evaluating the degree of "representativeness" and "involvement" of 10 books self-selected from their bookshelves. The results show that there is a high correlation between "representativeness' and "involvement", a well-established construct in marketing. Book similarity networks for every participants was generated based on book co-ownership data extracted from aNobii. Two social network analytical (SNA) metrics: coreness and connectivity, were then applied to measure a book's "representativeness" relative to the individual bookshelves. Results show that there were significant correlations between the SNA metrics and the user's self-assessed "representativeness" and "involvement" of the books. Furthermore, it was found the correlations were stronger among bookshelves owned by users who have low reading diversity.

Keywords: User profile · Recommender system · Coreness · Representativeness · Involvement

1 Introduction

Recommender system can greatly complement searching as a means of information access in two ways: firstly, they are particularly effective when users' information needs are ill-defined and difficult to express by queries, such is often the case in searching for leisure readings or other imaginary works. Secondly, they greatly increase opportunities for serendipitous finds by proposing items that might otherwise be unknown to the user. It is often less satisfactory to use subject-based access for imaginative works such as movies and fictions as it is certain viewing or reading experience, rather than topical knowledge, that users are seeking (Ross 1999; Lancaster 2003).

© Springer International Publishing AG 2017
F.F.-H. Nah and C.-H. Tan (Eds.): HCIBGO 2017, PART II, LNCS 10294, pp. 424–433, 2017.
DOI: 10.1007/978-3-319-58484-3_33

Using users' past viewed or purchased items as their preference profile, collaborative filtering system rely heavily on similarity measures between items and users to generate recommendation lists. The success of recommender system therefore depends very much on the accurate construction of user profiles. Yet users' profile can be incomplete, due to lack of inputs, or erroneous, due to one-time consumptions that do not necessarily reflect their more stable or durable preference. For example, the users of Amazon.com are given the option to provide feedbacks such as "This is a gift", or "Don't use for recommendations" on the recommended items to rule out titles not representative of their actual preference. Or as the popularity of compiling one's "desert island albums" attests, there are certain works we hold dearer to heart than the rest, works we are particularly fond of that we would not want to live without when if we were to be cast away on a desert island. In other words, not all the items in users' profiles are created equal, some are more central to his or her reading preference than others. One wonders whether the representative of books in one's reading profile is graded and can be measured.

Indeed, a graded membership view of an item to a category has long been held by "prototype" and "exemplar" theories in cognitive psychology. The prototype view of concept, as opposed the traditional rule-based view, states that different member of the same category vary in how typical they are to a concept (Rosch 1975). The similarity between an item and its categorical prototype was found to correlate with the ratings given by the subjects about how good an example the item is of its category (Rosch 1975). On the same token, one might argue that each book can be measured by how good it is able to represent a user's reading profile. While sharing the emphasis on resemblance in categorization, the exemplar theory argues that a new stimulus is compared to multiple "exemplars," as opposed an abstract prototype, stored in one's memory (Smith and Medin 1981). The question is then, in our context of generating better recommendations, are there also "exemplars" in one's memory/profile of past consumptions that best represent his/her reading preference? Following the graded membership of item in a concept, items with high "representativeness" can be considered as exemplars of one's preference. If that is the case, a weighing scheme that take into account the "representativeness" of the items in the profile when computing item-item or user-user similarity might help generate better recommendation lists.

2 Problem Statement

The objective of this study is to explore the construct of "representativeness", which is defined as the degree to which an item in a user's profile is able to represent his/her central and enduring preference. Specifically, it seeks to find out, firstly, from the user's perspective, whether there are discernible differences in the proposed "representativeness" construct among books in their bookshelves. Secondly, we wish to examine how well a book's "representativeness" agrees with its perceived "involvement, a well-established consumer psychological constructs in marketing. This is based on the assumption that readers tend to be more knowledgeable and emotionally engaged with books highly representative to their preference. Thirdly, how can the construct of "representativeness" of a book be measured non-obtrusively by social network analytical measures?

Our approach to the third question involves generating item-item similarity networks composed of books in one's bookshelf in order to represent an individual's reading profile. Various centrality-based measures were then to be applied to test how well they agree with the proposed "representativeness" construct. While centrality has been used as an indication of power or prestige an actor enjoys in its sociological origin, it has also been applied in the bibliometrics context for the measurement of the importance of a publication. For example e, betweenness centrality has been used to measure the degree of interdisciplinarity of scientific journals (Leydesdorff 2007). PageRank was used as a centrality measure previously to test whether an item's PageRank influences its sale in the "consumers bought this also bought" network in Amazon.com (Oestreicher-Singer and Sundararajan 2012). We suspect that books of high representativeness should occupy the central or core position in the network generated by book-book similarity relations in one's reading profile, based on the assumption that they are somewhat similar with each other, with similarity being defined by their co-occurrences in all the bookshelves in aNobii. One can imagine books that meet one's preference do not necessary share one common essential feature, such as genre, topics, or style, but are still likely to interconnect with each other in a "family resemblance" manner by a series of overlapping similarities. It therefore stands to reasonable ground to infer that the more involved a book is in the relations that connect the network, the more likely it is representative to the user's reading preference.

An ancillary question related to the SNA approach to the measuring of "representativeness" is whether the centrality based measures are universally applicable in all network typologies. One can imagine that the item-item similarity networks in users' reading profile might vary in terms of their degree of centralization and how they resemble a core-periphery network structure (Borgatti and Everett 2000). In our context, a clear core-periphery structure suggests a single core of reading interest consisting of books densely connected with one another where the centrality based measure would perform better. A scattered network, on the other hand, might suggest a more diverse reading interests where books highly representative to one's reading interests might not necessarily be cohesively interconnected themselves. How diverse one's reading interests might be a moderator in the correlations proposed above. It is therefore hypothesized that the proposed centrality based measures can better predict a book's representative when users' reading interests are less diverse, without the presence of a clear "core."

3   Methodology

3.1   Platform and Subjects

The online bookshelf aNobii was chosen as the test site for our study for it has attracted a relatively large user community in Taiwan where the study was conducted. Subject recruiting information was posted in the aNobii social network and book related forums in a campus-based online bulletin board system popular among college students. A total of 35 regular aNobii users participated in the study, all of whom met the criteria of having at least five "friends" and eighty titles in their bookshelves. One of the bookshelf data file was damaged in the data extracting process therefore the results were based on 34 valid bookshelves.

3.2 Procedures

The participants were first asked to answer questions regarding their reading habits and diversity of reading interests in the entry questionnaire. They were then asked to select 10 books from their aNobii bookshelf, 7 of which they believed to match their reading preference, the rest 3 did not. An item-based questionnaire were administrated to the selected books in which they were to answer, for each book the question "how do you think this title is able to represent your reading interest?" as well as three other questions regarding their perceived involvement of each book selected, all based on a 1–7 scale.

With the participants' consent, the bibliographic data of the books in their bookshelves were downloaded, including title, author, as well as the ID of other aNobii users who also owned the books. All the books owned by the participants were retrieved and the owner list for each book were identified. By comparing the owner lists, a similarity network composed of all the books owned by the participants can then be calculated using the normalized Jaccard similarity coefficient (See Fig. 1). Using normalized interaction by the smaller of the two sets allows us to rescale the similarity values into the range between 0 and 1, however, it also causes "false" similarity in some case when two rare books are owned by only a reader resulting in a perfect score of 1 even though they might be very different from each other. To rectify this chance induced similarity, such cases were ruled out from further analyses. A "global" network was then constructed with the nodes being the titles, and the edge, the similarity score between pairs of books.

$$\left| \frac{A \cap B}{Min\ (A,B)} \right|, \quad A \cap B > 1$$

Fig. 1. Normalized interaction similarity. Where A, B stand for the set of owners how have included title A and B in their bookshelves.

With the global network in place, we were then able to extract "local" networks composed of books appearing in each participating user's online bookshelf, which was then used to represent his/her reading profile. Centrality-based analyses were applied to the individual local networks to ascertain the centrality scores of the books judged by the participants. Correlation analyses were then be performed between network-based metrics and the constructs of involvement and "representativeness."

4 Results

4.1 Descriptive Statistics

Participants. The majority of the participants are female (32 out of 35), with an average age of 24.83. They tended to be avid readers with regular reading habit. The number of books in the participants' bookshelves range from 80 to 2379, with a medium of 238.

Self-assessed involvement and "representativeness". A book "representativeness" was created based on the question "how do you think this title is able to represent your reading interest?" on a 1–7 scale in the item-based questionnaire. Table 1 gives the descriptive data of the representativeness scores in high and low representative groups judged by the participants. As for "involvement" with each title, the participants were asked to answer the following questions: "Reading this kind of book always brings me lots of joy", "I am very interested in this kind of books", and "This kind of books mean a great deal to me." The Cronbach's α for these involvement-related items was .901, indicating high scale reliability. The average of the scores for these questions was then used as the "involvement" score. A high correlation was found between these two constructs ($r = .789$, $p < .000$).

Table 1. Representativeness score in high and low representative groups

	Mean	SD
Non-representative	2.56	1.19
Representative	6.16	0.67

4.2 Correlation Between Self-assessed and Network-Based Metrics

Two network-based methods were used to measure the importance of a title in each individual bookshelf: coreness score and connectivity. According to Borgatti and Everett (2000) a core-periphery structure is made up of a subgroup of core actors who are densely connected and a group of periphery actors who are sparely connected. The numerical core/periphery procedure in UCIENT was performed as the edges were weighted (Borgatti et al. 2002) in order to determine which titles selected belong to the "core" and which are in the periphery. A binary coreness variable was created based on the partition output, with core being coded as 1. Likewise a binary variable was created based on the participants' judgment whether a title is or is not representative to their preference. As Table 2 shows, significant correlations were found between this binary representativeness score and coreness (.173, $p < .01$) and involvement scores (.192, $p < .01$), though the correlations are low (See Table 2).

The connectivity measure was created based on the strength of connection of each book to the main component. As the individual networks thus extracted constitutes a complete graph, for all the books in a bookshelf are co-owned as least once, namely, the bookshelves owner themselves. Proper threshold needs to be determined in order to filter out spurious linkages, i.e. books were linked based on global co-ownership but

Table 2. Correlations between SNA based measure and representativeness and involvement

	Coreness	Connectivity
Representativeness	.185**	.283***
Involvement	.191**	.282***

** $p < .01$, *** $p < .001$

were not truly similar to each other. By gradually raising the threshold at the intervals of .1, the network grows to be less cohesive as items less well-connected are separated from the main component. Books that are disconnected from the giant component at the lower thresholds are then considered less "centralized", or less representative to the user's reading profile. Thus the threshold at which a book was disconnected from the rest of the network was used as a measure for its "representativeness" with regard to one's reading profile. For example, if a book was found disconnected from the giant component at the threshold of .8, its "connectivity" value would be .8, which is assumed to occupy a more central position than a book that was separated at the threshold of, say, .2. Correlation analysis was then conducted between this "connectivity" value and the involvement and the representativeness scores (both of which are numerical). As Table 2 shows, "connectivity" was found to be significantly correlate with both constructs (See Table 2).

4.3 The Moderating Role of "Preference Diversity"

In the entry questionnaire, the participants were asked four questions designed to measure the construct of "preference diversity" (Tang 2014), which are: "My reading interests are rather stable", "I have wide reading interests", "I follow faithfully certain authors or genres", and "I actively search for authors or genres I am not familiar with." The Cronbach's α for these diversity-related items was .823 indicating high scale reliability. A self-perceived reading diversity score was generated by taking the average of the scores in the four items. Following (Ziegler et al. 2005; Zhang et al. 2012), we measured the diversity within a set of titles by averaging intra-list pair-wise similarity of books in each bookshelf. A significant negative correlation was found (r. $-.249$, $p < .05$) between the self-perceived reading diversity and the average similarities of pairs of books in the bookshelf, which lends support to the validity of the construct. As mentioned earlier, we suspect that the degree to which the centrality or coreness measures is able to reflect the representativeness of the title is conditioned on the individual's reading diversity. It is hypothesized that the more diverse the users' reading interests are, the lower the correlation between the self-accessed and

Table 3. Descriptive statistics of high and low diversity groups

	Diversity	
	High (N = 17)	Low (N = 17)
Diversity score	4.14 (SD = 1.28)	3.59 (SD = 1.01)
Average book similarity	0.09 (SD = 0.01)	0.16 (SD = 0.03)

Table 4. Correlation between self-assessed representativeness network metrics split by high and low reading diversity

	Coreness		"Connectivity"	
	High diversity	Low diversity	High diversity	Low diversity
Self-assessed representativeness	.053	.294***	.274***	.301***

* $p < .05$, ** $p < .01$, *** $p < .001$

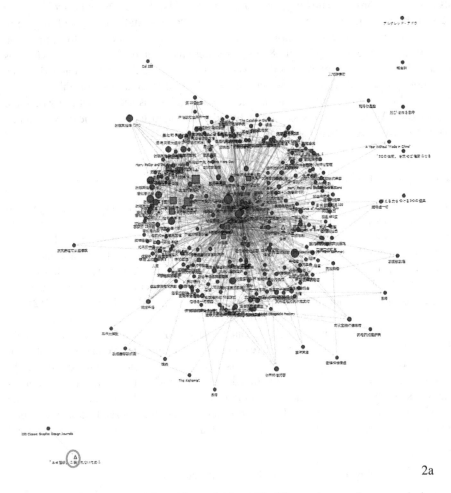

2a

Fig. 2. Comparison of network positions of titles with different degree of coreness in low vs high reading diversity bookshelves (Color figure online)

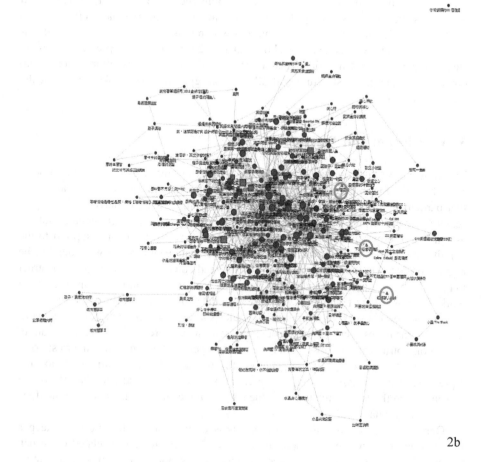

2b

Fig. 2. (continued)

network-based representativeness would be. To test the hypothesis, the participants were split into high and low preference diversity group by the overall mean (See Table 3 for descriptive statistics of the two groups).

Correlation analysis was then conducted between self-assessed representativeness and both coreness and connectivity based measures. For coreness, a significant correlation was found only in the low diversity (.300) but not the high preference diversity group (.047). As for "connectivity", a slightly higher correlation was found in the low diversity group (.301) compared to .274 in the high diversity group (See Table 4).

Two bookshelf networks, one belongs to reader with low reading diversity (Fig. 1a) and high reading diversity (Fig. 1b) were visualized to demonstrate the moderating effect of reading diversity. A threshold of .7 was set to dichotomize the edge values to improve readability of the graphs. The size of node signifies its coreness. The books selected to be representative to one's preference are in red square, and non-representative books, in yellow triangle. In both networks, non-representative books are much smaller in size, indicating low coreness score. A more clearly delineated core-periphery structure was shown in Fig. 2a, with a non-representative book clearly separated from the giant component. In Fig. 2b, on the contrary, there is no obvious core-periphery structure and all the non-representative books remain in the giant components.

5 Conclusion and Discussion

The construct of "representativeness" aimed to measure the degree to which a title in one's bookshelf is able to reflect his/her reading preference was proposed. It was shown that participants had no difficulty selecting titles from their bookshelves either representative or non-representative to their reading preference. They were equally able to assigning representative scores to the selected books, which lend some support to the validity of the construct. Furthermore, the "representativeness" score was found to be highly correlated to involvement, a well-established consumer psychological construct that, to the best of our knowledge, has yet to be used to apply in the realm of creative works such as leisure readings in our case. Another novel aspect of the study is to use item-similarity network to represent a reader's preference profile. Social network analytical measures were applied to explore way to capture a title's "representativeness" non-obtrusively by observe its network properties. Two network metrics: coreness and "connectivity" were shown to be significantly correlated to the representativeness measure though the correlations are low. We suspect that part of the reason behind the low correlation was the small sample size. Future study can be done with more user data.

One of the limitations is the completeness of the list, as the efforts to keep a thorough might vary greatly among users. Another user preference related construct, "preference diversity", was introduced to test its moderating role on the correlation between the self-report and network based "representativeness" measures. It was shown that, consistent with our hypothesis, the correlations between the two types of measures were higher in bookshelves whose owners had a lower reading diversity. The correlation between the coreness and "representativeness" measures becomes insignificant in bookshelves whose owners reported high reading diversity. Compared to coreness, connectivity based measure is less susceptible to the influence of reading diversity as its correlation with representativeness remain significant in both high and low reading diversity groups.

Future study can be done to explore other metrics that might be able to reflect the constructs proposed in the study. For example, clustering coefficient can be a candidate for measuring representativeness, on the ground that a high representativeness books are likely to be more heavily involved in the book similarity network therefore have a more densely connected ego network. Furthermore, besides intra-list similarity, modularity analysis can also be used to measure a bookshelf's diversity as the number of meaningful groupings is likely to be higher in highly diverse bookshelves.

References

Borgatti, S.P., Everett, M.G., Freeman, L.C.: Ucinet for Windows: Software for Social Network Analysis. Analytic Technologies, Harvard (2002)

Borgatti, S.P., Everett, M.G.: Models of core/periphery structures. Soc. Netw. **21**(4), 375–395 (2000)

Cattani, G., Ferriani, S.: A core/periphery perspective on individual creative performance: social networks and cinematic achievements in the Hollywood film industry. Organ. Sci. **19**(6), 824–844 (2008)

Lancaster, F.W.: Indexing and Abstracting in Theory and Practice, 3rd edn. University of Illinois Graduate School of Library and Information Science, Champaign (2003)

Leydesdorff, L.: Betweenness centrality as an indicator of the interdisciplinarity of scientific journals. J. Am. Soc. Inform. Sci. Technol. **58**(9), 1303–1319 (2007)

Oestreicher-Singer, G., Sundararajan, A.: Recommendation networks & the long tail of electronic commerce. MIS Q. **36**(1), 65–83 (2012)

Rosch, E.: Cognitive reference points. Cogn. Psychol. **7**(4), 532–547 (1975)

Ross, C.S.: Finding without seeking: the information encounter in the context of reading for pleasure. Inf. Process. Manage. **35**(6), 783–799 (1999)

Smith, E.E., Medin, D.L.: Categories and Concepts, p. 89. Harvard University Press, Cambridge (1981)

Tang, M.C., Sie, Y.J., Ting, P.H.: Evaluating books finding tools on social media: a case study of aNobii. Inf. Process. Manage. **50**(1), 54–68 (2014)

Zhang, Y.C., Séaghdha, D.Ó., Quercia, D., Jambor, T.: Auralist: introducing serendipity into music recommendation. In: Proceedings of the Fifth ACM International Conference on Web Search and Data Mining, pp. 13–22. ACM (2012)

Ziegler, C.N., McNee, S.M., Konstan, J.A., Lausen, G.: Improving recommendation lists through topic diversification. In: Proceedings of the 14th International Conference on World Wide Web, pp. 22–32. ACM (2005)

A Transaction Cost Equilibrium Analysis on Overlap Between Emergency Response Task Groups

Yun-feng Wang[(⊠)]

School of Economics and Management, Tongji University,
Shanghai, People's Republic of China
tjuwyf@tongji.edu.cn

Abstract. Nowadays a growing number of countries' emergency management mechanisms are based on the network governance mechanism. The task group such as emergency support function (ESF) of the United States is the basic component of emergency response network. How to share function units among task groups is a basic problem of network structure design. This paper proposes a model to decompose transaction cost structure of cooperation between groups and evaluate different choices of sharing units between groups. Through applying this model to the case with only two groups, it shows the equilibrium solution to both sides could be obtained by a bottom-up method.

Keywords: Transaction cost · Network governance · Emergency management · Inter-organizational relationship · Equilibrium analysis

1 Introduction

Task group is a national system often replicated by provinces and local governments in emergency governance of many countries. Governments use it to organize their agencies into groups. Each group focuses on some tightly related missions and groups can work together for some complex situations. However, how to form group programs seems significantly to depend on the personal experience of governmental officials. Even after the continual evolution of the system during many serious disasters, there are still very few studies on how to improve the design of task groups.

Emergency task groups take a key role in emergency network governance. The core idea of networked governance is that organizations are inter-dependent and should cooperate to achieve a commonly desirable goal [1]. Sharing organizations and resources between groups is a fundamental means to construct network. And it brings into groups various degrees of overlap.

According to the China official files on earthquake disaster emergency management (EDEM), in 2008 the overlap was fairly slight between the task groups at national level (Appendix 1: Table 1). In contrast, the overlap phenomenon of emergency support function (ESF) in the United States is much more obvious (Appendix 2:Table 2), where ESF corresponds to a task group. With 15 ESFs, National Response Framework 2008 introduced a mechanism of coordination from 47 federal agencies and the American

© Springer International Publishing AG 2017
F.F.-H. Nah and C.-H. Tan (Eds.): HCIBGO 2017, PART II, LNCS 10294, pp. 434–442, 2017.
DOI: 10.1007/978-3-319-58484-3_34

Red Cross. The National Response Framework was updated twice in 2013 and 2016 and maintained the 2008 version of structure for task groups.

Overlap between task groups takes structural embeddedness beyond the market and hierarchy framework. It seems like a hybrid of them. Yet there is still no dedicated exploration what has happened during the groups which develop the overlap relationship.

Most related studies are carried out in the framework of network governance of emergency management. They use network-based theory to analyze the topics of disaster response, in order to get more understanding on emergency networks. Some examples include interactions among organizations and information infrastructure supporting such interactions [2], coordination clusters in the response network [3], the relationship between planned networks, actual network and perceived influenced structure [4], network characteristics of inter-organizational collaboration [5]. Those studies are based on actual data and reach very convincing conclusions. They also provide insights into the features of network structure in real world that provide inspiration to set up our model in this study.

This paper intends to use transaction cost as a tool to explain the discrepancy among different degrees of overlap. As an application of the analysis framework, it discusses the equilibrium state of a case with only two task types and two corresponding groups.

2 Task Structure, Shared Unit and Transaction Cost

A task group could not just be regarded as some tightly related function units that often perform tasks together. What really decides the relationship between them is the task structure of emergency management. There are typically three types of role in certain kind of task: primary unit, support unit and coordinator unit. Task group completing a given task must include all primary units. Ownership of support units and coordinator units become the key issue of task group design.

Task group has some kinds of ownership of its function units. For units in the same task group, there is a complete set of mechanisms to improve efficiency, such as regular and interim meetings, reporting system, and positions for coordinator. And the emergency plans for units in one group are usually more detailed than those for groups. Besides, more often than not there are fund and authorization to help leaders unite the whole group.

Cross-group cooperation would bring transaction cost on synchronization between two or more parties. As all kinds of task need more than one unit, most missions have to be completed with the help from another group's units. In a network governance mode, the parties usually have relatively equal status. As far as the core task group is concerned, it seems to "borrow" units from other groups and has to "pay" for such an arrangement.

It is not always true that internal cooperation takes less transaction cost than cross-group cooperation does. The transaction cost of internal cooperation is proportional to the scale of a group, since synchronization takes many activities such as planning, communicating, and negotiating. Considering that hierarchy is the basic structure of public departments, bureaucracy will be more serious in bigger groups. Some kinds of delay are inevitable.

Besides internal and external function unit, there is a third option, namely, shared unit. One unit could be the member of different groups at the same time. For the shared unit, transaction cost not only comes from internal cooperation, but also from the arrangement of confliction from all its parent groups. It must make adjustments to fit into different plans and commands. This kind of transaction cost should rise with growing number of shared units.

Fortunately, the transaction cost could decline as the groups sharing more units. Shared units could play the role of coordination channels to eliminate difference and improve mutual understanding. For these reasons, the overlap extent of task groups affects transaction cost at both the unit level and the group level, even there is no shared units taking part in current cross-group actions.

The final program on task group setting usually highly correlated with groups' choice on transaction costs. In the emergency management, groups' professional opinions are easier to receive attention. The final solution should to some extent reflect their common choices. Of course in most cases, common choice may not be the optimal choice for each one.

Despite so many factors affecting the formation of a task group, transaction costs should be the dominant one. A deeper understanding of the causality could assist the government to greatly improve.

3   Model, Optimum and Equilibrium Solution

Set Θ_i contains all function units associated with task. There are two task group $\Omega_i \subset \Theta_i$ and $\Omega_j \subset \Theta_j$, $\Theta_i \subset (\Omega_i \cup \Omega_j)$. Let ρ_{ij} be the overlap rate between task group Ω_i and Ω_j, where $\rho_{ij} = \frac{k_{ij}}{w_i} \in [0, 1]$, $w_i = |\Theta_i|$, $k_{ij} = |\Omega_i \cap \Omega_j|$. Here $|\Theta_i|$ represents the number of elements in set Θ_i, and so for the others. Let $G_{ij} = |\Theta_i \cup \Theta_j|$ represent the total number of units.

Figure 1 demonstrates an example of two task groups with a total of 5 function units. The top half of the figure shows the distribution of units among sets. The bottom half counts the parameter values based on the distribution.

As discussed above, the transaction cost could be improved by properly sharing function units with other groups. There are three types of transaction costs that should be considered.

1. Cross-group cooperation cost,

$$M_i = (1 - \rho_{ij})\alpha_{ij}(w_i - s_{ij} - k_{ij}) \tag{1}$$

where $\alpha_{ij} \in (0, 1]$ is the cost parameter of cross-group cooperation, and $s_{ij} = |\Omega_i - \Omega_j|$. It is created by group Ω_i when it works with some unshared units in set $\Theta_i - \Omega_i$. The cooperation cost for each unit will drop as the two groups sharing more units.

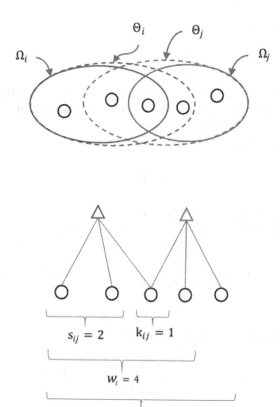

Fig. 1. An example of task groups and function units

Here $1 - \rho_{ij}$ represents the proportion of unshared units on all function units associated with task i. Even though there are a part of unshared units located inside the task group Ω_j, the set $\Theta_i - \Omega_i$, they cannot be taken as some channels of communication and coordination and thus cannot reduce the transaction cost like shared units.

2. Internal adjustment cost,

$$N_i = (1 - \rho_{ij})\beta_{ij}k_{ij} \tag{2}$$

where $\beta_{ij} \in (0, 1]$ is the cost parameter of internal adjustment. This formula contains two trends at the same time. One is shared units will take adjustment cost, because each shared unit has to adapt multiple leadership. The other is the average adjustment cost will fall with the rise of overlap rate.

3. Internal cooperation cost

$$O_i = \gamma_i(s_{ij} + k_{ij}) \tag{3}$$

where $\gamma_i \in (0, 1]$ is the cost parameter of internal cooperation. Internal cooperation will require more effort when the group grows in size. The subscript i of γ_i means this type of cost has no relationship with Ω_j.

As transaction costs cannot be negative,

$$\rho_{ij} \leq 1 - \frac{s_{ij}}{w_i} \tag{4}$$

should be satisfied in order to keep $M_i \geq 0$.

The total transaction cost of Task group Ω_i is calculated as

$$
\begin{aligned}
TC_i &= M_i + N_i + O_i \\
&= (\alpha_{ij} - \beta_{ij})w_i\rho_{ij}^2 - \left[(\alpha_{ij} - \beta_{ij})w_i + (\alpha_{ij} - \gamma_i)w_i - \alpha_{ij}s_{ij}\right]\rho_{ij} + \alpha_{ij}w_i - (\alpha_{ij} - \gamma_i)s_{ij}
\end{aligned}
\tag{5}
$$

The TC_i can reach the minimum value when

$$\rho_{ij}^* = 0, 1 - \frac{(\gamma_i - \beta_{ij})w_i + \alpha_{ij}s_{ij}}{2(\alpha_{ij} - \beta_{ij})w_i} \text{ or } 1 - \frac{s_{ij}}{w_i} \tag{6}$$

Specific value of ρ_{ij}^* depends on the relative sizes of α_{ij}, β_{ij} and γ_i. It shows that there is an optimal overlap rate for task group Ω_i which minimizes the transaction cost.

Unfortunately, the overlap rate between groups is not a unilateral decision. For example, another task group Ω_j can change k_{ij} and then s_{ij} by sharing some function units that belong to Ω_i but still in Θ_j. We should find the equilibrium solution for both sides and make sure no one wants to take the initiative to change k_{ij}.

In an equilibrium state, we can see some relationship between Ω_i and Ω_j. The overlap rate, ρ_{ij}^* and ρ_{ji}^* may not be equal but the shared function units should be the same. Then

$$\rho_{ij}^* w_i = \rho_{ji}^* w_j \tag{7}$$

where

$$\rho_{ji}^* = 0, 1 - \frac{(\gamma_j - \beta_{ji})w_j + \alpha_{ji}s_{ji}}{2(\alpha_{ji} - \beta_{ji})w_j} \text{ or } 1 - \frac{s_{ji}}{w_j} \tag{8}$$

The following condition should also be met when the two sets, Θ_i and Θ_j, overlap with each other,

$$\rho_{ij}w_i + s_{ij} + s_{ji} = G_{ij} \tag{9}$$

According to the Eqs. (6), (7), (8) and (9), the optimal solution of ρ_{ij}^*, ρ_{ji}^*, s_{ij}^* and s_{ji}^* can be obtained.

4 Discussion

Although this paper discusses a simple case of two task groups, we get some interesting and instructive findings. The most important one is the equilibrium state is closed. After we find the equilibrium state between Ω_i and Ω_j, the question becomes that whether or not Ω_i could get an equilibrium state with another task group, such as Ω_h, without breaking the equilibrium state with Ω_j.

In fact, the equilibrium state can only be broken by Ω_i and Ω_j themselves. Because the units shared with Ω_h will only come from the set of $\Theta_i \cap \Theta_h$, the choices of Ω_h will not change parameters in the cost formulas between Ω_i and Ω_j. And then the results of equilibrium will keep the same, such as s^* and ρ^*. If Ω_i or Ω_j desires to establish equilibrium with Ω_h and shares or gives up shared units belonging to $\Theta_i \cap \Theta_j \cap \Theta_h$, then ρ_{ij}^*, ρ_{ji}^*, s_{ij}^* or s_{ji}^* will be changed. These variables should be adjusted to restart a new equilibrium state.

The main conclusion is that the balance can only be destroyed by parties in the relationship. With this strategy one task group could keep the lowest transaction cost with one group when it builds equilibrium with the other one. As long as the group can carefully enough avoid the units possibly shared by multiple parties, it is capable of setting up a new equilibrium without breaking the previously established one.

Another important find is the equilibrium solutions do exist. Given some basic information we could get the best solution for both sides. Actually there are only three choices for any given group.

1. $\rho^* = 0$, there is not overlap with each other. Groups establish balance just by cross-group cooperation and internal cooperation;
2. $\rho^* = 1 - \frac{s}{w}$, it takes all related units internal firstly and then let the overlap to be determined by equilibrium;
3. $\rho^* = 1 - \frac{(\gamma-\beta)w + \alpha s}{2(\alpha-\beta)w}$, it is some solution between the above two.

Last but not least, it is worth noting that the basic assumption maybe challenged in some cases. That is all the tasks are independent of each other. In real practices, the capacity of a task group is very limited. Some parameters, such as α_{ij}, β_{ij} and γ_i, are difficult to maintain consistent when facing a growing number of tasks. And the final results will also suffer the impacts of parameter variations.

5 Conclusion

In this paper, the framework of transaction cost is used to analyze the mechanism of overlap phenomenon in emergency task groups. In order to reduce cost, task groups share units as an alternative to internalization and cross-group collaboration. It discloses micro-foundation of emergency network governance. The network structure is developed by disaggregating function units into three parts: unshared internal units, shared units and unshared external units. The third part is very important but is often neglected by existing studies.

We also use the bottom-up method to find the equilibrium overlap between groups. It is very useful in some scenarios that task groups need to change their composition to adapt to a dynamic environment. At first individual group finds the relationship between overlap rate and unshared units that could bring maximum transaction cost reduction. Then it could determine the parameters through building a balance relationship with the other group.

The future extensions of this study may come in two directions. First, a general model should be explored that could find the equilibrium solution for more than two task groups. As the interplay of groups' choice, it is very difficult to build balance between multi-groups. Some kinds of iterative algorithms should be introduced here. The second one is to measure the three types of transaction costs from real data. All kinds of models based on transaction cost have to face the challenge of finding evidence from empirical study. Taking advantages from the growing development of information systems in emergency management, we may try to estimate the costs by communication data in these systems.

Appendix 1

Table 1. Overlap between EDEM task groups of China, 2008

	DR	ML	EM	HEP	P	PR	ISPR	WC	SS	Average
DR	–	0	1	1	1	1	1	1	2	1.0
ML	0	–	0	2	1	4	5	4	0	2.0
EM	1	0	–	0	1	1	0	4	0	0.9
HEP	1	2	0	–	0	2	2	3	1	1.4
P	1	1	1	0	–	0	1	1	0	0.6
PR	1	4	1	2	0	–	6	3	0	2.1
ISPR	1	5	0	2	1	6	–	5	1	2.6
WC	1	4	4	3	1	3	5	–	0	2.6
SS	2	0	0	1	0	0	1	0	–	0.5

Source: [6]
DR: Disaster Relief, ML: Masses Life, EM: Earthquake
monitoring group, HEP: Health and epidemic prevention group,
ISPR: Infrastructure Support and post-disaster reconstruction, P:
Propaganda, PR: Production recovery, WC: Water conservancy,
SS: Social security

Appendix 2

Table 2. Overlap between ESF of United States

	T	C	PWE	F	EM	MC, EA, HHS	L, MRS
T	–	6	9	6	11	8	8
C	6	–	6	5	7	5	6
PWE	9	6	–	7	16	11	11
F	6	5	7	–	7	4	5
EM	11	7	16	7	–	15	13
MC, EA, HHS	8	5	11	4	15	–	9
L, MRS	8	6	11	5	13	9	–
PHMS	11	6	14	7	16	12	11
SR	6	5	7	5	9	7	8
OHMR	10	6	13	7	14	9	10
ANR	11	6	13	7	15	11	10
E	8	5	12	7	12	6	8
PSS	8	5	8	6	12	9	8
LTCR	7	5	12	6	14	13	9
EA	11	7	15	7	24	15	13
Average	8	5.3	10.3	5.7	12.3	8.9	8.6

	PHMS	SR	OHMR	ANR	E	PSS	LTCR	EA
T	11	6	10	11	8	8	7	11
C	6	5	6	6	5	5	5	7
PWE	14	7	13	13	12	8	12	15
F	7	5	7	7	7	6	6	7
EM	16	9	14	15	12	12	14	24
MC, EA, HHS	12	7	9	11	6	9	13	15
L, MRS	11	8	10	10	8	8	9	13
PHMS	–	9	13	15	10	10	11	16
SR	9	–	8	8	6	7	7	10
OHMR	13	8	–	13	11	8	10	14
ANR	15	8	13	–	10	9	11	14
E	10	6	11	10	–	7	9	12
PSS	10	7	8	9	7	–	8	13
LTCR	11	7	10	11	9	8	–	13
EA	16	10	14	14	12	13	13	–
Average	10.7	6.8	9.7	10.2	8.2	7.9	9	12.3

Source: [7]
T: Transportation, C: Communications, PWE: Public Works &
Engineering, F: Firefighting, EM:Emergency Management, L, MRS:
Logistics, Management & Resource Support, PHMS: Public Health &
Medical Services, MC, EA, HHS: Mass Care, Emergency Assistance,
Housing & Human Services, SR: Search & Rescue, OHMR: Oil &
Hazardous Material Response, ANR: Agriculture & Natural Resources,
E: Energy, PSS: Public Safety & Security, LTCR: Long Term
Community Recovery, EA: External affairs

References

Provan, K.G., Fish, A., Sydow, J.: Interorganizational networks at the network level: a review of the empirical literature on whole networks. J. Manag. **33**, 479–516 (2007). doi:10.1177/0149206307302554

Zhang, H., Zhang, X., Comfort, L., Chen, M.: The emergence of an adaptive response network: the April 20, 2013 Lushan, China Earthquake. Saf. Sci. **90**, 14–23 (2016). doi:10.1016/j.ssci.2015.11.012

Noori, N.S., Paetzold, K., Vilasis-Cardona, X.: Network based discrete event analysis for coordination processes in crisis response operations. In: 2016 Annual IEEE on Systems Conference (SysCon) (2016). doi:10.1109/SYSCON.2016.7490603

Guo, X., Kapucu, N.: Network performance assessment for collaborative disaster response. Disaster Prev. Manag. **24**, 201–220 (2014). doi:10.1177/0149206307302554

Wang, Y., Han, C., Liu, L.: Network analysis of the inter-organizational collaboration in emergency management system of China. In: 2013 IEEE International Conference on Systems, Man, and Cybernetics (2013). doi:10.1109/SMC.2013.220

The State Council of China: Notice of the composition of the earthquake relief headquarter task groups of State Council 关于国务院抗震救灾总指挥部工作组组成的通知 (2008). http://www.gov.cn/zhengce

The United States Department of Homeland Security. National Response Framework (NRF), Department of Homeland Security, Washington DC (2008)

Analyzing Load Profiles of Electricity Consumption by a Time Series Data Mining Framework

I-Chin Wu[1(✉)], Tzu-Li Chen[2], Yen-Ming Chen[3], Tzu-Chi Liu[3], and Yi-An Chen[2]

[1] Graduate Institute of Library and Information Studies,
National Taiwan Normal University, Taipei, Taiwan
icwu@ntnu.edu.tw
[2] Department of Information Management, Fu-Jen Catholic University, New Taipei City, Taiwan
[3] Industrial Technology Research Institute, Hsinchu, Taiwan

Abstract. Given the problems of gradual oil depletion and global warming, energy consumption has become a critical factor for energy-intensive sectors, especially the semiconductor, manufacturing, iron and steel, and aluminum industries. In turn, reducing energy consumption for sustainability and both tracking and managing energy efficiently have become critical challenges. In response, we analyzed electricity consumption from the perspective of load profiling, which charts variation in electrical load during a specified period in order to track energy consumption. As a result, we proposed a time series data mining and analytic framework for electricity consumption analysis and pattern extraction by streaming data mining and machine learning techniques. We identified key factors to predict the state of the annealing furnace and detect abnormal patterns of the load profile of their electricity consumption. Our experimental results show that the dimension reduction method known as piecewise aggregate approximation can help to detect the state of the annealing furnace.

Keywords: Energy consumption analysis · Load profiling · Piecewise aggregate approximation · Time-series data mining

1 Introduction

As a cornerstone of modern civilization and economic growth, electricity is critical for industrial and economic advancement, as well as a driving force for sustainable development. Indeed, social development correlates positively with power consumption, which in Taiwan, especially the consumption of electricity, has risen rapidly due to economic, industrial, and commercial growth.

In relation to total exports, Taiwan's manufacturing-oriented economy exports a considerable share of manufactured goods. Currently, most industries in Taiwan have replaced manual operation with machine operation during fabrication, which requires a sufficient but not excessive supply of stable electricity. In fact, too much or too little electricity can cause mechanical malfunctions and thereby reduce the efficiency of both production and electricity. As Table 1 shows, Taiwan Power Company's statistics from 2015 reveal that the industrial sector consumes an exceptionally large proportion of electricity—even up to more than 50% of the total consumed in Taiwan.

© Springer International Publishing AG 2017
F.F.-H. Nah and C.-H. Tan (Eds.): HCIBGO 2017, PART II, LNCS 10294, pp. 443–454, 2017.
DOI: 10.1007/978-3-319-58484-3_35

Table 1. Electricity sales in Taiwan, 2015

Industry sector	GWh	(%)
Industrial	114,241.9	55.3
Residential	42,196.6	20.4
Commercial	32,511.0	15.7
Other	17,541.8	8.5
Total	206,491.3	100.0

Source: Taiwan Power Company (http://www.taipower.com.tw/)

In response, manufacturers in Taiwan, is keen to identify the most cost-effective methods and techniques to increase electricity efficiency in their factories. In industries, many machines are highly energy intensive, and with machine data, we can analyze their tendencies regarding power and temperature, among other measures. We can also use anomaly detection to identify indicators of machine malfunction, which can then contribute to determining rules in order to explain the malfunctions. With such technologies, we can promptly correct abnormalities and thereby reduce the unnecessary waste of resources and improve the efficiency of electric consumption.

Without a doubt, energy is a vital resource for modern society, especially for long-term competitive sustainability. To reduce unnecessary energy consumption and improve energy efficiency, it is therefore critical to make informed decisions in real time. To that end, we collected data regarding energy consumption and information from the corresponding production and manufacturing domains from the plans of co-operating iron and steel manufacturers. Based on load profiles determined from data stream mining and machine learning techniques, we constructed an electric energy monitor and analysis framework, the kernel of which are a prediction model for identifying typical load profiles of each machine and a time series data-mining engine for analyzing and extracting typical patterns based on the load profiles. The objectives of our research were threefold:

1. To observe and analyze relationships among various attributes (e.g., electric power, temperature, and product weight) in a data warehouse framework to allow researchers to select and confirm key attributes based on the results of analysis and consult with domain experts.
2. To identify three states of the annealing process—heating-up, temperature retention, and cooling down—based on the temperature information of the operating machine and, following Keogh et al. [1], use piecewise aggregate approximation (PAA) to perform dimension reduction for data representation and, detect machine operational states according to energy load profiles that can inform real-time energy-optimization decisions; and
3. To propose and construct an electric energy monitor and analysis framework based on load profiles by data stream mining and machine learning techniques as a means to implement the proposed time series data-mining approach in co-operating iron and steel manufacture.

The overarching goal of the three objectives is to deploy a visualized decision-making support system and propose actionable energy-saving strategies for co-operating plants to solve real-world problems.

2 Time Series Data Mining

Time series data are easily obtainable from scientific, financial, and industrial applications, and given the deployment of numerous sensors and smart devices, the amount of accumulated time series data continues to expand rapidly. By extension, the increased generation and use of time series data have resulted in a great deal of research and developments in big data mining. Each time series database consists of sequences of values or events obtained over repeated measurements of time [2]. Time series data are large, as well as numerical and continuous in nature, which require continuous updating. Mörchen [3] has identified two chief research-related goals of time series analysis—to identify patterns represented by the sequence of observations and to forecast future values of time series data—both of which require the identification of patterns of time series data to enable the interpretation and integration of patterns with other data.

Kitagawa (2010) [4] classified time series analysis into four categories: description, modeling, prediction, and signal extraction. Sakurai et al. [5] have provided a comprehensive overview of key topics of time series analysis: similarity search and pattern discovery, linear modeling and summary, nonlinear modeling and forecasting, and the extension of time series mining and tensor analysis. In our study, we focused on the first. Popeangă [6] has proposed that energy production and consumption data recorded over a period at fixed intervals is a classic time (i.e., chronological) series data-mining problem. The entire process involves five steps: collecting data from various sources (e.g., the Internet, text, databases, data warehouses, sensors, and smart devices); conducting data filtering by eliminating errors or deploying a data warehouse to create an extraction, transformation, and loading (ETL) process in advance; selecting key attributes to be used in data mining for further analysis; detecting and analyzing new knowledge; and visualizing, validating, and evaluating results. The challenge of electricity consumption analysis is analyzing countless time series to find similar or regular patterns and trends with a fast or even real-time response. Accordingly, time series data mining techniques such as whole series clustering and classification, subsequent clustering and classification, time point clustering, anomaly detection, and motif discovery can be adopted for electricity consumption analysis and energy management.

Since time series are high-dimensional data, they are time consuming for computing and storage space cost. However, several techniques have been proposed that denote time series data with reduced dimensionality. Well-known dimensionality reduction techniques include discrete Fourier transformation [7], single value decomposition [8], discrete wavelet transformation [9], PAA [1], SAX [10], and indexable piecewise linear approximation [11]. We will adopt the intuitive method of PAA and discretized the PAA representation of a time series into a symbolic representation method SAX algorithm.

3   Time-Series Electricity Consumption Data Mining Framework

We collected energy consumption data and the corresponding product information of two annealing furnaces in 2014. Figure 1 shows the proposed time series data mining framework for electricity consumption analysis. The primary research questions were:

- What is a good attribute to identify the operational state of the machine?
- What is the best model to predict the operational states of machines (i.e., warm-up, heat retention, and cooling)?

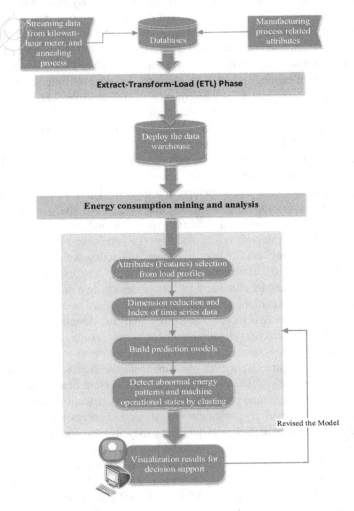

Fig. 1. Time-series data mining framework for electricity consumption analysis in industry

All tasks of analysis involved using the load profiles of the electricity consumption of the targeted machine. For the proposed framework, we preliminarily deploy the data warehousing framework to observe and analyze the load profiles of electricity consumption and the relationships among various attributes (e.g., electric power, temperature, and product weight). Next, we select and confirm key attributes to identify the state of the annealing furnace based on the results of analysis and consulted with domain experts. We confirm that either the electric power or temperature information of the operating machine can help to identify the entire machine operational process, which is 1,440 min on average. We use the temperature information of the operating machine to identify three states: warm-up, heat retention, and cooling.

We apply the PAA method to discretize streaming data into n segments with time-stamps in order to build the prediction model. We will refine the SAX algorithm, which is a symbolic representation of time series for dimensionality reduction and indexing with a lower-bounding distance measure to further extract subsequent patterns. It can help the system to detect abnormal energy patterns and machine operational states by symbolizing energy load profiles to make further energy-optimization decisions in real time. We will apply an agglomerative hierarchical clustering approach to discriminate normal and abnormal electric patterns—that is, to group the electric patterns for further analytical and prediction tasks. We plan to next conduct a series of experiments to construct a prediction model in order to identify their operational states (i.e., warm-up, heat retention, and cooling), the target annealing furnace, and abnormal energy patterns. We also included associated experiments of parameter selection of the PAA method in our experiments.

Ultimately, the goal of our series of studies is to deploy a visualized decision support system and propose actionable energy-saving strategies for co-operating iron and steel plants to solve real-world problems. We present the entire framework for electricity consumption analysis and detail some of the modules in the following sections.

4 Data Preprocessing and Data Warehousing Deployment

4.1 Data Preprocessing

Table 3 presents all of the attributes of the annealing furnaces related to electricity consumption analysis in our research. We adopted a data mart to visualize and observe the initial load profiles of electricity consumption. In general, data warehousing is fundamental to business intelligence, and data collection, data management, and data analysis techniques (e.g., data mart design with extraction, transformation, and loading tools) can help business analytics use data intelligently. Accordingly, we deployed the data warehousing framework to observe the load profiles of electricity consumption (Fig. 2) and analyzed the relationships among various attributes (e.g., electric power, temperature, and product weight. Figure 3 presents the fact table of our research. The data warehousing platform had two chief goals: to analyze the load profiles of each annealing process and to define annealing states based on the selected attributes of load profiles.

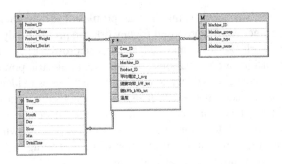

Fig. 2. Star schema of the data mart for EC Analysis

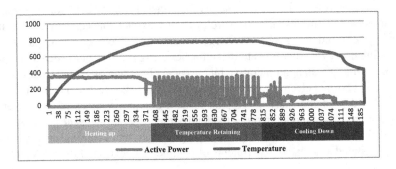

Fig. 3. Load profiles of active power and temperature

Data warehousing helped us to confirm the load profiles of each annealing process in order to preliminarily identify the normal or abnormal state of the machines. We confirmed that either the electric active power or temperature information of the operating machine can help to identify the entire machine operational process, which is 1,440 min on average. We used the data of annealing process from April 1, 2014, to December 31, 2014 to train and construct the prediction model to detect each machine's state and condition.

After selecting the attributes that were useful for periodical data analysis, we adopted the star schema to build the data mart (Fig. 2). The three dimension tables are the machine information table, the product information table with time information with different granularity table, and a fact table that shows the load profiles of current and temperature, among other things. Based on the analytical results of load profile, we used the temperature information of the operating machine to identify three states: warm-up, heat retention, and cooling. By extension, we could further identify the normal or abnormal states of each annealing process. We show one load profile of active power and temperature of one annealing furnace in Fig. 3 (Table 2).

Table 2. Electricity consumption analysis related attributes

Attributes	Data type
Logtime	Date yyyy/mm/dd hh:mm:ss
Current (I_avg)	Numeric
Voltage (V_avg)	Numeric
Active power (kW_tot), total active power (kWh_tot)	Numeric
Reactive power (kvar_tot), total reactive power (kvarh_tot)	Numeric
Apparent power (kVA_tot), total apparent power (kVAh_tot)	Numeric
Power factor (PF_tot)	Numeric
Temperature	Numeric
Product weight	Numeric

4.2 Time Series Representation for Constructing the Prediction Model

Time series representation. To represent time series data concisely and increase the index and processing times, we mainly adopted PAA in order to extract the primary features of time series data [1, 12].

We treated each annealing process as having streaming time series data that are divisible based on the differing granularity of time units, each of which is a feature point of the data stream. Accordingly, an annealing process entails several feature points with timestamps. Herein, we introduce two methods to extract feature points: a fixed interval method as a baseline method and the PAA of a time series. For the fixed interval method, if the length of the string was 1,000 and we aimed to extract 5 points, then we extracted the first, 250th, 500th, 750th, and 1000th points, in a method we dub the fixed feature point (FFP) method. Figure 4 shows an example of the FFP representation curve. For PAA, we averaged the values of points in a fixed interval to represent a feature point (Fig. 5). PAA is a non-data-adaptive representation model that transforms the time series into a different space and has the same transformation parameters regardless of features of the data at hand [13]. Put differently, the transformation parameters are preset without consideration of the

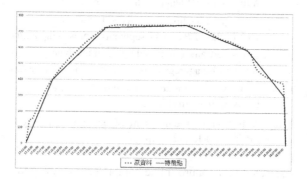

Fig. 4. FFP method for feature point extraction (temperature)

underlying data. We further adopted SAX after PAA to represent each feature point of the load profile symbolically. Due to the constraints of space, we report the results of the FFP method versus PAA for identifying states of the annealing process.

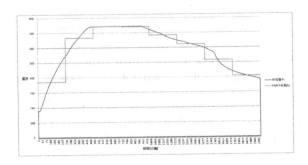

Fig. 5. PAA method for feature point extraction (temperature)

Feature frames of each annealing process. Based on the methods, we defined time series data and related notations (Table 3). We denoted time series data of an attribute i as S = (s1, s2,....sn), with the length of a time series in n and w as the dimensionality of the space to index the time series data. Put differently, a time series of length n can be represented in w dimensional space and each feature point by a feature frame of fix length (i.e., n/w). For PAA, the result is $\overline{S} = (\overline{s_1}, \overline{s_2}, \dots, \overline{s_w})$ – that is, w-dimensional space by vector $\overline{s}$. The ith feature point of $\overline{S}$ can be derived from Eq. (1).

$$\overline{s_i} = \frac{w}{n} \sum_{j=\frac{w}{n}*(i-1)+1}^{\frac{w}{n}*i} s_j \tag{1}$$

Table 3. Summary of notation used in PAA and SAX

Notations	Definitions
S_i	A time series of length n, $S_i = (s_1, s_2,....s_n)$
w	The dimensionality of the space, $1 \le w \le n$ That is, the *FFP* or *PAA* segments representing a time series S
FF (feature frame)	A feature frame composed by set of attributes
$\overline{S}$	A piecewise aggregate approximation of a time series
FP_A (feature point of active power)	A time series of the active power of length w after dimension reduction, FP_A = (fpa1, fpa2, ...fpa$_w$)
FP_T (feature point of temperature)	A time series of temperature of length w after dimension reduction, FP_T = (fpt1, fpt2, ...fpt$_w$)

The attributes selected in a feature frame comprised all extracted points of active power (FP_A) and the minimum, maximum, and average values of active power; all extracted points of temperature (FP_T) and the minimum, maximum, and average values of temperature; and (3) the weight of raw material information. The feature frame in Fig. 6 was the input of the training model. The specific notation, with a description of each attribute set of the feature frame, appears in Table 4. Attributes derive from the fact table shown in Fig. 2.

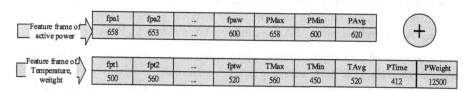

Fig. 6. An example of a feature frame as an input string for the prediction model

Table 4. Summary of the notation of the feature frame

Notations	Definitions
PMin	Minimum value of the active power of a state
PMax	Maximum value of the active power of a state
PAvg	Average value of the active power of a state
P_N	Number of extracted dimensions in a state of the active power
TMin	Minimum value of temperature of a state
TMax	Maximum value of temperature of a state
TAvg	Average value of temperature of a state
T_N	Number of extracted dimensions in a state of temperature
PWeight	Weight of materials for each operational process
PTime	Duration of each state of the entire operational process

5 Experimental Design and Results

5.1 Experimental Setup

We next conducted a series of experiments to construct a prediction model in order to identify operational states for the target annealing furnace. Notably, we discretized the streaming data into n segments with timestamps to construct the model. Based on our preliminary analytical results, we confirmed that either the electric power or temperature information of the operating machine can help to identify a machine's entire operational process, which is 1,440 min on average. We then used the temperature information of the operating machine to identify three states: warm-up, heat retention, and cooling. We collected energy consumption data and corresponding product information of two annealing furnaces from April 1, 2014, to December 31, 2014. Herein, we present the experimental results for one furnace. We explain the results of the two primary sets of experiments with the FFP method and PAA as feature extraction methods in what follows.

- Experiment 1 (FFP): The set of experiments included original stream data, data with the normalization process, data with the extreme value removal process, data with normalization, and the extreme value removal process—respectively, baseline_FFP, standardization _FFP, extreme_FFP, and hybrid_FFP.
- Experimental 2 (PAA): The set of experiments included original stream data, data with the normalization process, data with the extreme value removal process, data with normalization, and the extreme value removal process—respectively, baseline_PAA, standardization _PAA, extreme_PAA, and hybrid_PAA.

The purpose of data standardization with z-score standardization is to remove outlier data points and elucidate the relationship between a data point and the average value of all data points. The z-score converts all indicators to a common scale with an average of 0 and standard deviation of 1. The equation of the z-score method used appears in Eq. (2):

$$Normalized(e_i) = \frac{e_i - \overline{E}}{std(E)} \tag{2}$$

in which e_i represents the data points of the load profile, $std(E)$ is the standard deviation of the data points of the load profile, and $\overline{E}$ is the mean value of the data points.

The purpose of removing outlier values is to avoid excessive noise in the time series data. We removed feature points outside twice the standard deviation of the average value, $\overline{E}$, of the target load profile. Ultimately, the hybrid method involved removing outlier data points and adopting the z-score.

We adopted sequential minimal optimization, in which a multilayer perceptron (MLP) is a feedforward artificial neural network model, and a radial basis function (RBF). We tuned different learning rates to train the best MLP model and adopted five-fold cross-validation to evaluate the root mean squared error (RMSE) of the prediction results. The RMSE is the mean of the square of all errors, which is used to measure the differences between values.

5.2   Experimental Results for Identifying Operational States

Tables 5 and 6 show the average results of the three data mining approaches (i.e., MLP, radial basis function, and sequential minimal optimization) for the FFP method and PPA. We discretized the time series data into w points and listed the results of each variation method based on the FFP and PAA approaches. Note that when we set w to 50, for example, we extracted 50 feature points to represent the entire load profile of the active power.

Observation 1 (FFP). For the FFP approach, the worst method on average is *standardization_FPP*. However, the *hybrid_FFP* can achieve the minimum RMSE in comparison to the other three methods under various w value settings. By contrast, *hybrid_FFP* and *extreme_FPP* have similar results under various w values, which indicates that we can help to remove the extreme value and then perform standardization. Overall, the best results on average occurred when w was 100. It seems that a larger w

value (i.e., more feature points) with the FPP method does not generate better results in predicting states of machines.

Observation 2 (PAA). Like the FFP approach, the worst method for PAA is *standardization _PAA*. *extreme_PAA* and *hybrid_PAA* can achieve the minimum RMSE in comparison to the other two methods under various w values. Overall, the best results on average were with w at 150. The FFP method seems insensitive to p-values; however, more or fewer feature points does not yield better results in predicting states of machines.

Observation 3 (Comparison). Both dimension reduction approaches generated similar results between the methods. For example, after conducting data standardization without removing extreme values generated the worst results. When we compared the method between the approaches, we observed that the FFP method is worse than PAA, because the former is more sensitive to extract points in representing subsequent parts of the data stream. As such, we adopted PAA to further symbolize processing by the SAX algorithm and set w to 150 (i.e., 150 feature points to represent the entire data stream).

Table 5. Prediction the operational state by FFP method in terms of RMSE

Method/w	50	100	150	200	250	300	350	Average
baseline_FFP	0.070	0.086	0.108	0.085	0.086	**0.083**	0.100	0.088
standardization _FFP	0.340	**0.314**	0.497	0.337	0.344	0.365	0.422	0.374
extreme_FFP	0.082	0.081	0.072	**0.069**	0.0703	0.078	0.072	0.075
hybrid_FFP	0.065	**0.058**	0.062	0.059	0.065	0.060	0.064	0.062
Average	0.139	*0.135*	0.185	0.137	0.142	0.146	0.165	0.150

Table 6. Prediction the operational state by PAA method in terms of RMSE

Method/w	50	100	150	200	250	300	350	Average
baseline_PAA	0.121	0.136	0.126	0.150	0.211	**0.115**	0.129	0.141
standardization _PAA	0.397	0.218	**0.090**	0.109	0.164	0.104	0.126	0.173
extreme_PAA	0.115	0.097	**0.091**	0.099	0.091	0.125	0.100	0.103
hybrid_PAA	**0.083**	0.123	0.127	0.119	0.117	0.107	0.172	0.121
Average	0.179	0.143	*0.109*	**0.119**	0.146	**0.113**	**0.132**	0.134

6   Conclusions and Future Works

We proposed a time series data mining and analytic framework for electricity consumption analysis in energy-intensive industries. We deployed a data warehouse framework to analyze the load profiles of each attribute in order to select key attributes for further data mining tasks. We then compared the results of two dimension reduction approaches with various data preprocessing methods to predict the state of the annealing process of target furnaces. We preliminarily confirmed that PAA with data outlier removal and data standardization processing can achieve slightly better results than the FFP approach. In the future, we will finalize all modules mentioned in the framework and conduct a series of experiments to confirm the effectiveness of the proposed framework and approaches to identify electricity patterns and machine operational states in real time.

Acknowledgments. This research was supported by Ministry of Science and Technology of Taiwan under Grant MOST 105-2410-H-003-153-MY3 & Bureau of Energy of Taiwan is gratefully acknowledged.

References

1. Keogh, E., Chakrabarti, K., Pazzani, M., Mehrotra, S.: Dimensionality reduction for fast similarity search in large time series databases. Knowl. Inf. Syst. **3**(3), 263–286 (2001)
2. Han, J., Kamber, M., Pei, J.: Data Mining: Concepts and Techniques, 3rd edn. Morgan Kaufmann, San Francisco (2011)
3. Mörchen, F.: Time series knowledge mining. Ph.D. thesis, Philipps-University Marburg, Germany (2006)
4. Kitagawa, G.: Introduction to Time Series Modeling. Monographs on Statistics & Applied Probability. Chapman & Hall/CRC, Boca Raton (2010)
5. Sakurai, Y., Matsubara, Y., Faloutsos, C.: Mining and forecasting of big time-series data. In: Proceedings of the 2015 ACM SIGMOD International Conference on Management of Data, Tutorial, pp. 919–922, Melbourne, Victoria, Australia (2015)
6. Popeanga, J.: Data mining smart energy time series. Database Syst. J. **6**(1), 14–22 (2015)
7. Faloutsos, C., Ranganathan, M., Manolopoulos, Y.: Fast subsequence matching in time-Series databases. In: Proceedings of the 1994 ACM International Conference on Management of Data (SIGMOD), pp. 419–429 (1994)
8. Wall, M.E., Rechtsteiner, A., Rocha, L.M.: Singular value decomposition and principal component analysis. In: Berrar, D.P., Dubitzky, W., Granzow, M. (eds.) A Practical Approach to Microarray Data Analysis, pp. 91–109. Kluwer, Norwell (2003)
9. Chan, K.A., Fu, W.C.: Efficient time series matching by wavelets. In: Proceeding of the 15th International Conference on Data Engineering (ICDE), pp. 126–133 (1999)
10. Lin, J., Keogh, E.J., Wei, L., Lonardi, S.: Experiencing SAX: a novel symbolic representation of time series. Data Mining Knowl. Discov. **15**(2), 107–144 (2007)
11. Chen, Q., Chen, L, Lian, X., Liu, Y., Yu, J.X.: Indexable PLA for efficient similarity search. In: Proceeding of the 33rd International Conference on Very Large Data BaseS (VLDB), pp. 435–446 (2007)
12. Keogh, E.J., Pazzani, M.J.: A simple dimensionality reduction technique for fast similarity search in large time series databases. In: Terano, T., Liu, H., Chen, A.L.P. (eds.) PAKDD 2000. LNCS (LNAI), vol. 1805, pp. 122–133. Springer, Heidelberg (2000). doi:10.1007/3-540-45571-X_14
13. Kleist, C.: Time series data mining methods: a review, (Master's thesis, Humboldt-Universit¨at zu Berlin, Germany). http://edoc.hu-berlin.de/master/kleist-caroline-2015-03-25/PDF/kleist.pdf

Author Index

Printed in the United States
By Bookmasters